THE INSIDERS' GUIDE®

TO

Golf in the Carolinas

THE
INSIDERS'®
GUIDE
TO
Golf in the
Carolinas

by
Mitch Willard
&
Scott Martin

The Insiders' Guides Inc.

Co-published and marketed by:
Knight Publishing Company, Inc.
P.O. Box 31288
600 South Tryon Street
Charlotte, NC28232
(704) 358-5922

Co-published and distributed by:
The Insiders' Guides Inc.
The Waterfront • Suite 12
P.O. Box 2057
Manteo, NC 27954
(919) 473-6100

•

SECOND EDITION
2nd printing

•

Copyright ©1996
by Knight Publishing Company, Inc.

•

Printed in the United States
of America

•

Publications from The Insiders' Guides®
series are available at special discounts
for bulk purchases for sales promotions,
premiums or fundraisings. Special
editions, including personalized covers,
can be created in large quantities for
special needs. For more information,
please write to The Insiders' Guides Inc.,
P.O. Box 2057, Manteo, NC 27954 or
call (919) 473-6100 x 233.

ISBN 1-57380-008-2

Knight Publishing Company, Inc.
Subsidiary Publications Division

Director, Subsidiary Publications
Stewart Spencer

Manager
Linda Sluder

Advertising support from
the following companies:
**The Insiders' Guides® Inc.
By the Sea Publications
Great Direct Concepts
The Myrtle Beach Sun News**

The Insiders' Guides Inc.

Publisher/Editor-in-Chief
Beth P. Storie

President/General Manager
Michael McOwen

Affiliate Sales and Training Director
Rosanne Cheeseman

Partner Services Director
Giles MacMillan

Sales and Marketing Director
Julie Ross

Creative Services Director
Mike Lay

Online Services Director
David Haynes

Managing Editor
Theresa Shea Chavez

Fulfillment Director
Gina Twiford

Project Editors
**Dan DeGregory,
Beth Storie**

Project Artist
Elaine Fogarty

Foreword

by John Inman

Greetings and welcome to the great golfing states of North and South Carolina! Standing alone, each state would easily be one of the finest golf destinations in the world, but put them together, and you're talking about a golfer,s paradise. A lot of things make golf in the Carolinas special. Great land is the foundation for great golf courses, and the variety and quality of terrain here in the Carolinas is perfect.

The mountains of Upstate South Carolina and Western North Carolina are home to courses with mild summer temperatures and spectacular views, particularly in the fall and spring, when the trees and shrubs are in full color. The Piedmont region of North Carolina is rolling and wooded, and the courses you'll find in and around bustling cities such as Greensboro, Winston-Salem, Durham and Charlotte are classic parkland courses, often in majestic settings.

The Midlands of South Carolina, where the soil is sandy, is also an excellent region for golf courses, many of which attract visitors from out-of-state, most of whom are here to escape the brutal cold of northern climes. The coast of South Carolina is world-famous for its hospitality, its attractions and its literally hundreds of outstanding golf courses. Architects have used the rich land of the coastal plain to produce gems set hard by the ocean, in among the ancient oaks or meandering around salt marshes. It's no wonder that places like Charleston, Myrtle Beach and Hilton Head attract hundreds of thousands of golfers.

John Inman
—

The coast of North Carolina may not boast as many courses as the Palmetto state (how many coastlines do?) but don't be fooled into thinking that the coastal courses of North Carolina are anything less in quality. There are plenty of superb courses here, many of which are not quite as busy as their sisters in South Carolina.

I've left Pinehurst to last, because I think it's one of the most important and most beautiful golf destinations in the world. If you want epic nightlife, head to Myrtle Beach: Pinehurst is all about relaxation and golf in a truly classic and storied atmosphere. It's the cradle of resort golf in the United States, and all it takes is one walk down the hallway at Pinehurst's clubhouse to realize that Pinehurst is the home of competitive golf in the United States. How fitting that Pinehurst #2 will host the 1999 U.S. Open.

With all the great land around, it's no wonder that North and South Carolina boast some of the world's great golf courses, many of which are annually ranked in top-100 lists published by a variety of publications. One of the greatest golf course architects, Donald Ross, made his home in the Carolinas, and his work is everywhere. Other excellent craftsman have been busy here as well. Fazio, Maples, Nicklaus, Jones, Dye and Palmer are the big names. But there are plenty of lesser-known architects such as Gene Hamm, Russell Breeden, George Cobb and Tom Jackson who have produced fun, playable and justifiably popular courses.

Quite a few of these highly regarded courses are private, but just as many are accessible to the public. You don't have to be a millionaire to enjoy good golf in the Carolinas. There are plenty of courses where eighteen holes are yours for less than $25.

To top it all, the Carolinas offer excellent year-round weather for the golfer, even if it's a little sticky in the summer. All but a few weekends in the winter will find golfers enjoying time on the course. And if you've been to Chapel Hill, you know all about the magic of a Carolina Blue sky in the springtime. As a pro, I get to play golf all over the country and all over the world, but I'm always extra excited when I get a chance to play golf in my home state of North Carolina.

Hit it straight!

About John Inman . . .

Born in Greensboro, North Carolina, John Inman is a 1984 graduate of The University of North Carolina at Chapel Hill where his many accomplishments included winning the 1984 NCAA Championship, the 1984 Fred Haskins Award as the nation's best collegiate golfer, all in addition to being a three-time All-American.

John turned pro in 1985 and made it to the PGA Tour in 1986. He's won two tournaments: the 1987 Provident Classic and the 1993 Buick Southern Open. His other accomplishments include a 10th place finish at the 1993 Kemper Open, a pair of top 10 finishes in 1992 and four holes-in-one in the 1990s, all with a four-iron! He currently lives with his wife in Roswell, Georgia.

Preface

Welcome to the Carolinas!

Golf is played with a passion here, and we invite you to sample the Southern hospitality on and off the courses.

In North and South Carolina you have the best choices of golf courses in the world. We have studied and played them to provide this guide for choosing your own courses and for planning your golf vacation. The courses within each chapter are listed in alphabetical order for quick and easy reference. The chapters are organized to take you geographically from one end of each state to the other. We recommend enough variety of courses to suit every interest, whether you are a scratch golfer looking for the toughest challenges or a true beginner ready to learn. Even if you don't want to play, we recommend some tournaments that you can enjoy watching.

We wanted this guide to go beyond just providing great golfing information. We know that not everyone is a golf nut, so in each chapter we've given you details about other fun things to do. Plus, we've provided details about recommended accommodations and restaurants in each area to make planning your golfing getaway easier or to assure that you take fuller advantage of what each area has to offer.

Many of the accommodations we recommend at the end of each chapter will include golf in a package for you. Others may be more suitable for your non-golfing family or traveling companions with other interests (but don't worry — we've kept the recommended accommodations close to your courses for quick access).

We suggest restaurants suitable for any of the golfers we know, and we offer a medley of family activities in every location. Golf can be combined easily with other interests, and much is available to every visitor to the Carolinas.

The Insiders' Guide® to Golf in the Caroli-nas is intended to tempt you with enough basic information to help you understand our states' golfing mentality and add to your golfing pleasure. Please keep in mind that the greens fees for golf vary with the seasons, especially throughout much of the coastal area, with the more expensive golf being found during spring and fall. Also, rates typically increase a few dollars each year. We encourage you to call in advance for tee times and inquire about the cost as well as any special rates that may be available.

Although walk-ons are accepted at many Carolina courses, it's important to book tee times in advance if golf is the main purpose of your trip, especially if the choice of course or time of day is important to you.

Accommodations should be booked in advance to ensure availability, and be sure to inquire about golf packages, senior citizen discounts or other specials based on your length of stay. When calling for reservations, be sure to clarify the lodging's policy regarding cancellations. Unless otherwise noted, all accommodations accept most major credit cards.

The following price code key gives a general idea of the accommodation rates for the lowest charge for one room for two people for the places we note in each chapter.

Accommodations Rating Key

$50 to $75	$
$76 to $101	$$
$102 to $127	$$$
$128 to $153	$$$$
$154 and more	$$$$$

The following key explains the price range for an average meal for two at our recommended restaurants. As with accommodations, all restaurants accept at least MasterCard and Visa unless otherwise noted.

Restaurants Rating Key

Less than $20	$
$21 to $35	$$
$36 to $50	$$$
$51 and more	$$$$

We wish you par or better on your golfing excursions. And we hope all your non-golfing companions have (almost) as much fun as you golfers do. Let us know about your Insider experiences from following our recommendations in this guide so we can provide the best information possible in our annual updates.

How This Book Was Written

The authors of *The Insiders' Guide® to Golf in the Carolinas* visited each of the courses written about in this book. Inspections and reviews took place from February to October 1996. Scott Martin covered courses in North and South Carolina west of Interstate 95, and Mitch Willard covered courses to the east.

Courses were assessed either by playing a round or by riding a cart and surveying the layout. The positive aspects of the course were stressed in the belief that there's something commendable about every golf course, no matter how it may appear upon first inspection. It was physically impossible to review every public-access golf course in North and South Carolina (there are close to 600!), but we hope this book provides an excellent selection. We certainly tried!

As always, we welcome your comments and suggestions and encourage you to drop us a line:

The Insiders' Guides Inc.
P.O. Box 2057
Manteo, North Carolina 27954

Happy golfing!

About the Authors

Mitch Willard

. . . is a freelance writer in North Myrtle Beach, South Carolina. He plays golf every possible moment throughout the Carolinas, Virginia, Tennessee, California, Scotland or wherever an assignment or a whim may take him. He's steadily improving his game and fully intends to be good at it someday.

Mitch grew up in Lynchburg, Virginia, where he earned a master's degree in education and taught elementary school, then college, for more than 13 years. During that time he also learned to play golf and wrote numerous sports-related features for a variety of publications. The sports writing interest was born in high school when he was sports editor and photographer for the *High Times* newspaper.

A dedicated runner and fitness buff, Mitch enjoyed road racing for 17 years, then finally recognized that his aching feet would improve on the golf course but not on the road. When he moved to North Myrtle Beach more than three years ago, his love of golf intensified. Too many courses are readily available and affordable to deny the passion. He travels frequently for golf experiences and other business. Whenever an opportunity arises, a golf course always beckons. When not golfing or writing about it, he actually enjoys his real job as a Realtor, and he will talk to anybody about buying and selling property in any state.

His trip to St. Andrews, the home of golf in Scotland, during the research for this book, provided additional inspiration, if not reverence, for the game. Walking the links, seeing the home of the Royal and Ancient Golf Club and learning exactly how and where the phenomenon all began in 1400 CE brought an almost-religious experience into his life.

Mitch returned to his familiar courses in the Carolinas and to writing this book with renewed fervor and a true sense of belonging to the universal experience called golf.

Scott Martin

. . . was born in Cincinnati, Ohio, and raised in Montreal, Canada, and London, England. In 1984, he was awarded a Morehead Scholarship to the University of North Carolina at Chapel Hill where he took creative writing classes with Bland Simpson and Max Steele. He graduated from UNC with a BA in comparative literature. Following graduation, Scott spent almost a year in Denver, Colorado, where he coached a high school soccer team to an 0-15 record, accepted his first writing job and learned how to ski moguls without eating too much snow.

From Colorado, Scott moved to Charlotte, North Carolina, where he worked as a copywriter and typesetter. He then set out on his own as a freelance writer, specializing in preparing manuals for financial institutions such as Barclays American Mortgage and NationsBank. He also wrote articles for a number of local publications such as *Break* magazine and the *Charlotte Observer*. In 1992, he became editor of *SouthPark Update* magazine. And in 1995 he joined Knight Publishing's Subsidiary Publications department.

Scott took up golf seriously in 1992 and is a self-confessed addict. In four years, he has lowered his handicap from 28 to 10 and hopes to bring it down even further following his numerous travels and playing time as a golf writer for *The Insiders' Guide® to Golf in the Carolinas*. During the research for this book, Scott played golf at public and private courses throughout North and South Carolina and logged time on more than 730 miles of fairways and greens.

Outside work and golf, Scott is a member of the Charlotte Cricket Club and has twice completed the Charlotte Observer Marathon in less than four hours.

Acknowledgments

Mitch . . .

Writing *The Insiders' Guide® to Golf in the Carolinas* and updating it annually is a labor of love and a wonderful experience. What golfer would not want the opportunity to talk about and play some of the finest and best-known courses in the world?

First of all, I must thank my lovely wife, Liz, who constantly gave me encouragement and ideas that always seemed to come when they were needed the most. Without her, this book could not have been written so easily.

The staff and editors of The Insiders' Guides Inc. also need a special nod of thanks for all of their help. The atmosphere in their offices in Manteo, North Carolina, exudes information and ideas. Beth and Dan and the whole staff are ultimate professionals. Their help was tremendous. Let me also thank the *Charlotte Observer* for making the book possible.

This book could not have been written, of course, without the time and kindness of the club professionals, managers and staff at the golf courses. So many were as nice and helpful as they could possibly be. Some people really stand out for their courtesies to us and their knowledge and interest in assisting with our questions: Marcus Lund at Wild Dunes, Larry Snode at the Ocean Creek Course at Fripp Island, Marianne and Steve Harrison at Rhett House Inn, Gary and Sharon Groves at Cuthbert House Inn, Rebecca Scarborough at Scarborough Inn, Pam and Warren Bowen at Book and Spindle, Sharon and Don Neely at Park Avenue Inn, Dick Hester at Azalea Sands, the Myrtle West staff, Paul Kline at Tidewater, The Links Group and the Myrtle Beach National staff. They made the task of information gathering a joy.

Suffice it to say, everyone from the club professionals to the staff at the clubs and the rangers is very proud of their courses, and rightfully so. Most are glad to tell you about the course, and it gives them the perfect opportunity to do a little bragging about their home turf. After all, the Carolinas offer some of the best golfing opportunities in the world.

Many thanks also to my good friends — Fred Hickey, Rocky Burton, Jim Wilkes and Tom Hall — who gave me their constant encouragement and shared with me their knowledge and their time to talk and play golf. I am very lucky to have such supportive friends, and I thoroughly appreciate Sharon and Melvin Godfrey for helping me get a good start in the game of golf.

Scott . . .

Many, many, people throughout the Carolinas provided assistance with this book. I would particularly like to thank Holly Spofford Bell at Pine Needles, Luellen Cobb at Mid Pines, David Rucker at Myers Park Country Club, Peter Rucker at Hound Ears, Bill Hensley, Todd Smith at Charlotte Golf Links and The Divide, Beth Storie and Dan DeGregory at The Insiders' Guides Inc., Stewart Spencer and Linda Sluder at the *Charlotte Observer*, Tom Kirk-Conrad at Foxfire Resort, Dave Troupe, John Buckminster, Jeffrey Craig, Dave Tomsky and Dal Raiford at The Grove Park Inn, Ron Whitten at *Golf Digest*, Karen Miller, Melanie McGavran, Dennis Farley at The Squire's Pub in Southern Pines, David Craig, Chuck Cordell, Larry Williams (Bam!), Melody Dossenbach at Pinehurst Resort and Country Club, Irwin Smallwood, Dr. and Mrs. Walter Morris, Sylvain Blouin, Malcolm and Lauren Campbell, Chuck Lotz, Michael Pfaff, Steven Pandos, Sam Smith, Brian Laing, John Marks, Alan Knott, Jay Allred, Ron Green Jr., Dave Reece at Stoney Creek, Tom Jackson, Russell Breeden, H. C. Bissell, Ned Curran, James Fawcett, Americus "Max"

Lamberti at Pinehurst #2, Petie Miller, and Hector Ingram of Wilmington, North Carolina. And a special thanks to James J. Bissell for my back-cover photo.

I would also like to thank the numerous hard-working and amenable club professionals who graciously allowed me, often at a moment's notice, to play and review their golf courses. If there is a profession whose members are friendlier and more approachable, please let me know.

Throughout this book, you will find references to *Architects of Golf* (HarperCollins; 1981, 1993), researched and authored by Ron Whitten and Geoffrey Cornish. This 648-page volume is a must for any golfer interested in golf course architecture and design. It includes a history of golf course architecture, profiles of notable golf course architects from around the world and a list of their courses plus a comprehensive list of golf courses and their designers. It's a wonderful book that lovingly details the artists who create (and have created) the golf courses so many golfers enjoy every day.

Finally, I would like to dedicate this book to Thomas Martin as well as to the greenskeepers, golf course architects, entrepreneurs, pros, volunteers, rangers, manufacturers and others who work so hard and successfully to make excellent golf available to so many in North and South Carolina. Thank you all!

Table of Contents

Directory of Maps

Photo: Charles Slate, The Sun News

More than 90,000 people attended the SENIOR TOUR Championship,
played for the first time in Myrtle Beach in November of 1994.

Tournaments in the Carolinas

Tournaments come in every variety and take place at almost every course. You can probably play in some kind of tournament in the Carolinas any weekend you choose if you check around in advance. For instance, read about the International Summer Family Fun Tournaments, played all summer in Myrtle Beach, South Carolina, in our Family Golf Trips chapter.

If actually competing is more participation than you desire, join the galleries for some of the finest tournaments on spectacular scenic courses. Following are a few picks that we highly recommend.

SENIOR TOUR Championship

The Energizer SENIOR TOUR Championship will be played in Myrtle Beach every November for an indefinite number of years. It's the year-end tournament for the SENIOR TOUR's cream of the crop and an absolute grand finale for spectators who throng to the Grand Strand during the second week of the month.

This 72-hole tournament features the top 31 money leaders on the PGA SENIOR TOUR. In 1995, the top 16 Super Senior players (age 60 and older) were featured in a simultaneous but separate championship tournament. The largest purse of any PGA senior event and the largest combined purse of the super senior and senior tournaments were up for grabs.

This championship is played at the famed Dunes Golf & Beach Club where the 9th and the 18th holes (and almost all of the bars) overlook the ocean.

Anyone who loves to watch premium golf will go nuts over this tournament. Set against a sunny backdrop of warm and glorious fall days on one of the world's best-maintained and prettiest golf courses, spectators can watch the year's accumulation of champions vie for the top spot. Despite the tournament pressure and the tough course, players take time out for autographs and conversation and relax by the Atlantic while the world's television cameras tell their stories. If you're lucky, you can watch the tournament then shuttle back to your home or hotel and watch it again on ESPN. (Is that too much, or what?!) If you're really smart, you'll plan at least part of your vacation for early November. You can even play 18 holes a day (except at the Dunes Club, of course) then watch the seniors and super seniors finish their rounds.

We must admit that most of our favorite players are currently on the PGA SENIOR TOUR (does that mean we're getting older?!). It features the all-time greats — some who get better with age and many who have developed the personalities that attract loyal followers.

INSIDERS' TIP

Don't substitute lessons for practice. Lessons should guide your practice.

Any Golfer's Home Course

If you are reading this book you are undoubtedly a golfer — or planning to become one. If you are either, you owe it to yourself to visit the mecca of golf where the game was first played — St. Andrews' Old Course. With today's airfares, the trip might cost less than

you think if you plan ahead and check for special deals, and your adventures will be unforgettable. You will probably want to fly into Glasgow, Scotland, and hire a car for an easy drive to St. Andrews.

At St. Andrews, you will almost certainly feel that you are at your home course. Playing golf here is an unbelievable experience. Just walking the Old Course is incredible. It's a fabulous feeling to walk the course — or step down into one of the bunkers — that has played host to some of the most famous shots in golfing history. You *must* do this to truly appreciate the shot-making ability of Hogan, Nicklaus, Palmer or Watson.

According to John Philp, a professional with the Links Group at St. Andrews, ". . . no professional would say that the Old Course is the best links in the world. But it's the atmosphere that makes it."

You have easy access to the Old Course. It's on public land, and you can walk it any day after all play has finished. When you walk the fairways and greens of St. Andrews, you absolutely will be in awe of your surroundings.

Getting a tee time at the Old Course might seem like a hassle to those of us who are accustomed to calling the course a day or two before we want to play. A strict procedure must be followed. You may write the Links Management Committee, St. Andrews, Scotland KY169JA and request a tee time. Or, if you don't have any luck this way, you may want to show up at the course and put your name in the hat for any tee times open for that day. For assistance in booking your golf or accommodations in the United Kingdom or

The Royal and Ancient Golf Club of St. Andrews has
hosted many Open Championships.

neighboring countries, you will find all the help you need with Graeme Pook at Executive Golf & Leisure, 16 Melville Terrace, Stirling, Scotland FK8 2NE, telephone (44) 1786-451464. Don't leave home without plenty of money. Golf at the Old Course costs about $120, including a caddie (a major part of your game). Also, in order to play the Old Course, you must have a USGA handicap card. Ask your local pro about this.

If you don't succeed in getting a tee time at the Old Course, don't despair; you can play the adjacent New Course without too much trouble. If you play there and your golfing appetite is still not fulfilled, you have a number of other choices, one of which should go to the top of your list. Take a 30-minute drive to Angus. There, you'll find what Walter Woods, custodian of the Old Course for the last 21 years, calls "the number one course in the world" — Carnoustie Championship Course. Plus when you watch the British Open on television in 1999, you can tell all your friends you played there way back when. Getting a tee time at Carnoustie is less difficult than at St. Andrews.

A short drive down the coast is the Kirkcaldy District, with 11 courses in a 12-mile radius. Also nearby: Leven Links, Ladybank Golf Club, Lundin Golf Club and Scotscraig Golf Club. All of these are great courses; oftentimes, they're used during qualifying rounds for the British Open.

A final word to the wise: Don't go to Scotland thinking you may get a great deal on golf equipment. A set of name-brand golf clubs sells for about $1,400. For a sleeve of golf balls, you will pay about what Americans expect to pay for a box of 12 or 15 balls. But, be aware that you don't have to put up with the hassle of lugging your own clubs across the Atlantic; almost all courses and golf shops rent them.

So if your appetite has been whetted, don't hesitate. Make your reservations now for a golf excursion. Or better yet, plan on going to a future British Open. In 1997, it will be played at Royal Troon; in 1998, at Royal Birkdale; and in 1999, at Carnoustie.

Ticket information is available from the PGA by calling (803) 444-4STC.

Accommodations offering ticket packages are listed in Myrtle Beach Golf Holiday's *Vacation Planner*. To obtain a free copy, call (800) 845-GOLF. Myrtle Beach Golf Holiday is the host organization for the tournament.

Heritage Classic

The Heritage Classic has been played annually in April at Harbour Town Golf Links at Sea Pines Resort on Hilton Head, South Carolina, since 1969. The plaid winner's jacket has been donned by some of golf's true greats. The pros choose to play here because of the island's charm as well as the course's challenge, and the venue is the spectator's choice for the tradition and distinction that accompany this tournament.

The course, designed by Pete Dye and Jack Nicklaus in 1969, is continually listed in any ranking of top layouts. The greens are small and well-protected. The 18th hole is one of the country's most recognized, and the wind from the sound usually becomes a factor.

Call Sea Pines Resort at (800) 925-4653 for more information.

INSIDERS' TIP

At the practice range, shoot at a target. Employ a trial-and-error method, and don't be distraught if things don't always work out. You should expect to make mistakes in practice — that's what it's for. Use your imagination, especially with your short game, and find out what works for you.

DuPont World Amateur Handicap Championship

Anyone with an established handicap, no matter what it is, can play in this tournament. And anyone can win it!

The DuPont World Amateur Handicap Championship, the world's largest amateur golf tournament, is played the last week in August every year. It will be played for its 14th year in Myrtle Beach, South Carolina, in 1997, on more than 50 courses. It's a four-day, 72-hole flighted tournament open to any amateur with a verified USGA handicap (or foreign equivalent).

The DuPont Company of Wilmington, Delaware, is the title sponsor of the tournament, which is owned by Myrtle Beach Golf Holiday and managed by Golf Digest Sports Marketing.

All types of golfers from all locations compete in the World Am. It began with 680 golfers and has now grown to more than 4,000 players. Many participants return year after year to renew golfing friendships and play in a fun tournament. It's a true spectacle when they all bring their guests and gather in the convention center each evening to view scores and swap stories. Just the socializing alone, lubricated by lots of free-flowing drink, is enough to bring most folks back annually.

Players fly and drive to Myrtle Beach from every state and 20 or more foreign countries. The greatest number of golfers, of course, play in the men's division, although senior men and super seniors are loyal to the tournament, and the numbers of women increase every year.

Participants have been as old as 86 and as young as 16.

The grand prize is often something supersnazzy, such as a Lincoln luxury automobile. All entrants are eligible for the drawings, which include thousands of dollars worth of prizes.

For entry information, call (800) 833-8798.

In Connecticut or outside the United States, call (203) 373-7162.

PING Myrtle Beach Junior Classic

The PING Myrtle Beach Junior Classic will be played for the ninth year in June 1997. It's one of 34 tournaments nationwide conducted by the American Junior Golf Association (AJGA) and is one of the most popular stops on the tour.

Nearly 500 golfers between the ages of 13 and 18 apply annually, and 106 are selected by the AJGA. Another 14 are selected during the first-day qualifying round. Participants typically represent at least 17 states.

Myrtlewood Golf Club hosts the 54-hole tournament.

For information on this event, promoted by Myrtle Beach Golf Holiday, contact tournament chairman George Hilliard at (800) 845-GOLF.

Paine Webber Invitational Seniors Tournament

The PGA SENIOR TOUR makes one of its more lucrative stops in Charlotte at the TPC at Piper Glen. Arnold Palmer designed the course (with Ed Seay) and serves as tournament host. He personally invites some of the bigger names on the tour to participate. Past competitors include Chi Chi Rodriguez, Gary Player, Ray Floyd, Lee Trevino, Jim Dent, Bob Charles and Bob Murphy. The tournament is typically held in the first few weeks of summer — before it gets too hot.

The Paine Webber Invitational has been a popular event with Charlotte golf fans — and with good reason. It's a chance to see some players who, in their prime, were among the finest in the world. The course at Piper Glen is something to behold, as are

INSIDERS' TIP

If you're just beginning golf, find an easy or short course and play at times when it's not particularly busy.

How to Get Here

A car trip to the Carolinas is delightful from anywhere, because the road system is well-maintained and abundant nature can be seen from the roadways in each of these two states.

Interstate 95 traverses both states from north to south. Interstate 85 also runs north-south, passing through Greensboro and Charlotte in North Carolina and through Greenville in South Carolina. Interstate 40 bisects North Carolina east-west, giving drivers an opportunity to see Asheville in the western part of the state; historic Winston-Salem and Old Salem in the Piedmont; the well-known Triangle area, including Raleigh, Durham and Chapel Hill;

and Wilmington where the interstate ends near the coast. Interstate 77 goes north-south through western North Carolina, crosses I-40 and stops in Columbia, South Carolina. Interstate 20 crosses the South Carolina border at Augusta, Georgia, goes through Columbia and stops in Florence, South Carolina. Interstate 26 runs diagonally across South Carolina from Greenville in the Piedmont to the Lowcountry and Charleston.

Raleigh-Durham, Wilmington, Charlotte and Charleston boast international airports. Asheville and Greensboro in North Carolina and Columbia, Myrtle Beach, Florence and Greenville/Spartanburg in South Carolina all have domestic airports that offer various jet and connector flights daily. If you choose to travel by air, you will probably first arrive in Charlotte — a major hub. This is convenient, as Charlotte is on the border of the two states, and you can rent a car, enjoy the scenery and be almost anywhere in either state within 4½ hours.

No matter what mode of transportation you choose, the Carolinas offer you an opportunity to view all aspects of Mother Nature, from the Great Smoky Mountains of North Carolina to the Lowcountry and beaches of South Carolina. And the states' efficient interstate system will make it possible for you to get to your chosen golf courses easily.

the houses that surround the track. Most spectators watch the back nine, where you'll find some of the more difficult holes on the course. A great place to stake out a spot is the green on the par 5 16th, as most of the pros can reach the green complex in two shots. Then the short-game clinic take place. Most players get up and down (somehow) for birdie, proving why they are professionals — and reminding many of us spectators why we are amateurs.

Another fun place to watch is the par 3 17th. It's a short iron shot downhill to a multi-level green backed by water. The comment you'll hear the most from the gallery is, "Look how easily they swing — I'm going to swing less hard from now on!" Right. It's also reassuring to see the pros goof . . . you quickly realize that even those who play golf for a living are human.

As some of the bigger names on the regular tour are now playing the senior tour, this tournament is bound to grow in popularity. Most of the players seem to enjoy TPC at Piper Glen, Arnold Palmer is a big magnet, the money and extracurricular activities are good here, and the galleries are well-behaved, jovial and knowledgeable.

For more information, call (704) 543-9677.

Fieldcrest Cannon
LPGA Classic

The Fieldcrest Cannon Classic is a relatively new stop on the LPGA Tour. If all goes

Photo: Lake Norman Magazine

Spectators were numerous at the Fieldcrest Canon LPGA Classic,
played in September at The Peninsula Club.

well, tournament organizers and sponsors hope it will become an annual event. The inaugural 1995 tournament — the first LPGA event in Charlotte — was staged in the fall at The Peninsula Club on Lake Norman. Rees Jones designed this challenging private course.

Some of the stars of the LPGA Tour at this event: Nancy Lopez, Betsy King, Dottie Mochrie, Beth Daniel, Pat Bradley and Patti Sheehan. Quite a field.

For more information, call (704) 378-4410.

Chrysler Greater Greensboro Classic

Two weeks after The Masters, the professionals on what Insiders call the "Big Boys Tour" come to Greensboro for the Chrysler Greater Greensboro Classic. It's not a major, nor is it one of the biggest events on tour. Nonetheless, it's a popular tournament that attracts an excellent field.

Past winners include Sandy Lyle and Davis Love III.

The tournament is played at Forest Oaks Country Club near Greensboro. The course was designed by Ellis Maples and is set up as challenging as possible for the pros. You'll find the tees all the way back at the tips of the tee boxes. The rough is deep, and the greens are extremely fast. Despite these hurdles, the pros still manage to fire under par just about all day. If you've never attended a PGA tournament — and seen just how far the big boys hit the ball and how well they putt . . . well, you should check out the GGO in person.

For tickets and information, call (910) 379-1570.

Vantage Championship

On the last weekend of September each year, the top 78 money winners on the PGA SENIOR TOUR gather at the Championship Course at Tanglewood, in Clemmons, North

INSIDERS' TIP

Ask your friends to point you in the direction of a successful teaching pro in your area. If you can't get a lesson time very easily, take that as a good sign.

Carolina, to play in one of the richest and most popular events on that tour: the Vantage Championship. You'll see Trevino, Floyd, Irwin, Dent, Charles and other successful pros who are older than 50 and still able to play some serious golf.

It's worth attending this tournament to see the Seniors play on the difficult yet pictur-esque Championship Course at Tanglewood. It's a public course (see our Triad chapter), so you might want to play it a couple of weeks before the tournament then see how the pros approach the same hole on which you scored double bogey.

For ticket and other information, call (910) 766-2400.

The Outer Banks

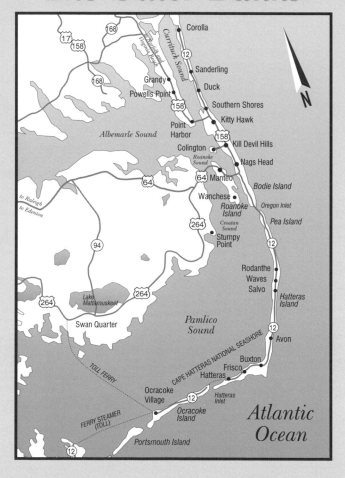

North Carolina's Outer Banks

The Outer Banks of North Carolina make us think of big sand dunes, fishing communities, hammocks, hang-gliding, windsurfing and glorious, relaxing family vacations. It's also the newest and best-kept secret of the golfing world. Popular and upscale as well as mid-range, courses here offer excellent golfing experiences, and the surrounding beach communities offer everything else for a complete vacation.

The Outer Banks north of Oregon Inlet include Corolla, Duck, Southern Shores, Kitty Hawk, Kill Devil Hills and Nags Head; Roanoke Island to the west includes Manteo and Wanchese; and to the south are Hatteras and Ocracoke islands. All of the golf courses are easily accessible from Manteo, Duck, Southern Shores, Kill Devil Hills, Kitty Hawk or Nags Head. Then go south to Hatteras or Ocracoke for some easy days of pure relaxation, maybe with a fishing pole or just a good book.

Currituck Club

N.C. Hwy. 12, Corolla
• 261-5261, 453-9400
Championship Yardage: 6800
Slope: No rating	**Par: 72**
Men's Yardage: 6490	
Slope: No rating	**Par: 72**
Other Yardage: 6170	
Slope: No rating	**Par: 72**
Ladies' Yardage: 5180	
Slope: No rating	**Par: 72**

Carolinas Golf Group created the Currituck Club, Corolla's only golf-resort community, as part of a 600-acre development. It promises the upscale ambiance appropriate for the Outer Banks gentry and like visitors. The land

has been used by a historic shooting club since the mid-1800s, and that will be preserved on one end of the development. The dense vegetation and several spectacular dunes provide an opportunity for a true links-style layout. It's the last available large tract of land of its kind along the Outer Banks.

The 18-hole Rees Jones course opened in July 1996. The club is offering a limited number of memberships, beginning with property owners. Public play is welcome daily. We recommend playing this course right away, as it is sure to be busy and popular once the surrounding homes are filled with golfers. The community will include a clubhouse and various amenities plus private beach access and 5 miles of bike trails that were not yet complete as we researched this place. Fees, any walking restrictions and slope ratings were not available when this book went to press.

Duck Woods Country Club

50 Dogwood Tr., Kitty Hawk • 261-2609
Championship Yardage: 6578
Slope: 132	**Par: 72**
Men's Yardage: 6161	
Slope: 129	**Par: 72**
Ladies' Yardage: 5407	
Slope: 127	**Par: 73**

This 18-hole country club is the oldest course on the Outer Banks; it boasts a pristine setting among tall pines and other foliage. The club aims to accommodate its 900 members, many of whom are non-locals, but will accept public play year round.

Housing surrounds parts of the course but does not inhibit play. You shouldn't be afraid

GOLF COURSES ON THE OUTER BANKS OF NORTH CAROLINA

Course	Type	# Holes	Par	Slope	Yards	Walking	Booking	Cost w/ Cart
Currituck Club	semiprivate	18	n/a	n/a	n/a	n/a	n/a	n/a
Duck Woods Country Club	semiprivate	18	72	129	6161	yes	2 days	$52
Goose Creek Golf & Country Club	semiprivate	18	72	109	5943	no	2 days	$28-$38
Nags Head Golf Links	semiprivate	18	71	126	5717	no	365 days	$75
The Pointe Golf Club	semiprivate	18	71	109	5426	yes	call	$37-$52
Sea Scape Golf Resort	semiprivate	18	72	123	6052	no	90 days	$40-60

to cut loose with a long shot; you won't find a window close enough to break.

Ellis Maples designed the course. Fairways are narrow, and water comes into play on 14 holes. Greens are bentgrass.

Warm up before playing Duck Woods because the course begins with a bang: a 481-yard par 5. Stay warm for the entire round because it ends with a 506-yard par 5. Shot placement is key on this course. For example, on the par 5 14th, you must lay up in front of the water bisecting the fairway.

Duck Woods is a friendly but unforgiving course; again, every shot must be placed carefully.

The driving range, putting green, target greens and a practice bunker are open to the public the day of play only.

Club rentals are available. The pro shop is stocked primarily with balls and tees but includes limited equipment and apparel as well. A clubhouse, locker rooms for men and women, a bar and restaurant are available to members. Beer and wine are sold to nonmembers, but no other alcoholic beverages are offered (the club does not hold a liquor license).

Walking is not allowed. Booking is accepted a week in advance for members and two days in advance for nonmembers. The greens fee, including cart, is $63 year round.

Goose Creek Golf and Country Club
U.S. Hwy. 158, Grandy
• 453-4008, (800) 443-4008
Championship Yardage: 6191
Slope: 114 **Par: 72**
Men's Yardage: 5943
Slope: 109 **Par: 72**
Ladies' Yardage: 5558
Slope: 116 **Par: 72**

Okay, technically speaking this course is not on the Outer Banks, but it's just minutes away across the Currituck Bridge on the mainland. Besides, we think Goose Creek has the

FYI

Unless otherwise noted, the area code for all businesses listed in this chapter is 919.

Also note that the MP found in many addresses in this chapter stands for milepost, a common location designator on the Outer Banks. Milepost 1 starts in Kitty Hawk, toward the northern end of the Outer Banks. The milepost markers end in South Nags Head, at MP 21.

right idea, the club's philosophy summed up on its score card: "Golf is a fun, relaxing, competitive sport. Enjoy Goose Creek to its fullest potential."

Goose Creek is one of the most player-friendly courses we have seen. The main objective is for golfers to have a good time and come back again. This is not a course where you will lose countless balls and go home frustrated. This *is* a course for the whole family. In fact, family golf outings are encouraged, and children are welcome during a recommended time frame conducive to young golfers who are learning the game.

The clubhouse is a former hunting lodge. The owners have converted the small bedrooms into private locker rooms for players. The homey atmosphere is derived from the owners' receptive attitudes as well as the ambiance of the pine-paneled lounge and snack bar — retaining the feel of the lodge living room and kitchen.

Steve and Bill Jernigan built the course four years ago from a Jerry Turner and Associates design. The Jernigans believe in their golfing concepts and are interested in the development of packages to bring golfers to the Outer Banks for the fun aspects of the game in a comfortable Southern-style atmosphere.

Bermudagrass greens and fairways grace the flat Goose Creek course, which is not a typical beach layout. The tree-lined fairways are relatively tight on the front nine and more undulating and open on the back. Greens are relatively small.

No. 13 is considered the signature. During fall and winter, the wind in your face presents the difficulty; during summer, the wind is at your back, thus the hole plays quite differently. A few water hazards exist and could come into play on five holes.

After playing Goose Creek, you should feel confident and upbeat about your game. It's a course for high-handicappers as well as seasoned golfers.

Photo: Village at Nags Head

Wind off the water presents an interesting challenge to Outer Banks golfers.

A driving range and practice green are available.

Walking is allowed for members only. Greens fees range from $35 during late afternoons to $40 for prime morning tee times. A three-day golf pass is offered for $99.

Nags Head Golf Links
Village at Nags Head

5615 S. Seachase Dr., off U.S. Hwy. 158, MP 15, Nags Head • 441-8073, (800) 851-9404

Championship Yardage: 6126
Slope: 130   Par: 71
Men's Yardage: 5717
Slope: 126   Par: 71
Other Yardage: 5354
Slope: 123   Par: 71
Ladies' Yardage: 4415
Slope: 117   Par: 71

This course offers enticing beauty along the Roanoke Sound. Views of the water are spectacular on almost every hole. Architect Bob Moore remembered not to mess with Mother Nature too much when he designed this course, and he left intact almost all of the wonderful natural setting.

With the wind whipping around the course, its proximity to the ocean and its design, this course could easily be mistaken for true Scottish links. If your ball travels out of the fairway, plan to spend time searching the dense undergrowth. The distance is fully realized because of the strength and influence of the constant winds. This is especially true on the 583-yard par 5 18th. It runs dangerously close to the Roanoke Sound and, therefore, truly tests your skills as a golfer. This course is difficult, and a less experienced golfer may want to play from the mid-front ("Other") tees. You also may want to leave your woods in the bag and play only with irons because, many times, your drive will get caught in the wind and blown offline.

In addition to the wind, water and wetlands present challenges, coming into play on all but four holes. Nags Head Golf Links requires both muscle and mind. Houses on the course may present a fear of breaking glass if you don't have control of your tee shots. After hitting each tee shot, you might need to look up and say a quick prayer that your shot lands somewhere near where you'd aimed.

Of the five par 3s, none is a "gimme." The

INSIDERS' TIP

Carry a current rule book (which, of course, you've read).

Alternative Routes to the Outer Banks

As golf courses of the Outer Banks become a dominant attraction, the need for several access routes is apparent. Let's face it, most of us want to know, "How long does it take to get there?" Well, improvements are in place as of May 1996. The Wright Memorial Bridge, the main access to the Outer Banks from points north, has been expanded from a single two-lane span to four lanes across two spans.

The Monitor-Merrimac Memorial Bridge-Tunnel (I-664), connecting Chesapeake and Newport News in Hampton Roads, is a time-saver. If you are coming from the Washington, D.C., area, take I-95 S. to I-295 north of Richmond, and follow signs to I-64 E. toward Norfolk and Virginia Beach. Follow I-64 E. until you get to Hampton. Go south on I-664 toward Newport News and through the tunnel; then take I-64 toward Norfolk/Virginia Beach; go south on U.S. Highway 17 at Deep Creek, Virginia, to South Mills, North Carolina. Pick up N.C. Highway 343 S. to U.S. Highway 158 E., which will take you directly to the Outer Banks.

An alternative from Hampton is to follow I-64 E. to Exit 290B (Battlefield Boulevard S.). Proceed past Chesapeake General Hospital (on the right) and exit right onto Va. Highway 168 S. Remain on Va. 168 into North Carolina; it eventually merges with U.S. 158 E. at Barco. Then follow U.S. 158 E. to the Outer Banks.

From points west and south, take I-95 to Rocky Mount, North Carolina, and pick up U.S. Highway 64 E. This route will take you to Manns Harbor, across the William B. Umstead Bridge to the north end of Roanoke Island and into Manteo. Follow U.S. 64 E. through Manteo and across the Manteo-Nags Head Causeway to access the beaches. At Whalebone Junction, take N.C. 12 south to reach Oregon Inlet, Hatteras Island and Ocracoke Island, or U.S. 158 to Nags Head, Kill Devil Hills, Kitty Hawk, Southern Shores, Duck and Corolla.

While there are currently just three vehicle access points to the Outer Banks — the Wright Memorial and William B. Umstead bridges and the ferry to Ocracoke — there are certainly alternate routes on the mainland, some of which may help you discover new and wonderful things. Who knows . . . you might find a way to take a couple of minutes off the trip back home.

cruelest par 3 is the 221-yard 15th. With one quick gust of wind, your ball could either be in sand on the right or in the pond in front of the green. This course changes almost minute by minute. You can be standing on the tee box with wind hitting you in your face, take a quick glance at the flag and notice the wind blowing the exact opposite direction on the green.

Nags Head Golf Links has a pro shop, bar, restaurant, driving range, putting green and rental clubs. The Links Grille overlooks the 9th green and Roanoke Sound.

Walking is not allowed. Greens fees, including cart, range from $50 to $75. A nine-hole shoot-

out is played every Sunday afternoon from May through September. Kids play free after 5 PM on Fridays and Saturdays. And tee times may be booked up to 12 months in advance.

This is a golfing experience that every golfer should appreciate, regardless of ability. A round here will make your visit to the Outer Banks unforgettable. It's also the place to remember: Golf is just a game. But golf on this beautiful course, regardless of your score, is a game worth playing.

Danny Agapion is a super professional, and you will be welcome at Nags Head Golf Links.

Pointe Golf Club

U.S. Hwy. 158 E., Powells Point • 491-8388
Championship Yardage: 6320
Slope: 120   **Par: 71**
Men's Yardage: 5911
Slope: 113   **Par: 71**
Other Yardage: 5428
Slope: 108   **Par: 71**
Ladies' Yardage: 4862
Slope: 110   **Par: 71**

Pointe Golf Club opened on July 1, 1995, and according to David A. Donovan III, the resident pro, it is as nice as any course in the country now. Donovan brings just the professionalism and personality the course deserves.

A Russell Breeden design, it's the first course in the country to have A1 bentgrass. This new disease-resistant, dense grass has been researched extensively at Penn State University, and Keith Hall, Pointe owner and president of United Turf, is a perfectionist when it comes to lush grass. The site of the course formerly was a turf farm, thus a special bit of attention was given these perfect greens. Hall and his friendly staff are devoted to providing the finest course conditions, including lush tifdwarf fairways.

No development surrounds this course, save the few scattered farmhouses that add to the character of this rural Carolina-mainland community.

Although built in an area known for links-style golf courses, the Pointe is more of a traditional-style course. The scenery is quite beautiful, as the Pointe overlooks the Currituck Sound. Strategically placed water hazards come into play on 15 holes, and generally windy conditions ensure that the course will never play the same way twice.

The signature hole is No. 6, a 457-yard par 4 with a carry over wetlands, a blind shot to the fairway, water, bunkers and slopes to the right.

The 18th hole plays an exciting 619 yards from the back tees. Your drive has to hit the fairway. Three perfect shots will make your birdie for the day.

A driving range, practice bunker, full-size putting green, clubhouse, pro shop and restaurant are available. The newness of the facilities is quite classy, and we think you'll appreciate the course's beauty.

Walking is allowed after noon from October 1 until May 24 for greens fee pass-holders. Call to inquire about options for couples, junior or individual passes. Greens fees are $52 in peak season (spring) and $37 after October. Packages are available through area rental companies.

Sea Scape Golf Club

300 Eckner St., off U.S. Hwy. 158 E.,
MP 2½, Kitty Hawk • 261-2158
Championship Yardage: 6408
Slope: 127   **Par: 72**
Men's Yardage: 6052
Slope: 123   **Par: 72**
Ladies' Yardage: 5536
Slope: 114   **Par: 73**

The Scottish links-style course is cut into the maritime forests of Kitty Hawk and the signature dunes of the Outer Banks. It was designed by Art Wall, with bentgrass greens and fairways. The fairways are somewhat wide.

Sea Scape is the second-oldest course on the Outer Banks, and it has aged beautifully since 1965. At Sea Scape, as at virtually all seaside courses, but particularly those on the Outer Banks, you not only play the course but also the wind. The course derives its character from the natural surroundings, with water views from almost every hole. If the wind is unforgiving and your shot lands in the rough, you will be looking for it in sand and sea oats as well as scrub.

The most challenging hole is No. 11. It's long and always plays against the prevailing wind. The par 3 141-yard 9th is aesthetically appealing from its elevated tee. Club selection is imperative here depending on the direction of the wind. Your shot easily could bounce off the road if you have a good tail wind. With its five par 3s and five par 5s, Sea Scape is a true test of your golfing ability as well as your patience. Housing along Sea Scape is sometimes close to the course and surrounded by woods.

Sea Scape is somewhat different this year following the addition of bulkheads and other structural changes on several holes, so you might want to try this course again if you haven't played it in 1996.

Sea Scape has a teaching center, club fitting, rental clubs, a driving range, bar, restau-

rant and a fully stocked pro shop. Bryan Sullivan has been Sea Scape's professional for many years. He has loads of knowledge about the course and always takes the time to discuss its intricacies.

Walking is not allowed. Greens fees range from $40 to $60, including cart. Advance tee times are available whenever you call, which means to call well in advance of your arrival if you plan to be here during the busy summer season.

Around the Outer Banks . . .

Tourism is king on these once barren, now booming barrier islands. As a result, the type, price range and selection of accommodations, restaurants and activities span the gamut. Regardless of your personal preferences and tastes, we think you'll find something here to satisfy you and yours.

Explore the options, especially in the off-season when locals' spirits rise and temperatures and lodging rates fall into a comfortable range. We suggest you pick up a copy of *The Insiders' Guide® to North Carolina's Outer Banks* to help in your search for a wonderful stay. These books are available in bookstores nationwide or through direct order — use the handy order form at the back of this book. Or, check out the Insiders' Guide Homepage on the Internet at www.insiders.com/outerbanks. And if you find yourself on Roanoke Island, stop by The Insiders' Guides Inc. headquarters on the Manteo Waterfront, meet the folks who help bring you these invaluable guidebooks and let them know how they're doing — they'll welcome your feedback.

Fun Things To Do

On the Outer Banks, you're sure to enjoy the beaches and the sand dunes, which are unlike any others anywhere else in the world. Looking for something truly unique? Try recreational clamming at **Hatteras Village Aqua Farm**, off N.C. Highway 12, just north of Hatteras Village, 986-2249. Rent a rake and bucket for $3 and sift the tidal flats of private clam beds to find your own dinner (22¢ per clam up to 100 in aggregate) at the only rake-your-own clam farm on the East Coast. If you

tire of harvesting mollusks, we suggest you follow Tony Bennett's advice: "When in Rome, do as the Romans do. . . ." On the Outer Banks, you must do some fishing, even on a golf trip; it's the greatest lure for most vacationers here, and many locals do it for a living, so there must be something to it, right? In fact, these barrier islands are renowned for offering some of the best fishing opportunities in the world. Call **Oregon Inlet Fishing Center**, N.C. 12 at the northern terminus of the Bonner Bridge, 441-6301, or **Pirate's Cove Marina**, Nags Head-Manteo Causeway, 473-3906, to get on a head boat or arrange a charter. Or stop by one of the many bait and tackle shops to get the gear you'll need for shore or pier fishing.

If angling isn't your activity, enjoy any one of the many quaint villages where biking or strolling is better than driving. Appreciate the native arts and crafts in the galleries, shops and boutiques prevalent all along the Outer Banks. You will find some enticing buys to remind you of your vacation here.

The **Wright Brothers Memorial**, U.S. Highway 158, MP 8, Kill Devil Hills, will teach you all about the world's first flight in a heavier-than-air plane. Plan on spending several hours at this educational and interesting site. National Park Service interpreters lead you through the historic events that started humankind's love affair with air travel, and the monument near the location of those first flights is a worthwhile stop. An entrance fee of $2 per person or $4 per car is charged. Call 441-7430 for information.

Dowdy's Amusement Park, U.S. Highway 158 (S. Croatan Highway), MP 11½, Nags Head is open from late spring through Labor Day, with a Ferris wheel and rides for the kid in all of us. Call 441-5122 for information.

Hang-gliding and windsurfing are important sports on the Outer Banks, for good reason: The wind here is as consistently good as anywhere on earth for related recreational activities. Surfers also find consistent seasonal breaks at a number of spots, especially on Hatteras Island. Shops to help get you catching the big one, be it wave or wind, are all over the place.

The *Lost Colony* historical drama tells the story of the first attempt at English settlement in the New World. Summer nights are enchanting when you enter the outdoor amphitheater and immerse yourself in the mystery. Call 473-3414 or (800) 488-5012 for information about tickets ($14 for adults, $7 for children younger than 12). Scheduled performances happen nightly except Saturdays, from early June through late August. Waterside Theatre, performance site of the *Lost Colony,* is off U.S. Highway 64/264 on the north end of historic Roanoke Island.

The **North Carolina Aquarium,** Airport Road, on the north end of Roanoke Island is open daily. Become acquainted with crabs, sharks, Loggerhead turtles and other marine creatures from the nearby Atlantic. The aquarium is open 9 AM to 6 PM Monday through Saturday and 1 to 5 PM on Sunday. Admission is $3 for adults, $2 for senior citizens and active military, $1 for kids ages 6 through 17 and free for children younger than 6. Call 473-3494 for more information.

The *Elizabeth II* is a representative 16th-century sailing ship, commemorating Sir Walter Raleigh's Roanoke Voyages. The **Elizabeth II State Historic Site** is a museum about life in the 16th century. It's easy to find on Ice Plant Island, across from The Insiders' Guides Inc. headquarters on the Waterfront in Manteo; it's worth a visit. Call 473-1144 for information on admission and changing hours.

The country's oldest-known grapevine grows off Mother Vineyard Road in Manteo. The Mother Vine is believed to be 400 years old. A small winery owned by the Etheridge family cultivated the vine on Baum's Point making the original **Mother Vineyard** wine until the late 1950s. Mother Vineyard Scuppernong is still produced, and the sweet pink wine is available locally.

The **Elizabethan Gardens** were initiated in 1951 by the state garden club as a memorial to the people of Sir Walter Raleigh's lost colony. Herbs, wild and native flowers and statuary combine with the history and mystery

> ## FYI
>
> Unless otherwise noted, the area code for all businesses listed in this chapter is 919.
>
> Also note that the MP found in many addresses in this chapter stands for milepost, a common location designator on the Outer Banks. Milepost 1 starts in Kitty Hawk, toward the northern end of the Outer Banks. The milepost markers end in South Nags Head, at MP 21.

for a fantastic and beautiful adventure. Admission is $3 for adults, $1 for youths ages 12 through 17 and free for children younger than 12. Call 473-3234 for information on seasonal hours. And, if you go, take a camera.

Want to pick up a few bargains? Check out **Soundings Factory Stores,** U.S. Highway 158, MP 16½, Nags Head, 441-7395, where you'll find discount prices everyday on major name brands such as Bass, Bugle Boy, Van Heusen, Corning, Pfaltzgraf and more. Browse through several collections of boutiques on the northern beaches from Corolla to Duck: Scarborough Faire, Wee Winks Square, Osprey Landing, the Waterfront Shops, TimBuck II and Corolla Light Village, to name just a handful.

The **Cape Hatteras Lighthouse,** off N.C. Highway 12, Cape Point in Buxton, is probably the most recognizable symbol of the Outer Banks. Explore the visitors center, with its interesting exhibits and gifts, or climb the 268 steps to the top of this 180-foot, black and white spiral-striped structure from. Climbing is permitted from May through Columbus Day. (Please note: It's a strenuous climb.) The light still flashes its warning to mariners, and a visit here will fascinate both young and old.

Where To Eat

Refer to our Preface for an explanation of the pricing code.

Corolla

Grouper's Grille & Wine Bar
$$$$ • TimBuck II, Corolla • 453-4077

This new restaurant offers recipes with influences from Thailand, India and Greece, among other locales. The pasta, chicken, steak and local seafood entrees are eclectic and tasty. The vegetarian offerings include wonderful things, such as an appetizer of our favorite Portobello mushrooms with vegetable

A Bird's-eye View

Standing on any tee box at almost any golf course along the Outer Banks, you can look around to see some of the most fantastic scenery in the world. The intrinsic beauty of the ocean is awe-inspiring.

Another way to capture the flavor of the area is to take a drive from the northern banks south along N.C. Highway 12 through Pea Island National Wildlife Refuge to Hatteras Village at the southernmost tip of Hatteras Island.

Then take advantage of the North Carolina ferry system, which will shuttle you to Ocracoke Island. Of course, ferries also run between Ocracoke Village and points on the North Carolina mainland, so visitors accessing the Outer Banks from points south can also utilize this service. It is truly a wonderful experience, and we think it will be one of the small but meaningful pleasures of your trip.

The North Carolina Department of Transportation Ferry Division operates seven routes within its system. It is not only a great excursion but a valuable service to Outer Banks citizens and visitors alike. The ferry service runs its fleet of more than 20 vessels year round. Some trips (Hatteras to Ocracoke) take as little as 45 minutes. Others (Ocracoke to Cedar Island)

---

pesto and a spinach lasagna with seasonal vegetables and a white wine tomato marinara sauce. Or, try the blackened shrimp salad with orange thyme vinaigrette dressing. Everything is fresh and original. Dessert is an experience all its own. We suggest the chocolate bag with white chocolate mousse and raspberry sauce garnished with fresh fruit. An extensive selection of wine and beer is available to accompany your meal, which is served on white tablecloths bathed in candlelight. Don't dress up if you feel casual. Reservations are recommended. Grouper's serves dinner only.

Duck

Duck News Cafe
$$ • N.C. Hwy. 12, Duck • 261-1549

Italian entrees, shrimp served three ways and creative local crab and tuna entrees are good choices here. The aged beef tenderloin is delicious, and the perfect evening topper is Key lime pie or the Lady Godiva, a sinful concoction of ice cream drowned in chocolate liqueur. Reservations are recommended for this family restaurant across from the Sanderling Inn. Dinner is served spring through fall, and lunch also is served during the summer.

Blue Point Bar & Grill
$$$ • The Waterfront Shops, Duck
• 261-8090

This is favorite locals haunt for imaginative, expertly prepared food, served in an atmosphere that doesn't take itself too seriously. The menu centers on what's fresh, rather than a set selection. Try a tuna entree, prepared in a way you never would have thought up yourself but will wish you could duplicate. Enjoy a steak and potato dinner that's anything but usual. And, if you usually don't have dessert, make an exception here. Reservations well in advance are an important idea, as is a visit to this waterfront bistro for lunch or dinner.

Elizabeth's Cafe & Winery
$$$ • Scarborough Faire, off N.C. Hwy. 12, Duck • 261-6145

As the name implies, wine is a primary focus here. If you like wine and want to learn a few things, you'll appreciate the choices at this warm and casual establishment, recognized from 1991 through 1995 by *The Wine Spectator* magazine. New in 1996 is a walk-in wine cellar, a retail sales area and expanded seating to accommodate additional patrons.

last as long as 2½ hours. Don't feel like you have to take these rides only in the daylight hours. We took the ferry ride from Cedar Island to Ocracoke on the last ferry of the day — 8:30 PM. Granted, it was a clear night, but the sky put on a great display of lights that can only be appreciated at sea.

The ferry system in North Carolina began on the Outer Banks in the 1920s and was run by a private enterprise. The first ferries took passengers across Oregon Inlet. After 13 years of subsidizing the privately owned ferry system, the state took over the service in 1947.

Call (800) BY FERRY for information about reservations, varying costs and schedules. The trip from Cedar Island to Ocracoke Island costs $10 per car, and the ferry from Ocracoke to Hatteras Island is free.

Photo: Phil Ruckle

Travelers on the ferry between Hatteras and Ocracoke experience close encounters of the feathery kind.

The changing menu offers eclectic country French and California dishes. Fresh seafood is prepared with fresh ingredients in creative and varied ways, and all desserts are homemade and delicious.

Dinner is served year round, and lunch is served as well in season. Reservations are recommended. Also, a new wine bar is open on summer afternoons, offering steamed shrimp, cheese and croissants, and microbrew beers in addition to the fine wines. Ask about the prix-fixe dinner for $75 per person, which includes six courses and accompanying wines. Elizabeth's has a strict no-smoking policy.

Fishbones Raw Bar & Grill
$$ • Scarborough Ln., Duck • 261-6991

Fishbones is in the Scarborough Lane Shoppes next to Scarborough Faire. It opened in the summer of 1995 and was immediately popular and successful. This restaurant has one of the best raw bars we've experienced in the area. The oysters are reasonably priced and icy cold. Some raw bars serve oysters plucked from a can and placed on a shell — not at Fishbones. You can sit at the bar and watch the bartender shuck them on the spot. You might want to initially ask for extra cock-tail sauce, because it's that good, as are the Bloody Mary's — hot and spicy. The raw bar is open all day, with more than a dozen selections.

Fishbones also serves the usual burgers and chicken entrees for lunch. However, for an alternative, you might give the veggie burger a try. It will make your mother happy . . . you'll have had your vegetables.

If you can't get there for lunch or the raw bar, don't fret: Fishbones also serves dinner. The tuna steak is fresh everyday, and it's great; or try lobster tails or pasta with fresh clam sauce. Evenings during the season, live music adds to the already nice atmosphere.

Before you leave, check out the array of T-shirts. You'll want one to remind you of your wonderful time here.

Kitty Hawk

Ocean Boulevard
$$$ • Beach Rd. (N.C. Hwy. 12), MP 2, Kitty Hawk • 261-2546

This restaurant was created by the same people who operate The Blue Point in Duck. Ocean Boulevard is in the former 1949 Virginia Dare Hardware Store building. The food is fresh and original. A good appetizer is poached oysters with horseradish risotto and fresh dill. The delightful entrees feature pasta, beef, shrimp, pork chops or fish, and you're sure to find a wine selection to accompany any dish. Reservations are recommended, and hours vary seasonally. This is a classy restaurant — popular with good reason.

Kill Devil Hills

Awful Arthur's
$$ • Beach Rd. (N.C. Hwy. 12), MP 6, Kill Devil Hills • 441-5955

Awful Arthur's is popular for steamed seafood and beer . . . lots of each. Locals keep it busy and even have their own specials offered all day Mondays. It's a casual and typical beach place, with some of the biggest fresh oysters shucked by fast and friendly bartenders who also serve a variety of drink. Landlubber sandwiches and platters are available if you're not a seafood lover.

Petrozza's Deli and Cafe
$$ • Dare Centre, U.S. Hwy. 158, MP 7, Kill Devil Hills • 441-2519

This is a casual place to eat in, or you can take good food home. Choose any of the deli sandwiches or salads served with fresh bread baked daily. Lunch and dinner specials offer variety at a great price. The sesame noodles, pasta salads and Italian standbys (meatballs, eggplant parmigiana, lasagna, stuffed peppers, etc.) are offered every day. Beer, wine, cappuccino and espresso are available too. Call 441-1642 for a recorded message listing the day's specials. Lunch and dinner are served during season; winter hours vary, so call first.

Goombay's Grille and Raw Bar
$$ • Beach Rd., MP 7½, Kill Devil Hills • 441-6001

Come to this fun spot if you're looking for a great time to go with your great food. It's noisy at times, but it's the sound of people having fun, so just join in. The food is built around a Caribbean theme (as is the colorful decor) and centers on fresh seafood and pastas. Our absolute favorite chicken-wing appetizer is served here. Or try the spicy crab balls

or sweet coconut shrimp. Daily specials also include some kind of stir-fry. There's a full line of beer, wine and spirits to wash it all down. And, of course, the Key lime pie (our favorite) is irresistible. For the price, quality of food and fun atmosphere, this place is hard to beat.

Chardo's
$$ • U.S. Hwy. 158, MP 9, Kill Devil Hills • 441-0276

Go during the winter for the pasta buffet, or anytime for the steak and pasta specials. Veal chops also are a specialty. Italian or California wine accompanies the entrees and salads. A coffee bar is available for after-dinner beverages. Desserts are made fresh here, and the cannolis, tiramisu or napoleons make for a great finish to any meal. Chardo's is open all year for lunch and dinner. Watch for cooking classes — great fun.

Nags Head

Kelly's Outer Banks Restaurant & Tavern
$$$ • U.S. 158, MP 10½, Nags Head • 441-4116

There are those people who feel their Outer Banks experience isn't complete without a visit to Kelly's. What keeps them coming to this place in droves? Well, it could be the great seafood or the extra-fun atmosphere or the bar where you can dance the night away to live bands. Maybe you see all your friends here. Go see for yourself. And tell Collis, the big guy who watches the bar entrance, that the Insiders sent you.

The raw bar is a great place to begin the meal. Dinner is the only meal served here, and choices include fresh seafood dishes, chicken, pasta or beef. You might like the sweet potato biscuits so much, you'll be full without the entree.

Penguin Isle Soundside Grill
$$$ • U.S. Hwy. 158, MP 16, Nags Head • 441-2637

Another place with an outstanding wine list — *The Wine Spectator* has heralded it "one of the best in the world" for the past four years — Penguin Isle also offers off-season wine dinners and full-time nice ambiance. The views of the Roanoke Sound are as soothing as the sunsets are spectacular. Fresh pasta, seafood, breads and creative pairings are delectable. Our favorite appetizers are seafood gumbo and black bean cakes. The desserts are also worth a taste. Penguin Isle is open from March through December. We highly recommend dinner here.

Soundside Pavilion
$$$ • U.S. Hwy. 158, MP 16½, Nags Head • 441-0535

All summer long, you will find a full surf-and-turf buffet here, and the view of the Roanoke Sound adds to the attraction. Fruits, salads, rolls, desserts and ice cream are included with such delectable items as fish, chicken, clams, barbecue, pasta, oysters and crab legs. A breakfast buffet is served daily in season, including pancakes, ham, corned beef hash, sausage, bacon, eggs, grits, French toast, fruit and all the coffee you can hold.

The Dunes
$ • U.S. Hwy. 158, MP 16½, Nags Head • 441-1600

Breakfast and lunch are popular here — especially the breakfast bar where you will see a big crowd being efficiently handled daily during the summer and weekends from February through November. If you don't like a buffet, try the crab omelette. Delicious seafood or steaks at moderate prices for dinner also are served with a salad bar, and everyone can find something good. Keep an eye out for the all-you-can-eat specials (we don't miss the soft-shell crab nights). The Dunes is also known for its friendly service.

Owens' Restaurant
$$-$$$ • Beach Rd., MP 16½, Nags Head • 441-7309

This restaurant is an Outer Banks tradition. In 1996, Owens' celebrated 50 years of fine dining and attentive service. It's the area's oldest restaurant continuously owned and operated by the same family. Seafood reigns supreme here, and it is prepared to perfection. Try the crab cakes — they melt in your mouth. Or pick a live Maine lobster from the tank for steaming. And beef tops the list if seafood isn't your choice. Homemade chowders are good beginnings, and homemade desserts are good endings. The wine list is substantial, or you can enjoy a drink from the upstairs piano bar. One visit to Owens' and we bet it will become a dining tradition for you too. Owens' is open for dinner only from mid-March through New Year's Eve.

Roanoke Island

1587
$$$ • At the Tranquil House Inn, Queen Elizabeth St., Manteo • 473-1587

Named after the year the English colonists attempted to permanently settle Roanoke Island, 1587 is one of the finest restaurants on the Outer Banks. The presentation is superb and meets the chefs' goals of standing apart from the mainstream. In fact, this is truly one of the best dining experiences we've had anywhere.

Savor some of the best-prepared delicacies at 1587, creations of Executive Chef Donny King who offers a constantly changing menu. For an appetizer, we like the grilled Portobello mushroom on a zucchini podium with balsamic-sauteed julienne vegetables. A great entree is the ocean panache of tiger prawns, mussels, scallops and fish tossed with vegetables and orzo pasta finished with feta cheese. A good selection of wine and beer is available, and brown bagging is allowed. Don't be in a rush. This is an experience, not just a meal. Reservations are suggested, and you should call for dinner hours, which change seasonally.

Full Moon Cafe
$$ • At the Waterfront, Queen Elizabeth St., Manteo • 473-MOON

A cozy cafe overlooking Shallowbag Bay from its second-story vantage point, this eclectic eatery opened in late 1995 and already is overflowing with local and visiting patrons. The cuisine here is creative and fun, featuring items we haven't seen on any other Outer Banks restaurant menu. Hummus spread, baked brie and crab dip are three of our favorites for appetizers. Lunch includes gourmet sandwiches, vegetarian offerings, seafood, chicken and homemade soups, such as Hungarian mushroom, curried spinach and spicy tomato, that change daily. Each entree is served with chips and Full Moon's own salsa. A separate dinner menu offers enticing seafood dishes, stuffed chicken breasts, roasted eggplant and nightly specials. All the desserts are delightful. Beer and wine are served.

You can eat inside the lovely little dining room, dine outdoors in the courtyard beside the soothing fountain or order any meal to go. Reservations are not accepted. Full Moon is open for lunch and dinner seven days a week in summer. Hours are more limited in the off-season, so call for specific schedules.

Weeping Radish Brewery & Bavarian Restaurant
$$ • U.S. Hwy. 64, Manteo • 473-1157

The most important thing here is the beer — varieties and flavors you'd never dream of. Enjoy some samples with a hearty Bavarian meal, or go during the afternoon for brewery tours. The Weeping Radish features an outdoor beer garden, separate pub, children's playground and two-story dining room. The traditional fare includes veal, spaetzle, sauerbraten and, of course, cooked red cabbage. It's open all year for lunch and dinner. The restaurant's name comes from the radish that is served in Bavaria with beer. It's cut in a spiral, sprinkled with salt, then put back together. The salt daws out the moisture and gives the radish the appearance of weeping.

Hatteras Island

The Froggy Dog Restaurant
$$ • N.C. Hwy. 12, Avon • 995-4106

Go to the Froggy Dog for a big breakfast, quick lunch or affordable dinner. Check out entertainment nightly in the Lily Pad Lounge and take home a T-shirt from the upstairs gift shop. And drop in daily for the happy-hour steamed shrimp. The restaurant is open every day year round, which is important on Hatteras Island: Not many establishments here stay open in winter. The steaks, burgers and

chicken are good if you ever tire of seafood. We like the broiled, fried or sauteed seafood entrees.

The Pilot House
$$$ • N.C. Hwy. 12, Buxton • 995-5664

This restaurant provides a lovely view of the Pamlico Sound, and the seafood, including a variety of shellfish, is fresh and well-prepared. Seafood bisque is a specialty. Oysters Rockefeller are as good here as anywhere we've been. The hand-cut grilled steaks are good too — but save room for the fresh fruit cobbler. The restaurant is open for dinner only from mid-April through late fall. Beer and wine are served in the upstairs lounge.

Ocracoke Island

Howard's Pub and Raw Bar
$ • N.C. Hwy. 12, Ocracoke • 928-4441

Probably the only place on Ocracoke Island open for a late-night visit in the off-season, everyone congregates here; it's a good destination for casual fun, occasional live music and dancing. The raw bar is good (and the only one around), and simple, tasty burgers and sandwiches are served day and night. Jalapeño poppers are good appetizers, and prime rib is a good entree. Beer and wine are served, including some 175 types of domestics, imports and microbrews as well as the owner's own label of red or white wines.

The Back Porch
$$$$ • 1324 Country Rd., Ocracoke • 928-6401

Owners John and Debbie Wells renovated this older building to blend with the natural landscape (note the waist-high cacti!). It's a quiet place to enjoy a first-class meal and comfortable conversation. Many folks don't think twice about the two-hour drive from Nags Head — including the free ferry ride — just to eat here.

The menu bursts with fresh herbs, vegetables and seafood, most of which is caught

---

INSIDERS' TIP

Count your clubs before beginning play and be sure to take the same number home with you.

nearby. All dressings, sauces, breads and desserts are made in the Wells' huge kitchen. Quality ingredients meld in each recipe in eclectic and sensational taste combinations. Sample the crab beignets or smoked bluefish appetizers. Enticing entrees include the Cuban black bean and Monterey Jack cheese casserole and the crab cakes with red pepper sauce. Fresh-ground coffee is served, and the wine list and beer selection are as ambitious as the rest of the menu. If you get hooked on the food — like we are — you may buy a copy of *The Back Porch Cookbook* and try your hand at some of the Wells' recipes at home. (After perusing this book, we're all the more impressed by the apparent culinary acumen needed to create such involved concoctions.) Dinner is offered nightly in season.

Where To Stay

Refer to our Preface for an explanation of the pricing code.

Duck

Advice 5¢
$$$$ • 111 Scarborough Ln., Duck
• 255-1050

This charming bed and breakfast inn opened in 1995 and offers four guest rooms and one suite, all with private baths, rocking chairs and decks. The suite includes color cable TV, stereo and Jacuzzi. The atmosphere is warm and inviting, as is the hospitality you'll receive from owners Nancy Caviness and Donna Black. Quiet-time activities, such as games, puzzles and books, are at hand. You may use locking storage for your gear — golf clubs, surf boards or fishing poles. A continental breakfast buffet of fresh-baked breads and fruit salad is served in the morning, and an afternoon tea tempts guests with homemade goodies and hot and cold drinks. The inn is open all year and is a non-smoking accommodation.

Sanderling Inn Resort and Conference Center
$$$$ • 1461 Duck Rd. (N.C. Hwy. 12), Duck • 261-4111, (800) 701-4111

The Sanderling Inn Resort occupies 12 acres of wilderness along the ocean. It's like an old beach home (a BIG one), with wooden siding and rocking chairs on the porch. The 86 rooms include robes for lounging, continental breakfast, afternoon tea and complimentary wine and cheese. The 28 rooms in the main building have kitchenettes. Another 32 rooms in the Sanderling Inn North are equipped with wet bars and refrigerators, and a newer south wing has 26 rooms with wet bars, refrigerators, microwaves, stereos with compact disc players, 1½ baths, king-size beds and double sleeper sofas. Two guests per room will have privacy and comfort here. Conference and meeting facilities are offered in another building. The beaches are private; the health club includes an outdoor pool, indoor pool, whirlpool, two exercise rooms, locker rooms, tennis courts and a walking/jogging trail. Ask about seasonal discounts or special holiday packages. Handicapped-accessible rooms are available at this year-round inn.

Kitty Hawk

Outer Banks Golf Getaways
$$-$$$$ • U.S. Hwy. 158, MP 2, Kitty Hawk • 255-1074, (800) 916-OBGG

This real estate company packages golf at four Outer Banks courses and offers private homes and condominiums from simple oceanside retreats to spacious homes for large groups. Tee times are confirmed in advance for you, and private or group lessons or club rentals can be scheduled. All packages include accommodations, a breakfast allocation, one round of golf per day, linens, towels and departure cleaning. Non-golfer rates also are available.

We recommend Outer Banks Golf Getaways if you travel with a group of golfers or possibly a large family. The ease of booking your golf and accommodations with one phone call is appealing for simple vacation planning.

3 Seasons Guest House
$$$$ • U.S. Hwy. 158, MP 2, Kitty Hawk • 261-4791, (800) 847-3373

This is a perfect bed and breakfast inn if you want to play Seascape Golf Course every day. The house overlooks the 9th green and is across the street from the clubhouse and pro shop. The ocean is just a few blocks away too. Bicycles, a common area, a Jacuzzi, complimentary cocktails and a full breakfast cooked to order add just about anything you could want for a great golf vacation. Other courses are only a few minutes away. Susie and Tommy Gardner offer five bedrooms — four of them for double occupancy. This inn is open April through November and is suitable for nonsmoking adults.

Beach Haven Motel
$$ • Beach Rd. (N.C. Hwy. 12), MP 4, Kitty Hawk • 261-4785

This is a small hotel with six semi-efficiency units across the street from the beach. Coffee makers, refrigerators, hair dryers and porch chairs are provided. A portable phone is available. Some units are large enough for up to four people. Croquet, grills and picnic tables and a putting green provide additional outdoor opportunities. It's open April through October.

Kill Devil Hills

Tanglewood Motel
$$$$ • Beach Rd. (N.C. Hwy. 12), MP 8¼, Kill Devil Hills • 441-7208

Eleven one- or two-bedroom apartments are available in this oceanfront motel. The one-bedroom units have a sleep sofa and accommodate four adults. One of the large apartments can accommodate up to 10 people. They have complete kitchens, cable televisions and full baths. A phone is available by request. Amenities include an outdoor pool, sun deck, outdoor bathhouse, boardwalk to the beach, picnic tables and grills. The motel is open April through October.

Cavalier Motel
$$$ • Beach Rd. (N.C. Hwy. 12), MP 8½, Kill Devil Hills • 441-5584

This oceanfront motel has 40 rooms with double and single beds. Six one-room efficiencies have two double beds and kitchenettes. Two pools, volleyball and shuffleboard

FYI
Unless otherwise noted, the area code for all businesses listed in this chapter is 919.

Also note that the MP found in many addresses in this chapter stands for milepost, a common location designator on the Outer Banks. Milepost 1 starts in Kitty Hawk, toward the northern end of the Outer Banks. The milepost markers end in South Nags Head, at MP 21.

courts are within the three one-story wings. Another 13 cottages are available as weekly rentals. Pets are allowed in the cottages. The Cavalier, a well-maintained family property, is open year round.

Colony IV Motel
$$$ • Beach Rd. (N.C. Hwy. 12), MP 9, Kill Devil Hills • 441-5581, (800) 848-3728

You can practice your putting at the nine-hole miniature golf course, then you can challenge your partners to a game of horseshoe at the pits here. Cindy and Tom Kingsbury run a nice family oceanfront motel with 87 units. They offer rooms with two doubles or one king-size bed. Fourteen units are efficiencies; one has a Jacuzzi. Some have direct beach access, and others have oceanfront balconies. The Colony is open April through November.

Cherokee Inn Bed and Breakfast
$$$ • Beach Rd. (N.C. Hwy. 12), MP 8, Kill Devil Hills • 441-6127, (800) 554-2764

This former hunting and fishing lodge across the road from the beach offers six rooms with private baths, remote control color televisions, ceiling fans and comfortable wicker furnishings. Five rooms have queen-size beds, and the other has a double and a twin bed. The atmosphere is homey, and guests may borrow bikes or gather on the porch for conversation. The inn is owned by Kay and Bob Combs, second-generation proprietors. This property has been an inn for 18 years and a bed and breakfast inn for nine. Continental breakfast is included. No smoking is allowed. The inn is open April through October.

Nags Head

Surf Side Motel
$$$$ • Beach Rd. (N.C. Hwy. 12), MP 16, Nags Head • 441-2105, (800) 552-7873

The friendly folks at this oceanfront hotel

will go out of their way to make your Outer Banks experience a good one. The rooms in this five-story structure all have ocean views, and some even have sound views also. All rooms have refrigerators, color cable TVs, phones and private balconies. Why not book the honeymoon suite (you can make this visit a second or third honeymoon!), with a king-size bed and private Jacuzzi? Complimentary coffee and sweets are provided for early-morning convenience, and an afternoon wine and cheese get-together is the perfect way to end a great day on the golf course. Indoor and outdoor pools, an indoor Jacuzzi and strolls on the beach are other recreation options.

The Nags Head Inn
$$$$ • Beach Rd. (N.C. Hwy. 12), MP 14, Nags Head • 441-0454, (800) 327-8881

This crisp, white oceanfront hotel is near the golf courses and the Oregon Inlet Fishing Center as well as Nags Head, Kill Devil Hills and Roanoke Island attractions. Amenities include an indoor/outdoor pool and refrigerators in every room plus a wide, inviting beach expanse. One suite includes a sitting room, wet bar and Jacuzzi.

Oceanfront rooms have private balconies; streetside rooms have sound views. Nonsmoking and handicapped-accessible rooms are available on each floor. The conference room accommodates up to 30 people. The inn is open year round.

Blue Heron Motel
$$$ • Beach Rd. (N.C. Hwy. 12), MP 16, Nags Head • 441-7447

This small family-owned motel is a fine choice for a well-managed beach front property. Double or king-size beds are available in 19 rooms, and 11 efficiencies provide full kitchens and sleep up to four people. All rooms have coffee pots, refrigerators, microwaves and televisions. One room is handicapped-accessible. Private balconies are available on the second- and third-floor rooms. The motel is open year round and offers weekly rates.

First Colony Inn
$$$$ • U.S. Hwy. 158, MP 16, Nags Head • 441-2343, (800) 368-9390

This landmark hotel has been moved and refurbished since it began in 1932. In 1988, the Lawrence family rescued the beachfront hotel from demolition, sawed it into pieces and moved it to undergo a three-year renovation. This Old Nags Head-style inn is listed on the National Register of Historic Places. The 26 rooms are now traditional and modern yet are enduring reminders of the old days at the beach.

Deluxe continental breakfast and afternoon tea are included in your stay. Classical or jazz background music in the reception area are reminders of earlier days, as are the English antique furniture and toiletries. A television, heated towel bars, tile baths, a telephone, refrigerator and individual climate control are standard in each room. Some rooms offer wet bars, trundle beds, Jacuzzis, VCRs and private balconies. The oceanfront gazebo across the street is a pleasant spot to while away some time after you leave the pool. The inn is open year round.

Roanoke Island

Scarborough Inn
$$ • U.S. Hwy. 64, Manteo • 473-3979

This is one of our favorite places to stay, especially when traveling without very young children or large groups of golfers. Furnished with authentic antiques, it's a charming and friendly atmosphere, carefully created and preserved by the family and managed by Fields and Rebecca Scarborough. Each room, piece of furniture and collectible holds a story that the family can relate. Although on the main street of this delightful village, the inn is tucked away and private, more so than the larger beach accommodations. Continental breakfast — muffins and a pot of coffee — is served to your room. Borrow a bicycle and explore historic Roanoke Island, or walk across the street for some food or drink. If Scarborough Inn is full, the Scarborough family also oper-

Photo: Phil Ruckle

Outer Banks golf courses are challenging and well-maintained.

ates Scarborough House in another nearby, lovely part of town. The inn is open year round.

White Doe Inn
$$$$ • Sir Walter Raleigh St., Manteo • 473-9851, (800) 473-6091

When you're looking for luxurious accommodations with the personal attention found at a bed and breakfast, look no further than the White Doe Inn. Bob and Bebe Woody, owners of this Queen Anne-style house, restored the property and added modern conveniences and niceties such as fireplaces (in every room), antique furniture, tile bathrooms (two with a Jacuzzi), stained-glass windows, lovely linens and finishing touches (Godiva chocolates on your pillow).

The inn is in a quiet neighborhood in Manteo — a perfect starting point for exploring all that Roanoke Island has to offer (see our "Fun Things To Do" section).

A full breakfast is served each morning, and tea and coffee with sweets are offered in the afternoon. Guests may take the inn's bicycles out for a spin on the 6-mile Manteo Bike Path or just sit in the front porch swing and watch the goings-on of this charming little town. The inn is open all year, and you should inquire about off-season rates.

Hatteras Island

Lighthouse View Motel
$$-$$$ • N.C. Hwy. 12, Buxton • 995-5680

The Hooper family has operated this establishment on the big curve in Buxton for more than 36 years. The 73 oceanfront and oceanside units include your choice of efficiencies, duplexes, motel-style rooms, villas or cottages. Amenities include an outdoor pool and a hot tub. Windsurfers, surfers and fishing vacationers all enjoy this motel, which is in close proximity to the landmark Cape Hatteras Lighthouse, renowned windsurfing mecca Canadian Hole and myriad restaurants and shops.

Cape Hatteras Motel
$$$$ • N.C. Hwy. 12, Buxton • 995-5611, (800) 995-0711

Owners Carol and Dave Dawson offer basic rooms as well as efficiencies that sleep six, with double beds as well as kings and queens. Part of the motel has been here for more than 30 years. Nearby Canadian Hole is a notable venue for windsurfers. The motel is also popular among anglers, beachcombers and surfers. Guests enjoy an outdoor swimming pool and spa. The motel is open all year.

Ocracoke Island

Berkeley Center
$$$, no credit cards • N.C. Hwy. 12, Ocracoke Village • 928-5911

This is a nine-room bed and breakfast inn, renowned for its hand-carved paneling of redwood, pine, cypress and cedar. Seven rooms have private baths, and the other two rooms share a bath. The manor house was built in 1860 and remodeled in 1950; the ranch house dates from the mid-50s. This inn is tucked away from everything, and the spacious rooms are furnished without telephones or televisions for the times you really want to escape. A television is available in the guest lounge if you suffer from withdrawal without one. The living and dining rooms, with their country estate-type atmospheres, are gathering spots for guests. Continental breakfast includes coffee and fresh breads and fruits served in the breakfast room of the manor house. The inn is open April through October.

Golf Equipment

Teed Off Discount Golf and Tennis, Three Winks Shoppes, U.S. Highway 158, MP 1, Kitty Hawk, 261-GOLF, offers major proline equipment, club repair service and custom clubs as well as supplies and apparel. Another option is **Smash Hit Tennis & Golf**, Scarborough Faire, Duck Road (N.C. Highway 12), Duck, 261-1138, which stocks a limited supply of golf clothing, equipment and accessories. These two places might have just what you're looking for. If not, you'll probably find what you need at the pro shops, especially those at Nags Head Golf Links and Sea Scape.

New Bern, Edenton, & Eastern North Carolina

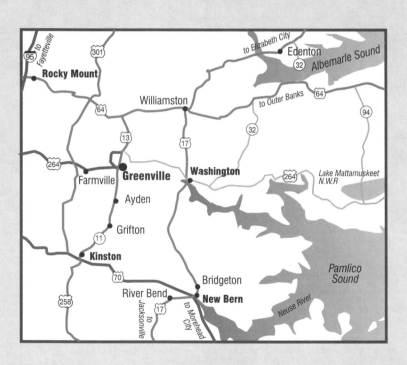

New Bern, Edenton & Eastern N.C.

Much of Eastern North Carolina is rural, and the scattered towns all have their own character that derives from their industries of agriculture, fishing, clothing manufacturing, boat building, cabinet making and, in the case of Jacksonville, Camp Lejeune military base. The area is not one you would primarily choose for a golf vacation, but you will find quality courses that are worth playing. The locale is quiet, and most courses are just enough off the beaten path to be appreciated by golfers who like to include a relaxing round with their vacations.

Bath is North Carolina's first town, founded in 1705, and the notorious pirate Blackbeard reportedly was one of the early residents here. Today, you can enjoy the historic district with the state's oldest church and three restored historic house museums from the 18th and 19th centuries.

The river town of New Bern is the second-oldest city in North Carolina, named by its Swiss settlers in 1710 after the Swiss capital of Bern. The black bear emblem emblazoned throughout the town also came from Bern. The city is at the confluence of the Neuse and Trent rivers, both of which influence most of the area's recreational pursuits. New Bern's downtown has been carefully restored to display a panoply of architecture, along with antiques shops, restaurants, specialty shops and art galleries. More than 200 homes here are listed on the National Register of Historic Places, and the 2,000 crape myrtles surrounding them are an attraction themselves. Tryon Palace, built by the royal governor in 1770, is open for tours and is the setting for summer re-enactments of historical events.

One of the city's many claims to fame: New Bern is where Pepsi-Cola originated.

Don't plan on too much wild nightlife or fast-paced activities. Just come to New Bern for some peace and quiet, and to appreciate its history — along with watersports and golf.

Historic Edenton is on Edenton Bay at the head of the Albemarle Sound, and it's home to a prestigious collection of 18th-century buildings. A guided tour of the historic district includes St. Paul's Church, Cupola House, Chowan County Courthouse National Historic Landmark, James Iredell House State Historic Site, Barker House and other outstanding examples of period architecture. Little has changed in this small town while centuries have crawled past; only the new golf courses, downtown shopping boutiques and modern conveniences will remind you of the date.

For more information on Eastern North Carolina, pick up a copy of *The Insiders' Guide® to North Carolina's Central Coast and New Bern* or *The Insiders' Guide® to North Carolina's Outer Banks* (also available online at www.insiders.com/outerbanks).

Ayden Golf & Country Club

Golf Club Rd., Ayden • 746-3389
Championship Yardage: 6784

Slope: 117	**Par: 72**
Men's Yardage: 6282	
Slope: 117	**Par: 72**
Ladies' Yardage: 5057	
Slope: 106	**Par: 72**

This is a straightforward, compact course — not extremely demanding. Water only comes into play on four holes. The 18-hole layout, designed by Clay Stroud, opened in

GOLF COURSES IN EASTERN NORTH CAROLINA

Course Name	Type	# Holes	Par	Slope	Yards	Walking	Booking	Cost w/ Cart
Ayden Golf & Country Club	semiprivate	18	72	117	6282	yes	1 day	$12-25
Carolina Pines Golf & Country Club	semiprivate	18	72	111	5845	yes	60 days	$24-28
Chowan Golf & Country Club	semiprivate	18	72	118	5921	yes	1 day	$30
Farmville Country Club	semiprivate	18	71	113	5640	yes	1 day	$18
Harbour Point Golf Links	public	18	72	113	5998	yes	4 days	$24-34
Indian Trails Country Club	public	18	71	118	6172	yes	1 day	$19-24
River Bend Golf & Country Club	semiprivate	18	71	109	6019	yes	5 days	$22-25
Rock Creek Country Club	semiprivate	18	72	110	6233	yes	no	$20-25
The Emerald Golf Club	semiprivate	18	72	124	6451	no	2 days	$37

1952. Bermudagrass covers the greens and fairways.

The front nine has narrow fairways, so accuracy counts from the beginning. No. 7 is a 515-yard par 5 with an extremely narrow fairway for your tee shot. It opens a bit, but the green is small.

The 18th is a long hole (618 yards) that doglegs slightly right. Bunkers surround the front of the green.

Amenities include practice greens, a driving range, pro shop, locker room, bar, grill and club rentals.

Walking is allowed. Year-round greens fees are $12 to walk and $20 to ride during the week and $17 and $25, respectively, on weekends. Tee times may be set up three days in advance.

Carolina Pines Golf & Country Club

390 Carolina Pines Blvd.,
New Bern • 444-1000
Championship Yardage: 6270
Slope: 115   Par: 72
Men's Yardage: 5845
Slope: 111   Par: 72
Ladies' Yardage: 4784
Slope: 108   Par: 72

Bermudagrass during the summer and winter rye during colder months grace this 18-hole course designed by Frank Marmarose, Ron Broissoit, Jim Stallings and Joe Hughes. It's not exceptionally long and, therefore, is often preferred by some of us who need all the help we can get to score well. This course wanders among residential areas and over lagoons near the Neuse River.

The signature 15th hole is a medium-distance par 5, reachable in two shots with a good drive. Trouble spots are left and right and behind the green, so the hole requires a decision and some straight shooting.

Carolina Pines has a pro shop, club rentals, a driving range and target greens. Also available are tennis courts, a pool and a clubhouse with lounge and patio.

Daily year-round greens fees, including cart, are $29 before noon and $25 after. Tee times may be booked a month in advance.

The staff is cordial, which always keeps us coming back, even though Carolina Pines is a bit off our routine path.

Chowan Golf & Country Club

1101 W. Soundshore Dr., Edenton
• 482-3606
Championship Yardage: 6392
Slope: 122   Par: 72
Men's Yardage: 5921
Slope: 118   Par: 72
Ladies' Yardage: 5062
Slope: 112   Par: 72

Although this 18-hole course has more than 300 members, the public is welcome. Fairways are bermudagrass; nine greens are bermudagrass and nine are bentgrass.

No. 3 is a par 4 that runs along S. Sound Drive, and a stream bisects the fairway 35 yards from the green. If you clear the stream, you still must contend with four bunkers in front of the green. Pine trees are widely spaced along the fairway.

The 4th hole is an unusual par 4. You have to play it like two par 3s because of the water that juts out in the path of your tee shot and flanks the fairway on the left and out-of-bounds on the right; water also juts into the landing area. Then you must hit to an elevated green.

No. 5, originally a par 5, has been changed to a par 4. It's a sharp dogleg right off the tee, with out-of-bounds to the right and water to the left. The green slants away from you and is not an easy receptacle for your shot.

Amenities include a practice green, driving range, pro shop, beer and beverage sales, club repair and regripping. Lessons are available.

The cost is $30 for greens fee and cart. Walking is generally allowed but is restricted

FYI

Unless otherwise noted, the area code for all phone numbers in this chapter is 919.

INSIDERS' TIP

Allow faster players to play through. You'll have more fun by observing proper etiquette and not feel rushed by someone waiting for you.

during the weekend morning hours. Tee times are first-come, first-served.

Chowan Golf & Country Club is a few miles outside historic Edenton. Mulberry Hill, a new upscale residential development along the sound, flanks the golf course.

Cypress Landing
600 Clubhouse Dr., Chocowinity
• **946-7788**
Championship Yardage: 6849
Slope: No rating	**Par: 72**

Men's Yardage: 6421
Slope: No rating	**Par: 72**

Other Yardage: 5976
Slope: No rating	**Par: 72**

Ladies Yardage: 4989
Slope: No rating	**Par: 72**

This course opened in July 1996. Weyerhaeuser Real Estate Company plans to develop a community with homes overlooking water or the tree-lined course. Cypress Landing is an 18-hole semiprivate club on the Pamlico River. Ault, Clark & Associates designed this course with bermudagrass greens and bentgrass fairways. Each hole offers four sets of tees, so golfers of any ability can enjoy a game here.

You'll find a driving range, putting green, rental clubs, pro shop and a beverage cart on weekends.

Walking is not allowed. Tee times may be booked two days in advance. Greens fees and cart range from $30 to $36.

The Emerald Golf Club
5000 Clubhouse Dr., New Bern • 633-4440
Championship Yardage: 6924
Slope: 129	**Par: 72**

Men's Yardage: 6451
Slope: 124	**Par: 72**

Other Yardage: 6123
Slope: 120	**Par: 72**

Other Yardage: 5441
Slope: 111	**Par: 72**

Ladies' Yardage: 4813
Slope: 114	**Par: 72**

Rees Jones designed this course in 1988 to attract golfers of all skill levels. It's placed among tall pines within a 700-acre residential community developed by Weyerhaeuser Real Estate Company. Greens are beautiful bentgrass, and fairways are bermudagrass. Additional tees recently were added and others adjusted to accommodate golfers' varying abilities. We appreciate the handicap specification on the score card, which leads us to the appropriate tees to make the course most challenging. Jerry Briele, PGA professional, and Jim Lanier, golf course superintendent, have done a fine job of upgrading this course.

Don't be intimidated by water here. Of the four par 3s on this course, three must carry over "the drink." The 5th hole (par 5) measures 521 yards. The fairway snakes beside the highway up to the green. Water borders the right, and trees line the entire left side. A bunker comes into play on any short approaches to the green.

The signature hole is the 18th, a delight for its characteristic rolling mounds on the left side and water lining the fairway on the right.

The first round of the PGA qualifying school was conducted here in 1992 and 1993. Emerald also is home to the Curtis Strange Shrine Classic.

A pro shop, driving range and lessons are available. Memberships entitle visitors to use tennis, swimming and club facilities as well as play golf.

The year-round cost Monday through Thursday is $37, including cart; Friday through Sunday and holidays, it's $42. Carts must stay on the path. Members are allowed to walk the course and may make reservations seven days in advance. Nonmembers must use a cart and may make reservations two days before they plan to tee off.

Farmville Country Club
300 Bynum Dr., Farmville • 753-3660
Championship Yardage: 6206
Slope: 115	**Par: 71**

Men's Yardage: 5702
Slope: 111	**Par: 71**

Ladies Yardage: 4759
Slope: 109	**Par: 71**

Farmville's front nine was built during the 1930s, and the back nine was added during the 1970s. The 18-hole course has bermudagrass greens and fairways. Small greens and tight fairways characterize the front nine; wider fairways and larger greens may surprise you on the back. Farmville is kept in

Grass is Grass

As you read *The Insiders' Guide® to Golf in the Carolinas*, you may notice at least two words in this book that are spelled and punctuated as you have rarely seen them: bermudagrass and bentgrass. Most times, they are spelled and punctuated "Bermuda grass" and "Bent grass," respectively. We must admit that we, too, used the words that way when we began developing this book. However, upon talking to professionals in the field, we learned that we were incorrect.

Of course, we felt compelled to verify this new information. After striking out at various attempts to dig up the correct answers, we finally called the United States Golf Association (USGA) in Far Hills, New Jersey. There, we talked to Annette Colbertaldo who confirmed that the two words in question were indeed spelled b-e-r-m-u-d-a-g-r-a-s-s and b-e-n-t-g-r-a-s-s (one word, lower case, in both instances).

This question answered, we went ahead with the task at hand, compiling information for this book. But a deep yearning to know more about bermudagrass and bentgrass kept gnawing at us. So it was back to research and more calls and questions about grass. Our calling and questioning turned out hot and cold, literally. Kimberly Erusha at the USGA said that bentgrass is a species of grass used mostly in the northern parts of the United States where the weather is colder. As you may guess, bermudagrass is used mostly in the southern climes where it is relatively warm year round.

Bentgrass is native to Europe. How it got to the United States is anyone's guess. Possibly because it was grown on the first golf courses (if it was good enough for the Scots, it's good enough for us). Bermudagrass, contrary to popular belief, is not from Bermuda; it's from the east coast of Africa. Spanish explorers indirectly introduced it to this country in the 1500s; they fed it to their horses, which in turn spread the seed as it passed through their digestive systems.

Courses throughout the Carolinas employ versions of bermudagrass, bentgrass and tifdwarf on their greens and fairways.

Both grasses form a good quality turf for golfing. Bermudagrass in the fairway allows the ball to sit up better. It also can survive long seasons of little rainfall. Bentgrass is an excellent quality turf at low mowing heights and has the toughness to take on cold winters in the North.

So, the next time you are out on the course and someone says, "That tree is blocking your shot, but your ball is really sitting up nicely," you can explain why. (Plus you can pass along the correct spelling!)

top condition, with good-quality greens and beautiful fairways.

This course demands accuracy. Every hole varies according to the natural landscape. A ditch runs through most of the front side, except on the par 3s. A creek crosses the 11th and 18th holes, and ponds add additional hazards on the back side. Except for the par 3s, you must continually contend with a ditch, creek or pond. Bring extra golf balls unless you can keep one in the air.

A practice green, chipping area, pro shop, locker rooms, a bar and grill are available. The short driving range is for warm-up purposes only. A cart path is provided for nine holes and planned for the additional nine.

The cost is $20 including cart. Walking is allowed. Only members may book a tee time in advance; for guests, it's first-come, first-served.

Harbour Pointe Golf Links
750 Broad Creek Rd., Bridgeton
• 638-5338
Championship Yardage: 6554
Slope: 117   **Par: 72**
Men's Yardage: 5998
Slope: 113   **Par: 72**
Ladies' Yardage: 5778
Slope: 110   **Par: 72**

Harbour Pointe is one of two 18-hole courses at the Fairfield Harbour resort community that are available to residents and time-share owners. Occasional overflow from Harbour Pointe is booked at Shoreline, Fairfield Harbour's private club.

Greens at Harbour Pointe are bentgrass, and fairways are bermudagrass. The course was designed by Tom Johnson and D. J. DeVictor. Sand and water combine to test players of every skill level.

The most challenging hole is No. 4. This par 4 measures 395 yards, with water from tee to green down the right side and a right dogleg.

The driving range is two-tiered. A pro shop, club rentals, a snack bar, lounge, tennis courts and a swimming pool round out the amenities.

Walking is allowed after 1 PM. Greens fees and cart range from $24 to $34. Tee times may be booked two days in advance.

Indian Trails Country Club
Country Club Dr., Grifton • 524-5485,
(800) 830-4822
Championship Yardage: 6634
Slope: 124   **Par: 71**
Men's Yardage: 6172
Slope: 120   **Par: 71**
Ladies' Yardage: 4796
Slope: 115   **Par: 71**

Part of this 18-hole course has been open since the early 1960s, and the rest has developed progressively. Many travelers are surprised to find a course like Indian Trails in such a small town. The public is welcome here, and member programs are under way to encourage junior and women's golf as well as executive networking. It's easily accessible from I-95 to N.C. Highway 11 and is one of the only area courses open to public play. Fairways and greens are bermudagrass.

The course is surrounded by forests on all sides. It's hilly, with frequent left or right doglegs and finger lakes wandering through the course that come into play on seven holes. The 1st tee is on the shoreline of what geologists believe was the ocean several million years ago, and the elevation varies significantly. The 9th hole is of special note. It's 440 yards from the back tees, has a pond on the right and trees on the right and left. The green is elevated and slopes from left to right — into trouble.

A putting green, driving range, pro shop, club rentals, a snack bar and beer sales are offered. A beverage cart is available occasionally on weekends. And a paved cart path complements the course.

Cost is $19, including cart, for weekdays; weekend fees increase to $15 plus $9 for a cart. Seasonal or twilight specials sometimes are offered, and the Golf Privilege Card is honored here on weekdays. Walking is allowed after 3 PM on weekends. You may book week-

end tee times a week in advance; weekday tee times are first-come, first-served.

Steven Mitchell, PGA professional, offers lesson packages. Call for information and reservations.

Ironwood Golf & Country Club
200 Golf Club Wynd, U. S. 43, Greenville
• 752-6659, (800) 343-IRON

Championship Yardage: 7069	
Slope: 124	Par: 72
Men's Yardage: 6625	
Slope: 119	Par: 72
Other Yardage: 5965	
Slope: 113	Par: 72
Ladies' Yardage: 5359	
Slope: 116	Par: 72

Ironwood Development created this first Lee Trevino signature golf course east of the Mississippi. The 18-hole course is private with daily nonmember play for a limited time. Members are given preference. The course is surrounded by a development with wooded lots and cluster home lots.

The club consists of a clubhouse, fitness room, grill room, dining room, bar, golf shop, men's and ladies' lounges. It's a prestigious community and the course is designed to match.

Greens fees including cart are $37 on weekdays and $42 on weekends.

River Bend Golf & Country Club
94 Shoreline Dr., River Bend • 638-2819

Championship Yardage: 6404	
Slope: 117	Par: 71
Men's Yardage: 5043	
Slope: 109	Par: 71
Ladies' Yardage: 5012	
Slope: 105	Par: 71

Greens and fairways are bermudagrass, and fairways are wide open on this Gene Hamm design. This 18-hole course (built in 1963) is open to the public and playable by the average golfer.

The signature hole is the 13th, a par 3 across water that plays 184 yards from the back tees. The green slopes away from left to

The clubhouse at The Sound.

right, with bunkers on the left and right front. Five holes on the back side have water. The front is tighter and weaves through a residential neighborhood. It's a fun layout, often referred to as player-friendly.

It has a driving range, practice green, club rentals, a snack bar, bar, pro shop, tennis courts and an Olympic-size pool.

Cart and greens fees range from $22 to $25. Walking is allowed, and the management is very helpful in booking advance tee times for out-of-towners; just call with your request.

Rock Creek Country Club
308 Country Club Blvd., Jacksonville • (910) 324-5151
Championship Yardage: 7108
Slope: 117   **Par: 72**
Men's Yardage: 6233
Slope: 110   **Par: 72**
Ladies' Yardage: 5389
Slope: 108   **Par: 72**

This 18-hole course, designed by Jerry Turner and built in 1971, is well-kept and playable. It's also well off the regular route (from

U.S. Highway 17, take N.C. Highway 1308, then N.C. Highway 1390), so it won't be as busy as many others during high season. Fairways are bermudagrass, and greens are bentgrass.

The signature hole is No. 15 — a par 4. Your tee shot must fly between water and a ditch.

Rental clubs and a restaurant are available here. Walking is allowed. Greens fees, including cart, begin at $20 and increase to $25 on weekends. Advance tee times are not required.

The Sound Golf Links
101 Clubhouse Dr., Hertford
• 426-5555, (800) 535-0704
Championship Yardage: 6504
Slope: 124   **Par: 72**
Men's Yardage: 5836
Slope: 119   **Par: 72**
Ladies' Yardage: 4665
Slope: 113   **Par: 72**

The Sound is an 18-hole course in Albemarle Plantation, a 500-acre world-class golfing and boating community outside Hertford. It's tucked away at the tip of Albemarle Sound, and the beautiful new clubhouse overlooks the water. You have to be familiar with the really good golf courses in the Carolinas to know about this Dan Maples original. Owner and designer Maples stamped his signature here. As with all Maples-designed courses, you get a break on the par 4s and 5s, but the par 3s are extremely difficult. It's a target golf course with a few similarities to a links course.

Fairways are wide, and marsh must be carried frequently. It's critical to hit where you aim. It's a fair course overall, but it's tough from the back tees. The pro's advice is, "Don't bite off more than you can chew."

On the 7th and 13th holes, the landing areas are extremely small. Both are par 4s.

This course is surrounded by undisturbed wetlands and tall pines. Enjoy the ride from the 16th green to the 17th tee over the wetlands. In fact, you'll probably enjoy all of the cart rides over the bridges. The three finishing holes stretch along the water and provide breathtaking views.

The 12,000-square-foot clubhouse has a pro shop and restaurant. A driving range and putting green also are available. The marina is the largest in the area. Amenities for members include a swim and fitness center and a separate recreation center.

Greens fees, including cart, range from $30 to $35. Walking is restricted, so call for details. Tee times may be booked up to nine months in advance.

Around New Bern, Edenton and Eastern North Carolina . . .

Fun Things To Do

Antiques shopping, historical tours and, of course, watersports are major interests for many golfers during their extra time in eastern North Carolina.

New Bern invites you to wear walking shoes or hop on the trolley and enjoy art galleries, gardens in bloom and especially restored homes, churches and stores reflecting internationally flavored 18th-century architectural influences. Sit on a park bench and watch the river, while every care of your 20th-century life flows away with it.

Visit the **Croatan National Forest** where deer, bears, alligators and Venus' flytraps are preserved. You can access the forest at 141 E. Fisher Avenue, just a few miles south of New Bern. Call 638-5628 for more information.

In town, browse through the **Firemen's Museum**, 410 Hancock Street, New Bern, 636-4087, or the **Civil War Museum**, 301 Metcalf Street, 633-2818. Be sure to leave an afternoon to amble through the **Tryon Palace Historic Site and Gardens**, Pollock and George streets; call 638-1560 for information about tour options and hours.

We suggest you plan a golfing vacation here each April so you can also attend the **Home and Garden Show**. This event is a must for garden lovers; the quiet, self-guided stroll through some of the town's most beautiful homes is enchanting, and you can get great decorating ideas for your own home.

Spend some quiet time in this small town. You won't hear the sounds of a big city. Talk to the people here — folks aren't shy about sharing their life stories with new friends who are here to enjoy local golf courses.

Visit this area during any festival, and you'll absorb some real flavor of the region and its people as well as be entertained and fed like royalty. Call (800) 437-5767 for general tourist information.

Call 482-2637 for information about **Edenton** or (800) 775-0111 for the **Tourism Development Authority**. And when you arrive here go straight to the **Visitors Center**, 108 N. Broad Street, for a genuinely warm welcome by the knowledgeable and courteous staff. Watch the introductory film, then take a guided tour of the more than 50 historic buildings along the tree-lined downtown streets. If you enjoy celebrations, visit Edenton during the September shrimp festival, the October peanut festival or the Christmas candlelight tour of private homes.

The 1730 **Newbold-White House**, North Carolina's oldest surviving home, is on N.C. Highway 1336 near Hertford, one of the state's oldest towns. Its medieval English architecture has been modified by Colonial touches. Call 426-7567 for tour information.

Nearby in **Bath**, the state's first town, you can tour three restored house museums. Go to the Historic Bath Visitor Center on Carteret Street (N.C. 92), 923-3971, for information on tours of the **Palmer-Marsh House**, the **Van DerVeer House** and **The Bonner House**. Here you can also get directions to **St. Thomas Episcopal**, the state's oldest church. Call 923-3971 for more information.

The prestigious **Albemarle Craftsman's Fair** at Knobbs Creek Recreation Center on Ward Street in **Elizabeth City**, one of the oldest demonstrating shows in the country, has been celebrated in October for 38 years. This event showcases myriad crafts of exquisite design and workmanship. Call the **Elizabeth City Area Chamber of Commerce**, 335-4365,

for information on events and nearby attractions. Also, make time for a walking tour through the historic district.

Lake Mattamuskeet National Wildlife Refuge, on N.C. 94 a mile north of U.S. 264 and east of Washington, encompasses 50,000 acres of marsh, lake, timber and cropland. The shallow lake is a winter refuge for various waterfowl, including more than 45,000 tundra swan and 150,000 birds. Also, thousands of snow and Canada geese and 22 species of ducks arrive for the season. Fishing and boating are popular here, including herring dipping and blue crab fishing. For information about the refuge, call 926-4021.

Pettigrew State Park, just off U.S. Highway 64 outside **Creswell** (follow signs once you've entered town), has 5 miles of trails through virgin forests and displays Native American dugout canoes along the trail. A new fishing pier and boat launch along the west side of the 16,600-acre lake provide for enjoyable activities, and a new hiking trail and a biking trail are under construction. Fishing, camping and nature programs are available. Call 797-4475 for information.

Somerset Place in Pettigrew State Park, 797-4560, presents hands-on educational programs about the plantation system and daily life during the antebellum period. The main house, a restored early Greek Revival-style coastal plantation home, is furnished with period pieces, and outbuildings include a smoke house, dairy, kitchen and the original Colony House where the family lived while the mansion was being built in the 1830s. This state historic site is open for tours year round, and admission is free, but groups planning to visit should call in advance for reservations.

The **Great Dismal Swamp Canal** is the oldest continually operating man-made canal in the country. You can view the **National Civil Engineering Landmark** from the visitors center here; call 771-8333. The **Dismal Swamp Wetlands Boardwalk** in northern Currituck

---

FYI

Unless otherwise noted, the area code for all phone numbers in this chapter is 919.

INSIDERS' TIP

After you hit, get your clubs and be ready to proceed to your ball.

County measures a half-mile and leads to 639 acres in the Dismal Swamp. An observation tower provides panoramic views of the area. Admission is free, but you must ask permission to go on the boardwalk or tower, which are owned by Elizabeth City State University. For information call 335-3375.

Hope Plantation, near **Windsor**, is the federal plantation home of Gov. David Stone. You can tour the entire complex for a glimpse at a statesman's life on a self-sustaining plantation in the early 1800s. Call 794-3140 for information.

The historic district of the small town of **Washington** (a.k.a. "Little Washington") is the site of 30 noteworthy structures dating from the late 1700s. This town is replete with restaurants and accommodations. Self-guided walking tours near the Pamlico River make for a full afternoon's activity. Call the **Washington-Beaufort County Chamber of Commerce**, 976-9168, or drop by the chamber offices, 102 W. Stewart Parkway, for information.

Where to Eat

Fresh seafood is fresh and abundant in eastern North Carolina restaurants. Country cooking is also prevalent, and you won't go home hungry. We believe in eating well when we're on golf trips; actually, we promote eating well all of the time. We recommend a few favorite spots offering variety, and you'll find others featuring local specialties and international cuisine. Unless otherwise indicated, the following restaurants accept most major credit cards. Refer to our Preface for an explanation of the pricing code.

New Bern

Annabelle's Restaurant & Pub
$-$$ • Twin Rivers Mall, Clarendon Blvd., U.S. 17, New Bern • 633-6401

You'll find a variety of food served in a casual atmosphere here. The lunch and dinner menus are the same and include something for almost any taste. Chicken, ribs, beef or seafood entrees are featured. Mexican dishes also are available. It's a great place to enjoy a quick soup, salad and a beer before your tee time.

Desserts are plentiful too, and we recommend hot fudge cake to finish any meal.

Anneliese's Surf & Turf
$$ • N.C. Hwy. 55 E., New Bern • 633-5828

Near downtown, this German restaurant offers all the standard fare, such as kielbasa, bratwurst, bockwurst, Wiener schnitzel, rouladen (sliced roast beef rolled around bacon, onions and carrots and topped with gravy) and, of course, outstanding Black Forest cake. Entrees are served with potato dumplings, red cabbage or your choice of cold salad or hot potato salad. Seafood dishes can be ordered fried or broiled and include local catches, such as shrimp, clams, flounder, scallops and crab. Try the soft-shell crabs, sea trout or other sauteed items. Anneliese's also prepares a variety of steaks, from filet mignon to rib-eye. And, as the name implies, you can order surf and turf.

The Berne Restaurant
$ • 2900 Neuse Blvd., New Bern • 638-5296

Menu selections include fried or broiled shellfish, trout, flounder and oysters (in season). We think the always full parking lot at this easy-to-find eatery (it's at a major intersection) is a sign of the good food served within. The Berne offers down-home country and seafood meals. Pork barbecue, a regional specialty, is featured; if that doesn't appeal to you, choose steak or seafood. Don't miss the breakfast buffet served each Saturday and Sunday. A traditional country breakfast is featured every day.

The Chelsea — A Restaurant & Publick House
$$-$$$ • Broad and Middle Sts., New Bern • 637-5469

Shellfish, steaks or sandwiches are good choices for lunch or dinner at The Chelsea. Regional cuisine wears a contemporary flair. Watch for the daily specials listed on the chalkboard, and enjoy the healthy house salad, vegetable, potato or rice and fresh bread that accompany every entree. The large bar is popular with locals and offers domestic and imported beers and mixed drinks. Live entertainers perform many nights.

Caleb Bradham first used this building as

his drugstore where he founded Brad's Drink, the original Pepsi-Cola. The colorful wall mural tells the story.

The Harvey Mansion
$$-$$$ • 221 Tryon Palace Dr., New Bern • 638-3205

This restaurant and lounge with a water view are in a restored building constructed by John Harvey in the 1790s. Before it became a restaurant in 1979, the building was a home, a mercantile establishment, a boarding house, a military academy and a community college throughout its history. Carolyn and chef Beat Züttel now own and operate the mansion and live there with their children.

Sunday brunch and gourmet dinners are served here, including fresh seasonal offerings of grilled, poached or sauteed seafood. The menu changes frequently and reflects the chef's heritage and influences from his native Bern, Switzerland. Homemade desserts are delicious. Downstairs, the cellar lounge boasts a copper bar, a pasta menu and an inviting atmosphere in which to relax before or after dinner.

The triple diamond rating, linens and candlelight encourage a dressy evening here.

Henderson House Restaurant
$$$ • 216 Pollock St., New Bern • 637-4784

This award-winning restaurant in a restored historic home is perfect for candlelight dining on a special occasion. Original art adorns the walls — a nice complement to your meal. And exquisite menu selections — creatively prepared veal, duck, lamb and pheasant — match the decor. The shrimp almandine is one of our favorites. The international wine list is extensive. Henderson House is open evenings from Tuesday through Sunday.

Latitude 35
$$ • 1 Bicentennial Park, New Bern • 638-3585

This restaurant in the Sheraton Hotel and Marina showcases fine dining, but don't avoid it because you're wearing golf attire. Come as you are and enjoy the views of the Neuse River and the marina. Locals enjoy the breakfast buffet, which includes eggs, grits, breakfast meat, waffles, muffins, fabulous biscuits, fresh fruits and cereals. Try a tasty salad or sandwich for lunch and seafood specialties in the evening. You won't be disappointed with the shellfish or other seafood, served broiled, baked, fried, grilled or blackened. If sea fare is not to your taste, order pasta, chicken or beef. A full salad bar is included with each entree.

Moore's Barbecue
$ • U.S. Hwy. 17 S., New Bern • 638-3937

No trip to North Carolina is complete without barbecue, and this is a good place to sample some. Pork, seafood or chicken and all the trimmings make for a fine Carolina-style lunch or dinner feast to eat in or carry out. Call for hours, which vary on weekends. If you're planning a big party, consider Moore's to cater a pig pickin'. You've not eaten real Southern food until you've tried this.

Pollock Street Delicatessen and Restaurant
$-$$ • 208 Pollock St., New Bern • 637-2480

If you are visiting and homesick for food from a New York deli, Pollock Street serves breakfast, lunch or dinner to please any Northern palate — and Carolinians love it too. Salads, bagels, quiche, pasta, sandwiches and other entrees are delicious and followed by great desserts. Call for hours, which vary daily.

Sandpiper Restaurant
$ • 2403 Neuse Blvd., New Bern • 633-0888

As soon as you sit down at Sandpiper, your hot hush puppies and butter will arrive. This gets your meal off to a good start, but don't fill up yet. You have many fried seafood platters from which to choose: fish, shrimp, oysters, deviled crab, scallops. We recommend the trout fillets or fried shrimp. Get a baked potato or fries and a hearty serving of cold

INSIDERS' TIP

On the driving range, use higher irons first and work up to the driver.

Springtime in the Carolinas means perfect golfing weather
plus blooming azaleas and dogwoods.

slaw. Oyster stew and clam chowder are specialties as well as shrimp or oyster cocktails.

Scalzo's
$$ • 415 Broad St., New Bern • 633-9898

Scalzo's huge variety of pastas with a choice of 18 sauces plus fresh lamb, seafood, beef, veal or chicken selections should please any palate. One of the best and most unusual sauces is the black olive and caper creation. Others include mixed seafood, red or white clam sauce or a standard marinara. Not a typical Carolina eatery, this place is more typical of an Italian restaurant. Choose a complementary wine and an Italian dessert and spend a memorable evening here.

Washington

No. 1 Chinese Restaurant
$-$$ • 1308 John Small Ave., Washington • 975-7445

Whether you prefer Cantonese, Szechwan or Hunan cuisine, you're in luck here, because this restaurant specializes in all three. We recommend the General Tso chicken, but be sure to ask for extra beverage to accompany this hot and spicy dish. This small restaurant in this equally small town offers one of the most extensive Chinese menus we have ever seen.

Many items can be ordered as a combination plate, such as chicken with garlic sauce, roast pork egg foo young or pepper steak. Combination plates include pork fried rice and egg roll. Other special dishes include spare rib tips, fried shrimp, chicken wings or half of a fried chicken. We also recommend Cantonese special No. 110 (a.k.a. subgum won ton), a combination of won ton, lobster, chicken and pork with vegetables and white rice.

PG's Creekside Restaurant
$-$$ • 1052 E. Main St., Washington • 946-9483

Whether outside in the gazebo or in one of the dining rooms (Patty's Porch, The Solarium or Grandpappy's Bedroom), you can enjoy good food from an entertaining menu at this restaurant near the Pamlico River. Featured menu items include the Annette Spinachello (spinach salad with tomatoes, eggs and bacon bits) and the Hugh Heffer (roast beef with cheddar cheese, onions and barbecue sauce on a honey wheat roll). Sweets for My Sweet desserts change daily.

Patty Lovely's vision of 35 years became a reality here. It's A Small World children's menu includes sandwiches dubbed by entrants in a sandwich-naming contest: That's A Bunch of Bologna, Nutter Butter Jelly Jubilee, Mexican

Puppy. Adult choices include several varieties of Fowl Play, Ham It Up, Beef Encounters and Chicken of the Sea; you'll find larger creative versions of some of the same items for dinner.

Edenton

The Dram Tree Restaurant
$$$ • 112 Water St., Edenton • 482-2711

Next door to the lovely bed and breakfast inn of the same name, this restaurant features entrees of beef, veal, lamb, poultry, pasta or seafood. A tasty beginning is the Dram Tree coconut shrimp or the seafood crepes. One of our favorite entrees is chicken colliers, a fricasseed breast of chicken over fettuccini with a sherry, creamy Dijon sauce with almonds. The vegetable ravioli combines our favorite eggplant and spinach with tomato and a roasted red pepper marinara sauce. Desserts made personally by Martha are special every day. The restaurant and inn take the name from the dram tree where the English captains of outgoing vessels during the 17th and 18th centuries partook of a dram of rum as a token of a safe voyage.

Lane's Family BBQ and Seafood
$ • E. Church St. Ext., Edenton • 482-4008

Fine authentic North Carolina barbecue with all the proper trimmings can be enjoyed here. In case you don't know, the main accompaniments to a chicken or pork barbecue (sliced or chopped) sandwich or plate are slaw and French fries or onion rings. Take home a pound or two of barbecue for another meal. You can also choose clam strips or a basic delicious hamburger. Daily specials also are offerings like chicken pot pie on Mondays or ham and collards on Wednesday. Don't miss the banana pudding or lemon meringue pie for dessert.

Where to Stay

The few major hotels in this part of the state are dependable, and the modest local motels are fine for a short stay. But, to sample the real flavor of eastern North Carolina, we suggest a bed and breakfast inn in a Victorian or Greek Revival-style restored home. If you're here for golf only, you'll want to consider an accommodation that offers a package and helps you book a tee time at your chosen course. Refer to our Preface for an explanation of the pricing code.

New Bern

The Aerie
$$$ • 509 Pollock St., New Bern • 636-5553, (800) 849-5553

This is a good place to talk to the locals at the on-site Tea Room, serving tea and coffee, scones and jam Wednesday through Saturday afternoons. A block from Tryon Palace, this 1880s Victorian home includes seven rooms with twin, queen- or king-size beds. Each room has a private bath and cable television. Complimentary wine, beer, soft drinks and light refreshments are provided, and a full gourmet breakfast is served daily.

Comfort Suites & Marina
$-$$$ • 218 E. Front St., New Bern • 636-0022, (800) 638-7322

Golf packages are a specialty at this new accommodation. The hotel is within walking distance of New Bern's downtown and historic area. Many of the 100 suites have waterfront balconies overlooking the beautiful Neuse River — perfect settings to reflect on your golf round. All suites have refrigerators, microwaves and coffee makers. Golfers can enjoy a complimentary continental breakfast prior to their daily round.

Fairfield Harbour
Rates vary • 750 Broad Creek Rd., New Bern • 638-8011

Timeshare units are available for twosomes or several foursomes, including small condominiums (for two) and two- to three-story houses. In addition to golf privileges at two on-site courses, amenities include tennis, pools, an exercise room, game room and miniature golf to practice your putting. Although the 237 units are time-shares, they're available for rent to the public.

Hampton Inn
$-$$ • 200 Hotel Dr., New Bern • 637-2111, (800) 448-8288

This hotel off U.S. Highway 17 at the U.S. Highway 70 bypass has 101 clean and comfortable rooms (maintaining this chain's national standards for quality). Guests have convenient access to golf courses and attractions. A continental breakfast is served daily; heartier breakfasts can be had at any of a number of nearby restaurants. Golf and historic district tour packages are available.

Harmony House Inn
$$-$$$ • 215 Pollock St., New Bern
• 636-3810, (800) 636-3113

Enjoy the interesting architecture, the antiques and the hospitality, including a delicious breakfast and afternoon social hour at this bed and breakfast inn in the downtown historic district. Golf courses and historic tours are nearby. The house was built in 1809. Around 1900, it was cut in half and the west side shifted to allow for an addition and a staircase; new porches also were added. Harmony House Inn has nine guest rooms and one suite; all are furnished with antiques or reproductions and include private baths and decorative fireplaces. A full breakfast is served daily in the dining room, and beverages are served in the evening.

The Magnolia House
$$$ • 315 George St., New Bern
• 633-9488

You'll think you are in Charleston, South Carolina, when you see this pink-painted bed and breakfast inn, just a short distance from Tryon Palace. Don and Kim Trudo's home is within walking distance of the town center and waterfront. The three guest rooms are cozy, and all have private baths. Family heirlooms, locally gathered antiques and local art adorn each room. Fresh-baked breads and muffins, seasonal fruits and fresh-ground coffee await guests each morning. Guests are invited to lounge and enjoy refreshments daily at 4 PM.

New Bern House Inn
$$ • 709 Broad St., New Bern
• 636-2250, (800) 842-7688

You can sit on the front porch swing and forget about your day if you didn't have a good round. The seven guest rooms in this bed and breakfast inn are air-conditioned; all have private baths and either twin, king or queen beds. You can't miss this Colonial-style home a block from the Tryon Palace complex. In case you didn't get enough exercise on the golf course, this inn provides a bicycle built for two to spin around historic New Bern. When you call for reservations, ask about the monthly mystery weekends. They are great fun for guests as well as the innkeeper.

The Sheraton Grand
$$-$$$ • New Bern Hotel and Marina,
1 Bicentennial Park, New Bern
• 638-3585, (800) 326-3745

Comfortable rooms overlook the Trent River and on-site marina. Packages include golf at your favorite course. A covered walkway leads guests to rooms, suites and minisuites (reminiscent of grand Southern hotels) with waterfront and city views. The hotel and inn have two restaurants for dinner and two lounges for relaxing. This is a one-stop choice if you don't want to venture any farther than the golf course and the hotel.

Vacation Resorts International
Rates vary • Broad Creek Rd., New Bern
• 633-1151

Condominiums at Fairfield Harbour overlook one of the golf courses, and rental packages for one- to three-bedroom units include golf, a pool, marina and other amenities. Units will accommodate six to 18 people. A three-day minimum stay is required.

Washington

Acadian House Bed & Breakfast
$ • 129 Van Norden St., Washington
• 975-3967

Leonard and Johanna Huber renovated this 1902 house and furnished it with antiques and local crafts, some of which are for sale. Acadian House is a block from the Pamlico River and a nice walk to the historic sites. It's also nearby good golf courses. True to their New Orleans roots, the innkeepers serve southern Louisiana specialties as well as tra-

> **FYI**
> Unless otherwise noted, the area code for all phone numbers in this chapter is 919.

Photo: S.C. Department of Parks, Recreation and Tourism

Carolina pines flank the fairways of this gem of a golf course.

ditional North Carolina eggs and meats for breakfast.

Pamlico House Bed & Breakfast
$-$$ • 400 E. Main St., Washington • 946-7184, (800) 948-8507

In the center of the historic district, this large turn-of-the-century home exudes the warmth and friendliness found so often in small Southern towns. The Colonial-style house, once the rectory of St. Peter's Episcopal Church, is appointed with period antiques and modern creature comforts. Guests awaken to a delicious breakfast each morning.

Edenton

Captain's Quarters Inn
$$$$ • 202 W. Queen St., Edenton • 482-8945

Phyllis Pepper offers golf-and-snooze or sail-and-snooze two-night packages. Hors d'oeuvres are served the first night, followed the next morning by an in-room continental breakfast and a three-course gourmet breakfast served in the dining room. After breakfast, go sailing or golfing for a few hours, then hurry back to Captain's Quarters for a two-hour guided tour of Edenton's historic district. Next, enjoy afternoon refreshments back at the inn. A four-course gourmet dinner rounds out the evening. A continental breakfast followed by a breakfast buffet is served the second morning. Sailing or golf at Chowan Country Club or The Sound at Albemarle Plantation, the aforementioned meals and refreshments all are included in the package.

Governor Eden Inn
**$$-$$$ • 304 N. Broad St., Edenton
• 482-2072**

Governor Eden Inn is just 1½ blocks from the visitors center in the historic district and seven blocks from the downtown shopping district. It's near Chowan Country Club, and The Sound at Albemarle Plantation is about 20 miles away. The turn-of-the-century Victorian inn includes four rooms with private baths. The wraparound porch and the upstairs balcony are inviting places to relax. As an added enticement, owner and operator Ruth Shackelford serves a hearty breakfast each morning.

The Granville Queen Themed Inn
**$$-$$$ • 108 S. Granville St., Edenton
• 482-5296**

Nine guest rooms are individually designed to carry out unique themes ranging from Egyptian to Italian, and furnishings, art and accessories are actually from Italy, China, Holland, Thailand and England. Choose this inn in the heart of historic Edenton when you want to experience a leisurely visit in an elegant setting. It is nonsmoking and not suitable for children or pets. Along with lodging the visit includes a five-course gourmet breakfast based around grilled chicken breast or filet mignon and accompanied by eggs folded with fresh basil and diced tomatoes. Weekend evening wine tastings also are enjoyable. Don't be in a rush for a morning tee time when staying here. Spend the morning lounging over breakfast and then touring the historic district.

Lords Proprietors' Inn
**$$$$$ • 300 N. Broad St., Edenton
• 482-3641, (800) 348-8933**

Three restored homes spread over an acre of ground in the historic district. The total of 20 rooms offer private bath, cable television, VCR and use of porches, parlors and library. Gourmet dinner and a hearty breakfast are included with the price Tuesday through Saturday nights, and rates are adjusted down to exclude dinner Sunday and Monday nights. Special historic preservation weekends during February and March include a reception Friday night before an elegant dinner. On Saturday afternoon private historic homes are opened for touring. Then enjoy another wonderful dinner and entertainment. It's a unique experience to visit here.

Trestle House Inn Bed & Breakfast
$$ • Soundside Rd. (N.C. Hwy. 1114), Edenton • 482-2282

This secluded inn is a wonderful hideaway just about 4 miles outside of historic Edenton. The owners will even pick you up from the Edenton Municipal Airport if you want to arrive on your private or corporate jet. This is an ideal setting for business meetings, with outstanding golf courses are nearby. The inn was built in 1972 as a private estate. It features massive exposed redwood beams milled from abandoned railroad trestle timbers, which came from trees estimated at 450 years old. Guest rooms are spacious and include private tiled bath, remote color TV with cable and HBO, ceiling fans and air conditioning. The complimentary breakfast is delicious and is accompanied by a view of the pasture and the private lake. Also, the exercise room, billiard table, shuffleboard and sundeck are suggested for a few relaxing hours.

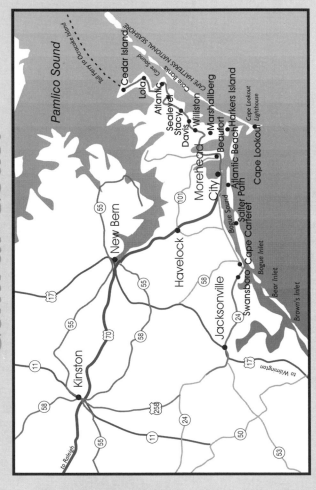

North Carolina's
Central Coast

North Carolina's Central Coast

North Carolina's Central Coast — known by some people as the Crystal Coast — is half-way between Myrtle Beach, South Carolina, and Norfolk, Virginia, or directly below North Carolina's Outer Banks. This 65-mile stretch of beaches comprising North Carolina's southern barrier islands is similar to little else in this world. It includes Atlantic Beach, Beaufort, Down East, Emerald Isle, Morehead City, Pine Knoll Shores, Salter Path and Indian Beach.

Bogue Banks is a 26-mile island stretching from Atlantic Beach (to the east) to Emerald Isle (to the west) and bordered by the Atlantic Ocean (to the south) and Bogue Sound and the Intracoastal Waterway (to the north).

This coast is known for its historic fishing villages and boat-building communities. Seafood festivals provide a background for some enjoyable family-oriented visits.

All other factors being equal, you wouldn't come here for a golfing vacation per se. But if you find yourself here for some other reason, you can find some nice greens and even golf packages offered by some accommodations.

Bogue Banks Country Club
152 Oakleaf Dr., MP 5, Pine Knoll Shores • 726-1034

Championship Yardage: 6008	
Slope: 116	Par: 72
Men's Yardage: 5757	
Slope: 113	Par: 72
Ladies' Yardage: 5075	
Slope: 116	Par: 73

This 18-hole, Morris Bracket-designed course is the only one on Bogue Sound in Atlantic Beach. It features narrow bermuda-grass fairways and lush bermudagrass greens.

Although relatively short, this course is deceptively tough to play. It runs between the sound and the ocean, and the back side includes three holes flanked by the sound; one green and one tee overlook the sound. It's a picturesque layout, and fowl and fauna abound.

The most challenging holes here are the 5th and 16th. No. 5 has a slight dogleg, with trees and bushes on the right and threatening water on the left. On the 16th, a slight dogleg leads to the narrow landing area. Water runs along the sides of many holes, patiently waiting for an errant ball.

The course has a pro shop, snack bar and tennis courts. Lessons are offered for golf and tennis.

Greens fees during the summer are $33 for walking or $45 for riding. During the off-season, from September to May, these rates are discounted; rates vary annually. Call up to one week in advance to book your tee time.

Brandywine Bay
U.S. Hwy. 70, Morehead City • 247-2541

Championship Yardage: 6609	
Slope: 119	Par: 71
Men's Yardage: 6150	
Slope: 115	Par: 71
Other Yardage: 5389	
Slope: 113	Par: 71
Ladies' Yardage: 5191	
Slope: 113	Par: 71

This 18-hole layout was designed by Bruce Devlin and revised by Ellis and Don Maples. Its 40 acres of rolling fairways and bentgrass greens are set among tall oaks and private residences. The front nine opened in 1980, and the back nine opened in 1983. It's a de-

GOLF COURSES ON NORTH CAROLINA'S CENTRAL COAST

Course Name	Type	Holes	Par	Slope	Yards	Walking	Booking	Cost w/ Cart
Bogue Banks Country Club	semiprivate	18	72	113	5757	yes	call	$33-45
Brandywine Bay	semiprivate	18	71	115	6150	yes	call	$20-35
Morehead City Country Club	semiprivate	18	72	110	6116	yes	3 days	$30
Silver Creek Golf Club	public	18	73	113	6030	yes	call	$35-40
Star Hill Golf and Country Club								
Lakes Course	semiprivate	9	35	56	2897	yes	365 days	call
Pines Course	semiprivate	9	36	53	2998	yes	365 days	call
Sands Course	semiprivate	9	36	56	2889	yes	365 days	call

manding course where water or woods come into play on every hole. Accurate tee shots and exacting approach shots are needed here.

The 2nd hole is noteworthy, with a winding lake guarding the fairway and green. Your tee shot must carry the lake; your second shot must be of equal accuracy. The 4th hole is a double dogleg right that requires an accurate tee shot followed by a lay-up to a small landing area guarded by water on the left and woods on the right. The green is somewhat elevated and guarded by water on the left. The par 3s are short but not necessarily easy.

Amenities include a pro shop, putting green and snack bar. A pool and two tennis courts are available to members.

Greens fees are $20 for walking or $35 with cart. Call at any time to set your tee time; folks are very accommodating here and will try to get you golfing when it's right for you.

Be sure to talk with ever-friendly Coy Brown, former head pro at Bogue Banks for nearly 19 years — now at Brandywine.

Morehead City Country Club
Country Club Rd., Morehead City
• 726-4917
Championship Yardage: 6345
Slope: 113   **Par: 72**
Men's Yardage: 6116
Slope: 110   **Par: 72**
Ladies' Yardage: 4991
Slope: 105   **Par: 72**

This 18-hole layout, built in 1952 by C.C. McCuisto, is somewhat flat and easily walkable. The county's oldest course roams along the Newport River. The club is private, but public play is accepted as time permits, particularly during the week. Bermudagrass greens and fairways are well-maintained.

Some holes are tight, and some are more open. The first hole is a good one, albeit a tough start. It's a position hole, with a dogleg left of 409 yards from the back tees, requiring you to draw the ball off the tee to get in better position. Several ditches run parallel to the fairways, but otherwise there's not much water to worry about.

The 18th is the signature hole, the only one where marsh comes into play. It's a par 5 of 509 yards from the back. The tee shot requires you to hit out of a chute to a fairly wide landing area. Then you have the option of trying to hit over the marsh or laying up short and leaving another 175 yards or more to the green. It's a beautiful hole, with the Newport River running behind the green.

Rental clubs, a driving range, bar and restaurant are offered.

Greens fees are around $35, including cart. Advance tee times aren't really necessary, but they'll happily accommodate you if you call early.

FYI

Unless otherwise noted, the area code for all businesses listed in this chapter is 919.

Also note that the MP found in many addresses in this chapter stands for milepost, a common location designator in the Bogue Banks area.

Silver Creek Golf Club
N.C. Hwy. 58, Swansboro
• 393-8058
Championship Yardage: 7005
Slope: 122   **Par: 73**
Men's Yardage: 6030
Slope: 113   **Par: 73**
Ladies' Yardage: 5526
Slope: 110   **Par: 71**

This 18-hole course, with bermudagrass fairways and bentgrass greens, was designed by Gene Hamm. It's open, flat and easy to walk. Stands of small pines dot the course but don't create much of a problem. Ponds come into play on 12 holes, but most are not extremely difficult. The toughest hole is No. 8, a par 3 measuring about 185 yards from the back tees, with a pond around the front and the right side.

You will encounter at least seven doglegs. No. 11 doglegs right over two ponds. It's a par 5 that requires a lay-up then a long iron over the water. On No. 2 it's also hard to position your drive over the lake, which runs down the hole from right to left. The farther left you go, the longer the carry. Then a trap on the right in the landing area makes it even tougher. No. 14 is a straightaway par 4 of 460 yards that usually plays tough with the wind in your face.

The 16th is another interesting hole, a par 3 of 145 yards, with terracing on the front and back of the green. And the 18th is a par 4 of 445 yards with a pond on the right of the green.

The clubhouse is inviting, and amenities include a locker room, driving range, putting greens, a pro shop, tennis courts, a swimming pool and a grill.

Greens fees, including cart, are $35 to $40. Walking is allowed after 2 PM. Advance tee times aren't required, but they'll be happy to book a reservation for you whenever you call.

Star Hill Golf & Country Club
Club House Dr., Cape Carteret • 393-8111

The 27 holes of Star Hill run more than 9000 yards. The three nine-hole courses are played as three 18-hole pairs, each set between the Intracoastal Waterway and the Croatan National Forest. They are flat, with narrow tree-lined fairways. All have bermudagrass greens. Russell Burney was the course architect.

Only about five holes have water.

A fully stocked golf shop, a driving range, rental clubs, a clubhouse, grill, tennis courts and a pool add to the desirability of visiting here. Corporate outings are welcome, and a banquet facility is available.

Greens fees, including cart, range from approximately $35 to $45. Walking costs from $25 to $35 and is sometimes restricted. There are no restrictions, however, on how far in advance you can book a tee time.

Lakes Course
Championship Yardage: 3254

Slope: 58	**Par: 35**
Men's Yardage: 2897	
Slope: 56	**Par: 35**
Other Yardage: 2662	
Slope: 52	**Par: 35**
Ladies' Yardage: 2507	
Slope: 52	**Par: 36**

No. 1 on the Lakes is considered the signature hole of this complex. From the back, it requires a 200-yard carry. You must cross the lake to the landing area then play over a creek that runs in front of the green.

Pines Course
Championship Yardage: 3194

Slope: 55	**Par: 36**
Men's Yardage: 2998	
Slope: 53	**Par: 36**
Other Yardage: 2497	
Slope: 49	**Par: 36**
Ladies' Yardage: 2390	
Slope: 52	**Par: 36**

On the Pines, you'll need a good tee shot on the par 5 No. 2. But don't leave your power

stroke at the tee; you'll need to follow up with two big shots.

Sands Course
Championship Yardage: 3107

Slope: 60	**Par: 36**
Men's Yardage: 2889	
Slope: 56	**Par: 36**
Other Yardage: 2672	
Slope: 52	**Par: 36**
Ladies' Yardage: 2279	
Slope: 56	**Par: 36**

No. 1 on the Sands requires a good tee shot, or you will need a long iron shot into a slight dogleg left surrounded by trees.

Around the Central Coast . . .

Fun Things To Do

In addition to golf, the best things to do here include fishing, swimming and sunning. It's a real getaway from busy resort areas, and you won't find a more beautiful spot for a quiet family vacation and easygoing fun. Eat plenty of seafood and spend sunny days beachcombing and ocean swimming.

Shop at the **Golfin' Dolphin**, Manatee Street, Cape Carteret, 393-8131, for golf equipment or apparel. Your big or little children can keep busy with arcade games, miniature golf and bumper boats at this family entertainment complex, while the golfers browse, buy and then break in their new accessories on the 50-tee driving range.

Children of all ages will enjoy amusements at **Jungleland**, Salter Path Road (N.C. Highway 58, MP 4.5), 247-2148, or **The Circle**, MP 2.25, both in Atlantic Beach, **Pirate Island Park**, Salter Path Road (N.C. Highway 58, MP 10.5), Salter Path, 247-3024, or **Playland**, 204 Islander Drive, MP 20.5, Emerald Isle, 354-6616. The boardwalks in Emerald Isle and Atlantic Beach also are must-stops on any beach trip.

If you crave some educational activity to give your trip a culturally redeeming quality, visit **Fort Macon State Park**, E. Fort Macon Road (N.C. Highway 58, MP 0), Atlantic Beach, 726-3775. On occasional weekends, you can

Brandywine Bay

Brandywine Bay Championship Golf Course invites you to discover 18 holes of the finest golfing experience on the North Carolina Coast! This course, designed by Bruce Devlin, boasts over 6600 yards of rolling fairways and bentgrass greens, the challenge of 40 acres of water, fast putting greens and the well known 555 yard par 5 hole #10. This is truly a golfer's paradise for the novice or seasoned veteran,

-PUBLIC & GROUPS WELCOME-

LESSONS AVAILABLE
BENTGRASS GREENS
FULLY STOCKED PRO SHOP

Tee Time Reservations:
(919) 247-2541

Brandywine Bay Championship Golf Course
Hwy. 70 West
Morehead City, NC 28557

witness militia musket firings and living history in the Civil War fortress at Fort Macon.

Check your map to differentiate between Beaufort, North Carolina, and Beaufort, South Carolina. Both cities are delightfully historic yet distinctly different, beginning with their pronunciations — in North Carolina, it's "Bowfort"; in South Carolina, "Beu-ford." **Beaufort Historic Site** (N.C.), 100 block of Turner Street, 728-5225, under the auspices of the Beaufort Historical Association, is the focus of, among other things, guided tours of a 21-block historic district that features homes, buildings and gardens dating from 1732. Seasonal celebrations revolve around the architecture and heritage included therein. Also in Beaufort, visit the **North Carolina Maritime Museum**, 315 Front Street, 728-7317, which celebrates the state's coastal heritage, maritime and natural history and natural resources. The museum maintains an impressive collection of watercraft models, including sailing skiffs and full-rigged ships.

In Pine Knoll Shores, enjoy the **North Carolina Aquarium at Pine Knoll Shores**, Salter Path Road (N.C. Highway 58, MP 7), 247-4004. Tucked away in the maritime forest of the Theodore Roosevelt Natural Area, the aquarium bustles with fun and educational activities between spring and fall, including films, talks, and workshops on coastal topics, on-board collecting cruises, canoe trips, snorkeling instruction, saltwater fishing and excursions to remote barrier islands. For a special treat, take a narrated sightseeing cruise on a paddlewheeler.

Enjoy outdoor drama presentations at the **Crystal Coast Amphitheater**, N.C. Highway 58, Pelletier (near Cape Carteret). The long-running professional production *Worthy Is The Lamb,* a passion play depicting the life and times of Jesus Christ, draws audiences from far and wide to its mid-June through September performances. Call (800) 662-5960 or 393-8373 for ticket and schedule information.

For a taste of regional culture, stop by the

Carteret County Museum of History, 100 Wallace Drive, Morehead City, 247-7533. Examine changing exhibits of American Indian artifacts and memorabilia of the county's settlers, some dating to 1722.

Small specialty shops dot the villages and tempt shoppers with antiques, art or local crafts. The fresh fare found at prevalent seafood markets will entice you to cook your own deep-sea delights, although world-class local restaurants will be happy to prepare their delectable bounty for you.

Festivals are based on such important leisure activities as kite flying, melon eating, fishing (of course) and the ever-shining convention of bald folks in Morehead City.

One of the year's greatest events — featuring entertainment as well as unsurpassed cuisine — is the **North Carolina Seafood Festival** on the first weekend in October on the Morehead City waterfront. It's a three-day celebration of the area's heritage and all that makes life delightful along the Central Coast. Call 726-6273 if you want more details. Other events revolve around boats, art, antiques, music, even sand castle building, and the welcome mat is always rolled out for visitors or newcomers.

Call (800) SUNNY NC or pick up a copy of *The Insiders' Guide® to North Carolina's Central Coast & New Bern* for complete Central Coast information.

Where to Eat

Refer to our Preface for an explanation of the pricing code.

Beaufort

115 Queen Street

$$$$ • 115 Queen St., Beaufort • 728-3899

Next door to Beaufort Grocery Co., you'll find an out-of-this-world dining experience with fine international cuisine. Each week, the menu offers new and different choices to tempt your

---

INSIDERS' TIP

In hot weather, drink plenty of fluids (especially if you're walking). Beer will only dehydrate you. Drink water *before* you feel thirsty.

palate. Four- or five-course dinners transport you away from the Carolinas for a change of pace. It might be German, African, Thai, Hungarian, French, Chinese — whatever direction the chef wants to go. Reservations are recommended and may be made at Beaufort Grocery Co. Don't be in a rush and don't worry about the steep cost — rest assured, it's worth it. Come here to relax and enjoy a leisurely evening.

Beaufort Grocery Co.
$$-$$$ • 117 Queen St., Beaufort
• 728-3899

The restored town grocery store is now famous for its fine cuisine, including salads, soups and sandwiches for lunch. Be adventurous and try the *gougeres*, which are herb pastries stuffed with wonderful salad things such as crab, shrimp, chicken or eggs. For dinner, try fresh seafood, choice steaks, chicken, duck or lamb with creative sauces. Definitely begin with a Carolina crab cake appetizer and end with a luscious dessert. Sunday brunch is great, and the small bar is well-stocked and invites conversations among locals and visiting golfers who all blend into the relaxed setting.

Clawson's 1905 Restaurant
$$ • 429 Front St., Beaufort • 728-2133

Old and new wares represent the atmosphere of the early days along the waterfront in Beaufort. Go early and expect crowds during the summer. Wonderful appetizers include battered and lightly fried vegetables. Entrees feature fried, grilled or sauteed seafood, chicken, pasta or steaks; and wine, beer or mixed drinks are available. For a great lunch, we recommend the hearty baked potato stuffed with seafood, vegetables or meat.

Finz Grill & Eatery
$ • 330 Front St., Beaufort • 728-7459

Finz offers seating on its great porch overhanging the creek as well as in the restaurant or the bar. Gumbo or black bean items

enhance the varied choices of seafood, such as flounder, Spanish mackerel or king mackerel. You could be eating next to the person who caught your meal, because the fresh seafood is caught by local fishermen. Seafood entrees can be ordered grilled, blackened or fried. Other dinner entrees include steaks and pasta. The lunch menu offers all sorts of sandwiches, subs, burgers and soups (we recommend the black bean). Finz is a friendly place to relax, with good food, nice people and all beverage permits for beer, wine or mixed drinks.

Net House Steam Restaurant & Oyster Bar
$$-$$$ • 133 Turner St., Beaufort
• 728-2002

Conch or clam chowder and every steamed mollusk plus other dinner choices and delectable desserts (did we mention the Key lime pie?) are enough to bring any golf group to this family-owned and operated establishment for lunch or dinner. The atmosphere is distinctly maritime; the restaurant is bedecked in weathered pine and nautical antiques.

Morehead City

Bogue's Pocket Cafe
$$-$$$ • 708 Evans St., Morehead City
• 247-5351

Special homemade delicacies include seafood, soups, salads, pasta, chicken, beef and definitely desserts. Hours vary, and the menu changes frequently. The owner also welcomes golfers to the Purple Pelican in Beaufort, 728-2224, overlooking the Intracoastal Waterway.

Calypso Cafe
$$$ • 506 Arendell St., Morehead City
• 240-3380

Creative cocktails and a tropical atmosphere welcome you into this world of fine food. We like to begin a meal with the black bean torta or the stuffed jalapeños. Then, move on to the entrees, which spotlight local seafood with an island taste of fruits and spices.

> ## FYI
> Unless otherwise noted, the area code for all businesses listed in this chapter is 919.
> Also note that the MP found in many addresses in this chapter stands for milepost, a common location designator in the Bogue Banks area.

Surfing for Golf

Everything and everyone is on the Internet these days, including Greg Norman whose page is sponsored by Reebok who probably paid an eight-figure sum for the worldwide Shark cyber-rights. The Norman page features a photo of Greg looking like he's just duck-hooked one into somebody's kitchen.

Thankfully, there are plenty of useful pages on the Internet, pages where you can find out about golf courses and tournaments, buy equipment and discover a cure for the yips or that terrible slice you've been fighting for the past 20 years. There's even a page on the Internet where Brad Pitt appears in his birthday suit. But that has nothing to do with golf even though I'm sure he's swung a club once or twice.

Part of the joy of Net surfing is wandering around aimlessly, trying to work out how to find things and jumping from page to page. This article is written by an Internet neophyte who would rather spend time on the course than in front of a computer screen, but I hope this points you in the right direction to find some great Net golf sites. I love reading about golf, and golf books are my favorite birthday and Christmas presents, thus I'm not terribly excited about the offerings on the Net. Based on my brief voyages, most pages offer a lot of pretty pictures but not a lot of meat (the obvious exception being the Insiders' Guide site, where this entire book is featured — see details below). You may find better pages than I found (and if so, let us know and we'll include your suggestions next edition).

If you have a search engine (see, I know the lingo) and you type in "golf," you're going to get about nine thousand entries, and eight thousand of them will link you to a real estate agent who would like to interest you in a stunning! home! next! to! a! golf! course!

Thankfully, golf on the Net features a number of golf links. This handy double entendre actually means there are plenty of golf courses you can research, but, more importantly, there are pages that can link you to golf pages. Hence the phrase: golf links. Geddit?

My favorite golf links page is, of course, the aforementioned Insiders' Guide Online[sm] site — www.insiders.com/carolina-golf. Though I'm clearly prejudiced, I now know a great golf Net site when I see one, and this is definitely one. Along with many of the other titles from this 35+-book series, this site gives you the entire content of the print version of *The Insiders' Guide® to Golf in the Carolinas*. It's hard to beat if you're looking for golfing details to North and South Carolina.

My second-favorite site is Thor's golf links at www.alto-oh.com/%7Ethor/pages/golf.html. Other good links pages include www.golflink.net; www.golf.com/links; www.well-com/user/ncifa/golf/links.htm and www.yahoo.com/Entertainment/Sports/Golf/. The latter is part of the powerful search engine. Any of these links will provide a list of just about everything that's out there plus a few pages that are really out there. One links page rates golf pages with a four-ball system: One golf ball means nothing special, while four balls means Excellent! Don't miss this.

If you've surfed the Net at all, you probably know that some pages are intricate, extensive and expensive, while others are quite basic. One of the extensive ones is Hillandale Golf Course in Durham, home to a fine Muni and one of the best golf shops in the country. You can buy stuff through their page: www.golflink.net/Hillandale/. It's a virtual catalog (see, I know the lingo).

Let's go from Durham to Maui. Type in www.maui.net/~gpsi/golf/index.html and you'll get a stunning and beautiful guide to some of the major golf courses on the island; this page has to be one of the most visually appealing (and slowest) on the Net.

If you're a left-handed golfer (like me) and you're tired (like me) of having right-handed idiots telling you that your problem is that you're hitting the ball from the wrong side, then you'll find intellectual and perhaps spiritual refuge with the National Association of Left-Handed Golfers at www.dca.net/golf/.

As you might expect, a number of golf periodicals are now available on the Net. *Golf Magazine* is at www.golfonline.com. *Golf Digest* and its affiliated publications can be found at www.golf.com/golfdigest. If your golf reading is more fiction than fact, you might find *Divot* interesting: It's a digest of golf fiction and opinion and can be reached at ubmail.ubalt.edu/~rnsmith/divot.html.

Two of the more useful sites are produced by two of golf's biggest and most important organizations: the United States Golf Association and the Professional Golfers Association. You can reach the folks in Far Hills, New Jersey, at www.usga.org. There's information about handicaps, rules, tournaments and other USGA bits and pieces. You can reach the PGA at www.pgaonline.com. Many local chapters of the PGA can be reached through the Net, allowing you to access your handicap and post scores, all from the comfort of your living room or office.

Once you've reached the golf links pages, you'll find that quite a few people have their own web pages, and many of them are dedicated to golf. The quality of these pages ranges from completely terrible to really excellent.

In rereading this Close-up, perhaps I've been a little too harsh on golf on the Internet. After all, the goal of the Internet (I think) is not to provide computer nerds with something to feel important about, but to be a global conduit for information.

There's a lot of important and useful golf stuff on the Net, but nothing beats the ultimate golf web site (see, I know the jargon). You can (and must) reach this site at www.ee.duke.edu/~ceh/caddy/caddy.html. Yes, that's right, this site is dedicated to the best movie of all time: *Caddyshack*. It features information about the movie as well as (get this) soundbites from the most popular movie never to be awarded an Oscar. While you're at the office, your computer will produce noises like "be the ball" or "NOONAN" or "I never slice" or "Oh honey! I'm hot today" or "the Dalai Llama; 12th son of the Llama." This site alone makes the Internet worthwhile.

Happy surfing! *Scott Martin*

Shrimp curry with tropical salsa and grilled fish with ginger salsa are two of our favorites. Pork, pasta, seafood fajitas and blackened or grilled seafood will also delight your taste buds. Don't leave without trying the paradise pie, which is a brownie and ice cream covered with strawberry puree. (You may be limited to one of these per customer.) Enjoy your meal at a table, at the bar or on the patio. We like the casual atmosphere as well as the food.

Capt. Bill's Waterfront Restaurant
$$-$$$ • 701 Evans St., Morehead City • 726-2166

Lunch and dinner on the waterfront have been a tradition here since 1941. Now owned by John and Diane Poag, Capt. Bill's continues its legacy as a place for good food in Morehead City. A daily lunch special, such as baked chicken, two vegetables and hush puppies, can cost less than $4. Specials change daily, but they're always good. Try the all-you-can-eat fish on Monday or all-you-can-eat fish and popcorn shrimp on Friday. Wednesdays and Saturdays feature conch stew. Desserts are made from family recipes and created from scratch; one of the best is the Down East lemon pie. By boat or by car, just get here quick and sample any of the 13 flavors of fudge made at the restaurant. And after your meal, you can visit the Ship's Wheel Gift Shop.

Nikola's

$$-$$$ • **Fourth and Bridges Sts., Morehead City**
• **726-6060**

Nikola's serves creative and delicious Italian fare in this Victorian house. Try the rack of lamb or any pasta or seafood entree for a delightful treat. The spinach soup is unsurpassed. Reservations are recommended for weekends.

Rapscallions

$$ • **715 Arendell St., Morehead City**
• **240-1213**

Locals and visiting golfers enjoy Raps' bar, with its popcorn and wide-screen television. Enjoy lunch or dinner in a casual atmosphere. The original Raps Burger is a good bet, or try the ribs and salads. Steamed clams and crabs are our favorite; they're fresh and make a great companion to a beer after your golf round.

Bogue Banks

Bistro By The Sea

$$ • **401 Money Island Dr., MP 1.25, Atlantic Beach • 247-2777**

You don't *have* to eat here, because the bar serves mixed drinks, beer and wine; just the same, we recommend that you dine at this small, casual restaurant — a local favorite — beside Sportsman's Pier. Seafood entrees vary nightly according to season, freshness and availability, including such tasty choices as cappellini with pesto, vegetables and scallops and eggplant Parmesan (a personal favorite). You won't be disappointed by the Caesar salad with chargrilled tuna or the leafy spinach salad with shrimp. If seafood is not your choice, we recommend the char-grilled steaks or the liver in orange liqueur (c'mon, your mom would be proud!). And if you're watching your cholesterol, try the stir-fried chicken with rice and wontons.

Bourbon Street Cafe

$$ • **MP 3, Atlantic Beach • 240-2811**

Look carefully in the Atlantic Station Shopping Center; this cafe is nestled in the corner. Always check the chalkboard at the front of this cafe to learn about the daily specials. If none tickles your fancy, try one of the many Cajun and creole temptations; we love the pasta jambalaya with chicken, shrimp and sausage. Try the seafood lasagna with shrimp, scallops and spinach. The conch fritters and gumbo ya-ya will transport your taste buds to New Orleans' original Bourbon Street. Chef Charles Deal's specialties include grilled and bronzed grouper, trigger fish and salmon. He is well-trained and experienced in New Orleans cuisine. Be sure to sample a Southern dessert, such as the yummy chocolate pecan pie.

Bushwackers Restaurant

$$ • **100 Bogue Inlet Dr., Emerald Isle**
• **354-6300**

Bushwackers is a great spot for broiled or steamed seafood and appetizers such as 'gator and shark bites. Entrees include prime rib and black Angus steaks. Try the rock 'n' roll cheesecake for a luscious dessert. Mixed drinks, beer and wine are served, and the lively atmosphere in the lounge will put a smile on your face. Enjoy the fun wait staff, the wonderful oceanfront view and the great decorations too.

Frank and Clara's Restaurant & Lounge

$$-$$$ • **MP 11, Indian Beach • 247-2788**

Locals love the crab cakes or anything made with fresh crab. Try any of the seafood offerings as well as the steaks. Relax in the upstairs lounge if there's a wait for a table at dinner, or return to the lounge for a nightcap. Locals and visitors, alike, feel at home here.

Mazzella's Italian Restaurant

$$ • **N.C. Hwy. 58, Cape Carteret**
• **393-8787**

You can't go wrong with this authentic, family-owned Italian restaurant where the pasta is fresh, the sauces are homemade and the

INSIDERS' TIP

You should buy a yardage book if one is available, especially if you're playing a course for the first time — just don't let it slow your play.

Photo: N.C. Travel & Tourism

The sun sets on another great day of Central Coast golf.

seafood and pizzas are scrumptious. To add to the positives, it's affordable and convenient to accommodations and golf courses to boot!

Rucker Johns A Restaurant & More
$$ • 140 Fairview Dr., MP 19.5, Emerald Isle • 354-2413

If you find a beach house to rent in Emerald Isle, you'll probably love the area so much that you won't want to venture any farther away than a golf course or this restaurant for all the excitement you could hope for in a vacation. If you're searching for fried calamari, you've found a home here; and it's just one of the special appetizers. Steaks and ribs are great, and we never tire of the crab cakes, shrimp entrees or seafood and pasta choices. The lounge doubles as a popular nightspot.

Tradewinds
$$-$$$ • Royal Pavilion, MP 5.5, Pine Knoll Shores • 726-5188

Sunday brunch is the best time to eat here. Sample the large selection of breads, entrees, fruits and desserts. Pasta, chicken, seafood and aged prime beef specialties are menu highlights, along with good soups and salads. We recommend the Jack Daniels rib eye — and maybe a drink of the same to go with it. Live entertainment often is featured.

Where to Stay

Since the Central Coast is becoming more of a year-round resort, it would be impossible to mention all of the area's accommodations. So we've listed some of our favorites in each price range. If our recommendations don't fit your needs, you can get good information about lodging from the **Carteret County Tourism Development Bureau,** P.O. Box 1406, Morehead City, North Carolina 29557, (800) SUNNY NC. The bureau staffs visitors centers at 3409 Arendell Street (U.S. Highway 70) in Morehead City and on N.C. Highway 58 just south of its intersection with N.C. Highway 24 near Cape Carteret.

Stay in Beaufort if you're looking for history and variety. You'll certainly find copious amenities and wonderful atmosphere at many accommodations, most of which are near golf courses. If you're comfortable with cut-and-dried lodging, some inexpensive local motels provide standard options, both in Beaufort and at the beach. Or, if you're looking for ocean access and fishing options coupled with convenient proximity to golf courses, stay at one of the islands' super beachfront resorts.

Refer to our Preface for an explanation of the pricing code.

Beaufort

Beaufort Inn
$$$ • 101 Ann St., Beaufort
• 728-2600, (800) 726-0321

Head into this historic town and you'll find the Beaufort Inn on Gallant's Channel. Enjoy the rocking chairs on the porch as well as a friendly welcome and the famous breakfast. The 41 guest rooms, all with private porches, feature early American decor created by local artists and craftspeople.

Captain's Quarters Bed & Biscuit
$$$-$$$$
• 315 Ann St., Beaufort
• 728-7711, (800) 659-7111

A complete English-style breakfast, featuring Ms. Ruby's famous "Riz" biscuits, and the traditional toast to the sunset, with complimentary light wines and fresh fruit juices served on the veranda or by the parlor fireplace, are among the reasons to enjoy the Captain's Quarters. The family atmosphere in this three-bedroom Victorian home will make you feel . . . well, like part of the family.

It's in the heart of the historic district, a block from the waterfront shops and restaurants. Rated "excellent" by the American Bed & Breakfast Association, the "home of hospitality with quiet elegance" is furnished with family heirlooms and antiques; yet Ruby and

Capt. Dick Collins are as modern as it gets, offering use of computer, modem and fax. If you're on the Information Highway, send them e-mail at captqtrs@abaco.coastalnet.com.

The Cedars Inn at Beaufort
$$$-$$$$ • 305 Front St., Beaufort
• 728-7036, (800) 732-7036

The inn is created from two period homes (c. 1768 and 1851). The Grady family offers 16 standard rooms and suites, all of which are en suite (private baths); some have sitting rooms or fireplaces. Second-floor porches include rocking chairs; sit back, relax and contemplate your next day's golf round. The hospitality is warm, and breakfast (included in your room rate) is a treat. The Cedars Inn is easy to find at the corner of Front and Orange streets.

FYI

Unless otherwise noted, the area code for all businesses listed in this chapter is 919.

Also note that the MP found in many addresses in this chapter stands for milepost, a common location designator in the Bogue Banks area.

Delamar Inn Bed & Breakfast
$$$ • 217 Turner St., Beaufort • 728-4300

The Delamar Inn (c. 1866) offers Scottish charm and homemade breads for breakfast plus afternoon cookies and refreshments. Mable or Tom Steepy will be glad to help you with tee times or arrangements for other activities, such as chartering a boat or exploring Beaufort by bike. Delamar is open all year. The three guest rooms have private baths and antique furnishings.

Inlet Inn Bed & Breakfast
$$$-$$$$ • 601 Front St., Beaufort
• 728-3600

Harborfront rooms with sitting areas, bars, refrigerators and ice makers; homemade continental breakfast; and afternoon wine are among the amenities at the Inlet Inn, which opened in 1985 on the same block as the 19th-century inn of the same name. Enjoy a little respite in the courtyard garden or in the rooftop lounge, with impressive views of the Atlantic Ocean, Morehead City Harbor, Cape Lookout Light, Fort Macon, the wild ponies on Carrot Island and the Beaufort waterfront. The inn is also near the North Carolina Maritime Museum and many fine restaurants and shops.

Photo: N.C. Travel & Tourism

For some golf is a way of life, and the Crystal Coast offers some of the area's best courses.

Langdon House

$$-$$$$, no credit cards • 135 Craven St., Beaufort • 728-5499

Fishing poles, beach baskets, arranged dinner reservations, full breakfast with Jimm's famous pecan waffles — these are a few of the treats here. All four rooms are comfortable and include private baths. Langdon House is open year round.

Pecan Tree Inn

$$$-$$$$ • 116 Queen St., Beaufort • 728-6733

Combine your honeymoon with your golf trip and you can enjoy the Jacuzzi in the bridal suite plus Susan's homemade muffins and special ground coffee in this charming historic home. The other six rooms effuse individual character, and each includes a private bath. The half-block walk to the waterfront is a treat. The Johnsons will help arrange tee times or other activities, including box-lunch excursions or bicycle rides through the historic district. In the morning, you can enjoy a continental breakfast on the wraparound porch or in the formal dining room.

Morehead City

Best Western Buccaneer Inn

$$ • 2806 Arendell St. (U.S. Hwy. 70), Morehead City • 726-3115, (800) 682-4982

Golf packages are arranged here for two nights or a week, with tee times booked on any area course. A full hot breakfast, comfortable accommodations, greens fees and cart are included in your price. The Buccaneer Inn is near shopping destinations and historical tours for fun in your spare time.

Bogue Banks

Atlantis Lodge

$$-$$$$ • Salter Path Rd., MP 5, Pine Knoll Shores • 726-5168, (800) 682-7057

Atlantis Lodge is one of the oldest hotels on Bogue Banks. It's situated among large live oaks on the ocean side of Salter Path Road. All of the units are efficiencies with kitchens

and separate dining, living and sleeping areas. Every unit also has either a patio or deck that faces the ocean. Lounge around the pool and psych yourself up for tomorrow's tee time. During fall and spring, the hotel offers package deals.

Harborlight Guest House

$$$-$$$$ • 332 Live Oak Dr., Cape Carteret • 393-6868, (800) 624-VIEW

Stay in one of the seven suites at this bed and breakfast inn. Once used as a restaurant by the ferry service, this three-story establishment is known for its beautiful views of more than 500 feet of shoreline and its choice setting close to Emerald Isle beaches. Enjoy your breakfast privately in your upstairs suite or have it served in the dining room or on the waterfront terrace. This guest house is open year round and is ideal for a 20-person conference.

Holiday Inn On the Ocean

$$ • Salter Path Rd., Atlantic Beach • 726-2544

On the oceanfront, with deep-sea fishing, sailing, pier fishing and golf courses nearby, this hotel is a convenient choice for outdoor enthusiasts as well as golfers. Amenities include a pool, restaurant and lounge. Hotel staff can customize golf packages and golf widow packages, including greens fees, a cart, daily full breakfast, golf towel and tees plus an oceanview or poolside room. The best deal is a two-night stay with two days of golf from early November until March.

Iron Steamer Resort

$$-$$$ • Salter Path Rd., MP 6.75, Pine Knoll Shores • 247-4221, (800) 332-4221

Families and anglers are welcome at Iron Steamer, open from Easter until Thanksgiving. The resort is named for a Civil War-era blockade runner; it's remains are visible from the on-site pier. Oceanfront rooms offer access to the beach, a pool and the pier. Request an in-room refrigerator or private balcony if you'd like.

Oceanana Resort Motel

$$-$$$ • E. Fort Macon Rd., MP 1.5, Atlantic Beach • 726-4111

This is a basic motel, with comfortable standard rooms, oceanfront rooms and suites. Amenities include a pool, children's play area (this place is great for families), fishing pier, picnic tables and grills and more. It's open from spring through fall only. Inquire about golf privileges.

Parkerton Inn

$$ • N.C. Hwy. 58 N., Cape Carteret • 393-9000

You'll have convenient access to the golf courses and the Crystal Coast Amphitheater at this somewhat new accommodation (less than two years old). Room options include efficiencies with kitchenettes. A complimentary continental breakfast is served daily. Be sure to inquire about golf packages.

Royal Pavilion

$$-$$$$ • Salter Path Rd., MP 5.5, Pine Knoll Shores • 726-5188, (800)533-3700

This is a familiar property to longtime visitors of Bogue Banks. Newly named after the John Yancey Motor Hotel was renovated, the Royal Pavilion currently offers oceanfront rooms and a conference center. The neighboring Tradewinds Restaurant will cater meals in the conference rooms — a perfect arrangement if a business meeting is part of your stay. The Pavilion's amenities include efficiency kitchens, an outdoor pool, private beach and arranged tee times.

Sheraton Atlantic Beach Resort

$$$-$$$$ • Salter Path Rd., MP 4.5, Atlantic Beach • 240-1155, (800) 624-8875

This full-service beach resort has a bar, restaurant, nightclub and pool, and a fishing pier is nearby. All rooms offer private balconies, refrigerators, microwaves and coffee makers, and suites include Jacuzzis.

Showboat Motel

$-$$ • Atlantic Beach Cswy., Atlantic Beach • 726-6163

Golfers who care to bring their fishing poles might want to stay here, since you can fish from the motel's wharf. You can cook your catch on a grill in one of the picnic areas that the motel maintains. If fishing isn't your thing, but you'd like an up-close and personal look at these creatures of the deep, take advantage of Wreckreational Divers, a complete on-site dive shop for golfers who want to go on a Sea Hunt. All rooms have refrigerators. The year-round property offers corporate and other special rates, so be sure to inquire.

Windjammer Inn

$$$-$$$$ • Salter Path Rd., MP 4.5, Pine Knoll Shores • 247-7123, (800) 233-6466

All of the Windjammer's rooms are spacious and oceanfront, with private balconies, cable TVs and refrigerators. Getting to your room via the glass-enclosed elevator offers a beautiful ocean view. No need to go out early for your cup of coffee — the Windjammer offers complimentary java each morning. There's a two-night minimum stay on summer weekends and a three-night minimum on holiday weekends; but, hey, it's a fun place to hang around for awhile.

Wilmington and The Cape Fear Coast

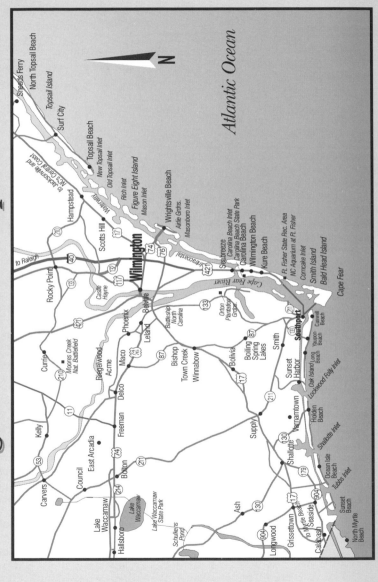

North Carolina's
Wilmington &
Cape Fear Coast

The Cape Fear Coast of North Carolina is a peninsula that takes its name from the river that flows to the nearby Atlantic Ocean. The area includes Wilmington, Carolina Beach, Wrightsville Beach and Kure Beach. Wrightsville Beach began as Wilmington's upper-class getaway — the quiet, quality vacationer's delight. Today it's a bustling beach, packed with sun worshippers during the summer. Carolina Beach flashes with more amusements and entertainment and less sophistication but provides more space for parking and beach use. Kure Beach is a peaceful bit of sandy village for the times you don't want to do much of anything except fish.

Topsail Island, a few miles north, is another significant fishing spot and is noted for the protection of sea turtles that regularly nest there.

Wilmington was an important port for its state when it was founded more than two centuries ago, and the Cape Fear River continues to flavor the city and its activities. The past and the present blend on the streets and in the countryside of Wilmington and the Cape Fear Coast. Many annual festivals revolve around the marlin, king mackerel, surf fishing or river-related activities. Jazz and art also are celebrated in the city where cultural events are surprisingly sophisticated for a seemingly sleepy Southern locale.

A college town and a film capital, Wilmington is a happening place, with shopping, dining, watersports and nightlife to please every modern taste. Also, it's a delight to antique and history lovers for its preservation of the past through extensive renovation efforts.

The Cotton Exchange and Chandler's Wharf are clusters among the 200 city blocks that comprise the state's largest historic district where shops and restaurants are housed in the restored buildings along the riverfront.

Golf is popular all year, and the moderate, comfortable climate lures travelers from the South during their hot summers and those from the North during their cold winters. We recommend courses that are good quality and fun to play; they are public or semiprivate and will make you welcome if you're a visitor or new resident here.

Courses in parts of the Brunswick Islands, which stretch south from the Southport area, are included in our Grand Strand chapter, as they are about halfway between Wilmington and Myrtle Beach and align themselves with the Myrtle Beach area for ease of identity with a major golf resort.

Contact the Wilmington Golf Association, (800) 545-5494, for information about packages from the leading hotels and golf courses. Greens fees vary with the seasons and are usually highest during spring and fall. Several courses in this area are less expensive during the week, and several offer senior or afternoon discounts. Advance booking is rec-

FYI
Unless otherwise noted, the area code for all phone numbers in this chapter is 910.

GOLF COURSES ON NORTH CAROLINA'S WILMINGTON AREA

Course Name	Type	# Holes	Par	Slope	Yards	Walking	Booking	Cost w/ Cart
Bald Head Island Country Club	semiprivate	18	72	136	6239	yes	7 days	$71
Beau Rivage Plantation	semiprivate	18	72	129	6166	no	30 days	$28-49
Brierwood Golf Club	semiprivate	18	72	121	6170	yes	call	call
Cape Golf & Racquet	semiprivate	18	72	125	6129	no	365 days	$20-40
Duck Haven Country Club	public	18	72	122	6053	yes	none	$20
Echo Farms Golf & Country Club	semiprivate	18	72	126	6073	no	24 days	$25-30
Fox Squirrel Country Club	semiprivate	18	72	123	6208	yes	2 days	$20-29
North Shore Country Club	semiprivate	18	72	123	6358	yes	14 days	$37-50
Oak Island Golf and Country Club	semiprivate	18	72	124	6135	yes	2 days	$35
Old Fort Golf Course	public	18	72	103	5773	yes	none	$20
Olde Point Golf and Country Club	semiprivate	18	72	120	6008	no	7 days	call
Porters Neck Plantation and Country Club	semiprivate	18	72	126	6818	no	60 days	$60-70
Topsail Greens Golf & Country Club	semiprivate	18	71	118	6010	yes	7 days	$22-28
Wilmington Municipal Golf Course	public	18	71	116	6267	yes	7 days	$15-20

ommended, particularly during the peak seasons.

Another good source for package information is Coastal Golfaway. The staff can arrange accommodations and tee times, giving you the choice of nearly 100 courses throughout various coastal areas including Wilmington and the Cape Fear Coast. Breakfast is usually included in their setups. Call 791-8494 or (800) 368-0045 for more information.

Bald Head Island Country Club
Bald Head Is., Southport • 457-7310
Championship Yardage: 6855
Slope: 143   **Par: 72**
Men's Yardage: 6239
Slope: 136   **Par: 72**
Other Yardage: 5536
Slope: 124   **Par: 72**
Ladies' Yardage: 4810
Slope: 132   **Par: 72**

This George Cobb course opened in 1975. Its bermudagrass fairways and greens provide 18 holes of hard work that is so much fun we call it a game. Exposed greens on the ocean side draw stiff wind to toy with your skill.

The signature hole is No. 16, a par 3 where you can see the ocean and Old Baldy from the elevated tee and remember you are miles away from anywhere. No. 8 is a par 3 similar to No. 16, although not as elevated. The maritime forest in which this course is set yields an almost subtropical vegetation not found on most other area courses. You will negotiate 15 freshwater lagoons and pause on top of dunes overlooking the Atlantic Ocean. The landscape is unspoiled and the turf excellent.

Amenities include a driving range, practice green, pro shop, locker room, bar, rental clubs, a beverage cart and snack bar. Two croquet greenswards, four tennis courts and a swimming pool are available. The club dining room and restaurants are popular and comfortable.

Greens fees average $71, including cart. It's best to stay here if you want to play here. Temporary club memberships include use of all club facilities and are provided with packages. Walking is allowed after noon. Advance tee times are accepted no more than seven days in advance.

A few words about Bald Head Island: It can only be reached by private boat or passenger ferry, a 20-minute ride from Indigo Plantation in Southport 2.5 miles across the water. No vehicles larger than electric golf carts are allowed here. Old Baldy is the 1817 lighthouse, oldest in the state. From its top, you get a view of the 2,000-acre island's dunes, marshes, creeks and beaches — home to abundant wildlife and a few human residents.

At the yacht harbor, you can spend several hours on the restaurant deck at Eb & Flo's — the island's gathering place for the general public. You'll fit right in if you drink your Heineken from cans and play cards while eating fresh seafood from paper plates with your fingers. You can be a yuppie while biking, golfing or socializing with old or new friends.

Beau Rivage Plantation
6230 Carolina Beach Rd., Carolina Beach
• 392-9022, (800) 628-7080
Championship Yardage: 6709
Slope: 136   **Par: 72**
Men's Yardage: 6166
Slope: 129   **Par: 72**
Other Yardage: 5610
Slope: 126   **Par: 72**
Ladies' Yardage: 4612
Slope: 114   **Par: 72**

This 18-hole championship course was built in 1988, designed by Eddie Lewis and features bentgrass greens and bermudagrass tees and fairways. It's considered a difficult course and somewhat resembles a desert around many holes. Except for the tricky sand traps, the course is situated on gently rolling

INSIDERS' TIP

Always check in 20 to 30 minutes before your tee time. You are expected to tee off at your scheduled time, not arrive at that time, then warm up and load your cart.

Photo: N.C. Travel & Tourism

Sea breezes and scenery add to the enjoyment of a round at Bald Head Island.

hills dotted with Carolina pines and live oaks draped in Spanish moss. It has unusually high elevations (it's the highest point in the city of Wilmington) and a unique character created by these rises. Water comes into play on eight holes, but the course is playable — not penal. The natural forest between the 3rd, 4th and 5th holes is a conservation area filled with wildlife, including alligators. If your ball goes in there for some odd reason, wish it well and leave it alone.

The 2nd hole is a 515-yard par 5 dogleg right, with trees flanking the right side. You may want to lay up for your third shot because the green has an obligatory bunker guarding the front side.

The 18th hole is a par 5 of special interest. It snakes to the right then cuts back to the left. This course is on rolling hills and holds a number of blind shots among its narrow fairways.

Amenities include chipping and putting greens, a driving range, club rentals and a clubhouse with bar, grill, restaurant, pro shop and locker rooms. Private and group lessons are offered. A pool, tennis courts and gourmet dining are available for lodge guests at this family-vacation destination, just a few miles outside Wilmington. Beau Rivage, French for Beautiful Shores, refers to the

beaches of the Atlantic, just minutes away from the golf course.

Greens fees range from $28 to $49; afternoon, group or senior rates are sometimes offered. Walking is not allowed. Tee times are accepted up to 30 days in advance.

Belvedere Plantation Golf & Country Club

2368 Country Club Dr., Hampstead • 270-2703
Championship Yardage: 6401
Slope: 128	**Par: 71**
Men's Yardage: 6021	
Slope: 120	**Par: 71**
Ladies' Yardage: 4992	
Slope: 113	**Par: 72**

This course was designed by Russell Burnie in the early 1970s and refurbished in 1991; it's 15 miles north of Wilmington and just north of Old Pointe Golf and Country Club (see the subsequent entry in this chapter) on U.S. Highway 17 N., convenient if you want to play 36 different holes in a day. Fairways are 419 bermudagrass, and greens are bentgrass. The course is set among 1,000 homesites, none of which are too close for comfort to the course, and the condos can be rented for an extended golf vacation.

The course is especially popular for its scenery, including the wildlife in the surround-

Photo: Porters Neck Company

Porters Neck, a Tom Fazio-designed course, opened in 1991 and was
voted by *Golf Digest* as the best coastal golf course in North Carolina.

ing forest. Osprey, gray heron or Canada geese often can be spotted among the tall pines, and the waterway view from No. 5 is peaceful.

Both No. 3 and No. 8 are considered signature holes. No. 3 is a par 3 requiring a first-shot carry over a lake. It's 180 yards from the back tees to an elevated green that slopes toward the lake. No. 8 is a par 5 that also requires a drive over a lake, which extends down the entire right fairway. A creek crosses the fairway in front of the small, elevated green. If you're a long hitter, you can go for the green in two. No yardage book is available, but the fairway markers are helpful. To reach the back nine, you must cross N.C. Highway 1675, but traffic isn't usually busy there.

Walking is allowed for members only. Tee times may be booked six months in advance. Greens fees, including cart, range from $18 to $43, and Wilmington or Hampstead residents should inquire about specials. A practice green and driving range are available. Tennis courts, a marina and a restaurant are on-site. The pro shop is limited, but the golf school offered there is first-class, as is PGA pro Tom Gibson.

Brierwood Golf Club

10 Brierwood Rd., Shallotte • 754-4660
Championship Yardage: 6607
Slope: 129   **Par: 72**
Men's Yardage: 6170
Slope: 121   **Par: 72**
Ladies' Yardage: 4812
Slope: 114   **Par: 72**

Dr. Ben Ward designed the first (now the back) nine holes, which opened in 1976. The second (front) nine opened in 1979, according to staff. This was the first course built in the South Brunswick Islands.

The course is set on flat terrain with houses bordering most holes. You'll find bermudagrass on the greens and in the fairways.

With water on 14 holes, Brierwood offers a challenging but fair test. Even from the back tees, the course is not a backbreaker; however, your wayward drives may find one of the ponds or may end up out of bounds and

in the back yard of someone's house. Even with all the water, you won't find many long carries. The emphasis is on accuracy, particularly off the tee. What few bunkers you'll find are around the greens, which are mid-size and somewhat flat.

Overall, your shots off the tee need to be sensible and straight. If your approach shot misses the green, you still have a good chance at getting up and down. But, if you reach the green in regulation, a good putt will yield a birdie — you can't ask for more than that!

Amenities include a putting green, bar, snack bar, pro shop, rental clubs and a beverage cart. Tennis courts are adjacent to the course, and we're told that the local fishing is excellent.

Walking is for members and members' guests only. You can book a tee time seven days in advance. Approximate cost, including cart, is $36 daily.

The Cape Golf & Racquet Club

535 The Cape Blvd.,
Wilmington • 799-3110
Championship Yardage: 6790
Slope: 133   **Par: 72**
Men's Yardage: 6129
Slope: 125   **Par: 72**
Other Yardage: 5629
Slope: 120   **Par: 72**
Ladies' Yardage: 4948
Slope: 118   **Par: 72**

This 18-hole layout by Gene Hamm encompasses an area on the peninsula between the Cape Fear River and the Atlantic Coast. Ponds, marsh and 24 lakes lend character and challenge to this course.

The 3rd hole is a 197-yard par 3. If your tee shot is short, you have a narrow landing area because of the water on the left and right of the hole. Woodland and bunkers back the green. The 13th hole is a notable par 3 (221 yards). You must cross two bodies of water from the championship (blue) tees — a deceptive shot with the wind in your face. The 15th and 17th holes are double greens. Water comes into play on 16 holes.

FYI

Unless otherwise noted, the area code for all phone numbers in this chapter is 910.

Private lessons and clinics are offered, and both traditional and corporate outings are easily accommodated. A driving range, practice putting and chipping greens, a pro shop, restaurant and lounge are on-site. A pool and tennis courts are adjacent to the clubhouse and available to members and guests.

Greens fees range from $26 Monday through Thursday to as much as $42, including cart, on weekends. Walking is not allowed. Booking is accepted up to a year in advance.

Duck Haven Country Club
1202 Wood Rd., Wilmington • 791-7983
Championship Yardage: 6506
Slope: 125   Par: 72
Men's Yardage: 6053
Slope: 122   Par: 72
Ladies' Yardage: 5361
Slope: 121   Par: 72

Raiford Trask designed this 18-hole course with bermudagrass fairways and greens. Pine trees line the fairways, only a few of which are wide open. Accurate tee shots are required, or you'll find yourself punching out from behind trees. The layout features 18 traps — fewer than on the average course.

A par 5 was added in 1995 to the back side, so if you have previously played this course, note the differences. This 525-yard hole (from the tips) is of special interest. You tee off over marsh, a tight shot requiring extra care and accuracy. Your second shot is over a small ditch to an elevated green.

Another interesting hole is No. 16, a straightaway par 3 that plays 180 yards from the back tees. The small green is hard to hit.

Practice greens are available but no driving range. A pro shop, locker room, snack bar, rental clubs and a beverage cart (on weekends) are offered.

Year-round cost is $20, including cart. Walking is allowed. Advance booking for tee times is not necessary.

Family Golf Trips

Family vacations and golf vacations once were mutually exclusive. But times are changing in that respect. Many Carolina resorts that cater to golfers welcome non-golfing family members, with pools, Lazy Rivers, planned activities akin to children's camps and show or tour packages to attract couples and groups after golfing is done.

Many families find the combination ideal. The golfing parent or couple can enjoy a few hours a day on the greens while the children enjoy some planned activities away from the folks. Then everyone can join in evening activities without being already tired of unaccustomed togetherness.

Close-up

Many golf courses welcome families as an investment in their futures, suggesting free golf for children or afternoon programs for kids and parents alike.

International Summer Family Fun Golf Tournaments are popular in the Myrtle Beach area during June, July and August. The one-day tournaments are designed for vacationing families, and 50 or more are played each summer on different golf courses. More than 4,000 golfers participate in these annual events, and many return every year for the same fun.

No minimum age is set for entrants. All winners are based on the Callaway Handicap System, so everyone has a good chance to be a winner. Two-person teams are standard, and Captain's Choice is the format. The cost is $20 per adult and $15 for youths 18 and younger, which covers all fees, prizes and cart. Preference is given to entrants who are vacationing with a Myrtle Beach Golf Holiday accommodation member. (Participating accommodations are listed in the *Myrtle Beach Golf Holiday*

Echo Farms Golf & Country Club

4114 Echo Farms Blvd., Wilmington • 791-9318

Championship Yardage: 6708

Slope: 131   Par: 72

Men's Yardage: 6073

Slope: 126   Par: 72

Ladies' Yardage: 5142

Slope: 121   Par: 72

Gene Hamm designed this 18-hole course in 1974 on a former dairy farm. It was improved in 1995, including some new tee boxes and features bentgrass greens, most of them large, and bermudagrass fairways. It is an open-hole landscape in the Scottish motif with great stands of hardwood trees. Freshwater lakes come into play on nine holes.

The 8th hole is a par 5 on which your sec-ond shot must account for a dogleg left (you have to lay up); the third shot must carry over a pond to an elevated green. The 16th is a long, straightaway par 5 with three fairway bunkers in the driving area. Play your drive to the right of the bunkers to avoid trouble. Wide fairways, but much water, characterize the course.

This course is well-maintained, and the staff is proud of its quality. Echo Farms is set in a residential community, and a large nature preserve within its boundaries is home to abundant and diverse wildlife.

Amenities include a driving range, practice greens, a pro shop, locker room, club rentals, a bar and a restaurant. Lessons and clinics are taught here.

Greens fees range from $25 to $30, in-

INSIDERS' TIP

Record your score at the next tee box or while driving to the next tee, not on or near the green.

Vacation Planner.) The accommodation's golf director will make the reservation for family tournament play.

To receive a vacation planner or for additional information, call (800) 845-GOLF.

Family golf vacations in the Carolinas can be easily combined with historical sightseeing tours that reflect the South's coming of age; many museums are close by golf destinations. From plantation tours in the primitive Lowcountry to state-run sophisticated high-tech aquariums and museums with touch displays and interactive learning, we have no dearth of delights for the young and the young at heart.

A festival is happening somewhere in the Carolinas any weekend you want to plan a trip. Festivals are a way of socializing outdoors with food, games, music and other entertainment, and they are suitable for every age group. Walk around and do nothing more than people-watch or find an activity and sample some delicious food.

Many Carolina golf courses are near amusements, arcades — and don't forget the hundreds of miniature golf courses. Any vacation can be planned to include exciting activities for everyone, even if golf remains the central focus for one or two members of your group.

The beaches of the coastal Carolinas and the mountains of the upcountry provide some of the best reasons for family golf vacations in the Carolinas. Whether you seek quietude and quality (if you're tired of the world's noises) or someplace loud and boisterous (if you crave big-city attractions), you'll find what you're looking for either at the beach or in one of our cities. Pick a spot that serves up your kind of family fun: We have year-round championship golf courses here to complement the ideal family vacation.

We recommend that you inquire with the respective chamber of commerce or tourism office, as well as your individual accommodation, for suggestions about nearby attractions and children's programs. Review our suggestions in each chapter for specific things to do in every location. Also, ask a local and you might well receive a plethora of ideas for seasonal family activities too numerous to describe in this book.

cluding cart. Walking is allowed only with a member. You may book a tee time up to 24 days in advance. Ask for Mickey Carey, and say that you read this book; he'll enjoy hearing how you learned of the course.

Fox Squirrel Country Club
591 S. Shore Dr., Boiling Spring Lakes • 845-2625
Championship Yardage: 6762

Slope: 125	Par: 72
Men's Yardage: 6208	
Slope: 123	Par: 72
Other Yardage: 5485	
Slope: 116	Par: 72
Ladies' Yardage: 5349	
Slope: 117	Par: 72

Bermudagrass greens and fairways blanket this course, which was designed by Ed Riccoboni. Water comes into play on the front nine on almost every hole. The fairways tighten on the back nine along corridors of tall longleaf pines.

The 2nd hole is an interesting par 3, 173 yards from the men's tees, and your tee shot must carry a lake.

The 9th hole is a difficult dogleg left with barrier trees that flank the left side and a ditch that runs about 80 yards in front of the green. The hole is 426 yards from the men's tees, and the prevailing wind is often in your face.

You won't find a single straightaway hole on the back nine, and the numerous doglegs make for interesting shots. Several of the doglegs on the back nine are fun because almost every one provides the chance for birdie or par. The 18th is a par 5, dogleg left, with large centered mounds in the fairway and natural white sand outlining the hole.

Wildlife is prevalent at Fox Squirrel, including (you guessed it!) North American melanistic fox squirrels as well as deer, alligators and birds in the wildlife preserve and bird sanctuary. The retirement-community atmosphere is quieter than many resort-type

Photo: N.C. Travel & Tourism

The golf course at Bald Head Island near Southport is a George Cobb classic.

courses, and the friendly staff will help make your visit enjoyable. The course's beauty makes it a favorite among locals.

Eagles Grille and Pub is in the newly remodeled clubhouse, with an outside deck overlooking the "big lake." This full-service facility is suitable for tournaments, outings, banquets or corporate functions.

Greens fees range from $20 to $32, including cart. Tee times are accepted seven days in advance. Walking is allowed anytime, so take advantage of it.

North Shore Country Club
Sneads Ferry • 327-2410, (800) 828-5035
Championship Yardage: 6866

Slope: 134	**Par: 72**
Men's Yardage: 6358	
Slope: 123	**Par: 72**
Other Yardage: 5636	
Slope 119	**Par: 72**
Ladies' Yardage: 5039	
Slope: 122	**Par: 72**

Bob Moore designed this 18-hole course, which opened in 1988. Relatively wide bermudagrass fairways are adorned with extensive mounding, tall pines and lakes. Greens are bentgrass.

Water and wind remind you that you're near the ocean and require a different game plan every round. Water comes into play on more than half of the holes. The course is scenic, with frequent views of the Intracoastal Waterway. It is always well-maintained.

The finishing holes on both sides are challenging and require a long carry over water off the tee.

The 18th hole emphasizes length; it plays 460 yards from the back tees, a slight dogleg left and usually into the prevailing wind. You tee off over water then must clear another pond to a large, slightly elevated green with two bunkers guarding the front. Drive down the right side and forget about those traps, but realize this adds length to the hole.

Amenities include a pro shop, driving range, practice green, rental clubs and a bar and grill.

Greens fees range from $37 to $50, including cart. Walking is allowed after 3 PM. Advance tee times are not necessary.

This course takes pride in its quality. As you finish each hole, look back and appreciate the magnificent view. Better yet, bring a camera, as photo opportunities abound (just don't let it slow your or anyone else's play). If you take home a photograph of every hole, you can imagine you're still at North Shore.

Oak Island Golf & Country Club
928 Caswell Beach Rd., Caswell Beach
• 278-5275
Championship Yardage: 6608
Slope: 128   **Par: 72**
Men's Yardage: 6135
Slope: 124   **Par: 72**
Ladies' Yardage: 5437
Slope: 121   **Par: 72**

This George Cobb course, completed in 1964, is one of the county's oldest. It was improved in 1995 and is inviting to golfers of all levels who enjoy its bermudagrass fairways and greens.

You'll need all your clubs to play Oak Island. The sea breezes are the challenge here. The wind may help you on one hole, then hurt you on the next. Water, sand, open fairways and the differences in individual hole layouts lend character to this course. You won't find adjacent fairways here. If you shoot wide of the fairway, you're in the trees.

One of the notable holes is the par 3 No. 7, which plays 191 yards from the back tees. You must carry over water to an inclined green (up about 35 feet), heavily trapped on both sides.

Both finishing holes are of interest. The 9th is a slight dogleg right with a trap in the corner. It measures 426 yards from the back tees and is played into the head wind; it can be 475 yards on some days.

The 18th is a par 5 that measures 553 yards from the tips. It's a straightaway shot, but you must hit into the same head wind. You must clear water on the third shot, which, depending on the wind, may require a 3-wood.

Amenities include a pro shop, rental clubs, a bar, restaurant and lounge, locker rooms, a driving range, putting green and a pool.

Cost is $35, including cart. Walking is allowed on weekdays after 1 PM. Tee times are accepted up to two days in advance.

In case you aren't familiar with this area, Caswell Beach is south of Bald Head Island on N.C. 211.

Old Fort Golf Course
3189 River Rd. S.E., Winnabow • 371-9940
Championship Yardage: 6311
Slope: 108   **Par: 72**
Men's Yardage: 5773
Slope: 103   **Par: 72**
Ladies' Yardage: 4580
Slope: 99   **Par: 72**

This 18-hole course, designed by the Trask Co., opened in 1990. Bermudagrass covers the greens and fairways. This wide-open layout has few trees and few traps. Fairways are wide, and greens are large. Water is a factor on about half of the holes — most of them on the back nine.

The owner's favorite hole, the par 3 196-yard 8th, is a toughie because of its length and small green with surrounding sand trap. The 17th, a par 4 measuring 433 yards from the back tees, requires tee and second shots that carry water.

Wind is also a factor on this course near the Intracoastal Waterway.

Practice greens, a driving range and rental clubs are available.

The cost is $20, including cart. Walking is allowed at the same price. The general public is welcome. Advance reservations for tee times are not necessary.

Olde Pointe Golf and Country Club

1300 Country Club Dr., Hampstead • 270-2403

Championship Yardage: 6913	
Slope: 136	Par: 72
Men's Yardage: 6253	
Slope: 123	Par: 72
Other Yardage: 6008	
Slope: 120	Par: 72
Ladies' Yardage: 5133	
Slope: 118	Par: 72

Jerry Turner designed this 18-hole course in 1974. Fairways are 419 hybrid bermudagrass, a big improvement from the previous coastal bermudagrass. The spacious greens are bentgrass. The rolling and scenic terrain ambles amid woods, lakes and streams.

FYI

Unless otherwise noted, the area code for all phone numbers in this chapter is 910.

The 12th, 13th and 14th holes are all considered signatures because of their scenic beauty on the lake. Tee-to-green concrete cart paths run continuously for 6 miles and accommodate Olde Pointe's fleet of carts.

The 11th hole is famous for its trickiness. It's a narrow par 5 of 589 yards, with a gradual dogleg right and a downward slope into the woods. It's hard to score par on this hole. The wind from the ocean will always affect your game.

A large putting green, driving range, chipping area, practice sand bunker, pro shop, snack bar and club rentals are available. Construction of a large member clubhouse is underway. The pro shop offers a good selection of gear, including women's clothing and accessories.

Lighted tennis courts and an Olympic-size pool are available to members. A boat ramp on the Intracoastal Waterway invites golfers to arrive by boat and is adjacent to a recreation area where tournaments can conclude with social functions.

Greens fees, including cart, are $35 on weekdays and $45 on weekends. Walking is allowed for members only. You may book tee times up to two weeks in advance.

Porters Neck Plantation and Country Club

1202 Porters Neck Rd., Wilmington
• 686-1177, (800) 423-5695

Championship Yardage: 7209	
Slope: 140	Par: 72
Men's Yardage: 6818	
Slope: 136	Par: 72
Other: Yardage: 6287	
Slope: 130	Par: 72
Ladies' Yardage: 5268	
Slope: 124	Par: 72

Porters Neck Plantation along the Intracoastal Waterway originated in 1732 when John Porter purchased 930 acres of King George II's original land grant from then-owner Maurice Moore. It remained a working plantation until a few years ago.

Today, it's a private country club community, but the golf course is available for public play. The course, homesites and amenities were carefully placed among the rolling hills and dogwood and pine forests, and a traditional ambiance has been preserved. Beautiful custom homes are mingled with patio homes and provide a distinctive air, yet they don't interfere with the golf course's playability.

The 18-hole bentgrass course was built in 1991 by Tom Fazio. The par 4 14th benefits the right-to-left player; water runs the length of the hole on the left side. The second shot must be well-placed on the green. If the pin's up front, aim short of the hole. With the flag to the rear . . . you'll probably want to look ahead to the 15th.

No. 8 favors the straight hitter. It's a par 5 measuring 506 yards. You do have a chance to reach the green in two with very well-played shots. The bunkers on the right side of the

green should be avoided at all costs. Also, a fairway bunker on the left could be deadly.

Rental clubs, a driving range and a bar are available. A sports complex includes lighted clay tennis courts, a heated lap pool, an aerobics studio and a fitness room. A new clubhouse is underway, as are big improvements to the pro shop, which offers quality items. The staff is friendly and helpful, and we heartily recommend this spectacular course. Frequent ladies' events are offered, and the course stays busy. It's minutes from Wrightsville Beach and convenient to downtown Wilmington.

Monday through Thursday, greens fees are $60 per person, including cart; weekend rates are higher and subject to change. No walking is allowed. You may call as many as 60 days in advance to set your tee time.

Topsail Greens Golf & Country Club

U.S. Hwy. 17 N., Hampstead • 270-2883
Championship Yardage: 6324
Slope: 121   **Par: 71**
Men's Yardage: 6010
Slope: 118   **Par: 71**
Ladies' Yardage: 5033
Slope: 113   **Par: 71**

Topsail Greens is more than 20 years old and was designed by Russell Breeden. This 18-hole course is tight and, as an ocean course, windy. Fairways and greens are bermudagrass. It's considered a shot-making course that requires thinking, not just swinging. Water comes into play on seven holes, and several greens are elevated.

The island green on the par 3 No. 8, the signature hole, plays 159 yards from the men's

INSIDERS' TIP

Lift and clean your ball only when necessary.

Photo: N.C. Travel & Tourism

Wilmington-area courses usually play close to the water.

tees. It's a test of accuracy as well as being a scenic beauty.

The 11th has a water hazard about 220 yards from the tee, which still leaves some 180 yards over a large lake to the green. It's a solid par 4.

The staff here is friendly, and the course is kept in quality condition. A new large practice green, driving range, pro shop, bar and restaurant, beverage cart and club rentals are available.

Greens fees range from $22 to $28, including cart. Twilight specials are offered for $10 to $12. Walking is allowed after 3 PM. Individuals may call seven days in advance to book a tee time. If you have a big group, just call; the staff is always helpful and will do whatever they can to accommodate you.

Wilmington Municipal Golf Course

311 S. Wallace Ave., Wilmington
• 791-0558
Championship Yardage: 6564

Slope: 118	**Par: 71**
Men's Yardage: 6267	
Slope: 116	**Par: 71**
Ladies' Yardage: 4978	
Slope: 114	**Par: 72**

This 18-hole Donald Ross design, which opened in 1926, has fewer water hazards and more flat terrain than most area courses. Fairways and greens are bermudagrass. Generally, fairways are relatively wide, and water hazards are not extreme.

One of our favorite holes is the 4th, a par 3 of 184 yards that plays from an elevated tee to an elevated green. A big valley in between leads to a big hill afterward if you shoot too long. To the right and left are woods. To the far right is a pond.

The clubhouse has showers and lockers for men. Practice greens, a pro shop, rental clubs and beer sales round out the amenities.

Greens fees are inexpensive: $7 to $8 for residents and $11 to $12 for nonresidents. The cart fee is an additional $8. Walking is allowed, and you may set a tee time seven days in advance. This is possibly the busiest 18-hole course in the Carolinas, hosting 80,000 golfers annually. It's popular for its playability and low cost, and the friendly staff is a big plus.

Around Wilmington and the Cape Fear Coast . . .

Fun Things To Do

The city of **Wilmington** is surrounded by attractions, and every day dishes up something to do. **The Riverwalk** is open for strolling along the Cape Fear River, and it's here you can appreciate the historic area's shopping and dining as well as the waterfront's leisure and commercial activities. We recommend walking, boat or horse-and-carriage tours for seeing the sights. Sunset, moonlight or dinner dance cruises offer a scenic view of the town from the *Henrietta II*, a stern-wheel paddleboat that's docked by the Wilmington Hilton on N. Water Street. It has an observation deck and a complete bar, and its dining salon is heated and air-conditioned. A knowledgeable guide with a straw hat and cane will lead your adventure walking tour from the foot of Market Street on the site of the old ferry landing. Call 763-1785 for information about group tours (including multilingual service). The horse-drawn carriage or trolley tour, narrated by costumed driver, departs from Water and Market streets. Call **Springbrook Farms**, 251-8889, to arrange private tours.

Our favorite time to spend a weekend in Wilmington is during the **North Carolina Azalea Festival** in mid-April. Call 763-0905 for information about the annual event, which includes a parade, a street fair and many activities in addition to fascinating home and garden tours. You don't even have to like gardens or historic walking tours to appreciate the multicolored spectacle in bloom throughout the city. Everyone else visits during this weekend too, so you will need advance reservations for accommodations and many restaurants.

The **Battleship *North Carolina***, across the river from downtown, is easily accessible at the junction of U.S. Highways 17 and 74. It is dedicated to veterans of World War II. The ship was the first modern U.S. battleship, and it carried a crew of 2,339 who made history in the combat zones of the Pacific from 1941 to 1945. It's open for tours every day and is a summer evening host to a spectacular sound and light show. The complex includes a gift shop, seasonal snack bar and riverside picnic area. Call 251-5797 for schedules, which vary with the seasons.

Enjoy live entertainment at **Thalian Hall**, home of the country's oldest community theater and current host to national touring companies as well as numerous local theater companies. Built between 1855 and 1858 as a theater and city hall, it continues to serve both purposes. It's at the corner of Chestnut and N. Third streets in downtown Wilmington. For more information, call 343-3664 or (800) 523-2820.

Art enthusiasts can view the permanent collections of 19th- and 20th-century North Carolina artists in the **St. John's Museum of Art**, 763-0281, 114 Orange Street, in downtown Wilmington. The three restored, architecturally distinctive buildings date from 1804 and are united by a sculpture garden. Some 80 contemporary North Carolina artists and craftspeople are represented in the sales gallery.

Wilmington Railroad Museum, on the corner of Water and Red Cross streets in downtown Wilmington, includes exhibits from the important rail era of the city's history. The railway system was once the largest in the world and an important contributor to Wilmington's economic development in the mid-1800s. For more information, call 763-2634.

The **Cape Fear Museum**, 341-7413, 814 Market Street, displays an interesting nautical exhibit and provides information about the social, cultural and natural history of the region. Changing exhibits and weekend programs offer diverse entertainment. The Michael Jordan Discovery Gallery offers a hands-on exploration of southeastern North Carolina where you can feed a Venus' flytrap or crawl through a beaver lodge.

The **Bellamy Mansion**, 5th Avenue and Market Street, is downtown's newest museum. This restored structure was built on the eve of the Civil War. Tours and changing exhibits on history and the design arts are offered. The antebellum home was originally the city home of a prominent planter, and all 22 rooms on four floors are open to the public. Call 251-3700 for information.

Shopping is a good way to spend a few hours in Wilmington. **The Cotton Exchange**, 321 N. Front Street, recalls the days when cotton was king and one of the world's largest export companies was located here. Eight restored buildings connected by brick walkways, open-air courtyards and gigantic heart-pine beams house 33 specialty shops and restaurants. **Chandler's Wharf**, nearby at Water and Ann streets, houses a variety of specialty shops as well as two fine restaurants with outdoor dining.

Airlie Gardens, 7 miles east of Wilmington on Wrightsville Sound off U.S. Highway 74, offers a walking tour or a 5-mile scenic drive. It was the estate of Pembroke Jones, a wealthy 19th-century rice magnate, and the grounds overlook Money Island on Wrightsville Sound where the infamous Capt. Kidd was believed to have buried his treasure. It's open to the public from March through October, and the 50-acre garden is enchanting for its grand display of azaleas and camellias among live oaks and tall pines. Call 763-4646 for information.

Poplar Grove Plantation is on U.S. Highway 17 outside Wilmington. It showcases an 1850 Greek Revival house on a 628-acre plantation. Costumed guides and scheduled events depict the history of the period. The **Southernaire Restaurant**, featuring family-style meals, is on the grounds. Call 686-9989 for information about prices and schedules.

Take the family to **Treasure Island Family Fun Park** in Sneads Ferry for go-cart racing, bumper boats, kiddie rides and miniature golf. It's a few minutes north of Topsail Island. Call 327-2700 for information. The **Jubilee Amusement Park** has go-carts, water slides, a Ferris wheel and other fun things you'd expect to find at an amusement park. It's on U.S. Highway 421, just over the bridge into Carolina Beach. Call 458-9017.

The **North Carolina Aquarium** at Fort Fisher on Kure Beach, 458-8257 or 458-7468, offers films, live animal exhibits and field trips. Other features include an alligator pond, touch tank, life-size whale sculpture, shark, stingray exhibits and other marine life of the Cape Fear Coast.

The **Fort Fisher Civil War Museum** on Kure Beach, 458-5538, is an earthen fort that

Photo: N.C. Travel & Tourism

Wind is almost always a factor at Bald Head Island.

kept the Cape Fear River and the port of Wilmington open to blockade runners, which delivered supplies to Confederate armies. It is the site of two major battles.

The **Southport Maritime Museum**, 116 N. Howe Street, 457-0003, houses a collection of nautical memorabilia of the lower Cape Fear area.

Fishing, swimming, sunning, sand-castle building, snorkeling, motor boating and sailing are always popular, and the Cape Fear River and the Atlantic Ocean welcome visitors year round. For serious beach or fishing time, visit any of the coastal villages. Surf fishing or pier fishing will yield bluefish, spot, flounder, trout, striped bass or pompano. Power boat rentals or guided kayak nature tours are easy to find on Topsail Island. Several good options are Turtle Island Ventures, (800) 64-KAYAK or 620-TOUR, on Topsail Island or Oak Island; Entropy Boat Rentals at 675-1877 for boat rental, ski and dive trips from Wrightsville Beach or Topsail Island; or Bateson's Charter Boats at 458-8671 in Caro-

lina Beach. Deep-sea fishing for Spanish and king mackerel, cobia, dolphin and grouper is popular from Carolina Beach.

For more information, contact the **Cape Fear Convention and Visitors Bureau**, (800) 222-4757 or 341-4030, or pick up a copy of *The Insiders' Guide® to Wilmington & the Cape Fear Coast.*

Where to Eat

Food in these parts is a Southern experience that attracts visitors from far and wide, and locals use mealtimes as gathering times, especially during sunny spring or fall days. Food plays a big part in outdoor socializing along Wilmington's downtown riverfront. And visitors and locals alike enjoy the glorious views, from indoors or outdoor decks overlooking the Cape Fear River or the Atlantic Ocean, in eateries throughout the villages dotting the Cape Fear Coast. Seafood is abundant and fresh, and other offerings reflect regional as well as international flair.

Restaurants accept most major credit cards. We recommend that you call for hours of operation, as varying schedules are common during different seasons. Refer to our Preface for an explanation of the pricing code.

Wilmington

Caffe Phoenix
$$ • 9 S. Front St., Wilmington • 343-1395

Don't complain about a short wait in line to dine here — it's worth it. Italian by nature, the restaurant's seasonal specials are always tasty, and this downtown luncheon or dinner spot provides atmosphere as well as delicious food. The decor is attractive, the staff attentive, and from appetizer to dessert, it's a treat.

Crook's by the River
$$-$$$ • 138 S. Front St., Wilmington
• 762-8898

The shrimp and grits is a local favorite, and many of the seafood or Southern specialties at this fine downtown restaurant are delicious. Fresh fish and wild game (sometimes alligator) are served based on seasonal availability. Reservations are suggested during the busy summer tourist season. It's a good spot for a late-night stop for a cocktail gathering or Sunday brunch as well as dinner. The Mt. Airy chocolate souffle cake, Princess Pamela's buttermilk pie and other recipes have acquired a national reputation, and we think you will help spread the word once you've sampled the fare.

Franko's Caffe & Trattoria
$$$-$$$$ • 10 Market St., Wilmington
• 763-8100

Authentic Italian dishes are prepared with fresh seafood and complemented by Italian wines. Prime rib and lobster are touted here, along with daily specials of risotto or pasta. Breads and desserts also are homemade and so tempting. We sample Italian cuisine in every city we visit and critique wine selections too, and this trattoria certainly measures up with the best. Reservations are a good idea. You can walk here from any part of downtown.

Front Street Brewery
$-$$ • 9 N. Front St., Wilmington
• 251-1935

This new addition to downtown Wilmington should be around for a long time to come, as it's popular with any age golfer or non-golfer for lunch, dinner or just good brew. It's a block from the Cape Fear River in the Foy-Roe building, an 1883 dry goods store and, later, a prominent menswear store. Tin ceilings and heart-pine floors are original, and the new woodwork has been specially crafted. Try a raspberry wheat ale in the spring or a spiced ale or oatmeal stout in the cooler months. Hand-crafted brews are the current rage and can satisfy a taste for variety in any size up to 24 ounce jumbos. The pub food complements the beer and can be selected from a before- or after-5 PM menu. For an appetizer, try the Southwestern stromboli, a spicy sausage and jalapeño jack cheese baked into a loaf of sourdough bread. Then try the artichoke ravioli pomodoro entree — flavored with fresh tomatoes, basil, garlic and olive oil.

FYI
Unless otherwise noted, the area code for all phone numbers in this chapter is 910.

The Pilot House
$$$ • 2 Ann St., Wilmington
• 343-0200

The historic Craig House is home to a riverfront restaurant that serves good seafood and pasta, including regional recipes such as seafood au gratin and flounder stuffed with crab meat, all prefaced by the seafood bisque. It also offers frequently changing specials. Try a huge burger or sandwich for lunch, and choose from the notable wine list to accompany your dinner selection. Lunch and dinner are served daily except Sunday. The atmosphere is casual for lunch and a bit dressier for dinner.

Roy's Riverboat Landing Seafood & Steaks
$$-$$$ • Foot of Market St., Wilmington
• 763-7227

In historic downtown, this restaurant is on one of the city's oldest building sites. The Eilers Building was constructed in 1857 as a dry goods warehouse. In the 1890s, the third story was used as one of the original U.S. Weather Bureau's Observation Stations. Now you can

Photo: N.C. Travel & Tourism

Accuracy is the name of the game here if you don't want big numbers.

choose from four dining rooms on two separate floors or a private balcony with a beautiful view of the riverfront and the Battleship *North Carolina*.

The signature dishes of the seafood specialist are Jefferson seafood turnover served with caviar; lobster imperial; grouper royale or Carolina clam chowder. Seasonal offerings may include quail, venison, lamb, veal or vegetarian dishes; and beef lovers will be happy with the New York strip or filet mignon. The beef marinade with herbs and spices is a specialty. Pastries and breads also are baked to perfection, and desserts include such delights as Miss Margaret's renowned four-layer coconut cream cheese pie.

Trails End Steak House
$$$ • Trails End Rd., Wilmington
• 791-2034

Beef and history are served here in equal portions. The view of the Intracoastal Water-

way adds to the interest of the old restaurant, which has many stories to tell. Call for reservations and directions here when you're ready for authentic broiled steak or prime rib, salad and appetizers. The hospitality bar includes salads and hors d'oeuvres with all entrees. The genuine hardwood charcoal-cooked entrees are always a treat, and beer, wine and cocktails are plentiful.

Water Street
$-$$ • 5 S. Water St., Wilmington
• 343-0042

This sidewalk cafe provides a nice view of the Cape Fear River. Good soups, salads, burgers and various entrees are available for lunch or dinner. Jalapeño poppers are tasty appetizers. Water Street seafood chowder is an unusually tasty combination of shrimp, scallops, clams, fish and fresh vegetables, which can be served in sourdough boule (sort of a bowl made of bread) and makes a fine meal. Pita pocket sandwiches can be filled with a choice of salad, such as herbed chicken, tabouli or hummus. Jambalaya or Greek-style scampi add flair to the entree selections.

The Beaches

Big Daddy's Seafood Restaurant
$$$ • 202 K Ave., Kure Beach • 458-8622

A trip to the beach isn't complete without a seafood platter, and Big Daddy's is a great place to enjoy one. Or try lobster tails or Alaskan snow crab. Have your seafood broiled, fried, grilled, steamed or however you like. Steaks and chicken also are available in this casual setting. If you're really hungry, get the all-you-can-eat buffet. This is a huge restaurant that has been dishing it out for many years, and we keep coming back.

Blackbeard's Quarters Seafood Restaurant
$$ • 108 N. Shore Dr., Surf City • 328-3803

Overlooking the Atlantic Ocean in the heart of Surf City, this eatery is open for Saturday breakfast buffet, Sunday brunch and weekday evenings for dinner. A seafood buffet is offered Monday nights. The atmosphere is beach casual, but the dining is fine. Try a shrimperoo appetizer (shrimp sauteed in beer and butter and seasoned). Lightly breaded and deep fried in peanut oil, the platters or seafood entrees are fresh and tasty. The landlubber section provides several choices of steak, chicken or pasta. Beer or wine go with any of it.

The Bridge Tender
$$$ • 1414 Airlie Rd., Wrightsville Beach • 256-3419

The view from here is of the Wrightsville Beach drawbridge over the Intracoastal Waterway. The decor is enhanced by lamp light and high, raftered ceilings. The food includes frequent specials of grilled seafood or Angus beef. The wine list is excellent and has been nationally recognized frequently. Our favorite entrees include any of the Cajun-spiced seafoods. Locals frequent this restaurant, and the atmosphere is welcoming to visitors, many of whom especially enjoy the lounge.

Gardenias
$$$ • 7105 Wrightsville Ave., Wrightsville Beach • 256-2421

Fresh pasta, fresh-baked bread, local seafood, Angus beef, vegetarian dishes and delectable desserts are well matched by fine wines at Gardenias. It's west of the Waterway and presents a dinner experience to suit any budget or taste. If you like wine and enjoy learning, the wine dinner specials are for you. Wine makers and chefs create complementary blends for each course and add commentary. Reservations are accepted but are only necessary for the wine dinners.

Mollie's
$ • Shore Dr., Surf City • 328-0505

Mollie's is casual and quick. It's right across the street from the ocean and easy to find as you drive into town. The home fries and biscuits are homemade, and the country ham or omelettes will start your day right. For lunch, the best sandwich for seafood lovers is the crab melt. If you're here for dinner, the captain's choice platter contains about all the seafood a big eater can handle . . . at a great price. Desserts are made daily.

One Eyed Parrot
$$ • Roland Ave. at Shore Dr., Surf City • 328-3326

It's casual and situated at a great shore location. For lunch, dinner or drinks and a snack, One Eyed Parrot is an enjoyable stop. Try the indescribable appetizer of pepper-seared scallops. Specialty sandwiches for lunch feature oysters, fish, shrimp, steak or chicken. For dinner, try the smoked and grilled baby back ribs made from a secret recipe. Or enjoy fried or broiled seafood entrees, grilled chicken breast or rib-eye steak with all the trimmings. Surf City is part of Topsail Island and is renowned for its relaxing atmosphere, which you're bound to notice.

Soundside
$$$ • 209 N. New River Dr., Surf City • 328-0803

Soundside is literally on the sound, and the views are enchanting. Seafood predominates the menu, but prime rib, chicken, soups

and salads are good too. Good wines accompany the fabulous dinners, which are creatively prepared and properly served by the courteous and well-trained waitstaff. Reservations are suggested. The Market, next door to Soundside, serves many of the same items, except entrees, with wine and followed by dessert.

Where to Stay

You'll probably want to stay near your favorite golf course. We recommend a few special accommodations that are nearby; most offer golf packages. Refer to our Preface for an explanation of the pricing code.

Wilmington

219 South 5th
$-$$$$$ • 219 S. Fifth St., Wilmington • 763-5539, (800) 219-SOFI

This bed and breakfast inn is a gracious Greek Revival structure built in 1871, restored and decorated for modern comfort. Rooms include king- or queen-size beds and fireplaces. Suites and efficiencies also are offered, all with private baths and access to common areas. A full breakfast is served, and golf packages are arranged at nearby courses. Also private walking tours of the historic district may be arranged. This inn advertises itself as "uniquely unpretentious."

Beau Rivage Plantation
$$$-$$$$ • 6230 Carolina Beach Rd., Wilmington • 392-9021, (800) 628-7080

Luxurious suites furnished with antique reproductions, balconies overlooking the golf practice facility, a pool and restaurant welcome you into the true plantation life, while you enjoy a golf vacation. Modern facilities are combined with old-fashioned elegance and Southern hospitality in the country club atmosphere. Golf packages are available, and family or business visits are a good idea.

Talk about a water hazard!

Catherine's Inn
$-$$ • 410 S. Front St., Wilmington
• 476-0723, 251-0863

A full breakfast and use of all of the inn's amenities are included during a visit to this classic Southern home. It's been restored to its 1883 splendor when the home was built by the Forshee family, and the rooms are comfortable and inviting, each with private bath. The spacious lawn overlooks a sunken garden and the Cape Fear River. Morning coffee is delivered to your room. Extras include complimentary afternoon refreshments, turndown service and bedtime liqueur.

The Curran House
$-$$ • 312 S. Third St., Wilmington
• 763-6603, (800) 763-6603

Vicki and Greg Stringer offer three uniquely furnished guest bedrooms with private baths, king- or queen-size beds, central air-conditioning and ceiling fans. This was the McKay-Green House built in 1837 in Wilmington's downtown. The exterior architecture is an unusual combination of Queen Anne and Victorian Italianate. Cable television and VCRs are available by request at no extra charge. A delicious full breakfast is included. The historic district's walking tours, shopping or dining are nearby, as are all area golf courses.

Front Street Inn
$-$$$$ • 215 S. Front St., Wilmington
• 762-6442

This is one of the few bed and breakfast inns we know that truly welcomes children. Stefany and Jay Rhodes have decorated with American art, which they say they gathered at galleries, fairs, auctions and attics, and each suite is spacious and inviting. Fireplaces, Jacuzzis, full kitchens and wet bars, VCRs, TVs and king or queen beds can keep you happy here for a long time. This historic downtown building is in a convenient location. Continental breakfast is fresh and emphasizes natural ingredients in muffins and breakfast pastries. The Sol y Solbra bar and breakfast room is the setting for breakfast or healthful beverages, beer, champagne and wine. Room service also is available.

The Inn on Orange
$-$$$ • 410 Orange St., Wilmington
• 815-0035, (800) 381-4666

Paul D. Marston and Thomas U. Renner offer luxury rooms and suites with private baths in a beautifully restored 1875 home downtown. A full country breakfast and complimentary beverages are included in the room rate. Each large room is furnished with antiques and reproductions and includes a fireplace, sitting area and either a king four-poster, queen or double brass bed. A spacious garden and pool add finishing touches.

Wilmington Hilton
$$-$$$$ • 301 N. Water St., Wilmington • 763-5900, (800) HILTONS

Overlooking the Cape Fear River, the restored downtown district and the Battleship *North Carolina*, this hotel is in an ideal spot for shopping, dining and a short drive to golf courses. Almost every amenity you could want is available, including a pool, restaurant, lounge, fitness center, conference space and courtesy van. You also can choose the concierge level for extra amenities, such as beverages and continental breakfast.

The Wine House
$$ • 311 Cottage Ln., Wilmington • 763-0511

The tiniest-ever bed and breakfast inn is this two-room cottage replicating an 1860s wine house. It's tastefully furnished with antiques, completely comfortable and located downtown, providing easy access to just about anything you'd need. The entire house is a private retreat tucked away behind a historic home and church. Breakfast is a varying delight of North Carolina traditional eggs and accompanying meats and bread.

The Beaches

Bald Head Island Resort
$$$$ • Bald Head Is. • 457-5002, (800) 234-1666

The management group here handles cottage, condo and villa rentals. This might be the farthest away from the real world you'll ever get, and it's no more than a 20-minute ferry ride. Golf carts and bikes are the only modes of transportation here faster than your feet, so imagine the noise and pollution levels dropping accordingly. Not the least expensive of resorts, this exclusive residential and vacation island will lure you into its luxurious golf course and yuppie-like atmosphere, and you can be part of it for a vaca-

tion or a lifetime. Golf packages include the round-trip ferry ride, cart and greens fees. Weekday fees are more affordable than weekend rates.

Blockade Runner Beach Resort and Conference Center
$$$-$$$$ • 275 Waynick Blvd., Wrightsville Beach • 256-2251, (800) 541-1161

Golf, sailing and children's packages are offered at this fine oceanfront resort, which overlooks the windsurfing and sailing center. The standard package includes waterfront accommodations and greens fees. The deluxe golf package includes room, greens fees, a cart fee and breakfast and dinner at the hotel's Ocean Terrace Restaurant where the gourmet choices are unlimited. Additional holes may be played regularly at no extra charge, except cart fee, on many Wilmington-area courses. A bar, restaurant, health center, pool, beach and comedy club provide choices of things to do during your visit — especially convenient if you're traveling with a family. The view is spectacular, and public beach access is great.

The Cottage
$$$ • 275 Waynick Blvd., Wrightsville Beach • 256-2251, (800) 805-2252

This remodeled 1935 boarding house is adjacent to the Blockade Runner Beach Resort at Wrightsville Beach. The 13 spacious rooms can be reserved individually or collectively — a good choice for large families or groups. Amenities at the Blockade Runner include a pool, health spa, Jacuzzi, lounges, live entertainment, oceanfront dining and children's programs. A golf director is on-site to arrange your tee times. The Cottage is reminiscent of years past when beach cottages were the only accommodations available.

Lois Jane's Riverview Inn
$$ • 106 W. Bay St., Southport • 457-6701, (800) 457-1152

A full breakfast, afternoon hors d'oeuvres and evening sweets are included for your stay in this beautifully restored 19th-century home overlooking the Cape Fear River. A room with a private bath is available by request. This is

Photo: N.C. Travel & Tourism

Oyster Bay Golf Links in Sunset Beach is one of the Carolina's beautiful courses.

a comfortable and charming bed and breakfast inn in the wonderful little village of Southport where you can stroll along the River Walk to antiques shops, restaurants or the Maritime Museum. Golf courses, especially Bald Head Island's, are easily accessible from here.

Seven Seas Inn
$ • 130 Fort Fisher Blvd., Kure Beach • 458-8122

Efficiencies, connecting rooms or two-room suites are offered here, along with cable television, refrigerators and coffee pots in the rooms. The whole family can enjoy the oceanfront and kiddie pools as well as a playground, picnic area with grills, ice cream parlor, game room and nearby amusement park, water slide and miniature golf. Laundry facilities also are available. Golf or fishing packages are offered.

The Surf
$-$$$$ • 711 S. Lumina Ave., Wrightsville Beach • 256-2275

Luxury oceanfront suites are convenient to golf courses as well as charter, surf or pier fishing and boating. Each of the 45 suites offers a combined living room/kitchen, cable television, queen-size sleeper sofa and a separate bedroom with queen-size bed. Meeting rooms and catering also may be arranged if you're here on business. The pool, sun deck and gazebo are oceanfront, and the Oceanic Pier and Restaurant are nearby.

Golf Equipment

Tee Smith Custom Golf Clubs, 1047 S. Kerr Avenue, Wilmington, 395-4008, is one place you will want to visit for the serious purchase of new clubs. Regripping service and various brands are available. Nearby **Pro**

Golf Discount, 914 S. Kerr Avenue, 392-9405, offers a large selection of major-brand equipment and accessories and provides professional club fitting, repair and regripping services on site. **The Golf Bag**, U.S. Highway 17 S., Hampstead, 270-2980, has a good selection of items, with emphasis on equipment and accessories for ladies. It's easy to find north of Porter's Neck Plantation and Country Club near Olde Pointe Golf and Country Club (see this chapter's previous entry).

The Sandhills

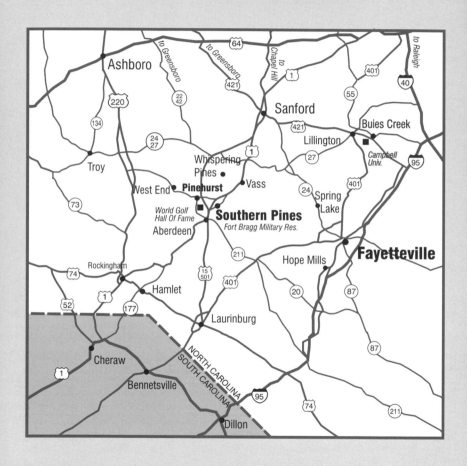

North Carolina's Pinehurst/Sandhills

Pinehurst is to golf what Aspen is to skiing, London is to fog, and the Sahara is to sand. If there's a finer, better, more fun *endroit de golf* than the Pinehurst area, please tell us, and we'll go there (at your expense) to see if you know what you're talking about. There are probably a few golf destinations that offer more courses, amenities, direct flights, restaurants or driving ranges with more balls, but nobody comes close to Pinehurst when it comes to tradition, history, ambiance, character and quality of golf. And don't geographically limit this zone: In the surrounding counties, there are plenty of excellent but lesser-known courses — so many so that you could easily play 36 holes a day for about a month and never play a poor track. An often overlooked aspect of this area is that there's something here for every budget; there are courses, restaurants and accommodations for the millionaire as well as for those of more limited means.

But the epicenter of it all is Pinehurst Resort and Country Club. This, after all, is the house that Donald built. "The Donald" is Donald Ross, the greatest golf course architect of all time. At least that's the opinion of the Donald Ross Society, a group of Ross fanatics. Pinehurst is where Ross settled and lived after a brief stint in the Northeast. This is also where he created his greatest course (Pinehurst #2) and based his design business. He owned and operated a small hotel, restaurant and bar: the Pine Crest Inn. Of course, other great architects have been ac-

tive in the area; you'll find courses by Ellis Maples, Dan Maples, Tom Jackson, Russell Breeden, Arnold Palmer, Gene Hamm, Jack Nicklaus, Jack Nicklaus II (yes, they're related), Tom Fazio, Rees Jones, J. Porter Gibson and a few others with whom you might not be familiar.

You could take any course in the Pinehurst vicinity, place it in any metropolitan area in the United States or Canada, and that course would instantly be one of the top two or three courses in that given zone. After seeing so many Pinehurst courses, you'll be numbed and spoiled. Golf is just not the same anywhere else.

Also special is the fact that just about every course here is accessible to the public in one way or another. Out of approximately 35 courses within 30 minutes of the traffic circle at the junction of U.S. highways 211 and 15/501, all but three or four are open to the public golfer. Some are more public than others. In other words, some courses are resort-oriented, and your chances of getting a choice tee time at a famous course are better if you're staying in a room that's just a few feet from the first tee. But, local knowledge includes the fact that, season permitting, you'll be able to play on almost every course.

The key to getting on the course you desire at the hour you desire here is getting to know the professional staff at a local club or, better still, at the resort where you're based. In the Pinehurst area, everyone in the business knows each other. The pro at resort #1 knows

FYI
Unless otherwise noted, the area code for all phone numbers in this chapter is 910.

GOLF COURSES IN NORTH CAROLINA'S PINEHURST AREA

Name	Type	# Holes	Par	Slope	Yards	Walking	Booking	Cost
Beacon Ridge	semiprivate	18	72	123	6143	restricted	anytime	$39-52
CC of Whispering Pines								
West Course	semiprivate	18	71	125	6007	restricted	anytime	$39-49
East Course	semiprivate	18	72	124	6406	restricted	anytime	$39-49
Cypress Lakes	public	18	72	118	6585	anytime	anytime	$25-27
Foxfire								
East Course	semiprivate/resort	18	72	123	6286	restricted	anytime	$45-64
West Course	semiprivate/resort	18	72	123	6333	restricted	anytime	$45-64
Hyland Hills	public	18	72	113	6111	restricted	anytime	$30-40
Keith Hills	public	18	72	124	6129	anytime	anytime	$29-34
King's Grant	semiprivate	18	72	118	6222	anytime	3 days	$29-36
Knollwood Fairways (9 holes)	semiprivate	18	72	121	5218	anytime	anytime	$22
Legacy	public	18	72	124	6505	no	anytime	$45-75
Little River Farm	public	18	71	n/a	6505	restricted	anytime	$40-60
Longleaf Country Club	semiprivate	18	71	110	6073	restricted	anytime	$42-67
Midland Country Club (9 holes)	semiprivate	18	70	n/r	5714	restricted	anytime	$25
Mid Pines Golf resort	resort	18	72	122	6121	restricted	anytime	$58-90
Pine Needles	resort	18	71	126	6318	restricted	anytime	$68-98
Pinehurst								
#1	resort	18	70	114	5873	caddies	anytime	$59-94
#2	resort	18	72	127	6334	caddies	anytime	$134-170
#3	resort	18	70	117	5593	caddies	anytime	$59-94
#4	resort	18	72	117	6396	caddies	anytime	$59-94
#5	resort	18	72	123	6357	caddies	anytime	$59-94
#6	resort	18	72	132	6603	restricted	anytime	$59-94
#7	resort	18	72	114	6692	restricted	anytime	$104-139
#8	resort	18	72	135	7092	caddies	anytime	$130-160
The Pit	public	18	71	128	6138	anytime	anytime	$45-80
Seven Lakes	semiprivate	18	72	122	6151	restricted	anytime	$45-60
Talamore at Pinehurst	public	18	71	134	6393	llamas	anytime	$42-82
Whispering Woods	semiprivate	18	70	n/a	6334	no	anytime	$30-42
Woodlake Country Club	semiprivate	18	72	129	6584	restricted	3 days	$45-70

the pro at resort #2 who can get a tee time at #2 because he knows the guy in the starting tower who, in turn, plays golf with the guy who used to caddie on tour for the friend of the pro at course #4 where the greenskeeper is friendly with the bartender at bar "A," which also happens to be Wayne Gretzky's favorite watering hole when he's down with family, friends and Marty McSorley for a week of 36 holes a day. You get the picture.

A lot of young and aspiring professional golfers come to Pinehurst to work, teach and hone their games for what they hope will be a life of professional golf on the big boys' tour. There are plenty of professionals and directors of golf whose knowledge and skills are excellent. What better place to be a professional than in Pinehurst, the capital of the golfing world? When it comes to playing certain courses, ask.

As with any resort area, seasons dictate operations. The first major "in-season" period begins at the end of February and extends through late May and early June. You'll find plenty of fine sunny days with perfect temperatures interspersed with days of rain and gloom. The summer months are primarily quiet on most of the courses. The intensity of the summer heat and humidity makes golf a chore, and the frequent late-day thunderstorms make it dangerous and wet. In deep summer the fairways are excellent, but the greens will be slow as the greenskeepers fight to save them from the heat and humidity. Fall brings a second season: You'll find the greens back to championship speed and the courses filling up. The fall season ends around Thanksgiving. The winter season is somewhat dead, but the courses are playable (unless the course has overseeded with rye, fairways will be brown and dull), and the rates can be at their lowest. Still, there can be plenty of wonderful and comfortable days in the winter season, and most courses offer outstanding rates.

Overall, Pinehurst offers some great values in any season; there's a course for nearly every budget. Low-cost but comfortable lodging options abound, and if you're on an eat-

If these llama caddies won't encourage your walking game, nothing will.

ing budget, Ronald McDonald has a secure presence here. You can spend a fortune in Pinehurst and get a lot in return, but you won't have to take out a second mortgage to have an excellent time here. Still, it's fun to have a couple of blowouts, and there are plenty of opportunities for that.

Whatever the size of your wallet or golfing desires, the key is to book and plan ahead as much as possible. Many, many courses host large outings and leagues, and there's nothing more depressing than showing up at a course only to find that you've arrived (without a tee time) smack dab in the middle of the annual tournament of the Mid-Atlantic Chapter of the Association of Undertakers and Mortuary Professionals. After your hour wait as the pro struggles to fit your foursome in, the pace of play will be best described as funereal. Just remember, the desk clerk at your hotel or the pro at your resort can be incredibly resourceful if you're polite.

Anyway, get to know people who work here, have fun and remember that it's always a beautiful day in Pinehurst.

Beacon Ridge Golf and Country Club
Seven Lakes W., West End • 673-2950
Championship Yardage: 6414

Slope: 125	Par: 72
Men's Yardage: 6143	
Slope: 123	Par: 72
Other Yardage: 5354	
Slope: 114	Par: 72
Ladies' Yardage: 4730	
Slope: 115	Par: 72

Beacon Ridge Golf and Country Club, a Gene Hamm design on rolling, wooded terrain, opened in 1988. This well-maintained course has bermudagrass fairways and bentgrass greens.

About 10 minutes outside the main Pinehurst area, Beacon Ridge offers some fine golf in a relaxed environment. It's part of a housing development, but houses don't interfere with play too much, if at all.

You'll find that the back nine is less undulating than the front and, therefore, a little less difficult by comparison. But overall, the course is challenging without being impossible — a happy medium that will satisfy golfers of all levels.

Perhaps what sets Beacon Ridge apart from a number of other courses in the area is its variety. Just about every hole has its own character. There isn't too much water to contend with, but when it comes into play, it will definitely affect your thinking. There are plenty of bunkers lurking to distract you as well — most of which are large and flat, with no face. The greens are mostly large and sloped. You'll find decent room off the tee, but if you miss the fairway, you'll end up in deep rough and pine trees and might not find your ball. Keep it in play and your score should be sensible.

Amenities include a practice green, range, chipping green, locker room, bar, restaurant, rental clubs and a pro shop.

The course is walkable for the extremely fit, but you'll be better off with a cart. You can book a tee time anytime you choose. Approximate cost, including cart, is $52 high, $39 low.

Country Club of Whispering Pines
2 Clubhouse Blvd., Whispering Pines
• 949-2311

The Country Club of Whispering Pines opened the East Course in 1959 and the West Course in 1970 — both Ellis Maples designs. The East Course is set on rolling terrain; the West Course is relatively flat. In the fairways, you'll find bermudagrass; on the greens, bentgrass.

The housing around the course is mostly owned by retirees who purchased the club from the developers a few years ago. There's a big membership push going on, so don't

INSIDERS' TIP

If you're going to play several golf courses and stay at a local hotel, go for the golf packages. This will save you the hassle of making telephone calls to several different courses and will often save you money off the advertised walk-up rates; plus you're more likely to get a preferred tee time.

be surprised if the club goes private within three to five years. The club offers a limited number of condos for rent.

Amenities include a practice green, range, chipping green, locker room, restaurant, rental clubs and a pro shop.

Both courses are walkable, but you must take a cart if you're not a member. You can book a tee time anytime. Approximate cost, including cart, is $49 high, $43 medium and $39 low.

West Course

Championship Yardage: 6340
Slope: 128	**Par: 71**
Men's Yardage: 6007	
Slope: 125	**Par: 71**
Other Yardage: 5525	
Slope: 118	**Par: 71**
Ladies' Yardage: 5135	
Slope: 121	**Par: 71**

Let's start with the West Course — newer, shorter and tighter than its sister track. There's also plenty of water to negotiate on the back nine, thus this course demands accuracy and sound judgment. There's a great variety of interesting holes and relatively few homes — the course is mature enough that tall pines tend to obscure the back porch of Ted and Millie Morris' place.

The key from the tee is to keep the ball in play on the tight fairways; the key to scoring from there is to avoid the many and mostly large bunkers that protect the large greens. If you miss the green and the rough is deep, then you're bound to have some scoring difficulties.

The back nine is definitely challenging, and just about every hole brings water into play. You'll really enjoy your good shots on the two par 3s. Overall, this is a fun course that will suit the player whose strength is accuracy, not distance.

East Course

Championship Yardage: 7110
Slope: 125	**Par: 72**
Men's Yardage: 6406	
Slope: 124	**Par: 72**
Other Yardage: 5943	
Slope: 117	**Par: 72**
Ladies' Yardage: 5542	
Slope: 123	**Par: 72**

Speaking of accuracy versus distance, perhaps the opposite could be said of the East Course, a track that's more than 7000 yards from the back tees. Of course, you don't have to play from the tips. The course will be somewhat more friendly from other tees. The fairways are mostly wide, and there seem to be quite a few of the epic and sweeping doglegs that made Ellis Maples famous. The track is really extremely fair and somewhat challenging, and most holes offer difficulties without gimmicks.

On the back nine, you'll find a couple of holes where water comes into play, but it's not as abundant as on the West Course. Still, it helps to be somewhat straight off the tee. You'll have plenty of chances to risk aiming for a certain segment of the fairway — the reward for a well-placed shot will be an easier approach. The greens are large, sloped and protected primarily by large bunkers. Once again, if the rough is grown up around the green, you'll have a difficult time finding your ball as well as getting up and down. There are also quite a few fairway bunkers. This fun and challenging course will test even the scratch golfer (from the back tees).

Cypress Lakes Golf Club

Cypress Lake Dr., Hope Mills • 483-0359
Championship Yardage: 7217
Slope: 126	**Par: 72**
Men's Yardage: 6585	
Slope: 118	**Par: 72**
Ladies' Yardage: 5060	
Slope: 116	**Par: 74**

We were told that Cypress Lakes opened in 1968, although we think (and we'll tell you why later) that it's much older. L.B. Floyd designed the course on rolling, wooded terrain, with bermudagrass fairways and bentgrass greens.

There are probably better golf courses in the greater Fayetteville metropolitan area, but this one stands out because it was previously owned by L.B. Floyd, father of golfing greats Raymond and Marlene Floyd. If you've ever read Ray Floyd's *From Sixty Yards In*, you know about young Raymond splashing about in the bunkers on his father's course. This is where we believe that the younger Floyd learned how to get the ball up and down so impressively . . . and so lucratively. Considering Raymond is fiftysomething, we think the course must have opened before 1968. The

The magnificent hotel at Pinehurst Resort and Country Club
is a destination for visitors from all over the world.

scorecard describes this as an "Open, Championship Course."

The course itself has been under new ownership for quite some time, and a renovation is almost complete. The layout is somewhat straightforward, and the obvious hazards or difficulties that need to be negotiated are easily visible from wherever you are. Still, it's a fun track that's well worth a visit if you're into finding out where the Floyds originally played golf.

Amenities include a practice green, range, chipping green, locker room, bar, restaurant, rental clubs and a pro shop.

You can walk your round and book a tee time anytime. Approximate cost, including cart, is $25 on weekdays and $27 on weekends.

Deercroft Golf and Country Club
U.S. Hwy. 15/501, Pinehurst • 369-3107
Championship Yardage: 6745
Slope: 125   **Par: 72**
Men's Yardage: 6185
Slope: 120   **Par: 72**
Ladies' Yardage: 5443
Slope: 113   **Par: 72**

The golf course at Deercroft Golf and Country Club opened in 1984. Gardner Gildy designed the track, which is set in wooded and undulating terrain.

Deercroft is roughly 15 minutes south of Aberdeen on U.S. Hwy. 15/501. As you approach the pro shop, a large sign tells you that Deercroft has been hailed by *Golf Week Magazine* as "One of America's Best Golf Courses."

Deercroft is a course cut out of some fine and mature pine forest, thus you'll always feel like you're far from civilization and all of its accompanying hassles and distractions. The preponderance of trees means you must keep the ball straight off the tee. Take whatever club you need to keep it out of the woods and away from the out of bounds markers that can often be quite close to the fairway. Adding to the fun are a number of deep and nasty fairway bunkers that may keep your ball from skidding into the woods but may also create an extra shot or two. There isn't a huge amount of water here at Deercroft.

Most of the greens are large and sloped and often surrounded by a series of flat bunkers with little or no significant face. A good player will probably not find it too difficult to get up and down on a regular basis. The real challenge here at Deercroft comes from keeping it straight off the tee, especially on some of the longer par 4s: There are six two-shotters of more than 400 yards from the tips, including the 18th, which is 470 yard par 4.

Deercroft is walkable for the fit, and you can walk anytime the course isn't too crowded. You can book a tee time at your convenience. Approximate cost, including cart, is $60 during the high season and $35 during the low season.

Foxfire Resort and Country Club
Hoffman Rd., Pinehurst • 295-5555

First, a note about the resort and accommodations. Plenty of people live all year at Foxfire, but many visit for a conference or just for golf. There are plenty of condominiums for rent, each with various bedroom/bathroom configurations. Call (800) 736-9347 for a brochure with all the details. Foxfire also specializes in conferences and golf tournaments/outings.

Once you've completed all your business, spend some quality time on the golf course. Then check out the restaurant, snack bar and bar, which we're told will stay open pretty much until you're ready to stop imbibing. Everyone here is warm and friendly; if you're looking for a relaxed setting for whatever sort of golf outing suits your fancy, you can't go wrong at Foxfire. With an advance call to the pro shop, the public can get a tee time on either course.

Now, about the golf courses. Both were designed by Gene Hamm. The East Course opened in 1968 and the West Course, in 1973. Both are set in rolling terrain, with pine forest bordering the bermudagrass fairways. Greens are covered with bentgrass.

Amenities include a practice green, range, chipping green, locker room, bar, restaurant, rental clubs and a pro shop.

Both courses are walkable for the fit, but you'll be encouraged to take a cart. You can

FYI

Unless otherwise noted, the area code for all phone numbers in this chapter is 910.

book a tee time anytime. Approximate cost, including cart, is $64 high, $55 medium and $45 low.

East Course

Championship Yardage: 6851
Slope: 130   **Par: 72**
Men's Yardage: 6286
Slope: 123   **Par: 72**
Other Yardage: 5864
Slope: 114   **Par: 72**
Ladies' Yardage: 5256
Slope: 119   **Par: 72**

Let's start with the East Course. You'll begin with the No. 1 handicap hole, a medium-length par 5. There's plenty of length from the back tees and plenty of width on most of the fairways. If you spray it a little off the tee, you'll find either deep rough or a nasty bunker, heavily infiltrated with love grass. You'll find some of those same bunkers around many of the greens. (By the way, the greenskeeper here is called Sandy Greens.) The greens are primarily large and sloped. You can push the ball a little, be pin high and still have a long putt for birdie. Water could prove irritating if you miss a shot badly. You might enjoy the back nine a little more than the front: It's completely undeveloped, and you really feel like you're away from it all. Some of the finest holes are on the back nine and require your best form and behavior.

West Course

Championship Yardage: 6742
Slope: 128   **Par: 72**
Men's Yardage: 6333
Slope: 123   **Par: 72**
Ladies' Yardage: 5273
Slope: 115   **Par: 72**

The West Course is fun, well-designed and perhaps a little easier in places than its counterpart, although it's plenty difficult in other places. Water comes into play on a few holes but shouldn't pose much of a problem unless you're particularly wayward. The greens are large and mostly flat, as are the bunkers. The challenges are evident; there's nothing tricked-up or artificial. If we had to choose between the two courses, we'd probably pick the East, but you'll be just as satisfied with the West. Foxfire is fortunate to have two good golf courses at its disposal.

Hyland Hills Golf Club

4100 U.S. Hwy. 1 N., Southern Pines
• 692-3752
Championship Yardage: 6726
Slope: 120   **Par: 72**
Men's Yardage: 6111
Slope: 113   **Par: 72**
Ladies' Yardage: 4677
Slope: 109   **Par: 72**

Hyland Hills Golf Club opened in 1973. Tom Jackson designed the course on rolling, wooded terrain bordered by houses and pine forest. Fairways are bermudagrass; greens, bentgrass.

Just north of Southern Pines, Hyland Hills offers a fine and fun golf course in a pleasant, primarily open setting. It's one of Tom Jackson's earlier designs and lacks some of the excesses of the modern Jackson era, such as huge mounds. But as you might expect from Jackson, this course offers well-designed holes. You won't find too much trouble off the tee, although wayward shots might find the deep rough in the summer, some nasty bunkers or the occasional small mound. Around the large and interestingly shaped greens are bunkers, more mounds and some greens with considerable slope and undulation. The greens pose the most difficulty, so bring your best putting game.

Overall, Hyland Hills provides outstanding variety. It's a good example of what made Tom Jackson such a sought-after designer. Mid- to low-handicappers should play the course from the back tees for the full effect and the most challenge. The course is an excellent value and justifiably popular.

Amenities include a practice green, range, chipping green, locker room, bar, restaurant, rental clubs and a pro shop.

INSIDERS' TIP

Plan now for a trip to the 1999 U.S. Open at Pinehurst #2. This should be a very special event, and if you enjoy golf tournaments, you'll love this one: the greatest golfers on the greatest Donald Ross course.

Profile: Donald Ross

Donald Ross is to golf course architecture what Elvis is to rock 'n' roll. No, that doesn't work. Donald Ross is to golf course architecture what Mozart is to opera. No, that doesn't work either. Donald Ross is to golf course architecture what Stradivarius is to violin making. That's it. That should give you the picture. And Pinehurst was his home for most of his life.

It's impossible to quantify Ross' influence on golf and golf course design. Word has it the first-ever biography about Ross is currently being written, although we were unable to discover when the book is due on the shelves or who will publish it. We do know that W. Pete Jones of Raleigh is the author.

Born in 1872 in Dornoch, Scotland, Donald Ross was the first son of Mundo and Lily Campbell Ross. At age 10, he began work as a caddie at Royal Dornoch Golf Club. He traveled to St. Andrews where he apprenticed as a clubmaker and professional under Old Tom Morris. It was here that he developed a love for golf and the understanding of what made a good golf hole. In 1899, Ross emigrated to Boston and became head professional and greenskeeper at Oakley Country Club where he improved the somewhat basic layout. It was at Oakley that he met members of the Tufts family. The Tufts were building Pinehurst, and they urged the young Ross to become the winter professional at their new resort.

At Pinehurst, Ross started to build his first great golf courses. Those courses — Pinehurst #1, #2, #3 and #4 — firmly placed Ross as the preeminent golf course architect in America, a country whose

Photo: The Architects of Golf

Donald J. Ross
—

population was just beginning its love affair with the game. From 1912 until his death in 1948, Ross was the busiest and arguably the best golf course architect in the United

---

The course is walkable for the extremely fit, but walking is restricted. You can book a tee time anytime you choose. Approximate cost, including cart, is from $40 down to $30.

Keith Hills Country Club

Keith Hills Rd., Buies Creek • 893-1371
Championship Yardage: 6660
Slope: 129   **Par: 72**
Men's Yardage: 6129
Slope: 124   **Par: 72**
Ladies' Yardage: 5535
Slope: 120   **Par: 72**

Keith Hills opened in 1977. Ellis Maples

designed the course and Dan Maples grabbed the assist. The course is set in primarily rolling, wooded terrain bordered by houses, with bermudagrass fairways and bentgrass greens.

Keith Hills is a well-regarded course that's owned and operated by Campbell University, so if you see a Camel wandering across the first fairway, you'll understand why (and if you don't understand — the university's mascot is a camel). The course is so well-regarded that it's often difficult to get a tee time during peak seasons. You can book a tee time just about anytime.

States. In 1925, more than 3,000 men were building courses designed by Donald J. Ross and Associates. The firm had winter offices in Pinehurst and summer offices in Rhode Island plus offices in North Amherst, Massachusetts, and Wynnewood, Pennsylvania.

Ross formed the American Society of Golf Course Architects. The society's jacket is Ross tartan. The award for contributions for furthering public understanding of golf is called the Donald Ross Award. There can't be a golf course architect in America who has visited Ross's best-known and least-known courses and come away without learning something.

Original and untouched Donald Ross courses incorporate a number of links touches from his native Dornoch and St. Andrews. He built fairway and greenside bunkers with steep faces and gave his greens a series of difficult undulations. Even though a Ross course always seems to play tougher than it looks, Ross never tricked up a course; he always made it playable and fair for all levels of golfer. The best place to see the finest original Donald Ross work is at Pinehurst's #1, #2 and #3.

A large number of Donald Ross courses were changed by other architects, yet many clubs are finding ways to restore their courses to original Ross form. A couple of architects are even making a good living in this line of work. As we've already mentioned, you'll see Ross' best efforts in the Pinehurst area, but examples of his work abound, from some of the most exclusive clubs in the country to munis where greens fees are $6 a round.

This portrait of Donald J. Ross, legendary golf course designer, was painted in oil by artist Anthony Franklin Weddington of Apex, N.C., and is part of the Pinehurst Resort and Country Club collection.
—

Artist: Anthony Franklin Weddington

The list of fine Donald Ross courses is endless, and you'll find a number of them in anyone's ranking of the top 100 courses in the country.

By the way, Ross fans might consider joining the Donald Ross Society. For more information, write to P.O. Box 403, Bloomfield, Connecticut 06002.

This beautiful course has the reputation for being kept in excellent condition. The fairways are wide, but the rough can get thick. The greens are large and sloped. A couple of elevated tees make for some dramatic tee shots. There's a reason why a course that's a little off the beaten track is so popular . . . it's not necessarily the hot dogs in the snack bar.

In October 1995, Keith Hills opened the largest practice facility in North Carolina, designed by Dan Maples. There's also an indoor teaching center. If you're in the Buies Creek or sandhills area, check out Keith Hills.

Amenities include a practice green, range, chipping green, locker room, snack bar, rental clubs and a pro shop.

The course is walkable, and you can walk anytime, although in the busy seasons you will be charged a cart fee whether you ride or not. You can book a tee time anytime, but make sure you call ahead; the course is very popular, as we've mentioned. Approximate cost, including cart, is $29 weekdays and $34 on the weekend.

King's Grant Golf and Country Club

198 Shawcroft Rd., Fayetteville • 630-1114
Championship Yardage: 6634
Slope: 125   **Par: 72**
Men's Yardage: 6222
Slope: 118   **Par: 72**
Other Yardage: 5814
Slope: 113   **Par: 72**
Ladies' Yardage: 5060
Slope: 115   **Par: 72**

Jim Holmes designed King's Grant Golf and Country Club, which opened in 1990. The course is set in rolling, wooded terrain bordered by houses. In the fairways, you'll find bermudagrass; on the greens, bentgrass.

Fayetteville is best known throughout the world as home to one of the largest army bases in the United States: Fort Bragg. This is where you'll find paratroopers and red berets. You'll also find King's Grant, a housing development course that's quite a challenge, particularly from the back tees. Many of the holes are extremely close to the houses, but if you ignore the back tees and the out-of-bounds markers, you'll find some fine, well-designed holes offering lots of challenge and interest.

Amenities include a practice green, range, chipping green, locker room, snack bar and a pro shop.

You can walk anytime. Book a tee time three days in advance. Approximate cost, including cart, is $29 on weekdays and $36 on weekends.

Knollwood Fairways Golf Club

1470 Midland Rd., Southern Pines
• 692-3572
Championship Yardage: 5398
Slope: 123   **Par: 70**
Men's Yardage: 5218
Slope: 121   **Par: 70**
Ladies' Yardage: 4730
Slope: 120   **Par: 70**

C.A. Pitts designed Knollwood Fairways. The course is set on flat terrain bordered by pine trees and condos. In the fairways, you'll find bermudagrass; on the greens, bentgrass.

Knollwood Fairways is a fun, short and entertaining layout that's great for a practice round or for the beginning or seasoned golfer who doesn't want to play a huge course. You start off with a short par 3 over water followed by a longer par 3 over land. Then you begin a series of short, tight par 4s. A local pro told us that he and his friends play the course with one rule: You must use your driver on every par 4. You might not have that same degree of control with your big stick, so take a little less club with you. There are a couple of full-length holes in the middle of the course. The massive driving range is popular with locals. Knollwood Fairways is a great place for an after-work practice round.

You can walk anytime (and you should walk here). You can book a tee time anytime you choose. Approximate cost, including cart, is $22 for 18 holes.

Legacy Golf Links

U.S. Hwy. 15/501 S., Aberdeen • 944-8825
Championship Yardage: 7008
Slope: 133   **Par: 72**
Men's Yardage: 6505
Slope: 124   **Par: 72**
Other Yardage: 594
Slope: 122   **Par: 72**
Ladies' Yardage: 5080
Slope: 128   **Par: 72**

Legacy Golf Links opened in 1992. Jack Nicklaus II, son of the Golden Bear, designed the course on rolling, wooded terrain, with bermudagrass fairways and bentgrass greens.

Jack Nicklaus II is perhaps best known as his father's son, but don't underestimate the design skill of the "second edition." Don't underestimate his golfing skill either: The younger bear won the North and South Amateur Championship in 1985. After graduating from the University of North Carolina, Jack II tried various pro circuits but soon decided to concentrate on working with his father's golf architecture business. His other efforts include Ibis Golf and Country Club in Florida and Hanbury Manor in England.

At Legacy, Jack II created a course that's extremely well-respected among locals who will not hesitate to recommend that their out-of-town friends visit this course. Legacy is a totally public course with an upper-market atmosphere. At the bag drop, an attendant takes care of placing your bag on the cart, and there's a shoe shine waiting for you after your round.

Photo: Bob Leverone

Arnold Palmer is just one of the many greats of the game to
have established his competitive reputation in Pinehurst.

The course itself is a good one — one of the better tests in the area, in fact — particularly from the back tees. Jack II and his design team built challenging, fun and playable holes. Water comes into play frequently and could lead to a big score if you're not careful. Off the tee, stick to the middle of the fairway; however, balls struck to the left and right sometimes come back to the middle due to favorable mounding. It's not death to miss the fairway, but you may find a bad lie or your view of the green obstructed by a pine tree. The course is not heavily bunkered. The greens are large and mostly sloped. Some of the par 3s are flanked by large slopes that could prove very nasty.

Golf Digest praised the layout and the course's value — a true rarity. If you like sensible and playable modern tracks, you'll enjoy Legacy. Play it and you'll understand why locals give it well-deserved kudos.

Amenities include a practice green, range, chipping green, locker room, bar, restaurant, rental clubs, a beverage cart, shoe shine and a pro shop.

Carts are required. Book a tee time anytime. Approximate cost, including cart, is $75 high, $50 medium and $45 low.

Little River Farm
500 Little River Farm Rd., Carthage
• 949-4600
Championship Yardage: 6931
Slope: 132   **Par: 71**
Men's Yardage: 6505
Slope: 125   **Par: 71**
Ladies' Yardage: 4705
Slope: 118   **Par: 71**

Little River Farm opened in 1996. Dan Maples designed the course. It's set in wooded terrain just north of Pinehurst on the road to Carthage. You'll find bermudagrass in the fairways and bentgrass on the greens.

Little River Farm is Dan Maples' third course in the Pinehurst area, and the three couldn't be much different. You'll find full descriptions of The Pit and Longleaf (his other Pinehurst courses) in this chapter. The big factor here is the soil; unlike the Pinehurst courses, the soil here at Little River Farm is Piedmont clay, thus there's more of a traditional park land feel to the track. There are more hardwood trees here than pines.

Little River Farm features some significant elevation changes, much more compared to other courses. The fairways vary in width, so be careful to leave some room for error on the tighter holes. In general, there's more room on the front nine, but the back nine gets tighter and a little more difficult. Difficulty off the tee comes in the form of ball-swallowing wetlands — make sure you know where they are.

Greens are not as large as some found on new courses, and they are more sloped than severely undulating. The greens are not tricked up in any way, and the head pro here thinks that these are Dan Maples' best greens. Unlike many courses, the shorter par 4s feature greens that are banked away from the fairway. The courses are not overly bunkered but are strategically placed around each green. We'd certainly take a look at Little River Farm, a brand new course and an interesting addition to the Pinehurst portfolio.

Little River Farm is walkable for the fit, and you can walk anytime. You can book a tee time anytime too. Approximate cost, including cart, is $69 during the high season and $40 during the low season.

Longleaf Country Club
1010 Midland Rd., Southern Pines
• 692-2114
Championship Yardage: 6600
Slope: 117   **Par: 71**
Men's Yardage: 6073
Slope: 110   **Par: 71**
Ladies' Yardage: 4719
Slope: 108   **Par: 71**

Dan Maples designed the golf course at Longleaf Country Club, which opened in 1988. The back nine is set in rolling, wooded terrain bordered with houses; the front is generally open. Fairways are bermudagrass, and greens are bentgrass.

As you drive down Midland Road for the first time, likely awed by the sheer number of golf courses concentrated on one road, you may pass Longleaf thinking it's a horse farm. Actually, the front nine is built on a former horse-training facility, and Dan Maples kept many of the old fences and hedges intact. The 100-, 150- and 200-yard markers are takeoffs on furlong markers. In case you're wondering why Dan Maples was chosen as the designer (aside from the fact that he's a darn good architect): He's part of the partnership that's developing this course. Ah, that explains it.

The front and back nines at Longleaf are quite different. It's sort of like Kyle Petty's hair: short front, long back. The front is so open, you would be excused for thinking it a links layout. The back is wooded and somewhat tight in places due to the intrusion of homes. There's a bit of water on the back nine, and one hole includes a tree right in the middle of the fairway — a Dan Maples eccentricity. There's plenty of room off the tee, and you should have lots of fun driving the ball. The greens are predominantly large, subtly undulating and well-guarded in places. The fairways feature some mounds and the occasional bunker. Overall, this fun course is suitable for all golfers.

Amenities include a practice green, range, chipping green, locker room, bar, restaurant, rental clubs and a pro shop.

The front nine is very walkable, and the back nine is walkable for the fit; you can walk anytime but still must pay a cart fee. You can book a tee time three months in advance. Approximate cost, including cart, is $67 high, $55 medium and $42 low.

Midland Country Club
2205 Midland Rd., Southern Pines
• 295-3241
Championship Yardage: 6186
Slope: 119   **Par: 70**
Men's Yardage: 5714
Slope: No rating   **Par: 70**
Ladies' Yardage: 5066
Slope: 113   **Par: 70**

Tom Jackson designed this nine-hole course on flat terrain bordered by houses. In the fairways, you'll find bermudagrass; on the greens, you'll find bentgrass.

Midland is owned by the same crew that's in charge of Knollwood, and you'll find the same ambiance and similar characteristics: fun, walkable, decently challenging, tight in places and excellent value. While this is not one of Jackson's extravaganzas, the course is wonderfully playable and well worth the approximately $20 per round. Before and/or after your round, challenge the Dunes Restaurant, just a lob wedge from the pro shop.

Amenities include a practice green, restaurant and rental clubs.

The course is extremely walkable, so walk if you can. Book a tee time whenever you choose. Approximate cost, including cart, is $25 for 18 holes.

Mid Pines Golf Resort
1010 Midland Rd., Southern Pines
• 692-2114
Championship Yardage: 6515
Slope: 127   **Par: 72**
Men's Yardage: 6121
Slope: 122   **Par: 72**
Ladies' Yardage: 5592
Slope: 128   **Par: 72**

The golf course at Mid Pines Golf Resort, a Donald Ross design, opened in 1921. The course is set in rolling, wooded terrain, with bermudagrass fairways and bentgrass greens.

First, a word or two about the resort: Mid Pines is well-known in the Carolinas as a great place for corporate meetings and conferences. Adjacent to the course are numerous houses available for rent; these wonderful old homes are a pleasant change from the typical hotel setting.

Should you want more of a hotel atmosphere, Mid Pines offers one of the most attractive and well-run facilities in the area. The rooms are traditionally appointed, many with

INSIDERS' TIP

Remember that Pinehurst was originally designed as a winter resort. The temperatures can be mild, the days sunny, and the rates for hotels and courses are at their lowest in winter. If you're looking for a way to enjoy the Pinehurst area at a reduced price, it's worth taking a risk with the weather and going in the off-season. Most courses overseed the fairways and, thus, they remain in excellent shape throughout the winter.

The Pit Golf Links in Pinehurst — you'll either love or hate this Dan Maples course that is one of the most unique and challenging in the Carolinas.

antiques. We can't think of a more wonderful setting for a conference or weekend getaway. There's also some wonderful food and drink. Other amenities include a lounge, outdoor deck, bikes, indoor game room, volleyball, babysitting services, outdoor swimming pool, tennis courts, a children's play area and shuffleboard. You can also organize or be part of a golf clinic.

Until recently, word was that the course was not in the best condition. That's all changed since Peggy Kirk Bell and some investors purchased Mid Pines in 1994. Bell also owns Pine Needles, and you can read more about her in the Pine Needles review. The end result is that the same superintendent who keeps Pine Needles in such great shape has been at work at Mid Pines. The result of this union: A great Donald Ross layout is enjoying a well-deserved renaissance.

Mid Pines offers classic, wonderful Ross resort golf. You'll find all the characteristics that made Ross so great: plenty of room off the tee, wonderful landscaping and tough greens and green complexes. It's exciting that such an excellent design is back on the map. And although you're more likely to get a good tee time if you stay at the resort, the track is open to public play.

If you're a fan of Donald Ross layouts and you enjoy a more traditional course, you'll really enjoy Mid Pines. And make sure you visit the locker room — one of the oldest, most traditional and untouched in the area; it's like stepping back into the 1920s.

Amenities include a practice green, range, chipping green, locker room, bar, restaurant, rental clubs, a beverage cart and a pro shop.

You may walk the course at any time. We suggest you book a tee time with your reservation. The public can book up to a week in advance in-season and anytime out-of-season. Approximate cost, including cart, is $90 high, $68 medium and $58 low.

Pine Needles Resort
Midland Rd., Southern Pines • 692-7111

Championship Yardage: 6708	
Slope: 131	Par: 71
Men's Yardage: 6318	
Slope: 126	Par: 71
Other Yardage: 6003	
Slope: 124	Par: 71
Ladies' Yardage: 5039	
Slope: 118	Par: 71

The golf course at Pine Needles Resort opened in 1927. Donald Ross designed the course on rolling, wooded terrain, with bermudagrass fairways and bentgrass greens. The course has hosted numerous significant tournaments and in 1996 was the site of the U.S. Women's Open.

Speaking of the resort, you'll need to stay here if you want to play Pine Needles during the spring and fall seasons. The course has opened its doors to the public during the summer. Like its relative, Mid Pines, Pine Needles is an excellent corporate retreat or weekend getaway. There are villas and apartments for rent, and you'll find the accommodations welcoming and well-appointed. Instruction is big here at Pine Needles: One of the finest teaching facilities in the Southeast is just seconds from the accommodations and is staffed by some fine instructors, including one of the most famous in the country: Peggy Kirk Bell. The course is also home to touring professional Pat McGowan, who is married to the former Bonnie Bell, a relative of Peggy Kirk Bell. A family atmosphere predominates; you'll feel right at home at Pine Needles. The place exudes golf, relaxation and Southern hospitality.

The golf course is magnificent. Like many Ross courses, the layout will not blow you away or drop your jaw; it will provide a stern but playable test with a lot of great golf holes. It's such a fair, fun and picturesque track, you'll be tempted to play it over and over again. Keep your ball out of the deep rough

adjacent to the fairways and greens, and play your approach shots to the right part of the greens. The rough isn't always grown up, and the greens aren't always fast, but you'll still find plenty of challenge. There's ample room off the tee on most holes, and a couple of water hazards come into play if you're not careful. Fairway bunkers on a few holes may envelop your ball. The greens are large and protected by a series of bunkers and small mounds and are somewhat more consistent than the putting surfaces on other Ross courses.

All potential problems are readily apparent, so keep your eyes open and you'll be OK. The layout features some extremely reachable par 5s, some long par 4s and some exciting par 3s where club selection is critical. But overall, there's no trickery, just pure golf in a wonderful setting — a true championship course with minimal "death or glory" shots.

It was great fun watching the U.S. Women's Open at Pine Needles; the USGA felt so good about the event here that it gave the nod to Pine Needles again for 2001. It's exciting that the resort has made the effort to host such an important event. We would rank Pine Needles as a must-play in the Pinehurst area; a lot of other people are going to find about how great Pine Needles is.

> **FYI**
> Unless otherwise noted, the area code for all phone numbers in this chapter is 910.

Amenities include a practice green, range, chipping green, locker room, bar, restaurant, rental clubs and a pro shop.

Walking is restricted primarily to the off-season. Book a tee time with your reservation. Approximate cost, including cart, is $98 high, $72 medium and $68 low. Special summer rates can be as low as $45.

Pinehurst Resort and Country Club
Carolina Vista Dr., Pinehurst
• 295-6811, (800) 487-4653

Here it is — the golf resort of golf resorts. If there's a resort that's more golf-oriented than Pinehurst, please show us. If there's a resort where golf is more celebrated and important, please take us there. If there's a resort with more high-quality courses, we'd love to see it. If there's a course with more history and prestige than Pinehurst, show us the book.

People come to the Pinehurst Resort and Country Club from the world over, and they're not coming for the logo golf towels in the golf shop or the gin martini (shaken not stirred) in the Ryder Cup Lounge. In fact, there's even a book about Pinehurst, by Lee Pace, entitled *Pinehurst Stories*. Even if you're not a golf history buff, pick up this volume; it's interesting reading.

The actual resort dates back to 1895 when Boston soda fountain magnate James Walker Tufts bought about 5,500 acres of former timberland in the middle of North Carolina. Tufts hired Frederick Olmstead to design and plan the resort and accompanying village. Olmstead designed New York City's famed Central Park as well as the grounds of the Biltmore Estate in Asheville, North Carolina (see our Mountains of North Carolina chapter).

The first golf course opened in 1897. Donald Ross was hired as the professional and greenskeeper in 1900, and it was from here that he built his reputation as the finest golf course architect ever.

The hotel that now dominates the scenery opened in 1901. The resort flourished and even stayed open during the Great Depression, when staff were compensated in coupons redeemable for merchandise in the Pinehurst Village General Store.

In 1943, the Holly Inn, the first hotel in Pinehurst, began year-round operations for the first time. In 1970, the Tufts family sold the resort to the Diamondhead Corporation, which in turn sold it in 1984 to present owners ClubCorp, Inc. For a better picture of the history of the course, take a stroll down the hallway on the first floor of the hotel where the staff have intelligently laid out the story behind the Pinehurst resort. There's more history in the clubhouse where the stories and pictures are more golf-oriented.

As soon as Donald Ross began sculpting great golf courses here, great golfers followed — coming here for tournaments and other events or just for pleasure. You'll see the names in the clubhouse. Palmer, Nicklaus, Snead, Hogan, Pavin, Love, Bobby Jones, Miller, Watson and Faldo are just a few of the greatest of the great who have come for the challenge, usually on course #2 — in Ross's opinion the greatest test of championship golf he designed. Others must think so too: Pick virtually any golf publication, and Pinehurst #2 is consistently ranked in the top 10 of all golf courses throughout the country.

Pinehurst #2 has hosted what has to be the most prestigious amateur tournament outside the U.S. Amateur: the North and South Championship. Some of the greatest names in the sport have won this tournament on their way to stardom as professionals. Once a professional tournament, it was Ben Hogan's first win. Other tournaments hosted by Pinehurst include the PGA Tour Championship, the PGA Championship, the Ryder Cup, the U.S. Senior Open, the PGA Junior Championship and the U.S. Amateur. In 1999, Pinehurst #2 will host the U.S. Open.

As part of Pinehurst's centennial celebration, the resort opened a new Tom Fazio-designed course, Pinehurst #8, in late 1995.

Golf amenities at Pinehurst include a range (called Maniac Hill), chipping and putting greens galore, a full golf school with some wonderful packages, restaurants, a bar called the 91st hole, locker rooms, shoe-shine service, rental clubs and pro shops. On course #1 through course #5, you can book ahead for a caddie. The cost will range from $25 to $50, depending on tip and the number of bags carried.

Unless you're a member of Pinehurst Country Club, you need to stay at the Pinehurst Hotel to play here. That's the official word. Some local hotels and some other resorts in the area offer access to Pinehurst courses, but you didn't hear that from us — OK? But why not get the full experience and stay at the hotel anyway: It's the centerpiece of Pinehurst hospitality, and it's well worth the price of admission, which fluctuates seasonally. The hotel offers several packages, many of which are good values, especially in the evergreen season (winter).

Pinehurst Hotel has 310 rooms in all. The Manor Inn, which is closer to the village, offers 49 rooms. And golf course condominiums are available as well.

The hotel provides ample meeting and exhibition space. In addition to the golf courses, which we promise to get to soon, there are 24 tennis courts, a lake for sailing and other watersports, swimming pools, a croquet court and a bowls lawn. A shuttle service can whisk you around the resort. And, of course, the hotel offers a full range of dining and drinking options, all serviced by staff dressed in britches. We think you'll love the hotel, and we're certain you'll love the golf courses. It's expensive but a great value if you believe in the tradition and excellence of a truly world-class resort. Go ahead! Get out the credit card, close your eyes, think of Donald Ross and have a great time. You won't regret it.

Pinehurst #1

Championship Yardage: 6102
Slope: 117   **Par: 70**
Men's Yardage: 5873
Slope: 114   **Par: 70**
Ladies' Yardage: 5307
Slope: 117   **Par: 73**

Pinehurst #1 opened with nine holes in 1899; a second nine opened in 1901. Dr. D. Leroy Culver, an amateur architect, designed the first nine. Donald Ross revised the first nine, added a second nine and made major changes to the course in 1913, 1937, 1940 and 1946. This rolling, wooded track has bermudagrass fairways and bentgrass greens.

As the number implies, #1 was the first course built at the Pinehurst resort and probably the first course that Donald Ross designed — unless you count the work he completed at Oakley Country Club near Boston. For Donald Ross fans, #1 is a shrine of sorts and a great example of his work. Although the course is not long by modern standards, it's still a fine test of golf: narrow fairways and tough, small greens. A couple of holes offer decent length off the tee. The fairways reveal examples of devilish Ross bunkers with steep grass faces — a true hazard for any golfer. Around the greens you'll see more grass-faced bunkers, and if you have a bad day with your short game, your score is likely to become larger than you'd care to admit. If you're a low handicapper, this course will provide a good tune-up for some of the other challenges that await you. If you're a mid- or high handicapper, you'll find this course pleasantly manageable if you keep the ball straight and putt well.

You must take a cart unless you take a caddie. You can book a tee time with your reservation at the hotel. Approximate cost, including cart, is $94 high, $72 medium and $59 low.

Pinehurst #2

Championship Yardage: 7053
Slope: 131   **Par: 72**
Men's Yardage: 6354
Slope: 127   **Par: 72**
Ladies' Yardage: 5863
Slope: 135   **Par: 74**

Pinehurst #2 opened with nine holes in 1901; an additional nine was completed in 1906. Donald Ross designed the course and made major changes in 1922, 1933, 1934, 1935 and 1946, although he constantly made minor improvements. Changes were made after Ross's death in 1948, but descendants of the Tufts family and others have brought the course back to its original form and shape.

So much has been said and written about #2 that it's somewhat unfair to summarize the course and the experience in just a few paragraphs. It's easily the finest golf course in the Carolinas as well as one of the best public-access courses in the world. And it's the reason why many golfers come to the Pinehurst. It's hosted several major and professional tournaments and is home to arguably the top amateur tournament in the country (behind the U.S. Amateur) — the North and South. For many professional golfers, this is the finest course anywhere. In summer and fall 1996, the course underwent a number of grassing changes to get ready for the U.S. Open.

So what makes #2 No. 1? At first, you might wonder. There are courses with better scenery and better views. There are courses with bigger clubhouses. And there are courses that will make your jaw drop more, that are more difficult. Yet for any apparent "shortcomings," Pinehurst #2 remains at the top of the list of the greatest golf courses. And in 1999, it will host the U.S. Open. Even with a somewhat moderate slope rating, par or worse will probably win the tournament. Still, what's the big deal?

Two things. First, this is the course that Donald Ross built and nurtured to what he thought was perfection. He eventually built a house next to the 3rd green near the confluence of the 3rd, 4th, 5th and 6th holes. He deemed Pinehurst #2 the greatest test of championship golf that he designed — that the person who won a championship here would be a golfer who had come as near as possible to all-around competence.

The terms "championship course" and "you'll have to use every club in your bag" have become well-worn clichés, but they apply at #2 perhaps more than anywhere in the Carolinas. Donald Ross built more than 400 courses in his lifetime — and this was his best.

Second, and perhaps more importantly, #2 is a golf purist's dream. Pinehurst #2 is a stunning example of what makes a great golf course: a designer who understands that a course is defined by the variety and fairness of the test.

Each hole here has its own set of difficulties and problems. Lose your concentration and your score will mushroom. In fact, it's a course where even the low to mid-handicapper will find that the score has somehow reached levels that mirror the national debt. From the back tees, we were humbled to the point of tears by the end of the round. Thankfully, on a second non-golfing visit, we spent two hours in the company of legendary starter and ranger Americus "Max" Lamberti, former curator of the PGA Hall of Fame.

Mr. Lamberti pointed out that many great golfers have been similarly humbled by #2. They may drive the ball well (you must) and hit their fair share of greens (you must), but it's the golfer with the creative and wizard-like short game who will ultimately prevail here. The fairways are generous, but it helps to be in the right place — and where you want to be often is where Ross placed a bunker or love grass. From there, your approach shot (often with a long iron) needs to hit the right portion of the green for a birdie putt. Often, the route to the correct portion

of the green is well-guarded by deep grass-faced bunkers or rough-infested hollows or a swale. And more often than not, the green plays smaller, and the less than perfect iron shot will roll off the edge. This is where the fun begins — and where the wizard of the short game will prevail.

To get up and down requires such a masterful touch that if you do so with relative ease you'll feel ready to give a short game clinic or write a book. But the severely undulating greens will give you nightmares. No putt is a gimme. And this is without all the gimmicks of modern golf course architecture. If you play to the top of your game, you'll be rewarded; but if you're "off," you'll be in for a long, frustrating round. What could be closer to the true spirit and challenge of the game?

Low handicappers will love the constant challenge and should play from the back tees. Mid-handicappers should play from the middle tees and hold on to their hats. High handicappers: Try to play within yourself, take in the experience, ignore the score and try not to impede the progress of the group behind you. Pinehurst #2 is a course you should play before you pass away. Despite the fee, you'll want to come back time and time again, constantly drawn by the addiction and timelessness of the greatest of all Donald Ross courses.

You must take a cart unless you take a caddie. Go ahead and take a caddie to experience the full effect and to keep you loose and limber. You can book a tee time with your reservation at the hotel. Approximate cost, including cart, is $170 high, $147 medium and $134 low.

Pinehurst #3

Championship Yardage: 5593
Slope: 117 | **Par: 70**
Ladies' Yardage: 5307
Slope: 117 | **Par: 71**

Pinehurst #3 opened in 1907. An additional nine was added in 1910. Donald Ross

---

INSIDERS' TIP

Several private courses offer tee times in tandem with golf packages. These courses include (designers in parentheses): Pinehurst Plantation (Ed Seay and Arnold Palmer), Pinehurst National (Jack Nicklaus), Pinewild (Gene Hamm) and Southern Pines Elks Club (Donald Ross).

Foxfire Resort boasts two solid Gene Hamm courses. It's just
one of the many excellent resorts in the Pinehurst area.

designed the course and made major changes in 1936 and 1946. The course is set on rolling, wooded terrain, with bermudagrass fairways and bentgrass greens. Pinehurst #3 is similar to #1: short and tight. And, like #1, it should not be discounted as too short to be interesting. It's a course where you must be straight off the tee and sharp with your short game to score well. The greens are small and crowned; there's plenty of trouble lurking off the tee in the form of deep grass-faced bunkers and irritating swales and hollows. Pinehurst #3 will be appreciated by those whose strength is accuracy, not distance. Many of the holes on #3 have been praised by avid Donald Ross fan Ben Crenshaw.

You must take a cart unless you take a caddie. You can book a tee time with your reservation at the hotel. Approximate cost, including cart, is $94 high, $72 medium and $59 low.

Pinehurst #4

Championship Yardage: 6919

Slope: 126	**Par: 72**

Men's Yardage: 6396

Slope: 117	**Par: 72**

Ladies' Yardage: 5696

Slope: 119	**Par: 73**

Pinehurst #4 opened nine holes in 1912 and nine more in 1919. Donald Ross designed the course, and Robert Trent Jones revised the layout in 1973, lengthening it and adding water. Rees Jones revised the layout once more in 1982. The course is set in rolling, wooded terrain. In the fairways, you'll find bermudagrass; on the greens, bentgrass.

Ross designed Pinehurst #4 as a short course well-suited to the high handicapper. The course was toughened to complement #2 in time for the World Open.

Enter the Jones clan.

Robert Trent Jones and son Rees designed a muscular track from the back tees. You can't help but be impressed with how the Joneses turned the course into a playable track for golfers of all levels. While #2 justifiably gets all the attention, #4 is well-deserving of its popularity. Gone are the grass-faced bunkers of the Ross era, which have been replaced and flattened. The re-

sult is a more aesthetically pleasing layout — but just as challenging. Overall, it's a super track.

You guessed it; you must take a cart unless you take a caddie. You can book a tee time with your reservation at the hotel. Approximate cost, including cart, is $94 high, $72 medium and $59 low.

Pinehurst #5

Championship Yardage: 6929

Slope: 130	**Par: 72**

Men's Yardage: 6357

Slope: 123	**Par: 72**

Ladies' Yardage: 5720

Slope: 131	**Par: 73**

Pinehurst #5, an Ellis Maples design, opened in 1961 on rolling, wooded terrain. Fairways are bermudagrass; greens, bentgrass.

This one of the lesser-known courses in the Pinehurst crown — perhaps, the most underrated. Maples lived in the Pinehurst area and supervised construction on Donald Ross's final design at Raleigh Country Club. Maples was a fine golfer who once shot 62. But he was also a teacher of the game and understood the needs and desires of the average golfer. Maples became one of the most sought-after architects in the Southeast. It's fitting that Pinehurst tapped Maples to design a course; he provided the resort with one of his finest efforts.

This course plays long from the back tees. But it's still fair and fun — though more so for the average player from the forward tees. Ironically, although Maples is sometimes considered the master of the long, sweeping and majestic dogleg, you won't find much of that here. Instead, you'll find some wonderful straightaway holes that demand accuracy. There's plenty of variety, from long and short par 4s to par 5s where the long-hitter will feel somewhat inclined to gamble. Pinehurst #5 is a tremendously playable course as well as being just plain fun to play.

As is typical at Pinehurst, you must take a cart unless you take a caddie. You can book a tee time with your reservation at the hotel. Approximate cost, including cart, is $94 high, $72 medium and $59 low.

Pinehurst #6

Championship Yardage: 7157
Slope: 139   **Par:** 72
Men's Yardage: 6603
Slope: 132   **Par:** 72
Ladies' Yardage: 5430
Slope: 125   **Par:** 72

Pinehurst #6 opened in 1979. George Fazio and nephew Tom Fazio tag-teamed the design here. The course is set in rolling, wooded terrain, with bermudagrass fairways and bentgrass greens.

Although it has been ranked as one of North Carolina's better golf courses, Pinehurst #6, like #5, is underrated. This course is "off-campus," and you'll have to drive or take the shuttle bus to get here. It's away from the main bulk of the Pinehurst courses, and its topography is more undulating. Fazio did not want to compete with the Ross designs, thus you'll find #6 quite different from its counterparts. The site is more dramatic, and there are some significant elevation changes.

When #6 opened, many felt Fazio had created the most difficult Pinehurst course. You have to keep the ball in play here; if you miss the course, you'll end up in thick vegetation or water or on steep fall-offs, and you may have to negotiate some mounds and swales. It doesn't look difficult, but as we all know, looks can be deceiving. Better golfers will have all they can handle from the back tees.

Tom Fazio returned to the course in 1991 to soften some of the green contours, but it's still possible to shoot some big numbers here. For a kinder, gentler ride, shoot from the forward tees; it's still an exciting track from there.

The course is walkable for the fit, but walking is restricted. You can book a tee time with your reservation at the hotel. Approximate cost, including cart, is $94 high, $72 medium and $59 low.

Pinehurst #7

Championship Yardage: 7152
Slope: 117   **Par:** 72
Men's Yardage: 6692
Slope: 114   **Par:** 72
Ladies' Yardage: 4996
Slope: 117   **Par:** 72

Pinehurst #7 opened in 1986. Rees Jones designed this lengthy course on rolling, wooded terrain, with homes bordering some of the holes. In the fairways, you'll find bermudagrass; on the greens, bentgrass.

Pinehurst #7, like #6, is another off-campus golf course. It's been consistently rated as one of the top 10 golf courses in North Carolina and as one of the best resort courses in the country since it opened.

Rees Jones is one of the most in-demand golf course architects in the nation, and he's created a significant course here. Some golfers are not excited about Jones's work, and a few locals feel there are too many uphill or blind shots. Still, it's impossible to describe the course without being positive. There's simply too much variety, interest and natural beauty to ignore.

Pinehurst #7 blends elements of links golf with elements of Pine Valley (as if we will ever play at Pine Valley!). There are lots of downhill tee shots, mounds and severely tiered, undulating greens to make life extra-interesting. There's also quite a bit of water as well as bunkers of all shapes and sizes. Some truly challenging holes are laid out in a "come get me" fashion.

If you're a traditionalist, perhaps you'll enjoy some of the older Pinehurst courses. But if you're a fan of Rees Jones and modern architecture, you'll absolutely love #7. We found Pinehurst #7 to be a spectacular course, deserving of its high ranking. It's worth a visit if you're in the Pinehurst area. It will certainly challenge you.

You must take a cart, although efforts are being made to introduce walking on the course. You can book a tee time with your reservation at the hotel. Approximate cost, including cart, is $139 high, $117 medium and $104 low.

Pinehurst #8

Championship Yardage: 7092
Slope: 135   **Par:** 72
Men's Yardage: 6692
Slope: 125   **Par:** 72
Ladies' Yardage: 4996
Slope: 112   **Par:** 72

Pinehurst #8 opened in late 1995. Tom Fazio designed the course on typical sandhills terrain: slightly undulating land replete with sandy waste areas and pine forest. In the fairways, you'll find bermudagrass; on the greens, a new strain of bentgrass called G2, which is supposed to let the greens remain firm and fast in hot weather.

The owners of Pinehurst Resort and Country Club hired Tom Fazio to design and build the course that would celebrate the 100-year anniversary of their great golfing destination. Quite an honor and challenge for Fazio, who stepped up to the plate and hit a home run with #8. There are so many excellent golf courses in the Pinehurst area that it's difficult for one track to stand out among all the others, but #8 succeeds in making the statement "I want to be one of the top resort courses in the world even though I'm just a year old." Apart from Pinehurst #6, which is really the work of his uncle, #8 represents a rarity — a public-access Fazio course in the Carolinas. And in case you didn't know, Tom Fazio is regarded as probably the top golf course architect in America.

Pinehurst gave Fazio a pretty good piece of land with which to create #8. It's certainly spacious, and, thankfully, there are no houses or condos bordering the fairways. If you enjoy the feeling of being away from everything, you'll really like #8.

But you've paid the significant fee for the golf, right? During your first tussle with this golf course, several things will strike you. From the tee, the best place to aim is not easily discerned: There's a bunker here and there, a clump of trees close to the fairway or a waste area or a swale. You want to bang it down the middle with your driver, but sometimes it's not always clear exactly where you'll find the hallowed ground of the center cut of the fairway. Also striking are the excellent variety of the challenges and the holes. No two holes are the same, and each hole boasts a unique set of challenges and all of this is achieved without being artificial and without water hazards. There are short par 3s and extremely long par 3s. There's a brutally long par 5 and a reachable one. And there's no easy way to summarize and characterize the par 4s.

The fairways here are wide, and bunkers often lurk near the best position for your approach shot. But perhaps the greatest challenge exists in and around the green complexes, which seem like a tribute to Donald Ross, only harder and larger. Many of the greens are simply enormous, but many play much smaller, what with some severe slopes

near the edges — edges that can send your ball into a swale or a bunker with a 5 foot grass face. It's all rather intimidating at times, thus you'll need to bring your very best short game to shoot anywhere near your handicap. With five sets of tees, #8 helps the higher-handicap golfer . . . at least from the tee box.

Memorable holes. The first: a downhill short par 4 of just 361 yards from the tips. The landing area narrows a bit from 150 yards in, and there are woods and a bunker on the left-hand side that could cause difficulty. Approach shots must be hit to a large green that slopes away from the fairway. The sixth: a monster par 5, 604 yards uphill from the tips; third shot is a wedge or shot iron to a green that features complete death if you go over it.

Over the years, you'll find that #8 will certainly be rated as one of the best golf courses in the Southeast. It's quirky and fun and quite a test. If you're wealthy enough to play it over and over again, you'll find that #8 will provide a different challenge each time out. It's not #2, but it's certainly a wonderful golf course and a fitting tribute and addition to the cradle of American golf.

This course is walkable for the fit, and you can walk anytime. See if you can take a caddie with you. Book a tee time with your reservation at the hotel. Approximate cost, including cart, is $149 during the high season.

The Pit Golf Links
N.C. Hwy. 5, Pinehurst • 944-1600
Championship Yardage: 6600

Slope: 139	**Par: 71**
Men's Yardage: 6138	
Slope: 128	**Par: 71**
Other Yardage: 5690	
Slope: 120	**Par: 71**
Ladies' Yardage: 4759	
Slope: 121	**Par: 72**

Dan Maples designed The Pit Golf Links, which opened in 1984. The course is set in pine barrens, with bermudagrass fairways and bentgrass greens.

Ask locals, even good golfers, what they think about The Pit and there's a sudden moment of silence . . . followed by a slightly glazed look and punctuated with "I hate that course," "It's quite a track" or "It's awesome." You'll either love or hate The Pit.

Photo: Pine Needles Lodge and Golf Club

The 375-yard 11th at Pine Needles is a fun driving hole.

Oddly, The Pit has its devotees among the mid- to high handicappers. We say "odd" because The Pit, in addition to being one of the most daring golf courses in the area, is the most penal. If you miss the fairway, that's it. Lost ball. Game over. As soon as a foursome of duffers arrives and pays the greens fee, you can see Titleist's stock shoot up. You're going to lose a lot of balls if you're not hitting it straight, so be prepared.

You know something's wrong when the back tees are called the screw tees. You know something is wrong, or different, when you drive up to the course through the rear end of Southern Pines past industrial plants. Word is The Pit was an excavation site for sand eventually used to build roads in the Great North State.

The result is a true test of target golf. Maples shows you the landing area (in most cases) and says "hit this or else." It's a truly penal course in an area known for it's less-than-penal tracks. Some compare it to Pine Valley. The Pit isn't a beautiful track by any stretch of the imagination. In fact, it might be the least attractive course in the Pinehurst area. But it makes for great and exciting golf.

There are some truly unbelievable holes

where par seems almost impossible. Take the par 5 15th, for example — the No. 1 handicap hole. From the back tees, at 550 yards, it demands that you bang it straight down the middle. Your approach shot to the small green must tumble through two massive mounds. The next hole, a 100-yard par 3 from the middle tees, features a green where there is no such thing as a flat pin placement.

But by far the most goofy hole is the par 5 No. 8. It's just 480 yards from the back, and it plays from an elevated tee. Keep it dead straight or you'll lose your ball. (A recurring theme.) A solid 3-wood might leave you just 200 yards from the green. However, the green is nearly 20 yards deep, and a tree to its left makes the hole completely inaccessible if the pin is on the left-hand side. It must be the most puzzling golf hole anywhere. Yet the course begs repeat visit after repeat visit; there is simply nothing like it.

Amenities include a practice green, range, chipping green, locker room, bar and a pro shop.

The course is not very walkable, but you can walk anytime. You can book a tee time anytime too. Approximate cost, including cart, is $80 high, $50 medium and $45 low.

Seven Lakes Country Club

Seven Lakes Dr., West End • 673-1092
Championship Yardage: 6927
Slope: 133   **Par: 72**
Men's Yardage: 6151
Slope: 122   **Par: 72**
Ladies' Yardage: 5186
Slope: 128   **Par: 73**

Seven Lakes opened in the early 1970s. Peter Vail Tufts designed the course on rolling, wooded terrain flanked with houses. In the fairways, you'll find bermudagrass; on the greens, bentgrass.

You won't find seven lakes, but you will find a sound course designed by Donald Ross's godson. When the Tufts family decided to sell the Pinehurst resort, Peter Vail established Seven Lakes as a housing development built around a golf course. It should come as no surprise that someone so close to Donald Ross produced such a fine golf course. We didn't see a rip-off of a Ross design. Rather, we saw a well-conceived, challenging, yet playable course, with a good reputation among local golfers.

Water comes into play here and there. The fairways are relatively wide, but it will help to play your shot carefully. A few bunkers lurk in the fairways, ready to create trouble. There are also some greens that require daring shots over water from uneven lies. Overall, this fun and thoroughly worthwhile course probably would have made Tufts' godfather proud.

Amenities include a practice green, range, chipping green, locker room, bar, restaurant, rental clubs and a pro shop.

The course is walkable for the fit, but walking is restricted; call for details. You can book a tee time anytime. Approximate cost, including cart, is $60 high, $50 medium and $45 low.

Talamore at Pinehurst

1595 Midland Rd., Southern Pines
• 692-5884
Championship Yardage: 7020
Slope: 142   **Par: 71**
Men's Yardage: 6393
Slope: 134   **Par: 71**
Other Yardage: 6058
Slope: 126   **Par: 71**
Ladies' Yardage: 4995
Slope: 125   **Par: 72**

Talamore at Pinehurst, a Rees Jones design, opened in 1991. The course is set in rolling, wooded terrain. Fairways are bermudagrass, and greens are bentgrass.

Yes, this is where you'll find the llama caddies. Perhaps this is a publicity stunt, but so what; it's a fun addition to a course, and it means that some people are out there walking. And golf needs more walking. The llamas go out about 30 times each year, and it will set you back an additional $100 per person for the luxury of having one of the beasts carry your bag for you. The service is only available from late fall through early spring. Llamas are social creatures, so you must bring them out in pairs or not at all. Book well ahead for llama service, and make sure that you are quite fit: Talamore is not a particularly walkable course, and you'll have to negotiate about 6 miles of undulating terrain.

Let's meet the llama caddies. Dollie Llama (no relation) is the first-known llama caddie in the world; her hobbies include tree pruning and mud wrestling. Jack began caddying in August 1993 and is the quiet and somewhat reserved type. Sir Hogan (no relation) is fond of apples and carrots and takes the game fairly seriously. Freddie loves kids and prefers a bad day on the golf course to a good day at the office. Reg the Wonder Llama is still in the opening credits of *Monty Python and the Holy Grail* and is unable to caddie at this time.

We've discussed the llamas, now what about the golf course? It's been highly rated and touted and is a fine example of Rees Jones's work. Rees apparently wanted to make this a thinker's course rather than a muscle layout. Well, he made the course a par 71 that plays more than 7000 yards from the back tees. Of course, you won't have to play the track from there, but you will find plenty of length, even from the front; the course seems to play a bit longer than the card.

As you might expect with a Rees Jones layout, the course is very picturesque. The bunkers and mounds are attractively shaped and visually appealing — unless your ball happens to be in the bunker or on top of the mound. The greens are undulating and can be particularly difficult if fast. Plenty of trouble lurks, and you'll find that Talamore offers a serious challenge, whatever your ability.

Amenities include a practice green, range,

Only Practice Makes Perfect!

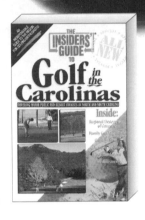

- *A new comprehensive book featuring the 400 best public and semi-private courses to play in the Carolinas.*

- *Helpful information on accommodations and restaurants in each area.*

- *Great golf tips and other great ideas on fun things to do.*

- *Fun family vacation ideas.*

- *Where to buy golf supplies.*

- *Rundown of pro tournaments in each state.*

Name _____

Street Address _____

City _____ State _____ Zip _____

☐ Visa　　☐ Mastercard　　☐ American Express　　☐ Discover

Account No. _____ Exp. Date _____

Signature_____ Phone No. _____

Quantity____ x $20.99 (price includes S&H)　　$ _____

N.C. residents add 6% sales tax ($1.08 per book)　$ _____

Mail to: The Charlotte Observer
P.O. Box 37269, Charlotte, NC 28237-7269　　Total _____

Payment in full (check, money order or credit card no.) must accompany this order form.　g

Mid Pines is an excellent Donald Ross course that's enjoyed a renaissance in the past few years under new ownership by Pine Needles.

chipping green, locker room, bar, restaurant, rental clubs, a beverage cart and a pro shop.

The course is not walkable (without a llama), so you'll want to take a cart (if you're not taking a llama). You can book a tee time anytime. Approximate cost, including cart, is $82 high, $55 medium and $42 low.

Whispering Woods Golf Club
26 Sandpiper Dr., Whispering Pines
• 949-4653
Championship Yardage: 6334
Slope: 122   **Par: 70**
Men's Yardage: 6006
Slope: No rating   **Par: 70**
Ladies' Yardage: 4924
Slope: No rating   **Par: 70**

Whispering Woods opened in 1974. Ellis Maples designed the course on rolling, wooded terrain bordered with houses. In the fairways, you'll find bermudagrass; on the greens, bentgrass.

This fine and relatively mature design is going through somewhat of a renaissance. Whispering Woods has sometimes been confused with the Country Club of Whispering Pines, just a few doors down the way. The new owners of Whispering Woods have pumped a lot of cash into the course, and the result is consistent conditioning and improved play.

Don't let the lack of length fool you. There's plenty of heft from the back tees, particularly if the course is wet. Whispering Woods is more difficult than it looks — and it looks plenty difficult in places. It's probably one of the area's most underestimated courses; and its final hole, one of the most interesting in the area. It's a severe dogleg to the left where the second shot is a short iron over water to a smallish green. Hit the tee shot too far to the left and you must negotiate a steep bank. If you're looking to play a good course in the Pinehurst area at a very affordable price, Whispering Woods is an excellent venue.

Amenities include a practice green, locker room, snack bar, rental clubs and a pro shop.

You must take a cart but may book a tee time anytime. Approximate cost, including cart, is $42 high, $38 medium and $30 low.

Woodlake Country Club

150 Woodlake Blvd., Vass • 245-4686
Championship Yardage: 7012

Slope: 134	**Par: 72**
Men's Yardage: 6584	
Slope: 129	**Par: 72**
Other Yardage: 6144	
Slope: 120	**Par: 72**
Ladies' Yardage: 5080	
Slope: 128	**Par: 72**

The golf course at Woodlake Country Club opened in 1969. We bet you didn't know the course was originally called Lake Surf Country Club. Dan and Ellis Maples tag-teamed the design on mostly flat terrain next to a lake. Fairways are bermudagrass; greens, bentgrass.

Actually, there are 27 holes at Woodlake. The most recent nine opened in 1992, exclusively designed by Dan Maples. That nine is being blown up, and the owners have hired the Arnold Palmer design firm to rework the Dan Maples nine and add an additional nine. This new course should be open in early 1997.

The original nine, designed by Maples and Maples, is an outstanding course and well worth the short drive from Pinehurst. Its reputation among Pinehurst golfers is excellent. The first few holes border a lake, and you'll have to be accurate. The lake is not a large man-made pond but a seriously grand lake that generates significant wind on occasion. Thus the first few holes can be very difficult, and the wind will play havoc with shot selection and shot making.

After this potentially brutal introduction to Woodlake, the course leaves the lake and heads for the woods where the wind is not quite as much a factor. In the woods you'll find plenty of sweeping doglegs the likes of which gained Maples notoriety. There's decent room off the tee, but your ball might find a tree or two if you're not careful. The greens are well bunkered and large. These "inland"

holes offer great variety and challenge, but you'll be glad to know that the course returns to its lakeside location for the final three holes.

The 18th, a wonderful par 5, begs you to go for glory with a second shot over water to a small, well-protected green. Are you gutsy enough? This course is certainly worth the price of admission. We look forward to the new course too.

One notable item here is an aquatic driving range. You actually hit balls into the water, and a large subsurface net shags them.

Amenities include a practice green, range, chipping green, locker room, bar, restaurant, rental clubs and a pro shop.

The course is walkable for the fit, although walking is restricted. You can book a tee time three days in advance. Approximate cost, including cart, is $70 high, $50 medium and $45 low.

Around Pinehurst and Southern Pines . . .

FYI

Unless otherwise noted, the area code for all phone numbers in this chapter is 910.

Fun Things To Do

So you're in Pinehurst and you're not playing golf. What's wrong? It must be raining to the point where even the Japanese golfers are off the courses. Or perhaps it's snowing. Or dark. That's it. It's dark and raining, and even the Japanese are looking for other entertainment.

The village of Pinehurst, built by the original owner of Pinehurst and laid out by Frederick Law Olmstead, is quaint and picturesque with its New England feel. Even the owner of the local bookstore has a New England accent, but she's become Southern enough to greet you with a smile as you walk in.

The village offers some excellent shopping and dining. If you're looking for a unique golf-oriented gift, take a few minutes to visit **Burchfield's Gallery**, (800) 358-4066. Take away a chess set made of golf figurines, a map of Pinehurst #2 in a solid frame, a personalized golf ball, framed golf cartoons, a hole-in-one memento, Pebble Beach bookends — even a ball drying rack. Perhaps what you'll find most amusing are some of the framed sayings, including "I once gave up golf; it was the most terrifying weekend of my life." If you're looking for a great gift for the golfer who has just about everything, then you'll love Burchfield's.

For those of you who are more culturally inclined, check out the **Performing Arts Center**, 250 N.W. Broad Street, Southern Pines, 692-3611; call for information about upcoming events.

One of the most interesting and least publicized attractions in Pinehurst is the **Tufts Archives** in the Given Memorial Library, which is located right in the heart of Pinehurst Village. The Tufts Archives are wonderfully arranged and the result is a presentation that provides the visitor with a comprehensive history of the development of Pinehurst. Call 295-6022 for more information. If it's too wet to play golf, then the Tufts Archives provide an interesting diversion, and it's five minutes walk from the main Pinehurst Hotel.

Those of you who enjoy gardening and gardens should head towards the **Sir Walter Raleigh Historical Garden**, which is part of **Sandhills Community College** located on Airport Road in Southern Pines. You can reach the garden at 695-3882. The lush wonderland is designed to resemble the type of garden you might have seen when Sir Walter was alive.

For comprehensive information about Pinehurst, contact the **Pinehurst Area Convention and Visitors Bureau**, P.O. Box 2270, Southern Pines, North Carolina 28388, (800) 346-5362.

Where to Eat

You'll find plenty of great places to eat in the Pinehurst vicinity. And you'll find that most of the better hotels still believe in the importance of matching the quality of the accommodations with the restaurant — somewhat of a rarity these days. Anyway, there's a better variety of cuisine than you might expect in Pinehurst and close surrounds (Southern Pines and Aberdeen), and we've included but a few of the many fine establishments. We also give you a couple of good choices in the Fayetteville area.

It's worth noting that many of the options we give you for accommodations sport excel-

lent restaurants on their premises. Round out your dining choices by perusing these selections. Refer to our Preface for an explanation of the pricing code.

Beefeater's
$$ • 672 W. Broad St., Southern Pines • 692-5550

As the name implies, Beefeater's is an outstanding place for beef, from filet mignon to prime rib. There's more, however, in the form of seafood, chicken and lamb chops, the latter being somewhat of a rarity in these parts; serve it up with mint jelly and a big baked potato and you're in fine fettle. The ambiance is low ceilinged and white tableclothed but not stuffy — and more casual than you might think. Get dressed up if you want, but feel free to visit the lounge after a round and still dressed in shorts.

According to our waitress, Beefeater's is popular with those who hail from climes north of the Mason-Dixon line. Evidently, the bartender is just a little rude to those folks, but no one seems to mind too much: He's not particularly conservative when it comes to pouring mixed drinks.

The restaurant is busy on most nights, particularly so on the weekends and during the season. It's the type of restaurant where golfers in the area for a week come over and over again.

The Coves
$-$$ • In Market Sq., Pinehurst • 295-3400

Just opposite the Holly Inn and right in the thick of the village of Pinehurst is The Coves, an eatery and drinkery with two distinct characters.

Upstairs, you'll find a restaurant where the atmosphere is on the casual side of formal; and downstairs, you'll find a subterranean bar that looks like it could become a touch raucous in the later hours of the evening.

The restaurant is open for lunch and dinner.

For lunch, go downstairs and ask the bartendress to pull you a pint of Bass ale, then order a hamburger — one of the best around. For dinner, impress your better half with the varied menu and the better-than-average selection of wine. Then head down-

Peggy Kirk Bell

Peggy Kirk Bell is one of the best known female golfers in the world and one of the most prominent promoters of golf in the Sandhills and in North Carolina. She is the owner of Pine Needles and Mid Pines. In 1996, Pine Needles hosted the most successful U.S. Women's Open to date.

Born and raised in Findlay, Ohio, Ms. Bell graduated from Rollins College in Winter Park, Florida, with a degree in physical education. Ms. Bell enjoyed an outstanding professional and amateur career. In 1950 she represented the United States as a member of the Curtis Cup team. She was a charter member of the LPGA and was the first professional to fly her own plane.

In 1953, she married Warren "Bullet" Bell and in the same year, they purchased the golf course at Pine Needles with Julius Boros and the Cosgrove family. Two years later, they bought out the partners and began to develop the buildings around the course.

Photo: Peggy Kirk Bell

Peggy Kirk Bell

Today, Ms. Bell and her staff have turned Pine Needles into one of the foremost teaching centers in the country. The Pinehurst area owes an enormous debt to Ms. Bell for bringing so many great tournaments to Pine Needles and for making the area friendly to women golfers of all levels. It's a great testament to Ms. Bell and her family that the U.S.G.A awarded the 2001 Women's Open to Pine Needles.

stairs for a game of Putt-Putt, another Bass ale, a shag on the dance floor and a game of darts.

The Coves is a locally owned gem that's, dare we say it, not quite as stuffy as some of the other eateries in and around the village. Perhaps that's why it's so popular.

Henning's Restaurant
$$ • U.S. Hwy. 1, Southern Pines • 692-8585

A local favorite pops up in a somewhat unlikely place: the Southern Pines Holiday Inn. We're told that "All Dishes are Personally Supervised by Mrs. Henning," but that may just be an advertising slogan. Still, the menu is strong and varied with such excellent fare as Veal Scallopini Alla Drew, Broiled Baby Flounder with Crabmeat, North Carolina Rainbow Trout, Steak and Oysters and the always popular Fresh Fruit au Kirch (sic). On Sundays, march over to the extremely famous Sunday Buffet. Even if you're not staying at the Holiday Inn, Henning's is worth a visit if you are hungry for a big meal at a moderate price.

The Lobster House
$$$ • 448 Person St., Fayetteville • 485-8866

The Lobster House is so well-known that it's almost a landmark. As the name implies, the Lobster House is the place to go for live

Maine lobster — if you're into that sort of thing. If lobster is not your game, sample other fresh seafood entrees. If beef is your taste, try the prime rib or charcoal steaks. It's closed on Mondays and is only open for dinner.

The Pine Crest Inn Restaurant

$$$ • Dogwood Rd., Pinehurst • 295-6121

The Pine Crest Inn is a place where a lot of people stay, but more still come to the excellent restaurant that serves breakfast and dinner. Breakfast is a hearty affair complete with fresh fruit, eggs cooked to your liking, waffles, pancakes and other such goodies. After a round or two of golf, dinner is a slightly more formal affair served in one of two elegant dining rooms adjacent to the bar. Once again, there's a lot to eat. Start out with some fried button mushrooms in horseradish then follow it up with entrees like rack of lamb, prime rib or filet mignon. Finish it all off with the greatest of all English desserts: trifle. Afterwards, return to the bar where there is usually much merriment to be found.

Raffaele's

$$ • 1550 U.S. Hwy. 1, Southern Pines • 692-1952

Raffaele's is situated at the northern end of the main business district in Southern Pines. The cuisine is Italian, and you'll find a real attention to detail in the preparation of the food.

Raffaele's is a local favorite, so much so that one local told us not to write about it so it won't become too full of tourists. That's probably as good a recommendation as you can find in the Pinehurst area.

Begin your meal with stuffed mushrooms; move on to spaghetti with Italian sausage; and complement everything with a beefy bottle of Valpolicella. The menu isn't massively extensive, but we feel confident that you'll find something you really enjoy.

Roma Gourmet Italian Restaurant

$$ • 3729 Sycamore Dairy Rd., Fayetteville • 864-1313

At Roma Gourmet you'll find a menu including live lobster, steaks, seafood and Roma's brand of Italian cuisine. With ad-

vance notice, Giovanni Giannone will prepare anything your stomach desires. In addition to cooking, Giovanni will sing any of your old Italian favorites — although he doesn't necessarily need advance warning for this. For your information, Giovanni came to America from Sicily, Italy, more than 25 years ago, jumped ship and ended up in Fayetteville.

The Squire's Pub

$$ • 1720 U.S. Hwy. 1 S., Southern Pines • 695-1161

Squire's is a fun watering hole and restaurant that's popular with locals and out-of-town golfers. The ambiance approaches that of an English pub, and you'll certainly find the same sort of friendliness. When the professional tours are in town, Squire's is a magnet. For instance, when the LPGA cruised through, long-hitting Laura Davies arrived with an entourage of 10 and proceeded to fill up the bar. The manager quantified the final bill as "plenty." If you're going to see a famous golfer enjoying a drink and meal, this is a place where this might happen.

Squires is a fantastic place to enjoy a drink. There are more than 40 beers available, most of them from England, and if you're in the mood for something stronger, how about a martini? (Two of these, and your handicap is five strokes less; three, and you'll be telling everyone that you just took £20 off Laura Davies.)

Thai Orchid

$$ • 1404 Sandhills Blvd., Aberdeen • 944-9299

And now for something completely different. . . . Thai Orchid is the only restaurant that serves good Thai food in an unpretentious setting. You won't be coming here for the atmosphere necessarily, but if you're a devotee of Thai food and you need a fix while golfing in Pinehurst, you'll want to come here.

Try the Thai grilled steak, Bangkok duck or spicy and sour fish. Start with koong da bog (shrimp roll) and wash the whole meal down with a cool Singha beer from Thailand. You can have your food prepared Thai hot, extra hot, medium or mild. The restaurant also

Photo: N.C. Travel & Tourism

Longleaf is a course with two different nines. The front is primarily flat and open, while the back is wooded and undulating.

offers excellent lunch specials: You'll leave with change from a $5 bill.

Where to Stay

As we've mentioned, one of the attractions of Pinehurst is the fact that there's something here for everyone's budget. You can spend a lot of money here on places to play, or you can spend a lot less on your hotel room and spend what you save to play on the better golf courses. If you want tradition, service and amenities, you'll find it here (for a price); if all you want is a basic room with Clint Eastwood movies and a shower, you'll find that here as well.

It should be noted that most of the following hotels have excellent restaurants and wonderful dining rooms. They are all worth visiting for their restaurants, even if you are not staying there as a guest. Refer to our Preface for an explanation of the pricing code.

Fairfield Inn by Marriott
$$ • 562 Cross Creek Mall, Fayetteville • 487-1400

Fayetteville's Fairfield Inn by Marriott is by the All-American Freeway at U.S. Highway 401 — one of the city's busiest intersections. The inn offers 135 clean and comfortable rooms at reasonable rates. You'll get free cable TV and local calls plus access to an outdoor pool. Children 17 and younger stay for free.

Foxfire Resort and Country Club
$-$$$ • Hoffman Rd., in Foxfire Village, Pinehurst • 295-5555

We've already told you that Foxfire has two fine Gene Hamm golf courses, but even if that were not so, you should consider staying at Foxfire anyway, particularly if you're looking for great value in a setting that's relaxed and secluded. Foxfire is also well suited for conferences.

At Foxfire, you'll stay in a condominium equipped with fireplace, telephone, TV (with ESPN and the Golf Channel), a living room, ample sleeping space and facilities to allow you to do your own cooking. Or wander over to the lodge for breakfast or dinner. There's also a lounge where the bartender will stay as late as you do.

Play at other fine courses in the area can be arranged by the courteous and well-connected staff. You'll really enjoy the hospitality and value at Foxfire.

Hampton Inn
$$ • 1675 U.S. Hwy. 1, Southern Pines
• 692-9266

The Hampton Inn is a modern motel-style accommodation that's always popular with golfers and visitors. There are 126 guest rooms. The price of admission includes free continental breakfast. Amenities include a pool, cable TV (with HBO), meeting room, guest laundry room and fax service. Local phone calls are free. There are golf packages with access to 18 local golf courses. The Hampton Inn's location could not be better.

The Holiday Inn
$$ • U.S. Hwy. 1 Bypass and Morganton Rd.,
Southern Pines • 692-8585

As you enter Southern Pines from the north, you can't help but notice the Holiday Inn — it will be on your right just before you enter the "main drag." For years the Holiday Inn has been a local stalwart and a popular place to stay among the golfing public. The hotel offers more than 160 guest rooms and suites. Enjoy the pool, room service, cable TV (with HBO) and four tennis courts plus a game room and fitness center. Golf packages are available, and most packages include free breakfast. Meeting and exhibit space is available as well.

On-site Hennings restaurant offers three meals a day and serves a surprising variety of dishes plus a sizeable breakfast buffet. But most importantly, there's TAMS lounge, where, a few years ago, *The Insiders' Guide® to Golf in the Carolinas* coauthor Scott Martin served notice of his karaoke prowess with his show-stopping rendition of George Strait's "All My Ex's Live in Texas."

The Holly Inn
$$-$$$ • Cherokee Rd., Pinehurst
• 295-2300

The Holly Inn was the first hotel in Pinehurst, and it lives on today as one of its finest. There's a wonderful and understated charm to the place that's both relaxing and timeless. You'll feel like you're stepping back in time as soon as you pass through the doors.

The restaurant is worth mentioning because it's one of the best in Pinehurst. The dining room, with its cupola roof, is like a scene out of *The Great Gatsby*; check out the intricate molding. Feast on duck with a smoked salmon appetizer; wash it down with a robust claret.

The rooms are all quite different: wonderful and traditionally appointed with antique furniture. The inn offers a number of golf packages and the golf course access is excellent. Once you've finished your round, relax with a gin and tonic in the garden, under a shade tree or on the veranda. The inn is part of the Historic Hotels of America and the National Trust for Historic Preservation.

Mid Pines Inn and Golf Club
$$-$$$ • 1010 Midland Rd., Southern Pines
• 692-2114

If you've read the description of the course at Mid Pines, you know the inn has always been a popular spot for meetings — and for good reason. Pinehurst Hotel notwithstanding, there might not be a more charming and stately building in the area.

All 118 guest rooms are graciously furnished with period antiques. Other amenities are geared toward business meetings and include full conference facilities that are perfect for small to midsize groups. The inn actually dates back to 1921. The cuisine in the restaurant is wonderful, and you'll feel like you're getting away from it all in the traditional atmosphere.

Golf packages are available, and the staff will work to get you a tee time at a course of your choosing other than Mid Pines or its sister course, Pine Needles.

The Pinehurst area is one of the world's top golf destinations.

The Pinehurst Hotel at Pinehurst Resort and Country Club
$$$-$$$$ • Carolina Vista Dr., Pinehurst
• 295-6811, (800) 487-4653

We've already gone through what makes the golf courses at Pinehurst so special, and golf is what Pinehurst is all about — so read about the courses before you read about the hotel. Driving through the Village of Pinehurst, you will surely stumble across the grand and magnificent Pinehurst Hotel. It has hosted all the great golfers in addition to some of the most famous people in the universe. And it's been an award-winning accommodation 13 years in a row.

As soon as you enter the hotel, your bags will be handled by a bell hop in plus fours. Enjoy this new and wonderful experience as you're taken care of in 1920s fashion. The rooms are traditionally appointed but offer all modern conveniences. In addition to the golf courses, the hotel offers children's programs, a swimming pool, a lake, tennis courts, croquet, lawn bowls and historical tours. You'll find a variety of restaurants as well as the Ryder Cup Lounge, where you can have a drink and discuss whether Lanny should have picked Curtis as the wild-card choice (he shouldn't have). It's a place for a blowout, so

get out the Osmium credit card . . . you'll enjoy every second of it.

The Pine Crest Inn
$$-$$$ • Dogwood Rd., Pinehurst
• 295-6121

Donald Ross purchased the Pine Crest Inn in 1921 and owned it until his death in 1948. Thus, for the golfing purist, the Pine Crest Inn is a special place — almost hallowed territory.

Today's Pine Crest Inn is known as one of the most popular and famous places to stay, eat and drink in Pinehurst. It's also one of the most fun and, at time, rambunctious — but in a polite way.

The rooms are wonderfully appointed and offer modern amenities — in-room telephones and color TV (with the all-important Golf Channel). The atmosphere is like being at home. The inn's excellent restaurant serves traditional cuisine. But perhaps the most famous part of the Pine Crest is Mrs. B's Bar where, since the inn's inception, golfers have come to recount their day of adventure and calamity on the links. The bartender, in addition to dispensing adult beverages, also flows with wit and wisdom about golf. And did we mention the occasional well-directed barb? One employee has said: "We have no featured or specialty drinks as such, but whatever the golfers drink, they usually end up singing."

There's nothing pretentious about the Pine Crest; it's pure fun and pure golf. If there's a hotel with better access to local golf courses, please let us know. In addition to all the Pinehurst Courses (including #2), the folks at the Pine Crest can get you on just about anywhere, often at a special rate.

Pine Needles
$$-$$$Ridge Rd., Southern Pines
• 692-7111

For a full description of the magnificent course at Pine Needles, see the entry earlier in this chapter. The course is reserved for hotel guests only. There are 71 sleeping rooms in Swiss-style lodges. Room amenities include full bathrooms and showers, cable TV (with ESPN and the Golf Channel) and a great view of the enormous practice facility. Guest services include a heated pool, grass tennis courts, sauna, dining rooms, a lounge and learning center. The golf packages include unlimited greens fees on the Pine Needles course. The staff can arrange tee times for you at other courses in the area as well.

Prince Charles Hotel and Conference Center
$$$ • 450 Hay St., Fayetteville • 433-4444

In historic downtown Fayetteville, the Prince Charles Hotel and Conference Center is an elegantly restored 105-room hotel that's one of the finest in the region. Luxurious suites with wet bars are available. You'll find conference space for up to 350 people. Ask about corporate rates as well. Chloe's restaurant features continental cuisine and is a great place to indulge in Sunday brunch. The Prince Charles is also home to Babe's, a nostalgic sports bar that serves an express lunch.

Golf Equipment

A number of courses have excellent golf shops where you'll find just about everything you'll need. And it's here that a number of PGA pros have been trained in the art of personal club fitting. Three prominent golf shops are in Southern Pines near the junction of

U.S. highways 1 and 15/501. **Spoon and Mashie**, 944-1982, on U.S. 1 is one the largest and best-equipped golf stores in the Carolinas and carries just about every type of club made. The store can custom fit clubs and offers full repair services as well. **Robert's Golf and Tennis**, 944-2757, offers a full range of gear and clubs in a friendly atmosphere; it's on U.S. 1 in Aberdeen. And at **Carolina Custom Golf**, behind the Chamber of Commerce on U.S. 15/501, Southern Pines, 695-1670, you'll find a massive store as well as a range with mats where you can pay $5 and hit balls all day.

Golf Instruction

As you might expect, Pinehurst is a great place to learn how to play or to improve your technique. Just about every course has excellent practice facilities, many of which have been specially designed by well-known architects. And most courses have PGA professionals who are qualified to help you with your game. A couple of courses boast teaching professionals who are sought after by the better golfers in the Sandhills and the Carolinas. Probably the two best-known golf schools are at Pinehurst and Pine Needles.

The **Golf Advantage School** at Pinehurst Resort and Country Club, Carolina Vista Drive, Pinehurst, is designed to help golfers of all skill levels improve their games. The school is supervised by former PGA president Don Padgett. The maximum student/teacher ratio is 5-to-1, and you'll get a chance to test your improved game on any of the eight great Pinehurst courses. If you really want to get serious, you can stay for a week's worth of school. Or, if you haven't got the time, stay for the weekend. Either way, the program includes lodging for the entire stay, three meals a day, daily greens fees and carts, unlimited range balls, personal video analysis, personalized club fitting, access to all the amenities and a graduation cocktail party. Quite a gig! Call (800) 795-4653 for the brochure and rates. Junior programs are also available.

At Pine Needles, on Midland Road in Southern Pines, Peggy Kirk Bell and her staff will lead you on a **Golfari**. Either Bell or PGA touring pro Pat McGowan will begin your day with an instructional session before helping you on an individual basis with your swing. After lunch, play golf all afternoon on the great Pine Needles course. The facilities at Pine Needles are excellent, and there aren't many instructors with a better reputation than Peggy Kirk Bell. For more information about instruction at Pine Needles, call (800) 747-7272.

Taking a slightly different approach is the **Woodlake Total Performance Golf School** at Woodlake Country Club, 150 Woodlake Boulevard, in Vass. In addition to a full instructional program and access to a wonderful golf course, your instruction includes fitness and nutrition evaluations. Call (800) 334-1126 for more information.

The Triangle Area

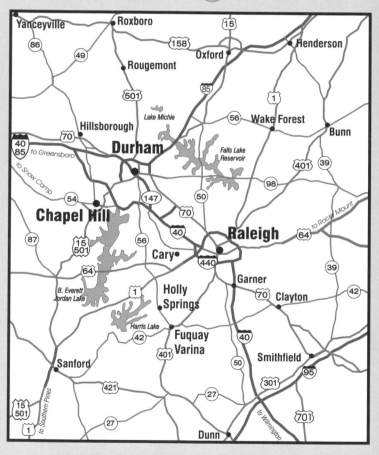

North Carolina's Triangle

Raleigh/Durham/Chapel Hill

The Triangle is best known for three major institutions of higher learning: the University of North Carolina at Chapel Hill, North Carolina State University in Raleigh and Duke University in Durham. The area is also well known nationally for the Research Triangle Park, a collection of research facilities owned and run by large industrials like IBM and Glaxo. The concentration of individuals with Ph.D.s to their names is greater here than in any other place in the country. Thus, it can be safely said that your chances of an intelligent conversation are greater here than in just about any part of the Carolinas. We can't decide if that means golfers here have better thought processes or course-management prowess.

In the counties that surround Raleigh, Durham and Chapel Hill, life is less high-tech and less academically oriented. The plentiful fields of eastern North Carolina are overflowing with a crop that's been the mainstay of agriculture in the great north state for centuries: tobacco. In these rural areas, a few golf courses have been built where the golden-leafed plant once grew. You'll be able to smoke wherever you feel like it in these outlying areas. Ask the people what they think about Californian-style thou shalt not smoke anywhere laws and you'll probably receive a answer that we would not dare print in a family-oriented book like this one.

In the heart of the Triangle, it's difficult, but not impossible, to avoid the influence of the universities. This is particularly true in Chapel Hill, less so in Durham, and even less so in Raleigh — a city perhaps more dominated by the state government than by N.C. State.

The Triangle has figured prominently in a number of "best places to live" surveys, and the number of people moving to the area seems to increase each and every year. Many come for the high-tech jobs, others to service those with the high-tech jobs, and others still to enjoy the wonderfully rich and diverse cultural life, inspired in part by the universities. Like other spots in North Carolina, the Triangle is increasingly home to retirees who want to relocate anywhere but Florida.

All this growth has meant that a number of new and very modern courses have sprung up in the area and that other older tracks are popular, successful and well-maintained. In the past few years, the weather has been unkind to many area courses. A big freeze burned many bermudagrass fairways three years ago, and several courses are still recovering from that shock. Then, of course, Hurricane Fran caused quite a bit of damage to the entire Triangle area in September of 1996, and some courses were harder hit than others.

Meteorology aside, you'll find an excellent variety of public courses in the area. There're plenty of old traditional designs plus some ultramodern moundfests that will test the patience of every golfer from scratch to 36. A couple of courses are family-owned and maintained, and there are some fine courses designed by architects no one has ever heard of.

Although it pains true-blue Tarheels to say it, the golf course at the Washington Duke Golf and Country Club, after its renovation by Rees Jones, might be one of the most mag-

GOLF COURSES IN THE TRIANGLE OF NORTH CAROLINA

Name	Type	# Holes	Par	Slope	Yards	Walking	Booking	Cost w/ Cart
Caswell Pines	public	18	72	114	6270	restricted	5 days	$20-25
Cheviot Hills	semiprivate	18	71	107	5975	restricted	anytime	$24-30
Crooked Creek	public	18	72	116	6028	restricted	7 days	$28-36
Devil's Ridge	semiprivate	18	72	127	6430	restricted	7 days	$34-44
Duke University's Washington Duke Golf & CC	semiprivate	18	72	129	6721	restricted	anytime	$50-60
Eagle Crest	public	18	72	n/r	6038	anytime	anytime	$23-30
Finley Golf Course (UNC)	public	18	72	117	6102	anytime	2 days	$26-32
Hedingham Golf Club	semiprivate	18	72	116	6276	restricted	anytime	$29-38
Hillandale Golf Club	public	18	71	118	6100	restricted	anytime	$25-29
Kerr Lake	semiprivate	18	72	118	6185	anytime	2 days	$23-28
Lake Winds Golf Course	semiprivate	18	72	n/r	6008	anytime	anytime	$22-26
Lochmere Golf Club	semiprivate	18	72	116	6156	restricted	7 days	$30-40
The Neuse Golf Club	semiprivate	18	72	129	6626	restricted	7 days	$32-38
Occoneechee Golf Club	semiprivate	18	71	119	5692	anytime	3-4 days	$24-26
The River	semiprivate	18	72	n/a	6116	anytime	14 days	$20-30
Roxboro Country Club	semiprivate	18	70	113	5364	anytime	2 days	$22-28
Sourwood Golf Club	public	18	72	112	6285	anytime	anytime	$16-20
Wake Forest Country Club	semiprivate	18	72	129	6525	restricted	7 days	$25-38
Washington Duke Golf & CC	semiprivate	18	72	129	6721	restricted	anytime	$50-60
Willowhaven	semiprivate	18	72	117	6342	anytime	3-5 days	$31.50-37.50

nificent in the Southeast. We believe the golfing world will soon discover this course as one of the best public-access tracks in the Carolinas. Don't be surprised if Washington Duke slides into *Golf Digest's* top 100 before the end of the century. Two ultramodern courses, Devil's Ridge and The Neuse, were recognized by *Golf Digest* as top new courses. These are show-stopping tracks built around housing developments. A couple of golf course management companies have recently purchased or developed courses in the area.

In the May 1996 edition of *Golf Digest*, the magazine ranked public-access golf courses in two categories. One rated courses with a daily fee less than $50; the other rated courses above that threshold. Duke's course and The Neuse in Clayton both made the top 75 in the country for those courses with greens fees less than $50.

A number of fine and well-known architects have been at work in the area, including George Cobb, Russell Breeden, Ellis Maples, John LaFoy and Gene Hamm.

One annoying aspect of golf in the Triangle is that many courses have a special Friday greens fee that's more than the weekday rate but less than the weekend rate. Most of us have to play hooky from work to play golf on Friday, so why should we be penalized? Makes no sense: Friday is still a school day. Sadly, most of the better courses employ this policy.

Caswell Pines Golf Club

**2380 County Home Rd., Yanceyville
• (910) 694-2255, (800) 694-1888
Championship Yardage: 6651**

Slope: 120	**Par: 72**
Men's Yardage: 6270	
Slope: 114	**Par: 72**
Other Yardage: 5720	
Slope: 108	**Par: 72**
Ladies' Yardage: 5145	
Slope: 111	**Par: 72**

Caswell Pines, a Gene Hamm design, opened in 1993. The course is primarily open, but woods and homesites border some holes. In the fairways, you'll find 419 bermudagrass; on the greens, you'll find bentgrass.

Built on what was previously a tobacco farm, Caswell Pines is an exciting and challenging course with a fine design in a pleasant setting. The Gene Hamm courses we've seen tend toward the traditional; this one leans toward the modern: earth-worked and mounded.

The course offers excellent variety and some truly outstanding holes, including a number with significant elevation changes. Off the tee, you'll have a decent amount of room: Big hitters will want to play from the back tees and use the driver. The great thing about Caswell Pines is that it makes you think. You'll need to keep your golfing wits about you if you plan to score well. The greens here are typically large, with plenty of subtle and not-so-subtle breaks; two-putting is quite a feat on many holes. Large bunkers around a number of greens make life even more difficult. And did we mention the significant amount of water? . . . Anyway, it's well worth the visit to Yanceyville to play this course.

Amenities include a practice green, range, snack bar, restaurant, rental clubs and a beverage cart.

The course is walkable for the very fit, but walking is restricted; call for daily details. You can book a tee time five days in advance. Approximate cost, including cart, is $20 weekdays and $25 on weekends.

Cheviot Hills Golf Club

**7301 Capital Blvd., Raleigh • 876-9920
Championship Yardage: 6475**

Slope: 116	**Par: 71**
Men's Yardage: 5975	
Slope: 107	**Par: 71**
Ladies' Yardage: 4965	
Slope: 114	**Par: 71**

Cheviot Hills Golf Club opened in 1930. *Architects of Golf* lists Harold Long as the original designer. Gene Hamm came along later to remodel and probably redesign. The course is set in rolling wooded terrain without a house in sight. In the fairways, you'll find bermudagrass; on the greens, bentgrass.

As you walk up to the 19th-century clubhouse, you'll be greeted by the pro-shop attendant who expertly combines friendliness with brusqueness. You'll feel like you're at a country

FYI

Unless otherwise noted, the area code for all phone numbers in this chapter is 919.

club, standing among people who have been friends for 50 years. The course itself is a masterpiece of understatement and traditionalism. There's nothing tricked up, nothing silly. Mounds are few and far between, and the only house you might see belongs to the couple who own the course. The only thing missing here is a knowledgeable caddie to carry and clean your clubs and help you read putts. The staff here at Cheviot Hills is justifiably proud of the course — and woe betide you should your cart stray from the path. The aforementioned pro-shop attendant, equipped with binoculars and a sound system that can be heard in Virginia, will let you know that "CARTS MUST BE KEPT ON PATHS AT ALL TIMES."

Interestingly, you'll find some short par 5s and some long par 4s, most with plenty of room off the tee. The staff informs us that you'll be using all your clubs and hitting all your shots. The course offers particularly good value if you walk. And you should. The exercise will be good for you.

If you're thinking about skipping Sunday morning services at your chosen house of worship and sneaking onto the course while you should be singing hymn 315, think again. The course doesn't open until 12:30 PM on Sundays.

Amenities include a practice green, range, chipping green, locker room, snack bar, rental clubs and a pro shop.

The course is walkable and you can walk almost anytime (two cheers!). You can book a tee time whenever you choose. Approximate cost, including cart, is $24 Monday to Thursday, $26 on Friday and $30 on weekends.

Crooked Creek

4621 Shady Greens Dr., Fuquay-Varina
• 557-7529
Championship Yardage: 6704
Slope: 120   **Par: 72**
Men's Yardage: 6028
Slope: 116   **Par: 72**
Other Yardage: 5296
Slope: 112   **Par: 72**
Ladies' Yardage: 4978
Slope: 114   **Par: 72**

Chuck Smith designed Crooked Creek, which opened in late 1995. Fairways are 419 bermudagrass, and greens are bentgrass.

Crooked Creek offers a traditional design that demands accuracy off the tee. The greens are midsize and undulating, with a few bunkers to catch those wayward iron shots you thought you had cured. The course also boats a number of interesting and well-designed dogleg holes. The greens, on the back nine especially, are rolling. Crooked Creek (have you ever seen a straight one?) is a good addition to the portfolio of courses in the eastern section of the Triangle and is worth a reconnaissance mission if you're in Raleigh and you're interested in surveying a new course.

Amenities include a practice green, range, chipping green, locker room, snack bar, rental clubs and a pro shop.

Walking is permitted Monday through Friday. You can book a tee time seven days in advance. Approximate cost, including cart, is $16 Monday through Thursday, $18 on Friday and $24 on weekends.

Devil's Ridge Golf Club

5107 Linksland Dr., Holly Springs
• 557-6100
Championship Yardage: 7002
Slope: 138   **Par: 72**
Men's Yardage: 6430
Slope: 127   **Par: 72**
Other Yardage: 5852
Slope: 120   **Par: 72**
Ladies' Yardage: 5244
Slope: 121   **Par: 72**

The golf course at Devil's Ridge opened in 1991. This John LaFoy design is set on undulating terrain, and many holes are bordered by houses. In the fairways, you'll find bermudagrass; on the greens, you'll find bentgrass.

John LaFoy is a well-known architect and former associate of George Cobb. LaFoy made frequent trips to Augusta National with Cobb, and when Cobb was slowed by illness in his later years, LaFoy took over a number of the design responsibilities; in fact, he was most responsible for Linville Ridge Country Club in the mountains of North Carolina. LaFoy began his own design business in 1986.

Here at Devil's Ridge, LaFoy created a tough track with all the trappings of a modern course: mounds, severely undulating greens, tough tee shots, extensive bunkering, eleva-

Photo: NC Travel & Tourism

A beautiful fall day is the perfect backdrop for a day of golf in the Triangle.

tion changes, more mounds, backbreaking length from the back tees and still more mounds. It's interesting to see how different this course is from many Cobb designs. You'll certainly want to spend a couple of dollars for the excellent yardage book, especially if you're playing this course for the first time. Keep your cart speed down on the front nine, as a state trooper lives next to one of the greens.

Excessive velocity aside, the course is well-designed, greatly varied and interesting. However, if you're not a fan of modern courses, steer toward something more traditional than Devil's Ridge. A good score requires hitting just about every club in your bag — and hitting crisply. Particularly interesting are the shapes of the greens: Many look like amoebae on steroids.

We think Devil's Ridge is a must-play course in the Raleigh area, even if you only play it once. Perhaps this description of the 17th hole from the yardage book best describes the course:

"This is the hole for which Devil's Ridge got its name. Not too long, not too narrow, not too hard. However, don't miss any shot or you'll post a BIG (their caps) number. Favor the left on your tee shot. If you miss the green to the right and look for your ball, you

may never be heard from again." Enough said.

Amenities include a practice green, range, chipping green, snack bar, rental clubs, a beverage cart and a pro shop.

Walking is restricted, although we wouldn't recommend it anyway. You can book a tee time seven days in advance. Approximate cost, including cart, is $34 Monday to Thursday, $38 on Fridays and $44 on weekends.

Duke University Golf Club
**N.C. Hwy. 751 and Science Dr., Durham
• 681-2288**
Championship Yardage: 7045

Slope: 137	**Par: 72**
Men's Yardage: 6721	
Slope: 129	**Par: 72**
Other Yardage: 6207	
Slope: 119	**Par: 72**
Ladies' Yardage: 5505	
Slope: 124	**Par: 72**

The golf course at Washington Duke Golf and Country Club opened in 1957. Robert Trent Jones designed the original course; Rees Jones redesigned and renovated it in 1993. At the time of the renovation, Jones' daughter was a student at Duke, and she persuaded her dad to perform the work for free. This picturesque track has 419 bermudagrass fairways and bentgrass greens.

This is Duke University's golf course, and it's the most magnificent course in the Triangle — and one of the finest layouts in North Carolina. Robert Trent Jones cut the original course out of Duke Forest; thus, just about every hole is bordered by wonderfully pretty woods replete with towering trees. Rees Jones must have kept the original routing; however, he blew up the tee boxes and green complexes, and the result is nothing short of stunning. The targets are wonderfully defined, and some of the holes are breathtaking. A lot of money was pumped into this course and it shows.

There's subtle mounding in the fairways and quite a few gaping fairway bunkers. You won't always have an even stance in the fairway. And water comes into play on a few holes. But it's the attention to detail around the green complexes that makes the course so spectacular. You'll see large, tiered greens, undulations and obvious slopes. Two-putting any green on this course is an achievement. Many greens are flanked by embankments; but, more importantly, each features a dizzying array of bunkers — some large, some small, but all potentially difficult and score-destroying. And as if the challenge wasn't great enough, the course finishes with two long and difficult uphill par 4s; you'll have to bust the ball off the tee if you want any chance of reaching the green in regulation. Make sure you play this course before you lose your swing.

We're not sure you'll want to play the course often if you're a high-handicapper. If you get into trouble, particularly around the greens, then you'll be faced with some difficult short-game challenges.

Amenities include a practice green, range, chipping green, locker room, bar, snack bar, restaurant, rental clubs, a beverage cart and a pro shop. You can also spend a night at the well-appointed Washington Duke Inn (see this chapter's subsequent "Where to Stay" section) adjacent to the course.

The course is walkable for the physically fit, but walking is restricted; call ahead for daily details. (You'll see lots of students walking out here.) You can book a tee time whenever you choose. If you're neither a Duke student nor a member of the university's faculty or staff, the approximate cost, including cart, is $50 weekdays and $60 on weekends.

Eagle Crest
4400 Auburn Church Rd., Garner
• 772-6104
Championship Yardage: 6514
Slope: No rating   **Par: 72**
Men's Yardage: 6038
Slope: No rating   **Par: 72**
Ladies' Yardage: 4875
Slope: No rating   **Par: 72**

Eagle Crest opened in 1968. This John Baucom design is set on rolling and primarily open terrain, with bermudagrass fairways and bentgrass greens.

We found a fun, straightforward, relaxing and soundly designed country course at Eagle Crest. You won't find any sand traps, so if you hate the beach, you'll love it here all the more. Water comes into play on four holes. Fairways are predominantly wide, although approach shots must hit small greens, some of which are crowned. If the ground is hard, you might be able to run the ball up to the hole with a low running hook. Feel free to use your Texas wedge. You'll find mounds, swales and grass bunkers around some of the greens. If you enjoy a no-frills course with a minimum of fuss and tricks, you'll enjoy the laidback setting we found here.

Amenities include a range, snack bar and rental clubs.

You can walk this course anytime; book a tee time whenever you choose as well. Approximate cost, including cart, is $13 weekdays and $20 on weekends.

Finley Golf Course
Finley Golf Course Rd., Chapel Hill
• 962-2349
Championship Yardage: 6580
Slope: 122   **Par: 72**
Men's Yardage: 6102
Slope: 117   **Par: 72**
Ladies' Yardage: 5277
Slope: 118   **Par: 73**

The University of North Carolina's Finley Golf Course, designed by George Cobb, opened in 1950. It's a mostly flat track with some minor undulations on the back nine. In the fairways, you'll find bermudagrass; on the greens, bentgrass.

Designer Profile: Gene Hamm

Gene Hamm served in the U.S. Navy during World War II. Using the GI bill, he studied golf management in Pinehurst. He worked with Ellis Maples before Maples took up architecture full time. In the mid 1950s, Hamm left his professional job to supervise the construction of the original Duke course designed by Robert Trent Jones. After this project, Hamm started his own design firm and was active in the Carolinas and Virginia.

An excellent golfer, Hamm won the 1978 and 1979 Carolinas Seniors on courses he designed. How 'bout that for fairness?!

Photo: The Architects of Golf

Gene Hamm

Quite a few well-known students, professors and coaches have graced this course. Michael Jordan started to play the game here under the tutelage of Davis Love III, a member of the UNC golf team at the time. And you might run into Dean Smith here too. Yes, there's strong level of stardom and tradition at this course adjacent to Siler's Bog.

The course itself is a fine and mature George Cobb design and one of the better courses in the Triangle area. The front nine is flat, and its fairways are bordered by woods filled with old hardwoods and majestic pine trees. The back nine is just as wooded but features a few holes on undulating terrain. There's plenty of variety here, and the difficulties on this course come from the bunkering, trees and subtly undulating putting surfaces. If the bermudagrass rough is grown up around the greens, finesse recovery shots will be difficult. If you're a fan of well-designed traditional-style golf courses, play at Finley. The course often hosts tournaments, team practice and other such events, so it's extra important to call ahead of time to make sure there's a tee time available for you.

Amenities include a practice green, range, chipping green, snack bar, rental clubs and a pro shop.

You can walk anytime and can book a tee time two days in advance. Approximate cost, including cart, is $26 weekdays (same for Friday) and $32 on weekends.

Hedingham Golf Club
4801 Harbour Town Dr., Raleigh
• 250-3030

Championship Yardage: 6675	
Slope: 121	**Par: 72**
Men's Yardage: 6276	
Slope: 116	**Par: 72**
Other Yardage: 5565	
Slope: 107	**Par: 72**
Ladies' Yardage: 4845	
Slope: 107	**Par: 72**

Hedingham Golf Club opened in 1992. David Postlethwait designed the primarily open track, although the course is part of a residential community, and houses border some holes. Fairways are bermudagrass, and greens are bentgrass.

We're not familiar with David Postlethwait, but based on the evidence here at this popular Raleigh course, he is in the modern-architecture camp. Locals tell us the course is fair — not overly demanding. It's tight off the tee, with out-of-bounds lurking on many holes. So keep the ball in play. Let's say that again. Keep the ball in play.

INSIDERS' TIP

If you're playing a course for the first time, or if you're on a particularly difficult course, don't be afraid to play from the mid-front tees. You won't have to use your driver quite as often and you'll probably enjoy your day a lot more.

The greens are medium-size to large, not overly undulating and boast some potentially difficult subtleties. A few small changes are being made to the course to make it more playable. And as with most modern courses, you'll find plenty of mounds in the fairways and around the green complexes.

Amenities include a practice green, range, chipping green, locker room, snack bar, rental clubs and a pro shop.

You can only walk at the end of the day (the exact time you can start walking varies depending on the season, so ask when you call for reservations). You can book a tee time six days in advance. Approximate cost, including cart, is $29 Monday through Thursday, $32 on Friday and $38 on weekends.

Hillandale Golf Course

Hillandale Rd., Durham • 286-4211
Championship Yardage: 6445
Slope: 122   Par: 71
Men's Yardage: 6100
Slope: 118   Par: 71
Ladies' Yardage: 5555
Slope: 113   Par: 74

Hillandale opened in the early 1900s. *Architects of Golf* lists Donald Ross as the original designer and Perry Maxwell and George Cobb as redesigners. You'll find information about Ross and Cobb throughout this book. Maxwell was a former banker who took to golf course architecture after World War I. We'll wager you're unaware that he built the first grass greens in the state of Oklahoma. He was known for designing wildly undulating greens and has rebuilt the putting surfaces at such mega-famous courses as Augusta National, Pine Valley and the National Golf Links. Maxwell eventually designed about 70 courses and remodeled 50 others. Thus, Hillandale boasts a fine architectural heritage. The terrain varies between flat and rolling. Bermudagrass covers the fairways, and bentgrass blankets the greens.

With more than 50,000 rounds of golf played here every year, Hillandale is probably one of the most popular golf courses in North Carolina. The track is owned and operated by The Durham Foundation, Durham's Community Trust and the Central Carolina Bank and Trust Company. So you might refer to Hillandale as Durham's muni.

The course is fun and relatively straight-forward and has the ambiance of an Old World course. Maxwell didn't get too wild with the greens — crowned and midsize to large. On the back nine, three holes have dual greens to accommodate the sheer volume of play. The fairways are relatively wide and open, but water comes into play on a few holes. The course is not overly bunkered, and chipping areas are mowed around the greens, so your ball might roll off if it hits the edge.

The golf shop at Hillandale is one of the best-stocked and largest of any golf course in North Carolina. In 1993, the golf shop was voted the Nation's Most Outstanding by the PGA of America.

Amenities include a practice green, range, chipping green, locker room, snack bar, rental clubs and a pro shop.

You can — and should — walk anytime; same goes for booking a tee time. Approximate cost, including cart, is $25 Monday through Thursday, $27 on Friday and $29 on weekends.

FYI
Unless otherwise noted, the area code for all phone numbers in this chapter is 919.

Kerr Lake Country Club

N.C. Hwy. 3, Henderson • 492-1895
Championship Yardage: 6430
Slope: 122   Par: 72
Men's Yardage: 6185
Slope: 118   Par: 72
Ladies' Yardage: 4799
Slope: 111   Par: 72

The golf course at Kerr Lake Country Club opened in the 1960s. A group of agricultural types designed this open layout, with bermudagrass fairways and bentgrass greens.

Here at Kerr Lake you'll find a fun, entertaining and relaxed course. This well-designed track follows the lay of the land faithfully, and its challenge is due in part to the decent length from the back tees. Locals feel Kerr Lake appears easier than it plays. There isn't a great deal of trouble off the tee, but you'll rarely have an even lie in the fairway. The recent installation of a sprinkler system increased the

Photo: Carolinas Golf Group, LLC

Devil's Ridge — a must-play course in the Raleigh area.

length of the course. The greens are medium-size and undulating, and their designs mandate good club selection.

Kerr Lake added its first-ever bunker in the spring of 1995! Curiously, the clubhouse at this popular country course resembles a bomb shelter. But, so what? You don't play golf in the snack bar, right?

Amenities include a practice green, range, snack bar, rental clubs and a pro shop.

The course is walkable and you can walk anytime. Call on Thursday for a weekend tee time. Approximate cost, including cart, is $23 weekdays and $28 on weekends.

Lake Winds Golf Course
1807 Moores Mill Rd., Rougemont
• 471-GOLF
Championship Yardage: 6365
Slope: 120	**Par: 72**
Men's Yardage: 6088	
Slope: No rating	**Par: 72**
Ladies' Yardage: 5388	
Slope: No rating	**Par: 72**

Lake Winds opened in 1982. Don Mason designed the course on rolling terrain, with bermudagrass fairways and bentgrass greens.

A few miles north of Durham, Lake Winds is an example of how good a family-owned, operated and maintained country course can be. The layout meanders around and through tranquil, rolling wooded terrain. The fairways offer decent width, and the greens vary in size and shape. There are some good driving holes. Most of the greens are protected by bunkers whose influence will vary greatly depending on pin placement. You'll find some surprisingly wonderful golf holes here. Senior PGA Tour professional Jim Thorpe holds his annual charity golf tournament at Lake Winds. Mr. Thorpe also holds the course record: 61. The closing three holes are exciting — perfect for those who like to wager while they play, which, of course, is against the law and not condoned by the authors, Knight Publishing Company, Insiders' Guides Inc., etc. We're told that the amount of postgame money exchanged will be greatly influenced by these three holes.

Amenities include a practice green, rental clubs and a pro shop.

The course is walkable, and you can walk anytime. You can book a tee time whenever you choose. Approximate cost, including cart, is $22 weekdays and $26 on weekends.

Golf for Women in the Carolinas

It's different from probably anywhere else in the world.

Those of us who live and play in the Carolinas are accustomed to the absolute fact that women are present, allowed and, yes, welcome . . . the same as male golfers.

Women golfers here possibly take this acceptance for granted until they are asked about it by visitors, usually from northeastern states, who are not accustomed to women being allowed on private courses every day, let alone any time of day. Women are welcome on all of the public or semiprivate golf courses that we researched for *The Insiders' Guide® to Golf in the Carolinas*.

More than 5 million women in America play golf, and social acceptance has changed dramatically since the 16th century when Mary Queen of Scots was criticized for taking a liking to the sport of the male nobility.

A recent book by Marcia Chambers, *The Unplayable Lie*, tells of the discrimination that exists in American golf today and of options that help both men and women understand how and why rules can change. The Carolinas, thankfully, are not the setting for any of the cases cited in Chambers' book.

Our differences probably stem from the fact that the vast majority of Carolina courses are public or semiprivate and not country clubs of the type found in many other locations. Also, with a plethora of courses, everyone's business is wanted and needed.

Many clubs do not have women's locker rooms, which might be somewhat annoying, but equal access has been considered for all of the newer clubhouses.

The **Executive Women's Golf League** has chapters in several cities throughout the Carolinas. It's part of a national movement including nearly 10,000 members in

Lochmere Golf Club

2511 Kildaire Farms Rd., Cary • 851-0611
Championship Yardage: 6867
Slope: 124   **Par: 72**
Men's Yardage: 6156
Slope: 116   **Par: 72**
Ladies' Yardage: 5052
Slope: 113   **Par: 74**

The golf course at Lochmere Golf Club is predominantly flat and laid out in woodlands, with 419 bermudagrass fairways and bentgrass greens. This Gene Hamm-designed track opened in 1985.

Lochmere offers a fun and challenging round in a picturesque setting, even though some holes are bordered by homes. For a modern course, the track is a little short; but don't think that makes it any easier. Many holes are tight off the tee, particularly if the rough is up. Once you've banged your ball down the middle of the fairway with your titanium super-mama, you'll have to deal with water, bunkers, mounds, embankments and swales. And once you've hit the green, you'll be faced with a sloping putt with all sorts of subtle breaks. Lochmere definitely will test your accuracy and short-game prowess.

Cary, North Carolina, is a booming and trendy suburb of Raleigh and is quite busy with traffic and construction. Amid the trendiness and bustle, Lochmere is amazingly peaceful and relaxed — part of what makes it so attractive. It's a challenging but fair track that we recommend you try. It's also host to a couple of minor professional tournaments.

Amenities include a practice green, range, locker room, snack bar, rental clubs, a beverage cart and pro shop.

more than 100 chapters. The league intends to promote golf by providing a nurturing atmosphere so women will not be intimidated while learning the game. It also emphasizes familiarizing women with the business etiquette of golf as part of professional networking. In fact, the organization pushes etiquette and training to such a point that women might be more conscious of their proper manners, and even of some rules of golf, than many men.

The camaraderie, including business and social networking, is spoken about among the league's members as an important part of their association. Women new to an area find immediate acceptance among a group with common interests, and those new to golfing find encouragement to learn how to buy clubs and get on a real course.

The leagues in any city welcome visitors from other chapters and invite new members — whether beginning or experienced golfers. For more information, call any of the Executive Women's Golf League Carolina chapters.

Val Skinner, Katie Peterson-Parker and Nancy Lopez exemplify the talent and grace of today's women golfers.
—

In North Carolina:

Charlotte	(704) 892-9274
Pinehurst	(910) 245-3270
Raleigh	(800) 326-3418
	(919) 781-5552
Wilmington	(910) 799-0132

In South Carolina:

Charleston	(803) 881-2014
Hilton Head	(803) 689-1300 Ext. 223
Myrtle Beach	(803) 448-5942 Ext. 18

The course is walkable for the dedicated, and you can walk anytime except before 2 PM on weekends. You can book a tee time seven days in advance. Approximate cost, including cart, is $30 Monday through Thursday, $34 on Friday and $40 on weekends.

The Neuse Golf Club
918 Birkdale Dr. • Clayton • 550-0550
Championship Yardage: 7010

Slope: 136	**Par: 72**
Men's Yardage: 6626	
Slope: 129	**Par: 72**
Other Yardage: 6027	
Slope: 123	**Par: 72**
Ladies' Yardage: 5478	
Slope: 126	**Par: 72**

John LaFoy designed the Neuse Golf Club, which opened in 1994. The course is set in rolling terrain, with houses bordering the fairways. In the fairways, you'll find 419 bermudagrass; on the greens, bentgrass.

The Neuse is a sister club to Devil's Ridge and, like its sister, is owned by Carolinas Golf Group. You can read about LaFoy in the Devil's Ridge write-up. *Golf Digest* rated the course as one of the best new tracks in the country when it opened, and it's also rated by the same magazine as one of the top 75 public-access courses in the country where you can play for less than $50 a round.

Yes, you might want to think about this course as The Noose — and after a round here, you might want to bind, gag and tie Mr. LaFoy to the nearest flagstick. This course appears to be more difficult than Devil's Ridge. The mounds seemed bigger here, the elevation changes bigger, the undulations on the green bigger, the bunkers steeper and deeper and the green complexes more menacing. The Neuse River flanks the course and comes into play on the 4th and 17th holes. The difficulties are easily visible from the tee boxes and fairways. The most amazing hole is, in fact, called "The Noose," a tortuous 192-yard par 3, with water and bunkers to the right of the green and a rock the size of a basketball court on the left. It's quite unlike any golf hole in the Triangle.

Other holes offer just as much challenge and difficulty. Here's what could happen: Your slightly pushed tee shot ricochets off a mound and ends up out-of-bounds — next to the Smiths' gas grill on their large back deck. Or it might land in one of the deep bunkers. Plop your ball in the middle of the fairway and you might have a lengthy walk from the cart path down a slope only to find that your lie is a foot above your feet. Your approach shot might hit a mound next to the green and bounce into a grass swale or down an embankment or into a pot bunker. Your first putt might have a 3-foot break — or it might end up rolling down a slope to the base of the green. Or you might bang it down the middle of the fairway, hit the middle of the green, one-putt and tell your friends that the course is not as difficult as it looks. Just remember that throwing clubs or smashing them on the cart path won't improve your score.

The Neuse provides an excellent example of an architect strutting his heroic and penal stuff. It's certainly a statement: "I'm going to make this course a challenge. But if you have a good round here and you conquer the challenge, you should feel extremely pleased with yourself."

And that's the point of a modern and challenging golf course. A lot of locals like The Neuse and rate it as the best option in the area. We highly recommend you play this course for the experience — even if you play just once.

Amenities include a practice green, range, chipping green, locker room, snack bar, rental clubs, a beverage cart and pro shop.

The course is not walkable. You can book a tee time seven days in advance. Approximate cost, including cart, is $32 Monday through Thursday, $34 on Friday and $38 on weekends.

Occoneechee Golf Club

1500 Lawrence Rd., Hillsborough
• 732-3435

Championship Yardage: 6062	
Slope: 124	**Par: 71**
Men's Yardage: 5692	
Slope: 119	**Par: 71**
Other Yardage: 4936	
Slope: 106	**Par: 71**
Ladies' Yardage: 4681	
Slope: 113	**Par: 71**

Occoneechee Golf Club opened in 1963. Marvin Ray designed the course, and James Ray, whom we believe to be related to Marvin, renovated it. Set on rolling terrain, you'll find bermudagrass fairways and bentgrass greens.

What a great name for a golf course! Too many tracks have mundane natural or town-oriented names. Nomenclature aside, Occoneechee is a fine and fair track laid out in a pleasant country setting. Frankly, there are more challenging courses out there, but there are less challenging courses as well. This one is set up to provide some interest to the big hitting flat-belly but is best suited for the mid-level golfer who wants to play on a good course without losing numerous balls in the woods, without having to hit it 275 yards over water, or without carrying it over a morass of bunkers and/or mounds.

The fairways are medium-width, although out-of-bounds areas make a couple of holes play a bit narrower. The greens are slightly raised and crowned — harder to hit than they appear. There are plenty of pretty trees, some of which might come into play — especially if you're wayward off the tee. Water comes into play on some holes and will affect your strategy if not your shot — ample proof that you don't have to hire a big-name architect to produce a fine and playable golf course. Dare we say the course has an Ellis Maples feel to it? An ongoing course renovation is under way. Overall, Occoneechee provides good value for your golfing dollar and boasts a pleasant and relaxed setting that's free of the houses and condos that have turned modern golf courses into the domain of Realtors rather than golfers.

Amenities include a practice green, range,

chipping green, locker room, bar, snack bar, beverage cart and pro shop.

The course is walkable, you should walk, and you can walk anytime (hooray!). You can book a tee time three to four days in advance. Approximate cost, including cart, is $24 weekdays and $26 on weekends.

The River Golf and Country Club
Sledge Rd., Bunn • 478-3832
Championship Yardage: 6407
Slope: 122   Par: 72
Men's Yardage: 6116
Slope: No rating   Par: 72
Other Yardage: 5870
Slope: No rating   Par: 72
Ladies' Yardage: 4483
Slope: No rating   Par: 72

The golf course at the River Golf and Country Club opened in 1990. We tried to find out who designed the course, but no one knows. Most of the holes are bordered by woods. Fairways are bermudagrass; greens, bentgrass.

The River Golf and Country Club is a serious "find." Bunn, North Carolina, is not as remote as you might think, and the course is well worth the drive. For our money, this is one of the best courses in the Triangle. Each hole is well-designed and thought out. The setting is both peaceful and magnificent. The fairways vary in width, and there are some fun tee shots from a couple of the elevated tees. The green complexes feature bunkers of various sizes and shapes plus some large undulating greens. There's even a double green on the back nine. Water comes into play on a number of holes in the form of streams and ponds. There's a distinct lack of housing — rare for a newer course.

Although recently built, the River possesses a traditional feel well beyond its years. Students of golf course architecture might leave the course wondering who is responsible for this outstanding track. The course is also a good value.

Amenities include a practice green, range, snack bar and pro shop.

Walk anytime except weekends before 2 PM. You can book a tee time two weeks in advance. Approximate cost, including cart, is $20 weekdays and $30 on weekends.

Roxboro Country Club
260 Club House Dr., Roxboro
• (910) 599-2332
Championship Yardage: 5663
Slope: 114   Par: 70
Men's Yardage: 5364
Slope: 113   Par: 70
Ladies' Yardage: 4425
Slope: 113   Par: 70

Roxboro Country Club opened in 1945. Ellis Maples rerouted the course (we think) and added nine holes in 1969. The course is set amid rolling, slightly wooded terrain, with fairways of bermudagrass and bentgrass greens.

Roxboro Country Club is a fine country club course. It's not the longest course in the world, but it might rate as one of the prettiest in the area. There are plenty of super holes, although those around the turn, which might have been part of the original nine, are not as pretty as the others. As with many Ellis Maples courses, you'll find beautiful sweeping doglegs, excellent use of the land, plenty of room off the tee, deep undulating greens and large bunkers protecting half or two-thirds of the green. You'll find plenty of examples of how Maples matches design elements with the length and pitch of the hole: Long holes have big greens; short holes have smaller greens with more protection. Water comes into play on a few holes and this adds a great deal visually to the course.

Amenities include a practice green, range, snack bar and pro shop.

You can walk anytime. You won't need a tee time during the week; call Thursday for a weekend tee time. Approximate cost, including cart, is $22 weekdays and $28 on weekends.

Sourwood Golf Club
8055 Pleasant Hill Church Rd.,
Snow Camp • (910) 376-8166
Championship Yardage: 6862
Slope: 117   Par: 72
Men's Yardage: 6285
Slope: 112   Par: 72
Ladies' Yardage: 5017
Slope: 106   Par: 72

Sourwood Golf Course was designed by Elmo Cobb (no relation to George) and opened in 1991, with a mix of open and wooded terrain. In the fairways, you'll find bermudagrass; on the greens, bentgrass.

We found Sourwood to be a fine owner-designed country course; Cobb easily could have made a good golf course architect based on the soundness of this layout. The course is named after the sourwood tree that still shows up in places but, sadly, is disappearing. Most holes are relatively straightforward — neither too easy nor overly difficult, just very playable. There's decent enough room off the tee, so use your driver liberally. The greens are sloped and midsize.

Even though the course is somewhat remote, it's worth the drive for a break from the city and a fun round of golf in a pleasant country setting on a playable track. Elmo Cobb is reputedly one of the better greenskeepers around, and many area golfers cite Sourwood as a course with good greens.

Amenities include a practice green and snack bar.

You can walk anytime except before 1 PM on weekends. Book a tee time whenever you choose. Approximate cost, including cart, is $16 weekdays and $20 on weekends.

Wake Forest Country Club
13239 Capitol Blvd., Wake Forest
• 556-3416
Championship Yardage: 6956
Slope: 135	**Par: 72**
Men's Yardage: 6525	
Slope: 129	**Par: 72**
Other Yardage: 6109	
Slope: 126	**Par: 72**
Ladies' Yardage: 5124	
Slope: 122	**Par: 72**

Wake Forest Country Club opened in 1968. Gene Hamm designed this course on undulating wooded terrain, with bermudagrass fairways and bentgrass greens.

Wake Forest Country Club is unrelated to Wake Forest University, which is more than an hour's drive to the west. The course is well known for its opening "world's longest par 5," a 711-yard behemoth on which you'll be happy to reach the ladies' tees on your first shot. If you don't reach the ladies' tees, the normal penalty (whatever *yours* is) does not apply: Please, just keep it in. Play it from the white

tees and it's an ample 526 yards. And to make matters more difficult, the stream that bisects the hole close to the green easily could destroy your early-round confidence if you're not careful.

The course was recently purchased by GolfSouth, and improvements to the track and its adjoining facilities are in progress. The absurd length of the 1st hole aside, Wake Forest should be better known for the quality of the layout. You'll find an excellent example here of a fine and playable traditional track that provides plenty of visual attraction and challenge. Attack this course and you'll be rewarded for sound execution, but realize that you'll be penalized proportionally for poor and wayward shots. Occasional trouble off the tee is augmented if the rough has grown up above an inch or two. The greens vary in size, shape, slope and waviness, but we're told that they are true and can get wonderfully fast. Water provides a hazard on a few holes. If you prefer mature, challenging courses, make the trip to Wake Forest Country Club.

Amenities include a practice green, range, chipping green, locker room, bar, snack bar, rental clubs, a beverage cart and pro shop.

Walking is restricted to after 2 PM on weekends; the course is walkable but hilly in places. You can book a tee time seven days in advance. Approximate cost, including cart, is $25 Monday through Thursday, $29 on Friday and $38 on weekends.

Willowhaven Country Club
253 Country Club Dr., Durham • 383-1022
Championship Yardage: 6655
Slope: 120	**Par: 72**
Men's Yardage: 6342	
Slope: 117	**Par: 72**
Other Yardage: 5721	
Slope: 111	**Par: 72**
Ladies' Yardage: 5436	
Slope: 117	**Par: 75**

The golf course at Willowhaven Country Club opened in 1957. George Cobb designed the course on rolling wooded terrain. In the fairways, you'll find bermudagrass; on the greens, bentgrass.

The course is approaching its 40th birthday, so it's definitely a mature track. It's one of Cobb's earlier efforts, one that clearly shows his skill in taking a pretty piece of land and turning it into a playable and attractive course. At Willowhaven, Cobb has created variety and challenge without anything tricked-up or fancy.

There isn't a lot of trouble off the tee, although it helps to be in the right sector on many of the doglegs. Trouble around the greens comes in the form of large sloped putting surfaces, swales, embankments and basic bunkers. The better golfer won't think that the course offers a huge amount of challenge, but there's easily enough from the back tees. If you're fond of traditional courses, you should make your way to Willowhaven.

Amenities include a practice green, range, snack bar, rental clubs and a pro shop.

Walk anytime; you can book a tee time three days prior to a weekday, five days prior to the weekend. Approximate cost, including cart, is $31.50 weekdays and $36.50 on weekends.

Around the Triangle . . .

FYI
Unless otherwise noted, the area code for all phone numbers in this chapter is 919.

Fun Things To Do

Raleigh is North Carolina's state capital as well as home to St. Mary's College, Peace College, Meredith College, St. Augustine's College, Shaw University and the North Carolina State University. Take the time to visit the **Governor's Mansion**, on 200 N. Blount Street, home to Gov. James B. Hunt and his family. It's an outstanding example of Queen Anne Cottage Victorian architecture. Call 733-3456 for tour information. You can also tour the **State Capitol** building in downtown Raleigh on Edenton Street; call 733-4994.

For more information about state government sites, contact the **Capital Area Visitor Center**, 301 N. Blount Street, 733-3456, or the **Greater Raleigh Convention and Visitors Bureau**, 225 Hillsborough Street, (800) 849-8499.

North Carolina State University Arboretum, 4301 Berry Road, is worth a visit, especially in the fall and spring; call 515-2011. The **North Carolina Symphony** is based in Ra-

leigh and plays concerts in various locations around Raleigh and the Triangle; call the Symphony office at 733-2750 for information on upcoming concerts.

The **North Carolina Museum of Art**, 2110 Blue Ridge Avenue, houses permanent displays of the state's art collection, as well as a number of changing exhibitions. There's a gift shop and cafe on site. Call 833-1935 for more information. Admission is free, and daily tours are offered at 1:30 PM.

Durham is perhaps best known for tobacco processing and as the location of the best movie ever about minor-league baseball: *Bull Durham*. The movie starred Kevin Costner, Tim Robbins and Susan Sarandon. Sadly, the ball park where the movie was filmed is no longer used. But fans of the **Durham Bulls**, who play rookie-league ball as a farm team for the Atlanta Braves, can cheer the team on in their new stadium at 200 Willard Street in Durham; call 688-8211 for information. Other minor-league play is presented by the **Carolina Mudcats**, who play AA ball in Zebulon at Five County Stadium, 269-2287.

If you're not in the mood for baseball or golf, then start with a visit to **Duke University** (for general information on touring campus sites, call 684-8111). You can take in the *faux* Gothic architecture (the chapel is modeled after Princeton University's) in addition to the Sarah P. **Duke Gardens**, located adjacent to the campus, a 55-acre bouquet of daffodils, pansies and students from New Jersey (who seemingly comprise a disproportionate amount of Duke's enrollment); call the Duke Gardens Office at 684-3698. You might also want to visit the **Duke Homestead and Tobacco Museum**, a state historic site. This attraction is housed in the former home of Washington Duke, father of the tobacco trade, and is located at 2828 Duke Homestead Road; you'll learn a lot about the influence of tobacco on the local economy. Call 477-5498.

West Point on the Eno, on Cole Mill Road, is part of the Eno River City Park and is a pleasant and quiet retreat from the city. The park covers 400 acres and is full of wildlife. You can enjoy camping, fishing, rafting, picnicking, hiking and general solitude. Call 471-

1623. Another excellent museum is the **North Carolina Museum of Life and Science** where you'll find hands-on exhibits, live experiments and wildlife. Call 220-5429. The museum is located at 433 Murray Avenue.

Durham is also a major center for medicine; naturally, we hope that you've come to Durham for golf and not for a visit to one of the area's healthcare facilities.

Chapel Hill is where author Scott Martin spent four extremely studious and serious years at the University of North Carolina, flagship institution of the University of North Carolina system. You should visit **Morehead Planetarium**, one of the finest in the country; call 549-6863. You'll find the building on E. Franklin Street; look for the lovely rose garden out front. While you're in the vicinity, cruise down Franklin Street to take in the general ambiance of one of the prettiest and most eclectic college towns in America. If you want to tour the campus of the **University of North Carolina**, call 962-2211.

Those of you who love flowers, trees and shrubberies should visit the **Coker Arboretum** in the North Carolina Botanical Garden on the N.C. 15-501 By-pass. Call 962-0522 for more information. Art lovers should visit the **Ackland Art Museum** on S. Columbia Street near the junction of Franklin Street. There's a permanent collection of European and American art in addition to a fine collection of sculpture dating from the Renaissance to the present.

For more information about Chapel Hill and Orange County, contact the **Chapel Hill and Orange County Visitors Bureau**, 105 N. Columbia Street, 968-2060.

Where to Eat

As far as urban areas go in North Carolina, it's probably tough to beat the Triangle for flair and variety. There's plenty of downhome Southern cooking to go around, but the diverse tastes brought here by the universities mean that food lovers are well taken care of

here. You'll find plenty of the chain-style eateries you might find at home, but while you're here, why not try something different: There's plenty to sample. The establishments we list here all take major credit cards unless noted otherwise. Refer to our Preface for an explanation of the pricing code.

Raleigh

Angus Barn
$$$$ • U.S. Hwy. 70 at Airport Rd., Raleigh • 781-2444

OK, so we'll start with something a little more traditional. Something that will stick to your ribs. This is one of the busiest and most popular steakhouses in North Carolina and has been — in the same location — for more than 30 years. The restaurant is popular with business people. Bring a big appetite and leave room for a desert. Don't even think about the word "diet."

In addition to the excellent steaks here at "Beefeaters' Haven," the Angus Barn features seafood, chicken and salads. Top it all off with a fudge sundae and they will be carting you out in a wheelbarrow.

The atmosphere at the Barn, as locals call it, is country elegant — we know that seems contradictory, but you'll see what we mean. While you don't have to really dress up, you'd probably feel somewhat conspicuous if you didn't gussy up at least a little bit.

Est Est Est Tratoria
$$ • 19 W. Hargett St., Raleigh • 832-8899

Enter on Salisbury Street. The restaurant is popular at lunch and has become even more so in the evenings. This place is perfect for the romantic in you — and, hopefully, your current or prospective better half too. Pasta is made on the premises. Choose a fine bottle of house wine to wash down your meal. You'll find a variety of entrees that change daily, but the basic menu components include pasta, seafood and lighter meats.

INSIDERS' TIP

Many professional golfers are very happy to score par on a hole. They shoot for the middle of the fairways and greens to avoid trouble and big numbers.

Greenshield's Brewery and Pub

$$ • 214 E. Martin St., Raleigh • 829-0214

For fine hand-crafted beer, you can't go wrong here. The pub is so authentic, it's frequented by Anglophiles, real English people (who only drink real beer), rugby players and darts-throwers. When hunger replaces thirst, try the fish and chips or pot pies.

Margaux's

$$$ • 8111 Creedmore Rd., Raleigh • 846-9846

French cuisine in northern Raleigh? In the land of new houses and shopping centers? Two well-educated chefs turned a sporting goods store into a restaurant that's been acclaimed in print and by word-of-mouth. Check it out and be sure to ask about the specials, which might range from Carolina quail to crab casserole.

Durham

Anotherthyme

$$ • 109 N. Gregson St., Durham • 682-5225

We know locals who call this place home. The menu is varied — French, Italian, Spanish, Chinese — so you never get bored. And besides, all your friends are here, so how could you have anything but a good time. The food is prepared with always-fresh ingredients. Count this one in for lunch, dinner or even a late-night snack. You'll have a great meal at a great price.

Bullock's Bar-B-Cue

$ • 3330 Wortham St., Durham • 383-3211

There just had to be an establishment with the word "Bull" in it, and this is it. Don't come here for the decor or to be coddled and "waited-on." Do come for the variety and quality of the barbecue, the hush puppies and tea so sweet your spoon stands at attention.

Darryl's 1890

$$ • 4603 Chapel Hill Blvd., Durham • 489-1890

Part of the Darryl's chain, this version offers plenty of food and plenty of ambiance in the form of secluded booths and interesting knick-knacks on the walls. The multi-page menu offers everything from seafood to chicken to prime rib to massive desserts and liver-threatening frozen drinks. The restaurant is significantly popular after football games and other events in Chapel Hill or Durham. Note that there is also a Raleigh location on U.S. Highway 70, just a few miles west of Crabtree Valley Mall.

The Fairview

$$$ • 3001 Cameron Ave., Durham • 490-0999

You'll find The Fairview inside the Washington Duke Inn, which is adjacent to the majestic Duke Golf Club — a must play in the Triangle area. Appetizers include mixed baby green salad, crab cakes and stone-baked pizza of the day. Proceed to your entree, which might be pan-seared large sea scallops, grilled breast of chicken, Colorado rack of Lamb or veal chop, all served with fresh vegetables and the latest joke about Dean Smith.

Magnolia Grill

$$$$ • 1002 Ninth St., Durham • 286-3609

When you just had your best golf day ever and it's time to celebrate, do so at the Magnolia Grill. This is one of the area's best restaurants, and it has the loyal customers to prove it. Your dining pleasure will depend on what's fresh and what's on the chef's ever-changing, always-innovative menu. The menu changes daily, but there's usually a vegetarian dish, steaks, a poultry dish and two or three seafood specialties. You should definitely leave room for dessert. The pastry chef here makes all the ice creams, sorbets and baked goods at the restaurant.

Make reservations here so you won't miss the opportunity to see why the Triangle is raves about this fine establishment.

Chapel Hill

Aurora

$$$ • 200 N. Greensboro St., Chapel Hill • 942-2400

Trendy, and justifiably so, Aurora is not a place to be seen, because you can't be — it's very dimly lit, especially at night. You'll find some of the most-acclaimed Italian food in the Triangle. Complement your veal, lamb, poultry or seafood with fresh pasta and dizzying sauces. Match it all with a hearty Italian wine and you're in for a great evening. Make a reservation here.

Carolina Brewery
$$-$$$ • 460 W. Franklin St., Chapel Hill • 942-1800

In the now super-trendy atmosphere that befits the western section of Franklin Street, it's only appropriate that a microbrewery should set up shop. Carolina Brewery's decor is a little upscale for a brewpub, with shiny metalwork to complement the equally shiny copper kettles and other devices designed to produce that most silken and sylvan of beverages: beer. The beer here is pretty good. You might try the Copperline Amber Ale, the Franklin Street Lager, the India Pale Ale or one of the select guest beers from other microbreweries around the country. The great thing about the microbrewery is freshness, so you'll find the beer here especially palatable and varied.

The food matches the ambiance and is symptomatic of the latest in microbrewery fare. You might find the cheesy creole pizza — made with fresh focaccia dough — to your liking. Or, try the marinated citrus chicken sandwich or Louisiana sausage po' boy — either, a perfect complement to your brew. The person with the slightly larger appetite might go for the duck trap river smoked red trout pasta or the jambalaya with andouille sausage smothered with spicy creole tomato sauce.

Crook's Corner
$$$ • 610 W. Franklin St., Chapel Hill • 929-7643

Crook's offers one of the most unique and subtly intense dining experiences anywhere. The restaurant itself, which looks like a cross between a hair salon and a former service station, is crowned with a statue of a pig. Wooden animal statuary rounds out the decor. The menu changes so rapidly, you'll never be disappointed. It might be something South American; it might be something like shrimp 'n' grits. It's always praiseworthy — and usually loud and fun. Crook's Corner is a great place for reunions of sorts.

The Fearrington House
$$$$ • 2000 Fearrington Village Center, Pittsboro • 542-2121

One of Chapel Hill's hottest restaurants (and it's been this way for years) isn't in Chapel Hill, it's just down U.S. 15-501 in Pittsboro. The menu changes monthly, but you'll find such mildly exotic fare as boneless leg of rabbit, free range veal loin, baked snapper, roasted guinea hen, or how about the Chilean sea bass. When this author attended Chapel Hill, taking your date here was more impressive than anything, even if you were left with no money for beer for the next month. It was worth the extravagance.

Pyewacket
$$ • 431 W. Franklin St., Chapel Hill • 929-0291

Pyewacket has been a Chapel Hill fixture with the old Volvo and tweed jacket academic crowd for years. Or at least that's how it's reputed. Actually, its popularity base has increased to include sorority women on "girls' night out" as well as business people in town to close a deal. The food is the key, and it's mostly within a vegetarian bent. Somehow, it seems light and hearty at the same time. Special entrees vary almost daily, but you can't go wrong with the seafod curry or the vegetarian lasagne. But, what we frequently find ourselves craving the most is their Morning Star salad, a worthy meal in itself. The wine list is also excellent.

The Rathskeller
$ • 157-A Franklin St., Chapel Hill • 942-5158

"The Rat," in its own subterranean fashion, exudes fumes of Chapel Hill past and present. It's a major student hangout, with a

Once or twice a year, enter a tournament and play tournament rules.

major and passionate following among alumni who line up after football games for spaghetti and tea and other such basics. It's not a place for the claustrophobic, but it is a place for those whose blood runs Tarheel blue. A must.

Where to Stay

Refer to our Preface for an explanation of the pricing code.

Raleigh

Courtyard by Marriott
$$ • 1041 Wakestowne Dr., Raleigh • 821-3400

The Courtyard by Marriott concept is popping up all over the country and is popular with business travelers. This version might look like some of the others you've seen, but there are some important amenities to note, including an on-site gym, whirlpool room and outdoor pool. Guests also have free access to a full-scale gym with extensive facilities across the road. When you're through working out, drop by the restaurant, serving breakfast and light dinners, and the bar. Staff members are quite friendly here. Due to the large volume of business travelers in the area, you should definitely book ahead for a room.

Hilton Convention Center
$$$-$$$$ • 3415 Wake Forest Rd., Raleigh • 872-2323

Convenient to Raleigh Community Hospital, and very near the Beltline (I-440), this popular and glitzy hotel boasts 338 rooms and quite a few large-scale political parties.

On the special executive floor, you'll have access to a private cocktail bar; your room will be a little larger than a regular room, plus you'll have an ironing board and a few other bells and whistles at your disposal. The standard rooms are comfortable as well, and all are equipped with coffee makers. Guests receive a free copy of *USA Today* daily.

Other amenities include a workout room, an indoor pool and a whirlpool. If you're in the mood to boogie, venture forth into Bowties night club where the price of admission is free if you're staying at the hotel. Enjoy the full-service restaurant; otherwise try one of the 30 restaurants within an hour's drive of the hotel.

Durham

Arrowhead Inn
$$$ • 106 Mason Rd., Durham • 477-8430

This wonderful bed and breakfast inn features eight guest rooms and is convenient to everywhere in Durham. Relax in the parlor with a game or some light TV. You'll also get a hearty breakfast when you awaken from a peaceful slumber.

Brownstone-Medcenter Inn
$$$ • 2424 Erwin Rd. • Durham • 286-7761

As you enter Durham, the signs tell you that Durham is the City of Medicine; it's also the city of cigarettes. Go figure. Anyway, here's a hotel that has developed to serve those visiting the extensive and well-known medical center. It's also a good place for golfers visiting Durham's golf courses. Here at the Brownstone, you'll find 140 elegant Colonial design rooms, extensive dining facilities, a banquet room with space for you and 129 of your closest friends, an indoor pool, cable TV (with ESPN) sauna, whirlpool, beauty and barber shop and, when you've had enough healthy living for the day, Burley's lounge featuring beer, wine, vodka, gin, whiskey, rum, tequila and other medicinal potions.

Holiday Inn Durham
$$ • 3460 Hillsborough St., Durham • 383-1551

Part of the worldwide chain, the Holiday Inn Durham offers 168 comfortable rooms

---

INSIDERS' TIP

At least once a year, spend a day at a golf tournament. You might want to follow a golfer whose play you enjoy. Or, camp out next to a reachable par 5 and watch the pros demonstrate their short game prowess.

Many Triangle-area courses require accurate placement.
Expect unhappy consequences if you miss your mark.

(and two suites) with a full range of amenities. Included in your bill is cable TV (with HBO, Showtime and ESPN) access to the swimming pool, plus access to Jamie's Restaurant and Lounge. The hotel also offers services for the business traveler, including fax and copy service and a meeting room that can contain (well, maybe) 200 business people.

Washington Duke

$$$ • Inn and Golf Club, 3001 Cameron Blvd., Durham • 490-0999

This 171-room hotel cost roughly $16 million to build, so it had better be nice, right?

Well this is one of the finest places in Durham. We've already raved about the golf course, so why not rave about the hotel that dominates the 9th hole, a dangerous par 5.

Service is a key at Washington Duke — room service, turndown service and just the right touches of white-glove style to keep you content. You can relax in their acclaimed restaurant, The Fairview, and enjoy an after-dinner drink in the Bull Durham Lounge. If golf is not your game, you can play tennis, take to the Duke Forest jogging trails or try out the swimming pool. For the business traveler, suites and meeting facilities also are available.

Chapel Hill

The Carolina Inn
**$$$ • W. Cameron Ave., Chapel Hill
• 933-2001**

Venerable and storied, this is the inn of the University of North Carolina. In 1995, this accommodation underwent a series of changes and improvements to equip it for latter part of the 20th century and prepare it for the 21st. The inn opened in 1924, so it needed some work. You'll love the architecture, designed to resemble Mount Vernon.

Amenities in the completely renovated rooms include coffee machines, cable TV and desks. The inn is within walking distance of downtown Chapel Hill and all of its attractions.

Fearrington House Country Inn
$$$$ • 2000 Fearrington Village Center, Pittsboro • 542-2121

Okay, we know this inn isn't in Chapel Hill proper, but it's less than 10 minutes away, and the experience you'll have at this charming spot is more than worth the drive. The 15 suites at Fearrington House are the definition of luxury but are presented without any of the highbrow attitude that too often accompanies an accommodation of this quality. Each room is unique, with beautiful antiques collected by the owners during trips to Europe. And the surrounding landscaping takes full advantage of the relaxing countryside that once was home to a dairy farm.

You'll also enjoy afternoon teas and a complimentary breakfast served in the on-site restaurant that has been commended by both *Gourmet* and *Food and Wine* magazines. Dinner here is an experience you'll want to add to your list.

Holiday Inn of Chapel Hill
**$$ • U.S. Hwy. 15/501 Bypass, Chapel Hill
• 929-2171**

Looking for a clean, comfortable hotel that won't take up all your golf money? This is a great choice. It's near a shopping mall and the UNC campus, and this location offers easy access to I-40, so scooting around the Triangle is convenient. Teddy's restaurant is on-site, and plenty of other good eateries are also nearby. During warmer months, relax in the outdoor pool after your golf round.

The Triad Area

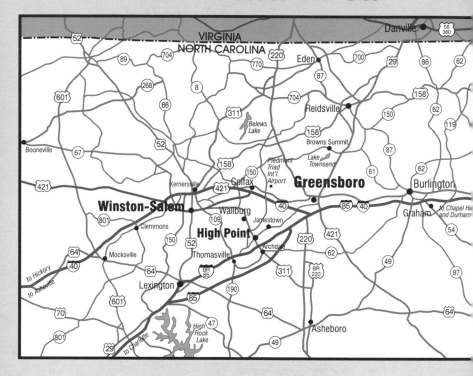

North Carolina's Triad

The Greensboro, Winston-Salem, Burlington and High Point areas are best known in the Carolinas for their industrial base. R.J. Reynolds, Sara Lee and Guilford Mills boast large manufacturing plants and administrative offices in the area. Wachovia Bank, one of the nation's largest financial institutions, is based in Winston-Salem and maintains its relatively new headquarters downtown. There are numerous fine cultural organizations and four well-known midsize universities: North Carolina A&T, Winston-Salem State, UNC-Greensboro and Wake Forest. There's also plenty of minor-league ice hockey in the area: Winston-Salem began play in the fall of 1995, and the Greensboro Monarchs have played in Greensboro for a number of years. So if it's too cold outside for golf, take solace in the fact that hot dogs, beer and glove-dropping are close at hand.

Golf-wise, there's more public golf in the Triad than you can shake a 4-iron at. The May 1996 edition of *Golf Digest* ranked the best public-access golf courses in the United States and divided the 150 courses into two groups: daily fees more and less than $50. The list included Oak Hollow in High Point, the Champions Course at Bryan Park and the Championship course at Tanglewood. Stoney Creek in Burlington has been recognized as a top new course, and *North Carolina Magazine* named Mill Creek the best new public course in the state in 1995.

With its small-town atmosphere and the predominance of rolling country terrain, it's difficult to describe the Triad as an urban area. For the sake of argument, however, let's say

that it's an urban area. Let's go one step further and say that the Triad offers the best public-access golf of any urban area in the Carolinas. Let's be even bolder and say that if you include all the recent additions to the current portfolio, the Triad rivals Pinehurst in terms of quality, variety and big-name architects. And Pinehurst is only about an hour away by car! In our minds, this makes golfers in the Triad some of the most fortunate in the United States, let alone the Carolinas.

Can you have too many public courses in a given geographic zone? We noticed that the excess supply means that prices are generally lower in the Triad than in other urban areas. This means less money for the owners; it can also mean less money for maintenance and, on many tracks, it shows. Given favorable climatic conditions, many courses are fine. Given poor natural conditions, you won't always find magnificent greens and fairways. It's difficult enough to grow anything on all this Piedmont clay, let alone lush bermudagrass. We should stress that in 1995 the courses were hit with a winter freeze-out of the fairways and a summer that began with floods and ended with baking heat. With Hurricane Fran ripping a swath through the middle of the state in September, Mother Nature obviously was not kind to these courses in '96 either.

But economics and conditioning aside, the Triad is stacked with good public courses. The municipal governments have, with the help of significant donations of free land, invested heavily in fine golf facilities with national reputations. Tanglewood, in Clemmons, hosts a

GOLF COURSES IN THE TRIAD OF NORTH CAROLINA

Name	Type	# Holes	Par	Slope	Yards	Walking	Booking	Cost w/ Cart
Bryan Park								
Champions Course	public	18	72	125	6622	restricted	30 days	$30-32
Players Course	public	18	72	120	6499	anytime	30 days	$30-32
Grandover Resort	resort	18	72	n/a	7100	restricted	anytime	$35-45
Greensboro National	public	18	72	n/a	6922	restricted	anytime	$35-40
Hickory Hill Country Club	semiprivate	18	70	110	5902	restricted	3 days	$22-28
Holly Ridge Golf Links	public	18	72	127	6121	restricted	anytime	$21-27
Jamestown Park	public	18	72	122	6186	restricted	7 days	$22-24
Lexington Golf and Country Club	public	18	70	116	5703	anytime	7 days	$18-20
Lynrock Golf Club	public	18	70	109	5538	anytime	2 days	$19-21
Maple Leaf	public	18	71	n/r	5655	restricted	7 days	$21-24
Meadowlands	public	18	72	n/a	6706	restricted	7 days	$35-40
Mill Creek	semiprivate	18	72	127	7004	No	7 days	$35-40
Monroeton Golf Club	public	18	70	103	5428	anytime	anytime	$11-16
Oak Hollow Golf Course	public	18	72	118	6090	anytime	2 days	$23-26
Oak Valley	public	18	72	n/a	7058	restricted	7 days	$34-40
Pine Knolls	semiprivate	18	72	110	5923	restricted	anytime	$22-28
Pine Tree	semiprivate	18	71	107	6046	restricted	10 days	$24-28
Pudding Ridge	semiprivate	18	70	123	6234	restricted	7 days	$24-28
Reynolds Park	public	18	71	118	5923	restricted	7 day	$22-28
Sandy Ridge Golf Course	semiprivate	18	72	n/r	5645	restricted	5 days	$21-25
Silo Run	public	18	71	n/a	6751	No	7 days	$22-28
Southwick Golf Course	public	18	70	111	5431	restricted	anytime	$12-20
Stoney Creek Golf Club	semiprivate	18	72	132	6573	restricted	7 days	$30-35
Tanglewood Park								
Championship Course	public	18	72	135	6638	restricted	7 days	$45-63
Reynolds Course	public	18	72	120	6061	anytime	7 days	$30

PGA SENIOR TOUR event and in 1974 hosted the PGA Championship won by Lee Trevino. Bryan Park's Champions Course in Brown Summit is probably a good enough layout to host a significant professional event. And each year, two weeks after the Masters, the big boys of the PGA Tour come to the area for the Greater Greensboro Open (see our Tournaments in the Carolinas chapter). In addition to these professional events, the area is host to a number of top-quality amateur tournaments. Wake Forest University has one of the most successful golf programs in the country; its alumni include Jay Haas, Arnold Palmer and Curtis Strange. Notable architects whose work graces this area include Jack Nicklaus, Arnold Palmer, Ed Seay, Robert Trent Jones, Rees Jones, Pete Dye, Gene Hamm and Tom Jackson. Plus there are numerous courses designed by "no-name" architects: Their efforts are worthwhile, interesting and justifiably popular. If you live in the Triad area, count your blessings. If you're visiting the Triad, schedule some time to visit one or more of the tracks listed in this chapter.

Triad Golf Today, an excellent monthly newspaper, gives timely updates on course developments, tournaments and other pertinent information for the Triad golfer. It's available in most pro shops.

Bryan Park and Golf Club
6275 Bryan Park Rd., Brown Summit
• 375-2200

The populace of the Triad area is fortunate that most of its municipalities have invested in fine golf complexes. Here in the Greensboro area, it's Bryan Park — a complex as fine as any public golf facility in the Carolinas. Fine architects designed the two courses. A state-of-the-art practice facility was completed on schedule in January 1996 and is now open.

If you're looking for a couple of public courses with real difficulty and serious challenge, visit Bryan Park; you won't be disappointed on either track and you'll be rewarded

if you travel a decent distance to play here. Both courses also provide excellent value for your golfing dollar and have been recognized for this by *Golf Digest*.

Amenities include a practice green, range, chipping green, snack bar, rental clubs and a pro shop.

Both courses are walkable for the fit; you can walk anytime on the Players and after 4 PM on the Champions. You can book a tee time one month in advance. Approximate cost for either course, including cart, is $30 weekdays and $32 on weekends.

Champions Course
Championship Yardage: 7135

Slope: 130	**Par: 72**
Men's Yardage: 6622	
Slope: 125	**Par: 72**
Other Yardage: 5977	
Slope: 118	**Par: 72**
Ladies' Yardage: 5395	
Slope: 123	**Par: 72**

Rees Jones designed the Champions Course, which opened in 1990 and is set in open terrain bordered by woods on some holes. Fairways are bermudagrass; greens, bentgrass.

The Champions Course offers some wonderful and difficult holes. Jones made good use of the natural landscape, including several acres bordering Lake Townsend, which comes into play on a number of holes. Rees Jones is the son of Robert Trent Jones, and both father and son demonstrate an annoying penchant (from a players perspective) for bunkering en masse. The younger Jones likes them deep and somewhat irregularly placed — some make us wonder whose ball would ever find these traps, they're so out of the way. Perhaps these bunkers exist solely for your viewing pleasure.

There's usually plenty of room off the tee. Wayward drives may end up in woods or bouncing like a pin ball around the many large mounds. You might find a bunker. Water comes into play a lot here in the form of the

INSIDERS' TIP

When the course you're playing is busy, spend a maximum of two or three minutes looking for your ball. Or, better still, take a little less club off the tee and concentrate on hitting it straight.

Photo: N.C. Travel & Tourism

Thousands of golf enthusiasts attend the Chrysler Greater Greensboro Classic.

lake, ponds and streams. The greens are large, sloped and flanked by many bunkers and a few embankments. You'll have trouble getting to most of the greens and just as much trouble getting up and down. The Champions Course is so-named for a reason. If you're a high-handicapper, you might be in for a long day, even if you play from the white tees.

Players Course
Championship Yardage: 7076
Slope: 128   **Par: 72**
Men's Yardage: 6499
Slope: 120   **Par: 72**
Other Yardage: 5925
Slope: 115   **Par: 72**
Ladies' Yardage: 5260
Slope: 120   **Par: 72**

The Players Course at Bryan Park, designed by George Cobb, opened in 1974. The bermudagrass fairways and bentgrass greens are set in open terrain, with woods flanking some holes. Rees Jones made some changes to the Players Course when he built the Champions, but it retained much of its "Cobb feel."

Even from the front tees, the Players Course is difficult; as the scorecard reads, it's "recognized as one of the best public tests of golf."

The Players Course is the more mature of the two, and if you're familiar with the work of George Cobb, you'll recognize this as one of his signature efforts. Rees Jones' modifications likely account for the addition of mounds and some new bunkering. But don't think that the Players Course is an easier version of its sister. From the back, there's still more than 7000 yards of tough golf ahead of you. There isn't nearly as much water, but you'll still find difficult greens and extensive bunkering. If the Champions Course looks crowded, think about trying the Players; it's still an excellent challenge and one of the best golfing values in North Carolina.

Grandover Resort
One Thousand Club Rd., Greensboro
• 294-1800
East Course
Championship Yardage: 7100
Slope: 140   **Par: 72**
Men's Yardage: 6600
Slope: 132   **Par: 72**
Ladies' Yardage: 4924
Slope: 121   **Par: 72**

The East Course at Grandover Resort opened in early 1996, and all 18 holes of the West Course will be finished in late 1996. David Graham and Gary Panks teamed up to design the course, which is set in rolling terrain bordered by woods in a few places. You'll find

419 bermudagrass fairways and bentgrass greens.

You can see Grandover Resort from Interstate 85 just south of Greensboro and might notice that the overall plans for the resort are quite grand. At press time, all 18 holes of the East Course were open and ready for play, and nine of the 18 on the West Course were open. But for now, we'll focus strictly on the East Course.

The Graham-Panks tandem is a proven combination that's designed some well-respected courses in Arkansas, Arizona, Virginia, Australia and Thailand. Here at Grandover, they've created a course that emphasizes variety. The setting is wonderful, and the golf experience is enhanced by some significant elevation changes that contribute to the flow of the layout.

The fairways are moderate in width, and some have been shaped to keep the ball in play if it's headed for the woods. The greens are generously sized and do not undulate significantly. But once again, let us emphasize, the key here is variety: No two holes or greens are alike. If the East Course is anything to go by, then the West Course should be just as good. Just another couple of great courses in the Triad. When will it stop? Will it ever stop?

Walking is restricted and, even when allowed, only for the fit. Amenities include a 40,000-square-foot clubhouse, meeting rooms, a range, putting green, restaurant, lounge, rental clubs and a pro shop. Approximate cost, including cart, is $35 weekdays and $45 on weekends. Bookings may be made a week in advance.

Greensboro National Golf Club

330 Niblick Dr., Summerfield • 643-4653
Championship Yardage: 6922
Slope: No rating   Par: 72
Men's Yardage: 6417
Slope: No rating   Par: 72
Ladies' Yardage: 4991
Slope: No rating   Par: 72

Greensboro National Golf Club opened in late 1995. The course is set in rolling terrain bordered mostly by woods. In the fairways, you'll find bermudagrass; on the greens, you'll find bentgrass with zoysia collars. Don and Mark Charles designed the course.

Set amid rolling farmland in horse country north of Greensboro, Greensboro National is a wonderful new course that's likely to become one of the more popular tracks in the area. The layout winds through a wonderful piece of land that's as pretty as any in the Piedmont. But more importantly, the designers, staff and developers created the course to be relatively easy to maintain and very golfer-friendly. With its four sets of well-spaced tees, the course is laid out to provide a fun challenge for all levels of golfer.

The layout of most holes is traditional and unassuming — there are few blind shots and no tricks. There are no significant elevation changes. The challenges are in plain view for all to see. Water and wetlands come into play on 10 holes. The strategically placed bunkers need to be avoided if you're going to score well. The greens are large and steadily sloped — there are no significant or awkward undulations. The fairways are wide enough to let you use your driver on many holes — particularly the longer par 4s.

Overall, we think you'll enjoy this track, which is best described as a golfer's golf course; it's a thoroughly well-designed and fair test. There are no houses on the course — yet. We also think you'll enjoy the fine amenities and facilities in the unique clubhouse, which looks a lot like a stealth fighter jet . . . really!

Amenities include a range, practice green, snack bar, rental clubs and a pro shop.

You can walk after 3 PM, but you'll find some significant distances between greens and tees. Bookings may be made a week in advance, with approximate cost, including cart, at $35 weekdays and $40 on weekends.

Hickory Hill Country Club

U.S. Hwy. 64 E., Mocksville • 998-8746
Championship Yardage: 6537
Slope: 116   Par: 70
Men's Yardage: 5902
Slope: 110   Par: 70
Ladies' Yardage: 4973
Slope: 109   Par: 70

The Golf Course at Hickory Hill Country Club, a Russell McMillan design, opened in 1970. Typical of courses in the Triad, Hickory Hill is primarily open but bordered by woods on a few holes. In the fairways, you'll find bermudagrass; on the greens, you'll find bentgrass.

Although Hickory Hill is not a terribly old course, it has what might be described as a pre-war design. The layout is an excellent example of minimalist architecture in a pretty, relaxed setting. You'll find good room off the tee and a few lonely grass or sand bunkers. Most of the green complexes are not raised, thus you can play all the run-up shots you want; the greens are mostly flat. There's no irrigation system in the fairways, so from 50 yards in, one of your options may be the putter.

A new pro/course manager arrived in 1995, and he is in the process of improving the club. If you're looking for an ultra-modern moundfest with severely undulating greens, look elsewhere. Hickory Hill harkens back to the early days of golf when every good player knew how to run the ball up to the green from almost anywhere. Where's my mashie?

Amenities include a practice green, range, chipping green, locker room, snack bar, rental clubs and a pro shop.

This course is a good one to walk, and you may walk anytime during the week and after 2 PM on weekends. You can book a tee time three days in advance. Approximate cost, including cart, is $22 weekdays and $28 on weekends.

Holly Ridge Golf Links

7727 U.S. Hwy. 311, Archdale • 861-GOLF
Championship Yardage: 6579
Slope: 135   **Par: 72**
Men's Yardage: 6121
Slope: 127   **Par: 72**
Other Yardage: 5727
Slope: 121   **Par: 72**
Ladies' Yardage: 4754
Slope: No rating   **Par: 72**

Holly Ridge Golf Course opened in 1994. Jim Bevins designed the course on rolling and open terrain, with bermudagrass fairways and bentgrass greens.

Holly Ridge offers an interesting addition to the Triad golf scene. The course is predominantly open, but some holes are bordered by woods and cow pasture. A lake comes into play on several holes and poses quite a challenge in places. Jim Bevins may not be a big

name, but he's provided a golfing test that demands intelligence to conquer. Like many modern courses, you'll find a lot of mounds at Holly Ridge — but you won't find any holly. You'll also find some tough driving tests, large bunkers, sloped greens and decent variety from hole to hole. Many greens are flanked by potentially nasty embankments. Perhaps the back nine is prettier for the moment than the front. Grow-in went well here; in time, Holly Ridge will be a good course for all levels of golfer. The course wins the prize for the most rakes per sand trap.

Amenities include a practice green, range and chipping green.

Walking is permitted on weekdays only, and the course is walkable. You can book a tee time whenever you choose. Approximate cost, including cart, is $21 weekdays and $27 on weekends.

Jamestown Park Golf Course

200 E. Fork Rd., Jamestown • 454-4912
Championship Yardage: 6665
Slope: 126   **Par: 72**
Men's Yardage: 6186
Slope: 122   **Par: 72**
Ladies' Yardage: 5298
Slope: 118   **Par: 72**

No one is sure when the golf course at Jamestown Park opened, but it is known that John V. Townsend designed it. The course is set in rolling terrain and flanked by woods. In the fairways, you'll find bermudagrass; on the greens, bentgrass.

We're not sure what the "V" in John V. Townsend stands for. In fact, no one is sure who Townsend is; we're told that he may have been a local politician. However, he might have made a fine golf course architect. The course here is pleasant, challenging, sensible and thoroughly well-designed. You won't find a lot of trouble off the tee. The fairways are relatively wide. The greens are large to huge, with the occasional bunker providing a challenge. Three of the par 3s are fronted by gaping bunkers running the entire length of each putting complex. On other greens, you'll be able to run the ball up to the hole. A bit of water comes into play on the back nine, though it's nothing to lose sleep over.

The front nine is pretty enough, but the

back nine is more interesting, varied and fun. Dare we say it, but John V. Townsend may have been a fan and imitator of Ellis Maples, for a couple of holes would have made Maples quite happy.

The course here at Jamestown Park is well worth a visit if you're looking for something relaxed yet challenging. And it's a good value.

Amenities include a practice green, range, chipping green, locker room, snack bar and pro shop.

You can walk anytime except before 12:30 PM on weekends. You can book a tee time seven days in advance for the week and on Thursday for the weekend. Approximate cost, including cart, is $22 weekdays and $24 on weekends.

Lexington Golf and Country Club
200 Country Club Blvd., Lexington • 246-3950
Championship Yardage: 5703
Slope: 116   **Par: 70**

Dugan Aycock designed Lexington Golf and Country Club, which opened in 1936. Set on rolling terrain and flanked by houses, Lexington boasts bermudagrass fairways and bentgrass greens.

You may not have heard of Dugan Aycock, which is a shame . . . he was quite a character. Aycock played on the U.S. Army golf team during World War II, was friends with the likes of Trevino, Nicklaus and Palmer, encouraged the great Bobby Locke to come to America from South Africa, raised enormous sums of money for charity and was a golfing partner of Bill "Earthquake" Smith, an officer of the law, former football player at the University of North Carolina at Chapel Hill and an excellent golfer. You can read the full story about Aycock in the men's locker room. Ladies, please knock before you enter.

If times had been different, perhaps Aycock would have been a designer. His product here in Lexington is a quirky and fascinating track, with enormous character and variety. The course is set on what must be fewer than 100 acres, thus the course is somewhat tight and short. This makes for quite a test of shotmaking and accuracy. Big numbers await the even slightly wayward golfer. There aren't many bunkers, but they should be avoided at all costs. The greens are flat and smallish, and you'll be able to run the ball up on a few holes — just like in the 1930s. There are more than a couple of holes that would catch the attention of almost any golf course architect. Play this one if you're in the area and, after your round, devour some Lexington-style barbecue for a real treat.

Amenities include a practice green, locker room, rental clubs and a pro shop.

Walk anytime and book a tee time seven days in advance for the weekend and anytime for the week. Approximate cost, including cart, is $18 weekdays and $20 on weekends.

Lynrock Golf Club
636 Valley Dr., Eden • 623-6110
Championship Yardage: 6046
Slope: 114   **Par: 70**
Men's Yardage: 5538
Slope: 109   **Par: 70**
Ladies' Yardage: 4913
Slope: 109   **Par: 70**

Jim Wilson designed Lynrock Golf Club, which opened in 1959. The course is set on mostly flat terrain, with bermudagrass fairways and bentgrass greens.

Lynrock offers fun and reasonably demanding country golf on a pretty track that winds around the valley floor immediately adjacent to the confluence of the Dan and Smith rivers. The river is remarkably wide here and comes into play on a couple of holes. This is most noticeable on the par 3 No. 2, which plays 150 yards from the tips. You tee off on one side of the river to a shallow green on the other side. Park it on the dance floor and you have to cross one of the most picturesque and longest bridges on any golf course in the area — perhaps in the Carolinas. A wonderful start to your round.

The rest of the course will not disappoint. The fairways are not overly wide, although they are fairly open. The greens are large and sloped; some are crowned and, thus, will play a little smaller if the greens are firm. Many of the green complexes include a series of medium-size bunkers, and you'll have to fly some of them. On other holes, you'll be able to run the ball up to the pin with a well-executed half-shot or some creative use of your Texas wedge.

Amenities include a practice green and rental clubs.

The course is walkable, you should walk and you can walk anytime. You can book up to two days in advance. Approximate cost, including cart, is $19 weekdays and $21 on weekends.

Maple Leaf Golf Club

4070 Hastings Rd., Kernersville
• 769-9122

Championship Yardage: 6028	
Slope: No rating	Par: 71
Men's Yardage: 5655	
Slope: No rating	Par: 71
Ladies' Yardage: 4643	
Slope: No rating	Par: 71

Maple Leaf Golf Club opened a front nine in 1981, designed by Ellis Maples, and a back nine in 1988, designed by Don Charles. The course is set in rolling wooded terrain, with bermudagrass fairways and bentgrass greens.

You won't find many Canadians here, but you will find a fine secluded course with an outstanding design pedigree. Anyone who has played golf in the Carolinas has heard of the great Ellis Maples. Charles is lesser-known, although he assisted with the renowned Legends complex in the Myrtle Beach area.

The result is a course with great interest and variety. It's not long from the back, but the narrowness of the fairways, in places, makes up for it. On the front nine, the 5th is a fun hole. Hit a decent drive downhill and you'll have a short iron over water to a small green set on a peninsula. But don't let this hole make you think the course is overly penal. On most holes you can recover from slightly errant shots. Extremely errant shots will have you dipping into your pocket for an extra ball.

You'll find a variety of options off the tee as well as in the size, shape and structure of the green complexes. With its challenge, picturesque setting, subtleties and sensible pricing, Maple Leaf offers one of the best low-cost golfing venues in the Triad.

Amenities include a practice green and snack bar.

You can walk anytime during the week and

after 4 PM on weekends. You can book a tee time seven days in advance. Approximate cost, including cart, is $21 weekdays and $24 on weekends.

Meadowlands

582 Motsinger Rd., Winston-Salem
• 769-1011

Championship Yardage: 6706	
Slope: 123	Par: 72
Men's Yardage: 6323	
Slope: 119	Par: 72
Ladies' Yardage: 4745	
Slope: 114	Par: 72

Meadowlands opened in late 1995. The course is set in beautiful terrain that's rolling and framed with woods. In the fairways, you'll find bermudagrass; on the greens, you'll find bentgrass. Hale Irwin and Stan Gentry designed the course.

No, Dorothy, we're not in New Jersey, we're in bucolic hardwood forests just south of Winston-Salem on the road to Thomasville. Just when you thought there couldn't possibly be any more great golf courses in the Triad, here comes Meadowlands — a fun and playable course in a magnificent setting that's absolutely free of houses. In terms of setting, Meadowlands rivals Tanglewood.

FYI

Unless otherwise noted, the area code for all phone numbers in this chapter is 910.

Hale Irwin is one of the greats of the modern era of professional golf. He holds the course record at Pinehurst #2, and in addition to winning tournaments on that course, he's won at such difficult and treacherous courses as Winged Foot, Inverness, Medinah, Harbour Town, Butler National and Pebble Beach. There are few players in the game who are more athletic or more consistent. Unlike some of his contemporaries who have ventured into the golf course design game, Irwin (based on the example here at Meadowlands) produces a golf course that mostly follows the lay of the land and is not overly demanding. You won't find excessive carries over water or swamp. You won't find wildly undulating greens. You won't find deep and almost inescapable bunkers lurking near the greens.

Here at Meadowlands, you'll find a relatively straightforward track where most of the

The Slope Story

We see those numbers on almost every score card at every golf course. We give it however many grains of salt we care to that day. But what do those slope and course ratings mean, and who assigns them to the course?

The United States Golf Association has committees all over the country who go to member courses to evaluate and assign each course a rating and slope. It is not an arbitrary number the USGA assigns — it's not meted out just because the officials think the course is tough, or the wind was blowing and taking most shots out of bounds on a given day.

The course rating is based on a course's difficulty for a scratch golfer, and the slope rating is the measure of difficulty for a non-scratch golfer. In many cases the rating committee will not even play the course.

The committee meets with the club pro or general manager to gather information such as total course length, length of the holes into the wind and length of holes downwind. They measure the speed of the greens, the height of the fairways, the height of the rough and the roll on the fairway. They also view and evaluate the tees, the landing areas and greens.

Topography, bunkers, out of bounds areas, water hazards and presence or absence of trees, naturally, also come into play when determining the rating and slope. Other factors include target areas, blind shots and holes that force the golfer to lay up. After all variables are accounted for, the numbers are calculated and the course rating and slope are assigned.

What does all of this mean to you and me? If you have a 10 handicap and a USGA index of 12.5 (you have an index if you have a handicap) and you traveled to another course with a higher rating and slope than your home course, your handicap would be adjusted. At the tougher course your 12.5 index factored into a handicap computer results in a higher handicap on that course.

A consistency problem can arise if your home course — where you established your 10 handicap — happens to be very difficult. Your friend might have a handicap of 10 that was established on an easier course. The catch? If you put your respective indexes into the handicap computer at the same course, both of you will have the same adjusted handicap. Although the system is imperfect, it is the best one that we have so far. Many have suggested alternative formulas, but so far none has USGA approval.

So, for good or for ill, those rating and slope numbers on the scorecard are not just pulled out of the hat and applied to the course. Time, effort and calculations have been put into making the playing field as level as possible for all golfers.

problems are easily seen and easily avoided with sound execution. Water comes into play on a few holes, most noticeably the par 4 No. 10, where you'll need to smack the ball about 200 yards over water to reach the fairway from the back tees. It's probably the only really intimidating shot on the course. Irwin routed the course to include a number of fine driving holes.

Apart from the sound design work, you'll enjoy Meadowlands for the setting. As we've mentioned, there are no houses on the course, and you really feel like you're miles away from all the clutter and clamor of today's fast-paced lifestyle. Golf should be an escape from the real world, and Meadowlands provides a rare example of a modern course that's designed to follow this belief.

We think you'll find Meadowlands a must-play course in the Triad area. Even though 6703 yards is relatively short for the tips these days, Meadowlands should provide the low-handicapper with a sensible challenge. From the middle and forward tees, Meadowlands will challenge the mid- to high-handicapper. Definitely give this one a try.

You can walk after 3 PM, but the course is not really designed to be walkable. You can book a tee time a week in advance. Approximate cost, including cart, is $36 weekdays and $40 on weekends.

Mill Creek Golf Club
1700 St. Andrews Dr., Mebane
• (919) 563-GOLF
Championship Yardage: 7004
Slope: 141	**Par: 72**
Men's Yardage: 6387	
Slope: 127	**Par: 72**
Other Yardage: 5711	
Slope: 122	**Par: 72**
Ladies' Yardage: 4884	
Slope: 113	**Par: 72**

The Golf Course at Mill Creek opened in late 1995. The course is set in rolling terrain bordered by woods and homesites. Rick Robbins and Brian Lussier designed the course in association with Gary Koch. You'll find bermudagrass in the fairways and bentgrass on the greens.

In 1995, *North Carolina Magazine* voted Mill Creek the best new public course in North Carolina. It's a well-designed course that's going to be an excellent challenge for the low-handicap golfer. The course is part of a large and extensive new-home community, and there are plenty of spots where this creates difficult out-of-bounds situations.

Overall, the course is full of serious difficulties. For starters, the rough here is rough. It's probably unlike any other rough we've ever seen. You know the thick long grass that grows so well in your back yard? Well, golf fans, that's the rough you'll find at Mill Creek. Miss the fairway here and your ball is 4 inches deep in stuff that will not yield to a weed-eater, let alone a golf club. In most cases, your only real option is to chip out and take your medicine. Of course, if you can keep it really straight and really long all the time, then you'll be just fine.

If the suicide rough doesn't cause enough problems, then the course offers plenty of other difficulties in the form of water, streams, out of bounds in difficult spots, woods, blind driving holes, large bunkers and some severely sloping greens. If you're having a bad day, then things are really going to be awful, and you might end up losing a lot of golf balls and throwing a lot of clubs around. However, once you reach the green, you're going to be really excited. The greens here are magnificently manicured and amazingly fast — especially for a public course that gets a lot of play.

There's ample variety at Mill Creek plus a number of really challenging holes. The 428-yard par 4 finishing hole features a unique touch in the form of a split fairway. It's an interesting aesthetic feature, but it was difficult to discern what it really added to the hole's playability. With all the great courses in North Carolina, it's definitely worth a visit to the one voted best new course — in anyone's poll. However, you might find Mill Creek unnecessarily difficult and better suited to the seasoned golfer. Have fun and bring a lot of balls!

Walking is restricted, and as you might expect from a brand-new housing development course, there are some significant distances between a few of the greens and the subsequent tees. You can book a tee time a week in advance. Approximate cost, including cart, is $35 weekdays and $40 on weekends.

Monroeton Golf Club
213 Monroeton Golf Course Rd., Reidsville
• 342-1043
Championship Yardage: 5729
Slope: 106	**Par: 70**
Men's Yardage: 5428	
Slope: 103	**Par: 70**
Other Yardage: 4955	
Slope: No rating	**Par: 70**
Ladies' Yardage: 4282	
Slope: 105	**Par: 70**

According to local legend, there was a golf course here when golfers still played on sand greens. Estimates of the date of origin indicate sometime in the 1940s, but the real date play began here might be even earlier. No one is sure who designed this course, which is bordered by woods and houses amid a rolling landscape. In the fairways, you'll find a combination of bermudagrass and native grasses; on the greens, you'll find bentgrass.

You might think that Monroeton Golf Club is a bit of an anachronism . . . it is. This classic country track probably has been untouched since the first golfer teed off here. The fairways are wide and somewhat undefined. Bunkers, there are not. The greens are sloped, crowned and large. If the ground is hard, you'll have to run the ball up to the green because it's unlikely your approach shot will hold. If you want to see what it was like playing golf before earth was moved and sands shifted, you need to play here. Besides, is there a lower cost for 18 holes, including cart, in the Triad? No way. Now you know why you bought this book!

If you're having some sort of legal dispute either on or off the golf course, you'll be pleased to know that the firm of Griffin and Crapse, with offices adjacent to the 3rd tee, will be more than willing to help you (for a fee, of course). If you call and the secretary says Mr. Crapse is on the golf course and he'll be back in a minute, it's probably true.

Amenities include a practice green, range, locker room and snack bar.

You can walk this course anytime. You won't need a tee time during the week; call on Tuesday for your weekend slot. Approximate cost, including cart, is $11 weekdays and $16 on weekends.

Oak Hollow Golf Course

1400 Oak View, High Point • 883-3260
Championship Yardage: 6483

Slope: 124	**Par: 72**
Men's Yardage: 6090	
Slope: 118	**Par: 72**
Ladies' Yardage: 4796	
Slope: 114	**Par: 72**

Oak Hollow Golf Course opened in 1972. Pete Dye designed the course on rolling, primarily open terrain, with a lake bordering many holes on the front nine. Fairways are bermudagrass, and greens are bentgrass. *Golf Digest* ranked the course as one of the best in the United States for less than $50 a round.

Yes, *the* Pete Dye designed the course. And what a course it is, especially for a public track. After the Robert Trent Jones era of golf course architecture came the Pete Dye era,

and you'll see many of the features that made Dye (and his sons) some of the most in-demand architects in the universe. Dye began life as a successful life insurance salesman, and there must be many a befuddled golfer who wishes that he had stuck to explaining the difference between term and life. During the '60s, Dye and his wife, Alice, herself an accomplished course designer, toured Scotland in between designing moderate-cost courses in the Midwest. Oak Hollow was built before Dye's career really took off and Japanese developers began lining up with bunkers-full of cash just to have a Dye course. Oak Hollow is the only Pete Dye course in North Carolina that's open to the public.

Although Dye incorporated a number of Scottish features into his work, this is not a links course. There isn't a great deal of trouble off the tee on most holes. The real work begins around the green complexes, which feature bizarre slopes, bunkers and shapes. It's quite possible to hit a green and still work extremely hard for a par. One of us hit the green on the perilous 6th hole — a 420-yard par 4 — found a grassy mound between the ball and the hole and had to get up to the pin with a wedge. On many holes, Dye brings Oak Hollow Lake into play in spectacular fashion, particularly on the aforementioned 6th hole where the tee box sits right in the middle of the lake. Other golf course architects spend time creating subtle shapes and nuances in an effort to create aesthetically pleasing layouts. Dye uses his imagination to create golf holes that are bizarre, penal, wonderful and somewhat mind-bending. His goal is to get you thinking; of course, that's when the trouble begins. If you're a student of golf course architecture, make the effort to play this course. It's quite an experience. And at less than $30 per round, it's a Dye course that won't increase your overdraft. It's a must-play in North Carolina.

Amenities include a practice green, range, chipping green, locker room, snack bar, rental clubs and a pro shop.

The course is walkable (can you believe it?) and you can walk anytime (also hard to believe). You can book a tee time two days in advance. Approximate cost, including cart, is $23 weekdays and $26 on weekends.

Oak Valley Golf Club

261 Oak Valley Blvd., Advance • 940-2000
Championship Yardage: 7058
Slope: 134   **Par: 72**
Men's Yardage: 6684
Slope: 127   **Par: 72**
Ladies' Yardage: 5197
Slope: 115   **Par: 72**

Oak Valley Golf Club opened in late 1995. The course is set in open and gently rolling terrain. In the fairways, you'll find bermudagrass; on the greens, you'll find bentgrass. Arnold Palmer and Ed Seay designed the course. The course is part of a housing development.

Just minutes from Tanglewood, Oak Valley is already vying to be one of the top golf course layouts in the quality-rich Triad. It helps that one of the greatest golfers ever attached his name and considerable design reputation to the course. For years, Palmer's designs have been ably led by Ed Seay who oversees an extremely capable group of architects, one of whom probably supervised the actual work.

Here at Oak Valley, you'll find some of the trademarks of a Palmer/Seay course. The greens undulate gently, and the green complexes feature an artistic combination of bunkers and swales — all designed to make getting up and down a considerable challenge. If you're on the wrong side of a green, a three-putt is a definite possibility. The architects made great use of the land to produce a number of excellent driving holes; these define the course and make it stand out from others in the Triad.

From the tee, you'll find plenty of difficulty lurking in and around the fairways, which are of sensible width. Palmer and Seay like to tempt golfers into "going for it" off the tee. Make the shot and you're in great shape; miss it and you're in a trap, out of bounds or in wetlands. The experts call it strategic golf, and you'll find some classic examples of this school of design. Making life just a little more difficult at Oak Valley is a stream that meanders through nine holes.

If you like a fine and serious test of golf, try Oak Valley. Once it's had time to mature, it's going to rival some of the other Palmer courses in the state, such as TPC at Piper Glen in Char-lotte or Pinehurst Plantation in Southern Pines. Oak Valley looks tough enough to test the professional from the tips yet provide a fun challenge from the forward tees. The course is owned and operated by Carolinas Golf Group, so the quality of your golfing experience should be safely assured. Try this course at least once — you may be tempted to challenge it over and over again.

You can walk on weekdays, but walking is really only for the fit. You can book a tee time a week in advance. Approximate cost, including cart, is $34 weekdays and $40 on weekends.

Pine Knolls Golf Course

1100 Quail Hollow Rd., Kernersville
• 993-5478
Championship Yardage: 6287
Slope: 121   **Par: 72**
Men's Yardage: 5923
Slope: 110   **Par: 72**
Ladies' Yardage: 4480
Slope: 92   **Par: 72**

Pine Knolls Golf Course opened in 1969. Most holes are open, and others are bordered by woods or houses. Bermudagrass blankets the fairways; bentgrass, the greens.

Yet another Triad golf course with the word "Pine" in its name, Pine Knolls offers a fun and mostly straightforward golf outing. The setting is pleasant and relaxed. You won't find a lot of bunkers, but you will find plenty of variety and a decent amount of challenge. The layout is sensible and not overly penal, although really bad shots will yield really bad results. Off the tee, you must think about and choose the correct weapon; use the driver wisely, perhaps sparingly. Around the medium-size greens, you'll find slope and some undulation. A few greens allow you to run the ball up from the fairway. One touch we especially liked was the path cut through the rough from the tee boxes to the fairways. It's a statement from the management that says: "yes, we like walkers." Pine Knolls is clearly popular; it's also a good value.

Amenities include a practice green, range, chipping green, locker room, snack bar, rental clubs and a pro shop.

Walk Pine Knolls anytime during the week and after 1:30 PM on weekends. You can book

The Piedmont of North Carolina features a number of nationally ranked courses. Most of these are set in rolling woodland.

a tee time whenever you choose. Approximate cost, including cart, is $22 weekdays and $28 on weekends.

Pine Tree Golf Club
1680 Pine Tree Ln., Kernersville
• (919) 993-5598
Championship Yardage: 6604
Slope: 113   Par: 71
Men's Yardage: 6046
Slope: 107   Par: 71
Ladies' Yardage: 4897
Slope: 110   Par: 71

Pine Tree Golf Club opened in 1971. Gene Hamm designed the course on rolling, wooded terrain. In the fairways, you'll find bermudagrass; on the greens, bentgrass.

Pine Tree is a course with challenge, scenic beauty and excellent variety. There are virtually no houses, so you'll be pleasingly far away from the hassles of urbanite civilization.

You'll find a great deal of room off the tee on most holes. Feel free to take out the big stick — you'll need it on many of the longer par 4s. The greens are large and sloped. The green complexes boast an abundance of large and flat bunkers: Avoid them. Quite a few greens are flush with their respective fairways; they're not built up in any way. So, despite all the bunkers, you can run the ball up to the pin on a few holes if you choose. Water comes into play here and there but should not cause too much of a problem. Occasional trees near or in the fairways will make you think twice about your next shot.

The general feeling of being away from it all is what we liked best about Pine Tree. Combine the peaceful setting with a challenging and varied course and you should be in for a good round. It's definitely a good value.

Amenities include a practice green, range, chipping green, locker room, snack bar, restaurant and pro shop.

You can walk Pine Tree only on weekdays. You can book a tee time up to 10 days in advance. Approximate cost, including cart, is $24 weekdays and $28 on weekends.

Pudding Ridge Golf Club
224 Cornwallis Dr., Mocksville • 940-4653
Championship Yardage: 6750
Slope: 128   Par: 70
Men's Yardage: 6234
Slope: 123   Par: 70
Ladies' Yardage: 4709
Slope: 111   Par: 70

Pudding Ridge Golf Club opened in 1994. The course is set in open, rolling terrain, with bermudagrass fairways and bentgrass greens. Mark Charles and Don Bowles teamed up on the design.

Pudding Ridge takes the cake for the most intriguing golf course name. According to local sources, Gen. Cornwallis' troops coined the name during the American Revolutionary War. The troops thought that the soil looked like pudding, which, as you may know, is the British word for a dessert that looks like local soil.

Pudding Ridge is a brand-new course with an interesting design. The owners of the property took the architectural duties upon themselves, and their work is admirable. Pudding Ridge needs some maturity to reach its aesthetic peak, but its openness is unique and in stark contrast to the Triad's many wooded courses. The openness also gives the course a links feel.

You'll find a lot of room off the tee, some sloping medium to large-size greens and assorted sizes of bunkers that come into play in varying degrees based on pin placement. One of the great aspects of Pudding Ridge is that, unlike many modern courses, there's an absence of mounds. We like the abandoned grain silo in the 5th fairway — a unique hazard. The question of what happens if the ball falls in the silo is best left to the rules gurus in Far Hills, New Jersey (at USGA headquarters).

Amenities include a practice green, chip-

INSIDERS' TIP

Take the time to learn something about golf course architects and architecture. Many fine books have been written on the subject, and you'll understand (and probably enjoy) a course more if you're familiar with the architect's style.

ping green, locker room, snack bar, restaurant, rental clubs and a pro shop.

The course is walkable for the physically fit, and you can walk anytime during the week and after 3 PM on weekends. You can book a tee time seven days in advance. Approximate cost, including cart, is $24 weekdays and $28 on weekends.

Reynolds Park Golf Course
2391 Reynolds Park Rd., Winston-Salem
• 650-7660
Championship Yardage: 6320
Slope: No rating   Par: 71
Men's Yardage: 5923
Slope: 118   Par: 71
Ladies' Yardage: 5538
Slope: No rating   Par: 75

Reynolds Park Golf Course opened in 1940. Perry Maxwell designed the original layout, and Ellis Maples revised the track in 1966. The course is primarily open, although woods border a few holes. Fairways are bermudagrass; greens, bentgrass.

Here at Reynolds Park, you'll find a fine old municipal course that's justifiably popular. Maxwell is not a big name in North Carolina, but he's known for another extremely popular municipal course: Hillandale in Durham. He was quite a character, and you can read about him in the Hillandale review in our Triangle chapter.

The course is laid out on a relatively small tract of land, thus some of the fairways are pretty tight. But the course is open, so you won't be out of bounds very often even if your drive strays somewhat. It's certainly an entertaining course. There are some holes where it seems like Maples left well enough alone. These holes are somewhat featureless and bunkerless but challenging. Other holes reveal Maples' influence, featuring large bunkers and sloped greens. The result is a lot of variety and a need for accuracy with approach shots. You'll also notice some fine views of

downtown Winston-Salem. The course is evidently quite popular with local golfers — low- and high-handicappers alike.

Amenities include a practice green, range, locker room, snack bar, rental clubs and a pro shop.

You can walk the course anytime during the week and after 1 PM on weekends. Book a tee time seven days in advance for a weekday and on Thursday for the weekend. Approximate cost, including cart, is $22 weekdays and $28 on weekends.

Sandy Ridge Golf Course
2055 Sandy Ridge Rd., Colfax • 668-0408
Championship Yardage: 6021
Slope: No rating   Par: 72
Men's Yardage: 5645
Slope: No rating   Par: 72
Ladies' Yardage: 5175
Slope: No rating   Par: 72

Sandy Ridge Golf Course opened in 1972. Gene Hamm designed this course amid rolling wooded terrain. In the fairways, you'll find bermudagrass; on the greens, you'll find bentgrass.

Just to the south and west of Greensboro near Piedmont Triad International Airport is the tiny town of Colfax and its one golf course — Sandy Ridge. You're greeted by a docile and somewhat geriatric dog of mixed breed who sniffs at your golf shoes with comforting approval.

A new greenskeeper arrived in 1995 and just after the commencement of his employment, we heard distinct murmurs of approval from golfers with whom we spoke. The design is interesting and varied. Most of the time you'll find plenty of room off the tee, although the back nine seems a little tight in spots. The greens vary in size, are only slightly sloped and, on some holes, are surrounded by small mounds. There are no bunkers, so you'll be able to play some run-up shots if you're a long way from the green and can't land your

INSIDERS' TIP

For a mid- to high-handicapper, bogey is not a bad score, particularly on the more difficult holes. Don't be too disappointed with an occasional bogey. If you're in trouble early off the tee, cut your losses and find the easiest way to make bogey.

shot like a well-thrown dart. The terrain is pretty, the golf is relaxed and the dog is well-fed and amiable.

Amenities include a practice green, locker room, snack bar and dog (again, friendly). You may walk this course anytime during the week or after noon on weekends. You can book a tee time whenever you choose for the week and on Monday for the weekend. Approximate cost, including cart, is $21 weekdays and $25 on weekends.

Silo Run Golf Course

4040 Rockford Rd., Boonville • **367-3133**
Championship Yardage: 6751
Slope: 123   **Par: 71**
Men's Yardage: 6116
Slope: 116   **Par: 71**
Ladies' Yardage: 4990
Slope: 118   **Par: 71**

Silo Run opened in 1995. The course is set in rolling terrain adjacent to farmland. In the fairways, you'll find bermudagrass; on the greens, you'll find bentgrass. Thomas H. Peagram designed the course.

About 20 miles west of Winston-Salem, Silo Run is in territory that could be described as the foothills of the Blue Ridge Mountains. Thus, you'll find more than a couple of holes that will introduce you to the joys of mountain golf; perhaps the defining feature of Silo Run is the elevation change on most holes. It makes for picturesque scenery and some very interesting and demanding golf play. Take advantage of the elevation changes on the 9th and 16th holes, which are 631 and 623 yards, respectively, from the back tees. Occasional bunkers (primarily flat) lurk in the fairway and protect many of the greens. Greens are medium-size and not overly undulating.

Silo Run is somewhat different from the big-budget new courses that have recently arrived in the Triad. You won't find any houses on the course, but you will find a pleasant, challenging and friendly country layout that provides decent value for your golfing dollar. To enjoy the course to its fullest, you'll need to keep it as straight as you can and pull out the correct club.

Amenities include a practice green, snack bar, rental clubs and a pro shop.

With some extremely steep elevation changes between some greens and tees, you'll find this course virtually impossible to walk. Approximate cost, including cart, is $22 weekdays and $28 on weekends. Bookings may be made one week in advance.

Southwick Golf Course

3136 Southwick Dr., Graham • **227-2582**
Championship Yardage: 5778
Slope: 116   **Par: 70**
Men's Yardage: 5431
Slope: 111   **Par: 70**
Ladies' Yardage: 4413
Slope: 108   **Par: 70**

Southwick Golf Course opened in 1960s. Elmo Cobb designed this well-maintained course on predominantly open land, with woods bordering a few holes. In the fairways, you'll find bermudagrass; on the greens, bentgrass.

Don't let the yardage fool you. Let's just call Southwick a Dudley Moore course: short yet entertaining. Truly, it can be plenty tough from the back tees, especially considering the need to play it straight with the driver. The rolling terrain may cause some difficulty with club selection on your approach shots. Call it the "Witches of Southwick" effect (apologies to John Updike). You won't find Cher here, nor will you find Jack Nicholson, but you will find greens that vary in size, shape and slope, quite a few bunkers and some water.

Overall, Southwick offers good variety, plenty of doglegs and plenty of entertainment. A section of the county amateur tournament is held here, and the staff in the pro shop tells us that scores for that event are always highest here.

Amenities include a practice green, range, snack bar, rental clubs and a pro shop.

You can walk anytime, save weekends before 3 PM in the summer. You can book a tee time anytime. Approximate cost, including cart, is $12 weekdays and $20 on weekends.

Stoney Creek Golf Club
911 Golf House Rd. E., Burlington
• 449-5688
Championship Yardage: 7063
Slope: 144   **Par: 72**
Men's Regular Yardage: 6573
Slope: 132   **Par: 72**
Men's Yardage: 6179
Slope: 129   **Par: 72**
Other Yardage: 5546
Slope: 109   **Par: 72**
Ladies' Yardage: 4737
Slope: 123   **Par: 72**

Stoney Creek Golf Club opened in 1992. Tom Jackson designed the course, which is set in rolling terrain and bordered by woods and houses. Fairways are bermudagrass; greens, bentgrass.

The slope of 144 from the back tees is as high a rating as you'll find most anywhere in North and South Carolina. Consider that the rating from the back tees for the Ocean Course at Kiawah (South Carolina) is about 149. According to the staff in the pro shop, Stoney Creek from the tips is every bit as difficult as its muscular slope rating. If you're not a scratch golfer and you're not up for more than 7000 yards of Tom Jackson, consider the other more forgiving tees: There are four sets for your golfing enjoyment.

Ask Tom Jackson about some of his favorite self-designs, and Stoney Creek makes the list. Perhaps this is because Jackson was allowed to lay out the course before the housing development was initiated. If you're going to have houses around a golf course, Stoney Creek is a rare example of the proper way to do it.

You won't find the large numbers of mounds that you might find on other Jackson courses, but you will find plenty of bunkering off the tee and around the green complexes. The 1st hole, a tortuous par 5, is probably one of the most difficult starting holes in the area. Many of the bunkers are of the large cloverleaf-shape variety; others are a little smaller but no less penal. Many of the greens are flanked by steep embankments.

Stoney Creek — the creek itself — is not as much a factor as it might seem. The putting surfaces on this course are mostly sloped and large, although some are quite undulating.

Perhaps what separates this Jackson course from others is the excellent variety. Jackson manages to incorporate a number of different looks in most of his courses, but at Stoney Creek he offers increased interest and mental challenge on a playable and not overly penal design. The setting is also remarkably peaceful — given the proximity of houses to many holes.

Just five minutes from I-40/85 between Burlington and Greensboro, Stoney Creek is an accessible course; it's also an excellent value. Local golfers know how good the course is, but outside the Triad, word has yet to spread, which is why we're spreading it here.

Amenities include a practice green, range, chipping green, snack bar, restaurant and pro shop.

The course is walkable for the physically fit, and you may walk anytime during the week and after 3:30 PM on weekends. You can book a tee time seven days in advance. Approximate cost, including cart, is $30 weekdays and $35 on weekends.

Tanglewood Park
U.S. Hwy. 158 W., Clemmons • 766-5082

Tanglewood Park boasts two formidable Robert Trent Jones courses: the Championship, which opened in 1959 and was redesigned in 1973, and the Reynolds, which opened nine holes in 1965 and was completed in 1970. Both tracks are set in rolling wooded terrain, although the Championship Course is slightly more open; both offer bermudagrass fairways and bentgrass greens.

But let's talk about Tanglewood Park. Just west of Winston-Salem, in bucolic and ancient woodlands, you'll find this magnificent setting. The land, once part of the Reynolds estate, was donated by the Reynolds family. You may have heard of their company: R.J. Reynolds. In a day at Tanglewood, you could play golf, attend a corporate picnic, get married in the wedding chapel, go horseback riding, attend a steeplechase, play tennis, jog, go camping and then be buried in the graveyard adjacent to the 18th green on the Championship Course. There can't be many park complexes like Tanglewood.

But we're here to talk about golf, not

parks. There are two wonderful and nationally recognized courses here, both of which have been ranked in *Golf Digest's* list of the Top 100 Public Courses. In 1974, the Championship Course hosted the PGA Championship — won by Lee Trevino. Each fall, members of the PGA SENIOR TOUR gather here for the richest event of the year, the Vantage Championship (see our Tournaments in the Carolinas chapter). The $1.5-million purse typically brings out the best players on the tour, including Palmer, Trevino, Charles, Rodriguez and Floyd.

During the rest of the year, the course brings out people from across North and South Carolina who feel motivated to attack one of the least vulnerable golf courses anywhere. Estimates vary, but Tanglewood "boasts" somewhere between 120 and 140 bunkers. It just depends on who you ask. You could ask the maintenance supervisor, but he's probably too busy maintaining the sand to notice your query. We'll get to the bunkers later.

The only problem here, in our minds, is the architecture of the clubhouse, which looks more like a East German chiropractic clinic than a structure befitting two of the prettiest and finest public golf courses in the Carolinas. Anyway, who cares what the clubhouse looks like — as long as the burgers and hot dogs are worth their mustard (and they are).

Amenities include a practice green, range, chipping green, locker room, snack bar/grill, rental clubs, a wedding chapel and a pro shop.

The Championship Course is more walkable than the Reynolds; ironically, you can walk the Reynolds Course anytime but may only walk the Championship Course in December, January, July and August. You can book a tee time seven days in advance. Approximate cost, including cart, is $45 weekdays and $48 on weekends for the Championship and $30 every day for the Reynolds. If you live outside North Carolina, the cost for the Championship Course is upwards of $63.

Championship Course

Championship Yardage: 7022		
Slope: 140		Par: 72
Men's Yardage: 6638		
Slope: 135		Par: 72
Other Yardage: 6014		
Slope: 130		Par: 72
Ladies' Yardage: 5119		
Slope: 130		Par: 74

This might be the prettiest and most challenging public course in the Southeast. If it's not No. 1, then it's got to be in the top three. The course is long and plays even longer. The fairways are as wide as the rough will allow, meaning it can play both narrow and long at times. The greens are large and undulating to the point where a two-putt is an accomplishment. But it's the excessive bunkering that makes this course so difficult. It's Bunkers R Us. Just about every shot you play from the tee, and certainly every approach shot, will be influenced by the beach. If you're shooting for a green, it's safest to aim for the middle and hope for the best. Adding insult to injury is the inconsistent condition of the bunkers: Some are full of sand; others are concrete-hard at the bottom. No course will test your bunker play and patience like Championship at Tanglewood.

If Verdi were alive and still writing operas, he might write one about the saga that's surrounded the condition of the greens here. In this book, we've gone out of our way not to discuss course conditioning because it can vary so much from season to season, and not even the best greenskeeper can beat the worst the Mother Nature can create. Let's just say that there's many a Senior PGA pro who loves the course but hates the greens. It's tough with a public course and a limited budget.

Even if your ball is finding the bunkers more than the greens, you can't help appreciating the wonderful setting and ambiance. With its pristine ponds and lakes, its large and mature trees, its chutes and its tranquility, this

FYI

Unless otherwise noted, the area code for all phone numbers in this chapter is 910.

outstanding layout feels like an exclusive country club. In fact, there are probably plenty of country clubs that would gladly trade courses with Tanglewood. You'll find magnificent hole after magnificent hole. It's a must-play course in North Carolina, even if the weather preceding your visit has made course maintenance difficult. Play here before you pass on to the great sand trap in the sky.

Reynolds Course

Championship Yardage: 6469

Slope: 125	Par: 72

Men's Yardage: 6061

Slope: 120	Par: 72

Ladies' Yardage: 5432

Slope: 120	Par: 72

Don't think of the Reynolds Course as the poor sister of the Championship Course. Robert Trent Jones, bless his heart, blessed Reynolds with far less bunkering. The challenge here comes from the dense woods surrounding many of the holes. From the back tees, all the trees make driving the ball a serious challenge. Even if you avoid the trees, you may end up in the deep rough. The greens on this course are predominantly massive, so note the pin position and feel free to fire at it. Even if you miss the green, you'll have a good chance at par if you chip well out of the rough. Water comes into play in the most awkward places, such as right in front of the green on a 214-yard par 3. Thank you, Mr. Jones. While some of the greens are slightly sloped, others offer dramatic elevation changes, making putting all the more difficult.

When we visited the course, several greens were in need of serious help, although this may have been caused by the inclement weather preceding our inspection. The course is undergoing a long-term renovation supervised by the head of maintenance. If you can't get on the Championship Course, or if you're in the mood for slightly less bunkering and difficulty, try the Reynolds Course. It would be walkable, except for the fact that the distance between the 9th green and the 10th tee is nearly a mile. Again, it's a wonderfully pretty and peaceful course, just like its sister.

Around the Triad . . .

Fun Things To Do

After you've played the courses, you will find plenty of opportunities for fun in the Triad. On sunny days, which are plentiful, outdoor entertainment abounds. The natural beauty of the Triad lends itself to many green city parks — perfect spots for picnics — and beautiful gardens. The Triad is also home to historical sites and several battlegrounds. If rain is keeping you off the course, visit one of the numerous museums or retail establishments in the area. Greensboro and Winston-Salem boast several shopping malls; Burlington is home to a large number of factory outlet stores; and High Point is a renowned furniture mecca.

Reynolda Gardens of Wake Forest University, 100 Reynolda Village, Winston-Salem, 759-5325, was made possible by tobacco magnate R.J. Reynolds who gave this wonderful land to the city; it's now home to some of the most magnificent and extensive gardens in the Triad. Reynolda Gardens is a must-visit for anyone interested in flora.

If you've never been on a brewery tour, you'll definitely want to tour the **Stroh Brewery**, 4791 Schlitz Avenue, Winston-Salem, 788-6710. This is one of the largest breweries in the United States. You'll be able to see all that goes into producing a can or bottle of beer; at the end of the tour, you can sit down and enjoy a cold one.

By American standards, **Old Salem**, Old Salem Road, Winston-Salem, 721-7300, offers a slice of history. This Moravian village dates back to the 18th century. More than 80 buildings from the original village have been restored. Re-enactors dressed in period costume act out the daily events of the 18th century in museums and shops along the streets of Old Salem. Don't leave without trying the Moravian sugarcake.

After a hot summer day of golfing, or if you have the kids with you, a trip to **Emerald Point Waterpark**, 3910 Holden Road, Greensboro, 852-9721, may be in order. The 45-acre waterpark features 30 rides and attractions, including a wave pool, several waterslides and bodyslides, and kiddie pools. For the adventurous, the Skycoaster offers an airborne thrill: This huge swing, attached to an arch by steel cables, launches you, secure in your body harness, horizontally 115 feet into the air and swings you back and forth under the arch like Superman.

Greensboro Historical Museum, 130 Summit Avenue, Greensboro, 373-2043, is housed in a former church that dates back to the turn of the century. Exhibits trace the many and varied religious and racial groups that built the city of Greensboro into what it is today. Learn about military history, early transportation and decorative arts.

Those interested in American military history may want to visit the American Revolution battleground sites in Greensboro and Burlington. The **Guilford Courthouse National Military Battleground Park**, 2332 New Garden Road, Greensboro, 288-1776, was the site of a 1781 battle in the American Revolution. The site features a museum, walking trails, 28 monuments, musket demonstrations and guided tours. The **Alamance Battleground**, 5803 N.C. Highway 62 S., Burlington (Exit 143 off I-85), 227-4785, was the site of a 1771 battle that preceded but was an early part of the Revolutionary War. Re-enactments of the battle, which pitched the Regulators (country farmers) against the troops of Royal Gov. William Tryon, are held periodically at the battleground. An audiovisual program and tours of the battlefield, monuments and the historic 1780 Allen House make for an interesting day of learning about the 18th-century battle.

High Point touts itself as "the furniture capital of the world," so if you need furnishings, you might as well check out the bargains. Don't worry about lugging a settee around for the rest of your visit to the Triad; the store will ship it home for you. More than 50 furniture stores, including Rose, the Atrium, Furniture Land South and Young's, are scattered around the city; call the **High Point Convention and Visitors Bureau**, 889-5151, for information. The **Furniture Discovery Center**, 101 W. Green Drive, High Point, 887-3876, is a museum dedicated to the art of furniture-making.

Where to Eat

Refer to our Preface for an explanation of the pricing code.

Greensboro

J. Butler's Bar and Grille
$$ • 3709 Battleground Ave., Greensboro • 282-8080

Across from Brassfield Cinema and Brassfield Shopping Center, J. Butler's offers a feast of sandwiches, gourmet burgers, salads and entrees to enjoy before or after taking in a movie or tackling a shopping expedition. Couple this with a fully stocked bar and you also have a really fun and relaxed place to unwind after a rough day on the links.

Kyoto Fantasy
$$ • 1200 S. Holden Rd., Greensboro • 299-1003

There's always something fun, funny and bizarre about going to an authentic Japanese steakhouse. The chef comes to your table, and you bear witness to his wizardry as he slices and dices with surgical knives. You'll get the full treatment here at Kyoto Fantasy: Take your shoes off and sit down for your session. Make sure you change your socks before you go. There's also a sushi bar for raw fish fans or the extremely trendy.

Longhorn Steaks Restaurant and Saloon
$$$ • 2925 Battleground Ave., Greensboro • 545-3200

Longhorn was a pioneer in the introduction of Texas-style steakhouses in the Carolinas. You'll find a large yet friendly environment, with a rustic Western-looking decor. There's a bar, and you may have to wait a few minutes here while a table is readied for your appetite. Once you sit down, indulge in a big steak — washed down with a couple of beers. Or try the salmon if you're not a steak person. The atmosphere is relaxed, and it's almost essential to wear jeans. You can wear a cowboy hat if you like, but there's no discount for this type of behavior.

Sunset Cafe

$$$ • 4608 W. Market St., Greensboro
• 855-0349

The Sunset Cafe offers a solid alternative to the chain-style restaurants that dominate the local scene. This restaurant specializes in vegetarian, seafood, poultry and lamb dishes served in a warm, cozy atmosphere.

High Point

Barracuda Bistro

$$ • 2801 N. Main St., High Point • 869-1010

A new and unique concept, especially for High Point, the Barracuda Bistro offers a West Indian feel and menu. At the raw bar, the decor is supposed to make you feel like you're underwater, looking up at the clear blue sky of the Caribbean. And then you hoover a couple of oysters and sink a Red Stripe and you listen to the reggae, mon, and you're suddenly far from the madding crowds of raging downtown High Point.

The menu is definitely fish oriented, even though the red meat eating among you should try the double-cut pork chops or West Indian ribs. But it's sub-aquatic fare that should prove most attractive. There's grilled salmon with papaya relish and plantation chips or seared rare tuna with a West Indian vinaigrette or Caribbean gumbo or blackened grouper. With the tropical murals and the abundant banana and mango trees, the ambiance here is tropical and, who knows, maybe you'll catch a fish and maybe it will be a Barracuda. A good value for fresh fish and ambiance.

Noble's

$$$ • 114 S. Main St., High Point • 889-3354

Noble's is a "dressy casual" restaurant with a fine and varied menu that changes daily. All sauces and desserts are made on the premises, and all the meat and fish is cut that day. The restaurant is well-known for its oyster salad, which is a popular appetizer. Diners are also fond of the veal tenderloin and free range chicken, a true rarity in the Carolinas. If you're a fish eater, you should definitely try the salmon, tuna or grouper. When you're finished with your main course, try the apple tart or some of Noble's home-made ice cream. The restaurant sits on two

levels: street and basement. There's a jazz trio on Thursday, Friday and Saturday for your further entertainment.

Note that you'll also find a Noble's in Winston-Salem.

Sugar Magnolia

$$$ • 126 E. State Ave., High Point
• 883-1668

No, it's not the song by the Grateful Dead, but one of High Point's newest and most popular restaurants. The menu changes after each High Point furniture show (there's one in the fall and spring), but the establishment boasts enough regular diners that the chef prepares a wide range of specials. Ambiance here is supplied by a wide patio, a bar with a fireplace and a nonsmoking dining room.

Appetizers include baked brie or a special dish called Three Musketeers, which is marinated beef tips. Once you've disposed with D'Artagnan and shouted "One for all and all for one," it's time to choose a main course. How about angel hair pasta with garlic and wild mushrooms? Or baked sea bass? Or crabcakes? The fish and veal specials change every night, plus there's a solid variety of beef and chicken.

Round everything off with an espresso or glass of port or a stirring rendition of the song named after this eatery. "Takes the wheel when I'm seeing double; pays my ticket when I speed."

Winston-Salem

Par-3 Bistro

$$$ • Bethania Station Rd., Winston-Salem
• 924-9485

One of the most remarkable restaurants in the world, the Par-3 Bistro expertly combines two of America's favorite pastimes: golf and eating. The nine-hole par 3 course features bermudagrass greens and quite a bit of water. The restaurant is fine dining all the way. Try the roast duck or one of the many veal or beef dishes, all created by chef Michel Claire who has served up fine culinary fare in California, Altanta and France. It's probably the only place in the world where you can play golf and eat rack of lamb for less than $25.

Szechwan Palace
$$ • 3040 Healy Dr., Winston-Salem
• 768-7123

Tucked away in a somewhat innocuous strip mall in the Hanes Mall area is one of Winston-Salem's best Chinese restaurants. The decor is somewhat predictable, with a dominant theme of meandering scenes of the Great Wall of China interspersed with red dragons. The menu, however, is less predictable; you'll find some unique creations that go well beyond your typical sweet-and-sour fare — even the name implies some hot and spicy entrees. You can also sip a Chinese beer, although the Chinese are not especially renowned as world leaders in the production of quality adult malt beverages.

Twin City Diner
$$ • 1425A W. First St., Winston-Salem
• 724-4203

Twin City Diner is a relaxed and fun neighborhood restaurant where locals meet and mingle. There's a well-stocked bar where you can swap stories or watch a sports event on the discreetly placed televisions. The menu is extensive. The wings, served in multiples of five, are excellent. Sample some traditional pub fare — hamburgers and sandwiches — or delve into a more substantial entree, such as Cajun salmon.

Vincenzo's
$$ • 3449 Robin Hood Rd., Winston-Salem
• 765-3176

Vincenzo's is one of those great institutions where you feel right at home the second you walk in the door. The restaurant has been serving up Italian dishes since 1964. There's veal parmigiana, spaghetti, eggplant parmigiana, lasagna, veal marsala, a delightful clam sauce and steamed clams. Plus there's lots of Italian vino to help you wash down all that great pasta.

Where to Stay

Refer to our Preface for an explanation of the pricing code.

Greensboro

Best Western Windsor Suites
$$$ • 2006 Veasley St., Greensboro
• 294-9100

Best Westerns are best known for clean and pleasant but basic motel-type rooms and good locations. The Windsor Suites is a step-up from the usual — it feels more like a fine hotel. Rooms are elegantly decorated, and there's lots of faux wood paneling. Unlike many hotels, you can actually open the window to the outside world. You'll find plenty of restaurants just around the corner as well as easy access to I-40.

In addition to your larger than usual room, amenities here include a separate sitting area, microwaves and refrigerators in the rooms, a complimentary breakfast, a TV with thirty-eight channels, free HBO and ESPN, plus an exercise room with sauna.

Courtyard by Marriott
$$ • 4400 W. Wendover Rd., Greensboro
• 294-3800

If you've seen a Courtyard by Marriott before, then you won't be surprised to find this clean, well-kept hotel in a convenient location and run by an efficient staff. Suites boast two TVs and a separate second bedroom with a pullout couch. Amenities include an outdoor pool, an indoor whirlpool and an exercise room. A restaurant on the premises serves breakfast daily.

Embassy Suites
$$$ • 204 Centreport Dr., Greensboro
• 668-4535

Enormous and efficient, the Greensboro Embassy Suites is everything you'd expect from the hotel chain that popularized the free breakfast concept. As the name implies, at Embassy Suites you get a suite, and there are 221 of them here, 118 of them nonsmoking. This is a great choice if you're taking a family golf vacation so you all have room to spread out. There's a restaurant, lounge, cable TV in every suite and a large indoor swimming pool with an adjacent Jacuzzi. If you're the fitness type, we'd recommend a trip to the well-appointed exercise room.

Holiday Inn Four Seasons
$$$$ • 3121 High Point Rd., Greensboro
• 292-9161

With 522 rooms, the Holiday Inn Four Seasons is one of the largest and most impressive hotels in Greensboro. As you drive by on I-40, you can't miss the place — it's about 30 stories tall. This hotel offers meeting and convention facilities in addition to a nightclub with live entertainment, a weight room and other amenities, including an indoor/outdoor pool to keep you active. You'll also find four restaurants on site, including Stinger's Bar & Grill and Joseph's — serving Italian cuisine. Shoppers will enjoy the nearby mall as well.

High Point

Holiday Inn - Market Square Convention Center
$$$ • 236 S. Main St., High Point • 886-7011

Large and extremely busy during the two annual furniture markets, High Point's Holiday Inn is primarily a business hotel, featuring plenty of meeting rooms. There's an outdoor pool, a restaurant offering three meals a day and a lounge where you can hoist a quick one after a hectic day at the market. Rooms feature coffee machines and full cable TV with free Showtime.

Radisson Hotel High Point
$$$$ • 135 S. Main St., High Point • 889-8888

Located right downtown adjacent to the Furniture Market, the large Radisson is targeted at the business traveler who might really enjoy the eighth floor Business Class level. Here, in addition to all the regular amenities, you get free local phone calls, free fax service, free access to the special lounge and free breakfast for two. So, when you're in town for business but also to get in a round or two on the area's great courses, here's your home base. If you're just a regular traveler, the hotel is still pretty spectacular, offering indoor swimming, a Jacuzzi, cable TV (with ESPN) plus a full-service restaurant.

Super 8 Motel
$ • 400 S. Main St., High Point • 882-4103

You'll find 44 fully renovated rooms here at High Point's outpost of the popular chain.

There's a host of amenities here including satellite TV (with HBO), swimming pool, complimentary breakfast, available waterbeds and a choice of king- or queen-size beds. The convenient location is just a mile from the Furniture Market and there are AAA rates, commercial rates, family rates, senior rates and special furniture market rates, which are just a hair above regular rates. Right.

Winston-Salem

Adam's Mark
$$$ • 425 N. Cherry St., Winston-Salem
• 725-3500

One of Winston-Salem's biggest hotels with 315 rooms, the Adam's Mark offers all the amenities you might expect from a top hotel, including an indoor pool, an outdoor sundeck, 24-hour room service, two restaurants, a lounge and a gift shop.

Hampton Inn
$$$ • 1990 Hampton Inn Ct.,
Winston-Salem • 760-1660

This Hampton Inn exemplifies the trademark quality that has gained this chain a reputation for clean, well-appointed rooms and friendly service. We recommend the Jacuzzi suites on the third floor as a pleasant and slightly more spacious version of the standard rooms. There's nothing better than a hot bath with swirling jets of water to relax you after a hard day on the links. And once the muscles are loosened up, head for the workout room to tighten them again. Business travelers will appreciate the meeting facilities as well. The hotel is convenient to I-40.

Regency Inn
$$ • 128 N. Cherry St., Winston-Salem
• 723-8861

You probably have seen plenty of Best Westerns around the country on your travels, but this one is a little different from others: It's not the typical motel-style that defines the chain. The Regency Inn is a downtown hotel that's a great place to stay at a sensible price, with color cable TVs in every room and a full range of amenities. Enjoy the outdoor pool when the weather is right, and don't miss the complimentary continental breakfast.

The Charlotte Area

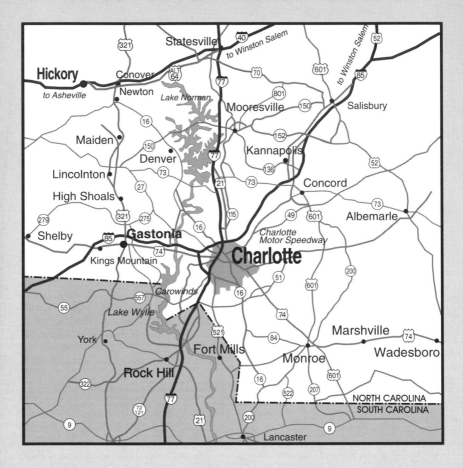

North Carolina's Charlotte Region

Charlotte is one of the most talked-about cities in the country — and usually for all the right reasons. Economic success in the Queen's City of the South has been strong and steady. Drive past downtown Charlotte (locals call it Uptown) and you'll see signs of prosperity in the form of grandiose skyscrapers usually seen in larger cities like New York, Los Angeles and Chicago. Much of the success has been created by NationsBank, First Union and the other significant financial institutions that employ a lot of men in heavily starched white shirts and a lot of women in blue suits. Depending on whose figures you use, Charlotte is the number two financial center in the United States, surpassing Chicago, Los Angeles, San Francisco and Atlanta. So stuff that in your safe deposit box and smoke it!

The big banks have grown in part through the acquisition of other banks, but much of their success is the result of the strong economy in Charlotte and its surrounding counties. Charlotte is also a major distribution and trucking center. Surrounding towns such as Gastonia, Kannapolis and Concord are home to some massive and prosperous textile mills. But perhaps the most visible sign of the arrival of the Charlotte area is the construction of the Charlotte Panthers' stadium next to the Charlotte Observer building.

All this success has meant that the Charlotte region has seen an influx of new resi-

dents from all over the country and all over the world. (Believe it or not, Charlotte even boasts a strong cricket team!) Sadly, the public golfing scene in the Charlotte region has been languishing behind Charlotte's success. As recently as 1990, if you were an avid golfer, you would have to travel a good 45 minutes to an hour to find a course worthy of your weekend golfing investment. But, with apologies to Bob Dylan, the times, they are a-changin' — and golfers regionwide have plenty of reasons to sing and swing. In 1995 and 1996, eight public or semiprivate courses are due to open or have opened. Most of the new public courses are connected to housing developments.

Some big names in golf course architecture have built or are about to open courses in the Charlotte region. Arnold Palmer and Ed Seay are designing Birkdale. Tom Jackson is designing and building Olde Sycamore to the east of Charlotte. Russell Breeden, the venerable octogenarian, designed Charlotte National. The Charlotte area isn't Pinehurst and it isn't the Triad, but the situation is definitely improving.

The Charlotte area is excellent territory for the golf course architect. There's an abundance of wonderful hardwood trees in addition to numerous streams, ponds and other natural hazards. The sticky red clay makes life difficult at times for grasses, but modern turf maintenance and construction methods

GOLF COURSES IN NORTH CAROLINA'S CHARLOTTE REGION

Name	Type	# Holes	Par	Slope	Yards	Walking	Booking	Cost w/ Cart
Birkdale	public	18	72	n/a	n/a	n/a	n/a	$45-50
Charlotte Golf Links	public	18	71	121	6220	restricted	anytime	$35-44
Charlotte National	semiprivate	18	72	n/a	7227	restricted	3 days	$36-45
Eagle Chase Golf Club	semiprivate	18	72	122	6103	anytime	5 days	$28-33
Fort Mill Golf Club	semiprivate	18	72	118	6373	restricted	3 days	$29-32
Gastonia Municipal	public	18	71	110	5671	anytime	7 days	$25-27
Glen Oaks Country Club	semiprivate	18	70	n/r	6026	restricted	7 days	$24-34
Highland Creek Golf Club	semiprivate	18	72	124	6505	no	3 days	$42-48
King's Mountain	semiprivate	18	72	118	6143	anytime	3-4 days	$23-30
Larkhaven	public	18	72	n/a	6464	restricted	5 days	$29-35
Lincoln Country Club	semiprivate	18	72	121	6017	anytime	anytime	$25-31
Mallard Head	semiprivate	18	72	116	6442	restricted	2-3 days	$23-28
Monroe Country Club	semiprivate	18	72	116	6310	restricted	5 days	21-26
Mooresville Golf Course	public	18	72	121	6102	anytime	3 days	$18.50-21.50
Piney Point	semiprivate	18	72	n/a	6710	anytime	3 days	$22-33
Regent Park Golf Club	public	18	72	n/r	6478	no	4-7 days	$37-43
Renaissance Park	public	18	72	121	6880	anytime	7 days	call
River Bend Golf Club	semiprivate	18	72	117	5956	restricted	3 days	$25-32
Rock Barn Club of Golf	semiprivate	18	72	128	6318	anytime	6 days	$36-40
The Tradition	public	18	72	n/a	n/a	n/a	n/a	n/a
Westport Golf Course	semiprivate	18	72	118	6291	restricted	3 days	$20-26
Woodbridge Golf Links	semiprivate	18	72	121	6156	restricted	5-7 days	$26-35

mean that good clubs can maintain their courses to high standards all year. Golfing weather is best in fall and spring. But there are plenty of good days for golf in the winter. Summer can be exceedingly hot at times, and the greens can be exceedingly slow as a result. But it's still bearable if you avoid the midday sun, the mad dogs and the Englishmen posing as golf-book writers.

Birkdale

8600 Sam Furr Rd., Huntersville
• 895-8038
Championship Yardage: Not available
Slope: Not available Par: Not available
Men's Yardage: Not available
Slope: Not available Par: Not available
Ladies' Yardage: Not available
Slope: Not available Par: Not available

The golf course at Birkdale is scheduled to open in fall 1996 and was still under construction at press time. This explains why we don't have any yardage or course rating. Arnold Palmer and Ed Seay are designing the course in wooded terrain that will also be home to a number of houses, condos and apartments.

Birkdale is a production of the Harris Group, a Charlotte commercial real estate company headed by Johnny Harris, one of the most influential and prominent people in the area. Harris is a member of a number of famous golf clubs, including Augusta National. He's a close friend of Arnold Palmer and a keen and good golfer in his own right. If there's one thing that you should know about Johnny Harris, it's this: If Johnny Harris is going to do something, then it's going to be done properly, whatever the cost.

So what does that mean for Birkdale? The plans are quite grand. The Arnold Palmer and Ed Seay design should be magnificent, and the Palmer course will be daily-fee. The Palmer courses we've seen feature a number of strategically placed bunkers and water hazards that end up creating a risk-and-reward type of golf course. Whatever your level or ability, the course should provide quite a challenge, and it will probably be one of the most talked-about and popular public courses in the Charlotte region.

Golfers likely will talk about the wonderful facilities too, including a state-of-the art lighted range, 18-hole putting course and instruction from PGA professionals. The anticipated fee structure is in the $40 to $50 range. Once the course is open, it should be well worth the visit — it's only 20 minutes north on I-77 from Uptown Charlotte.

Charlotte Golf Links

11500 Providence Rd., Charlotte
• 846-7990
Championship Yardage: 6700
Slope: 127   Par: 71
Men's Yardage: 6220
Slope: 121   Par: 71
Ladies' Yardage: 5279
Slope: 117   Par: 72

Charlotte Golf Links, designed by Tom Doak, opened in 1992. The course is mostly flat and open. Fairways are bermudagrass; greens are pennlinks bentgrass.

Doak is a young architect who, after graduating from Cornell University, spent several months touring Scottish links courses and even spent some time as a caddy at the Old Course at St. Andrews. He authored two books about golf courses, including *Anatomy of a Golf Course*, a must-read for anyone interested in golf course architecture and design. Doak is also an expert golf course photographer. He apprenticed himself to Pete Dye. Doak is quite opinionated about design and is, not surprisingly, at his most positive when discussing his favorite type of course: the links (his passion and specialty).

Charlotte Golf Links is a challenging course and a must-play for the golfing purist. Much of the land here is open. With the wind blowing and a light rain coating the course, you're going to feel like you're in Scotland — or at least that's the idea. The fairways are wide in places, narrow in others, but they boast a number of subtle slopes and undulations just like the genuine article. Each hole has been designed to reward the successful risk-taker more than the conservative. However, with risk comes the potential for poor results, and there's always a chance that your ball might find the long native grass that borders many holes. Locals have a name for this "stuff" — it's a scatological word that we can't publish in this book.

The green complexes feature a number of small pot bunkers with grass faces and coarse sand. The greens don't pitch or roll much, but you'll find that some of the shortest putts are some of the most difficult. In really hot weather, be prepared to bang the ball toward the hole with a degree of authority: the greens can be slow.

Charlotte Golf Links, along with Highland Creek, marked the beginning of a new era in public golf in Charlotte, and it's exciting that one of the newest courses is also one of the most traditional and walkable. Todd Smith and his staff run a tight ship here, and the course is well-organized.

The best time to see and play Charlotte Golf Links is late on a sunny day when the shadows bring out all the subtle shaping in the fairways and the grass faces of the bunkers are dark and menacing. It's a special place. And it's very accessible to southeast Charlotte.

One interesting amenity worth noting is the electronic yardage system that's hooked up to the carts. The system tells you the yardage to the hole, the length of your drive, the total yardage of the hole and other useful information. The system is designed to take the guesswork out of figuring how far you might be from glory. One of the system's main benefits is potentially speeding up play quite a bit.

Amenities include a practice green, driving range, chipping green, locker room, snack bar, rental clubs, a beverage cart and pro shop.

You can walk Charlotte National Golf Club course weekdays and weekends after 2 pm. The course is very walkable. You can book a tee time whenever you choose. Approximate cost, including cart, is $35 Monday through Thursday, $39 on Friday and $49 on weekends.

Charlotte National

6920 Howey Bottoms Rd., Charlotte
• 882-8282
Championship Yardage: 7227
Slope: 134   **Par: 72**
Men's Yardage: 6700
Slope: 129   **Par: 72**
Ladies' Yardage: 5423
Slope: 121   **Par: 72**

Charlotte National opened in spring/summer 1996. Russell Breeden designed the course, which is set on primarily flat land bordered by mature woods. Fairways are bermudagrass; greens are bentgrass.

As soon as you step onto the first tee at Charlotte National, it's clear that you're on a Russell Breeden course. The fairways are mostly wide. The bunkers are large and flat. Most of the greens are large and sloped, with the occasional subtle undulation. There are no tricks, and the challenges of the course are laid out in front of you — what you see is what you get. In today's era of golf course architecture, where good courses are defined by the difficulty of the test, the amount of earth moved, and the layers upon layers of severity, Charlotte National is a welcome step back to relative minimalism. The course proves the fact that you don't really have to do too much to produce a course that's fun and playable — and still challenging.

And you'll find the course to be fun and playable so long as you don't play from the tips — a backbreaking 7227 yards. That's longer than any course we've seen. However, it's more pleasing for the short hitter from the forward tees. The course is built on some fine Union County farmland and winds through some fine woodland; thus, it boasts a pleasant and relaxed air — free of houses and other urban encroachments. Water comes into play on some holes but should not prove too hazardous to your score or overall golfing health.

Like many Breeden courses, this track will not make you say "Wow!" or "Gee whiz, this

A driver with more loft (at least 11 degrees) is better for the average golfer.

The Custom Publishing Department of The Charlotte Observer can help you save money on all the printing needs relating to your golf course.
We produce and print:
- Scorecards
- Yardage Books
- Yardage Sheets
- Brochures
- Marketing Materials

If you're in the golf business and want to spend less on printing, call Scott Martin at 704/358-5935 for more information.

custom publishing
The Charlotte Observer

Photo: David Ramsey, The Harris Group

Arnold Palmer introduced the Birkdale Golf Course at a reception in Huntersville just north of Charlotte. Palmer's golf course architecture group designed this and many other courses in the Carolinas.

is amazing!" but you'll probably appreciate its ambiance and playability.

Amenities include a practice green, driving range, snack bar and pro shop.

You can walk this course anytime during the week and on weekend afternoons. The course is very walkable. You can book a tee time on Wednesday for Saturday or Thursday for Sunday. Approximate cost, including cart, is $36 during the week and $45 on weekends.

The Divide Golf Links

2200 Divide Dr., Matthews • 882-8088
Championship Yardage: 6973
Slope: 137   **Par: 72**
Men's Yardage: 6587
Slope: 127   **Par: 72**
Other Yardage: 6145
Slope: 121   **Par: 72**
Ladies' Yardage: 5213
Slope: 121   **Par: 72**

The Divide opened in fall 1995. John Cassell designed the course, which is set on gently undulating terrain and is currently surrounded by woods, although houses will eventually border some holes. Fairways are 419 bermudagrass, and greens are pennlinks bentgrass.

The Divide is brought to you by the same group who built Charlotte Golf Links, one of Charlotte's better public courses. So it comes as no surprise that the Divide, despite its youth, is already shaping up as a fine public golf facility. The Divide marks John Cassell's entry into the noble profession of golf course architecture. Judging by The Divide, there should be plenty of other public golf course owners who will want to use his services. Cassell designed the track with the help of Todd Smith and the staff and ownership of the course, thus the emphasis is playability. If you're an average public golfer, then you'll find the course has been built with you in mind. However, if you're a stronger player, this course still should give you a stern test from the back tees (note the 137 slope from the tips).

The fairways are mostly wide, and occasional bunkers lurk, although they tend to be on the small side. On many holes, a wayward drive might find the woods. The green complexes feature mildly undulating greens, pot bunkers, flat bunkers and embankments. You'll need to bring a strong short game to get up and down successfully. A brook wanders through some of the layout and poses a serious hazard on quite a few holes.

Perhaps what we liked most about The Divide is that it's straightforward but interesting:

It lacks the excesses that make too many public courses too difficult and time consuming. The course clearly has been designed to keep your round less than 4 hours, and most importantly, it's clearly been designed to put the fun back into public golf. We think that The Divide will ultimately become one of Charlotte's most popular public golf courses. You'll also find that it's one of the prettiest once all the housing and construction work is finished.

Amenities include a driving range, putting green, chipping green, bar, restaurant, snack bar, pro shop and beverage cart.

With 8 miles of cart path, you'll need to take a cart. You can book a tee time three days in advance. Approximate cost, including cart, is $33 weekdays and $39 weekends.

Eagle Chase Golf Club

3215 Brantley Rd., Marshville • 385-9000
Championship Yardage: 6723
Slope: 128   **Par: 72**
Men's Yardage: 6103
Slope: 122   **Par: 72**
Ladies' Yardage: 5139
Slope: 121   **Par: 72**

Eagle Chase Golf Course opened in 1994. Tom Jackson designed this rolling and mostly open course. Bermudagrass covers the fairways, and bentgrass covers the greens.

To most Charlotteans, Marshville is well known as a town you pass through on the way to the beach. Doze off for a few minutes and you've missed it. It's the home of musician Randy Travis and numerous poultry processing plants: These two facts are not necessarily related. Marshville is also home to this outstanding new golf course. It's well worth the 45-minute drive from downtown Charlotte. Eagle Chase is home to a semipro event and, more importantly, the Charlotte Checkers annual golf tournament, where one of us won a shirt for being closest to the pin on the extremely treacherous par 3 12th hole. We're sure you wanted to hear about that.

The most talked-about hole on the course is No. 2, a mid-length par 4 where the elevated tee gives you a great look at the treacherous shot before you: water to the left and right. Much of the course features significant elevation changes. For the most part, you'll find a decent amount of room off the tee with very few long, forced carries. The bunkers are large and cloverleafed as you might expect from an architect who spent a couple of years under the tutelage of Robert Trent Jones. The greens also are large but not particularly undulating. The course also features a number of interesting and difficult par 3s on which par is a good score.

Even though Eagle Chase is not very close to Charlotte, it can still be counted as one of the best public courses in the Charlotte area. It's quite a challenge from any of the tees and a lot of fun for golfers of all levels.

Amenities include a practice green, driving range, locker room, bar, rental clubs and a pro shop.

We do not recommend walking this course, but you're allowed to anytime. You can book a tee time five days in advance. Approximate cost, including cart, is $28 weekdays and $33 on weekends.

Ed. note: The following course is in South Carolina. While you might expect to find it in our Midlands chapter, we've included it in the Charlotte Region because of its proximity to the Queen's City and the volume of Charlotte-area golfers who play here.

Fort Mill Golf Club

101 Country Club Dr., Fort Mill, S.C.
• (803) 547-2044
Championship Yardage: 6865
Slope: 133   **Par: 72**
Men's Yardage: 6373
Slope: 118   **Par: 72**
Ladies' Yardage: 5448
Slope: 123   **Par: 72**

The front nine at Fort Mill Golf Club opened in the 1947. The back nine opened in the 1970s. Donald Ross designed the front nine just before his death in 1948, and George Cobb designed the back. The front nine is open, and the back is set in rolling terrain. In the fairways, you'll find bermudagrass; on the greens, you'll find bentgrass.

Fort Mill has long been a well-known favorite of Charlotte golfers. The club is part of a triumvirate of Springs Industries-owned courses, all of which are popular and well-run; the others are in Chester and Lancaster, and each is worth a visit. You'll find write-ups in our Midlands chapter. Ross also designed the course in Lancaster.

It's difficult to find a golf course that has enlisted two better architects than Ross and Cobb. The result is a fine and mature course that's more challenging than it looks. This is a country-club caliber design.

The front nine, designed by Ross, offers plenty of room off the tee. If you're wayward with your driver, the most significant hazards are posed by the large trees. As you might expect with a Ross course, the trouble begins on and around the greens, where there are plenty of small bunkers and difficult putts. If you're playing for money, never give your opponent a gimme on this nine — make 'em drop it in the hole. Watch as a two-foot putt is rammed three feet past or ends up two inches short. (Hit it, Alice.) It's part of what makes Ross's designs so timeless (and irritating).

The back nine is a genuine Cobb championship-caliber test. Many of the holes are truly long and seem to play even longer. The greens are large and not quite as undulating as the Ross greens, but no less difficult. The bunkers are larger and the fairways wider on this nine. Water is sparse, but you'll discover that wayward shots will find the hazard if you're not sensible. Have fun here and buy textiles made by Springs Industries out of gratitude for their excellent contributions to public golf in South Carolina.

Amenities include a practice green, snack bar and pro shop.

You can walk anytime on weekdays and after 2 PM on weekends. You can book a tee time three days in advance. Approximate cost, including cart, is $29 weekdays and $32 on weekends.

Gastonia Municipal Golf Course
Niblick Dr., Gastonia • 866-6945
Championship Yardage: 6474

Slope: 115	**Par: 71**
Men's Yardage: 5671	
Slope: 110	**Par: 71**
Ladies' Yardage: 4344	
Slope: 110	**Par: 71**

Gastonia Municipal Golf Course opened in the 1930s, although there's no real record of who designed it. The course is set on open and rolling terrain. Fairways and greens are covered with bermudagrass.

Gastonia Muni offers a fun and playable track that's a great value for Gastonia residents. If you live in this lovely town just west of Charlotte, you can walk as many holes as you're able on a weekday for just $8. You can't beat that deal anywhere.

Muni courses have a charm and quality that's somewhat hard to define or describe. Many munis were built on land that was once open countryside. Thus as a metropolis expands, its municipal golf course often becomes an oasis of green in the middle of urban sprawl. That is the case at Gastonia Muni. A couple of power lines traverse the course in a few places, but for the most part you still feel like you're out in the country.

The front nine is open, and the fairways are a little tight in places. The greens are small and sloped, and you can run the ball up to the pin on quite a few holes. You'll find an average of one bunker per green on both the back and front nines. A stream wanders through the track in a couple of places.

The back nine offers a bit more room off the tee, and many of the holes are more strategic — especially around the green complexes. Still, the setting is pleasant and relaxed, and the course provides a fun and potentially rewarding challenge for all levels of golfer. The more than 40,000 rounds of golf played here per annum prove that Gastonia Muni has something going for it besides sensible greens fees.

Amenities include a practice green, chipping green, locker room, restaurant, beverage cart and pro shop.

The course is walkable anytime. You can book a tee time seven days in advance. Approximate cost, including cart, is $25 weekdays and $27 on weekends. As we mentioned before, the rates are less if you're a resident of Gastonia, which you should at least think about.

Glen Oaks Country Club
245 Golf Course Rd., Maiden • 428-2451
Championship Yardage: 6430

Slope: 116	**Par: 70**
Men's Yardage: 6026	
Slope: No rating	**Par: 70**
Ladies' Yardage: 4953	
Slope: No rating	**Par: 70**

The golf course at Glen Oaks Country Club opened in 1967. This Bill McRee design is set on flat terrain with many open holes. Bermudagrass covers the fairways, and bentgrass covers the greens.

Glen Oaks presents a remarkably interesting and challenging course in a country setting. The strength of the course is its variety, although the routing of the holes is a little bizarre. The course is intelligently bunkered. The front nine tends to be a little more wooded than the back and is a little tighter off the tee. The greens are mostly flat and midsize, and many are flush with the fairway, making run-up shots possible and advisable if the fairways and greens are hard. There's quite a bit of water on the back nine, and you'll find your golfing skills tested by a number of approach shots requiring accurate club selection and shot execution. There's even an island green — perhaps a tip of the hat to Pete Dye. You might arrive at the 18th with your best score ever only to find the closing hole one of the most difficult on the course. Clearly, Glen Oaks is popular with the local population — for good reason.

Amenities include a practice green, driving range, locker room, bar, snack bar, restaurant, rental clubs and a pro shop.

The course is walkable for the fit and dedicated, and you can walk on weekdays. You can book a tee time seven days in advance. Approximate cost, including cart, is $24 weekdays and $34 on weekends.

Highland Creek Golf Club
7001 Highland Creek Blvd., Charlotte
• 875-9000
Championship Yardage: 7008
Slope: 133   Par: 72
Men's Yardage: 6505
Slope: 124   Par: 72
Other Yardage: 5947
Slope: 122   Par: 72
Ladies' Yardage: 5080
Slope: 128   Par: 72

Highland Creek Golf Club opened in 1993. Lloyd Clifton and Ken Ezell designed the course, which is set in rolling wooded terrain bordered with houses. In the fairways, you'll find bermudagrass; on the greens, bentgrass.

When it opened, Highland Creek was almost universally acclaimed as the greatest thing for public golf in the Charlotte area since the invention of public golf. Along with Charlotte Golf Links, it certainly marked the end of a drought for Charlotte's public golfer. Here at last was a modern and well-designed course, well-kept and within sensible driving distance of Charlotte. Since then, the course has maintained its popularity and is one of the most played tracks in the area.

The Clifton-Ezell team hasn't completed a lot of work in North and South Carolina — Highland Creek is their only course in the Carolinas, in fact — but the firm has been active for years in Florida. At Highland Creek, they produced one of the most challenging and demanding public golf courses in the western section of the Carolinas. In places, it's also one of the prettiest and most varied.

FYI

Unless otherwise noted, the area code for all phone numbers in this chapter is 704.

On quite a few holes, the course is tight off the tee. The locals will tell you that it's essential to be in just the right place in the fairway; thus, you need to be accurate with whatever you like to use off the tee. Should you spray your shots around somewhat, you'll find your ball in Highland Creek, someone's back yard or the woods. If it seems like Highland Creek comes into play on just about every hole, it's not an illusion. The creek poses quite a hazard, and it's no fun having to fish for your ball.

Once you've navigated the hazards off the tee, you must play an accurate approach shot. The greens are predominantly large, as are the bunkers and embankments that flank many of the green complexes. You'll certainly leave here with memories of many holes — and with an opinion about the layout. We think you'll want to come back and challenge this exciting course again and again. Despite all the new courses opening in the Charlotte region, Highland Creek should remain one of the most difficult and exciting.

You'll find a fun and friendly staff at Highland Creek. Coauthor Scott Martin took golf lessons here from Mark McLaughlan, the head pro and a man of great patience whom we highly recommend as an instructor. The new clubhouse is large and magnificent and offers rooms for corporate meetings and other such events.

Current amenities include a practice green, driving range, chipping green, locker room, bar, restaurant, rental clubs, a beverage cart and pro shop. Walking is not a viable option here. You can book a tee time three days in advance. Approximate cost, including cart, is $42 weekdays and $48 on weekends.

King's Mountain Country Club
Country Club Dr., Kings Mountain
• **739-5871**
Championship Yardage: 6483
Slope: 121   **Par: 72**
Men's Yardage: 6143
Slope: 118   **Par: 72**
Ladies' Yardage: 5019
Slope: 119   **Par: 72**

King's Mountain Golf Course opened its first nine holes in the 1940s; the second nine opened in the 1970s. The course is set in rolling wooded terrain. In the fairways, you'll find bermudagrass; on the greens, you'll find bentgrass.

King's Mountain offers a couple of varied and thoroughly interesting nines. The front is the original nine and is built much like many courses of its day. The greens are somewhat small and sloped, and there's plenty of room for run-up shots from just about anywhere. Your chipping game will be seriously tested. There are a few bunkers — enough to wreck a potentially good score. Many of the greens are flanked by steep embankments. What you'll probably notice most about the front nine are the towering pine trees that delineate the fairways. They create quite a frame for many holes.

On the back nine, there's a little more room off the tee. Many of the holes are bordered by thick woods that create quite a hazard. The greens are still relatively flat and somewhat small. It's still possible to run the ball up to many of the holes due to the lack of bunkers

fronting the greens. There are also some fun tee placements on a few holes. Overall, it's a relaxed yet challenging course, exhibiting a maturity rarely seen on many modern courses.

Amenities include a practice green and snack bar.

The course is walkable anytime. You can book a tee time whenever you choose for the weekdays and on Wednesday for the weekend. Approximate cost, including cart, is $23 weekdays and $30 on weekends.

Larkhaven Golf Club
4801 Camp Stewart Rd., Charlotte
• **545-GOLF**
Championship Yardage: 6464
Slope: 121   **Par: 72**
Men's Yardage: 6042
Slope: 115   **Par: 72**
Ladies' Yardage: 4645
Slope: 110   **Par: 72**

Larkhaven Golf Club opened in 1959. A.B. Connell designed the course, which is set in undulating terrain bordered by woods. You'll find bermudagrass fairways and bentgrass greens here at Larkhaven.

Larkhaven has long been a popular golf course among Charlotte-area public golfers. The course is relatively straightforward; the challenges here come from a couple of water hazards and the tightness of the fairways in places, particularly on the front nine. The key to scoring well here is doing whatever it takes to keep the ball in play.

A couple of holes you'll really enjoy include the par 4 1st, a 262-yard par 4 that tempts you to bang it onto the green with the driver. All you have to do is smack it into a large bank and hope it rolls up to the green. It's a unique opening hole. The 9th, a 207-yard par 3 over water, is an exciting way to finish the front nine.

The greens here at Larkhaven are relatively small and sloped. A few bunkers lurk here and there, but getting up and down from within them should not be too difficult. Overall, we think you'll enjoy your round here at

INSIDERS' TIP

Always keep an eye on the group in front of you and the group behind. Keep up with the group in front if the course is busy. Let faster players play through.

Larkhaven. It's a fun course in a relaxed setting where the premium is accuracy, not length.

Amenities include a practice green, locker room, snack bar and pro shop.

The course is walkable and you can walk during the week. You can book a tee time on Monday for the weekend. Approximate cost, including cart, is $29 weekdays and $35 on weekends.

Lincoln Country Club
2108 Country Club Rd., Lincolnton
• 735-1382
Championship Yardage: 6467

Slope: 125	**Par: 72**

Men's Yardage: 6017

Slope: 121	**Par: 72**

Ladies' Yardage: 5011

Slope: 118	**Par: 72**

The current back nine at Lincoln Country Club opened in 1949, and the front nine opened in 1993. Peter Tufts is credited with Lincoln's recent design. The course is set on rolling wooded terrain. Lincoln has bermudagrass fairways and bentgrass greens.

There are two distinct nines here. The front is newer, though not particularly modern or penal in design; it's not a tricked-up course. You'll find some mounds, but they're not of the massive variety. The terrain is somewhat flat, and many holes are bordered by trees. Thankfully, there's decent width off the tee. You'll find a number of tough but short par 4s, each with an interesting and unique feature. The greens are midsize and sloped.

The back nine is older and more traditional in design. If the fairways are hard, you'll be able to play a variety of run-up shots to the greens, which are flush with the fairways. You'll also find a fair amount of sensible bunkering. All in all, it's a fun and playable track that's justifiably popular with the local population.

Amenities include a practice green, driving range, chipping green, locker room, snack bar and pro shop.

Walk this course anytime and book a tee time whenever you choose during the week and two days before the weekend. Approximate cost, including cart, is $25 weekdays and $31 on weekends.

Mallard Head Country Club
Brawley School Rd., Mooresville
• 664-7031
Championship Yardage: 6904

Slope: 121	**Par: 72**

Men's Yardage: 6442

Slope: 116	**Par: 72**

Other Yardage: 6233

Slope: 113	**Par: 72**

Ladies' Yardage: 5469

Slope: 121	**Par: 72**

The golf course at Mallard Head Country Club opened in 1979. J. Porter Gibson designed this course, which is set in rolling terrain. Houses border some of the holes. Fairways are bermudagrass, and greens are bentgrass.

Mallard Head is a popular and reasonably priced golf course that has long attracted golfers from Charlotte and the eastern shores of Lake Norman. There are some interesting and diverse golf holes with plenty of challenge, particularly from the back tees. The greens are large to medium-size and flanked by bunkers and the occasional embankment. The front nine is more wooded than the back. Water comes into play on a few holes, and its influence varies in intensity. On most holes, you'll find enough room off the tee to pull out the big stick and take a big whack. Overall, Mallard Head is a fun course that's popular with the locals; it's well worth a visit if you're in the area.

Amenities include a practice green, locker room, snack bar, rental clubs and a pro shop.

The course is walkable for the physically fit, and you can walk anytime during the week. You can book a tee time whenever you choose for weekdays and on Thursday for the weekend. Approximate cost, including cart, is $23 weekdays and $28 on weekends.

Monroe Country Club
U.S. Hwy. 601 S., Monroe • 282-4661
Championship Yardage: 6759

Slope: 118	**Par: 72**

Men's Yardage: 6310

Slope: 116	**Par: 72**

Ladies' Yardage: 4964

Slope: 117	**Par: 73**

The golf course at Monroe Country Club opened in 1936 with nine holes, and a second nine was added in 1984. Tom Jackson

Rock Hill: Charlotte's Bedroom Community

While you're in the Charlotte area for golf, you might want to forget about staying in the usual big hotels downtown and instead stay in Charlotte's bedroom community: Rock Hill, South Carolina. It's not like you will be blazing any trails. Two of Charlotte's professional sports teams, the football Carolina Panthers and the basketball Charlotte Hornets, have training facilities in the area.

Close-up

Two bed and breakfast inns in Rock Hill are second-to-none when it comes to comfort, accessibility and convenience. **The Book & The Spindle**, 626 Oakland Avenue, is a lovely, luxurious 1930s home restored by Pam and Warren Bowen. Each of the two suites has its own breakfast

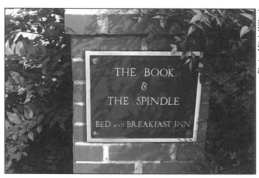

THE BOOK
&
THE SPINDLE

BED and BREAKFAST INN

The Book & The Spindle offers grace and charm in Rock Hill, South Carolina.

Photo: Mitch Willard

nook. Two additional rooms are smaller but still comfortable. All have private baths. Our favorite spot in the whole house is the piazza in the Charleston suite. The Bowens call it a porch dummy. It's a bright little sun room where you can read, work or relax in a wicker chair while communing with the redbirds perched on a branch outside the window. The Camden suite features its own private canopied rooftop patio. With the proper

designed the newer front nine, and Donald Ross, the back. The course is set on rolling wooded terrain. You'll find bermudagrass on the greens and fairways.

There can't be many better Carolina-based architectural combinations than Donald Ross and Tom Jackson. Both have worked extensively in the area, and their efforts here at Monroe Country Club make this course worth playing. It's also an excellent value.

The Jackson nine is tight and challenging. There are very few mounds. The greens are large and somewhat flat. The bunkers aren't quite as demonic as those on other Jackson layouts. Anyway, the length from the back and the tight fairways will give you all

the challenge you want — and then some. Particularly remarkable is the maturity of the front nine: It looks as though it's been there as long as the original nine.

We're constantly awestruck by the quality and timelessness of a Donald Ross track; the back nine here is no exception. The simple yet sensible layout might lead you to believe that you'll run away with a low score. But the intelligent placement of bunkers and the small crowned greens make the course more difficult to play than it looks. There's no such thing as a gimme on a Ross course, and with the added element of grainy bermudagrass greens, you'll be praying that your two- and three-footers for bogey somehow find the bottom of the cup. The setting is pretty, and many weather, this could be another favorite spot. Each room has a different theme at this charming English-style inn with modern amenities.

Before you go to bed, leave a message with Pam as to what time you want your breakfast served — as long as it's before 10 AM. Promptly at the time you ordered, your breakfast is brought upstairs on a tray. This may be a welcome change from inns where breakfast is served in the din-ing room, especially if you like to linger in the morning with your significant other. The suites also have full kitchens if you'd prefer to stay in and prepare a meal.

Photo: Mitch Willard

The Book & The Spindle has myriad antiques and fine reproductions displayed about. Rooms overlook the beautiful campus of Winthrop University.

Just a few blocks away at 347 Park Avenue is **Park Avenue Inn**. Sharon and Donny Neely will make you feel right

You will feel right at home at the Park Avenue Inn in Rock Hill, South Carolina.

at home with their Southern hospitality; they open their hearts and home to the fullest. Their tons of knickknacks include antique toys and glass. Also, collections of family memorabilia hang on the walls, creating a homey atmosphere. Breakfast is served between 7 and 9 AM at the dining room table. We think you'll appreciate both the breakfast and the table, a 10-foot-long primitive piece of furniture made from four large boards. The house includes three guest rooms and three baths, and the rooms are quite comfortable.

Rates at both of these inns are no more than you would pay for one of the nationally recognized hotels in the city. For reservations, call The Book & The Spindle, 328-1913, or the Park Avenue Inn, 325-1764.

---

of the holes have an Ellis Maples-like look with a couple of sweeping doglegs. The back nine is wider off the tee. If you're a fan of good golf course architecture, take some time to visit this course.

Amenities include a practice green, driving range, snack bar, restaurant and pro shop.

You can walk anytime during the week and after 2 PM on weekends. You can book a tee time five days in advance. Approximate cost, including cart, is $21 weekdays and $26 on weekends.

Mooresville Golf Club
W. Wilson Ave., Mooresville • 663-2539
Championship Yardage: 6528
Slope: 124   **Par: 72**
Men's Yardage: 6102
Slope: 121   **Par: 72**
Ladies' Yardage: 4976
Slope: 115   **Par: 72**

The front nine at Mooresville Golf Club, designed by Donald Ross, opened in the 1940s. The back nine, designed by Porter Gibson, opened in 1978. The front nine is

INSIDERS' TIP

If your group is one of the first on the course, it's all the more important to practice fast play.

open, and the back is set on rolling terrain. In the fairways, you'll find bermudagrass; on the greens, bentgrass.

There aren't many low-cost public-access Donald Ross courses in the Carolinas, but Mooresville Golf Club is one of them. As with many Ross courses, the layout is excellent. There's plenty of room off the tee. The difficulties include some awkward bunkers and mounding around small greens with numerous minute and irritating undulations. Donald Ross perfected the art of the heart-attack-inducing two-foot putt, and you'll see many examples of that here. Each hole has a character and challenge all its own. The subtle shaping and innuendoes become magnificently apparent late in the day.

To score well on the front nine, you'll need to be precise with club selection and control. You'll also need to drive the ball well and in the right part of the fairway. Believe it or not, the front nine here at Mooresville is something of a rarity — a relatively untouched and unmolested Donald Ross design.

The back nine is no less interesting. It's quite tight in places, and some of the holes require a decent thump off the tee if you're going to score well. The greens are larger, as are the bunkers and the embankments that flank some of the greens. Mooresville is a fun and challenging course, a great value and one of our favorites. Some of the older greens get a bit beaten up during the summer, but you won't find better fairways anywhere — especially for the investment.

Amenities include a practice green, driving range, snack bar and pro shop.

Walk anytime you wish. You can book a tee time three days in advance. Approximate cost, including cart, is $18.50 weekdays and $21.50 on weekends.

Piney Point Golf Club

Piney Point Rd., Norwood • 474-3985
Championship Yardage: 6710
Slope: 118   **Par: 72**
Men's Yardage: 6385
Slope: 115   **Par: 72**
Ladies' Yardage: 4955
Slope: 111   **Par: 72**

Piney Point Golf Club opened in 1964. Porter Gibson designed the course. The course is mostly open, with woods bordering a few holes. Fairways and greens are bermudagrass.

This mature golf course, close to Lake Tillery, is justifiably popular among local golfers. The pace and overall ambiance of the course are relaxing and unassuming. The course offers countrified golf in a relaxed setting.

But don't be fooled into thinking that Piney Point is a bit too countrified to be serious. The layout offers a fun and playable challenge that will keep you on your toes from the 1st tee to the 18th green. The course is laid out on a tract of old farmland, and you can tell very little earth was moved to construct it.

Despite the minimalist architecture, the course offers a number of interesting and difficult golf holes — there's plenty to keep your head on your game.

Characteristically a throwback to earlier times, the fairways and greens get hard and dry when there isn't much rain. Try to fire the ball like a dart on this course and it might scurry over the green, leaving you with a difficult chip shot back to the hole. When the course is dry, you have to let the ball roll up to the hole, often by landing it short of the green. In these days of major irrigation, this situation is somewhat rare.

The course features a number of mid- to long par 3s, a variety of par 4s and four reachable par 5s. A mid-handicapper should par all the par 5s but will be quite seriously tested on the longer par 4s. Par is a good score on all the par 3s, where you'll probably have to use a mid- to long iron to reach the green.

We think you'll really enjoy the relaxed atmosphere at Piney Point. It's less than an hour's drive from east Charlotte — well worth the trip if you want to play a fun course far-removed from the mayhem of the city. It's also a good value.

Amenities include a practice green, driving range, chipping green, snack bar, rental clubs and a pro shop.

You can walk this course anytime. The course is very walkable, and lots of people walk here. You can book a tee time three days in advance of the weekend if you're not a member. Approximate cost, including cart, is $22 Monday through Thursday and $33 on weekends.

Photo: Lake Norman Magazine

The Fieldcrest-Cannon Classic at the Peninsula Club, just
north of Charlotte, is a popular stop on the LPGA tour.

Ed. note: The following is a South Carolina course; however, its proximity to Charlotte and the fact that it is frequented by Charlotte golfers makes it a natural addition to this Charlotte Region chapter.

Regent Park Golf Club
3000 Heritage Pkwy., Fort Mill, S.C.
• (803) 547-1300
Championship Yardage: 6861

Slope: No rating	**Par: 72**
Men's Yardage: 6478	
Slope: No rating	**Par: 72**
Other Yardage: 6083	
Slope: No rating	**Par: 72**
Ladies' Yardage: 5258	
Slope: No rating	**Par: 72**

Ron Garl designed Regent Park Golf Club, which opened in 1995. The course is set on rolling wooded terrain. In the fairways, you'll find bermudagrass; on the greens, bentgrass.

Regent Park has risen from the ashes of what used to be Jim and Tammy Bakker's PTL empire just south of Charlotte in Fort Mill. Close to the clubhouse, you'll find all sorts of evangelical theme park items that are worth a quick look — if you're fascinated by that sort of thing.

The new owners of Regent Park, a group of Malaysian money-magnates, have created a stunning golf course as the centerpiece of what will eventually be a large housing development. They have also built a top-quality, state-of-the-art practice facility that includes a place to practice the uphill and sidehill shots you'll need on this course.

Playing at Regent Park, you can't help being staggered by and impressed with the money that must have been poured into its construction and design. It's a golfing extravaganza the likes of which you won't find on any public course in the immediate area. The result is a number of beautiful golf holes flanked by serious hazards and difficulties. You'll find large bunkers, mounds, water, swamp, tricky lies in the fairway and the type of problems normally reserved for professional and low-handicap golfers. It's as stern a test of golfing skill and patience as you'll find on any top-quality public or private course. Many of the greens are sensible and sloped, while others make you feel like you've landed on a Putt-Putt course with a few too many under your belt. You'll see what we mean when you visit this course — something you definitely should do.

There's a serious emphasis at Regent Park to make this a top-quality public facility. Tee times are spread out at 10 minute intervals, and your tee time is secured by a Visa card. Show up for your tee time! As you leave the course, your clubs are cleaned and carried to your car . . . talk about service.

You won't find a larger testament to modern golf anywhere in the Charlotte region than at Regent Park. You must use a cart at Regent Park.

Amenities include a practice green, driving range, chipping green, snack bar, rental clubs, a beverage cart and pro shop.

You can book a tee time four to seven days in advance for an $8 service charge; otherwise it's three days in advance. Approximate cost, including cart, is $37 weekdays and $43 on weekends.

FYI
Unless otherwise noted, the area code for all phone numbers in this chapter is 704.

Renaissance Park Golf Course
1525 Tyvola Rd. W., Charlotte • 357-3373
Championship Yardage: 7525

Slope: 126	**Par: 72**
Men's Yardage: 6880	
Slope: 121	**Par: 72**
Other Yardage: 6270	
Slope: 115	**Par: 72**
Ladies' Yardage: 4606	
Slope: No rating	**Par: 72**

Renaissance Park Golf Course opened in 1987. Michael Hurdzan, a well-respected architect and agronomy expert, designed the course on a mix of open and wooded terrain on what used to be a landfill. In the fairways, you'll find bermudagrass; on the greens, you'll find bentgrass. The course is owned by the City of Charlotte and Mecklenburg County.

At the time of writing this chapter, a renaissance was underway at Renaissance Park — a $1 million renaissance to be exact. The goal is to redesign a number of absurdly difficult holes in an effort to make the course more playable. Most of the course is built on land that formerly served as a garbage dump; sadly, this means that the clubhouse is cur-

Photo: KPC Photography, Inc.

The par 5 12th hole at Highland Creek Golf Club in Charlotte is the #1 handicap hole and is one of the most challenging par 5s in the Carolinas.

rently closed due to potentially lethal levels of methane buildup in the basement. On certain days, particularly during the hot summer months, Renaissance boast a remarkable smell. It should be interesting to see what the course looks like once refinished.

One reason for Renaissance's popularity is the proximity to Charlotte-Douglas International Airport and the Charlotte Coliseum, each just a 5-minute drive away, as well as Uptown Charlotte (10 minutes).

River Bend Golf Club
Longwood Dr., Shelby • 482-4286
Championship Yardage: 6555
Slope: 130	**Par: 72**
Men's Yardage: 5956	
Slope: 117	**Par: 72**
Ladies' Yardage: 4920	
Slope: 102	**Par: 72**

River Bend opened in 1965. Russell Breeden designed the course, which is open and set on rolling terrain. In the fairways, you'll find bermudagrass; on the greens, bentgrass.

River Bend has a local reputation as a playable track that's usually in good condition. It's exactly what you'd expect from a Russell Breeden course. You won't find a ton of trouble off the tee, and your approach shot will be hit to a medium-size green flanked by a series of bunkers that are not too penal. The owner of

the course talks wistfully about Russell Breeden cruising around, building the course with the help of his personal earth mover. He also talks proudly about the conditioning. The course is definitely worth a visit, and it's a good value.

Amenities include a practice green, driving range, chipping green, snack bar and pro shop.

The course is walkable, and you can walk on weekdays. You can book a tee time three days in advance. Approximate cost, including cart, is $25 weekdays and $32 on weekends.

Rock Barn Club of Golf
Rock Barn Rd., Conover • 459-9279
Championship Yardage: 6778
Slope: 132	**Par: 72**
Men's Yardage: 6318	
Slope: 128	**Par: 72**
Other Yardage: 5921	
Slope: 122	**Par: 72**
Ladies' Yardage: 4812	
Slope: 117	**Par: 72**

Rock Barn Club of Golf opened in 1968. Russell Breeden designed the course. The club recently added an additional nine holes, designed by Tom Jackson. The course, which is convenient to I-40, is set on rolling terrain, with woods bordering many of the holes. In the fairways, you'll find bermudagrass; on the greens, bentgrass.

In the northern reaches of the Charlotte

region, Rock Barn Club of Golf has long had an excellent reputation for its sound design and great conditioning. We found this to be true. Rock Barn Club of Golf is, perhaps, one of Breeden's finest efforts — a course with outstanding variety and playability, laid out in a peaceful setting. Should anyone accuse Breeden of being a cookie-cutter architect, bring them here: There are some wonderful and imaginative holes on this excellent layout. You'll find decent room off the tee, though it helps to be in the right part of the fairway with your drive. The greens are large and sloped. Three-putts are an annoying possibility; there's just enough slope and undulation to make even the shortest putt an adventure. As with many Breeden courses, the large bunkers vary in intensity, depending upon pin placement. You should definitely take time to play here.

Jackson's nine is new — and modern in design. The architect unleashed some of his most venomous features, and you'll find plenty of major elevation changes, large mounds, nasty bunkers and severely undulating greens. It's certainly a stunning and entertaining track — a strong contrast to Breeden's more mature and less penal 18. After your round on the main course, take a few beers to the new nine and you'll have had all the golf you could possibly want — and more.

Amenities include a practice green, driving range, locker room, snack bar, rental clubs and a pro shop.

The original course is walkable for the fit, and you can walk anytime, but we don't recommend you walk the Jackson nine. You can book a tee time six days in advance. Approximate cost, including cart, is $36 weekdays and $40 on weekends.

The Tradition

3800 Prosperity Church Rd., Charlotte • 549-9400
Championship Yardage: Not available
Slope: Not available Par: Not available
Men's Yardage: Not available
Slope: Not available Par: Not available
Other Yardage: Not available
Slope: Not available Par: Not available
Ladies' Yardage: Not available
Slope: Not available Par: Not available
The Tradition is slated to open in late 1996

or early 1997. John Cassell is designing the course. Fairways will be bermudagrass, and greens will be bentgrass.

At the time of writing, The Tradition was still under construction. However, due to our inside sources, we learned that the course is going to be, as the name implies, a traditional layout.

The Tradition is being developed by the same group that owns two new and successful public courses in the Charlotte region — The Divide and Charlotte Golf Links. We're told that The Tradition will be a parkland-style course that's similar in design and feel to a country club course in the area. The property is relatively hilly and wooded. In keeping with the true tradition of the game, the course is designed to be walkable, and you'll be allowed to walk. We can't tell exactly what this course will be like once it's finished, but based on the ownership and the people involved, The Tradition should be worth a visit and an interesting addition to the portfolio of courses in the Charlotte region.

No word yet on amenities or specific walking policies. The cost, including cart, for 18 holes will be in the $30 to $40 range.

Westport Golf Course

7494 Golf Course Dr., Denver • 483-5604
Championship Yardage: 6805
Slope: 123   Par: 72
Men's Yardage: 6291
Slope: 118   Par: 72
Ladies' Yardage: 5597
Slope: 118   Par: 72
Westport Golf Course opened in 1968. Porter Gibson designed the course, which is set on rolling wooded terrain. Bermudagrass blankets the fairways, and bentgrass covers the greens.

Westport has been popular for quite some time with the droves of Charlotte golfers who gladly make the 30-minute trek to the western shores of Lake Norman in search of a fun round at a sensible price on a well-designed course.

Even though Lake Norman is close by, it does not come into play, and water is a factor on only a few holes. What makes Westport a popular course is the pretty setting combined with the ample variety and challenge. There's decent room off the tee on most holes, and the greens are medium-size, predominantly sloped and not excessively bunkered. Gibson placed some light mounding around the green complexes as well. For many years, the course was famous (or infamous) for its 4th hole, a 424-yard par 4 where you had to lay up with a mid-iron off the tee; you then had to hit a long-iron or fairway wood off a tight downhill lie over a lake and uphill to a large green, where three-putting was a distinct possibility. The most popular score on the hole was "X." The State of North Carolina recently forced the course to dredge part of the lake (why, we're not sure), and the result was that the hole evened out, making it slightly less difficult.

With all the new courses under construction closer to Charlotte, it will be interesting to see how Westport fares. If courses like Westport are going to prosper, it will be important to maintain the track to consistently high standards year round.

Amenities include a practice green, driving range, locker room, snack bar, rental clubs and a pro shop.

You can walk the course anytime during the week and after 2 PM on weekends. You can book a tee time whenever you choose for the weekdays and on Wednesday for the upcoming weekend. Approximate cost, including cart, is $20 weekdays and $26 on weekends.

Woodbridge Golf Links

**1007 New Camp Creek Church Rd.,
Kings Mountain • 482-0353, 338-9024
Championship Yardage: 6743
Slope: 131   Par: 72
Men's Yardage: 6156
Slope: 121   Par: 72
Ladies' Yardage: 5054
Slope: 127   Par: 73**

Woodbridge Golf Links opened in 1971. Porter Gibson and Bob Toski designed the course, which is set on rolling, partially wooded terrain. The fairways are blanketed with bermudagrass; on the greens, you'll find bentgrass.

J. Porter Gibson is a well-known and respected Charlotte-based golf course architect. He has worked with the likes of Sam Snead and, for a while, Bob Toski, the re-nowned instructor who still plays in the Paine Webber Seniors Tournament at Piper Glen. Gibson was a leader in the development of wastewater irrigation systems for golf courses. Bet you didn't know that!

Woodbridge is owned by the same people who own the Beck Mercedes auto dealership in Charlotte. The solid ownership has meant that the course has developed a reputation for good maintenance. This reputation has in turn meant that the course has attracted numerous golfers from the Charlotte and Gastonia areas. It's always been a popular and challenging course with a sound design. Woodbridge also has hosted a women's collegiate golf tournament.

The front nine is set in open terrain and features a number of holes where water comes into play. The course is at its prettiest on the back nine, where several holes dip into woodland next to a rivulet. A wooden bridge crosses the rivulet after the 600-yard par 5 No. 13 (hence the course's name). The greens are large enough that club selection becomes a significant issue on many holes. There's plenty of room off the tee, so you'll be fine taking the big stick out and giving the ball a good thump. Water comes into play in a number of instances and could really irritate you and lead to some big numbers.

Woodbridge is a fun and playable course that stands a good chance of remaining popular in the face of all the competition from the new courses coming on line in the Charlotte area.

Amenities include a practice green, driving range, locker room, snack bar, rental clubs, a beverage cart and pro shop.

The course is walkable for the fit, and you can walk anytime during the week. You can book a tee time seven days in advance for the week and on Monday for the weekend. Approximate cost, including cart, is $26 weekdays and $35 on weekends.

New Courses in the Charlotte Region

In the first edition of *The Insiders' Guide*® *to Golf in the Carolinas*, we discussed a number of courses now included in this chapter's

"Golf Courses" section. However, a handful of courses are pending.

Charlotte real estate magnate B.V. Belk (no relation to the retailers) is building a new course east of Charlotte to be named **Olde Sycamore**. Tom Jackson is the architect. The course should open in spring 1997 and will feature a lot of the touches that make Jackson one of the foremost golf course architects in the Carolinas. According to our sources, the owners gave him a great piece of wooded land near Mint Hill. Look for this course to be one of the best in the Charlotte region once it's matured and grown in.

Charlotte is well known as a hub of NASCAR activity. Charlotte Motor Speedway is the engine that drives much of this activity, and the speedway is slated to build and develop a golf course. There's no news of exactly when this might happen.

The same can be said of **Waterford** and **Crystal Lakes**, two courses originally scheduled for completion in 1996 or 1997.

Fox Den near Statesville promises to be an accessible course to Charlotte golfers. It's a 45-minute drive from Uptown on I-77. The course is being built in tandem with a housing development. Clyde Johnston is designing the course, and it's scheduled to open in late 1996. Johnston is well-known as a former associate of Willard Byrd, one of the finest architects in the Carolinas. According to owners, Fox Den promises excellent variety. Some holes will remind you of mountain golf; others will remind you of beach-type courses.

The next few years are going to be great ones for the long-suffering Charlotte public golfer. Stay tuned for details.

In and Around the Charlotte Area . . .

Fun Things To Do

Charlotte is a working town, so you're not going to find a large number of really touristy things to do and see. You will, however, discover some major attractions that draw people from all over the city and surrounding counties.

As Charlotte is the retailing epicenter of the Carolinas, **SouthPark Mall**, 4400 Sharon Road, Charlotte, 364-4411, is the retailing epicenter of Charlotte. In addition to Belk, Hecht's and Dillard's, there are more than 100 retail stores, including a Warner Brothers Store, two Victoria's Secret shops, Pea in the Pod, the Nature Conservancy and Brooks Brothers. The mall is well-run, clean and an excellent place for those who love to shop. Amid the myriad retail stores, you'll find a number of interesting eateries. Besides SouthPark, there are three other malls in this area offering a fine collection of specialty shops: Specialty Shops on The Park, Morrocroft Village and Sharon Corners.

Discovery Place, 301 N. Tryon Street, Charlotte, 845-3882, is a nationally known state-of-the-art science museum. It's a hands-on type of place that will fascinate children of all ages. Wander around the numerous displays and well-designed exhibits. Learn about subjects such as the rain forest, electricity, weather and moon exploration. This is a great place to spend hours discovering the nature of the world around you.

Once you've finished your museum tour, step over to the Charlotte Observer Omnimax theater. Watch a movie in a special surround-sound environment that truly has to be seen to be believed — it's like watching a movie on all four walls of the theater while sitting in a dentist's chair.

Charlotte is successfully on the map as a sports town. The **Charlotte Hornets** of the National Basketball Association's Eastern Conference play in the Charlotte Coliseum on Tyrola Road W. and come close to selling out each and every home game. NBA action Hornets-style is a never-ending barrage of noise and off-court entertainment. If you're a fan of excellent dancing, you'll enjoy the cheerleading squad, affectionately known as the Honeybees. For ticket information, call 357-0252.

The **Carolina Panthers** franchise is one of the two newest entrants in the National Football League. The Panthers began their existence in the NFL with a startlingly successful season and have now moved into a state-of-the-art home: Ericsson Stadium on S. Mint Street. Call 358-1644 for more information.

The 1996-97 season marks the **Charlotte Checkers** fourth ice-hockey campaign at Independence Arena, 2700 Independence Boulevard, Charlotte, 342-4423 — known to locals as the "Big I." The Checkers play in the East Coast Hockey League — the hockey equivalent of Class AA baseball. The team is affiliated with the Boston Bruins and New York Rangers of the NHL and the Chicago Wolves of the IHL. The season starts in October and lasts until mid-April. In 1996, the Checkers won the Riley Cup as champions of the league.

There's nothing quite like minor league ice hockey. The Checkers were popular in the 1950s, '60s and early '70s until the league folded. The revamped Checkers feature youthful players who hope that their stay in Charlotte lasts but a season. ECHL teams can only have three players with three or more years of professional experience on the roster. Plenty of players are eager to prove themselves worthy of a better league, so the action is always fast, furious and hard-hitting. And, yes, there is the occasional incident where players drop their gloves and engage in fist-to-fist combat. It's part of the game. In the Checkers' first season the team mascot, a 7-foot-tall bear named Chubby, got into a fight with player Sebastien LaPlante of the Greensboro Monarchs over the use of a water pistol.

Yes, there's never a dull moment at a Checkers game. Plenty of home games sell out. As you enter the Big I, turn left and say hello to the ticket-taker named Betty.

Opened in 1992 in tandem with the tallest building in the Carolinas — the NationsBank Corporate Center — the **Blumenthal Performing Arts Center**, 130 N. Tryon Street, Charlotte, 372-1000, is a testament to Charlotte's commitment to the arts. The Blumenthal Center is home to the Charlotte Symphony Orchestra, Opera Carolina and numerous other arts groups. The main performing hall seats about 2,000 patrons.

In the course of a recent year, events included an opera, a symphony, a rock 'n' roll performance, Carol Channing in Hello Dolly and a major dance production. The adjacent state-of-the-art Belk Theater seats about 400 in a warm

Charlotte's Renaissance course is one of the more popular public courses in the region. Extensive changes are planned in 1996.

and intimate setting. Consult a copy of the *Charlotte Observer* to see what's playing.

Charlotte Motor Speedway, N.C. Highway 49 N., Concord, 455-2121, is the place for stock-car racing, or NASCAR as it is more commonly known. It's a major industry in the Charlotte region, and many of the top racing teams are headquartered just a smooth 3-wood from the speedway. There are three major races at CMS — the Winston Select and the Coca-Cola 600 in May and the Mello-Yellow 500 in the fall. Each race event is replete with "extracurricular activities," so come prepared for long days in the sun — the local population provides much of the entertainment. During the year, there are many ancillary events including auto fairs, demonstrations, non-NASCAR races and exhibitions. Call to arrange a tour of the facility. For motorsports fans, a trip to Charlotte is not complete without a stop at CMS.

Paramount's Carowinds, south of Charlotte, just off I-77 on Carowinds Boulevard, Fort Mill, South Carolina, 588-2600, has been one of the Charlotte region's biggest attractions for years. It was called simply "Carowinds" until corporate giant Paramount bought the theme park.

It must be one of the most entertaining places in the Carolinas: from long, screaming roller coasters and water rides to smaller-scale carousels designed for smaller-scale people. The larger, more involved roller coasters are some of the most radical in the Southeast. You'll be turned upside-down at high speeds on The Vortex, a stand-up roller coaster. In addition to the rides, Carowinds' Palladium is a great place to see pop-music concerts in the summer months.

The **Mint Museum of Art**, 3730 Randolph Road, Charlotte, 337-2000, is housed in the city's former 19th-century federal mint, a fact that in part explains why the town is such a banking center today.

For an art museum nestled in one of Charlotte's oldest neighborhoods, the Mint is a pretty hopping place. Various auxiliaries and affiliated organizations spend a lot of time and energy keeping the museum alive and funded, so it's quite a social center as well. There's always at least one exhibit going on in addition to the regular collection, including one of the world's best accumulations of pre-Columbian art.

The museum is closed on Mondays.

Where to Eat

Refer to our Preface for an explanation of the pricing code.

Charlotte

Dilworth Brewing Company

$ • 1301 East Blvd., Charlotte • 377-2739

Dilworth Brewing Company, or Dilworth Brewery as it's better known, has been a stalwart on the Charlotte restaurant scene for a number of years. All the beer is brewed on the premises — it's all excellent. There's nothing like good fresh beer, and the brewmaster at this wonderful establishment has been improving his ales for some time. The place has been open for a while — it has a wonderful lived-in feel and coziness usually reserved for an old pub. The food also has improved over the years to the point where you can complement your pint with anything from chicken wings to a burger or a fresh fish entree. It's also an excellent value.

La Bibliotheque

$$$ • 1901 Rexford Rd., Charlotte • 365-5000

La Bibliotheque has become one of Charlotte's best fine restaurants. You'll want to wear a coat and tie for dinner at this award-winning establishment. Owner Adam Kantback runs the restaurant as if it's his home, and he greets you with a hospitality and grace that you won't find in many places. Although located in an office building, its ambiance is that of a fine French restaurant. The service is impeccable, and the menu is diverse and exciting but rooted in French cuisine.

La Bibliotheque is open for a remarkably reasonable lunch, but things are at their best during dinner. This place is best suited to a full-course meal, and you need to take your time, have an appetizer, clear the palate, order a good bottle of wine and then indulge in some dessert. Round out the meal with a glass of port and you'll be in heaven until you wake up. Don't leave without trying the marinated salmon.

FYI

Unless otherwise noted, the area code for all phone numbers in this chapter is 704.

La Paz

$$ • 523 Fenton Pl., Charlotte • 372-4168

La Paz is off Providence Road in Eastover — one of Charlotte's oldest and most venerable neighborhoods. La Paz used to be a house, so the ambiance steers well away from the cookie-cutter type of restaurant so prevalent today. The drinks are generous, and the large selection of Mexican beers is always kept ice-cold. You'll probably find a greater diversity of imaginative Mexican dishes at La Paz than at most Mexican establishments. It's a lot of fun and always popular with old-money locals.

Manzetti's

$$ • 6401 Morrison Blvd., Charlotte • 364-9334

In the SouthPark area's Specialty Shops on the Park, Manzetti's has long been a popular stop on the drinking and dining scene. It's a pretty trendy place, so come expecting to see a number of slightly aging yuppie-types dressed to kill. The atmosphere is definitely "fern bar," with bright brass rails and dark wood predominating. The food is outstanding; menu items include fun appetizers and a number of traditional American entrees. There's plenty to drink at the bar, and it's always crowded with fun people. It's a great place for a relaxed outing with friends.

Providence Cafe

$$ • 110 Perrin Pl., Charlotte • 376-2008

If you're looking for an excellent meal for your dollar, then look no further than Providence Cafe, just off Providence Road near the intersection of Providence and Queens. If you get lost in this area of Charlotte, don't worry — you're not the first and certainly not the last. As you enter Providence Cafe, you might be fooled into thinking that you're going to spend a lot of "cashola," but don't worry — your bill for a big session will be less than you think. In addition to a fine array of beverages, the mildly eclectic menu features a number of interesting selections that won't increase your overdraft.

Cornelius

Kobe Japanese House of Steak and Seafood
$$$ • 20465 Chartwell Center Dr., Cornelius • 896-7778

If you've never been to a Japanese steakhouse, here's your chance. It's all here and it's all good. There's the sushi bar, where the expert sushi chef will prepare your California Roll along with that green radioactive horseradish that's guaranteed to clear out your sinuses no matter how bad your head cold. Then there's the show itself. The authentic Teppan-Yaki show where the ambidextrous chef dices and slices the meal right before your eyes, sizzling the rice, making the shrimp dance and the steak do the fandango. Wash it down with some sake and you've received the full Japanese steak house experience. It's best to go in a party of 10 so you can dominate a table and have a chef all to yourself.

Davidson

North Harbor Cafe
$$-$$$ • 181 North Harbor Dr., Davidson Landing • 892-3855

Literally inches from Lake Norman, it's possible to drive your boat right up to the North Harbor Cafe then drive it back to your lakeside mansion. Because of its accessibility to the lake and its fine views of the water, this ranks as one of the area's hot spots, especially if you dine outside in the middle of a midsummer day. Call ahead for reservations. The menu includes fresh fish, steaks, chicken dishes, fajitas, burgers, sandwiches, soups, salads and a full list of great desserts. It's sounds like pretty standard fare, but the quality of the preparation and the lakeside feel make North Harbor Cafe one of the most popular spots on the eastern shores of Lake Norman.

Denver

Jones Fish Camp
$ • N.C. Hwy. 16, Denver • 483-2480

For more than 43 years, Jones Fish Camp has been serving up the stuff that fish camps

are all about — great fish and down-home, nothing-fancy ambiance. In addition to broiled and fried seafood, you'll find ribeye steaks, prime rib and chicken dishes. So there's more to Jones Fish Camp than just fish. But you will also find a staple fish camp specialty here: iced tea that's so sweet and so strong and so iced that a spoon will stand to attention in it.

Gastonia

El Cancun
$ • 516 E. Garrison St., Gastonia • 853-2855

Take a tasty trip to Mexico at one of the Charlotte region's greatest venues. If you like Mexican food but don't want to spend a fortune on it, head for El Cancun. Your waiter or waitress (always Mexican) will bring you chips with excellent salsa. After that, you should skip reading the menu and indulge in the cream burritos. But all the choices on this extensive menu are wonderful. Wash it all down with a Dos Equis or two.

Hillbilly's Bar-B-Que and Steaks
$$ • 930 E. Garrison Blvd., Gastonia • 861-8787

Yer invited for supper here at Hillbillys, which describes itself as a "cook-out inside." You'll find some of the best pit barbecue in town, in addition to hickory-cooked rib eye and New York Strip steaks. Also enjoy ribs, chicken, pork, beef, sizable hot dogs, hamburgers and a pretty extensive kids menu as well. Hillbillys will also cater anything from family reunions to shotgun weddings.

Where to Stay

Refer to our Preface for an explanation of the pricing code.

Charlotte

The Dunhill Hotel
$$$ • 237 N. Tryon St., Charlotte • 332-4141

The Dunhill is in Uptown Charlotte near the new NationsBank tower. It's in an old building with the ambiance of an Old World bed

Former PGA SENIOR TOUR player Gordon Jones practices for the annual Paine-Webber Seniors at the TPC at Piper Glen.

and breakfast inn that makes it a great alternative to the larger chain-style hotels. Yet it's extremely convenient to the central business district, library and Discovery Place (see our "Fun Things To Do" section). You'll find a restaurant on the ground floor, in addition to services tailored to the business traveler.

Hilton at University Place
$$-$$$ • 6929 JM Keynes Dr., Charlotte
• 547-7444

Just off I-85 near the University of North Carolina at Charlotte, the Hilton at University Place is a fully appointed 240-room hotel. The Hilton is convenient to the university area (hence its name), but it's also near Charlotte Motor Speedway, all the new office developments in the area, a couple of fine golf courses (including Highland Creek) and the new hospital. So should you be suddenly hit by a flying golf ball and need some stitches to your head, the Hilton will be a convenient place to recuperate.

The Park Hotel
$$$ • 2200 Rexford Rd., Charlotte
• 364-8220

In the heart of SouthPark, with some of the best shopping in the Southeast just a short walk away, the Park offers great location and excellent service. The Park is well-known in Charlotte as one of the best hotels in the city. In fact, it's where the players in the Paine Webber Senior PGA tournament stay. With nearly 200 rooms, the Park boasts a European feel. Morrocroft's Restaurant, on the first floor, is an outstanding place to eat. Amenities at The Park Hotel include several meeting rooms, an outdoor swimming pool with a whirlpool, two ballrooms and a newsstand plus full meeting and banquet facilities. Wayne Shusko is one of the friendliest, most helpful and most experienced hotel managers in Charlotte. The Park enjoys tremendous repeat business, with good reason.

Radisson Plaza Hotel
$$$ • 2 NationsBank Plaza, Charlotte
• 377-0400

The Radisson Plaza in Uptown Charlotte was one of the city's first large hotels with connections to a large chain. It's a magnificent accommodation, with close to 400 rooms

and a bunch of meeting rooms and entertainment suites. If you're in Uptown and you're looking for a first-class hotel with every amenity under the sun, then you won't go wrong here.

Concord

Holiday Inn Express
$$ • 1601 N.C. Hwy. 29 N., Concord
• 786-5181

Convenient to I-85 and Concord, this Holiday Inn Express offers a comfortable place to stay at a comfortable rate. You get free local and Charlotte calls, free breakfast bar, free newspaper and free cable with HBO and ESPN on a 26-inch color TV with remote control. There are in-room refrigerators, nonsmoking rooms and free 18-wheeler parking. In addition, you'll get a discount on your room if you're a member of AARP, and there's fax and copy service.

Cornelius

Holiday Inn Lake Norman
$$ • I-77 and N.C. Hwy. 73, Cornelius
• 892-9120

On the east side of Lake Norman, the Holiday Inn is convenient not only to the lake but to the entire Charlotte region. The hotel has 119 guest rooms, offers a free breakfast buffet, a restaurant and lounge, a pool and a fitness room as well as meeting and banquet facilities. If you're someone who can't survive the day without a cup of coffee, rest easy here: You'll find an in-room coffee maker at your disposal.

Gastonia

Comfort Inn
$$ • I-85 and N.C. Hwy. 161, Gastonia
• 739-7070

Convenient to West Gastonia and I-85, this new and friendly Comfort Inn boasts a number of amenities including in-room microwaves and refrigerators, free deluxe continental breakfast, cable TV with HBO and ESPN, fax and copy service and a laundry room. If you really want to splash out, spend the extra cash for the executive Jacuzzi room.

Econo Lodge

$$ • I-85 and N.C. Hwy. 274, Gastonia
• 867-1821

Just seconds from the always bustling I-85, Gastonia's Econo Lodge offers a swimming pool, free cable TV (with HBO), free local calls, continental breakfast and meeting rooms. Inquire about seniors' and other discounts.

Golf Equipment

One of the leaders in golf retailing in Charlotte is **Pro Golf Discount**. The three stores in Charlotte offer an outstanding variety of equipment for players of all levels. If you want the latest state-of-the-art clubs custom fitted to your swing, you can find that here as well. If your golfing budget is limited, Pro Golf offers playable clubs perfect for those who are just starting the game. Pro Golf stocks a variety of putters and utility clubs that you won't find anywhere else. You'll also find a good selection of name-brand accessories, including gloves, shoes, shirts, balls and bags. Stop by any of the three locations in Charlotte: Central Avenue, 536-9021; South Boulevard, 523-7262; and Pineville, 541-6950.

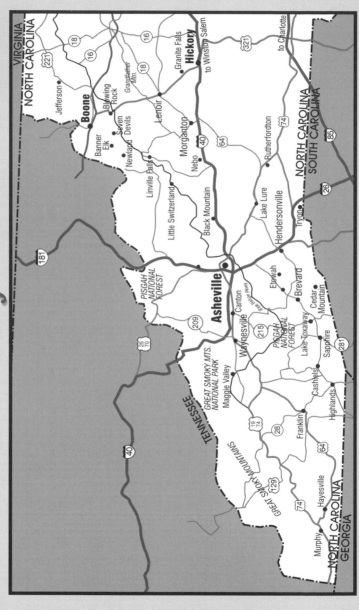

The Mountains of North Carolina

North Carolina's Mountains

Stretching from the deep valleys around Murphy to the foothills around Hendersonville and North Wilkesboro, the North Carolina mountains offer some spectacular scenery and excellent opportunities for rest and relaxation. Basically, the entire western section of North Carolina is one big mountainous forest populated with a wonderful variety of hardwood trees, plants and flowers. It's where the Appalachians begin, and it's where the Appalachians might be at their prettiest and most dramatic.

For more than a century and a half, the North Carolina mountains have been a year-round haven for vacationers from all over the eastern seaboard and beyond. Many of said visitors bring their golf clubs. In the early part of this century, golf was mostly limited to the resorts, where guests were the only people allowed on the adjoining course. In the 1920s, architects built courses for private memberships. It's only in the past 20 years that a number of purely public and semiprivate courses have opened. Today, due in part to the lack of population in the mountains, many courses don't appear quite as crowded as their counterparts to the east.

The steep wooded hillsides of the mountains and the lush and verdant valleys have provided magnificent canvases for some of the world's greatest golf course architects. Donald Ross, Jack Nicklaus, Tom Fazio (who lives in Hendersonville), Fred Hawtree, Martin Hawtree, Tom Jackson, George Cobb and Ellis Maples have produced fine work in the mountains, although many of their courses are private.

The line between public and private courses is sometimes somewhat ill-defined in the mountains. At quite a few private courses, you can play if you rent a house, condo or apartment for a week. In our minds, that still means they're private, so these courses have not been reviewed or included in this chapter. However, we've included a number of courses where you can get a tee time if you stay at an accompanying hotel or inn. But if a tent or Winnebago is more your style, we've included a number of courses where you can strap on your golf shoes in the parking lot, plunk down some cash in the pro shop and play away to your heart's content.

Natural and moderate undulations in the land often provide the golf course architect with the best sites for golf courses; obviously, the mountains present some wonderful landscapes. And with the arrival of the golf cart and modern earth moving equipment, many sites that would not have been viable in the past have been used to create stunning courses.

It's interesting to see how designers have adapted their styles to the mountainous terrain. For example, if your home course is designed by George Cobb, it's probably a difficult layout, lengthy and trying. Here in the mountains, Cobb may have realized that many golfers are probably on vacation, so he turned down the difficulty meter and produced tracks that are a little more user-friendly. The key to a good course in the mountains is a good

FYI

Unless otherwise noted, the area code for all phone numbers in this chapter is 704.

GOLF COURSES IN NORTH CAROLINA'S MOUNTAINS

Name	Type	# Holes	Par	Slope	Yards	Walking	Booking	Cost w/ Cart
Apple Valley Golf Club	public	18	72	130	6297	no	30 days	$40
Bald Mountain	public/resort	18	72	121	6125	restricted	30 days	$40
Black Mountain Golf Course	semiprivate	18	71	n/r	5780	restricted	6 dats	$25-30
Blue Ridge	semiprivate	18	72	n/a	6862	restricted	anytime	$39-41
Boone Golf Club	semiprivate	18	71	112	5859	restricted	7 days	$40-45
Buncome County Muni	public	18	72	107	5929	anytime	3 days	$23
Chatuge Shores	public	18	72	118	6269	restricted	3 days	$24
Cleghorn Plantation	public	18	72	126	6313	no	anytime	$22-30
Crooked Creek Golf Club	public	18	72	n/r	6267	restricted	2 days	$25
Cummings Cove Golf and CC	semiprivate	18	70	n/r	5720	restricted	anytime	$25
Etowah Valley Country Club								
South/West Course	resort	18	72	123	6880	restricted	anytime	$43
West/North Course	resort	18	73	122	6700	restricted	anytime	$43
North/South Course	resort	18	73	121	6604	restricted	anytime	$43
French Broad Golf Center	public	18	72	115	6313	restricted	7 days	$36-38
Glen Cannon	semiprivate	18	72	121	6272	no	3 days	$50
Granada Farms	semiprivate	18	72	112	5835	restricted	anytime	$20-23
Grassy Creek Golf and CC	public	18	72	116	5774	restricted	7 days	$32-35
Great Smokies Hilton	public/resort	18	70	117	5131	restricted	anytime	$26-32
Grove Park Inn	semiprivate/resort	18	71	119	6033	restricted	anytime	$60
Hawksnest Ski and Golf	semiprivate	18	72	110	5953	restricted	7 days	$32-36
High Hampton Inn	semiprivate/resort	18	71	120	6012	anytime	1 day	$37-48
Hound Ears Club	resort	18	72	120	6036	restricted	anytime	$48
Jefferson Landing	semiprivate/resort	18	72	115	6424	no	anytime	$39-49
Lake Junaluska Golf Course	public	18	68	n/r	4579	anytime	anytime	$21

Name	Type	# Holes	Par	Slope	Yards	Walking	Booking	Cost w/ Cart
Lake Toxaway	resort	18	71	116	5594	anytime	anytime	$62
Lenoir Golf Course	semiprivate	18	71	106	5886	anytime	anytime	$22
Linville Golf Club	resort	18	72	n/a	6780	restricted	anytime	$50
Maggie Valley Resort and CC	resort	18	72	118	6031	restricted	anytime	$48
Marion Lake Club	semiprivate	18	70	n/r	5710	anytime	anytime	$39-49
Meadowbrook Golf Club	public	18	72	105	5850	anytime	anytime	$20-25
Mill Creek	semiprivate	18	72	113	5775	restricted	2 days	$38
Mountain Aire	semiprivate	18	71	n/a	5571	anytime	anytime	$28-32
Mountain Glen Golf Club	semiprivate	18	72	119	6195	anytime	7 days	$35
Mount Mitchell Golf Club	public	18	72	116	6110	restricted	14 days	$40-45
Olde Beau Golf Club	semiprivate	18	72	129	6264	no	14 days	$40-50
Orchard Hills Golf Club	semiprivate	18	72	106	5673	restricted	4 days	$22-26
Quaker Meadows Golf Course	public	18	71	108	6133	restricted	anytime	$20-24
Red Fox Country Club	semiprivate	18	72	124	6393	no	anytime	$30-35
Reems Creek Golf Course	semiprivate	18	72	127	6106	no	anytime	$38-42
Sapphire Mountain Golf Club	public	18	70	118	5690	no	30 days	$25
Springdale Country Club	semiprivate/resort	18	72	121	6437	anytime	anytime	$35
Village of Sugar Mountain GC	public	18	64	91	4198	yes	5 days	$29-30
Waynesville Country Club Inn								
Carolina/Dogwood Course	semiprivate/resort	18	70	100	5395	restricted	anytime	$41
Dogwood/Blue Ridge Course	semiprivate/resort	18	70	100	5258	restricted	anytime	$41
Blue Ridge/Carolina Course	semiprivate/resort	18	70	100	5493	restricted	anytime	$41

layout, and the better designers make use of the hazards and difficulties produced by Mother Nature. Thus, you'll find plenty of elevation changes on many courses in addition to potentially annoying small streams.

One of the great golfing difficulties in the mountains is judging distance. You'll be faced with plenty of shots where you're shooting straight uphill or downhill. A decent rule of thumb is to take two extra clubs for an uphill shot and one less if it's seriously downhill. Learn how to play the steep embankments that you'll find on many mountain courses. At courses where the elevation is above 4,000 feet, your golf ball may fly a little farther.

The most noticeable difference between the older and newer courses is the layout. Older courses tend to meander around valley floors, while the modern ones venture forth into the hills and, with the help of your golf cart, you'll be able to smack the ball from mountaintop to mountaintop. Almost.

The seasons and climate are quite different from the plains of North and South Carolina. Summers can be warm or even hot. Spring and fall boast temperate days when you might need a sweater or rain gear, while winter life can include snow, sleet, wind, rain, crisp temperatures and bright sun. Some courses choose to stay open all year, while others close up shop. Thus, in winter it's essential to call a course before you leave the driveway or hotel parking lot. The cooler summer temperatures mean that courses can use bentgrass or bluegrass in the fairways. Is there a prettier sight on a golf course than a crosscut bentgrass fairway on a bright autumn day in the North Carolina mountains? On the greens, you'll find bentgrass greens almost exclusively. Cooler temperatures mean that golf courses can keep their greens wonderfully fast, so keep your ball below the hole whenever possible.

Fall and spring bring a fair share of visitors to the mountains, but no season is quite like summer, when it seems that most of Florida moves here for at least three months. Many of these migratory birds are part of the older generation of Americans, and they live to play golf. They venture forth onto the course with no other agenda for the day apart from having a great time and perhaps a vodka and tonic at cocktail time (ahhh — what a life!).

After the monotonous flatness of almost every golf course in Florida, our golfing brothers and sisters really enjoy the undulation changes and bentgrass greens.

Enjoy golf in the mountains, and don't let the terrain bother you too much. Remember that most people are playing golf as part of a getaway from the real world, so take the leisurely pace in stride, enjoy the fine views, the relaxing ambiance and the fine and varied challenges that some of the greatest golf architects in the world have produced for your golfing pleasure.

Note that we've divided this chapter geographically into three sections: the Asheville area west, the Boone/Blowing Rock area and the Hickory/Lenoir area. We realize the tourism bureaus probably wouldn't divide things this way. But the Mountains region is widespread enough that we thought it helpful to write about the courses that are in your general vicinity, no matter where in the mountains you may be.

Asheville Area

Generally the courses we profile for you in this section are west of Asheville, but we do include a few, such as the Black Mountain Golf Course and Meadowbrook in Rutherford, that lie east of the city. We felt these areas were more closely allied with greater Asheville than our other mountain regions.

Apple Valley Golf Club
201 Boulevard of the Mountains, Lake Lure • 652-2888

Championship Yardage: 6726	
Slope: 138	**Par: 72**
Men's Yardage: 6297	
Slope: 130	**Par: 72**
Other Yardage: 5511	
Slope: 118	**Par: 72**
Ladies' Yardage: 4661	
Slope: 114	**Par: 72**

Apple Valley opened in 1985. Like its sister course, Bald Mountain, Apple Valley is part of the Fairfield Mountain Golf Resort. Dan Maples, son of Ellis Maples, designed the course. Some holes are flat; others are set in rolling terrain. Fairways are bermudagrass, and greens are bentgrass.

Apple Valley is a fine mountain course. Interestingly, you'll be hard pressed to understand why the slope rating is so high from the back tees. We must assume that the course is a lot tougher than it looks. Play it from the middle or front tees if you're a mid to high handicapper.

The course boasts a number of interesting holes. We particularly enjoyed the par 4 12th that plays 369 yards from the back tees. A mountain stream bisects the hole. From the tee, you'll have to decide whether to lay up or try to smack it over the stream. Go for it successfully, and the approach shot is less fraught with difficulty. Many of the holes are bordered by woods. The greens are fairly large and sloped, with the occasional buried elephant in the green complex. A couple of holes feature interesting blind shots where local knowledge is a big plus. Water frequently comes into play. Overall, Apple Valley is a fun and interesting course designed by one of the finest and most respected architects in the Carolinas. We'd play this one over Bald Mountain, although if you're at the resort for two days, play both courses.

Amenities include a practice green, range, locker room, snack bar, rental clubs and pro shop.

You must take a cart here. You can book a tee time 30 days in advance. Approximate cost, including cart, is $40 weekdays and weekends.

Bald Mountain
201 Boulevard of the Mountains, Lake Lure • 625-3040
Championship Yardage: 6575
Slope: 125	**Par: 72**
Men's Yardage: 6125	
Slope: 121	**Par: 72**
Other Yardage: 5208	
Slope: 108	**Par: 72**
Ladies' Yardage: 4808	
Slope: 112	**Par: 72**

Bald Mountain, a Willie B. Lewis design, opened in 1974. Most of the holes are bordered by woods. The rolling fairways are covered with bermudagrass, the greens with bentgrass.

Bald Mountain is part of the Fairfield Mountain Golf Resort. We found a genuine and challenging mountain track that's fun from any of the tees. If you're a movie buff or a fan of Patrick Swayze, you'll enjoy the 16th green, where part of the cinematic masterpiece *Dirty Dancing* was filmed. In fact, a good bit of the movie was filmed in and around the resort town of Lake Lure. Great movies aside, the course is worth playing, particularly in tandem with Apple Valley, its sister course.

You'll need to keep the ball straight off the tee and away from the hazards, including several bunkers and a mountain stream.

Amenities include a practice green, range, locker room, bar, snack bar, restaurant, rental clubs, beverage cart and pro shop.

The course is walkable for the physically fit, and you can walk after 2 PM. You can book a tee time 30 days in advance. Approximate cost, including cart, is $40 weekdays and weekends.

Black Mountain Golf Course

17 Ross Dr., Black Mountain • 669-2710
Championship Yardage: 6181
Slope: 129   **Par: 71**
Men's Yardage: 5780
Slope: No rating   **Par: 71**
Ladies' Yardage: 4959
Slope: No rating   **Par: 71**

The front nine at Black Mountain opened in the 1930s, and a back nine opened in the 1960s. Ross Taylor designed the course, which mixes open holes with those bordered and framed with woods. In the fairways, you'll find a combination of bluegrass and bentgrass; on the greens, you'll find bentgrass.

Here at Black Mountain, we found a playable and justifiably popular course, with good variety and interest. Locals inform us that the back nine is more difficult than the front. The front provides significant difficulties in the form of streams, small greens, small mounds, bunkers and narrow fairways. Difficulties on the back come from some longer par 4s, plenty of creeks, undulating greens plus the world's longest and perhaps only par 6 — the 747-yard 17th. With the small greens here, you'll need to plan your approach shots and manage your short game with a degree of precision.

Amenities include a practice green, snack bar, rental clubs and pro shop.

The course is walkable for the fit and you can walk anytime except weekend mornings. You can book a tee time six days in advance. Approximate cost, including cart, is $25 weekdays and $30 weekends.

Buncombe County Municipal Golf Course

226 Fairway Dr., Asheville • 298-1867
Championship Yardage: 6356
Slope: 115   **Par: 72**
Men's Yardage: 5929
Slope: 107   **Par: 72**
Ladies' Yardage: 4897
Slope: 109   **Par: 72**

Buncombe County Municipal Golf Course opened in 1927. Donald Ross designed the course. Fairways are bermudagrass, and greens are bentgrass. The front nine is flat and open, while the back nine is wooded, tighter and much more rolling.

Quick, how many counties have a municipal course designed by the famed Donald Ross? Answer, not many. Here at Buncombe Municipal, you'll find a fine and straightforward Ross layout that doesn't look like it's been touched since it opened. We found a sensible layout, with small and flat bunkers fronting large crowned greens. The significant difference in layout between the back and the front nines makes the course all the more interesting. We were told that the course is host to close to 50,000 rounds a year. If you've got a twenty spot burning a hole in your pocket, and if you've never played a Donald Ross course, you

INSIDERS' TIP

If you're a mid- or high handicapper, time spent practicing your short game will help you avoid big blowups and big numbers. Once your short game has improved, you can plan your approach shots to maximize the effectiveness of your short game.

Golf in North Carolina's mountains features spectacular scenery and mild weather.

should stop by for a round. Just be careful on the 9th hole: If you airmail your approach shot, you'll hit a car in the parking lot . . . no free drop from the front seat of a Jaguar, even if you've just smashed the windshield.

Amenities include a practice green, snack bar, rental clubs and pro shop.

The course is walkable, you can walk anytime, and you should walk. You'll only need a tee time on weekends and holidays, and you can book three days in advance. Approximate cost, including cart, is $23 on weekends and weekdays.

Chatuge Shores Golf Course
Myers Chapel Rd., Hayesville • 389-8940
Championship Yardage: 6687
Slope: 123	**Par: 72**
Men's Yardage: 6269	
Slope: 118	**Par: 72**
Ladies' Yardage: 4950	
Slope: 120	**Par: 72**

Chatuge Shores Golf Course, designed by J. Townsend, opened in 1969. Some holes are flat, but most feature some undulation. In the fairways, you'll find bermudagrass; on the greens, you'll find bentgrass. Water comes into play on some of the holes.

Chatuge Shores offers a fun, friendly and mature course, presenting challenges for golfers of all levels. The layout is fairly straightforward. Some of the fairways are wide, some are on the narrow side. Trees delineate the fairways. The greens are primarily small and slightly rolling. Bunkers will make you think about the safest approach shot on a number of holes. The main interest comes from the variety in the shape and size of the greens. There aren't many public courses in the immediate area, so Chatuge Shores is definitely worth a visit. It's clearly a popular track, so you won't be alone.

Amenities include a practice green, range, chipping green, snack bar, rental clubs and pro shop.

The course is walkable. You can book a tee time three days in advance. Approximate cost, including cart, is $24.

Cleghorn Plantation Golf and Country Club
200 Golf Cir., Rutherfordton • 286-9117
Championship Yardage: 6903
Slope: 134	**Par: 72**
Men's Yardage: 6313	
Slope: 126	**Par: 72**
Other Yardage: 5679	
Slope: 115	**Par: 72**
Ladies' Yardage: 4751	
Slope: 111	**Par: 73**

The golf course at Cleghorn Plantation, a George Cobb design, opened in 1969. The course is set amid rolling terrain, and many holes are bordered by homes or woods. In the fairways, you'll find bermudagrass; on the greens, bentgrass.

Cleghorn Plantation is a real find. The course may originally have been planned as a private track, but financial hard times in the 1980s probably facilitated the change. A number of recent improvements have been made, and it looked to us like the course is shaping up to be one of the finest in the North Carolina foothills. Many of Cobb's resort/vacation courses are less demanding than his more serious efforts. Cleghorn is not a vacation course.

Play the tips and you're in for a long day unless you can hit the ball a country mile off the tee. Play it from the men's or forward tees for a more sensible outing. The course features a number of epic sweeping holes, including elevated tee shots followed by uphill approach shots to large and heavily bunkered greens, which pitch and roll significantly.

The attraction of the course is the excellent layout, great variety, playability and sensible combination of natural and manmade hazards. It's excellent news for area golfers that this outstanding golf course is on the way up in the world. If you're visiting the area, this is the course to play. If you live in western North Carolina and you're up for a serious challenge, Cleghorn is a must-play for you too. And right now, it's an excellent value as well.

Amenities include a practice green, range, snack bar and pro shop.

A cart is required to play Cleghorn; you may book a tee time whenever you choose. Approximate cost, including cart, is $22 weekdays and $30 on weekends.

Crooked Creek Golf Club
764 Crooked Creek Rd., Hendersonville
• 692-2011
Championship Yardage: 6652
Slope: No rating   Par: 72
Men's Yardage: 6267
Slope: No rating   Par: 72
Ladies' Yardage: 5546
Slope: No rating   Par: 72

Alex Guin and Stewart Goodin designed Crooked Creek Golf Club, which opened in

1968. The course has a wide-open feel; many of the holes are flat and others are set in rolling terrain. Fairways are bermudagrass, and greens are bentgrass.

First, a note about the clubhouse. It was built in World War II by Warner Brothers executives, afraid that the Japanese might invade California, necessitating a move to the East Coast. So if Bugs Bunny shows up unexpectedly and says "What's up, Doc?" right in the middle of your back swing, you'll know why.

This is one of the earliest examples of a course set in a housing development. Homes and out-of-bounds provide potential threats on many holes. You'll find good variety on this course. Some of your tee shots must negotiate narrow fairways. Some of the greens are small, others are midsize to large. Many greens are crowned and sloped, others offer significant undulations. There isn't a lot of water on the course. The most omnipresent hazards are the bunkers around the green complexes; they come in an interesting variety of shapes and sizes. Overall, it's a fun and straightforward track that will provide a decent challenge from the back tees.

Amenities include a practice green, range, snack bar and pro shop.

The course is walkable, although walking is restricted. You can book a tee time two days in advance. Approximate cost, including cart, is $25.

Cummings Cove Golf and Country Club
3000 Cummings Rd., Hendersonville
• 891-9412
Championship Yardage: 6008
Slope: No rating   Par: 70
Men's Yardage: 5720
Slope: No rating   Par: 70

Cummings Cove Golf and Country Club, which originally was called Horseshoe Country Club, opened in 1986. Robert Cupp, a man with an interesting background, designed the course. Cupp is certainly a prolific architect, having designed courses in almost every state in the Union. In the North Carolina

FYI
Unless otherwise noted, the area code for all phone numbers in this chapter is 704.

Profile: Dan Maples

Dan Maples, son of Ellis Maples, lives in Pinehurst. Dan was born in 1947 and was president of the American Society of Golf Course Architects in 1990. Before Dan had his driving license, he was handling earth-moving equipment, helping his father build golf courses.

He attended Wingate Junior College and earned a bachelor's degree in landscape architecture from the University of Georgia in 1972. During the summer months, when he was not studying, Dan helped his father build golf courses. After two years as a professional at Palmetto Country Club, Dan joined the family firm and became a full partner after two years. In the early 1980s, he began his own firm based in Pinehurst.

One of Dan's first designs, Oyster Bay Golf Links, was chosen by *Golf Digest* as the best new resort course in 1993. Dan's hobby is researching the history of course construction in Pinehurst.

Dan is part of the ownership group at Longleaf, a course he designed. In Pinehurst, he also designed The Pit Golf Links. The two courses couldn't be more different, so it's difficult to characterize Dan's design philosophy — although both courses are challenging and fun. (Some would disagree that The Pit is a fun golf course.) Dan seems to enjoy, on just one hole, placing a tree right in the middle of a fairway or anywhere it's likely to cause the most trouble. He has designed a number of well-known courses in the Carolinas, including Cramer Mountain, Keith Hills, Marsh Harbour Golf Links, The Pearl Golf Links, Woodlake, Heritage Plantation and The Witch. He has also designed courses in Alabama, Georgia, Hawaii, Spain, Germany, Virginia and Tennessee.

Dan Maples is in mid-career now, but you can be sure that by the time he's finished designing courses, he'll be rated as one the best.

Photo: The Architects of Golf

Dan Maples
—

---

mountains, he assisted Jack Nicklaus in the design of Elk River, one of the state's most revered private courses. Cupp's resume includes a Master's of Fine Arts degree from the University of Alaska, advertising experience, pro shop management, an associate's degree in agronomy and a significant stint as an associate in the Jack Nicklaus design firm. Cupp has worked with a variety of touring pros, including Tom Kite and Fuzzy Zoeller.

Cupp produced a challenging course here at Cummings Cove. Your tee shots need to be precise though not always very long. Your approach shots must hit small and undulat-

ing greens with little or no bailout potential. Many of the greens are flanked by embankments. The course is bordered by woods and homes.

You'll probably remember two holes in particular. The 10th, a 370-yard par 4 bordered by a lake, provides one of the smallest tee shot landing areas of any course around. And the green on the par 5 No. 5 is horseshoe-shaped; hit the ball to the wrong level of this green and you may have to bring out the lob wedge to get it close to the hole.

Take the challenge of this course if you get the chance. There's an awful lot of target golf here, so keep it straight and you'll have a good round.

Amenities include a practice green and snack bar.

The course is not easy to walk, but you may anytime during the week and after 2 PM on weekends. You can book a tee time whenever you choose. Approximate cost, including cart, is $25.

Etowah Valley Country Club
Brickyard Rd., Etowah Resort
• 891-7022, 891-9412
South/West Course
Championship Yardage: 7108
Slope: 125   Par: 72
Men's Yardage: 6880
Slope: 123   Par: 72
Other Yardage: 6287
Slope: 118   Par: 72
Ladies' Yardage: 5480
Slope: 119   Par: 72
West/North Course
Championship Yardage: 7003
Slope: 124   Par: 73
Men's Yardage: 6700
Slope: 122   Par: 73
Other Yardage: 6215
Slope: 121   Par: 73
Ladies' Yardage: 5319
Slope: 117   Par: 73
North/South Course
Championship Yardage: 6909
Slope: 124   Par: 73
Men's Yardage: 6604
Slope: 121   Par: 73
Other Yardage: 6156
Slope: 118   Par: 73
Ladies' Yardage: 5391
Slope: 115   Par: 73

The South and West courses at Etowah Valley opened in 1967. The North course opened in 1988. Edmund B. Ault designed all three. Ault's credits include only two courses in North Carolina and one full 18-hole course in South Carolina. However, he was a prolific designer who built and redesigned more than 100 courses, primarily in Maryland, Arkansas, Pennsylvania and Virginia. He was a scratch golfer at one stage and played in the national amateur championship. (Bet you didn't know that!)

These well-maintained courses have bentgrass fairways and greens. Overall, all three courses are playable, fun and laid out in a picturesque and mostly flat setting. All of your approach shots will be influenced by large bunkers of varied shapes. On the longer par 4s, you'll often have a chance to run the ball up to the green. All of the green complexes offer bailout areas; if you're a good chipper, head for these areas and avoid the bunkers.

The South Course is primarily flat and somewhat narrow. Water comes into play on quite a few holes in the form of a large pond or mountain stream. The greens are primarily midsize and sloped. Play from the back tees and you'll have a long course to negotiate. If you want a more sensible outing and you're not a long hitter, play from the other (white) tees.

The West Course is also primarily flat, although three holes offer elevation changes. From the tips, the course is even longer than the South Course. The greens might be a little larger, but so are the bunkers!

The newest nine is the North Course. The terrain is more rolling, giving the course a more open feel. A stream will come into play on most holes. The greens are large and undulating. Once again, bunkers will make you think about the most sensible approach to the green.

There's a lodge where you should stay if you definitely want to play Etowah Valley. If you don't stay here, you may be able to get on this course if you call in advance, although resort guest and member play take priority. So there will be times when you'll be told "Sorry, members and guests only." Your chances of playing here if you're not a guest at Etowah Resort are best out of season.

INSIDERS' TIP

A lesson from a PGA professional demonstrating the proper technique for playing out of a sand trap is well worth the small investment.

Amenities include three practice greens, a range, bar, snack bar, restaurant, beverage gazebo, rental clubs and pro shop.

Walking is restricted, although the first two nines are walkable, and you should walk. You can book a tee time with your reservation or two days in advance. Approximate cost for 18 holes, including cart, is $43.

French Broad Golf Center

5 French Broad Ave., Asheville • 687-8545
Championship Yardage: 6857
Slope: 120	**Par: 72**
Men's Yardage: 6313	
Slope: 115	**Par: 72**
Other Yardage: 5881	
Slope: 111	**Par: 72**
Ladies' Yardage: 5082	
Slope: 113	**Par: 72**

The golf course at French Broad Golf Center opened in 1993. Karl Litten designed the course. The layout is remarkably flat and wide open, with woods bordering the course. In the fairways, you'll find rye; on the greens, you'll find bentgrass. The course sits directly in the path of Asheville's airport, so if a 737 cruises by less than 100 feet over your head while you're in the middle of a testy three footer that your opponent should have given you, you still have to drain the ball — you've been warned.

Okay, so who is this Karl Litten guy? Apart from the fact that he's a graduate of Steubenville College, he's an accomplished architect who apprenticed under the flamboyant Robert von Hagge, surely the greatest and most prolific architect who never designed a course in South Carolina. Litten formed his own firm in 1979 and, like his teacher, was very busy in Florida in the 1980s. Litten formed a design partnership with Gary Player in 1987 that continued through 1989. His design here, just south of Asheville, is remarkable in that the ground is almost totally flat — just like in Florida. Trees have been planted, but they shouldn't come into play for years. The result is an interesting and subtly varied design with a links flavor. Play the course in a fresh wind and you might feel like you're in Scotland.

Off the tee, the fairways are relatively wide, with mounds presenting most of the trouble. Upon initial inspection, you might be tempted to think that the green complexes have a certain similarity. But upon closer inspection, you'll find that Litten has used the flatness to produce approach shots that require a great deal of thought and strategy. On some holes, for instance, a low, running bounce-up shot is possible — even advisable — if the course is dry and there's a hearty wind. The greens are typically medium-size and mostly flat or slightly sloped. Bunkers provide most of the problems around the green. Water comes into play on the majority of holes on the front nine and is a factor on the back nine on a few holes. Interestingly, the final three holes provide excellent scoring opportunities for the better player. Overall, French Broad is a fine course that you should make an effort to play.

Amenities include a practice green, range, chipping green, snack bar, bar and restaurant, rental clubs, beverage cart and pro shop.

The course is walkable after 1 PM on weekdays, and you should walk here. You can book a tee time seven days in advance. Approximate cost, including cart, is $36 weekdays and $38 on weekends.

Glen Cannon Country Club

Wilson Rd., Pisgah Forest • 884-9160
Championship Yardage: 6548	
Slope: 124	**Par: 72**
Men's Yardage: 6272	
Slope: 121	**Par: 72**
Ladies' Yardage: 5172	
Slope: 117	**Par: 72**

Glen Cannon Country Club opened in 1966. According to *Architects of Golf*, Willie B. Lewis of Greenville, South Carolina, designed the course. Lewis used to be an associate of George Cobb. For a mountain track, this course has a remarkably wide-open feel; also remarkable is its flatness. Fairways are bermudagrass; greens are bentgrass.

Locals tell us that Glen Cannon is one of the more private semiprivate courses in the area, so make sure you call for a tee time.

Glen Cannon offers a fine, playable and relatively straightforward mountain course that winds around a lush and wide valley floor. The fairways are mostly spacious and delineated by trees and shrubs. The greens are medium-size to large. The grass around the greens is mostly bentgrass: If it's a couple of inches deep, plan to avoid it at all costs. Most of the greens are sloped and not overly rolling. Water hazards come in the form of several branches of a mountain stream . . . watch out for it. Bunkers provide frequent hazards, and many are grass-faced; some are in the fairway, others are around the greens. The back nine is a little hillier and offers fine views from some tee boxes. Particularly appealing is a small but beautiful waterfall that complements the 2nd hole.

If you're looking for a good course in the Brevard area with a sound design and plenty of variety, try Glen Cannon. You'll likely have an enjoyable round. Just make sure you ring the bell before venturing towards the 17th hole. The bell alerts those on the driving range that you're about to cross their line of fire.

Amenities include a practice green, range, chipping green, locker room, bar, snack bar, restaurant, rental clubs, beverage cart and pro shop.

The course is walkable, but you must use a cart if you're not a member. You can book a tee time three days in advance. Approximate cost, including cart, is $50.

Great Smokies Resort

1 Hilton Inn Dr., Asheville • 254-3211
Championship Yardage: 5600
Slope: 118   **Par: 70**
Men's Yardage: 5131
Slope: 117   **Par: 70**
Ladies' Yardage: 4502
Slope: 112   **Par: 70**

The golf course at Great Smokies Resort opened in 1975. According to *Architects of Golf*, Willie B. Lewis designed the course. The course is somewhat tight, particularly on the front nine, with woods bordering many of the holes. You'll find bluegrass and fescue in the fairways and bentgrass on the greens.

Corporate takeovers and changes have affected, if not the course, at least the name of the hotel attached to this interesting mountain track. The course opened as Great Smokies Hilton, but the Holiday Inn chain took over and renamed the complex as the Great Smokies Resort. It's actually a Sunspree Resort, for what it's worth. Improvements to the hotel have been made recently.

The golf course is a truly challenging mountain layout with a solid design. While cruising around the course, we sensed that someone had redesigned the layout and perhaps some of the holes. You'll find plenty of elevation changes. Hazards come in the form of well-placed bunkers and potentially pesky mountain streams. You'll need to keep it straight off the tee and think about your approach shots. The course is not long, but don't think that this makes it easy: Errant tee shots mean lost balls. The greens are predominantly large and sloped. The first four or five holes seem particularly tight. When you arrive on the 5th tee, you're confronted with your mortality as you tee off next to a small graveyard. Hello! The course is also dotted with octagonal holiday chalets, and certain holes are dominated by the 279-room hotel whose aspects lie firmly in the East German school of architecture.

Amenities include a practice green, bar, snack bar, restaurant, rental clubs and pro shop.

The course is walkable for the fit and dedicated, and you can walk after 1 PM from Monday through Thursday. You can book a tee time with your hotel or octagonal holiday chalet reservation, although you don't need to stay here to play here. Approximate cost, including cart, is $26 weekdays and $32 on weekends (including Fridays).

The Grove Park Inn Resort

230 Macon Ave., Asheville • 252-2711,
(800) 438-5800
Championship Yardage: 6520
Slope: 125   **Par: 71**
Blue Yardage: 6033
Slope: 119   **Par: 71**
Ladies' Yardage: 4987
Slope: 111   **Par: 71**

The golf course at The Grove Park Inn opened in February 1899. Willie Park Jr., Herbert Barker, Donald Ross and Russell Breeden are the architects who have worked on or influenced the course. Ask the excellent staff here who has had the biggest influence and they'll tell you it was Donald Ross. The course is laid out on the hillside beneath the magnificent and storied Grove Park Inn. You'll find Vamont bermudagrass in the fairways and Penncross bentgrass greens.

Springtime in the mountains is a great time for golf.

Nearly a century old now, the golf course at The Grove Park Inn is steeped in history — the likes of which would fill a book with stories. But, first, let's investigate the Grove Park Inn. There's a book about this veritable lodge, and it's worth the small investment. Few resorts can rival the Grove Park Inn's legacy and physical appearance. From F. Scott Fitzgerald to George Bush, Beau Bridges and Tammy Wynette, the Grove Park Inn's list of guest luminaries is unsurpassed in its depth and variety. There's something extremely special about staying in a room just a corridor away from where Fitzgerald spent time with his pen in his hand. Today, guests come to The Grove Park Inn from all over the world to relax in the well-appointed rooms, eat in the fine restaurants, dance in the nightclub or relax with a drink on the balcony overlooking Asheville. If you're up for an amazing Sunday brunch, this is the place.

But this is a book about golf, not hotels, right? So let's talk about this wonderful course — a top 3 favorite of this author. If you're an architecture fan, the first thing you'll notice is that this track was built in a remarkably tight area — covering just 80 acres. Just as remarkable is the fact that very few of the holes are noticeably tight. The front nine is predominantly flat, while the back nine, which is closer to the hotel, makes greater use of the slope beneath the inn. The greens vary in shape, size and slope. Errant tee and approach shots risk landing in bunkers, but the course is not overly penal. Water comes into play mostly on the front nine. The yardage book is a useful guide if you're playing the course for the first time.

We've heard people complain that the course is too short to be interesting for the big hitter. While it may be true that the par 5s are mostly on the short side and there are three or four short par 4s, we'd still challenge the long hitter to score par or better on the short holes. Each of the short holes features a unique challenge that could lead to a bogey or worse. For example, the par 4 11th is only about 350 yards, but it's an uphill hole with a small green that slopes away from the fairway. Thus it's quite easy for a decently struck short iron to end up in the thick rough behind the green, leaving you with an almost impossible up and down.

For those who don't feel that the course is long enough, it boasts a couple of long par 3s and some par 4s that are longer than 400 yards. Combine this with the fact that the fairways usually offer very little roll and a number of difficult stances and you'll be pleased to score well on this course. If there's a course that proves you don't need a lot of length to be challenging, this is it. Another hole you'll enjoy is the par 4 18th, where you tee off literally right next to the walls of the inn. You drive downhill to an extremely narrow v-shaped fairway, where you're more than likely to have a difficult stance for your second shot, which you'll have to hit uphill to a large green flanked by trees and deep bunkers.

As you might expect from a course touched by the hands of Donald Ross, there's plenty of variety and interest. Every hole has its own character and charm, including the 9th, supposedly one of Bobby Jones's favorites. It's a lengthy and tight par 3 (more than 200 yards from the tips) with a long green fronted by three large and flat bunkers — a great way to finish the front nine.

But the layout is only a part of the story. Golfers who have played here include such greats as (the aforementioned) Bobby Jones, Ben Hogan, Jack Nicklaus, Arnold Palmer, Fuzzy Zoeller and Walter Hagen. There's a wonderful story about Ben Hogan scoring 11 on the par 3 7th and 4 on the par 5 8th; fable has it that his expression never changed.

From about the mid-'20s to the mid-'50s, the course hosted a stop on the PGA Tour. During that period, many of the pros would come to the inn for the summer and play for big bucks with the wealthy guests who were here to escape the heat of the cities. So when you play at The Grove Park Inn, you're walking in the footsteps of giants.

Finally, let's not forget that the course is closing in on 100 years; there are few courses with such magnificent views and maturity. One of the magnificent views will be you as you putt on the 17th green in full view of the guests in the Sammons Wing of the inn. You can play at the Grove Park Inn without staying at the hotel; but that's a lot like visiting the Metropolitan Museum of Art without taking a look at the Renoirs. Still, if you're in the Asheville area staying elsewhere, you must play this golf course.

Amenities include a practice green, rental clubs, locker room, bar, snack bar, restaurant, beverage cart and pro shop.

You can walk after 3 PM . . . if you're fit. You can book a tee time whenever you choose. Approximate cost, including cart, is $60 weekdays and weekends.

High Hampton Inn and Country Club

N.C. Hwy. 107 S., Cashiers Inn, Cashiers
• 743-2450, (800) 334-2551
Men's Yardage: 6012
Slope: 120   **Par: 71**

The golf course at High Hampton Inn and Country Club opened in 1923 and was originally designed by J. Victor East. However, the course has been redesigned twice by George Cobb; once in 1958 and again in 1980 with the help of John LaFoy. Some of the holes are flat, but most include undulations. Bentgrass covers the fairways and greens.

General public play at this fine old course is limited to after noon. Guests at the inn can play anytime.

High Hampton offers a mature track with plenty of variety. Its most remarkable feature is the variety in terms of length. For example, the par 5 No. 3 measures a significant 572 yards; next up is the par 4 No. 4, just 229 yards. This pattern is often repeated. But don't be fooled into thinking the short holes are easy. You'll be shooting to small crowned greens that probably become extremely fast in the spring and fall. On the longer holes, including two monster par 3s, you'll still find that the greens are not overly large. So, you'll need to be accurate to score well. The course presents a variety of fairway widths. You'll also find some imaginative tee sites. Interestingly, the course is devoid of bunkers, and water only comes into play on a few holes, most noticeably on the par 3 No. 8, where you might be tempted to take more club than you actually need.

Even if your golf isn't going too well, enjoy the setting; it has to be one of the finest of any public-access course in the mountains. Woods border a number of the holes, mountain streams crisscross the track and there are wonderful views of the surrounding peaks from the elevated tees. You might think that 6012 yards isn't the longest course, but there are some

significantly long holes where your drive through a chute has to be long and accurate. Don't be fooled by the distance; the course is tough enough for all levels of golfer. One throwback to the 1920s is the lack of yardage markers. You'll be on your own when it comes to choosing clubs — no cart-mounted laser-guided yardage aids here. Most holes offer a 150-yard marker, but that's it. It's rather interesting having to estimate yardage on your own.

Amenities include a practice green, range, chipping green, snack bar, bar, restaurant, locker room, rental clubs and pro shop.

The course is walkable, you can walk anytime and you should walk. If you're not staying at the inn, you can only book a tee time one day in advance. Approximate cost, including cart, is $48; it's $37 if you're staying at the inn.

Lake Junaluska Golf Course

19 Golf Course Rd., Waynesville
• 456-5777
Championship Yardage: 4962
Slope: No rating   **Par: 68**
Men's Yardage: 4579
Slope: No rating   **Par: 68**
Ladies' Yardage: 3792
Slope: No rating   **Par: 68**

There's evidence of the first nine holes of a golf course as far back as 1919; the course added a new nine in 1993. The architect of the front nine is unknown, but Jim Moulin produced the back. The course is well-maintained, and efforts are ongoing to improve it. It's primarily wide open and set in rolling terrain. You'll find bluegrass in the fairways and bentgrass on the greens.

Lake Junaluska Golf Course is owned and operated by a conglomeration of Lake Junaluska Assembly, SEJ Administrative Council and the United Methodist Church. So if you want a beer with your mid-round hot dog, forget it. In fact, the brochure clearly states that the course has a "No alcohol — no profanity" policy. Two retired ministers serve as part-time rangers and golf-course maintenance experts. We played with one of them who, at age 72, could still drive the ball more than 270 yards. And that's after having had surgery on three of the vertebrae in his neck!

This friendly course is an interesting old

track with small greens. If the ground is hard, you'll have to take one less club than normal and let the ball run onto the greens. If you miss a green, you'll have to negotiate a tough chip or pitch up an embankment. A small pond and the occasional mountain stream come into play. You'll especially enjoy the 135-yard par 3, where the winds can sweep off the lake and influence a short shot to one of the smallest greens in Christendom. You might be tempted to think that the course is too short to be fun, but think otherwise.

There's plenty of entertainment here, and if you're not satiated after your round, you can pick up a copy of *Tee-Ology*, a book by John Freeman about golf's lessons for Christians and other seekers . . . a bargain at $10. If you like unmolested old courses without any gimmicks or trickery, take a look at this track.

Amenities include a practice green, snack bar, rental clubs and pro shop.

The course is walkable anytime. You can book a tee time whenever you choose. Approximate cost, including cart, is $21.

Lake Toxaway Country Club
353 W. Club Blvd., Lake Toxaway
• 966-4020
Championship Yardage: 6234
Slope: 122   **Par: 71**
Men's Yardage: 5594
Slope: 116   **Par: 71**
Ladies' Yardage: 4627
Slope: 109   **Par: 71**

If you want to play on this course, you have to stay at the inn.

The golf course at Lake Toxaway opened in 1960. According to *Architects of Golf*, R.D. Heinitsh designed the original layout. However, John LaFoy redesigned the course. LaFoy is a well-known architect who has designed fine tracks throughout the southeast. LaFoy apprenticed under George Cobb and made frequent visits to Augusta National to study the design. When Cobb was slowed by illness, LaFoy took over many well-known Cobb projects, including Linville Ridge. Most of the holes on the course are bordered by woods. The layout is undulating, with a number of significant elevation changes. You'll find bluegrass in the fairways and bentgrass and poa annua on the greens.

Lake Toxaway's course is well-designed and in a beautiful environment.

The course starts with a bang: a 445-yard par 4 uphill to a raised green fronted by a mean bunker. Is there a more difficult opening hole in North Carolina? Things become a little more lenient on the rest of the front nine, but you'll find plenty of traps — some in the fairways, some around the greens. Most of the holes on the front boast just one bunker, but it's placed in a difficult spot and will force you to think about how heroic you plan to be on your approach shot: proof that you don't need a multitude of bunkers to make a hole interesting and challenging. Remember what Donald Ross said about there being no misplaced bunkers on a golf course. Some bunkers have steep faces. The greens are midsize to large, crowned and sloped, with subtle undulations. The fairways are of a sensible width. Some of the greens are flanked by steep embankments, usually on the opposite side of the bunker. Note the Astroturf cart path next to the green on No. 10: Is this still a free drop, or must you hit from the artificial stuff?

Things get more difficult on the back nine. First, there are more bunkers and some steeper embankments. On the 11th hole (where the Wards and their canine, Mulligan, live) you'll find a relatively gentle par 4. Then begins a long and treacherous series of holes, including a 429-yard par 4, a 659-yard par 5 and a 230-yard par 3. So don't be lulled into a state of semi-catatonic complacency when, upon first glance at the scorecard, you see a mere 6234 yards from the tips. There are some big holes here.

The course will be fun and entertaining for golfers of all levels. Go ahead and splurge on a night at the inn and enjoy yourself on this wonderful track. You'll love the golf as well as the opportunity to relax on the veranda overlooking the 10th tee as you recount the gory details of your round, tell a few lies, collect on the bet and sip a cold beer.

Amenities include a practice green, range, chipping green, locker room, bar, snack bar, restaurant, rental clubs, beverage cart and pro shop.

The course is walkable for the fit, and you can walk anytime. Book your tee with your room. Approximate cost, including cart, is $62.

Profile: Ellis Maples

Ellis Maples is one of North Carolina's greatest golf course architects. In fact, he may be one of the greatest in the country. Maples' father, Frank, was a construction superintendent for Donald Ross and the greenskeeper at Pinehurst Country Club.

Ellis attended Lenoir-Rhyne College and spent two years as assistant greenskeeper at Mid Pines and Pine Needles. In 1937, Ellis helped build a course in Plymouth, North Carolina. He remained at the course as greenskeeper and spent the war years as an engineer. In 1947, he redesigned the course at New Bern where he was the pro and the manager. After this, he remodeled and planned a number of layouts.

In 1948, he supervised the building of the last Donald Ross layout, at Raleigh Country Club. He stayed on as superintendent until 1953 when he opened a design firm. From 1953 until his death in 1984, Maples built close to 70 golf courses, including Forest Oaks Country Club and Grandfather Golf and Country Club, both top tracks in North Carolina. Forest Oaks is home of the Greater Greensboro Open. Maples hired Ed Seay who eventually became top designer in the firm of Arnold Palmer design. Son Dan joined Ellis's firm. Son Joe was the head pro at Boone Golf Club, and son David built courses.

Ellis Maples
—

Ellis Maples courses include Country Club of North Carolina, Country Club of South Carolina, Midland Country Club near Aiken (a favorite of this author), Boone Country Club, Greensboro Country Club, Pinehurst #5, Red Fox Country Club and Devil's Knob. Ellis Maples completed courses in Alabama, Georgia, Tennessee, Virginia and North and South Carolina.

Maggie Valley Resort and Country Club

340 Country Club Rd., Maggie Valley
• 926-1616

Championship Yardage: 6336	
Slope: 121	**Par: 72**
Men's Yardage: 6031	
Slope: 118	**Par: 72**
Other Yardage: 5344	
Slope: 111	**Par: 72**
Ladies' Yardage: 4645	
Slope: 105	**Par: 72**

The golf course at Maggie Valley opened in 1963. William Prevost Sr. designed the course, although Emmett Mitchell is also cred-

ited as a designer. The course is relatively open, with trees defining the fairways on which you'll find bluegrass; on the greens, you'll find bentgrass. You'll also find it easiest to get a tee time at Maggie Valley if you're staying at the resort.

The advertisements exclaim: "You gotta meet Maggie!" And indeed you should. The 2-mile stretch of tourist traps that defines the town of Maggie Valley may lead you to think that the course is similar in its attitude towards aesthetics. Don't worry; the golf course at Maggie Valley is one of the better and prettier courses in the area. It's hosted four N.C. Open Championships, the women's state senior championship, the Western North Carolina PGA Assistant Pro Championship and a host of other competitions. Tom Doak, a golf course architect and a noted golf course architecture writer, didn't see much here of interest, but we'd disagree.

The back and front nines are quite different. The front winds along the valley floor, while the back is much hillier and presents some fine views from some of the tee boxes. Perhaps the front nine is a little tighter off the tee, although you might not notice a big difference. Problems come in the form of the streams that crisscross the course; take a good look at the layout on the scorecard and make a note of where the streams are. The bunkers are large and flat and will influence your approach shots. The greens are rolling, and a few are two- or even three-tiered; on some of the putting surfaces, just the slope and pitch will give you fits. The scorecard gives you green depths, which is useful considering the vastness of some of the greens. Despite all the hazards and undulations, Maggie is not overly penal, and you'll be able to score well here if you keep your game under control. In any case, you'll find excellent variety and interest here at Maggie Valley. It's well worth a visit if you're in the area.

Amenities include a practice green, range, chipping green, locker room, bar, snack bar, restaurant, rental clubs, beverage cart and pro shop.

The course is walkable for the fit, and you can walk after 2:30 PM. Book your tee time with your stay at the resort. Approximate cost, including cart, is $48 (the highest mid-season rate).

Meadowbrook Golf Club

Meadowbrook Rd., Rutherfordton
• 863-2690
Championship Yardage: 6378
Slope: 110 **Par: 72**
Men's Yardage: 5850
Slope: 105 **Par: 72**
Ladies' Yardage: 5208
Slope: 108 **Par: 75**

Meadowbrook opened in 1964. The course is set on rolling terrain, with bermudagrass fairways and bentgrass greens. Some of the holes are open, others are bordered by woods.

This fun and relatively straightforward course has a mountain feel to it despite the fact that it's located a bit west of where the real mountains begin their ascent. If you hate bunkers, you'll love this course — there are none. Except for a few narrow fairways, you won't find a great deal of trouble off the tee. This is especially true on the front nine, which is more open than the back. Don't be fooled by the clubhouse: It looks like a hay storage facility. But the course is set in pretty surroundings and has a pleasant and peaceful ambiance not usually found on purely public courses. Credit the ever-underrated architect, Willie B. Lewis. The greens are predominantly midsize to large, with subtle undulations. There's plenty of water to contend with from a mountain stream as well as a pond on two holes. This track is certainly worth a look if you're fond of courses with a traditional feel.

Amenities include a practice green, locker room, snack bar, restaurant, rental clubs and pro shop.

You can and should walk anytime. You can book a tee time whenever you choose. Approximate cost, including cart, is $20 weekdays and $25 on weekends.

Mill Creek Country Club

100 Mill Creek Rd., Franklin • 524-6458
Championship Yardage: 6167
Slope: 115 **Par: 72**
Men's Yardage: 5775
Slope: 113 **Par: 72**
Ladies' Yardage: 4483
Slope: 113 **Par: 72**

Mill Creek Country Club opened in 1968. After numerous queries and additional research, we've discovered that no one knows who designed this course. (Do you? If so, please write us and let us know.) The layout is primarily wide open with some elevation changes. In the fairways and on the greens, you'll find bentgrass.

This Mecca of golf in Franklin is a fun and straightforward course with plenty of challenge for golfers of all levels and abilities. The fairways provide various widths. The greens are small to midsize and protected by flat bunkers that could prove disastrous if your bunker technique isn't up to snuff. The greens are sloped. The most notable landscaping feature is the preponderance of mature willow trees, some of which come into play. You'll have some fine mountain views, particularly from the elevated tees. If you're in the area, stop by the course for a fun round.

Amenities include a practice green, chipping green, snack bar, rental clubs and pro shop.

You can walk the course after 2 PM. Book a tee time two days in advance, if you wish. Approximate cost, including cart, is $38.

Red Fox Country Club

2 Club Rd., Tryon • 894-8251
Championship Yardage: 7104

Slope: 136	**Par: 72**
Men's Yardage: 6393	
Slope: 124	**Par: 72**
Other Yardage: 5705	
Slope: 111	**Par: 72**
Ladies' Yardage: 5286	
Slope: 118	**Par: 73**

Red Fox Country Club opened in 1966. Ellis Maples designed the course, a primarily open track, with woods and houses bordering some holes. In the fairways, you'll find bermudagrass; on the greens, bentgrass.

Red Fox is an excellent example of Ellis Maples' architectural talent. Maples took a pretty piece of land and turned it into a fine and tough country golf course. The fairways are wide, and the greens are large and sloped; there are plenty of bunkers, mostly around the green complexes. (These are basic details that match many of Maples' courses.) The beauty of the course comes from the layout — the sweeping doglegs, the variety of shots you have to play and the subtle shaping of the large flat bunkers. Ellis Maples courses often feature a number of uphill approach shots that tend to be on the blind side. Some people don't like this. Still, we've heard a number of better golfers rave about this course as one of the best undiscovered secrets in the foothills of the mountains. At least it's been a secret until now, right?

It's difficult to describe the essence of this fine old course, so we recommend you play it and take in its attractions and challenges. Play

it from the Red Fox tees (the tips), and you'll be in for a long day. If you're in for less of a challenge, play it from one of the other sets. We have a feeling you'll go out of your way to play this course over and over again.

Amenities include a practice green, range, locker room, snack bar, rental clubs and pro shop.

You must take a cart here, but you can book a tee time whenever you choose. Approximate cost, including cart, is $30 weekdays and $35 on weekends.

Reems Creek Golf Course

Pink Fox Cove Rd., Weaverville • 645-4393
Championship Yardage: 6477

Slope: 130	**Par: 72**
Men's Yardage: 6106	
Slope: 127	**Par: 72**
Other Yardage: 5357	
Slope: 119	**Par: 72**
Ladies' Yardage: 4605	
Slope: 114	**Par: 72**

Reems Creek Golf Course, a Martin Hawtree design just to the north of Asheville, opened in 1989. This is a mountain track, and you'll find plenty of significant elevation changes. Most of the holes are open, and a few are bordered by woods. Bentgrass blankets the fairways and covers the greens.

Martin Hawtree is from England and is the third generation of the Hawtree family, famous for its fine and prolific golf course designs, most of which are in the British Isles. Martin Hawtree has a doctorate in Land Planning from Liverpool University. His father, Fred, designed nearby Mount Mitchell Course. European PGA Tour player Simon Gidman was an assistant in the design of Reems Creek.

Reems Creek is Martin Hawtree's only golf course in America. After playing it, you might be thankful there isn't a second effort anywhere. It's a challenging track that's a sort of hybrid mountain/links course. The result is an extremely challenging course that will test every aspect of your game and make you use every club in your bag.

The serious elevation changes mean you'll often have to negotiate a serious up-

FYI

Unless otherwise noted, the area code for all phone numbers in this chapter is 704.

Photo: Grove Park Inn Resort

The Grove Park Inn is an old and storied hotel in Asheville.

hill or downhill shot. The lack of length means you'll be playing some target golf as well. If the weather has been hot and the greenskeeper has saturated the fairways, the course will be a little wider than it looks. Hit a straight drive and you're still not out of trouble. Your approach shots to the mostly large greens need to be placed just right if you're going to score par. Some of the greens, particularly on the back nine, must slope up to six or seven feet from back to front: Take our advice and do everything you can to stay below the hole. In fact, in our opinion some greens verge on being unfair. So make sure you check the pin placement and hit your approach shots to the sensible portion of the green. Oh, you'll also find plenty of mounding to help define the fairways and green complexes. Bunkers are everywhere as well, and Hawtree has taken a page out of Robert Trent Jones's book and made them cloverleaf-shaped. There are some grass bunkers around some of the greens as well.

Reems Creek seems to be a much admired and talked about course among the local golfing population. If you're looking for a very challenging modern course in the Asheville area, you'll get all you can handle at this impressive track.

Amenities include a practice green, range, snack bar, grill, rental clubs and pro shop.

You must use a cart at Reems Creek. You can book a tee time whenever you choose. Approximate cost, including cart, is $38 weekdays and $42 on weekends.

Sapphire Mountain Golf Club

30 Slicers Ave., Sapphire • 743-1174
Championship Yardage: 6147
Slope: 119   **Par: 70**
Men's Yardage: 5690
Slope: 118   **Par: 70**
Ladies' Yardage: 4515
Slope: 112   **Par: 70**

The course used to be called Holly Forest. The management attributes the current design to Ron Garl, although *Architects of*

Golf attributes the design to Tom Jackson. Most of the holes are bordered by woods. The course is owned and operated by LinksCorp. You'll find bentgrass on the greens and in the fairways.

There are two other courses in the Cashiers area with the name Sapphire. Sapphire Mountain is the only course bearing the Sapphire nomenclature that's open to the public. The first thing you'll notice about the course is the somewhat bizarre routing, which must have been changed from the original. As your round progresses, you'll see that perhaps the rerouting was completed to produce the remarkable par 3s that define this course. Each one has its own character, and each is quite dramatic. For example, on the 203-yard 4th hole, you'll smack your tee shot to a green with a large rock on the left and a steep embankment to the right and front; and it's only the No. 14 handicap. Go figure. The 15th hole, just 138 yards, features an undulating island green. Although the par 3s are worth the price of admission, the 401-yard par 4 No. 14 is surely one of the most dramatic and difficult golf holes in North Carolina. You have to drive from an elevated tee to a narrow landing area with a stream on the left-hand side. Your approach shot will travel to a significantly elevated two-tiered green. Miss the green to the right and your ball will be swallowed by a waterfall. A dramatic and difficult hole, par here is a good score. Overall, good variety, bizarre routing, tricky greens and some large bunkers will make your golfing life difficult and interesting. Oh, and if the greenskeeper lets the rough grow then finesse shots become more difficult. In an area where most of the courses are private, Sapphire Mountain provides a modern public course in a pleasant setting.

Amenities include a snack bar, rental clubs, a locker room, bar, restaurant, beverage cart and pro shop.

Walking is not permitted here. You can book a tee time 30 days in advance. Approximate cost, including cart, is $25 weekdays and weekends.

Springdale Country Club

200 Golf Watch Rd., Canton • 235-8451
Championship Yardage: 6812
Slope: 126   **Par: 72**
Men's Yardage: 6437
Slope: 121   **Par: 72**
Other Yardage: 5734
Slope: 113   **Par: 72**
Ladies' Yardage: 5421
Slope: 121   **Par: 74**

All 18 holes at Springdale Country Club opened in 1970. Joseph Holmes laid out the original course, and according to the staff at Springdale, Fred Tingle revised the track. Most of the course is set in rolling terrain and includes some decent elevation changes. You'll find rye grass fairways and bentgrass greens.

The fairways vary in width. The greens vary in shape, but most are fairly large and undulating. A number of changes were completed recently, including the construction of a new practice putting green, the renovation of the practice range and the redesign of all bunkers. Springdale also recently hired a full-time PGA professional as Director of Golf.

You don't have to stay at one of the guest cottages or at the inn to play here, but we recommend it. The resort is family-owned and operated and, according to the staff, enjoys strong repeat visits. The focus here is golf. As the brochure firmly states: "Here, the game of golf reigns supreme; no pools, spas or tennis courts." Way to go!

The golf course is a challenging mountain track with plenty of variety. Play it all the way from the back and you're in for a long day. Play it from the front and the course is kinder and gentler. Some fairways are narrow and bordered by woods while others are wide and more forgiving. The back nine is more open than the front. You'll enjoy driving the ball from some of the elevated tees. The greens are midsize and sloped. Streams come into play on some of the holes. Overall, Springdale is a beautiful and fun course that will provide a challenge for any golfer.

And just in case you're worried about playing too slowly, each golf cart is equipped with an egg timer. If it dings, then you've spent too much time on that hole and need to go the next.

Amenities include a practice green, range, chipping green, locker room, snack bar, restaurant, rental clubs, beverage cart and pro shop.

You can walk anytime (if you can hack it . . . it's not advisable!). And you can book a tee time whenever you choose. Approximate cost, including cart, is $35.

Waynesville Country Club Inn
Country Club Dr., Waynesville • 452-4617
Carolina/Dogwood Course
Championship Yardage: 5798
Slope: 103	**Par: 70**
Men's Yardage: 5395	
Slope: 100	**Par: 70**
Ladies' Yardage: 4927	
Slope: 103	**Par: 70**

Dogwood/Blue Ridge Course
Championship Yardage: 5803
Slope: 105	**Par: 70**
Men's Yardage: 5258	
Slope: 100	**Par: 70**
Ladies' Yardage: 4565	
Slope: 100	**Par: 70**

Blue Ridge/Carolina Course
Championship Yardage: 5943
Slope: 104	**Par: 70**
Men's Yardage: 5493	
Slope: 100	**Par: 70**
Ladies' Yardage: 5002	
Slope: 104	**Par: 70**

Golfers started swinging at Waynesville Country Club Inn in 1926, and the course has an interesting design history. Little known is the fact that Donald Ross designed the initial routing. John Drake finished the construction of the course. Ross Taylor revised the layout. Then Tom Jackson arrived to add the third nine and revised the course in 1989. If you ask in the pro shop who designed the course, they'll tell you it was Tom Jackson. In the fairways, you'll find bluegrass; on the greens, you'll find bentgrass.

The inn here is a magnificent structure. You can get on the course even if you're not staying here, but you'll probably find it easier to get a tee time if you're a guest. You can

also rent a condo or vacation cottage, or whatever it's called these days. All sorts of packages are available.

You won't find tremendous "let's let it rip with the titanium driver" length on any of the three nine hole courses, but you'll find a bit more room off the tee on the Carolina nine, which is flatter and a little more straightforward than the Dogwood and Blue Ridge courses. The latter two courses are placement tracks where judgment is more important than brute strength. We think you'll find that all three courses are much more user-friendly than some of today's modern earth-moving impossibilities: There's very little that's unfair about any of the three courses, at least from the tee to the green. A few mountain streams provide the water hazards, and the courses are only moderately bunkered. But it's on and around the greens where the courses become trickier. We're in a valley here, thus reading putts is extremely difficult and likely to add to your score. Such are the joys of mountain golf. The setting is super, and you'll enjoy a round on any of the courses, particularly if your strengths are putting and hitting it straight but not especially far.

Amenities include a practice green, locker room, bar, snack bar, restaurant, rental clubs and pro shop.

Walking is restricted. You can book a tee time with your reservation or one day in advance. Approximate cost for 18 holes, including cart, is $41.

Boone/Blowing Rock Area

Blue Ridge Country Club
N.C. Hwy. 181, Linville Falls • 756-7001 *4013*
Championship Yardage: 6862
Slope: 128	**Par: 72**
Men's Yardage: 6362	
Slope: 123	**Par: 72**
Ladies' Yardage: 5203	
Slope: 116	**Par: 72**

Blue Ridge Country Club opened nine holes in 1995 and opened all 18 in the spring of 1996. Ken Ezell and Lloyd Clifton designed the course, which is set on the side of a mountain near Linville Caverns on the way to Linville and Boone. Greens are bentgrass, and the

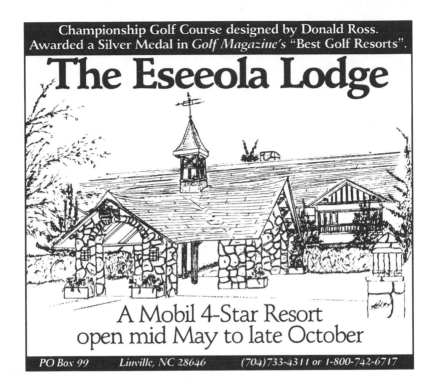
fairways are a mixture of bluegrass, rye and fine fescue. Many of the holes feature significant elevation changes.

We know you've just read the Charlotte chapter of this book, and thus we know you're familiar with the design team of Lloyd Clifton and Ken Ezell. They produced one of Charlotte's most popular and challenging public courses, Highland Creek. They also designed a significant number of courses in Florida. Thus this new course boasts a fine design pedigree.

The course here at Blue Ridge Country Club is both challenging and picturesque. On most holes, you don't have to drive the ball a long way, but you mustn't spray it; if you do, you've probably lost your ball for good. Also, if the rough is grown up, you'll find it to be extremely difficult and tough.

The greens here are mostly large and quite undulating, and they are flanked by a series of bunkers and embankments that could make

getting up and down quite difficult. Something you'll really like about the course is that it's been designed so that almost all of the problems and challenges are easily seen from wherever you are. A lot of tee boxes are elevated, so you're provided with an abundance of downhill tee shots. This effect is created by the excellent routing of the course. We think you'll really enjoy the ambiance here, the pretty setting and the variety of challenges that are presented to you for your golfing enjoyment. Just leave that driver in the trunk of your car unless you're able to hit it very straight.

There's quite an emphasis here on making the course a destination with a resort-type atmosphere: You'll find a number of well-appointed rooms at the small inn, which also features a pleasant restaurant. The facility is proving popular as a corporate retreat. Retirees are already purchasing lots adjacent to the golf course, so you're going to find a lot of houses being built quite soon.

Amenities include a practice green, range, restaurant, snack bar, meeting room, rental clubs and pro shop.

You can walk here at anytime, but you'll find it quite a hike. You can book a tee time whenever you please. Approximate cost, including cart, is $39 weekdays and $45 on weekends.

Boone Golf Club

Fairway Dr., Boone • 264-8760

Championship Yardage: 6401	
Slope: 120	**Par: 71**
Men's Yardage: 5859	
Slope: 112	**Par: 71**
Ladies' Yardage: 5172	
Slope: 103	**Par: 75**

Boone Golf Club, an Ellis Maples course, opened in 1959. The course is flat in places, rolling in others, with bentgrass fairways and greens.

At Boone Golf Club we found a formidable and mature Ellis Maples design that's close to Boone and well worth a visit. It's one of Maples' first courses, and it's one of his first in the mountains. One of Maples' sons, Joe, was formerly the head pro here. Ellis Maples had been an architect for just six years when the Boone club was built, and you'll see many of the features that later came to be standards on his other fine courses.

You probably won't experience a great deal of trouble off the tee, but it will help to be long from the tips. Trees border many of the fairways. The greens are midsize and undulating — in fact, we noticed some buried elephants on a couple — so make sure your approach shots are well-placed. You'll also find some intelligent and sneaky bunker placements around the greens. A couple of small tributaries of the New River come into play on some holes.

If you're in Boone and looking for a fine Ellis Maples' design, drop by for 18 holes. You won't be disappointed. The club boasts about 500 members.

Amenities include a practice green, restaurant, rental clubs and pro shop.

Nonmembers can walk after 2 PM. You can book a tee time seven days in advance. Approximate cost, including cart, is $40 weekdays and $45 on weekends.

Hawksnest Ski and Golf

2058 Skyland Dr., Seven Devils
• 898-5135, (800) 822-4295

Championship Yardage: 6244	
Slope: 117	**Par: 72**
Men's Yardage: 5953	
Slope: 110	**Par: 72**
Other Yardage: 5181	
Slope: 102	**Par: 72**
Ladies' Yardage: 4799	
Slope: 120	**Par: 72**

Hawksnest opened in 1965. A committee of local residents designed the course. Most of the holes are bordered by woods. In the fairways, you'll find bluegrass; on the greens, you'll find bentgrass. If you arrive at the course and it's dumping snow, leave your sticks in the car, strap on your skis and head for the slopes above the first tee.

Standing on the area just outside the pro shop, with the course spreading out below, you might think this layout is wide open. It isn't. Leave your driver in the trunk of your Porsche or Rolls unless you can keep the ball extremely straight: If you miss the fairway, you're in the thick woods and reaching into your bag for a fresh ball. Narrow fairways aside, Hawksnest proves that designing a golf course by committee can work successfully in places. With the mountainside above you and magnificent views from some of the tees, this course is surely one of the most striking in the mountains. You'll find a pleasant mix of flat holes and those with elevation changes, which include terraced fairways. The greens are medium-size and sloped just enough to make for some tricky putts. Miss the green and you may find your ball in a bunker, but it's more likely that you'll be playing from the well-prepared chipping areas. It's always nice to find a course that rewards and encourages skillful chipping. To score well here, choose less club than you think you'll need off the tee, keep your ball in play and shoot for the middle of the greens.

Amenities include a practice green, range, chipping green, locker room, snack bar, rental clubs and pro shop.

You can walk after 6 PM if you've got the stamina. You can book a tee time seven days in advance. Approximate cost, including cart, is $32 weekdays and $36 on weekends.

Hound Ears Club

N.C. Hwy. 105 S., Blowing Rock • 963-5831

Championship Yardage: 6165

Slope: 122	Par: 72

Men's Yardage: 6036

Slope: 120	Par: 72

Other Yardage: 5639

Slope: 115	Par: 72

Ladies' Yardage: 4959

Slope: 110	Par: 73

The golf course at Hound Ears Club, designed by George Cobb, opened in 1963. We found a pleasant mix of open and wooded holes. The fairways are covered with bluegrass; the greens, bentgrass.

You can't walk off the street and play at Hound Ears; you must stay at the well-appointed lodge. It may be worth your while if you're looking for a first-rate mountain resort, away from it all in a peaceful and pampered setting. Both the course and the lodge seem to be extremely popular with the well-to-do seasoned-citizen set. And with good reason: The golf course is a fine example of an excellent mountain track. Some of the holes are flat, while others offer dramatic elevation changes. The fairways are predominantly wide, and the greens are large and undulating. The three-tiered 12th green, a par 5 hole, must surely be one of the most difficult in western North Carolina; a three-putt is an accomplishment. There's an interesting story that accompanies this hole. In 1995, Peter Rucker, the head pro, scored consecutive double eagles. You may be interested to know that Peter Rucker is the brother of David Rucker who is the head pro at Myers Park Country Club in Charlotte and the person who attempts to teach this author how to strike a golf ball so that it lands somewhere near the anointed target.

Most of the greens here at Hound Ears are built-up and protected by bunkers that should only be a hazard if the pin is placed nearby and you play for it. Hit your approach shot to the middle of the green and you'll be fine. As for water, there's the Watauga River and a tributary stream; both come into play on a number of holes. There's also a pond on the back nine that could prove irritating. Make sure you look at the card if you've never played the course before.

We would be remiss if we failed to describe, or at least try to describe, the general ambiance of the course. The mountains rise above you, streams burble as you pull your club back, you drive your cart under ancient and cool rhododendron bushes and you feel relaxed and at ease with the world. Until, sadly, you pull your tee shot into the woods. It's a wonderful resort course, and it's a great place to be pampered.

Amenities include a practice green, range, snack bar, rental clubs and pro shop.

The course is walkable for the fit, and you can walk before 8 AM and after 6 PM. Book your tee time in conjunction with the lodge reservations. Approximate cost, including cart, is $48 weekdays and weekends.

Jefferson Landing

N.C. Hwy. 16-88, Jefferson
• (910) 246-5555

Championship Yardage: 7111

Slope: 121	Par: 72

Men's Yardage: 6424

Slope: 115	Par: 72

Other Yardage: 5720

Slope: 109	Par: 72

Ladies' Yardage: 4960

Slope: 103	Par: 72

The golf course at Jefferson Landing opened in 1991. Dennis Lehmann and Larry Nelson designed the course; you may know Dennis Lehmann as the associate of Jack Nicklaus responsible for Elk River in Banner Elk — a private course rated as one of the finest in North Carolina. The course, for a mountain track, has a remarkably wide-open feel; also remarkable is its occasional flatness. In the fairways, you'll find an interesting combination of bluegrass and fescue; on the greens, you'll find bentgrass.

First, a note about the resort and the development. At Jefferson Landing, you can purchase a pre-existing home or homesite, stay at the well-appointed lodge or rent a townhouse for a week . . . it's up to you. And you can enjoy an adult beverage or two. We mention that because the course is situated in Ashe County, which is as dry as the Sahara Desert when it comes to adult beverages.

You can, of course, play golf. The lay-

Whatever It Takes

In the course of my travels as I investigated and researched golf courses, I played golf with a lot of interesting characters, some of whom I enjoyed, some of whom I'll be happy not to see again. One person who is part of the former category is an assistant pro at one of the larger resorts in Pinehurst. He used to be a caddie on the pro tour. Apart from his

ability to play golf very well and his ability to recite most of the words from one of the best movies ever made, *Caddyshack*, this golfer told me about the players on the PGA tour, where the big boys play.

"The pros do whatever it takes to be in the middle of the fairway. After that, every iron is going right where it needs to go and every chip and putt looks like it's going in."

Personally, this advice or method of playing golf strikes me as excellent, if you can practice enough to get there. If you can follow this general game plan, then you'll probably enjoy the game a lot more, even if your scoring average isn't 69.23. Doing whatever it takes to be in the fairway means taking a fairway wood or even a mid-iron off the tee. You may hit the ball only 150-200 yards, but that's a lot better than being in the woods or in a stream or in the back yard of somebody's house — someone who, despite spending all the money to own a house next to a golf course, is amazed when golf balls and golfers appear in their back yards.

A second shot where it needs to be may be short of the green and thus short of all the trouble that often surrounds the green complex. After these two good shots, a well-executed pitch or chip and two (or even one) good putts means no more than bogey on even a long par-4. One less than 18 bogeys and you've shot in the 80s.

So take the advice of a caddie who's seen the best in the world play golf. Let the course come to you instead of stretching to do something you can't do and you'll enjoy golf a lot more . . . and save money on golf balls to boot. *Scott Martin*

out, while relatively fresh, is straightforward and well-designed. There are no trick holes; there are no frivolously designed holes. There's plenty of water in the form of streams and ponds, but it doesn't always come into play. Quite a few tee boxes provide dramatic downhill tee shots. From the back tees, at a whopping 7111 yards, the course will give you all the challenge you want and then some: Water comes into play more often from the tips than from the forward tees.

The strength of the course lies in its tremendous variety — again, not in tricks or gimmicks. What you see is what you get from the tee as well as with respect to your approach shots. The well-kept Penncross bentgrass greens provide an excellent example of why this type of green should be the grass of choice on putting surfaces in the next cen-

tury: It's true, resilient, fair and easier to maintain than pure bentgrass. The greens are medium-size, as are the bunkers protecting them, and are flattish and tricky. The management is in the process of planting a large number of trees on the course to help define the fairways. Overall, Jefferson Landing is worth a visit if you're looking for a fine mountain golf course with good amenities and pleasant surroundings. Aim for the middle of the fairway and the middle of the green and you'll enjoy your round.

Amenities include a practice green, range, chipping green, snack bar, rental clubs, beverage cart and pro shop.

The course is not walkable. You can book a tee time whenever you choose. Approximate cost, including cart, is $39 weekdays and $49 on weekends (including Fridays).

Linville Golf Club

N.C. Hwy. 221, Linville • 733-4363
Championship Yardage: 6780

Slope: 132	**Par: 72**
Men's Yardage: 6279	
Slope: 126	**Par: 72**
Other Yardage: 5437	
Slope: 113	**Par: 72**
Ladies' Yardage: 5086	
Slope: 117	**Par: 72**

A golf course called Tanglewood opened adjacent to the current course in 1892. The old course no longer exists (a victim of the Great Depression) although a portion is used as the driving range. Donald Ross designed the new course in 1924. Linville Golf Club is set among majestic and wonderful wooded scenery in the well-heeled retirement and second-home town of Linville. In the fairways, you'll find bentrgrass; on the greens, you'll find poa annua. Linville Golf Club is private; you must play as the guest of a member or be a guest at the excellent Eseeola Lodge. The course is open from May to October.

Among golfers in North Carolina, Linville Golf Club is well-known as one of the best mountain golf courses and maybe as one of the best courses in the Carolinas. Most golfers would happily choose this course over one of the more modern earth-moving extravaganzas with houses bordering (and interfering with) almost every hole on the golf course. A lot of factors make the course particularly interesting and particularly good.

For starters, Linville is somewhat of a rarity: a true Donald Ross course that looks like it's relatively untouched. Richard S. Tufts, who died in 1980 and who used to own Pinehurst Resort, revised the course a little, but for the most part, it's pure Ross. This means that the layout is excellent: There are no silly or poorly conceived holes on the course. You'll also find plenty of those Ross greens that play smaller than they look; getting up and down from a greenside bunker is no easy task, and we'll give you a short game proficiency certificate if you can get up and down from behind the green. Like many great Ross courses, you need to let the course come to you, and you

FYI

Unless otherwise noted, the area code for all phone numbers in this chapter is 704.

need to stay below the hole on your approach shots, chips and pitches.

From the tee, many of the holes are relatively wide, while others are somewhat narrow; spray the ball off the tee and you're probably going to be in the woods or on an adjacent fairway. From the middle tees, a well-struck 3 wood may be your best and wisest choice.

Ross courses (in North Carolina, at least) don't usually feature a lot of water, and Linville is a little bit of an exception in that a couple of streams often come into play, although they shouldn't really bother a good shot. If your other favorite pastime is fly fishing, you'll wish you could bring your rod; giant trout wander around in the streams, just waiting to be hooked, safe in the knowledge that they are protected by a no fishing sign.

The course boasts a number of magnificent holes, most notably the par 4 third that measures 449 yards from the tips. The aforementioned stream bisects the hole at about 150 yards from the front of the turtlebacked green, which is perched on a small knoll. Most of the fairway slopes significantly downhill from right to left, making the approach short even more difficult. Par here is a great score. Golf course architect and golf writer, Tom Doak, believes this hole is one of the greatest par 4s in the world. We'd have to agree; we haven't seen a lot of better and more difficult golf holes anywhere. But don't think that the third hole is the only great one on the course. We think you'll find the 2nd, 8th, 11th, 12th and 18th to be fine and testing challenges. Linville is mostly a placement golf course. You don't have to hit the ball a mile to score well here. You just need to be in the right place at the right time and let the course come to you. Even if things are going badly here for you, remember that you're in a special place.

One other notable feature are the poa annua greens. Most course superintendents hate the stuff, due to the theory that it can take over and ruin the consistency of a good bentgrass green. We think you may find the greens here are some of the best you'll ever play and some of the trickiest to putt in the early and late season. It's simply crucial to stay beneath the hole; otherwise, you're going to find yourself with an almost impossible downhill putt. One of the great things about the greens is that they are so true; a well-struck putt is rewarded with a great result.

With its fine architectural pedigree and its majestic setting, Linville proves that a basic layout can be a great layout. If you're a fan of really good, old golf courses, you should bribe a member to let you on or stay at the Eseeola Lodge and invest in a golf package. It's well worth the cashola.

Amenities include a practice green, range, chipping green, snack bar after the 11th hole, rental clubs and pro shop.

The course is walkable, but, sadly, you're not allowed to walk before 4 PM; it's a tragedy that such a great old course won't let you strap your bag to your shoulder or that of a caddie. You can book a tee time when you reserve at the Eseeola Lodge, which offers golf packages. Approximate cost, including cart, is $50 weekdays and weekends.

Mountain Aire Golf Course

1104 Golf Course Rd., West Jefferson
• (910) 877-4716

Championship Yardage: 6107	
Slope: No rating	**Par: 71**
Men's Yardage: 5571	
Slope: No rating	**Par: 71**
Other Yardage: 4935	
Slope: No rating	**Par: 71**
Ladies' Yardage: 4143	
Slope: No rating	**Par: 71**

Strangely, no one seems to know when Mountain Aire opened or who designed the course. It is known that the course is primarily open in design and features some dramatic topography. In the fairways, you'll find bluegrass; on the greens, you'll find bentgrass.

Deep in the heart of Jefferson County, you'll find Mountain Aire perched on the side of a significant and pretty mountain. The result is a course with stunning elevation changes, most noticeably on the 452-yard par 4, where you tee off from what seems like the top of a cliff. The left side of the fairway features an embankment dotted with grassy pot bunkers — a unique hole. Also interesting is

the 2nd hole, a par 3 listed as 89 yards, although it may be even less.

We looked hard to find a hole here that's flat . . . we couldn't find one. Thus expect to hit either uphill or downhill on just about every shot. The greens are predominantly small and slightly sloped. Overall, Mountain Aire is a pleasant course, affording fine views and some challenging holes.

Amenities include a practice green, range, snack bar and rental clubs.

The course is walkable for the physically fit, and you can walk anytime. You can book a tee time whenever you choose. Approximate cost, including cart, is $28 weekdays and $32 weekends.

Mount Mitchell Golf Club

7590 N.C. Hwy. 80 S., Burnsville
• 675-5454

Championship Yardage: 6475	
Slope: 121	**Par: 72**
Men's Yardage: 6110	
Slope: 116	**Par: 72**
Ladies' Yardage: 5455	
Slope: 117	**Par: 72**

Mount Mitchell Golf Course opened in 1975. Fred Hawtree designed the course on a valley floor, thus it's predominantly flat. You'll find bentgrass in the fairways and on the greens.

Fred Hawtree is the son of Frederic George Hawtree, well-known in the United Kingdom as one of the great designers in the first half of the 20th century. Fred Hawtree continued his father's design excellence. After a distinguished record in World War II, including a stint as a POW in a Japanese camp, Hawtree designed and built numerous courses in England and France in addition to a few in Germany, Iran, the Netherlands, South Africa, Spain, Switzerland and Wales. Mount Mitchell is his only course in the United States. Fred Hawtree's son, Martin, continued the architectural firm and is, himself, a prolific designer. You can see an example of Martin's (demonic) work at Reems Creek Golf Course just north of Asheville in Weaverville (see the write-up in this chapter).

Comparing Reems Creek to Mount Mitchell is like comparing the musical artist formerly known as Prince to Mozart. Whereas

Reems Creek is a masterpiece of modern earth-moving prowess, Mount Mitchell is a kinder, gentler course. Rumor has it that Ben Wright and Charlie "Choo-choo" Justice had houses on the course at one stage. Justice would sit on his porch and let golfers know how the putts were breaking.

The routing is magnificent. There are no bad holes, and each shot requires thought and a degree of precision. The holes have a gentle shape and appearance yet are quite challenging, due mostly to the tightness off the tee and the potential for big score disasters posed by mountain streams and several bunkers. It's probably one of the prettiest public courses in the mountains. As you drive up to the course through the winding mountain road and come upon the crosscut fairways, you can't help drooling a little at the sight.

The key to scoring well here is keeping the ball in play. If you're wild with your driver, lock it in the trunk and rely on your short game to keep you out of the big number dog house. The greens offer a great deal of variety. Some are sloped, others are tiered, others still are undulating.

Even though the course is a little remote, take time to get here, particularly in the fall, when the greens are probably very fast and the trees blaze magnificently with color.

Amenities include a practice green, locker room, snack bar, restaurant, rental clubs and pro shop.

The course is walkable for the fit, and you can walk after 1 PM Monday through Thursday. You can book a tee time two weeks in advance. Approximate cost, including cart, is $40 weekdays and $45 on weekends.

Mountain Glen Golf Club
N.C. Hwy. 194, Newland • 733-5804
Championship Yardage: 6723

Slope: 129	Par: 72
Men's Yardage: 6195	
Slope: 119	Par: 72
Ladies' Yardage: 5506	
Slope: 110	Par: 72

Mountain Glen Golf Course opened in 1964. This George Cobb design features rolling, relatively open terrain, with trees delineating the bluegrass fairways. The greens are bentgrass.

Mountain Glen is an example of a Cobb resort/vacation course with excellent routing. Cobb believed this type of course should be more straightforward and less fraught with difficulty than a country club course that a member might play many times a year. After all, you're on vacation! If you still want a challenge, play it from the back tees. Actually, the course is quite long from the Ladies' tees.

The fairways are medium-width, and the greens are medium-size and sloped, with subtle breaks. Mountain streams comprise most of the water hazards. There's plenty of bunkering around the greens, so plan your approach to avoid them. Most of the bunkers are built to catch shots that are wide and short. If you don't like the look of a bunker, take an extra club or two. This is a fun and relatively challenging course that's worth the price of admission. An interesting local rule is that no beginning golfers are allowed on the course on weekends and holidays before 4 PM. A good move.

Amenities include a practice green, chipping green, locker room, snack bar, rental clubs and pro shop.

The course is pleasantly walkable, and you can walk anytime (hooray!). You can book a tee time seven days in advance. Approximate cost, including cart, is $35 weekdays and weekends.

Olde Beau Golf Club
U.S. Hwy. 21, Roaring Gap
• (910) 363-3333
Championship Yardage: 6705

Slope: 131	Par: 72
Men's Yardage: 6264	
Slope: 129	Par: 72
Seniors Yardage: 5720	
Slope: 120	Par: 72
Ladies' Yardage: 4960	
Slope: 118	Par: 75

The golf course at Olde Beau opened in 1990. Billy Satterfield designed and owns the course and the surrounding development. Olde Beau features some significant elevation changes, and woods border most of the holes. In the fairways, you'll find a combination of bluegrass and rye; on the greens, you'll find bentgrass.

Olde Beau is named after Beau the dog,

the former and now passed-away apple of Mr. Satterfield's eye. There's a memorial to this K9 next to the 15th green. Satterfield must have enjoyed Beau's company because the course named in honor of his four legged and very ugly friend is one of the most magnificent testaments to golf and golf course architecture in the mountains. It's open for limited public play; once all the lots have been developed, it may become members only. It's actually easier to get to the course from Charlotte and the Triad than from the central mountains. Go ahead and make the trip from wherever you are.

Mr. Satterfield is not a well-known designer; in fact, this may be his only course. But Olde Beau is certainly evidence that you don't have to be a big-name architect to produce a stunning course. You'll be faced with a variety of shots off the tee and an even wider array of approach shots. The fairways vary in width; the green complexes, vary in size, shape and bunkering. Each shot requires thought and planning. Our advice is to steer clear of the trouble and take the bailout options . . . where they exist!

The front nine is challenging enough to make you happy after just nine holes. But the course really begins on the 10th tee, when you leave the snack bar with hot dog and adult beverage in hand. The 12th, 13th, 14th and 15th holes are breathtaking in their intensity, design, complexity and views. These holes are literally built on the side of a mountain. The panorama from the 15th green, where Olde Beau rests in peace (save the occasional "Fore!"), is unlike any other in the mountains. It's worth the price of admission to say that you scored a par on this tough target hole. The 17th hole, a severe dogleg left with a severe drop off, is a memorable par 5. After your round, relax with a drink in the fine clubhouse and reflect on the memory of Olde Beau and his amazing legacy.

Amenities include a practice green, range, chipping green, locker room, bar, snack bar, restaurant, rental clubs and pro shop.

The course is not walkable, and you must use a cart. You can book a tee time two weeks in advance. Approximate cost, including cart, is $40 weekdays and $50 on weekends (including Fridays).

The Village of Sugar Mountain Golf Course

Village of Sugar Mountain, Banner Elk • 898-6464

Championship Yardage: 4488
Slope: 94   **Par: 64**
Men's Yardage: 4198
Slope: 91   **Par: 64**
Ladies' Yardage: 3470
Slope: 90   **Par: 64**

The golf course at Sugar Mountain opened in the early 1970s, according to local legend. The staff here did not know who designed the course, and we couldn't glean any information from our typically reliable text sources; but if we could warrant a guess, it might be Russell Breeden. Some holes are set in open terrain, while others are wooded. The course is primarily flat, with some minor elevation changes. Fairways are bluegrass; greens, bentgrass.

Sugar Mountain is best known as one of the largest ski areas in the Southeast. It's still small by Western standards, but it's very popular and often very crowded. A large, multistory concrete-sided building, which looks like an East German government building, is annoyingly perched on top of the mountain and must surely win the prize for the structure most deserving of the wrecking ball.

Architectural snafus aside, the Village of Sugar Mountain offers a fine and somewhat unique golf course. This par 64 course is defined by its nine varied, interesting and thoroughly hazardous par 3s. The other holes offer decent length and width off the tee, although a few are tighter. It looks like little earth was moved during construction. A couple of streams provide hazards, as do some large bunkers. The greens are built-up and medium-sized; they are primarily sloped and slightly undulating. This friendly course is a good place for the beginner and interesting enough for the better and more experienced player who will be happy to keep the score close to par. Overall, Sugar Mountain is a course where residents and visitors alike will have a lot of fun.

Amenities include a practice green and rental clubs.

The course is walkable, and you should walk here; we were told that several octoge-

Photo: N.C. Travel and Tourism

Spectacular views abound on many golf courses in North Carolina's mountains.

narians keep themselves atrophy-free by walking the course on a regular basis. Hey, maybe it'll work for you. You can book a tee time five days in advance. Approximate cost, including cart, is $29 weekdays and $30 on weekends.

Hickory/Lenoir Area

Granada Farms
10 River Dr., Granite Falls • 396-2313
Championship Yardage: 6661
Slope: 121   **Par: 72**
Men's Yardage: 5835
Slope: 112   **Par: 72**
Ladies' Yardage: 4821
Slope: 103   **Par: 72**

According to *Architects of Golf*, Granada Farms opened in 1978, although the pro shop staff cite a somewhat earlier date. Tom Jackson designed the course on rolling terrain. Some of the holes have an open feel, while others are bordered by woods and houses. Bermudagrass blankets the fairways; bentgrass covers the greens.

A well-struck 4-wood from the textile mills of Granite Falls sits Granada Farms Country Club, a housing development with one of Tom

Jackson's first solo designs. Since this effort, Jackson's stock has risen: The houses around his golf courses are bigger, the mounds around the greens are more ominous, the greens are more demonic and the distance from the back tee has increased.

Granite Farms is a good example of why Jackson became such a hot and well-respected designer in the Carolinas. You'll also see the links elements that have continued to define Jackson's work since the construction of Granada Farms. The fairways here are mostly wide, with bunkers and the occasional mound coming into play. The greens are midsize to large, and the green complexes include a multitude of bunkers, mounds and hollows. Water comes into play on a few holes and is ingeniously employed. The course is certainly worth a look if you're in the area, especially if you're a fan of Tom Jackson.

Amenities include a practice green, range, locker room, snack bar and pro shop.

The course is walkable (amazing for a Tom Jackson course), and you can walk after noon on weekends and anytime during the week. You can book a tee time whenever you choose. Approximate cost, including cart, is $20 weekdays and $23 on weekends.

Grassy Creek Golf and Country Club

101 Golf Course Rd., Spruce Pine
• 765-7436
Championship Yardage: 6277
Slope: 120   **Par: 72**
Men's Yardage: 5744
Slope: 116   **Par: 72**
Ladies' Yardage: 4797
Slope: 109   **Par: 72**

Grassy Creek opened the first nine holes in 1956 and the next nine in 1966. The course is laid out on rolling terrain. Fairways combine bluegrass and bentgrass; greens are bentgrass.

At Grassy Creek we found a fine, mature course that's more challenging than it looks. Hit a long or wild hook off the first tee and your ball will land smack in the middle of a McDonald's drive-through. After this, the course becomes a lot prettier. It's predominately tight off the tee, although you can escape by hitting onto the adjacent fairway. The greens are sloped, sometimes crowned, small to midsize on the front nine and slightly larger on the back. Many of the greens are protected by bunkers of various sizes and shapes. Some are flanked by steep embankments. A mountain stream comes into play on some holes. Have a go here if you're looking for a relaxed outing.

Amenities include a practice green, range, chipping green, locker room, snack bar, restaurant, rental clubs and pro shop.

You can walk this course anytime except Saturday before noon. You can book a tee time seven days in advance. Approximate cost, including cart, is $32 weekdays and $35 on weekends.

Lenoir Golf Course

N.C. Hwy. 18, Lenoir • 754-5093
Championship Yardage: 6385
Slope: 112   **Par: 71**
Men's Yardage: 5886
Slope: 106   **Par: 71**
Ladies' Yardage: 4943
Slope: 103   **Par: 71**

Lenoir Golf Course, a Donald Ross design, opened in 1927. Lenoir is not only open, but it's also one of the flattest courses you'll see anywhere outside the coastal plains. You'll find bermudagrass on the fairways and bentgrass on the greens.

This course has a strong membership, so much so that it restricts public play on weekends. Our advice is to take a sick day and spend some time at this fine old course. The staff in the pro shop said that a few changes have been made to the original design. Nevertheless, you'll find plenty of examples of what made Ross "The Man" when it came to golf course architecture and why so many of today's modern earth-moving designs seem superfluous. There's tremendous beauty in simplicity and plenty of difficulty as well. Ross designs have stood the test of golfing time, and this course is an excellent example.

This course is so open, in fact, that wayward drives will find the next fairway and still leave you a shot at the green. The greens are small and sloped and often flanked by one or two simple, flat bunkers. We challenge you to get up and down from one of them! There aren't that many relatively unmolested Ross designs around and even fewer that are open to the public. If you're a Ross fan, you'll want to play this course. It's also a great value.

Amenities include a practice green, locker room, bar, snack bar, restaurant and pro shop.

You can walk anytime, and you won't need a tee time during the week. Approximate cost, including cart, is $22.

Marion Lake Club

N.C. Hwy. 126, Nebo • 652-6232
Championship Yardage: 6110
Slope: No rating   **Par: 70**
Men's Yardage: 5710
Slope: No rating   **Par: 70**
Ladies' Yardage: 4826
Slope: No rating   **Par: 74**

The first nine at Lake Marion opened in 1923; the second nine opened in the early 1970s. The track is set in rolling terrain. In the fairways and on the greens, you'll find bermudagrass. No one is certain about who designed this course, although a staff member said many knowledgeable golfers believe the layout of the original nine smacks of

Donald Ross, and the second nine is the work of Russell Breeden.

Here at Lake Marion, you'll find a country course in a pleasant setting. The older holes, on the back nine, feature small greens, and you can run the ball up to the hole if the ground gets hard. The greens are generally medium-size on the front and often flanked by steep embankments that you'll want to avoid. The back nine features some pretty views of the lake. The 14th hole features a tee shot near a very pretty house just 30 yards from the tee. This popular course is worth a visit.

Amenities include a practice green, range, locker room, snack bar and pro shop.

You can walk this course and book a tee time whenever you choose. Approximate cost, including cart, is $39 weekdays and $49 on weekends.

Orchard Hills Golf Club
Colony Springs Rd., Granite Falls
• 728-3560
Championship Yardage: 6134
Slope: 111   **Par: 72**
Men's Yardage: 5673
Slope: 106   **Par: 72**
Ladies' Yardage: 4803
Slope: 105   **Par: 74**

W. Pitts designed Orchard Hills, which opened in the 1950s. The course is set on undulating terrain, with bermudagrass fairways and bentgrass greens.

At Orchard Hills, we found a mature, sloped and predominately open course, with a number of uphill shots. You won't find a lot of trouble off the tee. There is a small stream that comes into play on a few holes, and a pond could affect one hole. The greens are midsize and sloped, and you'll find some bunkers protecting them.

Amenities include a practice green, range, chipping green, locker room, snack bar and pro shop.

You can walk anytime during the week and after 2 PM on weekends. You can book a tee time as early as Tuesday for the following weekend. Approximate cost, including cart, is $22 weekdays and $26 on weekends.

Quaker Meadows Golf Club
N.C. Hwy. 181, Morganton • 437-2677
Championship Yardage: 6704
Slope: 111   **Par: 71**
Men's Yardage: 6133
Slope: 108   **Par: 71**
Ladies' Yardage: 5625
Slope: No rating   **Par: 71**

The golf course at Quaker Meadows opened in 1969. This Russell Breeden design is open and primarily flat, with bermudagrass fairways and bentgrass greens.

We failed to find any Quakers, but we did find a fine, well-designed Breeden course. Typical of a Breeden track, we found little trouble off the tee, save the occasional stream or out-of-bounds area. The greens are classic Breeden: large, undulating, sloped and flanked by well-shaped and strategically placed bunkers which vary in intensity depending on pin placement. The course is clearly popular with the local golfing population and with good reason — it's playable, fun and challenging without being tricked up. At par 71, the course offers significant distance from the tips. Only one hole presents a water hazard to be feared.

Amenities include a practice green, range, locker room, snack bar, restaurant, rental clubs and pro shop.

You can walk this course anytime except weekends before 2 PM. Book a tee time whenever you choose. Approximate cost, including cart, is $20 weekdays and $24 on weekends.

Around the Mountains . . .

Fun Things To Do

North Carolina's mountains present a playground unlike any other. It's perfectly possible to do anything but play golf here and still find plenty to do.

Hang on. Did we really say that?

Let's try again. You'll find plenty to do here once you've finished playing golf.

That's better.

Once you've finished playing, try mountain biking, antique hunting, roller coastering and horseback riding. In fact, there's enough going on to fill a rather large book, and may we be so bold as to suggest *The Insiders' Guide to North Carolina's Mountains* as an excellent resource. Look for it at fine bookstores, call (800) 716-1388 to order a copy or use the handy order form at the back of this book.

Here are just a few major attractions that you shouldn't miss if you're in the mountains:

In Boone, check out **Horn in the West**, 264-2120, off N.C. 105 and U.S. 321 and 421, an outdoor drama depicting the trials and travails of those who settled the North Carolina mountains, including Daniel Boone. It's two hours of history and entertainment rolled into one. The season lasts from mid-June to mid-August.

Tweetsie Railroad, between Boone and Blowing Rock on U.S 321/221, is a great place to take the family. In addition to the 100-year-old locomotive, there's much to see, do and sample, including a petting farm, Mouse Mine #9, caramel apples and a Ferris wheel and other rides. Call (800) 526-5740 for more information. The season runs from May to Labor Day.

If you're not particularly claustrophobic, **Linville Caverns** is an entertaining option. The caves were initially discovered by Native Americans in the 1820s. The limestone caverns also served as hideouts for Civil War deserters. It's a great place to see some serious caves and experience total darkness when the guides cut the lights. The caves are between Linville and Marion, 4 miles south of the Blue Ridge Parkway on U.S. 221. Call 756-4171 for more information.

For those of you who prefer life in the fast line to life underground, the **New Asheville Speedway** in Asheville (surprise!) at 219 Amboy Road will satisfy your need for speed. This short track used to be a regular NASCAR stop; despite the present-day absence of the big boys, there's still plenty of competition. Enjoy racing action every Friday night from April to September. The speedway's clever tag line, "Each year, 80,000 fans buy seats, but they only use the edge," sums it up. Call 254-4627 for more information.

There are quite a few "touristy" spots in the North Carolina mountains, and Maggie Valley might be the most touristy of them all. One of the major attraction here is the well-known **Ghost Town in the Sky**, Soco Road (U.S. 19), 926-1140 or (800) GHOST TOWN. You must take the incline railroad or a chair lift to get here. The Wild West theme is accentuated by gun fights, jail breaks, bank robberies, country music and Indian dances. You'll also find more than 20 rides, including the Red Devil roller coaster. There is also tons of food to eat, most of it deliciously loaded with calories. Ghost Town in the Sky is open 9 AM to 6 PM from May to October.

No trip to Asheville is complete without a visit to what many must consider North Carolina's premier attraction, the **Biltmore House**. The aforementioned *Insiders' Guide to North Carolina's Mountains* devotes an entire chapter to the Biltmore Estate, and justifiably so. George Vanderbilt completed this magnificent chateau in 1895, and the home is still in the possession of his descendants who graciously open it to the public. In addition to the house, check out the estate's winery; some currently produced wines are gaining significant praise from wine connoisseurs. The Biltmore House itself boasts more than 225 rooms, 50 of which are open to the public.

Biltmore plans plenty of annual events, but perhaps the best time to see the estate is during the Christmas holidays when the house is decorated in a fashion that will drop your jaw and make you happy that you chose the Biltmore House over the golf course. You'll also find four places to eat: Deer Park Restaurant, the Stable Cafe, the Winery Cafe and The Bistro. For more information about the Biltmore Estate, call (800) 543-2961. It's located off N.C. 25 at the junction of Hendersonville Road and McDowell Street..

Waterfalls

No trip to the mountains is complete without a trip down a waterfall. Or if you're not the type to envelop yourself in a barrel and take the plunge, at least you should go see one. It's probably safer. A number of golf courses in the mountains feature waterfalls of various shapes and sizes — often where you least expect them. Following is a selection of non-golf course waterfalls:

Avery County: **Elk Falls**' 65 feet of power

cascade into one of the largest post-waterfall pools in the mountains. Travel north on U.S. Highway 19 E. to Elk Park (just inside the North Carolina-Tennessee border). Turn right on Elk River Road and proceed 4 miles to a parking area next to the Elk River. Hike the short trail to the falls.

Burke County: One of the best-known of all mountain waterfalls, **Linville Falls** tumults down the deep Linville Gorge. The upper and lower falls are equally dramatic. Access Linville Falls at milepost 316.3 on the Blue Ridge Parkway, where there's a visitors center for your convenience.

Transylvania County: One of the most accessible of all mountain waterfalls, **Looking Glass Falls** is also one of the prettiest. It's on U.S. Highway 276, 5.5 miles into Pisgah Forest and the junction with U.S. Highway 64 near Brevard. Your total hike from car to view and back may be less than 30 feet.

Jackson County: You're an eight-hour drive to the beach, so take what you can get and lounge and sunbathe on the sand next to the pool at the foot of **Silver Run Falls**. Why not bring your 60-degree wedge and practice getting out of bunkers? Drive south from Cashiers on N.C. Highway 107 for 4 miles. Park at the gravel-covered pull-off on the left. Follow the short path to the falls.

Blue Ridge Parkway

One of the most remarkable attractions, if we could call it such, is the Blue Ridge Parkway. Construction began in 1935, part of a government project designed to employ then-unemployed people during the Great Depression. The roadway links Great Smoky Mountains National Park in North Carolina and Shenandoah National Park in Virginia. Thus a large portion of the Parkway winds through the North Carolina mountains. In some cases, it's a useful if somewhat circuitous route to some of the golf courses. Mount Mitchell Golf Course, for example, is just a few miles from the Parkway.

Cruising this picturesque roadway provides some of the greatest motoring pleasure anywhere. As you enter, a sign reads "No Commercial Vehicles;" thus, your journey will not be cluttered by the inevitable fast food joints and tourist traps that are sadly all too common on other mountain roads. It's the sort of road that makes you wish for an Italian sports convertible with a close-ratio stick shift, a rocket under the hood and a suspension so tight you go around curves like you're on rails. This is real motoring.

Regularly during your trip, you'll be tempted to stop at one of the wonderful overlooks to take in the view. There are also numerous trails and picnic tables for your convenience. Like the mountains themselves, the Parkway changes dramatically by season. Enjoy the colorful fall. Get up early in the morning and rise above the clouds. Dip into morning fog so thick you can't see five feet in front of you. But drive safely; if you're in the driver's seat, keep your eyes on the road and your hands upon the wheel. Catch the views at the overlooks, not from behind the wheel.

The Parkway emergency number is (800) 727-5928. For general Parkway information, call 298-0398.

Skiing

It's actually quite a good idea to plan a trip with both golf and skiing in mind — if you're that ambitious. If it's cold, then it's quite likely that the course you came to play will be closed. If it's warm, then you won't be able to ski, but you'll be able to play golf.

Skiing in the North Carolina mountains is not like skiing in the West. Most of the time, 99 percent of the snow is manmade and the slopes get icy. If there's real snow, it may be wet, which will turn icy in the late-afternoon shadows. About once every five years a winter of big storms will create optimal snow conditions, even if the runs tend to be a little short. We're sure you've heard that a bad day on the golf course is better than a good day in the office. Well if you take the same attitude about skiing to the North Carolina mountains, you'll have lots of fun.

The major ski areas include:

Hawksnest Golf and Ski Resort, 1800 Skyland Drive, Banner Elk, 963-6561, offers 11 slopes: two beginner, five intermediate and four advanced, with a 619-foot vertical drop. The golf course here is interesting too (see our review in this chapter).

Beech Mountain Ski Resort, Beech Mountain, 387-2011, is the highest ski resort in eastern North America, at approximately 5,500 feet. It's got quite a complex attached to it, including shops, ski rental, restaurants, an ice rink and a nursery. There are 14 slopes in all with a vertical drop of 830 feet. Ample accommodations are available at the resort.

Sugar Mountain, Banner Elk, 898-5421, is 5,300 feet above sea level, and there are 18 slopes. Tackle the whopping (for North Carolina) 1,200-foot drop over and over again until the lactic acid buildup makes your quadriceps scream "No more!" Plenty of chair lifts assure you won't have to wait too long between runs. Ski rentals, lessons, lockers, a nursery and a cafeteria are available.

Appalachian Ski Mountain, Blowing Rock, 295-7828, is a family-owned resort that's been in business since 1962. There are eight slopes with a vertical drop of 365 feet. Check out the giant fireplace in the Bavarian-style lodge overlooking the slopes.

Where to Eat

There are hundreds of excellent restaurants in the mountains. While we're confident the head pro at the golf course you're visiting can provide a sound dining recommendation, here are a few places you might want to go to celebrate that 76 you just posted (even if it was for nine holes). Be aware that America's bout with temperance lives on in full force in a number of counties in the North Carolina mountains. If you're in the mood for a bottle of claret to wash down your steak, you might be out of luck. In vino non veritas. Refer to our Preface for an explanation of the pricing code.

Asheville Area

Boston Pizza
$ • 501 Merrimon Ave., Asheville • 252-9474

Boston Pizza is about a John Daly drive away from the University of North Carolina at Asheville. There's a sort of college-campus beer-and-pizza ambiance to the place, which is also well-suited for families. When school's in session, and the weather is a little chilly, you'll probably run into a few students who look like they're right out of the Seattle "grunge" scene, donning oversize faded sweaters and Kurt Cobain look-alike three-day beard growth.

Alternative music scene aside, the pizza at Boston Pizza is wonderful. You can also devour subs and other Italian staples. This is a student hangout: Adult beverage is never in short supply.

The Grove Park Inn
$$-$$$$ • 290 Macon Ave., Asheville • 252-2711

Even if your taste in accommodations is on the lower end of the scale, we recommend you splurge on the culinary delights at the Grove Park Inn, in part because there's a strong chance (particularly if you ask) that your table may overlook the golf course. You'll be dining next to a Donald Ross masterpiece. And you'll be dining in the hotel with the greatest golf history outside of Pinehurst.

There are other places for blowouts in Asheville, but this one has golf attached to it. You can eat just a stone's throw away from where golfing giants once smacked the ball around.

You'll find three restaurants: Blue Ridge Dining Room, Sunset Terrace and Horizons. Book a tee time on Sunday afternoon and precede your best-ever round with the awe-inspiring brunch in the Blue Ridge. Or have lunch at the Sunset Terrace, with its wonderful views, after an early morning round. Perhaps you're entertaining guests for golf and dinner at Horizons . . . it's hard to miss here.

Louie Michaud's Mountain Brook Center
$$-$$$ • Mallard Sq., Highlands • 526-3573

We'll risk the cliche, but there's something for everyone here at Louie Michaud's: pasta, steak, ribs, lamb, chicken and big salads. Try the prime rib buffet on Wednesday and the seafood buffet on Friday. There's also a belly-bulging brunch buffet on Sundays.

> **FYI**
> Unless otherwise noted, the area code for all phone numbers in this chapter is 704.

Relia's Garden Restaurant
$-$$ • U.S. Hwy. 19-74, Bryson City
• 488-9186

Relia's is just 20 minutes from Bryson City at the Nantahala Outdoor Center. You must cross a steel bridge over the Nantahala River to get to the restaurant. If the weather's right, you should sit on the open-air porch overlooking the herb and vegetable gardens that supply the restaurant. Talk about seeing what you're eating! Thus, you'll find a fresh touch here that few other restaurants can match. Go for the trout or one of the many vegetarian dishes.

Boone/Blowing Rock Area

Famous Louise's
Rock House Restaurant
$-$$, no credit cards • U.S. Hwy. 221, Linville Falls • 765-2702

Louise's Rock House sits right on the border of three counties: Burke, McDowell and Avery. While this might lead to an intra-county identity crisis, it also leads to good food in a storied atmosphere. The building used to be a Prohibition-era roadhouse before becoming a restaurant.

The food here is primarily down home. Menu items include pork loin, country-style steak, roast beef, turkey with all the fixins', fried chicken and a full complement of side dishes. There's also seafood delivered three times weekly from the coast.

Pepper's Restaurant
$-$$ • 2066 Blowing Rock Rd., Boone
• 262-1250

Pepper's has been well known in Boone for more than 20 years. It's particularly popular due mainly to the light, airy interior with its wooden floors and comfortable booths. The specialties here include seafood, pasta and sandwiches. Or try the mountain trout served à la Pepper.

Tumbleweed Grill & Microbrewery
$-$$ • 122 Blowing Rock Rd., Boone
• 264-7111

Tumbleweed serves up a great combination of fine Mexican food and excellent handcrafted beer in an intimate atmosphere. The restaurant is popular and small, so you might want to make a reservation if you're on some sort of official schedule (but who is in the mountains?). Otherwise, enjoy an ale while you wait for your table.

At your table, why not enjoy another beer with your chipotle shrimp Caesar salad or Anasazi chicken sauteed with ancho chiles and goat cheese and rounded off with a Madeira wine sauce and tobacco onions. Yum! Have another beer, and the excess nature of your caloric intake will soon match the excess nature of the lies you'll be telling about how you got up and down for birdie from the stream on the back nine at Boone Golf Course. Yeah, right.

Hickory/Lenoir Area

1859 Café
$$$ • 443 2nd Ave. S.W., Hickory
• 322-1859

In the heart of bustling downtown Hickory is the 1859 Café. We wouldn't wear shorts, but you won't have to walk in wearing black tie. Dinner is served nightly except Sunday and features an outstanding selection of beef, seafood, duck, lamb and a variety of pasta dishes. One of our favorite items on the menu is the Sesame Salmon with Ginger Soy Sauce. If the temperature is pleasant, you might enjoy the outdoor patio. The restaurant also features periodic live entertainment.

Ham's Restaurant
$$ • 204 U.S. 321, Hickory • 326-4267

Ham's is part of a small and good chain of well-run restaurants in North Carolina. There's one in Chapel Hill as well. The restaurant offers breakfast, lunch and dinner and boasts all ABC permits. Ham's provides good basic food in a relaxed atmosphere where you are welcome to show up in whatever clothes you feel like wearing; the restaurant is particularly good at deli-style sandwiches. Ham's is an excellent place to go when there's a sporting event going on that you'd like to watch on their big-screen TV with a couple of friends over a couple of pitchers of beer and a few meaty hamburgers with stacks of french fries and onion rings.

Where to Stay

The variety of accommodations in western North Carolina is as massive as the mountains themselves. All the major chains have built a significant presence here. In addition, there are some wonderful old inns and hotels that date back to the 19th century. Numerous small and intimate bed and breakfast inns dot the pastoral landscape. Many of the places to stay are affiliated with a golf course and can help you secure a tee time. Refer to our Preface for an explanation of the pricing code.

Asheville Area

Best Western Mountainbrook Inn
$$-$$$ • U.S. Hwy. 19, Maggie Valley • 926-3962, (800) 752-6230

In this busy tourist town, the Best Western offers a range of amenities including a pool, hot tub and your own personal rocking chair where you can sit, relax and watch the mountains. You're within walking distance of many of Maggie Valley's attractions.

Cedar Crest
$$$$ • 674 Biltmore Ave., Asheville • 252-1389

Just north of the Biltmore Estate entrance lies this wonderful Victorian bed and breakfast. Asheville businessman William Breese built the home in 1891, but after his death, the house fell into disrepair. Jack and Barbara McEwan came all the way from Wisconsin to renovate the house and open the inn. Their renovation efforts are nothing short of astounding. If you stay at one of then guest rooms, you'll find yourself back in the 1890s. All rooms feature personal telephones (a plus in our opinion, since many b&bs have only central phones), and there's even a croquet court out back. Cedar Crest is open all year.

Inn on Main Street
$ • 88 S. Main St., Weaverville • 645-3442

You can't miss the Inn on Main Street. It's the big, blue house on (you guessed it!) Main Street. The house dates back to 1900, when it was built as a combination office and home for Dr. Zebulon Richardson, a physician who may have left his practice every Wednesday afternoon for his customary and sacred 1:34 tee time. Who knows. The inn has been renovated recently, and the rooms are elegantly furnished with fine antiques.

The Phelps House Bed & Breakfast Inn
$ • W. Main St., Highlands • 526-2590

You'll find lots of charm in this modestly priced B & B that's close to all the fine golf courses in the area. The house dates back to 1885. Each room has a private bath. You'll get a massive and hearty breakfast to push you along while you walk your 18 holes of choice.

The Lion and the Rose
$$$$ • 276 Montford Ave., Asheville • 255-7673

Located right in the middle of Asheville's historic district, the Lion and the Rose also features a witch and a wardrobe — just kidding. In fact, this friendly bed and breakfast features six Victorian guest rooms, each with private bathrooms, and a Southern-style breakfast with all sorts of bacon and ham and jam and other such delights.

The Plaza Motel
$$ • 111 Hendersonville Rd., Asheville • 274-2050

Built in the 1940s but completely refurbished, the Plaza Motel is a comfortable, clean, reasonably priced place to stay that's convenient to Biltmore Village and the Biltmore Estate. Many of the other motels in the area are more expensive.

Richmond Hill Inn
$$$$ • 87 Richmond Hill Dr., Asheville • 252-7313

This superb 12-room bed and breakfast inn was built in 1889 and used to be the home of diplomat Richmond Pearson. Facing the bulldozer in the 1970s, the inn survived extinction and flourished under the ownership of a Greensboro businessman, Albert Michel, who spent three years renovating it. The rooms are beautifully furnished in the Victorian style and feature cable TV, with ESPN. If a room at the inn isn't available, then it's best to try the Croquet Cottages, which, even

Photo: Hound Ears Club

The 15th hole at Hound Ears Club is a short, beautiful yet treacherous par 3 that's one of the most picturesque one-shotters in the North Carolina mountains.

though they were built in 1991, complement the main house. The Richmond Hill Inn is open all year, and your visit will not be complete without a visit to the wonderful restaurant, one of Asheville's best.

Boone/Blowing Rock Area

The Burgiss Farm Bed and Breakfast
$$ • N.C. Hwy. 18, Laurel Springs • (910) 359-2995

Innkeepers Tom and Nancy Burgiss have created a fun atmosphere and offer great hospitality. Additions to this 1897 farmhouse mingle Old World charm with modern conveniences like private baths, a massive great room, a wet bar and a large Jacuzzi room. All this means great privacy, which makes the inn quite popular with honeymooners.

Enjoy select items from Nancy's breakfast menu, which must be one of the most creative around. It features such delicacies as Hawaiian pancakes and baked fruit.

Days Inn - Blowing Rock
$$-$$$ • U.S. Hwy. 321 Bypass, Blowing Rock • 295-4422

This Days Inn offers a good value in an area replete with golf courses. Choose from a variety of configurations among the 118 guest rooms. Also enjoy the enclosed atrium with hot tub.

Eseeola Lodge
$$$$ • U.S. Hwy. 221, Linville • 733-4311

The original Eseeola Lodge, destroyed by fire in 1936, opened somewhere near the turn of the century, and thus there's a great deal of history and tradition associated with this well-known establishment. The railroad made this remote section of the mountains somewhat accessible, and well-heeled vacationers made Eseeola a fine establishment frequented by the well-to-do of the Southeast. The rates, which in the middle of summer are upwards of $250 per night (including dinner and breakfast), are still geared toward the monied, so be prepared to shell out some serious plastic if you're going to stay here.

Still, it's well worth it if you enjoy excellent service, fine food and wonderfully appointed rooms. There are 29 rooms in all, most with private porches, surrounding a large main room with an inviting fireplace. Next to this main gathering room is the Lodge dining room. Gentlemen must wear a jacket and tie for dinner.

One of the biggest benefits of being a guest at the Lodge is access to one of the best golf courses in the Carolinas — Linville Golf Club (see the description earlier in this chapter). Golf packages are only available in May, June, September and October and are quite popular due to the quality of the course and accommodations.

If golf is not your game, Eseeola offers tennis on clay courts, swimming and croquet. There are 2,000 acres for hiking and fishing and special recreation programs for children as well.

Maple Lodge
$$-$$$ • Sunset Dr., Blowing Rock • 295-3331

If you're looking for a wonderful and homey place to stay in the mountains, look no further than the Maple Lodge. You'll find a place that's graceful, simple, elegant and convenient to Main Street in Blowing Rock and to the Blowing Rock Stage Company, which performs in the summer months.

There are 12 guest rooms at the Maple Lodge, and each room is named after a flower. Each room offers a private bath, and some even come complete with crocheted canopies — how about that for elegance! Your room fee includes a large breakfast that will set you up perfectly for the rest of the day. The spread includes muffins (homemade) and other breads, egg dishes and fresh fruit. The meal is served in the sun room, overlooking the flower garden. Innkeeper Marilyn Bateman will make sure your stay here is memorable and relaxing.

The Ragged Garden Inn
$$-$$$ • Sunset Dr., Blowing Rock • 295-9703

The first thing you'll notice at the Ragged Garden Inn is the stunning stone staircase in the grand hall. You'll also notice the English-style flower gardens and the chestnut bark siding found on older homes in this region.

Innkeepers Joyce and Joe Villani tap into their extensive experience as restaurateurs in Connecticut and Florida to produce a sumptuous breakfast. Each of the inn's five guest rooms has a private bath. The inn is open from April to January; a good time to be here is in the spring when the garden is at its best.

The Switzerland Inn
$-$$$$ • Blue Ridge Pkwy., Mile Post 334, Little Switzerland • 762-2153, (800) 654-4026

Just a well-struck 5-iron from the Blue Ridge Parkway, this fine old inn offers 55 rooms and an outstanding view of the mountains. Enjoy fine dining here as well. It's a friendly place, and you'll end up meeting and mingling with other guests, perhaps even sharing a tee time at a local course. Fall is the peak season.

Hickory/Lenoir Area

Holiday Inn Express
$$ • 142 Wilkesboro Blvd., Lenoir • 758-4403

The Holiday Inn Express of Lenoir offers clean, comfortable and sensibly priced lodgings in an area where there aren't many hotels. Your room price includes continental breakfast, access to the outdoor swimming pool, cable TV (with HBO and ESPN) plus free access to a local gymnasium where you can further develop your golfing muscles.

The Hickory Bed and Breakfast
$$$ • 464 7th St. SW, Hickory • 324-0548

A half-mile from downtown Hickory, you'll find The Hickory Bed and Breakfast, which is run by Bob and Pat Lynch. Bob spent 30 years serving his country in the Coast Guard and has augmented the charm of his already charming 1908 Georgian house with a unique collection of collectibles from around the world. The Lynch's offer four rooms, all with queen-size beds and adjoining bathrooms. Being near all the furniture factories, the inn also features fine antiques. Before you leave for your daily business or pleasure, the Lynch's will cook you up a large breakfast.

Howard Johnson Hotel
$$ • 483 Hwy. 70 SW, Hickory • 322-1600

Convenient to I-40 and all of Hickory's major thoroughfares, the Hickory Howard Johnson offers a full range of amenities and goodies including a restaurant and lounge, banquet facilities, family rates, senior rates, cable TV (with ESPN and free HBO), swimming pool, fitness center, sauna, laundromat and a fax service.

The Grand Strand of South Carolina

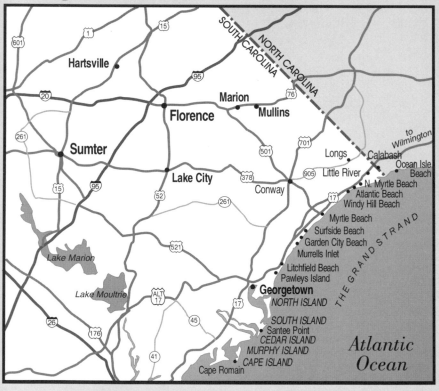

SOUTH CAROLINA

NORTH CAROLINA

to Wilmington

601
1
15
95
20
261
95
15
52
521
ALT 17
26
176
41
45
17
261
378
501
701
905
76
17

Hartsville

Marion
Florence
Mullins

Sumter

Lake City

Conway

Longs
Calabash
Ocean Isle
Beach
Little River
N. Myrtle Beach
Atlantic Beach
Windy Hill Beach
Myrtle Beach
Surfside Beach
Garden City Beach
Murrells Inlet
Litchfield Beach
Pawleys Island

THE GRAND STRAND

Lake Marion

Lake Moultrie

Georgetown
NORTH ISLAND

SOUTH ISLAND

Santee Point
CEDAR ISLAND
MURPHY ISLAND
CAPE ISLAND

Cape Romain

Atlantic
Ocean

South Carolina's Grand Strand

The Grand Strand is a 60-mile stretch of coast which extends from Southport, North Carolina, to Georgetown, South Carolina. Anchored by the booming tourist resort of Myrtle Beach, the area includes more than 100 golf courses . . . yes, actual championship golf courses. Almost 4 million rounds are played here every year.

In addition to Myrtle Beach, the Grand Strand includes North Myrtle Beach and Little River in the northern part of South Carolina and Calabash and the Brunswick Island area in the southern part of North Carolina. Also, the Grand Strand stretches south from Myrtle Beach to Surfside, Murrells Inlet, Litchfield, Pawleys Island and Georgetown.

Golfing on the Grand Strand

The golf season on the Grand Strand is year-round, with the busiest and most expensive peaks in spring and fall. However, the busiest, thus most expensive, hotel season is summer, when families and students of all ages throng to the clean white sands of the public beaches along the Atlantic.

At least a hundred hotels offer golf packages that include accommodations, tee times and usually breakfast. Some will also package theater tickets or dinner if you are interested in a simple plan for the family's vacation. The golf package usually is the way to go, unless you live here or own your own condo for annual golf vacation stays. In addition to the cost savings of a hotel's golf package, the convenience is built in. You can re-quest that the golf director of the hotel book the room and the tee times. Hotels specializing in golf packages do staff a golf department where knowledgeable employees can book via computer on courses of your choosing or, on your first trip here, you may want to ask for the golf director's recommendations of the most convenient, most challenging, easiest or something in a particular price range.

We've listed most of the best courses; however, everyone's definition of the best course differs. Other courses are available, and still more will open over the next year; we'll review them in our next edition.

All courses on the Grand Strand have eight or more different rate periods during the year. Within those periods, summer and winter specials, afternoon and twilight deals, coupon discounts, locals' rates or short-term memberships sometimes are offered. The greens fees listed here indicate the widest price range. The time of year and day will be reflected in each course's daily fees, and we recommend that you ask for details when you book your tee time directly. If you book through a hotel as part of a golf package, you will pay less than the daily fee. Several of the top-rated courses carry surcharges that are not itemized in packages; be sure to inquire when booking your golf package. The package prices may not include that surcharge for certain courses, and you don't want any surprises taking a bite out of your budget. Most courses welcome walk-ons, yet they are sometimes so full that tee times are not available. Tee times are accepted up to a year in advance by most courses, and pre-booking is recommended if you are picky about the course, day or time you play.

GOLF COURSES ON THE GRAND STRAND OF SOUTH CAROLINA

Course Name	Type	# Holes	Par	Slope	Yards	Walking	Booking	Cost w/ Cart
Angels Trace								
North Course	public	18	72	129	6216	call	anytime	$50
South Course	public	18	72	132	6442	call	anytime	$50
Arcadian Shores Golf Club	resort	18	72	131	6485	no	365 days	$20-78
Arrowhead Country Club								
Lakes/Cypress Course	public	18	72	122	6242	no	365 days	$23-79
Azalea Sands Golf Course	public	18	72	116	6287	yes	365 days	$20-54
Bay Tree Golf Plantation								
Gold Course	public	18	72	128	6390	yes	365 days	$34-55
Green Course	public	18	72	126	6492	yes	365 days	$35-55
Silver Course	public	18	72	122	6363	yes	365 days	$35-55
Beachwood Golf Club	public	18	72	117	6344	no	365 days	$2
Belle Terre	public	18	72	n/r	6666	no	395 days	$54-71
Blackmoor	public	18	72	118	6217	no	365 days	$32-81
Brunswick Plantation & Golf Links	semiprivate	18	72	124	6215	no	7 days	$30-55
Buck Creek Plantation								
Cypress/Tupelo Course	public	18	72	126	6306	no	365 days	$25-68
Meadow/Cypress Course	public	18	72	119	6211	no	365 days	$25-68
Tupelo/Meadow Course	public	18	72	119	6115	no	365 days	$25-68
Burning Ridge								
East Course	semiprivate	18	72	119	6216	no	365 days	$20-58
West Course	semiprivate	18	72	114	6237	no	365 days	$20-58
Caledonia Golf & Fish Club	public	18	70	115	6104	no	365 days	$51-96
Carolina Shores Golf & Country Club	public	18	72	122	6231	no	3 days	$25-55
Colonial Charters Golf and Country Club	semiprivate	18	72	119	6337	no	365 days	$24-49
Cypress Bay Golf Club	public	18	72	110	6101	yes	365 days	$20-58
Deer Track Golf resort								
North Course	semiprivate	18	72	121	6511	yes	365 days	$24-55
South Course	semiprivate	18	71	119	6143	yes	365 days	$24-55
Dunes Golf and Beach Club	private	18	72	130	6565	no	365 days	$100

Course	Type	Holes	Par	Slope	Yardage		Open	Price
Eagle Nest Golf Club	public	18	72	116	6417	yes	365 days	$42
Eastport Golf Club	public	18	70	111	5400	no	365 days	$24
Heather Glen Golf Links								
1 Red/2 White Course	public	18	72	110	6337	no	365 days	$25-81
2 White/3 Blue Course	public	18	72	109	6510	no	365 days	$25-81
3 Blue/1 Red Course	public	18	72	126	6427	no	365 days	$25-81
Heritage	public	18	71	122	6575	no	365 days	$52-72
Indigo Creek Golf Club	semiprivate	18	72	120	6185	yes	365 days	$20-38
Island Green Country Club								
Dogwood/Holly Course	semiprivate	18	72	111	5847	yes	365 days	$23-42
Holly/Tall Oaks Course	semiprivate	18	72	111	5864	yes	365 days	$23-42
Tall Oaks/Dogwood Course	semiprivate	18	72	111	5705	yes	365 days	$23-42
Legends								
Heathland Course	public	18	71	121	6190	no	365 days	$87
Moorland Course	public	18	72	130	6125	no	365 days	$87
Parkland Course	public	18	72	127	6425	no	365 days	$87
Litchfield Country Club	resort	18	72	130	6342	yes	365 days	$40-69
Long Bay Club	public	18	72	130	6565	no	365 days	$50-97
Marsh Harbour	public	18	71	121	6000	no	anytime	$52-72
Myrtle Beach National Golf Club								
North Course	public	18	72	109	6033	yes	365 days	$25-50
South Course	public	18	72	118	6089	yes	365 days	$25-50
West Course	public	18	72	113	6113	yes	365 days	$25-50
Myrtle West Golf Course	semiprivate	18	72	118	6191	no	365 days	$25-58
Myrtlewood Golf Course								
Palmetto Course	semiprivate	18	72	118	6495	no	365 days	$24-62
PineHills Course	semiprivate	18	72	119	6112	no	365 days	$24-62
Ocean Harbour Golf Links	resort	18	72	127	6592	no	7 days	$25-76
Ocean Isle Beach Golf Course	public	18	72	122	6146	yes	365 days	$20-43
Ocean Ridge Plantation								
Lion's Paw Golf Links	public	18	72	130	6457	no	anytime	$30-80
Panther's Run Golf Links	public	18	72	134	6706	yes	anytime	$30-80
Oyster Bay Golf Links	public	18	71	130	6560	no	365 days	$87
Pawleys Plantation Golf & Country Club	public	18	72	132	6522	no	365 days	$47-82

Course Name	Type	# Holes	Par	Slope	Yards	Walking	Booking	Cost w/ Cart
Pearl Golf Links								
East Course	public	18	72	132	6543	no	365 days	$69
West Course	public	18	72	131	6738	no	365 days	$69
Pine Lakes International Country Club	semiprivate	18	72	118	6522	no	365 days	$47-110
Possum Trot Golf Course	public	18	72	113	6388	yes	365 days	$32-57
Quail Creek Golf Course	semiprivate	18	72	116	6331	yes	365 days	$20-58
River Club	semiprivate	18	72	125	6240	yes	365 days	$40-74
River Hills Golf and Country Club	public	18	72	123	6400	no	365 days	$25-60
River Oaks Golf Plantation								
Bear/Fox Course	public	18	72	118	6314	no	365 days	$20-55
Fox/Otter Course	public	18	72	118	6345	no	365 days	$20-55
Otter/Bear Course	public	18	72	119	6425	no	365 days	$20-55
Robbers Roost Golf Club	public	18	72	129	6725	no	365 days	$29-40
Sea Trail Plantation & Golf resort								
Byrd Course	resort	18	72	126	6263	no	365 days	$34-58
Jones Course	resort	18	72	126	6334	no	365 days	$39-63
Maples Course	resort	18	72	117	6332	no	365 days	$34-58
Surf Golf and Beach Club	semiprivate	18	72	119	6360	no	365 days	$43-70
Tidewater Golf Club and Plantation	public	18	72	126	6000	no	365 days	$63-98
Tradition Club	public	18	72	n/a	6500	yes	365 days	$43-61
Waterway Hills								
Lakes Course	public	9	36	115	3001	yes	365 days	$29-54
Oaks Course	public	9	36	118	3080	yes	365 days	$29-54
Ravine Course	public	9	36	112	2579	yes	365 days	$29-54
Wicked Stick	public	18	72	n/r	6156	no	365 days	$30-65
Wild Wing Plantation								
Avocet Course	public	18	72	119	6614	no	365 days	$100
Falcon Course	public	18	72	117	6674	no	365 days	$100
Hummingbird Course	public	18	72	123	6310	no	365 days	$100
Woodstork Course	public	18	72	111	6598	no	365 days	$100
Willbrook Plantation Golf Club	semiprivate	18	72	127	6077	yes	365 days	$33-63
The Witch Golf Links	public	18	71	121	6011	no	365 days	$46-83

Ladies are welcome on all courses any day. Walking is permitted on certain courses, but not every day, so you should inquire specifically if that is your interest.

Refer to this chapter's "Where to Stay" section for information about a few hotels that offer golf packages. For a complete listing, call **Myrtle Beach Golf Holiday** at (800) 845-GOLF. Do make reservations before your arrival. Maybe you remember the days of driving to the beach on a whim, arriving in the middle of the night and finding a room. Well, those days are long gone, folks. During certain weeks, which you might not even suspect, every single bed is full. In addition to the beach, the golf courses, the theaters and retail shops that attract tourists, conventions of all shapes and sizes bring the remainder of the area's 12 million annual visitors.

Getting around on the Grand Strand is fairly simple. Myrtle Beach itself is just a long, skinny island bordered on the east by the Atlantic Ocean and on the west by the Intracoastal Waterway. U.S. Highway 17 stretches the length of the coast, and you can find a multitude of golf courses, restaurants and accommodations right on this route without any possibility of getting lost. U.S. 17 is also called The Bypass where it branches and attempts to circumvent the main part of Myrtle Beach; and U.S. Highway 17 Business is called Kings Highway where it runs through the city. Both roadways run back together, so you still can't get lost no matter which north-south route you choose. Both route you by golf courses, as does almost any turn you take. Other main routes to the beach area from the west are S.C. Highway 9 and U.S. Highway 501. Many major golf courses also line these routes. And that's about all you need to know of our geography to get around just fine.

The greatest confusion tourists encounter is in learning that Myrtle Beach and North Myrtle Beach are two different cities, and both have their east-west streets labeled numerically and geographically. For instance, 17th Street could exist in four different places — north or south in either city. Remember to pay attention to exact addresses in that respect.

One location you will need to find that isn't labeled is Restaurant Row. It's a 2-mile strip of some of the best restaurants around, just north of Myrtle Beach on U.S. Highway 17. Nowhere does a sign proclaim that you are there, but you'll know it; otherwise, any local can direct you. Refer to our "Where to Eat" section for some favorite places to eat all along the Strand, and feel free to try others. Plenty of good food is a staple of the area's Southern hospitality.

If you should encounter heavy traffic, seemingly standing still on occasion, don't worry; it will be a problem only for a couple of miles, and probably only during happy hour and dinner hour, when locals just want to get home and visitors want to eat. You're probably on vacation anyway and don't need to rush to get anywhere. That same traffic is nowhere to be found when you're on the way to your early morning tee time. The minor traffic congestion, which is the major topic of locals' conversation, is nothing like that of a big city.

FYI

Unless otherwise noted, the area code for all N.C. phone numbers in this chapter is 910; the area code for all S.C. numbers is 803.

What to Bring

Bring your golf clubs, and that's all that matters, because that's the most important activity along the Grand Strand. Just wait — you'll see that golf really is the consuming passion. If you don't bring your clubs, or if a companion decides to take up the game while here, rental clubs are available at almost all courses.

Golf in the Carolinas is a vacation in more ways than one. The pace is slow, and the way of life is relaxed. You can pack casual attire and bathing suits for the summer. Or just buy it in the pro shop or at virtually any corner shop once you've arrived. You won't ever doubt the prevalence of beachwear shops after one drive along the Strand. Wear golf shirts and Bermuda shorts for golfing. Pack sweaters or jackets for winter trips. Don't worry about dressing up for dinner along the coast, because everyone is in resort mode. Casual wear, even shorts, is acceptable at most restaurants.

You might need your camera, because no

one will ever believe the story about the alligator unless you can prove it.

You need to bring your family for sure. Even if you're planning a "strictly golf" trip, so much is available for the non-golfers in your family that everyone can have a good time. The beach is the most important attraction from sometime in March through November, with only a few cool days scattered throughout. Water parks and miniature golf are plentiful for the children's entertainment. World-class shopping abounds from basic malls to outlets and specialty shops. And country music performances and dinner shows of many varieties delight visitors young and old.

For complete information on the area, pick up a copy of *The Insiders' Guide® to Myrtle Beach & the Grand Strand*, available in bookstores nationwide or through the convenient order form in the back of this book.

Angels Trace Golf Links
1215 Angels Club Dr., Sunset Beach, N.C.
• 579-2277, (800)718-5733

Both Angels Trace courses offer a pro shop, club rentals, snack shop, driving range and putting green. Walking is not allowed.

North Course
Championship Yardage: 6640	
Slope: 139	**Par: 72**
Men's Yardage: 6216	
Slope: 129	**Par: 72**
Other Yardage: 4524	
Slope: 115	**Par: 72**
Ladies' Yardage: 5316	
Slope: 111	**Par: 72**

This public, 36-hole complex opened in November 1995. It's near The Pearl and a number of other popular courses on the southern edge of North Carolina where scenic courses and seafood restaurants are sprinkled throughout Calabash, Sunset Beach and Ocean Isle Beach. No houses are around the courses, and no noise or distractions will hinder your golf game here.

This Clyde Johnston course follows the lay of the land, with natural streams running through it. Gentle mounds and a few manmade ponds add to the character. Nos. 5 and 9 are bulkheaded. No. 5 is the signature: a par 4 dogleg left. The first shot is a placement shot, and the second must carry over water. Traps are inside the fairway; two are in front and one on the side of the green, which is on a hill surrounded by oyster shells. Water comes into play on at least nine holes. You'll find some good long par 5s that require accurate shot placement. Tees, fairways and rough are bermudagrass, and greens are bentgrass. Fairway width varies from wide to narrow. It's a tough course, but popular for its playability. The average golfer will enjoy it.

Greens fees with cart cost an average of $50. Rates will vary during eight different seasons for the area's courses. Ladies are welcome anytime.

South Course
Championship Yardage: 6876	
Slope: 139	**Par: 72**
Men's Yardage: 6442	
Slope: 132	**Par: 72**
Other Yardage: 5590	
Slope: 119	**Par: 72**
Ladies' Yardage: 4811	
Slope: 122	**Par: 72**

Also designed by Clyde Johnston, this course shows similarities to the North Course. Water is a factor on 15 holes. You have a chance of losing your ball on at least 10 of these. No. 4 is a par 3 — 147 yards from the men's tees. Your tee shot is downhill to a large green with bunkers in front and back. The green slopes from back to front, so you must stay below the hole to have a good chance for birdie. The challenging finishing hole is a par 5 of 465 yards that doglegs right. You can really let it fly here because of the wide hitting area. The best approach to the green is from the left side of the fairway; however, you must be careful not to be too far left; be aware of

INSIDERS' TIP

Proper attire is required on most golf courses. Wear collared golf shirts and Bermuda shorts of standard length for summer dress. Socks are optional on most courses. Jeans, T-shirts, tank tops, short shorts and bathing suits are inappropriate attire.

water on that side. Conversely, don't be too far right, because trees will block your approach shot. The green is wide and well protected by three small bunkers at its front and one large bunker in the back that runs the entire length of the green.

Greens fees with cart average $50. No restrictions are placed on ladies' play.

Arcadian Shores Golf Club

701 Hilton Rd., Myrtle Beach • 449-5217, (800) 248-9228

Championship Yardage: 6446	
Slope: 131	Par: 72
Men's Yardage: 6028	
Slope: 116	Par: 72
Other Yardage: 5636	
Slope: 113	Par: 72
Ladies' Yardage: 5113	
Slope: 117	Par: 72

This 18-hole course was designed by Rees Jones in 1974. It was refurbished during 1994 and was in excellent condition and quite popular for the 1995 and 1996 seasons. Arcadian Shores includes 64 creatively placed sand bunkers among natural lakes and elevated lush bermudagrass greens. Water comes into play on eight holes. The fairways are wide and beautifully tree-lined. A challenging hole is No. 2, a 178-yard par 3. Your shot must travel over water and up a small hill to a fairly large green. The par 4 13th hole is one of the prettiest on the course. If your drive is lucky enough to make it to the top of a knoll, your ball will roll, leaving a relatively easy second shot over water to the green.

The course offers rental clubs, a driving range, practice green, pro shop, bar and restaurant. Ladies are welcome and encouraged by twilight clinics and discounted greens fee offered one afternoon each week during the summer. Also, locals are eligible for a special rate.

Greens fees range from $43 to $86 depending on season and include a cart. Walking is not allowed. Arcadian Shores accepts tee times 365 days in advance.

Arcadian Shores is affiliated with the oceanfront Hilton Hotel, and the golf course is across the street. The course is bisected by Hilton Road, which connects to U.S. 17 from the oceanfront.

Arrowhead Country Club

1201 Burcale Rd., Myrtle Beach
• 236-3243, (800) 236-3243

Lakes/Cypress Course

Championship Yardage: 6666	
Slope: 130	Par: 72
Men's Yardage: 6242	
Slope: 122	Par: 72
Other Yardage: 5713	
Slope: 115	Par: 72
Ladies' Yardage: 4812	
Slope: No rating	Par: 72

Cypress/Waterway Course

Championship Yardage: 6644	
Slope: 130	Par: 72
Men's Yardage: 6183	
Slope: 122	Par: 72
Other Yardage: 5559	
Slope: 115	Par: 72
Ladies' Yardage: 4624	
Slope: 116	Par: 72

Lakes/Waterway Course

Championship Yardage: 6612	
Slope: 130	Par: 72
Men's Yardage: 6179	
Slope: 122	Par: 72
Other Yardage: 5560	
Slope: 115	Par: 72
Ladies' Yardage: 4698	
Slope: 116	Par: 72

Raymond Floyd and Tom Jackson unveiled this creation in November 1994. The first 18 of 27 holes opened with large bermudagrass greens and unique bermudagrass fairways due to numerous undulations, an unusual feature for a lowlands course, according to Floyd.

The nine-hole Lakes Course measures 3317 yards from the championship tees. The nine-hole Cypress Course measures 3349 yards among hardwoods standing in coastal wetlands.

The signature 13th hole is a beautiful 355-yard par 4 that crosses water twice and overlooks the Intracoastal Waterway. Mounds, pristine woodlands and lakes, which come into play on 17 holes, makes the Lakes/Cypress 18 a challenging course. One particularly tough hole is No. 2 on the Cypress, a narrow par 5. Water flanks the left side of the tee shot, which is followed by a lay-up, then another shot across water to a green sitting at its edge.

The nine-hole Waterway Course opened

in fall 1995. You guessed it; it also wraps along the snaking Intracoastal and calls upon all your skills to avoid water hazards.

The national trend toward 27-hole courses is growing, and Arrowhead's owners are delighted to have more to offer. They also emphasize their proximity to the airport for visiting golfers in a rush.

Arrowhead Country Club is the first Floyd signature course in South Carolina. Floyd won the GOLF MAGAZINE SENIOR TOUR Championship played in Myrtle Beach in November 1994, a very good year for him. He previously won three major U.S. championships, 22 events on the regular PGA tour and nine tournaments in less than two full years on the PGA Senior Tour.

Jackson has been involved with 75 golf course projects, including design and construction of six Myrtle Beach area courses.

Rental clubs, a driving range, putting green, pro shop, locker room, bar and restaurant are available. The upscale country club atmosphere is classy and comfortable. No restrictions are placed on ladies' play. Frequent summer specials are organized to invite family or junior play.

Walking is not allowed at Arrowhead. Greens fees include cart and average $79. Tee times may be booked up to a year in advance.

Azalea Sands Golf Club
U.S. Hwy. 17 S., North Myrtle Beach • 272-6191, (800) 253-2312
Championship Yardage: 6902

Slope: 123	**Par: 72**
Men's Yardage: 6287	
Slope: 116	**Par: 72**
Ladies' Yardage: 5172	
Slope: 119	**Par: 72**

This 18-hole course, designed by Gene Hamm, was built in 1972. It's 6902 yards of golfing pleasure, according to Manager Dick Hester. Tifdwarf greens are set among lakes, bunkers and trees. One of the toughest holes is the 18th, a 540-yard par 5. Another challenging hole is a 195-yard par 3. The 5th hole requires a shot over a lake to a green well guarded by bunkers.

Amenities include practice greens, bar, snack bar, beverage cart, pro shop and rental

clubs. No driving range is provided. No restrictions are placed on ladies' play.

Greens fees, including cart, range from $20 to $54. The 12-month VIP membership for $25 is a great deal; with membership, a round costs $20. Azalea Sands accepts tee times 365 days in advance. Walking is allowed certain times of year, and a pull cart costs $3.

The course is just minutes from several of the largest golf equipment shops and a couple of miles from Barefoot Landing, a popular destination for lunch or dinner.

Bay Tree Golf Plantation
S.C. Hwy. 9, North Myrtle Beach • 249-1487, (800) 845-6191

You can't miss this golf course on S.C. Highway 9 because of its gigantic golf ball, which doubles as a water tower for the Little River area. Bay Tree has three 18-hole courses, all designed by George Fazio and Russell Breeden. In 1972, Bay Tree Golf Plantation was the first to build three courses simultaneously at the same site. It's a popular club for local memberships among the North Myrtle Beach crowd. All three courses have plentiful water hazards and bermudagrass fairways, which are overseeded with rye during the winter.

The clubhouse offers a comfortable and scenic bar and restaurant at the 55th hole, a well-stocked pro shop and large men's and ladies' locker rooms. A driving range, practice green and rental clubs are available. Nearby, you'll find condominiums for rent — a great option when you want to be on three great golf courses and a bit away from the beach and its traffic.

Greens fees range from $20 to $40, and carts are an additional $15. Check for afternoon or summer specials as well as three- or seven-day memberships. All three courses accept tee times 365 days in advance, and walking is allowed.

Gold Course
Championship Yardage: 6942

Slope: 135	**Par: 72**
Men's Yardage: 6390	
Slope: 128	**Par: 72**
Ladies' Yardage: 5264	
Slope: 117	**Par: 72**

The No. 1 handicap hole is the par 4 No. 5, which plays 455 yards from the championship tees, 409 yards from the men's tees. Heavy hitters may choose to lay up short of the water — 265 yards out. If you are in control of your drive, you can hit into a narrow landing area approximately 160 yards from the pin. Shots too far right will land in the woods. The green is guarded by a trap on the left that should not come into play, but the green is undulating and pin placement is crucial to making par or birdie here. The 16th tee and fairway flank S.C. 9 in front of the towering golf ball. A birdie is a real possibility here if you carry the water and cut the dogleg. Several fairway bunkers might come into play with errant tee shots. If you do score birdie here, you won't have long to enjoy it; No. 17, a 189-yard par 3, plays longer than it appears. The green is encircled by water and bunkers.

The LPGA championship played on this course in 1977 was the first nationally televised tournament from the Grand Strand. This course was named to *Golf for Women* magazine's Top Fairways list of the country's 100 most women-friendly golf courses. The 1995 list — the first of its kind — was compiled by a panel of experts from all facets of the golfing community.

Green Course

Championship Yardage: 7044

Slope: 135	**Par: 72**
Men's Yardage: 6492	
Slope: 126	**Par: 72**
Ladies' Yardage: 5362	
Slope: 118	**Par: 72**

The Green Course features narrow fairways. You're immediately initiated to its difficulty on No. 1, a 563-yard par 5 where you must traverse water to reach a narrow green. Water comes into play on many holes, including the par 4 11th, where a hazard intersects the fairway. Your tee shot must lay up short of the water. The green is guarded by bunkers in front and back.

Silver Course

Championship Yardage: 6871

Slope: 131	**Par: 72**
Men's Yardage: 6363	
Slope: 122	**Par: 72**
Ladies' Yardage: 5417	
Slope: 116	**Par: 72**

Bay Tree rebuilt and reshaped its Silver Course and reopened it in fall 1995. Greens, tees and traps were restructured and senior tees added. The fine George Fazio design and undulations didn't change. The greens were made much larger, and some trees were removed. Target mounds behind some of the greens are helpful for approach shots. Many believe it to be the locals' favorite, and it's often preferred by women. Since Bay Tree opened its 54 holes, no major changes were made until the 1995 restructuring of the Silver Course; the Gold and Green courses are slated for overhaul over the next few years.

The Silver course starts with a difficult 388-yard par 4. It's a slight dogleg right on a narrow fairway with woods on both sides. The lone fairway bunker shouldn't pose a problem for long hitters. You should constantly stay right on this hole and have a good approach to the large undulating green. The back nine includes the tough par 5 12th hole, which is 518 yards. In order to have a good approach, drives and second shots must be from the center of the fairway left, but beware of a small pond. Reach here safely and you'll have a nice short iron shot to a triangular green that is well guarded by three sand traps.

Beachwood Golf Club

1520 U.S. Hwy. 17 S., North Myrtle Beach
• 272-6168, (800) 526-4889
Championship Yardage: 6825

Slope: 120	**Par: 72**
Men's Yardage: 6344	
Slope: 117	**Par: 72**
Other Yardage: 5817	
Slope: 115	**Par: 72**
Ladies' Yardage: 5052	
Slope: 111	**Par: 72**

The 18-hole course, set between the Intracoastal Waterway and the Atlantic Ocean — as are many Grand Strand courses — was designed by Gene Hamm and built in 1968. Its lush fairways and bermudagrass greens meander through tall pines and lakes and host abundant native wildlife. The signature finishing hole, a par 3, plays 239 yards and calls for a long, accurate shot to reach a green protected by three bunkers.

The practice facility is multifaceted, with two large greens, a driving range with multiple target areas, a chipping green and practice bunker. A complete pro shop, snack bar and lounge welcome you.

Greens fees, including cart rental, range upward from $22. The course accepts tee times 365 days in advance. Walking is not allowed.

Belle Terre
U.S. Hwy. 501, Myrtle Beach • 449-4470, (800) 340-0072
Championship Course
Championship Yardage: 7013
Slope: 134	Par: 72
Men's Yardage: 6672	
Slope: 127	Par: 72
Other Yardage: 6368	
Slope: 123	Par: 72
Other Yardage: 5880	
Slope: 113	Par: 72
Ladies' Yardage: 5049	
Slope: No rating	Par: 72

Rees Jones Par 58 Course
Back Yardage: 3201
Slope: 93
Front Yardage: 2802

Belle Terre is planned as a 54-hole complex. Two championship courses and an 18-hole executive course all were designed by Rees Jones. One championship course and the executive course opened in fall 1995. The executive course includes par 3s and 4s for an overall par 58. A new feature here is the motorized pull-cart for golfers who desire walking.

The name Belle Terre (beautiful earth) came from Jones' description of the property. The Championship Course, with tifdwarf bermudagrass, measures more than 7000 yards. The front nine has water and sand on six holes. The back nine has sand and protected wetlands. The combination of water, sand and protected wetlands makes this a tight course where course management, club selection and ball placement are paramount.

"The soil and natural shape of the land allow for subtle elements of an old-style, classic design, giving the holes clear definition so that a player can stand on the tee and have a clear perspective without using gimmicks. The subtleties make the course different every time you play it," Jones said.

The driving range is lighted and features rolling terrain and tees on each end. The pro shop is fully stocked, and the clubhouse has a nice bar and restaurant as well as a collection of Jimmy D'Angelo's memorabilia. (D'Angelo is one of the consultants for the course and is well known as the first pro in Myrtle Beach.) Walking is not allowed on the Championship Course. Greens fees, with cart, are $54 to $71. Ball cleaners are on the carts. The staff is ex-

We're No. 1

South Carolina is the leading golf vacation destination in the country, according to *Golf Digest* subscribers.

To the state's leaders as well as the golf community, this designation, achieved in 1995, is a giant leap toward reaching the destiny they've envied. The Grand Strand

area, sprawling around Myrtle Beach, is home to half the state's courses. It dubbed itself "America's favorite golf resort" years ago and waited with some degree of impatience and a steady pace of construction and marketing for a study to prove the assertion accurate.

The latest study by the South Carolina Department of Parks, Recreation and Tourism (PRT) reported that the state's economy gained more than $644 million from golf course operations alone in 1992-93. When transportation, hotels, restaurants and other expenditures are factored in, the figure rises to $1.5 billion.

"Golf is a key example of what this state has to gain by aggressively and intelligently marketing its best resources," said Grace Young, PRT director, who is happy to recognize a good thing for her state when she sees it.

"Attracting more golfers means more jobs, more income and more tax revenue for the state," said Gov. David M. Beasley in announcing that the state will continue to promote itself internationally by focusing attention on its outstanding golf at more than 200 courses.

All of this is supporting evidence that you're welcome here in South Carolina, whether to play a round of golf or to relocate and enjoy a new lifestyle. It didn't get to be the golfers' top choice by being anything less than the best.

Photo: HLA Advertising and Public Relations

With such outstanding courses and the comfortable year-round climate, is it any wonder South Carolina courses rank at the top?

tremely friendly here. At the end of your round you are asked to complete a questionnaire — for which you earn a beer.

Blackmoor

S.C. Hwy. 707, Murrells Inlet • 650-5555
Championship Yardage: 6614

Slope: 126	**Par: 72**
Men's Yardage: 6217	
Slope: 118	**Par: 72**
Other Yardage: 5774	
Slope: 111	**Par: 72**
Ladies' Yardage: 4807	
Slope: 115	**Par: 72**

This 18-hole course was built in 1990 and was the first in the Myrtle Beach area designed by Gary Player. Bermudagrass greens and fairways are always perfectly maintained. Several blind shots to the green complexes will remind you to study the course layout. As with several on the southern end of the Grand Strand, Blackmoor was built on the site of a rice plantation along the Waccamaw River. The natural lakes, cypress trees and moss-draped oaks lend tranquility to the course. From the back veranda of the clubhouse, you can oversee the finishing hole, listen to the birds and commune with nature.

The course includes a bar, snack bar, beverage cart, pro shop and rental clubs. Blackmoor offers a practice green and a chipping area as well as a driving range.

Greens fees range from a $32 summer rate to $81, including cart, during prime spring and fall golfing seasons. Walking is not allowed. Tee times are accepted 365 days in advance.

Brick Landing Plantation

N.C. Hwy. 2, Ocean Isle Beach, N.C.
• 754-5612, (800) 438-3006
Championship Yardage: 6482

Slope: 140	**Par: 72**
Men's Yardage: 6154	
Slope: 132	**Par: 72**
Other Yardage: 5792	
Slope: 122	**Par: 72**
Ladies' Yardage: 4835	
Slope: 114	**Par: 72**

This 18-hole course, designed by H. M. Brazeal along the Intracoastal Waterway, features ocean views. Hardwood forests and saltwater marshes also characterize this South Brunswick Island layout, easy to reach from either Myrtle Beach or Wilmington.

The first two holes and the last two play along the waterway. Four holes on the back nine are adjacent to Sauce Pan Creek which is a saltwater marsh filled with wildlife. Villas along the fairways and homes along the water or among the hardwoods present no problem to the golfer.

Complete practice facilities include putting greens, practice bunkers, a wide driving range with target greens and instructors. Rental clubs are available. Greens fees including cart rental range from $37 to $65.

Brunswick Plantation & Golf Links

U.S. Hwy. 17, Calabash, N.C.

• 287-PUTT, (800) 848-0290

Championship Yardage: 6779	
Slope: 131	Par: 72
Men's Yardage: 6215	
Slope: 124	Par: 72
Other Yardage: 5791	
Slope: 118	Par: 72
Ladies' Yardage: 5210	
Slope: 115	Par: 72

The links-style course was designed by Willard Byrd and opened in 1992. Fairways are bermudagrass, and greens are bentgrass.

The signature hole is the 15th, a par 3 surrounded by oyster shells and water. It's a carry of 197 yards off the back tees over water. No. 4 is a long dogleg right, with water on one side and sand on the other.

Amenities include practice greens, driving range, pro shop, bar and snack bar, beverage cart and rental clubs.

Greens fees range from $30 to $55. Walking is not allowed.

Buck Creek Golf Plantation

S.C. Hwy. 9, North Myrtle Beach

• 249-5996, (800) 344-0982

Cypress/Tupelo Course

Championship Yardage: 6865	
Slope: 132	Par: 72
Men's Yardage: 6306	
Slope: 126	Par: 72
Other Yardage: 5744	
Slope: 115	Par: 72
Ladies' Yardage: 4956	
Slope: 124	Par: 72

Meadow/Cypress Course

Championship Yardage: 6751	
Slope: 126	Par: 72
Men's Yardage: 6211	
Slope: 119	Par: 72
Other Yardage: 5688	
Slope: 111	Par: 72
Ladies' Yardage: 4972	
Slope: 117	Par: 72

Tupelo/Meadow Course

Championship Yardage: 6726	
Slope: 128	Par: 72
Men's Yardage: 6115	
Slope: 119	Par: 72
Other Yardage: 5574	
Slope: 115	Par: 72
Ladies' Yardage: 4684	
Slope: 117	Par: 72

This club's three nine-hole courses are played as three 18-hole pairs. All are naturally beautiful and are kept in top condition. A recent ownership change brought improvements to the already popular complex. Upgraded equipment includes 100 new carts, improvements to the irrigation system and lightweight fairway mowing units that are adjustable within an eighth-inch for immediate impact on course presentation. The new hand-held digital caddy is available for measure to the cup within a yard's accuracy. It's expected to speed play as well as increase shot accuracy. Another feature unique to this course is the installation of a one-hour photo processing lab for an additional service to golfers who want to capture memories of their game. This 137-acre natural wetland sanctuary is home to many varieties of wildlife. All courses were designed by Tom Jackson, built by John McWhite and opened in 1990. All have bermudagrass greens and plentiful water hazards. The complex was designed to accommodate all levels of play and is exceptionally challenging for the low handicapper. Accuracy and shot placement are a must.

No. 9 at Tupelo and No. 2 at Cypress are tough holes. The 9th at Tupelo is a big dogleg left, and you easily can miss the green into traps or wetlands. The Cypress' No. 2 is a par 5 where long hitters off the tee must be aware of the water on the right. The second shot is crucial because it must carry water. Aim for the right side of the green; if you shoot left, you might be in another water hazard. If you get to the front of the green without getting wet, you will be in position for a pitch to the

INSIDERS' TIP

Limit conversation on the green. Concentration is critical to putting, and players should respect each other's time for mental preparation.

green. The Meadows' Nos. 1 and 4 were recently restructured, and the Tupelo's No. 5 had a facelift in 1996, so if you have previously played this complex, be prepared for changes and improvements.

A putting green, driving range, pro shop, rental clubs, a snack bar and bar are offered. Improvements to the clubhouse should be complete for the 1997 season and will include a classy look plus expanded locker rooms with showers. No restrictions are placed on ladies' play.

Walking is not allowed. The course accepts tee times 365 days in advance, and greens fees range from $25 to $68, including cart.

Burning Ridge
U.S. Hwy. 501,
Myrtle Beach • 347-0538,
(800) TEE-OFFS

Both the East and West courses of Burning Ridge are 18 holes. These adjacent courses were built in 1980 and 1987, respectively; both were designed by Gene Hamm. They incorporate numerous lakes and huge molded bunkers, and both feature bermudagrass fairways and greens.

The complex has a practice green, a practice sand trap, driving range, pro shop, bar and restaurant, beverage cart and rental clubs. No restrictions are placed on ladies' play. Walking is not allowed.

Greens fees range from $20 to $58, including cart. Free cart fees are available for juniors during the summer. Burning Ridge is part of the Links Group of courses, all of which accept tee times 365 days in advance from their central toll-free reservation number, noted above.

East Course
Championship Yardage: 6780

Slope: 132	**Par: 72**
Men's Yardage: 6216	
Slope: 124	**Par: 72**
Other Yardage: 5724	
Slope: 114	**Par: 72**
Ladies' Yardage: 4524	
Slope: 115	**Par: 72**

The par 3 No. 12 is 210 yards over water

from the men's tees. You must choose the right club, and you must be long and left because your tee shot must carry over water in front and on the right.

West Course
Championship Yardage: 6714

Slope: 122	**Par: 72**
Men's Yardage: 6237	
Slope: 114	**Par: 72**
Ladies' Yardage: 4831	
Slope: 118	**Par: 72**

No. 14, a 577-yard par 5, is a slight dogleg left and usually plays into the wind. If you want to play 36 holes in one day, this is an ideal place to be; as the saying at Burning Ridge goes: The first 18 was so good, we decided to stay. Any hooks or shanks will definitely find water — it's in view on every hole on this course. You must pick the spots to be aggressive because of this liquid hazard.

Caledonia Golf & Fish Club
King River Rd.,
Pawleys Island
• 237-3675, (800) 483-6800

Championship Yardage: 6503

Slope: 130	**Par: 70**
Men's Yardage: 6104	
Slope 115	**Par: 70**
Other Yardage: 5738	
Slope: 116	**Par: 70**
Ladies' Yardage: 4968	
Slope: 113	**Par: 70**

Caledonia opened in early 1994 and has drawn rave reviews from some of the country's most discriminating golfers. The 18-hole course was built on the site of a historic colonial rice plantation along the Waccamaw River. The centuries-old live oaks will capture your attention; you'll think you're driving onto a movie set. After your round, the rocking chairs beckon from the back porch of the antebellum-style clubhouse overlooking the 18th green. You just might want to live here if you could.

Mike Strantz, former assistant to Tom Fazio, was the architect who made a splash with Caledonia — his first course. Caledonia complements the surrounding natural landscape. Greens are tifdwarf; fairways are 419

> ### FYI
> Unless otherwise noted, the area code for all N.C. phone numbers in this chapter is 910; the area code for all S.C. numbers is 803.

Wild Wing's Wood Stork course was recognized by *Golf Digest* in the "Places to Play, 1994-1995" as a Top 100 Great Value Course in America and a four-star award winner.

bermudagrass. Tees are marked with replicas of the native waterfowl that inhabit the plantation's rice fields: wood duck, mallard, redhead and pintail. Gently sloping fairways with unique landing areas, vast waste bunkers and tough approach shots offer extreme challenges. The hunting and fishing retreat that predates the golf course maintains its old shed where Thursday night socializing remains a time-honored tradition.

The course offers a putting green, a driving net in lieu of a range, a nice pro shop, a three-hole Par 3 course, men's and women's dressing rooms and a comfortable bar and restaurant with good food. No restrictions are placed on ladies' play.

Summer greens fees, including cart, are $51; spring fees are $96. Tee times are accepted a year in advance. Walking is not allowed.

Carolina Shores Golf & Country Club

U.S. Hwy. 17 N., Calabash, N.C.

• 579-2181, (803) 448-2657, (800) 579-8292

Championship Yardage: 6783

Slope: 128	**Par: 72**

Men's Yardage: 6231

Slope: 122	**Par: 72**

Ladies' Yardage: 5385

Slope: 122	**Par: 72**

The 18-hole course opened in 1974. It was designed by Tom Jackson. The greens and fairways are tifdwarf bermudagrass.

The toughest hole, ironically, is the 1st — a long par 5 with a lot of sand and protected by water in front. The course is known for its challenge: Note the 96 sand bunkers and 10 lakes. The layout of the front nine definitely brings water into play.

Practice greens, a driving range, pro shop,

locker room, bar, snack bar, beverage cart and rental clubs are offered.

Greens fees range from $25 to $55, including cart. Walking is not allowed.

Colonial Charters Golf & Country Club
S.C. Hwy. 9, Longs • 249-8809
Championship Yardage: 6769
Slope: 124	**Par: 72**
Men's Yardage: 6337	
Slope: 119	**Par: 72**
Other Yardage: 6001	
Slope: 115	**Par: 72**
Ladies' Yardage: 5079	
Slope: 120	**Par: 72**

This course's most difficult hole is the 18th. It's been called so many names, ranging from one of the 10 toughest "Hell Holes" to the No. 1 hole in Myrtle Beach's "Dream 18." Go ahead and play it and tell us what you think. It always generates comments.

The 18-hole course was built in 1988, designed by John Simpson.

Swing analysis, lessons, club fitting and club repair are available here. Colonial Charters also has rental clubs, a practice green, driving range, bar, restaurant and locker room, and ladies' play is unrestricted. A special program encourages juniors to play free during the summer.

Greens fees are seasonal and range from $24 to $49. Walking is not allowed. You may book tee times 365 days in advance.

Cypress Bay Golf Club
U.S. Hwy. 17, Little River • 249-1025, (800) TEE-OFFS
Championship Yardage: 6502
Slope: 122	**Par: 72**
Men's Yardage: 6101	
Slope: 118	**Par: 72**
Ladies' Yardage: 5004	
Slope: 113	**Par: 72**

The Russell Breeden-designed, 18-hole course was built in 1972. Locals like it a lot for its ample supply of water and sand. The picturesque 8th hole challenges you with 180 yards over water.

No driving range is provided, but rentals clubs are. After your round, unwind at the bar and restaurant.

Greens fees range from $20 to $58, including cart. Cypress Bay accepts tee times 365 days in advance. Walking is allowed after 3 PM.

Deer Track Golf Resort
U.S. Hwy. 17 S., Surfside Beach
• 650-2146, (800) 548-9186

Both the Toski Links and the South courses (18 holes each) were designed by Bob Toski and Porter Gibson and built in 1974. Owner-operator Gary Schaal, past president of PGA of America, is better known in golf circles nationally and beyond than he is in Myrtle Beach.

The complex offers practice greens, rental clubs, a driving range, pro shop, bar, restaurant and beverage cart. Locker rooms are available for members only.

Greens fees range from $24 to $65, including cart. Walking is allowed after 1 PM. Tee times may be booked 365 days in advance.

Toski Links
Championship Yardage: 7203
Slope: 121	**Par: 72**
Men's Yardage: 6511	
Slope: 121	**Par: 72**
Ladies' Yardage: 5353	
Slope: 119	**Par: 72**

Bermudagrass fairways and elevated tifdwarf bermuda greens are featured here. No. 8 is a long and narrow hole that plays 458 yards from the back tees — beware of this one! The signature hole on this course is the 17th, a par 3 that requires a tee shot to a green guarded by water and bunkers on three sides. A million-dollar upgrade in 1996 returned the previously named North, now the Toski Links, to its original outstanding design.

South Course
Championship Yardage: 6916
Slope: 119	**Par: 71**
Men's Yardage: 6143	
Slope: 119	**Par: 71**
Ladies' Yardage: 5226	
Slope: 120	**Par: 71**

The South Course has bermudagrass greens, more water hazards and more narrow fairways than the Toski Links. It underwent design changes with rebuilt greens in 1994. The signature hole is No. 4, a 204-

yard par 3 that requires a tee shot to a peninsula green.

The Dunes Golf and Beach Club
9000 N. Ocean Blvd., Myrtle Beach
• 449-5914

Championship Yardage: 7165	
Slope: 138	Par: 72
Men's Yardage: 6565	
Slope: 130	Par: 72
Other Yardage: 6175	
Slope: 118	Par: 72
Ladies' Yardage: 5390	
Slope: 127	Par: 72

Robert Trent Jones Sr. designed this 18-hole course in 1948. It's the only private course in Myrtle Beach that you can play — if you stay with a member accommodation. Several major hotels maintain memberships with this premier course. When you book your golf vacation, check with several hotel golf directors to locate a member property if you want to get on the Dunes. Also, reciprocal agreements allow for members from other clubs to play here. The PGA seniors end their season here, and the Golf Writers Association of America has played its annual championship at the Dunes for 43 years. Everyone wants to play this course.

The Dunes features bentgrass greens and superior water hazards. Several holes overlook the Atlantic Ocean. The signature hole is the 13th, a par 5 that plays alongside a large lake. *Sports Illustrated* named it one of the best 18 holes in America. The championship tee on No. 18 was enlarged and realigned toward the drive-landing area, and another men's tee was added to change the angle of play and stretch the hole to 405 yards.

The clubhouse includes bar, grill room and dining room, and the pro shop was expanded in 1995. The food is always good, especially the pastry chef's creations. The club houses one of the last vestiges of the good-ole'-boy days: a men-only lounge.

Members enjoy a pool, tennis courts, memberships for juniors, weekly bridge and frequent dances. Locker rooms are spacious. Driving range and practice green are provided as well as rental clubs.

Greens fees are approximately $100, including cart. Tee times are accepted 365 days in advance. Walking is not allowed.

Eagle Nest Golf Club
U.S. Hwy. 17 N., Little River • 249-1449, (800) 543-3113

Championship Yardage: 6901	
Slope: 120	Par: 72
Men's Yardage: 6417	
Slope: 116	Par: 72
Other Yardage: 5594	
Slope: No rating	Par: 72
Ladies' Yardage: 5105	
Slope: 115	Par: 72

According to legend, it's actually an osprey nest tucked high in the tree on the way to the 8th hole. Don't worry about it too much; you'll keep busy enough looking for your own birdie. The course provides a wonderful guide to its birds as well as how to shoot for them. We haven't found ours yet, but we're willing to keep looking.

This 18-hole course, designed by Gene Hamm and built in 1972, is sprinkled among woods, water and marsh grass. It boasts three tough finishing holes. The 18th is the signature hole, a par 3 over water to a small green. Bermudagrass greens are perfectly kept and are a pleasure to play.

Rental clubs, a driving range and a restaurant are available.

Greens fees average $42, including cart. The course accepts tee times 365 days in advance and does allow walking.

Eastport Club
U.S. Hwy. 17 N., Little River
• 249-3997, (800) 334-9035

Championship Yardage: 6047	
Slope: 116	Par: 70
Men's Yardage: 5400	
Slope: 111	Par: 70
Ladies' Yardage: 4560	
Slope: 114	Par: 70

Architect Dennis Griffiths designed this track as a finesse course. He did not produce the typical beach layout when he created this 18-hole design, built in 1988. It has narrow bermudagrass fairways and large bentgrass greens and is bordered on the east by the Intracoastal Waterway.

Holes No. 1 through 15 are short, and the course lulls you up to this point. Then, the last three holes are uncharacteristically difficult. The course is mostly flat, with occasional uneven lies. Some tree-lined fairways have doglegs. On the 3rd hole, your second shot will vary depending on the placement of your tee shot over the lake. The friendly ducks sometimes try to help find the ball.

Rental clubs are available, as are a bar and restaurant. Eastport has neither a driving range nor a practice green.

Greens fees average $24, including cart. The course accepts tee times 365 days in advance. Walking is not allowed.

Glen Dornoch Waterway Golf Links
U.S. Hwy. 17 N., Little River • 249-2541, (800) 717-8784
Championship Yardage: 6905
Slope: No rating   **Par: 72**

A tribute to Dornoch, Scotland, where Donald Ross was born, this 260-acre site along the Intracoastal Waterway offers magnolias, pines, oaks, lakes, river, marsh and waterway views among a planned self-contained resort to include a hotel, condominiums and related facilities. The 18-hole course opened in September 1996 and was not complete for review when this book went to press. At least four holes are on the waterway, and dramatic elevation changes dropping some 35 feet to the waterway are spectacular. There are no wide open fairways.

Glen Dornoch was created by the owners of Heather Glen and designed by Clyde Johnston. Be sure to say hello to our friend Sam who was previously at Heather Glen. He, his laughing brogue and his kilts are the real thing.

Heather Glen Golf Links
U.S. Hwy. 17 N., Little River • 249-9000, (800) 868-4536

Inspired by Glen Eagles and St. Andrews, the Scottish tradition is unmistakable at this 200-acre historic site. The three nine-hole courses with bermudagrass greens are a collective masterpiece — designed by Willard Byrd and Clyde Johnston, built in 1987 and named America's top new course of that year

by *Golf Digest*. The 50-foot elevation changes, gigantic 100-year-old pine trees, pot bunkers and waste areas transport you from South Carolina to Scotland for a few hours. The 18th-century clubhouse, authentic Scottish pub and pro shop add to your day's pleasure here.

Rental clubs, a driving range, putting area, locker room and beverage cart are available.

Heather Glen accepts tee times 365 days in advance. Greens fees range from $35 to $90, including cart. Walking is not allowed.

1 Red/2 White Course
Championship Yardage: 6786
Slope: 130   **Par: 72**
Men's Yardage: 6337
Slope: 123   **Par: 72**
Ladies' Yardage: 5949
Slope: 117   **Par: 72**

2 White/3 Blue Course
Championship Yardage: 6791
Slope: 130   **Par: 72**
Men's Yardage: 6510
Slope: 126   **Par: 72**
Ladies' Yardage: 6200
Slope: 117   **Par: 72**

3 Blue/1 Red Course
Championship Yardage: 6791
Slope: 127   **Par: 72**
Men's Yardage: 6427
Slope: 126   **Par: 72**
Ladies' Yardage: 5959
Slope: 117   **Par: 72**

The Red Course's par 5 No. 3 has a large fairway bunker on the right. The sloping green also has three smaller pot bunkers behind and left of the green.

No. 8 on the White Course is a beautiful hole. You have a choice of playing it safe or going over the water. The right side of the fairway has mounds and bunkers, and the green has bunkers to the left and around the back.

No. 1 on the Blue Course is a par 4, with a beautiful view of the hole from an elevated tee. The fairway is tilted from left to right, and the drive must be slightly left of center. What makes this hole especially tough is a large but hidden green. No. 5 is a short par 3 with huge mounds on the right and pot bunkers placed in the mounds at right, behind and guarding the left side of the green.

The Heritage Club
Kings River Rd., Pawleys Island
• 236-9318
Championship Yardage: 7040
Slope: 137   Par: 71
Men's Yardage: 6565
Slope: 128   Par: 71
Other Yardage: 6090
Slope: 117   Par: 71
Ladies Yardage: 5325
Slope: 125   Par: 71

The Heritage Club opened in 1986. It was designed and developed by Larry D. Young and was ranked in *Golf Digest's* 1990 Top 50 Public Courses. It is part of a golfing community built on 600 acres of giant magnolias, 300-year-old oaks, freshwater lakes and marshes. An avenue of oaks also leads to the Southern colonial-style clubhouse that overlooks the Waccamaw River. The Heritage speaks of gracious Southern living and pays tribute to the rice culture of bygone days.

The 18 holes each have intriguing personalities. The par 3 13th requires a carry across water. The 4th hole features an avenue of centuries-old oaks alongside the fairway.

The driving range, putting green, pro shop, dining room and lounge are top-quality. Tee times may be booked any time.

Greens fees, with cart, range from $47 to $83. Walking is not allowed.

Indigo Creek
U.S. Hwy. 17 S., Surfside Beach • 650-0381
Championship Yardage: 6744
Slope: 128   Par: 72
Men's Yardage: 6185
Slope: 120   Par: 72
Ladies' Yardage: 4921
Slope: 120   Par: 70

This Willard Byrd 18-hole course was built in 1990. It sports bermudagrass greens, doglegs, bunkers and water. Note the 90-degree dogleg on No. 12 that crosses the same creek twice. Giant oaks draped with Spanish moss are standard in the Lowcountry, where time seems to stand still.

The course offers rental clubs, a driving range and a bar and restaurant.

Greens fees average $40, including cart. Walking is not allowed.

Island Green Country Club
455 Sunnehanna Dr., Myrtle Beach
• 650-2186
Dogwood/Holly Course
Championship Yardage: 6272
Slope: 118   Par: 72
Men's Yardage: 5847
Slope: 111   Par: 72
Ladies' Yardage: 4510
Slope: 115   Par: 72
Tall Oaks/Dogwood Course
Championship Yardage: 6123
Slope: 118   Par: 72
Men's Yardage: 5705
Slope: 111   Par: 72
Ladies' Yardage: 4996
Slope: 116   Par: 72
Holly/Tall Oaks Course
Championship Yardage: 6243
Slope: 118   Par: 72
Men's Yardage: 5864
Slope: 111   Par: 72
Ladies' Yardage: 4704
Slope: 115   Par: 72

This 27-hole course was built in 1980 and has recently undergone major improvements under the management of the Links Group. Bermudagrass greens are nestled among azaleas and dogwoods, which always seem to be in bloom in Myrtle Beach. All three 18-hole combinations are similar, with narrow tree-lined fairways and small greens. The Holly Course features an island green on the 9th hole.

These are not especially difficult courses, except for that island green; therefore they can be enjoyed by all levels of golfers.

Island Green is not among the most expensive places to golf either, ranging from $23 to $42, with carts included. Rental clubs are available as well as a bar and restaurant. There is no driving range however. Tee times are accepted 365 days in advance. Walking is allowed.

The Legends Golf Club
1500 Legends Dr., Myrtle Beach
• 236-9318

The three 18-hole courses are just off U.S. Highway 501. The Legends Golf Club consists of the Heathland, Moorland and Parkland courses. These courses have been designed in three distinctively different architectural styles.

The Legends Group is owned and operated by Larry Young, one of the major names in the country's golf industry. In addition to The Legends Golf Club, the group's Grand Strand courses include Marsh Harbour, Oyster Bay and The Heritage Club (see respective entries in this chapter).

The complex offers rental clubs, caddies, a driving range, bar, restaurant, pro shop and beverage cart.

Caddies are mandatory if you wish to walk. Greens fees range from $47 to $83, including cart. You may book any time.

Heathland at The Legends

Championship Yardage: 6785
Slope: 127   **Par: 71**
Men's Yardage: 6190
Slope: 117   **Par: 71**
Ladies' Yardage: 5060
Slope: 121   **Par: 71**

This 18-hole course is British-links style with bermudagrass greens — designed by Tom Doak and built in 1990. The first thing that may strike you upon approaching the three-course complex is the magnificent Scottish-style clubhouse, and you'll also notice the distinct absence of trees on the Heathland Course. In lieu of tree boundaries, Doak provided strategic bunkers and deep rough to make this course a challenge. Another difficulty comes from the presence of wind and its direction. Most of the bunkers that guard the greens are deep, in typical Scottish style, and shots from within them must be well-played in order to escape. No. 8 is the shortest hole on the course. Pin position is crucial here, since the front of the green has a severe contour. No. 14, a par 4, has one of the smallest greens on the course. The key here is to pick the right club.

Moorland at The Legends

Championship Yardage: 6799
Slope: 128   **Par: 72**
Men's Yardage: 6143
Slope: 121   **Par: 72**
Ladies' Yardage: 4905
Slope: 127   **Par: 72**

The 18-hole Moorland Course, with tifdwarf greens, was designed by Pete Dye and built in 1991. Dye created what is probably one of the most challenging golf courses on the East Coast. It has much natural growth, sand, water and waste areas combined with incredible undulations and many bulkheaded areas reminiscent of PGA West. This is a target golf course. The par 4 2nd hole has a sand trap running almost from tee box to green. No. 17, a par 3, has an island green with a twist: The green is an island in a sea of sand.

Parkland at The Legends

Championship Yardage: 7170
Slope: 131   **Par: 72**
Men's Yardage: 6460
Slope: 127   **Par: 72**
Other Yardage: 6230
Slope: 123   **Par: 72**
Ladies' Yardage: 5570
Slope: 125   **Par: 72**

These 18 holes were designed by The Legends Group and built in 1992.

The Parkland Course, with tifdwarf greens, is distinctly different from Heathland and Moorland because its fairways are tree-lined; it's not unlike the other two in that it has deep bunkers and undulating greens. Water and sand are dominant. The Parkland has a great finishing hole — a par 4 measuring 465 yards. The successful tee shot must be played on the right side of the fairway opposite two large traps. The most challenging hole is the par 5 15th, which has a big fairway. Wetlands cut this fairway into halves running lengthwise. The fairway leading up to the green has seven traps that can cause trouble. No. 11 must be played to the left side. This 515-yard hole is a par 5.

> ## FYI
> Unless otherwise noted, the area code for all N.C. phone numbers in this chapter is 910; the area code for all S.C. numbers is 803.

INSIDERS' TIP

If your area has a links-style course, play it one day in a howling gale or light rain to get a sense of what it's like to play in Scotland — where golf began.

More than 4,000 golfers participate in the DuPont World Amateur Handicap Championship played in Myrtle Beach.

To reach the green, the ball must carry over water; if your shot is too long, four sand traps await to catch your ball.

Litchfield Country Club

U.S. Hwy. 17 S., Pawleys Island
• 448-3331,
(800) 344-5590
Championship Yardage: 6752
Slope: 130   Par: 72
Men's Yardage: 6342
Slope: 124   Par: 72
Ladies' Yardage: 5917
Slope: 119   Par: 72
Other Yardage: 5264
Slope: 119   Par: 72

One of the area's oldest and most prestigious clubs, Litchfield, opened in 1966, was designed by Willard Byrd. Greens are tifdwarf bermuda, and fairways are bermudagrass on this challenging course. Its mature narrow fairways, lined with moss-draped oaks and large well-protected greens, wind through a former rice plantation to a traditional clubhouse. Although private, a limited number of guests are booked on this course.

The traditional layout is tough but fair; never tricky. Water comes into play on seven of the front nine holes, and water or marsh is in all of the back nine.

Country club cottages are available for vacationers. The course winds through a real estate development, and the scorecard reminds you that you may retrieve your ball from the backyard of a homeowner but must not play from there. The Lowcountry cuisine in the fine dining room is on par with the quality of the golf.

Greens fees range from $40 during the summer to $69, including cart. You may walk the course when you like, and you may also book a tee time 365 days in advance.

The Long Bay Club

S.C. Hwy. 9, Longs • 399-2222,
(800) 344-5590
Championship Yardage 7021
Slope: 137   Par: 72
Men's Yardage 6565
Slope: 130   Par: 72
Other Yardage: 6139
Slope: 126   Par: 72
Ladies' Yardage: 5598
Slope: 127   Par: 72

Jack Nicklaus' signature mounds can't be missed as you approach North Myrtle Beach from S.C. Highway 9. The 18-hole course was built in 1989 and meanders through a lovely residential area and forest. It's rated by *Golf Digest* in the state's top 10 courses. It has tifdwarf greens and fairways. Numerous waste bunkers dot the course, and the cart path goes through several of them.

Nos. 7, 8 and 9 are brutal finishes on the front nine. The signature hole is No. 10 — a par 4. Your drive must be straight on this hole because a left or right shot will be in sand. You're surrounded by sand from your second shot. This sand trap is so big that it runs three-fourths of the fairway. No. 13 is a par 3 of 123 yards with an island green. The abundance of lakes, mounds and bunkers is exciting on this course, which everyone wants to play.

The bar and restaurant are classy and comfortable with a wonderful view of the course. Don't leave home without you-know-what, because the soft drink machines on this course only take credit cards. The pro shop is well stocked. Rental clubs and a driving range are available.

Greens fees range from $50 to $97 and include cart. Walking is not allowed. Tee times may be booked 365 days in advance.

Man O' War

U.S. Hwy. 501, Myrtle Beach • 347-6600
Championship Yardage: 7027
Slope: 133   **Par: 72**
Men's Yardage: 6311
Slope: 126   **Par: 72**
Other Yardage: 5579
Slope: 118   **Par: 72**
Ladies' Yardage: 5025
Slope: 121   **Par: 72**

This 18-hole public course opened in January 1996. It is set on 94 acres and surrounds a breathtaking 100-acre man-made lake. The rustic red, ranch-style clubhouse is constructed partially over water and is reminiscent of Minnesota's northern fishing lodges. Sixteen holes feature water hazards. Three are considered signature holes. The 9th hole is an island, and two holes play to island greens. No. 14, a 354-yard par 4, and No. 15, a 126-yard par 3, similar to the famed Sawgrass No. 17, highlight the Dan Maples course. Greens are Crenshaw bentgrass; fairways are bermudagrass.

Amenities include a driving range, putting green, rentals and beverage carts. Greens fees including cart range from $35 to $82. Walking is not allowed.

Marsh Harbour

Marsh Harbour Rd., Calabash, N.C.
• 579-3161, (803) 249-3449, (800) 552-2660
Championship Yardage: 6680
Slope: 134   **Par: 71**
Men's Yardage: 6000
Slope: 121   **Par: 71**
Ladies' Yardage: 4795
Slope: 115   **Par: 71**

Marsh Harbour sits on the North and South Carolina borders just south of Calabash (thus the local phone numbers from both states). A good drive with a fade from the 10th tee in North Carolina will cross into South Carolina, then land on the fairway back in North Carolina.

Everyone seems to want to play Marsh Harbour — and its reputation is well-deserved. Salt marshes along the Intracoastal Waterway provide exciting scenery and exciting golf play. Larry Young built Dan Maples' design in 1980 and presented a rare combination of elevated ground skirted by low-lying marsh.

The famous hole is the par 5 17th, featuring three distinct targets. Picture trees on the left and large bunkers on the right. You can handle the tee shot; then the second shot must carry across the marsh to a landing area with water on three sides . . . a toughie. Cross the marsh again to a green beside the marsh. Not too many of us make par on this one.

Greens fees, including cart, range from $47 to $83. While walking is not allowed, you may book your tee time whenever it's convenient for you.

Myrtle Beach National Golf Club

U.S. Hwy. 501, Myrtle Beach • 448-2308, (800) 344-5590

This club has three 18-hole courses. All were built in the 1970s and designed by Arnold Palmer and Frances Duane. All feature bentgrass greens.

The Myrtle Beach National Golf Club owns another five courses on the Grand Strand, and their reservationist at Tee Time Central can quickly book your entire week for you with one easy phone call. They accept tee times 365 days in advance.

The course offers rental clubs, a driving range and bar and restaurant.

Greens fees change at least eight times a

year based on the season, not including occasional afternoon and other specials; prices range from $25 to $100. Walking is allowed.

King's North

Championship Yardage: 6759
Slope: 125 **Par: 72**
Men's Yardage: 6033
Slope: 109 **Par: 72**
Ladies' Yardage: 5047
Slope: 113 **Par: 72**

Built in 1973, this course was one of the beach's initial courses and one of the first anywhere to feature an island green. Arnold Palmer and the Palmer Design Group oversaw substantial changes to this course in 1995. It was previously called The North Course.

What began as a minor update evolved into total design and visual enhancement. The bentgrass greens were reshaped and enlarged and sodded with the new hybrid Crenshaw bent. Trees were removed to open the course. Several fairways now feature increased undulation, and bunkers and lakes were dramatically reshaped. The famous par 3 No. 3 includes SC-shaped traps, and it underwent a major enhancement with the addition of bulkheads and a new foot bridge. The par 5 No. 6 is called The Gambler — it was dedicated by Kenny Rogers in June 1996 shortly after the course reopened. Play it safe by going right into the fairway, or if you do have a little of the gambler in you, go for the island fairway — your tee shot must carry at least 225 yards from the back tees.

The time allotment is specified on your score card: You should go out in two hours and 15 minutes and back in two hours and 20 minutes; avoiding slow play is important on this course.

South Course

Championship Yardage: 6416
Slope: 123 **Par: 72**
Men's Yardage: 6089
Slope: 118 **Par: 72**
Other Yardage: 5710
Slope: 112 **Par: 72**
Ladies' Yardage: 4723
Slope: 109 **Par: 72**

This 18 hole course was built in 1975 and remodeled in 1990. It has flat fairways with some mounding. Compared to its counterparts, this course features the smallest greens and greenside bunkers.

No. 5 is a 355-yard par 4 dogleg, which is unintimidating unless you are short (your shot, not your person), and your second shot could be into a fairway pond that sits squarely in your line of fire. As you make the turn, No. 9 is a 390-yard par 4 where you must stay right because of the sand down three-fourths of the left side of the fairway. It's tough to make a birdie because of the small green. If you do hit the green, you'll probably be near the hole — it's that small. The 13th, a 166-yard par 3, could be unlucky, as you must shoot over a sea of sand to an island green.

West Course

Championship Yardage: 6866
Slope: 119 **Par: 72**
Men's Yardage: 6113
Slope: 113 **Par: 72**
Ladies' Yardage: 5307
Slope: 109 **Par: 72**

The 18-hole West Course, built in 1974, is the longest course at Myrtle Beach National. Although many tall pines line the fairways and can claim your ball, the course is considered wide open. No. 18 is the only hole on which you'll find a water hazard.

Myrtle West Golf Course

S.C. Hwy. 9, Longs • 249-1478, (800) 842-8390
Championship Yardage: 6787
Slope: 132 **Par: 72**
Men's Yardage: 6191
Slope: 118 **Par: 72**
Other Yardage: 5555
Slope: 108 **Par: 72**
Ladies' Yardage: 4859
Slope: 113 **Par: 72**

It's only a few minutes past the bridge over the Intracoastal Waterway from North Myrtle Beach. Drive across the covered bridge to the Southern-mansion clubhouse. Take plenty of balls in case the numerous water hazards claim some, and enjoy the beautiful holes set among Carolina sand and tall pines. The 18-hole course was built in 1990, designed by Tom Jackson. The entire course is bermudagrass.

Pick the right tee for your level of ability, the professionals advise. Don't think you have to play macho golf. Where you tee it up defines the difficulty around the greens. No. 17

is one of the most difficult — 457 yards and usually playing into the wind.

Amenities include practice putting and chipping greens, a sand bunker, driving range, rental clubs, a beverage cart during peak season and a bar and restaurant. When you visit the well-stocked pro shop, Chuck Qualey and John Galyean, club professionals, and Tim Cauley, general manager, will make you feel like you're at your home course.

Myrtle West accepts tee times 365 days in advance. A rental cart is included in the greens fee, which ranges from $25 to $58. Walking is not allowed.

Myrtlewood Golf Club

48th Ave. N., Myrtle Beach • 449-5134, (800) 283-3633

Myrtlewood offers back-to-back challenges, with two 18-hole courses along the Intracoastal Waterway. It's easily accessible on the U.S. Highway 17 Bypass from any part of the Grand Strand.

Amenities include a driving range, practice green, rental clubs, a beverage cart, pro shop, bar and snack bar.

Greens fees range from $24 to $62, including cart. The complex accepts tee times 365 days in advance. Walking is not allowed.

Palmetto Course

Championship Yardage: 6957	
Slope: 121	Par: 72
Men's Yardage: 6495	
Slope: 118	Par: 72
Other Yardage: 6098	
Slope: 115	Par: 72
Ladies' Yardage: 5305	
Slope: 117	Par: 72

The Palmetto Course was designed by Edmund B. Ault and built in 1973. Its bentgrass greens are smooth, and its bermudagrass fairways are on open, rolling coastal terrain. No. 15 is a tough hole, because the long par 4 with water on the right usually plays into the wind and demands a long second shot.

The signature hole is the 18th. Don't dare pull your tee shot; if you do, your ball will land at the bottom of the Intracoastal Waterway. In fact, the entire length of the hole runs along the waterway. The green is well guarded with bunkers to the front, left and right.

PineHills Course

Championship Yardage: 6640	
Slope: 125	Par: 72
Men's Yardage: 6112	
Slope: 119	Par: 72
Other Yardage: 5692	
Slope: 112	Par: 72
Ladies' Yardage: 4906	
Slope: 113	Par: 72

The PineHills course was the original Myrtlewood, built in 1966. It was rebuilt in 1993 — Arthur Hills' first design in Myrtle Beach. Bermuda fairways are full of plateaus, and bentgrass greens are situated in hollows or tucked into low hills. Bunkers are used sparingly, and water hazards are cleverly placed. No. 18 requires a good tee shot over water to a narrow green with bunker and water around it.

Ocean Harbour Golf Links

Sommersett Dr., Calabash, N.C.
• 579-3588, (803) 448-8398

Championship yardage: 7004	
Slope: 138	Par: 72
Men's Yardage: 6592	
Slope: 134	Par: 72
Other Yardage: 6148	
Slope: 127	Par: 72
Ladies' Yardage: 5358	
Slope: 126	Par: 72

An 18-hole course built in 1989, Ocean Harbour was Clyde Johnston's first design on the Grand Strand. It crosses the North Carolina-South Carolina border; so, like its neighbor, Marsh Harbour, Ocean Harbour has a local phone number for each state. On the 5th hole, you can drive from North Carolina into South Carolina, then return on the 9th tee.

The 532-yard par 5 No. 7 is the signature hole. The tee area is surrounded by a cedar grove. The marsh and waterway views are spectacular. On each shot you will have to clear marshland. As if that's not hard enough, the green's location in the middle of marsh makes it seem as if you are shooting at an island.

All 18 holes are tough; you'll encounter a lot of water. Fairways are bermudagrass, and greens are bentgrass. Saltwater marshes and natural elevation shape the course on 500 acres of grass bunkers and gentle rolling fairways. Sand bunkers and multiple ponds con-

Pier of Distinction

It's a combination country club and church, and you can arrive with or without a fishing pole. It's meeting the social, spiritual and recreational needs of many a soul. That's how Cherry Grove Pier is described by one of the regulars who frequents the North Myrtle Beach fishing spot.

Everyone knows everyone among a daily crowd, and they clearly get a lot more than fish from the experience. Cherry Grove is just across Hogg Inlet from the award-winning Tidewater Golf Club, and the vacationing anglers might fill the popular family-style motels quicker than the golfers if you aren't careful. It's another sport for the time left after golf.

Close-up

Margaret Prince and her son, Ed, who own the pier, the restaurant and neighboring motels, welcome everyone who enjoys the sea. The pier is popular with locals and tourists for its July 4 fireworks and various gatherings. For the fishing, for the social network of good people, or just for some quiet time alone with nature, the Cherry Grove Pier invites you for a breezy stroll on a hot day.

Photo: Liz Mitchell

The Cherry Grove Pier features a unique double-deck spectator area.

How many people are on the pier? Prince usually says, "elbow to elbow and shoulder to shoulder," and most days that's what you'll see. A unique feature of the pier is the octagonal two-story gazebo perched on the end. It's the only two-story pier in South Carolina. The top level is for spectators. The bottom is reserved for serious fishing, and during tournament time it can't be disturbed.

A walk to the end of the 900-foot pier makes even a non-angler ready to join the club, whatever its affiliation. It's jammed with interesting people who share a camaraderie washed up by the sea. The hospitality is as wide as the ocean itself.

tribute to the endless challenges. The panoramic views include rare combinations of the Calabash River, the Atlantic Ocean and the Intracoastal Waterway. The clubhouse is a fine finishing spot with its view of the confluence of the waterway and the river.

Practice greens, a driving range, pro shop, bar, snack bar and rental clubs are available.

Greens fees range from $25 to $76, including cart, and tee times are accepted up to a year in advance. Walking is not allowed.

Ocean Isle Beach Golf Course
Pearl Blvd., Ocean Isle Beach, N.C.
• 579-2610
S.C. number   **272-3900**
Championship's Yardage: 6626
Slope: 126   **Par: 72**
Men's Yardage: 6146
Slope: 122   **Par: 72**
Ladies Yardage: 5075
Slope: 116   **Par: 72**
This 18-hole course was designed by

Russell Breeden and opened in 1976. The bermudagrass greens and fairways are carved through rolling terrain, towering pines and live oaks. A tough hole is the 10th, where you have to hit over a ditch to a small green; the ball often will bounce off the back side. No. 10 is frequently a bogey hole. No. 16 is a dogleg right that plays 451 yards from the championship tees.

Greens fees range from $20 to $43, including cart. Amenities include practice greens, a driving range, pro shop, rental clubs, a bar and a snack bar. Walking is not allowed.

Ocean Isle is a quiet piece of golfer's paradise: No big city lights, but golf galore. While it's actually in North Carolina, the course aligns itself with the Myrtle Beach golfing scene. The Pearl (see subsequent entry) is the sister course to the Ocean Isle Beach Course, and you can spend many a vacation day trying to master the combination.

Ocean Ridge Plantation
U. S. Hwy. 17, Sunset Beach, N.C.
• 287-1717, (803) 448-5566, (800) 233-1801

Lion's Paw and Panther's Run comprise 36 holes at Ocean Ridge Plantation. The second nine of Panther's Run opened in October 1995.

Willard Byrd designed the first 18 holes, and Tim Nelson Cate designed the newer Panther's Run. All have bermudagrass fairways and bentgrass greens. Walking is not allowed.

Amenities include practice greens, a driving range, pro shop, bar, restaurant, beverage cart and rental clubs.

Greens fees range from $30 to nearly $80.

Lion's Paw Golf Links
Championship Yardage: 7003	
Slope: 138	Par: 72
Men's Yardage: 6457	
Slope: 130	Par: 72
Ladies' Yardage: 5364	
Slope: 118	Par: 72

The toughest hole on Lion's Paw is No. 3, a 204-yard par 3. Water comes into play on 15 of 18 holes. Fairways are somewhat narrow

on the front nine, and the second nine is links style.

Panther's Run Golf Links
Championship Yardage: 7089	
Slope: 140	Par: 72
Men's Yardage: 6706	
Slope: 134	Par: 72
Other Yardage: 6267	
Slope: 128	Par: 72
Other Yardage: 5546	
Slope: 118	Par: 72
Ladies' Yardage: 5023	
Slope: 116	Par: 72

On Panther's Run, the 4th hole is tough due to the great expanse of water to carry. The course, set along a nature preserve, offers pretty scenery, an interesting variety of elevations and marsh to clear on several holes. Five sets of tees allow every golfer to find a comfort zone. Wide fairways twist and turn around visually appealing lakes, brooks and waterfalls on the new nine. Deer, barn owls and waterfowl frequently are spotted along the course.

Oyster Bay Golf Links
Lakeshore Dr., Sunset Beach, N.C.
• 236-9318, (800) 552-2660
Championship Yardage: 6685	
Slope: 134	Par: 70
Men's Yardage: 6305	
Slope: 125	Par: 70
Ladies' Yardage: 4665	
Slope: 118	Par: 70

Oyster Bay is an 18-hole links-style course that is part of the popular Legends Group. It was designed by Dan Maples. Its trademark oyster-shell landscaping and walls have been incorporated into the design. Oyster Bay opened in 1983 and was recognized by *Golf Digest* as the best new resort course in the country that year and was ranked in the top 50 overall courses. It's one of the most beautiful courses anywhere.

The 15th and 17th holes are par 3s with island greens. The 17th hole is played from oyster shell-walled tees, and its island green is built on a mountain of shells. The 13th hole has a lake flanking the entire right side, its green guarded by a large cavernous bunker.

Walking is not allowed at Oyster Bay. Amenities include rental clubs, a pro shop, bar, restaurant, beverage cart, driving range and practice green. Tee times are accepted anytime. Greens fees range from $47 to $83 including cart.

Pawleys Plantation Golf & Country Club
U.S. Hwy. 17 S., Pawleys Island
• **237-1736, (800) 367-9959**
Championship Yardage: 7026

Slope: 132	**Par: 72**
Men's Yardage: 6522	
Slope: 127	**Par: 72**
Other Yardage: 6127	
Slope: 122	**Par: 72**
Ladies' Yardage: 5572	
Slope: 130	**Par: 72**
Other Yardage: 4979	
Slope: 126	**Par: 72**

A signature course by Jack Nicklaus, Pawley's Plantation offers exclusive play to members and guests of member hotels. Call the course or ask the golf director at one of the Sands Properties about how to get on this course. You may remember Pawleys Plantation best for the double green and dramatic split fairway. Lake and marsh views and bentgrass greens are spectacular, and similarly spectacular shots frequently are required to traverse the marsh.

The country club setting includes a clubhouse and lounge where breakfast, lunch and dinner are served. A pool and tennis court for guests are minutes from the beach.

Greens fees range from $47 to $82, including cart. Walking is not allowed. You may book your game at any time.

The Pearl Golf Links
1300 Pearl Blvd. S.W., Sunset Beach, N.C.
• **579-8132, (803) 272-2850**

The Pearl offers the East and West courses, both of which are 18-hole tracks, finely designed by Dan Maples and built on a 900-acre marsh preserve. Both courses were built in 1987 and feature bentgrass greens. The East Course is a traditional layout, and the West Course is links style. Both boast spectacular finishing holes: one, along the Calabash River; the other, on a bluff overlooking the Intracoastal Waterway.

No two holes are alike, and you will definitely use all your clubs. The marsh views and natural wildlife in the undisturbed area are a visual feast. On the West Course, water and/or marsh comes into play on every hole; on the East Course, you'll encounter water or marsh on every hole except Nos. 8 and 15.

A pro shop, driving range, bar, restaurant and rental clubs are available.

Tee times may be booked a year in advance, and greens fees average $69, including cart. Walking is not allowed.

East Course
Championship Yardage: 6749

Slope: 135	**Par: 72**
Men's Yardage: 6543	
Slope: 132	**Par: 72**
Other Yardage: 6250	
Slope: 127	**Par: 72**
Ladies' Yardage: 5125	
Slope: 129	**Par: 72**

No. 17 on the East Course is the signature hole. It's a slight dogleg left with three fairway bunkers, oyster beds and marsh down the left side. If you're long on approaching the green, a sand trap flanks the back side, not to mention more marsh.

West Course
Championship Yardage: 7008

Slope: 132	**Par: 72**
Men's Yardage: 6738	
Slope: 131	**Par: 72**
Other Yardage: 6419	
Slope: 129	**Par: 72**
Ladies' Yardage: 5188	
Slope: 127	**Par: 72**

On the West Course, No. 16 is the signature. It's a 604-yard par 5 that bends twice before you get to the green. No only do you have to put up with marsh running down the complete right side of the fairway and green, but trouble is compounded by the addition of oyster beds, sand and marsh also down the right. An abundance of love grass covers this course, especially on the 1st, 2nd, 9th, 11th and 12th holes. You don't need to know what it is; just stay out of it.

Pine Lakes International Country Club

5603 Woodside Dr., Myrtle Beach
• 449-6459, (800) 446-6817
Championship Yardage: 6609
Slope: 125   Par: 71
Men's Yardage: 6176
Slope: 121   Par: 71
Ladies' Yardage: 5376
Slope: 122   Par: 71

From the moment you walk into the clubhouse, you begin to soak up the tradition Pine Lakes exudes. It's called the Granddaddy. "When I die, take me to the Granddaddy," a well-known writer instructed.

Pine Lakes International was the first golf course in Myrtle Beach, built in 1927. Robert White, the first president of the PGA and a native of St. Andrews, designed this 18-hole course. It was meant as a playground to complement the million-dollar Ocean Forest Hotel, an elaborate resort for the wealthy. Sunday afternoon croquet matches on its lawn continue another of its age-old traditions. Invitations to members of the neighboring Dunes Club announce the introduction of a "new game."

Among the many significant events Pine Lakes claims, one of the biggest is that *Sports Illustrated* was born here in 1954 when Henry Booth Luce and 66 other Time-Life executives came for a game and left with a brainstorm.

In 1995, it was the first Grand Strand course to lease a million-dollar fleet of carts with the Rolls-Royce design.

Today it retains the prestige its heritage demands. Scottish flavor and Southern gentility are reflected in every touch, beginning with the tartan-dressed starters, continuing with the mimosa Thomas serves as you approach the 3rd tee, and culminating on cooler days with the signature clam chowder served at the turn. Its special Southern-style Manhattan recipe, heavy with red pepper, is said to add an extra 30 yards to your remaining drives. The cook will sign your score card if any of it is worth writing home about.

The fairways are wide, and while not overly tough, the course can be challenging, depending upon pin placements. Pine Lakes starts with a bang: a 563-yard par 3. The par 3 No. 7 is one of the country's most beautiful holes, according to the editors of *Golf Digest*. Greens are bermudagrass.

When your game is over, assistants will wash your clubs, shine your shoes and present your crying towel to remind you of this round.

Walking is not allowed. Booking tee times up to a year in advance is recommended. Rental clubs and a driving range are available. The bar, restaurant and pro shop are within the 60-room antebellum mansion, and a snack bar overlooks the pool.

Greens fees start at $47 during summer months and range to $110 in the high season. A cart is included.

Possum Trot Golf Club

U.S. Hwy. 17, North Myrtle Beach
• 272-5341, (800) 626-8768
Championship Yardage: 6966
Slope: 127   Par: 72
Men's Yardage: 6388
Slope: 113   Par: 72
Other Yardage: 5505
Slope: 108   Par: 72
Ladies' Yardage: 5153
Slope: 111   Par: 72

One of the older courses on the Grand Strand, this 18-hole layout was built in 1968. It was designed by Russell Breeden. Greens and fairways are bermudagrass. High handicappers welcome the course's openness; yet the 50 bunkers and nine lakes and ponds combine with the length and finesse to challenge any golfer. Watch out for No. 11 — 430 yards uphill and into the wind from the men's tees. This course's signature hole is No. 13, a 163-yard par 3 full carry over water.

The extensive practice facility includes a driving range, sand bunkers and separate pitching, chipping and putting greens. Other amenities include a pro shop, bar, beverage cart, snack bar, locker rooms for men and women and rental clubs.

Greens fees range from $32 to $57, including cart. Walking is allowed after noon.

FYI

Unless otherwise noted, the area code for all N.C. phone numbers in this chapter is 910; the area code for all S.C. numbers is 803.

The course accepts tee times 365 days in advance.

Quail Creek Golf Club

U.S. Hwy. 501, Myrtle Beach • 347-0549, (800) TEE-OFFS

Championship Yardage: 6812

Slope: 119	Par: 72

Men's Yardage: 6331

Slope: 116	Par: 72

Other Yardage: 5955

Slope: 114	Par: 72

Ladies' Yardage: 5287

Slope: 112	Par: 72

Gene Hamm designed this bermudagrass 18-hole course in 1968. It has extra-wide fairways, large greens and easy playing conditions. No. 11 is a 526-yard par 5 that doglegs left. The somewhat large green is guarded front, left and right by bunkers. Somewhat unique to this course, water comes into play on about six holes only.

The clubhouse, including a bar and restaurant, was recently renovated. A driving range and rental clubs are available.

Part of The Links Group, this club accepts tee times 365 days in advance. Greens fees range from $20 to $58, including cart. Walking is allowed.

River Club

U.S. Hwy. 17 S., Pawleys Island • 237-8755, (800) 344-5590

Championship Yardage: 6677

Slope: 135	Par: 72

Men's Yardage: 6240

Slope: 119	Par: 72

Ladies' Yardage: 5084

Slope: 120	Par: 72

The River Club is an 18-hole Tom Jackson design. Its fairways are wide and open, and the large tifdwarf bermudagrass greens are undulating. More than 90 bunkers and plenty of water offer challenges to all skill levels. Its par 5 finishing hole wraps around a lake. Long hitters may be able to reach the green in two; however, if you miss, you can put at least a bogey on your scorecard.

Amenities include a pro shop, small locker room, driving net and a restaurant. There are also nice facilities for your short game including practice putting and chipping areas along with a bunker.

Greens fees range from $38 to $75, including cart. Tee times are accepted up to a year in advance. Walking is not allowed.

River Hills Golf & Country Club

U.S. Hwy. 17 N., Little River • 399-2100, (800) 264-3810

Championship Yardage: 6829

Slope: 133	Par: 72

Men's Yardage: 6196

Slope: 123	Par: 72

Other Yardage: 5535

Slope: 113	Par: 72

Ladies' Yardage: 4861

Slope: 120	Par: 72

Tom Jackson designed this 18-hole course in 1988, with bermudagrass greens and fairways. Fairways are somewhat narrow, and water comes into play on 13 holes. The course is in a densely wooded setting and features 40-foot elevation changes. No. 5 is a challenge: a long par 4 uphill, with bunkers surrounding it.

A complete practice facility is available as are rental clubs, a pro shop, locker rooms for men and women, a beverage cart on busy days and a snack bar.

Walking is not allowed. The course accepts tee times 365 days in advance. Greens fees range from $25 to $60, including cart.

River Oaks Golf Plantation

831 River Oaks Dr., Myrtle Beach • 236-2222, (800) 762-8813

Bear/Fox Course

Championship Yardage: 6778

Slope: 126	Par: 72

Men's Yardage: 6314

Slope: 118	Par: 72

Ladies' Yardage: 5133

Slope: 116	Par: 72

Fox /Otter Course

Championship Yardage: 6791

Slope: 125	Par: 72

Men's Yardage: 6345

Slope: 118	Par: 72

Ladies' Yardage: 5043

Slope: 118	Par: 72

Otter/Bear Course

Championship Yardage: 6877
Slope: 125   Par: 72
Men's Yardage: 6425
Slope: 119   Par: 72
Ladies' Yardage: 5188
Slope: 118   Par: 72

Three nine-hole courses make up the three 18-hole combinations completed in 1990. Tom Jackson designed the Bear Course, and Gene Hamm designed the Otter and Fox courses. Fairways and greens are bermudagrass. Wildlife, undulating greens, mounded fairways, finger-shape sand bunkers and large lakes provide scenic beauty along the Intracoastal Waterway.

Water comes into play or at least is a major presence on the Bear Course, which many believe to be the most difficult of the trio. The 2nd hole on the Bear is . . . well, a bear . . . with water and sand prominently coming into play. Some doglegs on the Fox are difficult, although the course plays shorter than the others.

Practice greens, a driving range, pro shop, snack bar, rental clubs and beverage cart are offered.

Greens fees range from $20 to $65 and include cart. Tee times may be booked a year in advance. Walking is not allowed.

Robbers Roost Golf Club

U.S. Hwy. 17 N., North Myrtle Beach
• 249-1471, (800) 352-2384
Championship Yardage: 7148
Slope: 137   Par: 72
Men's Yardage: 6725
Slope: 129   Par: 72
Other Yardage: 6356
Slope: 120   Par: 72
Ladies' Yardage: 5387
Slope: 116   Par: 72

Designed by Russell Breeden, the 18-hole course opened in 1969, with tifdwarf bermudagrass on the tees, fairways and greens.

Breeden once said that No. 16 — a par 5 — was the greatest hole he had ever built. The par 5 is a slight dogleg left with a huge lake between the fairway and the green. If you hit a super tee shot, you have the option to go for it, but then you need a terrific second shot. Fairway bunkers are on the right,

and greenside bunkers are left, right and behind. No. 14 is another interesting hole. It's a par 4, 390 yards, but water butts up against the relatively small green, so the second shot is critical. There's no sand on this hole, but the landing area for your drive is extremely narrow.

Water provides a challenge on several holes, and the course's length is a challenge in itself.

The Southern plantation-style porch around the clubhouse is a fine place to unwind after you've finished your round.

A driving range, rental clubs and a bar and restaurant are available.

Greens fees begin at $29 and go to $40, including cart. Walking is not allowed. You may book tee times a year in advance.

St. James Plantation

U.S. Hwy. 211, Southport, N.C.
• 253-3008, (800) 247-4806
Championship Yardage: 7052
Slope: 142   Par: 72
Men's Yardage: 6428
Slope: 132   Par: 72
Ladies' Yardage: 5048
Slope: 119   Par: 72
Other Yardage: 5845
Slope: 124   Par: 72

P.B. Dye designed this course in 1991 with bentgrass greens and bermudagrass fairways. Views of the waterway are spectacular, and the course also plays along salt marshes. It is a challenge to golfers of all levels with its pot bunkers, bulkheads and shots that must carry water along with multi-level fairways that are trademarks of Dye's architecture. Good course management is a key here. If you have a bad shot, don't try to be a hero on your next one. Take the penalty and move on. The final three holes play into and over a series of marshes and lakes and offer a fantastic finish to a beautiful layout.

The signature hole is No. 17, a par 4 running along a tidal marsh. It's about 440 yards from the back tees and plays to a peninsula green in the marsh. The lake is along the left side, and the tidal marsh along the right. A 200-yard carry to the fairway is a challenge. The small green is surrounded by three bunkers.

Facilities include a pro shop, practice greens, a driving range, rental clubs, a restaurant, bar and sometimes beverage cart. Greens fees range from $40 to $65. Walking is not allowed.

Sea Trail Plantation & Golf Links
301 Clubhouse Rd., Sunset Beach, N.C.
• 287-1100, (800) 546-5748

Sea Trail Plantation is a classy resort community set on 2,000 acres and featuring 54 signature holes of championship golf on bentgrass greens. The three 18-hole courses were designed by Dan Maples, Rees Jones and Willard Byrd, respectively, and named as such. Meeting and conference space plus golf packages make this resort a choice for many golf parties who want their townhouse or villa accommodations right on the course.

Sunset Beach is a great little North Carolina community (right over the border), with no resemblance to the neon hustle and bustle of Myrtle Beach. Views include the golf courses or the river. The beach is about a mile away. Resort amenities include a bar, restaurant, pro shop, fitness room, pool, tennis club and biking and jogging trails. Walking is not allowed on these golf courses.

Dan Maples Course
Championship Yardage: 6751

Slope: 121	**Par: 72**
Men's Yardage: 6332	
Slope: 117	**Par: 72**
Other Yardage: 6035	
Slope: 112	**Par: 72**
Ladies' Yardage: 5090	
Slope: 108	**Par: 72**

This course was built in 1986 and promptly nominated by *Golf Digest* as one of the most outstanding resort courses in the country. Maples' Oyster Bay Golf Links is also within Sea Trail Plantation, and his Marsh Harbour course is nearby. You can stay and play here for a long time if you're looking for some really fine golf.

The par 3 No. 3 is an intimidating hole because of a pond on the right of the green. This hole must be played to the middle or left of the pin regardless of where it's placed. Play the dogleg-left par 4 7th hole in the center of the fairway. The second shot must go over water to a kidney-shape green. An island tee on the 13th is what makes this short par 4 interesting. Bunkers are on the left of the fairway. A good tee shot will leave a mid- to short-iron shot to a deceptive green.

Greens fees range from $34 to $58, including cart.

Rees Jones Course
Championship Yardage: 6761

Slope: 132	**Par: 72**
Men's Yardage: 6334	
Slope: 126	**Par: 72**
Other Yardage: 5716	
Slope: 118	**Par: 72**
Ladies' Yardage: 4912	
Slope: 115	**Par: 72**

The Rees Jones course opened in the spring of 1990. Water comes into play on 11 holes. The par 3 No. 5 has many obstacles. Besides playing over water, it is surrounded by seven sand traps, to the rear, right and left; thus, club selection is crucial. Par 5 No. 8 needs a long tee shot if you hope to reach the green in two; however, you must be careful of the water in front of the green. It's safer to lay up and hit the green in three.

Greens fees begin at $39 and go to $63, including cart.

Willard Byrd Course
Championship Yardage: 6751

Slope: 128	**Par: 72**
Men's Yardage: 6263	
Slope: 126	**Par: 72**
Other Yardage: 5590	
Slope: 116	**Par: 72**
Ladies' Yardage: 4717	
Slope: 121	**Par: 72**

The Byrd Course opened in fall 1990. It's built around lakes ranging from 14 to 20 acres. Shot-making finesse is called for here. The par 3 No. 2 is medium-length, but you must play over water. If possible, try to place your shot so you'll have an uphill putt. The par 4 No. 11 is a narrow dogleg right with four fairway traps. The green is long and narrow and slopes downward from back to front. Par 5 No. 18 requires a drive down the right-center; otherwise, you're in water. You can reach the green in two with a long iron shot. If the hole is on the front of the green, try to stay below the hole.

Greens fees are $34 to $58, including cart.

Surf Golf & Beach Club

1701 Springland Dr., North Myrtle Beach
• 249-1524, (800) 765-SURF
Championship Yardage: 6842

Slope: 126	**Par: 72**
Men's Yardage: 6360	
Slope: 119	**Par: 72**
Other Yardage: 5960	
Slope: 114	**Par: 72**
Ladies' Yardage: 5178	
Slope: 111	**Par: 72**

This George Cobb classic was Myrtle Beach's third course when it opened in 1961. The 18-hole layout was rebuilt and enhanced in 1992, then it received another facelift in 1996 with improvements to its bentgrass greens. The finishing hole is a dramatic par 3 over water. It's 219 yards, usually played against the ocean breeze.

The clubhouse opened in 1990 after a multi-million-dollar expansion and renovation. It's surrounded by an upper-class neighborhood just two blocks from the ocean. The bar, the food in the restaurant and the views are excellent.

Other amenities include a pro shop, driving range, practice green, locker rooms and rental clubs.

Tee times may be booked a year in advance. Greens fees range from $32 to $83, including cart. Walking is not allowed.

Tidewater Golf Club & Plantation

4901 Little River Neck Rd., North Myrtle Beach • 249-3829, (800) 446-5363
Championship Yardage: 7150

Slope: 134	**Par: 72**
Back Yardage: 6530	
Slope: 126	**Par: 72**
Men's Yardage: 6000	
Slope: 118	**Par: 72**
Other Yardage: 5090	
Slope: 132	**Par: 72**
Ladies' Yardage: 4665	
Slope: 127	**Par: 72**

Ken Tomlinson's 18-hole creation was named the top new course of 1990 by both *Golf Digest* and *Golf Magazine*. It continues to draw rave reviews for its bentgrass greens and bermudagrass fairways set on a wooded peninsula between the Atlantic Ocean and the Intracoastal Waterway. The 3rd, 4th and 12th greens are on the marsh, and the 13th is on Cherry Grove Inlet and the Atlantic. The 16th fairway affords a view straight to the waterway where you might see sailboats and barges passing.

This course can be difficult at times, but is forgiving at times and rewarding and enjoyable for all levels of players. Nothing is artificial here. All of the holes were designed to leave undisturbed the natural surroundings and the lay of the land. An intriguing aspect of Tidewater is the player's variety of choices. For instance, the 360-yard par 4 No. 4 requires a perfect drive close to the marsh; however, if the marsh is too intimidating, you can bail out with a shot to the right but must contend with two fairway sand traps. Then, your second shot must carry over the traps that surround the green.

You might feel intimidated by the extremely large sand trap right off the tees on No. 5, a par 4. The green also is guarded on the left and right by traps. When you arrive at the tee box of the spectacular par 3 No. 12, you will be immediately excited to notice that your tee shot must carry marshland that at high tide is filled with water and at low tide displays the failed shots of previous players. Par 3 No. 17 plays from a tee box with a view of the waterway over water to a green bordered by four sand traps. The signature hole is No. 13, from which you can see all of the Cherry Grove section of North Myrtle Beach.

Rental clubs, a driving range, putting greens, a pro shop, bar and grill and new clubhouse with restaurant are available.

Tee times may be booked 365 days in advance. Walking is not allowed. Greens fees range from $63 to $98, including cart.

The Tradition Club

1027 Willbrook Blvd., Pawleys Island
• 626-1658, (800) TEE-OFFS
Championship Yardage: 6717

Slope: No rating	**Par: 72**
Men's Yardage: 6500	
Slope: No rating	**Par: 72**
Other Yardage: 5554	
Slope: No rating	**Par: 72**
Ladies' Yardage: 4924	
Slope: No rating	**Par: 72**
Forward Yardage: 4148	
Slope: No rating	**Par: 72**

This stunning 18-hole course was crafted by Florida architect Ron Garl from acres of natural sand waste areas. It opened in fall 1995.

It includes an island par 3 as well as a par 3 strategically placed in the center of a vast waste area. Large rolling greens are set among the sand and towering Carolina pines. Garl created multiple teeing areas to determine the ideal ladies' yardage and to enable every level of golfer to play each hole equitably with the same clubs. This experiment has garnered national attention as has the Links Group's addition of this masterpiece to their collection along the Grand Strand. The 18th green is guarded by the 8,000-square-foot luxury clubhouse, which houses dressing rooms, men's and women's locker rooms, dining area, bar with fireplace and conversation areas, private members' room and large pro shop. The clubhouse is decorated with Italian marble, leather upholstery, imported designer pieces and original European artwork.

The elaborate world-class practice area includes a 43,000-square-foot putting green shaped like a clover with four individual locations for practice, a multilevel chipping and pitching area, practice sand bunkers and target greens framed by sand and water to make practice itself an unforgettable experience. Eighteen acres of the practice facility feature multiple greens at varying yardages, and individual coves sit on the left side of the driving range, allowing golfers to practice anything from wedge to full-iron shots.

Tee times may be booked a year in advance. Greens fees, including cart, range from $43 to $61. Walking is allowed after 3 PM.

Waterway Hills Golf Course
U.S. Hwy. 17 N., Myrtle Beach • 449-6488, (800) 344-5590

One of the most unusual to access, this club includes three nine-hole courses on the west side of the Intracoastal Waterway. You can only get to them by the lift over the waterway. If you're afraid of heights and the rocking ride of a ski lift, you won't know what you're missing. Wilderness surrounds these courses, which are especially popular for that reason. One of the pros says there's an advantage to having nothing but wildlife around.

These courses were built in 1975, designed by Robert Trent Jones Sr., with bermudagrass greens. The terrain is rolling, and water comes into play a great deal.

Amenities include a bar, restaurant, driving range and rental clubs.

Walking is allowed, and pull carts are available. Tee times are accepted a year in advance and may be reserved through the same toll-free number for bookings at Myrtle Beach National Golf Club.

Greens fees range from $29 to $54, including cart.

Lakes Course
Championship Yardage: 3190
Slope: 121   **Par: 36**
Men's Yardage: 3001
Slope: 115   **Par: 36**
Ladies' Yardage: 2490
Slope: 115   **Par: 36**

Hole No. 9 is a dogleg-left, 390-yard par 4. It has a nice wide fairway, but traps are left and right of your landing area. If you hit the landing area right, you have a nice iron shot to the undulating green, which is guarded on the right by two small traps.

Oaks Course
Championship Yardage: 3271
Slope: 119   **Par: 36**
Men's Yardage: 3080
Slope: 118   **Par: 36**
Ladies' Yardage: 2579
Slope: 118   **Par: 36**

Every single hole on the Oaks is straightaway. No. 3 is a par 4 (422 yards), which shoots straight (as you suspect it should), but halfway down the fairway you must contend with lakes on each side. If you go long on your drive either left or right, your ball will get wet.

Ravine Course
Championship Yardage: 2927
Slope: 121   **Par: 36**
Men's Yardage: 2579
Slope: 112   **Par: 36**
Ladies' Yardage: 2335
Slope: 112   **Par: 36**

The 8th hole, a 470-yard par 5, is straightaway. If you try to go for the green in two, a pair of bunkers could be a hindrance, as could

FYI
Unless otherwise noted, the area code for all N.C. phone numbers in this chapter is 910; the area code for all S.C. numbers is 803.

a greenside bunker in front. There's yet another bunker behind the green.

Wicked Stick Golf Links

U.S. Hwy. 17 S., Surfside Beach • 650-2146, (800) 548-9186

Championship Yardage: 7001

Slope: 129	Par: 72

Men's Yardage: 6507

Slope: 122	Par: 72

Other Yardage: 6080

Slope: 117	Par: 72

Ladies' Yardage: 4911

Slope: 123	Par: 72

John Daly's first-ever signature course, Wicked Stick opened in 1995, almost as a celebration of Daly's dramatic win of the British Open at St. Andrews that summer. Daly served as consultant to architect Clyde Johnston on this course, which was developed by Southpark Golf Group Ltd. Partnership, a group led by past president of the PGA of America Gary Schaal.

This 18-hole links-style course with bermudagrass features expansive dune fields, large sand waste areas with gorse-like vegetation, pot bunkers and strategically placed water hazards. A select number of Daly signature tees offer additional length and difficulty, but generous landing areas help the average player.

Amenities include a pro shop, rental clubs, driving range, putting green and beverage cart. Greens fees range from $30 to $65, including cart. Walking is allowed after noon.

Wild Wing Plantation

U.S. Hwy. 501, Myrtle Beach • 347-9464, (800) 736-WING

Wild Wing Plantation is a 72-hole golf reserve, and it is a showcase of Pennlinks bentgrass enjoyed by good golfers. Japanese-owned, it shows a distinct Oriental influence in the clubhouse and in its attention to detail and perfection. The plantation is set on 1,050 acres of natural beauty west of Myrtle Beach.

Almost every golfer loves the aesthetics and the variety of Wild Wing's courses; beginners might not excel on these tough layouts, but they will enjoy nature while they improve. Some golfers could spend a four-day golf trip just at Wild Wing and be more than content with the diversity of its four courses.

The bird names are not just incidental; all represented species have been sighted. On the Falcon Course, for example, a falcon sometimes just sits on a mound watching a hole, even when a foursome is approaching the green. The operations staff is studying the possibility of planting specific flora to attract the desired fowl to their namesake courses.

The pro shop, bar and restaurant are award winners. A beverage cart, driving range, practice greens and rental clubs are available.

Tee times are accepted up to a year in advance. Greens fees range from $42 to $93 at the Wood Stork and Hummingbird courses and from $54 to $108 on the Avocet and Falcon courses, including a cart in all cases. Each cart is equipped with a club and ball washer, computerized yardage system and water cooler; you may not take a personal cooler. Walking is not allowed.

Falcon Course

Championship Yardage: 7082

Slope: 134	Par: 72

Men's Yardage: 6697

Slope: 128	Par: 72

Other Yardage: 6089

Slope: 117	Par: 72

Ladies' Yardage: 5190

Slope: 118	Par: 72

The Falcon Course, 18 holes built in 1994, was designed by Rees Jones in a "modern traditional" style. With an abundance of mounding, narrow fairways and small bentgrass greens, the Falcon offers diversity in design and play while creating a visually exciting experience. According to the renowned Jones, "The natural appearing features help to contain errant balls and provide a variety of approach shots." Both nines feature large lakes. This course contains Wild Wing's most dominant feature, a 515-yard bunker, which separates the 12th and 13th holes. Now that's a bunker!

Avocet Course

Championship Yardage: 7127

Slope: 128	Par: 72

Men's Yardage: 6614

Slope: 119	Par: 72

Other Yardage: 6028

Slope: 114	Par: 72

Ladies' Yardage: 5298

Slope: 118	Par: 72

The Avocet course opened in 1993 and was recognized by *Golf Digest* as one of the

Top 10 Best New Resort Courses for 1994. It was designed as a signature course by Larry Nelson. Bentgrass greens are elevated, and one is a double green. Some fairways are double, and some tees are elevated.

Hummingbird Course

Championship Yardage: 6853

Slope: 131	**Par: 72**
Men's Yardage: 6310	
Slope: 123	**Par: 72**
Other Yardage: 5796	
Slope: 123	**Par: 72**
Ladies' Yardage: 5168	
Slope: 123	**Par: 72**

The Hummingbird Course — 18 holes designed by Willard Byrd — opened in 1992. It's a links-style course with bentgrass greens, native grasses around its perimeter, strategically placed lakes and open fairways. It has an array of pot bunkers and waste areas.

Wood Stork Course

Championship Yardage: 7044

Slope: 126	**Par: 72**
Men's Yardage: 6598	
Slope: 111	**Par: 72**
Ladies Yardage: 5409	
Slope: 121	**Par: 72**

The Wood Stork Course, its 18 holes also designed by Willard Byrd, opened in 1991. Its parklike setting features significant natural hazards: The first eight holes play through wetlands; the next 10, through a pine forest.

Willbrook Plantation Golf Club

U.S. Hwy. 17 S., Pawleys Island
• 237-4900,
(800) 344-5590
Championship Yardage: 6704

Slope: 125	**Par: 72**
Men's Yardage: 6106	
Slope: 118	**Par: 72**
Ladies' Yardage: 4963	
Slope: 118	**Par: 72**

Dan Maples designed this 18-hole course of bermudagrass on rice plantation wetlands between Litchfield Beach and Pawleys Island.

The par 4 No. 5 is a 383-yard hole. Your drive has to carry water onto the fairway, which has a nice landing area, and the second shot also has to carry water onto a small green that gives the appearance of an island green, surrounded by water on three sides. You won't

have to play the true island green until you get to the 127-yard par 3 No. 6.

Public play is limited, with members given preference. A new clubhouse opened in fall 1995. A driving range and putting green are available as well as rental clubs.

Greens fees are $33, including cart, with a summer coupon published regularly in Myrtle Beach's *The Sun News*, and $46 in the high season, with a $17 additional cart fee. Booking is accepted a year in advance. Walking is allowed, but varies by season.

The Witch

1900 S.C. Hwy. 544, Conway • 347-2706, 448-1300
Championship Yardage: 6702

Slope: 133	**Par: 71**
Men's Yardage: 6011	
Slope: 121	**Par: 71**
Ladies Yardage: 4812	
Slope: 109	**Par: 71**

The Witch is an 18-hole course built in 1989 and designed by Dan Maples, with bermudagrass fairways and bentgrass greens. This course was built in the middle of a swamp. Wetlands come into play on almost every hole, and bridges wind through the course for about 4,000 feet. The 15th hole is a par 4 requiring a carry over wetlands of as much as 200 yards. The 9th hole features an island fairway surrounded by wetlands; it requires a carry over wetlands on the tee shot and the second shot.

Practice greens, a pro shop, beverage cart, rental clubs, a driving range, bar and restaurant are available.

The course accepts tee times 365 days in advance. Greens fees range from $46 to $83 and include a cart. Walking is not allowed.

The Wizard

U.S. Hwy. 501, Myrtle Beach • 347-6600
Championship Yardage: 6813

Slope: No rating	**Par: 71**
Men's Yardage: 6206	
Slope: No rating	**Par: 71**
Ladies' Yardage: 5054	
Slope: No rating	**Par: 71**
Other Yardage: 5575	
Slope: No rating	**Par: 71**

This 18-hole course opened in fall 1996 across the lake from Man O' War and was not completed for review when this book went to press. It's another Dan Maples layout. It features the new bentgrass G-2 greens, similar to Crenshaw bent but developed to be more heat tolerant and able to be trimmed to a finer surface.

The clubhouse is a castle design with a snack bar and a huge lounge. Amenities include driving range, putting green and rentals. Walking is not allowed. Cost ranges from $39 to $82, cart included.

Around the Grand Strand . . .

Fun Things To Do

Entertainment comes in many forms along the Grand Strand. On those days when you're not playing golf, or if you and your family come here for golf combined with vacation, you have an almost endless choice of activities.

You only have to look at the **Atlantic Ocean** for the most obvious entertainment. If the sedentary life of sunbathing while reading a book isn't for you, you can rent a Jet Ski, take a sail boat ride out into the wild blue yonder or do a little Parasailing. All of these can be done for a minimal cost. Or rent a bike and pedal along the sand with the kids on funny low-slung, three-wheel banana bikes until you've seen it all. Of course, the ocean also provides fun in the form of fishing, whether from one of the many piers, in the surf or aboard a Gulf Stream charter boat in search of the big ones. Several charters are available in Murrells Inlet, Little River or Calabash.

Speaking of water, just wait 'til you see the giant water slides on a 10-acre water park at **Myrtle Waves**, off U.S. Highway 17 Bypass at 1001 10th Street N. in Myrtle Beach. This fun is dictated by the heat of the summer season, so call 448-1026 for information on hours and rates. Or visit **Wild Water Waterpark and Family Fun Center**, 910 U.S. Highway 17 S., 238-WILD, a 16-acre park in Myrtle Beach featuring 33 exciting rides, miniature golf, video arcade, food court, picnic facilities and much more. If you tire of the water, the place to race is **Myrtle Beach Grand Prix** with two loca-

tions: 3201 S. Kings Highway, Myrtle Beach, 238-2421; and 3900 U.S. Highway 17 S., in the Windy Hill section, North Myrtle Beach, 272-6010.

To combine some nature and education for another big splash of entertainment take a walk on the wild side to visit **Alligator Adventure** for live shows with exotic wildlife including albino American alligators, giant Galapagos tortoises, dwarf crocodiles of West Africa, enormous pythons, boas and anacondas. Call 361-0789 or (800) 631-0789. It adjoins Barefoot Landing, U.S. Highway 17 N., North Myrtle Beach.

When the sun goes down you don't have to sit around and clean your clubs to get ready for your tee time tomorrow. The fun, entertainment and enjoyment can continue when the moon comes out. The beach is alive with music at one of the many theaters. Calvin Gilmore's **Carolina Opry**, N. Kings Highway at U.S. Highway 17 Bypass, Myrtle Beach, was one of the first to bring country music fans to Myrtle Beach in lieu of Nashville, and his popularity continues. Call 238-8888 or (800) THE-OPRY for reservations. **Legends in Concert**, Third Avenue S., Surfside Beach, features Elvis, Marilyn Monroe, Michael Jackson, Whitney Houston and scores of other impersonators barely discernible from the original superstars in live, full-stage productions. Call 238-STAR. Dolly Parton's **Dixie Stampede**, N. Kings Highway at U.S. Highway 17 Bypass, Myrtle Beach, is an exciting dinner theater with horses and wagons and a friendly north-south rivalry entertaining you while you feast and applaud. Call 497-9700 or (800) 433-4401.

Fantasy Harbour, U.S. Highway 501 (behind Waccamaw Pottery), Myrtle Beach, also features live entertainment at **The Gatlin Brothers Theatre**, **Ronnie Milsap Theatre** and **Snoopy's Magic On Ice**. Call 236-8500 or (800) 681-5209 for information. **Medieval Times** dinner theater, 236-8080, provides a fine feast served by your own wench and a jousting tournament for knightly entertainment from another century.

The group **Alabama** appear several times each year in their namesake theater at Barefoot Landing, U.S. Highway 17 N., Myrtle Beach. Guest performers have included Barbara Mandrel, Waylon Jennings, Merle Haggard, Tammy Wynette and many more of the biggest names in country music. Call 272-1111 or (800) 342-BAMA for information.

The **Palace Theater** is a new attraction that will offer a varied list of entertainers reaching far beyond country styles. This venue at Broadway At The Beach, from 21st to 29th avenues N., off U.S. Highway 17 Bypass in Myrtle Beach, opened in 1995 with Bill Cosby, Kenny Rogers and The Righteous Brothers (not all together, of course). The Rockettes traveled here from New York City's Radio City Music Hall for a two-months-running Christmas show in 1996. From *Cats* to Sawyer Brown, The Beach Boys, Johnny Mathis and Jeff Foxworthy, big-name performers and performances comprise the entertainment du jour. Call 448-0588 or (800) 905-4228 for information.

You may want to add a little culture to your trip. If so, take a trip to **Brookgreen Gardens**, U.S. Highway 17 S., Murrells Inlet, the world's largest outdoor sculpture garden. This beautiful slice of Lowcountry landscape features more than 500 pieces of sculpture. Wildlife and botanical gardens boast more that 2,000 different plants. Children and adults, alike, will enjoy this natural attraction. Call 237-4218 for information.

Shopping is always on the agenda when you are visiting Myrtle Beach, and with the 1995 opening of the **Myrtle Beach Factory Stores**, U.S. Highway 501, west of the Intracoastal Waterway, Myrtle Beach, 236-5100, the variety is even larger. Other familiar places are the **Outlet Park at Waccamaw**, U.S. Highway 501, west of the Intracoastal Waterway, Myrtle Beach, 236-1400, and **Barefoot Landing**, U.S. Highway 17 N., North Myrtle Beach, 272-8349, still award winners for the bargains and variety plus proximity to theaters and children's entertainment. Another recent addition (1995) to that list is **Broadway At The Beach**, from 21st to 29th avenues N., off U.S. Highway 17 Bypass in Myrtle Beach, 444-3200, a unique place to eat, shop and be entertained (see previously mentioned Palace Theatre). The $250 million complex includes 100 specialty retail stores and 12 restaurants (including the Hard Rock Cafe). It also includes the IMAX theater, with a six-stories-tall screen and surround-sound that brings you feature films bigger than life.

The Grand Strand has much to offer va-cationers and residents who come here to play golf. It's possibly the miniature golf capital of the world, not to mention the ever popular **Pavilion Amusement Park**, 812 N. Ocean Boulevard, Myrtle Beach, 448-6456, which has been spinning its Ferris wheels for years and luring every kid to rides and amusements that delight the entire family. You might go home tired, but never bored.

Where to Eat

Dining along the Grand Strand is neither for the timid nor the dieter. The Myrtle Beach Area Chamber of Commerce has counted 1,400 restaurants and claims that the area has more restaurants per capita than San Francisco — usually considered the benchmark for abundant and noteworthy dining establishments. Personally, we haven't been able to keep count in Myrtle Beach, but we are diligently trying.

The food is outrageously delicious, no matter what your preference. Of course, fresh seafood is the local specialty, and you will encounter Calabash-style (lightly breaded and fried) cuisine throughout the area. Calabash is actually a little fishing village on the southern edge of North Carolina. Many seafood buffets throughout the area offer all-you-can-eat choices, predominantly Calabash-style. Please don't even think about cholesterol; anything so tasty just has to be good for you.

The other primary local specialty is Lowcountry cooking. The Lowcountry stretches from the southern end of the Grand Strand throughout the Charleston and Hilton Head areas. Wealthy plantation owners settled in the Lowcountry, and their style of cooking depended heavily on locally produced fish, fowl and vegetables. The preparation took its flavorful hints from slaves who brought their ancestral memories of Creoles, sauces and stews from the French.

Plenty of ribs, steaks, burgers and chicken are equally delicious if you don't want seafood. Also, vegetarian specialties, Italian and Oriental delicacies are equally superior.

Yes, as you might have guessed, we love food, and it's our distinct pleasure to tell you about it. Refer to our Preface for an explanation of the pricing code.

North Strand

The Brentwood Restaurant

$$$ • Luck and Mulberry Sts., Little River • 239-2601

Chef Bill Stublick and his brother Jim of Brentwood, New York, brought their unique culinary talents into the charming restored 1910 home where you'll be seated in one of several small dining rooms, then treated to desserts and after-dinner drinks in the upstairs salon. Fresh-baked bread, crisp house salads, vegetable du jour and a choice of wild rice pilaf or potatoes du jour will accompany entrees from the land or sea. Grilled ostrich or twin lobster tails might catch your attention. If not, try the rack of lamb or veal maison. This fine restaurant is out of the mainstream, but convenient to North Myrtle Beach and Calabash-area golf courses. You don't have to dress up to enjoy the dressy meal here.

Chestnut Hill

$$$ • 9922 U.S. Hwy. 17, North Myrtle Beach • 449-3984

Chestnut Hill offers fine dining in a casual atmosphere overlooking a beautiful marsh. Friendly service by the professional staff adds to the experience, and we think you'll want to come back often. Seafood, steaks, chicken and home-baked breads are the specialties. Be careful not to fill up on the wonderful sweet potato rolls before dinner. We choose the shrimpers platter as an entree again and again. It's cooked three different ways, so you don't have to make up your mind which is best. We try to finish with homemade Key lime pie.

Dick's Last Resort

$$ • Barefoot Landing, North Myrtle Beach • 272-7794

Yes, Dick's even serves golfers, and the same rough and rude service is dished out to all who want to be loud and crazy in this popular nightspot where the pork chops, catfish or chicken is served in a bucket and eaten with fingers. The food is actually pretty good too, but you have to drink a lot to appreciate (or overlook) the zany atmosphere here. If you can manage to get here for Elvis's birthday, you will know he's alive and well on the Strand like nowhere else on earth.

Hemingway's

$$$ • Barefoot Landing, U.S. Hwy. 17 N., North Myrtle Beach • 272-6118

A huge menu offers more than 30 exotic seafood selections plus beef, veal, duck, chicken and pastas. Sidewalk dining is a good place to watch the crowds pass by, but the dining room offers a nice atmosphere too. A delicious appetizer is salmon crepes au caviar or soft-shell crab Maryland. Our favorite fish dish is mahimahi San Tropez, although many choices are tempting. Maybe try the unusual surf and turf of duck and lobster. Everything here is tasty, and you'll be anxious to return on every trip.

Joe's Bar & Grill

$$$ • 810 Conway Ave. at U.S. Hwy. 17 S., North Myrtle Beach • 272-4666

The selection of beef, veal, seafood and poultry is good. Begin with an appetizer of scallops en bacon brochette or escargot en brie butter. Then think about the Lowcountry crab cakes, which are the real thing. Desserts are special every day. The atmosphere is golf shirt, but the meal is coat and tie. It's in a remodeled rustic home on a saltwater marsh among gnarled live oak trees. Joe's Bar & Grill is open for dinner. Just across the street — and easier to find — is Hamburger Joe's, which is open for lunch of barbecue sandwiches and beer.

The Old Pro's Table

$$$ • U.S. Hwy. 17 S., North Myrtle Beach • 272-6060

You'll find the area's only collection of golf antiques here as well as quality steaks or seafood for dinner. This famous haven of golf atmosphere across from Barefoot Landing is convenient and accessible from any golf course. On a good day, you won't have to wait too long. Good entrees include the famous baby back ribs, several varieties of fresh fish, barbecue chicken and shrimp and prime rib or steaks.

The Parson's Table

$$ • U.S. Hwy. 17 N., Little River • 249-3702, (910) 579-8298

The main dining room here was built in 1885 as the Little River Methodist Church.

When a new church was built, this became a community meeting place, then was moved to the present location and converted into a restaurant. The antique stained-glass windows, Tiffany lamp and chandeliers plus the flooring and doors have been combined from retained originals and other furnishings collected from various churches and farmhouses and added over the years. Enjoy the architecture and the antiques while you dine, but don't overlook the main reason to visit: the award-winning food.

Beef, seafood, pasta and a variety of duck, veal, pork or chicken dishes are offered. We also like the desserts: apple pie with hot vanilla cinnamon sauce, strawberries Romanoff or banana and pineapple praline. Petite dinners for light appetites and children's specialties also are offered. It's open for dinner only any day except Sunday.

Myrtle Beach

Bagel Factory
$ • 2012 N. Kings Hwy., Myrtle Beach • 626-4717

The old-fashioned bagels promise no fats, oils or cholesterol. This bakery, deli and cafe offers a variety of breakfast or lunch omelettes, sandwiches, burgers, platters and bagels flavored with anything you can imagine — and, of course, all the trimmings and stuffings to accompany them. Fresh, quick, casual — it's great food to grab on the run. You can choose a Reuben of corned beef, pastrami or turkey with the standard Russian dressing and sauerkraut on rye. You can also take home eclairs, cannolis or brownies to round off your meal.

Carolina Roadhouse
$$ • 4617 N. Kings Hwy., Myrtle Beach • 497-9911

The Roadhouse is patterned after the supremely popular California Dreaming restaurants in Charleston and Columbia. It smells like the fresh cedar of its rafters combined with honey-drizzled fresh rolls and fries you can watch being prepared in the show kitchen. For lunch or dinner, try the ribs or one of the giant seafood platters. Slow roasted prime rib and huge salads with special house dress-

ings are also trademarks. We love the baked potato soup and the fresh fish of the day — try it blackened. It's a fun place for a big crowd to gather. And if you're into shellfish, Carolina Roadhouse has some of the best oyster shooters around.

Carolinas Grill & Specialties
$$$ • Kingston Plantation, 9800 Lake Dr., Myrtle Beach • 497-7300

In the Radisson resort, this upscale oceanfront setting is home to unique delicacies including fresh grilled seafood, beef and chicken. An outstanding starter is fried lobster medallions. Then try a sautéed grouper or salmon filet, which will melt in your mouth.

Along with the views, the pastry chef's creations are our favorite part of this visit. Ask about the chocolate espresso Charlotte or the peanut butter pie. Be sure to wind your way upstairs to the lounge for an after-dinner drink and superb look at the ocean too. This is not the resort's main restaurant (which also is a good choice), but a small, intimate (almost hidden) dining room available by reservation only.

Collectors Cafe
$$$ • 7726 N. Kings Hwy., Myrtle Beach • 449-9370

A flavor of Europe greets you in the art galleries of Collectors. Also you will notice about 100 selections of wine and 20 different coffee roasts from all over the world. Handpainted tables, chairs and tiles are scattered among the original art of the owners, all of which is for sale if you can tear your attention from the Mediterranean food long enough to shop. Open for dinner only, the superb menu features grilled Thai shrimp or lobster zucchini pancake for appetizers. Enjoy an original pasta entree or, perhaps, lamb loin and pesto wrapped in phyllo dough. Desserts are decadent but appropriately matched with cappuccino or espresso to finish a special evening. Reservations are suggested.

Croissants Bakery & Cafe
$ • 504-A 27th Ave. N., Myrtle Beach • 448-BAKE

This wonderful bakery has the best muffins in town to grab on the run and also serves a good sit-down breakfast, including quiche or country grits and eggs casserole. For lunch, try a salad in a French-bread bowl, quiche or deli sandwich with a fresh croissant. It's convenient to shopping, beach and many golf courses.

Giovanni's – A Touch of Italy
$$$ • 504-H 27th Ave. N., Myrtle Beach • 626-8995

Giovanni's menu is based on the regional specialties of Italy's Piedmonte, Vald'Aosta and Liguria. The pasta, shellfish over pasta, beef, veal and seafood specialties are all delicious. From tagliatelle to tortelloni to cappelletti to fuzzoletti to buccatini, it's all here — and you'll feel like you're in Italy. You'll even find Italian coffees and fresh-baked pastries. In a lovely setting, this restaurant's service and menu will never disappoint.

Key West Grill
$$ • Broadway at the Beach, between 21st and 29th Aves. N., Myrtle Beach • 444-3663

The Cuban, Spanish and Calusa Indian influences from the Keys are in the tropical atmosphere and unique recipes of this spicy and popular new restaurant. Try the garlic crawfish or coconut shrimp to start. We can't resist the Key West conch chowder. Blackened fish specialties of the day or frog legs will transport your taste buds to another place. Pasta is plentiful, and rice with black beans accompanies some entrees. Several lobster combos are tempting. The view of the lake is relaxing while you look around at the sky blue ceiling and unique architecture in this restaurant within the city's newest shopping complex.

Rossi's
$$$ • 9600 U.S. Hwy. 17 N., Myrtle Beach • 449-0481

Italian food is the specialty here, including homemade pasta, but any menu choice is fine; we've never had a bad meal here. Golfers will find their own special corner, and everyone will have fun. A loud crowd usually waits around the bar until seating is available. The cheese and crackers on the bar make the wait worthwhile. Try one of the daily specials for a unique appetizer — or maybe the oysters Rossi, a slight deviation from oysters Rockefeller. Veal, chicken and steak also are good if you tire of our recommended seafood or pasta. If you wish, wait staff can suggest an appropriate wine to suit your entree choice.

Sam Snead's Tavern
$$ • 9708 N. Kings Hwy., Myrtle Beach • 497-0580

Sam Snead's serves good food for dinner only. The sporty atmosphere is pleasing for a casual meal. As good as the food is the memorabilia collected by Snead, one of the greatest golfers of all time. The fourth such restaurant in the country to open, this is a real museum. Snead occasionally greets visitors with his homespun philosophy explaining his self-taught golfing success.

You might tee off with hot cheese and spinach dip. Then go around the greens with the crispy fried pecan chicken salad. It's too much for one person. The short course includes tavern onion soup or a burger; then the long course offers blackened chicken pasta or a pasta with four cheeses. Specialties such as oak-fired shrimp Carolina or oak-grilled tuna mignon are as good as the sirloin or tenderloin available here and in the neighboring and upscale Thoroughbred's. If you can stay for the chip shot, you should try the chocolate sack. It's large enough for four people and an outrageous chocolate delight any dessert lover won't soon forget.

Sea Captain's House
$$$ • 3002 N. Ocean Blvd., Myrtle Beach • 448-8082

This is one of the oldest and best local establishments. All the recipes are special Southern secrets. During early breakfast, you can watch the dolphins play while you enjoy specialties of eggs Benedict or traditional eggs, bacon and home fries. A long wait for a dinner table is common (no reservations are taken), but you can add your name to the list and enjoy watching the waves break and the sea

---

FYI
Unless otherwise noted, the area code for all N.C. phone numbers in this chapter is 910; the area code for all S.C. numbers is 803.

gulls flocking to the lights. Lunch and dinner are experiences to remember. The menu choices are predominantly seafood, but you'll find plenty of chicken or salad choices as well. This restaurants serves our favorite she crab soup. Think about splurging on a special dessert. You'll be hard pressed to find anything remotely comparable.

Shenanigan's
$$ • U.S. Hwy. 17, Myrtle Beach • 272-1171

Aged steaks, slow roasted prime rib, fresh seafood and pride in detail characterizes this spot, open for dinner only. Any choice is good, but we prefer such specials as the prime teriyaki steak. The accompanying hoppin' johns is a typical choice too. A tempting appetizer is the Savannah spinach and artichoke dip. Kids pay what they weigh, so don't be alarmed by the big scale when you enter the restaurant. You can take home a pint-size souvenir golf bag beer mug to remember your Myrtle Beach round later during the year.

Villa Mare
$$ • 7819 N. Kings Hwy., Myrtle Beach • 449-8654

Please don't tell all of your friends about this fabulous Italian restaurant. Don't tell anyone the food is some of the best around, served in large portions and quite inexpensive. This is a secret place among locals, and we don't want it to get so crowded that we can't get our table. Lunch and dinner are real treats in this refreshing little spot. Pasta, soup, salad and bread accompany any entree from seafood to our all-time favorites eggplant parmesan or lasagna. The house red wine goes well with these selections.

Vintage House Cafe
$$ • 1210 N. Kings Hwy., Myrtle Beach • 626-3918

An eclectic surprise in the midst of old Myrtle Beach, this lovely cafe provides a gourmet menu for lunch and dinner. A favorite luncheon choice is salmon and grits. Dinner entrees include Mediterranean grilled chicken breast over linguine with black olives, tomatoes and feta cheese or grilled New Zealand rack of lamb marinated in olive oil and fresh herbs. Tom and Trina O'Brien specialize in the use of herbs and sauces for their homemade delicacies. Desserts include homemade cheesecakes and similar goodies, with various teas, cappuccino, espresso or wines.

South Strand

Bovine's
$$ • U.S. Hwy. 17 Bus., Murrells Inlet • 651-2888

Right on the water in the middle of the fishing village of Murrells Inlet, this restaurant's menu is eclectic and its view a magnet to bring you back often. One tempting daily special is the honey-crust pizza from the wood-fired brick oven. From the wood-fired grill come great steaks or roasted prime rib. A delicious entree is the mesquite-grilled free-range chicken breast stuffed with pancetta, goat cheese and wild mushrooms. Check out the desserts too.

Bovine's, open for dinner only, is popular with locals as well as traveling golfers.

Conch Cafe
$$$ • 1482 N. Waccamaw Dr., Garden City • 651-6556

Jimmy Buffet would be at home here — maybe he *was* here when he wrote some of his tunes. Don't come here in a rush. Come after a round of morning golf on the South Strand and plan on languishing with a long, cool salty drink and a sandwich. Salads or sandwiches in any variety are good choices, and dinner promises seafood entrees concocted from local recipes.

Drunken Jack's Restaurant & Lounge
$$$ • U.S. Hwy. 17 Bus., Murrells Inlet • 651-2044

Plan to arrive long before you expect to be hungry, because the wait "in-season," as locals say, might be more than an hour or two. The downstairs lounge provides a view of the inlet fishing fleet at Snug Harbor Marina — and a drink. And if you can wait, the seafood choices upstairs are worth it. Alcoholic drinks are available any day except Sunday. We usually choose a fish special (caught today in the devil's triangle), which can be prepared many ways, or the crab casserole baked

Myrtle Beach Nightlife

It's the place for night life. Neon and noise are splashed across the middle of Myrtle Beach like you see in few other golf resorts. This town never rolls up the sidewalks; the party begins late at night and continues until early morning. You have to sample it, even if you have to manage with only a few hours of sleep to make your early tee time. It's boisterous and sometimes bawdy, but, hey, it's all in good fun.

The shag, the Southern-style jitterbug-type dance, which originated in North Myrtle Beach to the beach music of the 1960s, draws semiannual reunions of dancers and serious party-types from all over the world to North Myrtle Beach's Main Street at The Horseshoe. You can take lessons if you missed learning it when you were younger, or you can watch the regular competitions and cheer for your favorite shaggers.

For games, dancing and a good time including good food, try Yesterday's NiteLife at 1901 N. Kings Highway. It includes a sports bar section with games for golfers, race car drivers and other sports enthusiasts.

A nearby favorite spot for dancing to the tunes spun by Jumpin' Jack Flash (a local DJ) is Studebakers at 2000 N. Kings Highway. Or you can check out 2001, at 920 Lake Arrowhead Road. It's three clubs, with a piano bar, a disco and live performances, all in separate sections. This club almost always attracts a crowd of golfers and party people. Also for the extra-late party crowd, Jamaica Joe's is a favorite hangout.

Player's Sports Lounge in the Galleria Shopping Center on Restaurant Row hosts live bands, pool tournaments, Ping Pong tables, 20 televisions and more sports games than you can play in a night.

The newest excitement is Celebrity Square's collection of nine nightclubs at Broadway At The Beach, opened in late 1995, and promising to rival any big city's nightlife. Live music ranges from blues to jazz to pop to country (of course) to you-name-it. Dancin' in the street is literally encouraged here; for one admission ticket, you may mix and match any of the clubs, and street parties on summer weekend evenings are frequent.

---

in cheese. Word has it Jack might have traded his peg leg for the marinated chicken breast or steak and lobster from the charcoal grill.

Flo's Place Restaurant & Raw Bar
$$ • U.S. Hwy. 17 Bus., Murrells Inlet
• 651-7222

Flo's is one of the only places we know that offers alligator ribs. Flo's recipes, including the alligator and crawfish specialties, came from her childhood in Louisiana where her father regularly brought home such delicacies. Try the stewpot, with some of everything mixed in. Plan to hold on to your hat unless you want to find it hanging from the rafters where Flo's collection sports hundreds of them.

Flo's Place is fun and friendly, and it literally hangs over the marsh, creating a definite backwoods bayou feeling. Alcoholic drinks are served here every day except Sundays.

Island Cafe & Deli
$$ • U.S. Hwy. 17 S., Pawleys Island
• 237-9527

Locals frequent this cafe once a week for the Wednesday lobster night or the Monday shrimp night. Special price, special drink and seafood cooked to order will keep you coming back too. Reservations are recommended for dinner seven days a week. Everyone driving from one golf course to another on the South Strand stops here for a sandwich for lunch. Our favorite (plus the lobster special) is a big, cool salad with lots of toppings and crusty, hot bread with a glass of wine.

J. Edward's
$$ • 2300 S. Kings Hwy., Myrtle Beach • 626-9986

The tasty and tender ribs are local award winners in this casual dinner restaurant. If you can't choose which barbecue to eat, try the chef's sampler of ribs, chicken, a pork chop and shrimp. Bread, salad or slaw and baked potato, sweet potato or fries accompany the entree. You won't leave here hungry — nor as clean as when you arrived. Just dig in and enjoy. The people are friendly and the service good.

Where to Stay

Most of the major hotels on the Grand Strand offer golf packages. The following offers a variety of suggestions from basic golfer's accommodations to luxury resorts for a special family vacation. Refer to our Preface for an explanation of the pricing code.

North Strand

T-Time Tours
$$-$$$ • 505 Main St., North Myrtle Beach • 249-4545, (800) 458-8463

Try this vacation package company for golf, accommodations, entertainment, USAir and Budget car rental. Choose accommodations from one-, two- or three-bedroom fully equipped condominium units with views of the Intracoastal Waterway or the Atlantic Ocean. Golf on any of the area's championship courses, and choose country music or variety shows plus amusement parks, shopping or other attractions.

The Winds Clarion Inn
$-$$ • 310 E. First St., Ocean Isle Beach, N.C. • 579-6275, (800) 334-3581

It's not part of the North Strand, technically speaking, but this inn apparently prefers it that way. This lovely oceanfront hotel is part of the North Carolina Golf Coast Association, which is seeking to develop its own identity separate from the Myrtle Beach or Wilmington areas — its big-town neighbors to the south

and north, respectively. The 73 rooms include oceanfront rooms and one-, two- or three-bedroom suites overlooking subtropical gardens and a 7-mile-long island beach. Heated pool (enclosed in winter), whirlpools, exercise room, sauna, bikes, shuffleboard, malletpool, wetbars and refrigerators or kitchens in all suites are additional amenities. The four-bedroom spa houses (which sleep eight golfers) are ideal for golf groups. All five luxurious houses include full kitchens, great rooms and large Jacuzzis. Each bedroom also has a private bath, cable TV, wet bar with refrigerator, private telephone and balcony.

Golf packages with guaranteed tee times and discounted rates are offered on 20 high-quality Brunswick County courses within a five- to 15-minute drive and a total of some 86 championship courses in the Myrtle Beach area. Golfers are welcomed at a weekly reception during the prime golf seasons — spring and fall. Also, the continental breakfast buffet is more than the usual continental fare — it's pancakes, waffles or cereal.

If you aren't looking for the big-city lights and other attractions, come here for great golf and great beach access in the family-type Ocean Isle area.

Myrtle Beach

Bar Harbor Motor Inn
$$ • First Ave. N., Myrtle Beach • 626-3200, (800) 334-2464

This oceanfront property is convenient to the golf courses, and we think you'll enjoy the great views, the outdoor pool or indoor heated pool while traveling on your Southern Escape Golf package. Excellent package prices on any area course are offered year round. Call (800) 554-4546 for information on custom packages. This family-owned accommodation effuses a family-friendly atmosphere. Suites, rooms and efficiencies with private balconies are available.

Beach Vacations Inc.
$$ • 357 Lake Arrowhead Rd., Myrtle Beach • 449-2400, (800) 449-4005

One-, two- and three-bedroom accommodations are available in the way of oceanfront condominiums or golf course villas — part

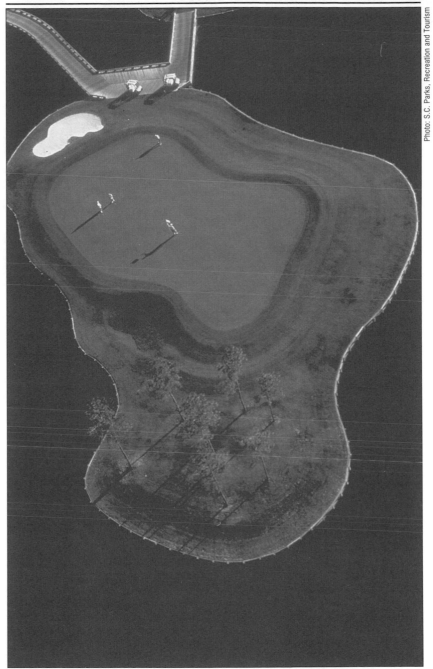

Photo: S.C. Parks, Recreation and Tourism

This hole at Man O' War is just one of many testing water holes in the Myrtle Beach area.

and parcel of the golf vacation this company will package for you. Properties feature pools, Jacuzzis, tennis, full kitchens and cable TVs. You'll enjoy the quality accommodations, especially if you like to overlook the fairways, and friendly and helpful staff will assist with your package booking.

The Caravelle

$$ • 70th Ave. N., Myrtle Beach • 449-3331, (800) 845-0893

One of the first to offer the golf package, this beachfront hotel offers 420 spacious accommodations including rooms, suites, efficiencies or condominiums. The indoor and outdoor pools and whirlpools, a Lazy River, sauna, game room and breakfast buffet will add interesting asides to your golf vacation. Tee times are available on the private Dunes Club as well as almost 100 other championship courses. A "golf widow" package is offered, and you might want to check out the "blizzard escape" winter package too.

The Caribbean Resort & Villas

$$$ • 3000 N. Ocean Blvd., Myrtle Beach • 448-7181, (800) 845-0883

Oceanfront suites in the tower sleep extra guests in the living room, and oceanfront and oceanview rooms and two- or three-bedroom condominiums with kitchen, living and dining room, washer and dryer are available. Golf packages are available on any area course including the private Dunes Club. The breakfast included with your golf package will give you the real flavor of a local Myrtle Beach favorite — the Sea Captain's House next door.

Amenities include indoor and outdoor pools, whirlpools and a Lazy River, which is covered during cooler months. Non-golfing family members hang out at the pool or roam a few blocks to the mall.

Coral Beach Resort Hotel

$$$ • 1105 S. Ocean Blvd., Myrtle Beach • 448-8421

Have you ever taken a group to the beach only to encounter an unusually rainy week with nothing to do outdoors? If so, consider staying at the Coral Beach Resort Hotel. Of course, it never rains on the golf course, but sometimes it rains on the kids' pool parties. This quality hotel has a bowling alley on the sixth floor, arcade games and a regular entertainment center of its own. It also caters to golf groups, as you'll surmise from the memorabilia adorning its version of the 19th hole plus the indoor putting green and indoor driving range. Golfers who take advantage of the package deal with area courses are invited to complimentary cocktail parties during the season.

The oceanfront suites sleep three golfers or a family of six. Suites and efficiencies include a kitchen with refrigerator, range, microwave, toaster and utensils, and suites feature living and dining areas as well. Suites are oceanfront, and rooms and efficiencies are oceanview, all with private balconies. Amenities include a general store and gift shop, the Atlantis restaurant, a lounge, two snack bars and a pool bar, three indoor whirlpools, two heated outdoor pools, a steamroom and saunas, an exercise room and suntan beds.

Dunes Village

$$ • 5200 N. Ocean Blvd., Myrtle Beach • 449-5275

The Dunes Village has the feel of a small family resort where everyone knows your name. Catering to golfers, and booking packages on any area course including the private Dunes Club, this oceanfront resort offers an attractive year-round pool and tennis courts and is a nice spot for the whole family to enjoy. All rooms are oceanfront with private balconies.

The breakfast here is legendary, and many guests return to this same home at the beach year after year.

Kingston Plantation – A Radisson Resort

$$$$$ • 9800 Lake Dr., Myrtle Beach • 449-0006

This is one of the classiest resorts if you want to splurge on a luxury oceanfront suite and spend some time; also two- or three-bedroom oceanview condominiums or lakeside villas of one, two or three bedrooms are practical if you're only here for golf. Golf packages get guests on many of the top-rated Grand Strand courses. Be sure to enjoy the oceanfront pool and bar plus the fine dining, especially the weekend dinner buffet. The Swan

Sea Conference Center is a convenient site for meetings and reunions. Tennis and racquetball courts, an indoor pool, sauna, whirlpool and health club also are on the property. The Arcadian Shores Golf Course is across the street, and many nightspots are an easy drive from the Radisson.

The Inn at Myrtle Beach

$$ • 7300 N. Ocean Blvd., Myrtle Beach
• 449-3361

This looks like a regular medium-size oceanfront motel and is priced accordingly, but it's far better quality than most, offering attractive furnishings and spacious rooms, mini-suites or efficiency apartments. If you bring a big family, consider the penthouse suite for its pleasant view, screened porch and plenty of rooms. The outdoor pool, whirpool and restaurant (open for breakfast and dinner) also will keep a family occupied. Golf packages include bookings on any area courses, and an on-site practice putting green is available to help you get ready.

Myrtle Beach Martinique

$$$ • 7100 N. Ocean Blvd., Myrtle Beach
• 449-4441, (800) 542-0048

One of Myrtle Beach's nicest oceanfront hotels, with exceptional attention to quality service, the Martinique splashes its tropical colors and hospitality across just about any size room, efficiency or suite. An indoor pool, oceanfront pool, whirlpool, exercise room, sauna and meeting and convention facilities are available.

The on-site Cafe du Port serves breakfast, lunch and dinner, and the Banana Boat lounge is a popular afternoon and evening spot for socializing. This accommodation is convenient to golf courses, and staff will book tee times on any area course for guests taking advantage of golf packages.

Ocean Creek

$$$$ • 10600 N. Kings. Hwy., Myrtle Beach
• 448-8446, (800) 443-7050

Choose the towers on the oceanfront, or choose a short walk back to a villa on the 57-acre resort that welcomes golfers. The variety

includes 400 studios plus one-, two- and three-bedroom condominiums.

The Four Seasons restaurant features a buffet breakfast and full-service dining plus banquets or receptions for private groups. A putting green is on site. The knowledgeable and friendly golf department will book packages with any area courses you choose. Seven pools include an indoor pool and whirlpool. A tennis complex and beach club with oceanfront pool also are available. The freshwater creek running through the property provides a unique change of scene for the golfer who doesn't prefer the ocean.

The family who doesn't golf can scoot across U.S. Highway 17 to spend a day at Barefoot Landing and Alligator Adventure, an award-winning entertainment, shopping and dining complex.

Ocean Dunes/Sand Dunes Resort

$$$ • 201 74th Ave. N., Myrtle Beach
• 449-7441

This oceanfront resort caters to golfers — it's convenient to any golf course. Packages are booked on any area course plus the exclusive private Dunes Club and Pawleys Plantation. Rooms, suites, efficiencies, villas and penthouses are available. All have private balcony, refrigerator, in-room movies, cable TV and private safe. Microwaves are available in suites and efficiencies.

The oceanfront Brass Anchor seafood restaurant and lounge offers live entertainment, and the Dolphin pool bar is oceanfront as well. A fitness center, indoor and outdoor pools, a sauna, whirlpools, a beauty salon and massage therapy round out the amenities.

Sands Ocean Club Resort

$$ • 9550 Shore Dr., Myrtle Beach
• 449-6461, (800) 845-2202

Suites or efficiencies in this oceanfront resort hotel are convenient to all major golf courses. Golfers are welcomed at a weekly reception and clinic. Exclusive play on Sands' Pawleys Plantation is a treat for guests here. Each unit has a private balcony, refrigerator,

FYI

Unless otherwise noted, the area code for all N.C. phone numbers in this chapter is 910; the area code for all S.C. numbers is 803.

in-room movies, cable TV and a kitchen with microwave. A poolside cafe, oceanfront restaurant and indoor and outdoor pools are available. A Lazy River, health club, gift shop, convenience store, covered parking and rain insurance round out amenities.

The area is popular during summer when Sandals lounge and the neighboring Ocean Annie's Beach Bar offer live music, and lots of fun folks dance away the days and nights here. Sands Ocean Club is an easy walk to a few shops. And during November, slip across the footbridge to the Dunes Club for the Energizer SENIOR TOUR Championship (see our Tournaments in the Carolinas chapter). Early reservations are recommended for packages that include tickets to the tournament.

Sea Mist Oceanfront Resort
$$ • 1200 S. Ocean Blvd., Myrtle Beach • 448-1551, (800) SEA-MIST

Sea Mist is one of the largest oceanfront resorts that caters to golfers, with customized packages for twosomes or large groups. Perfect for families too, this resort offers supervised and structured summer programs for children.

Accommodations for any size group or family vacation include single rooms, suites, multi-bed apartments and a lacy and romantic honeymoon suite with a red heart-shape Jacuzzi. Eleven pools (two indoor), a Jacuzzi, sauna, steamroom, lounge, cafe and ice cream parlor are on site. Discount theater tickets and limousine service round out the amenities. The Family Kingdom amusement park is nearby, and many other activities are within walking distance.

Sheraton Myrtle Beach Hotel
$$$$$ • 2701 S. Ocean Blvd., Myrtle Beach • 448-2518

The Sheraton is one of the truly nice spots to find a room, efficiency or suite. All have refrigerator, coffee maker, in-room movies, cable TV, plus microwave in suites and efficiencies. Golfers and their families will enjoy indoor and outdoor pools, whirlpool, health club, sauna, gift shop and good food and drink in a welcoming setting in Kokomo's beach bar or oceanfront restaurant and lounge. Golf packages are booked on any area course and include a weekly reception.

Swamp Fox Ocean Resort
$$ • 2311 S. Ocean Blvd., Myrtle Beach • 448-8373, (800) 228-9894

The Swamp Fox boasts more oceanfront footage than most hotels. A quality and experienced golf department will help you book any package, even on the private Dunes Club, and can include theater tickets if desired. Cocktail receptions for golfers are offered weekly during golf season.

Choose from efficiencies or suites in its new tower or rooms in the older motel. Take a group and enjoy a penthouse with plenty of space, cooking and dining facilities plus an outstanding view. Little ones will enjoy the Lazy River, and everyone will be pleased with indoor and outdoor pools, Jacuzzis, saunas and the adjoining Gabriel's Restaurant.

South Strand

Litchfield Beach and Golf Resort
$$$$$ • U.S. Hwy. 17 S., Pawleys Island • 237-3000, (800) 845-1897

If you or someone in your party plays tennis or racquetball, wants to find a spa and health club or simply wants to retreat from the busy resort area to the quiet marshes of the South Strand, this is the place for you. Everything you might need is here, and it's surrounded by Litchfield Country Club, River Club and Willbrook Plantation Golf Club; plus the resort offers booking on all of the area's other courses. The restaurant is great, entertainment is nearby, and specialty shops are easily accessible. Oceanview, marshview and fairway villas are available. At Litchfield, you could completely miss Myrtle Beach and still have the vacation of a lifetime.

Golf Equipment

You'll find anything you need on the Grand Strand. You won't have any trouble finding a store, and what you will find is bound to be bigger and better than anything you've seen elsewhere. If you're in the market for new clubs, wait until you get here to shop. In addition to the following suggested equipment shops, professionals at many of the golf courses offer custom fitting. Ask a local golfer if you have any questions.

When golf shopping on the Grand Strand, check out any or all (if you have a week or more to spend just shopping!) of the following golf equipment retailers: **Nevada Bob's**, 3100 N. Kings Highway, Myrtle Beach, 448-1779, or 2006 U.S. Highway 17, North Myrtle Beach, 272-4705; **Golf Dimensions**, 2301 U.S. Highway 17 S., North Myrtle Beach, 272-4630; **Martin's Golf and Tennis**, 1615 U.S. Highway 17, North Myrtle Beach, 272-6030; 2204 U.S. Highway 17 N., 448-7525, or U.S. Highway 501, 236-7878, in Myrtle Beach; or 1010 U.S. Highway 17 S., Surfside Beach, 238-1643; **Scottish Pride Golf**, 1500 U.S. Highway 501, Myrtle Beach, 946-9464; **Clubmaker's Golf**, 2016 N. Kings Highway, Myrtle Beach, 626-0099; **Wild Willie's**, U.S. Highway 501, Myrtle Beach, 249-9722 or (800) 249-9722; and **Sam's Discount Golf & Tennis Inc.**, 3300-C U.S. Highway 17 S., North Myrtle Beach, 272-6998.

Golf Instruction

Most of these golf schools offer any type of package you'll need to improve your golf game. Call for specific information or ask at any course you choose to play about private lessons taught by professional staff.

We recommend the following: **Legends Academy**, (800) 882-5121; **The Links Golf School** at The Tradition Club, (800) 833-6337; **Phil Ritson Golf School**, (800) 624-4653 or 237-4993; **The Classic Swing Golf School** at Deer Track Golf Resort, (800) 548-9186 or 650-2545; **Riley Golf School**, (800) 30-RILEY; and **Myrtle Beach Golf School**, (800) 94-SWING.

Charleston/Hilton Head/Beaufort

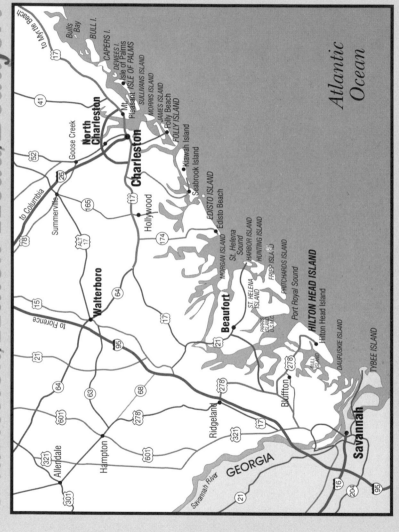

South Carolina's Lowcountry

Charleston, Beaufort and Hilton Head

The Lowcountry stretches south along the South Carolina coast from Georgetown to Hilton Head. Lowcountry defines the marshy terrain and is often used to define the golf courses, the food, the culture, the architecture and the lifestyle of this area.

Charleston speaks of history with an irresistible charm and beauty. Walking the cobblestone streets of downtown or taking a guided tour by water or by horse and carriage, you may believe it's still the 17th century. Wandering among the military sites, homes, churches and formal gardens is a great way to enjoy Charleston when your golf game is finished. You'll seldom see so many architectural treasures as the huge mansions of pastel colors, and all are preserved in their original antebellum splendor. Charleston is an important Southern city that was once one of the wealthiest cities in the country, and it displays faint touches of modernity and a California lifestyle in its street life.

As the home of the annual Spoleto Festival USA — the world's largest arts festival in terms of the actual number of events offered — each May, Charleston offers cultural entertainment opportunities unheard of in many Southern cities. Art, music, drama and dance are reflective of international influences, not of a Southern city torn by its country's Civil War. Yet the carefully preserved traditions of the African culture are proudly shared by Gullah presentations so moving that you may feel the prickle of goose bumps.

Be sure to sample some she-crab soup, shrimp and grits and other local seafood, as well as some Lowcountry recipes, including black bean specialties and frogmore stew (just so you'll know, it doesn't even have any frogs in it). In fact, more grits are sold in these low coastal plains than anywhere else in the world, and the small town of St. George capitalized on this by instituting the World Grits Festival, celebrated each April. If you really want to learn about some Southern food, watch for the frequent food-related festivals throughout the coastal Carolinas from spring through fall, featuring shrimp, Cajun specialties and other tasty regional fare.

FYI

Unless otherwise noted, the area code for all phone numbers in this chapter is 803.

Golf follows the gracious Southern style with tradition and quality. Many clubhouses return you to a veranda with wooden rocking chairs, where you can look out over the rolling fairways, sip a cool mint julep and recount your winning shots. Charleston was the home of Harleston Green and The South Carolina Golf Club, the first golf course and golf club in America, respectively, both established in 1786. Today the area offers more than 20 outstanding courses and a relaxing pace, well-known since the 1991 Ryder Cup put Kiawah's Ocean Course in the international spotlight.

Included in the Charleston area are North Charleston, Summerville, Mt. Pleasant,

GOLF COURSES IN CHARLESTON/HILTON HEAD/BEAUFORT, SOUTH CAROLINA

Course Name	Type	#Holes	Par	Slope	Yards	Walking	Booking	Cost w/ Cart
Callawassie Island Club								
Dogwood Course	semiprivate	9	36	n/r	3239	no	call	$52-73
Magnolia Course	semiprivate	9	36	n/r	3275	no	call	$52-73
Palmetto Course	semiprivate	9	36	n/r	3187	no	call	$52-73
Charleston Municipal Golf Course	public	18	72	110	6161	yes	7 days	$20-23
Charleston National Country Club	semiprivate	18	72	129	6482	PM	60 days	$34-56
Coosaw Creek Country Club	semiprivate	18	71	124	6068	yes	call	$38-44
Country Club of Beaufort at Pleasant Point	semiprivate	18	72	115	6112	yes	call	$24
Country Club of Hilton Head	semiprivate	18	72	128	6543	no	call	$55-73
Crowfield Plantation	semiprivate	18	72	120	6471	yes	call	$20-49
Dunes West Golf Club	semiprivate	18	72	125	6392	no	365 days	$42-72
Golden Bear Golf Course/Indigo Run	semiprivate	18	72	125	6643	no	call	$55-73
Hilton Head National Golf Club	public	18	72	119	6260	no	call	$40-66
Island West Golf Club	public	18	72	124	6208	no	call	$49-62
Kiawah Island								
Marsh Point Course	resort	18	71	126	5841	no	call	$94
Ocean Course	resort	18	72	139	6824	no	call	$110
Osprey Point Course	resort	18	72	124	6015	no	call	$100
Turtle Point Course	resort	18	72	132	6396	no	call	$100
Oak Point Golf Club	public	18	72	128	6468	yes	call	$40
Ocean Point Golf Links	resort	18	72	124	6060	yes	call	$39-54
Old South Golf Links	public	18	72	119	6354	PM	call	$48-75
Oyster Reef Golf Course	semiprivate	18	72	123	6440	no	call	$63-79
Palmetto Dunes Golf Course								
Arthur Hills Course	resort	18	72	120	6122	yes	call	$36-75
George Fazio Course	resort	18	70	123	6239	yes	call	$36-75
Robert Trent Jones Course	resort	18	72	119	6148	yes	call	$36-75

Course Name	Type	#Holes	Par	Slope	Yards	Walking	Booking	Cost w/ Cart
Palmetto Hall Plantation								
Arthur Hills Course	semiprivate	18	72	123	6582	yes	call	$36-75
Robert Cupp Course	semiprivate	18	72	126	6522	yes	call	$36-75
Patriots Point Golf Links	public	18	72	113	6274	call	call	call
Port Royal Golf Club								
Barony Course	resort	18	72	122	6038	yes	call	$32-76
Planters Row Course	resort	18	72	126	6009	yes	call	$32-76
Robbers Row Course	resort	18	72	129	6188	yes	call	$32-7
Sea Pines								
Harbour Town Course	resort	18	71	126	6119	no	call	$105-175
Ocean Course	resort	18	72	119	6213	no	call	$105-175
Sea Marsh Course	resort	18	72	117	6129	no	call	$105-175
Seabrook Island								
Crooked Oaks Course	resort	18	72	121	6387	yes	call	$50-75
Ocean Winds Course	resort	18	72	125	6395	yes	call	$50-75
Shadowmoss Plantation	semiprivate	18	72	117	6399	weekdays	call	$24-32
Shipyard Golf Club								
Brigantine Course	resort	9	36	n/r	2959	after 5 PM	call	$38-80
Clipper Course	resort	9	36	n/r	3132	after 5 PM	call	$38-80
Galleon Course	resort	9	36	n/r	3035	after 5 PM	call	$38-80
The Golf Professionals Club								
Champions Course	semiprivate	18	72	119	6430	yes	call	$22-25
Players Course	semiprivate	18	72	101	5659	yes	call	$22-25
The Links at Stono Ferry	resort	18	72	112	6085	no	call	$38-41
Wild Dunes								
Harbor Course	resort	18	70	117	5900	no	call	$35-75
Links Course	resort	18	72	121	6131	yes	call	$55-110

McClellanville and St. George. Also, the islands are important vacation spots away from the bustling city life: Edisto, Kiawah, Seabrook and Sullivans Island, Folly Beach and Isle of Palms. Each boasts its own character and attracts its own type of visitor or resident. Sample each until you find your own niche for seclusion or activity.

You'll also discover more than 20 courses in the Hilton Head and Beaufort areas. Beaufort (pronounced beu-ford) lies a few miles inland and on a bay on the way south from Charleston to Hilton Head. Beaufort's entire town is a historic landmark and a treasured find for any architecture, history or antiques buffs. Interested browsers should schedule extra time for roaming around here after the golf game, or families could spend their days here while the golfer does the golf thing nearby.

Golf, tennis and relaxing are the major activities on Hilton Head Island and Fripp Island, which is a few miles from there near Beaufort. Hilton Head is a 12-mile strand showcasing the white sands of the Atlantic beaches and the undisturbed natural beauty of flora and fauna. It is best known for the Heritage Golf Classic that was first played here on the Harbour Town Golf Links in 1969. Every spring, the party returns, and the plaid winner's jacket is passed to another of the world's best golfers. The lack of amusement parks, the unobtrusive shopping areas and a quiet way of life lead many to vacation or retire here. It's the most peaceful resort if you're looking for luxury, sophistication and good taste. Internationally known for its golf and tennis resorts and its fine quality, Hilton Head prides itself on catering to the crème de la crème rather than offering something for everyone. If that's your style, you will feel right at home here. Just don't expect anything too much more strenuous than a tennis match or a round of golf.

Additional information is available in *The Insiders' Guider to Greater Charleston* or by calling the Charleston Trident Chamber of Commerce, 577-2510; the Charleston Area Convention and Visitors Bureau, 853-8000; the Edisto Chamber of Commerce, 869-3867; the Greater Beaufort Chamber of Commerce, 524-3163; the Hilton Head Island Chamber of Commerce, 785-3653; or the Greater Summerville Chamber of Commerce, 873-2931.

Charleston Courses

Charleston Municipal Golf Course
2110 Maybank Hwy., Charleston
• **795-6517**

Championship Yardage: 6411	
Slope: 112	**Par: 72**
Men's Yardage: 6161	
Slope: 110	**Par: 72**
Ladies' Yardage: 5202	
Slope: 114	**Par: 72**

This 18-hole course, managed by the city, is Charleston's oldest course — built in 1929. It was designed by John E. Ademes. It's a well-run public course, with bermudagrass greens and fairways. Greens fees for visitors are $12 on weekdays and $15 on weekends, and carts are an additional $10; late-afternoon greens fees specials are offered for $5. The course hosts 54,000 rounds of play a year, in part because it has less water than many courses, the fees are affordable and booking a round is relatively easy. Calling a week in advance is recommended.

Practice greens, a driving range, rental clubs, a pro shop, snack bar and bar are available. On busy days, a beverage cart also makes the rounds.

Walking is allowed. The scenic 13th, 14th and 15th holes are on the marsh and the Stono River.

Charleston National Country Club
U.S. Hwy. 17 N., Mt. Pleasant • 884-7799

Championship Yardage: 6928	
Slope: 137	**Par: 72**
Men's Yardage: 6482	
Slope: 129	**Par: 72**
Other Yardage: 6061	
Slope: 122	**Par: 72**
Other Yardage: 5509	
Slope: 114	**Par: 72**
Ladies' Yardage: 5103	
Slope: 126	**Par: 72**

The existing 18-hole course was designed by Rees Jones and opened in 1990. (The original Jones-designed course was destroyed by Hurricane Hugo in 1989.) It is home to the

Photo: Hilton Head Island Resort

Aim at the lighthouse on the 18th when you're at Pete Dye's
course on Hilton Head Island, south of the Charleston area.

Citadel and the College of Charleston golf teams. Fairways and greens are bermudagrass. Marshland and bridges characterize this course.

One of the pro's favorite holes is the par 4 12th, a dogleg right with a big pond on the right and marsh on the left. It requires a fairly long but accurate tee shot. You have very little rough and are in a hazard if you shoot left or right. Your second shot (ostensibly) is to an elevated and undulating green surrounded by bunkers and backed by the Intracoastal Waterway, which usually wafts a gentle breeze over the green. Another challenging hole is No. 6, a par 4 — challenging not because of its length but because of its hazards. Your tee shot needs to hit a landing area to prevent hitting a second marsh that you can't see from the tee. Then your second shot will be over a marsh onto the narrow green.

A practice green, driving range, rental clubs, bar and restaurant are available. Members may access locker-room facilities, a pool and a tennis center. The pro shop staff is very cordial and ready to answer questions and meet golfers' needs.

Greens fees range from $34 on off-season weekdays to $56 on in-season weekends, including cart. The course is open to the public year round, and tee times are accepted 60 days in advance. Walking is allowed on a limited basis during afternoons only. Senior discounts are available to golfers age 65 and older. Dress code requires a collared shirt and no jeans, fairly standard for Carolina courses and enforced stringently here.

Coosaw Creek Country Club

4210 Club Course Dr., North Charleston • 767-9000
Championship Yardage: 6593
Slope: 129   Par: 71
Men's Yardage: 6068
Slope: 124   Par: 71
Ladies' Yardage: 5064
Slope: 115   Par: 71

Arthur Hills designed this 18-hole course that opened in 1993. It is situated on 645 acres of woods and wetlands and features bentgrass fairways and bermudagrass greens. A few holes have marsh and a bit of rolling ground somewhat unique to the Lowcountry. This course places a premium on accuracy rather than length, making the approach shot and the short game the keys to scoring well. The best opportunities for scoring are on the front nine, as the course takes charge on the back nine, with more of the water and wetlands coming into play.

Hole No. 11, a 224-yard par 3, requires your tee shot to cross water and wetlands three times. The tee shot on No. 12, a 596-yard par 5, must cross a lake then avoid a pot bunker in the middle of the fairway. The second shot must be played long and left to avoid pine trees on the right side of the fairway at the entrance to the green. The difficult No. 14 requires a perfect drive then still leaves another 200 yards over a marsh. The signature hole is the 16th, a 516-yard par 5 from the back tees, requiring a 3-wood off the tee to drive over a big pond. A 40-foot elevation change down, then back up, from tee to green provides a unique situation.

Two practice greens, a driving range and club rental are available. A pro shop, shower facilities and a grill room are on site. A beverage cart makes the rounds on weekends and holidays.

Greens fees range from $38 on weekdays to $44 on weekends year round, including cart. Walking is allowed with some restrictions, depending on how busy the course is. Tee times are accepted one week in advance.

Crowfield Golf & Country Club

300 Hamlet Cir., Goose Creek • 764-4618
Championship Yardage: 7003
Slope: 134   Par: 72
Men's Yardage: 6471
Slope: 120   Par: 72
Other Yardage: 6701
Slope: 128   Par: 72
Ladies' Yardage: 5682
Slope: 115   Par: 72

Tom Jackson and Bob Spence designed this 18-hole course in 1990 with bermudagrass greens and fairways. It's so popular that it's hosted the South Carolina PGA Championship three times.

They planned to take advantage of the wetlands and forests of an 18th-century plantation. Dense hardwoods surround every hole, and the layout has rolling terrain and plentiful bunkers. Accuracy is essential on this course. The signature 7th hole is a par 5, measuring 513 yards from the back tees, and mounds are abundant. All greens are elevated, and the course offers extraordinary character and subtleties for the Lowcountry. Every hole has three or more sand traps. Water hazards are small rather than large bodies of water.

Practice greens, a driving range, pro shop, bar and restaurant and rental clubs are offered. If you need personalized instruction, you can get it at the driving range.

The cost ranges from $25 to $59, including cart. Walking is allowed during the week or after 2 PM on weekends. Out-of-towners trying to make vacations plans can call at any time to book an advance tee time; otherwise, if you're in town, count on an advance booking of one week.

Dunes West Golf Club

S.C. Hwy. 41, Mt. Pleasant • 856-9000, (888) 955-1234

Championship Yardage: 6871	
Slope: 131	**Par:** 72
Men's Yardage: 6392	
Slope: 125	**Par:** 72
Ladies' Yardage: 5278	
Slope: 118	**Par:** 72

This Arthur Hills design is an 18-hole course that opened in 1991 and has received national attention for its bermudagrass-covered dunes along the Cooper River, set among ancient oaks draped with Spanish moss. It's part of a residential community 10 miles northeast of Charleston. The clubhouse was built on the foundations of an old plantation house.

As with all Lowcountry courses, marshland is dominant — although it doesn't always come into play. The course is some-

Marlene Floyd Golf Schools for Women

Women are different. They play golf differently. They need to be taught differently, says Marlene Floyd, Ladies Professional Golf Association member, tour player and women's instructor extraordinaire.

The North Carolina native and several other female professionals from the Carolinas teach 12 schools for women only each year at Palmetto Dunes in Hilton Head. The two-day sessions allow only 10 or 12 students and begin indoors with lectures and photographs of good golfers in action. Then, they progress outdoors with gimmicks and weighted clubs that teach the students ex-

Close-up

actly how to tilt, how to swing, how to grip, what to do and, more importantly, what to feel.

Floyd teaches golfers to understand the swing and, thus, to become more proficient at the game. She explains exactly how centrifugal force works and what the body should be experiencing during the actions required of golf. She demonstrates where the elbows should be, what the wrist should do and what else it takes to reach the green.

"A woman has to be more proficient than a man because of lack of muscle, lack of wrist, hand and forearm strength," Floyd said. She emphasizes the difference between men and women, explaining the different center of gravity and the changes in forearm and hand action.

Floyd's father and mother and her famous brother Raymond Floyd, a star on the regular and now the senior PGA tours, all played, and finally Marlene began the game when she was in her 20s and dating a golf pro. She began her schools for women in 1993 and had previously taught for 14 years. The family was named "Golf Family of the Year" in 1988 by the New York Metropolitan Golf Writers Association.

For information on Marlene Floyd Golf Schools for Women, call (800) 637-2694.

what open. High rough and copious sand give trouble around the greens. The signature hole is 18th, a straightforward par 4 with two different greens. A short green that plays about 420 yards is in the marsh; the far green plays at 454 yards from the back tees and requires a shot over the marsh to the green for the second shot. Live oaks line the right side of the fairway, and woods are on the left.

Amenities include practice greens, a driving range, rental clubs, a pro shop, bar, restaurant and beverage cart.

Tee times are accepted a year in advance. Fees range from $42 to $72, including cart. Walking is not allowed.

Kiawah Island
S.C. Hwy. 700, Kiawah
• **768-2121, (800) 654-2924**
Marsh Point
Championship Yardage: 6334

Slope: 126	**Par: 71**
Men's Yardage: 6007	
Slope: 120	**Par: 71**
Ladies' Yardage: 4944	
Slope: 122	**Par: 71**

Gary Player places a premium on accurate shot placement, and that is reflected in this 18-hole course, opened in 1976. Undulating greens and narrow marsh-lined fairways are well guarded with water on 13 holes but offer a good game to players of all levels. It's a short course but one not to be considered too easy.

Dramatic contouring within the putting surface makes precise iron play a prerequisite to good scoring. A halfway house is at No. 10.

Greens fees are $94, including cart, and should be booked through the resort. Walking is prohibited.

The Ocean Course
Tournament Yardage: 7371

Slope: 149	**Par: 72**
Championship Yardage: 6824	
Slope:141	Par:72
Men's Yardage:6244	
Slope: 134	**Par: 72**
Ladies'Yardage:5327	
Slope:133	Par:72

Pete Dye's 1991 course gained immediate fame when it hosted the 1991 Ryder Cup,

and you'll most certainly feel like part of a great tradition when you play here. It's simply one of the best, one of the toughest and one of the most scenic courses in the area. The second hole is difficult, and if you can par it with a five, you should take the score card home to show your friends. After your drive you have two options: lay up short of the marsh or try to carry the marsh leaving a wedge shot to the green. Hole No. 4 is a 453-yard par 4 and is the toughest hole on the course. You are required to carry over two marshes. Whatever you do, don't go too far left on this hole; club selection is important on the approach here. The 17th hole requires a check of the wind to be sure you can carry the 197 yards to the green. If the wind is in your face, don't be embarrassed to return to your bag to choose a longer club.

All 18 holes offer panoramic views of the Atlantic Ocean, and 10 play directly along the ocean. Dunes, marshes, water, sand bunkers and rolling greens all make you work at playing, but you'll never complain given such beautiful surroundings.

Make bookings through the resort for an all-inclusive package with every amenity. Greens fees are at least $110, including cart. Sorry, fitness buffs — walking is not an option.

Osprey Point
Championship Yardage: 6688

Slope: 124	**Par: 72**
Men's Yardage: 6015	
Slope: 118	**Par: 72**
Ladies' Yardage: 5122	
Slope: 120	**Par: 72**

Tom Fazio used four lakes to challenge you on 15 holes, and moguls will determine the route of your golf ball past marshes and lagoons, sometimes into forests of pines, palmettos, magnolias and oaks. This 18-hole course, opened in 1988, is wider and more forgiving than the other Kiawah courses.

Strong holes include the 453-yard par 4 No. 9 and a pair of par 3s longer than 200 yards. Also, strategic short par 4s tempt the big hitters.

Greens fees are more than $100, including cart. Book tee times through the resort for the best prices. No walking is allowed.

Aim at the lighthouse on the 18th when you're at Pete Dye's
course on Hilton Head Island, south of the Charleston area.

Turtle Point

Championship Yardage: 6914
Slope: 132   Par: 72
Men's Yardage: 6025
Slope: 122   Par: 72
Other Yardage: 6489
Slope: 127   Par: 72
Ladies' Yardage: 5285
Slope: 122   Par: 72

Jack Nicklaus designed this 1981 course with a spectacular finishing hole. Two other holes along the Atlantic are also beautiful. Lagoons, oak-lined fairways, the ocean and the winds blowing off the Atlantic all contribute to the difficulty here. A keen eye and deft touch are required to master the gentle breaks of this course. Turtle Point is always on any list of top resort courses.

Greens fees are more than $100, including cart, and can be booked through the resort as part of a fine package including many amenities. Walking is not allowed.

Oak Point Golf Club

4255 Bohicket Rd., Johns Island
• 768-7431
Championship Yardage: 6759
Slope: 137   Par: 72
Men's Yardage: 6468
Slope: 132   Par: 72
Other Yardage: 5996
Slope: 126   Par: 72
Ladies' Yardage: 4671
Slope: 121   Par: 72

Clyde Johnston designed this 18-hole course with fairways and greens of bermudagrass. Wildlife is prevalent on this course.

Water comes into play on 16 of the 18 holes. The 3rd hole is a 90-degree dogleg with an island green, measuring 367 yards from the back tees. The 11th is a 193-yard par 3 from the back tees with a narrow driving area flanked by water on the right and left; there's water just left of the green as well.

Rental clubs, pro shop, practice green and driving range round out the amenities package.

Cost is $55 year round, including cart. Walking is permitted after 2 PM, and you can book up to 60 days in advance.

Patriots Point Links

U.S. Hwy. 17 Bus., Mt. Pleasant • 881-0042
Championship Yardage: 6838
Slope: 118   Par: 72
Men's Yardage: 6274
Slope: 113   Par: 72
Ladies' Yardage: 5582
Slope: 115   Par: 72

This is an 18-hole public course just across the Cooper River bridges from Charleston into Mt. Pleasant. It was designed by Willard Byrd and opened in 1981. The views of the ocean are amazing as are the panoramas of Shem Creek, James Island, Patriots Point and Sullivans Island. The wind coming in from Charleston Harbor is a factor on most shots here, and it adds multiple dimensions to the course.

The signature hole is the par 3 17th, 139 yards from the back tees, with the green stretching into the harbor itself. This is a real test for a birdie.

Amenities include a pro shop, rental clubs, a large driving range, grill and snack bar. Group or individual instruction is provided.

Patriots Point's rates vary seasonally and range from $30 on weekdays to $42 on weekends, including cart, all a great value. Walking is generally allowed except on weekends before noon. Call whenever you wish for an advance tee time, and they'll do their best to accommodate you.

Seabrook Island

1002 Landfall Way, Seabrook Island
• 768-2529, (800) 824-2475

This resort includes a medical center, boat docking and an equestrian center that will rent you a ride to the trail or the beach. Other resort amenities are clay tennis courts and an excellent beachfront with sailing and fishing arrangements. Babysitters are registered at Seabrook, and you can ask the front desk personnel for assistance with scheduling one.

Golf packages arranged through the resort are recommended for great family vacations. These courses are only available to resort guests or island residents. Amenities include a clubhouse with a large pro shop and private instruction.

Walking is allowed on both courses during afternoons. Appropriate golf attire is a

must. Greens fees are $50, and high-season rates elevate to $75, including carts.

Crooked Oaks

Championship Yardage: 6862

Slope: 126	Par: 72

Men's Yardage: 6037

Slope: 117	Par: 72

Ladies' Yardage: 5250

Slope: 119	Par: 72

Other Yardage: 6387

Slope: 121	Par: 72

Crooked Oaks is an 18-hole Robert Trent Jones Sr. course that opened in 1981. The course is placed in the forest and the black water lagoons, and the greens are small. Crooked Oaks is true Scottish style in that the clubhouse is not at the turn; you play nine out and nine back, and restroom facilities are provided at the 9th hole. As you make the turn, you'll find No. 9, a 170-yard par 3 with a large bunker guarding the front left of the green. The 18th hole, a par 4 of 427 yards, requires that you carry a large body of water before reaching the fairway.

Ocean Winds

Championship Yardage: 6805

Slope: 130	Par: 72

Men's Yardage: 6027

Slope: 120	Par: 72

Other Yardage: 6395

Slope: 125	Par: 72

Ladies' Yardage: 5524

Slope: 127	Par: 72

Ocean Winds, opened in 1973, offers 18 holes designed by Willard Byrd. The greens are large, the layout is flat and the breeze at this oceanside course is prevalent (hence its name). Only five holes on Ocean Winds do not have water. The 3rd is a 516-yard straightaway par 5, and you must avoid the sand on the entire right side of the green. The 6th hole is another par 5, with water bordering the entire left side of the fairway . . . so play to the right. Also be aware of the bunker on the left side of the green.

Shadowmoss Plantation

20 Dunvegan Dr., Charleston • 556-8251, (800) 338-4971

Championship Yardage: 6701

Slope: 123	Par: 72

Men's Yardage: 6399

Slope: 117	Par: 72

Other Yardage: 6129

Slope: 112	Par: 72

Ladies' Yardage: 5169

Slope: 120	Par: 72

Russell Breeden designed this course with bermudagrass greens and fairways. It opened in 1970 and was extensively renovated in 1986 with the addition of several water hazards.

Beware of the par 5 8th hole, 533 yards from the back tees, with water lining both sides of the fairway and cutting across the path of your second shot. It's a dogleg right with bunkers surrounding the green. The two par 3s on the back are tough also. Water hazards are primarily off to the side, and they don't come into play if your ball is anywhere near where it should be.

A pro shop, locker room, bar, snack bar, beverage cart, club rental, driving range and practice green make your golfing experience nice. Tennis courts and a swimming pool plus a meeting room are available for a business trip combined with your golf.

Greens fees are $24 during the week, $30 on weekends; during the spring and fall seasons, fees increase to $28 and $32, including cart. Walking is allowed Monday through Friday only. If you're an out-of-towner, you can book your tee time up to three months in advance.

Wild Dunes

Isle of Palms • 886-6000, (800) 845-8880

Just a 20-minute drive east of Charleston on the northeastern tip of the Isle of Palms lies this special resort that features two championship 18-hole courses designed by Tom Fazio. It's also a top-rated tennis resort, and the white, sandy beach runs for more than 2 miles. A fitness center, marina and 20 pools round out the resort amenities. The drive over the causeway to the isle — the new connector to which you will hear locals refer — is a prelude to the treats that await you on this tropical paradise. You can really feel the transition into modern-day resort mode as you drive onto the isle and leave behind any ideas of historical tours or city traffic. Villas and homes for vacation rental have views of the golf course, the ocean, woods or marsh.

Though the rates vary slightly for the two courses, the advance reservation policy is the same for both:

If you're staying at the resort, you may book a tee time through them up to a year in advance. If you're not a guest and are calling for weekend play, do so seven days in advance; for week days, call 30 days in advance.

The Harbor Course

Championship Yardage: 6446

Slope: 124	Par: 70

Men's Yardage: 5900

Slope: 117	Par: 70

Ladies' Yardage: 4774

Slope: 117	Par: 70

A target golf course, Harbor involves water or marsh on 17 holes and is peppered with heavy bunkering. Fazio claims this 1986 course as one of his favorites. It's laid out similar to a Scottish design at St. Andrews, with eight holes out and 10 back in. Instead of a clubhouse at the finish, a halfway house is located in the middle of everything between the 4th and 5th holes as well as between the 12th and 13th. Bermudagrass greens and fairways are popular. The signature 17th is a 460-yard par 4 that traverses the marsh at Morgan Creek. Marshland and water are mixed on this winding course.

Practice greens, club rental, a pro shop, bar, deli and pizzeria add to the pleasant atmosphere.

Rates range from $35 during off-season afternoons to $75 during spring and fall, including cart. Walking is not allowed on this course.

The Links Course

Championship Yardage: 6722

Slope: 131	Par: 72

Men's Yardage: 6131

Slope: 121	Par: 72

Ladies' Yardage: 4849

Slope: 121	Par: 72

Other Yardage: 5280

Slope: 125	Par: 72

This course opened in 1980. No. 1 is an enjoyable introduction to the course espe-

An Inviting Island

The Native Americans left a legacy for us to enjoy on the 10 miles of wide, sandy Kiawah Island. It's close enough to Charleston for easy access, yet it's worlds apart from everything. Its name came from the Indians who lived here during the 1600s and used the island resources for hunting and fishing. The Kiawahs disappeared, as did most tribes that inhabited the Carolinas during that period.

George Raynor, who was believed to be a pirate, was given title of the land by the Lords Proprietors. The island passed to daughters, granddaughters and husbands of that family during the next 50 years.

Then the Vanderhorst family acquired the island and kept the property for 200 years. During the Revolutionary War, sick and wounded junior officers were allowed passes to rest on Kiawah Island. Soldiers from the War of 1812 were located on the  island to protect the city of Charleston. During World War II, U.S. Army teams patrolled the island's coast with horses and jeeps. After the Civil War, Arnoldous Vanderhorst IV returned home, and many of his former slaves returned to the island, enabling planting to resume. He was killed in a hunting accident, and his ghost has been reported on the island on many occasions, but the family rarely returned.

In 1951, a lumberman, C.C. Royal, purchased Kiawah Island, and in 1974 it was developed into a world-class resort and residential area. The undisturbed Atlantic beach has been preserved in a natural state as much as possible for the sake of the sea life. Dolphins play along the coast, and beachcombers can unearth a wide variety of shells. Sea turtles frequently come to the shore at night during nesting season, and each lays up to 150 eggs.

The resort includes four golf courses, two tennis complexes, three pool complexes, the 150-room Kiawah Island Inn, four restaurants and lounges. Also, 350 villas and 22 private homes are for rent. Regional influences are noticed in the cuisine, such as fresh seafood, locally grown vegetables, herbs and spices.

Kamp Kiawah is a supervised program for half-days or full-days for children ages 3 to 11, and it offers a fun-filled day while parents enjoy their time on the golf course. A teen program includes late-night movies, photo scavenger hunts, basketball and volleyball tournaments, dance contests, billiard tournaments and pizza parties. Families find sand sculpture contests, movies, jeopardy, bingo, ice cream socials and aqua aerobics planned. Interpretative nature excursions are guided by staff biologists. They include off-island tours by boat or tractors, marsh creek canoe excursions, birding walks, night beach walks and bike tours. A full marathon is enjoyed each December by more than 3,500 runners. An annual triathlon takes advantage of the beach and trails of the island. The Charleston Symphony Orchestra plays twice a year. Need we say more? This island entices the vacationer with any level of relaxation or excitement that is wanted.

Call 768-2121 for complete information.

cially if the wind is not in your face. It's a par 5 of 501 yards from the back tees. Not a single fairway bunker is on this first hole. You can have a safe lay up, and then your wedge shot to the green will give you a chance at a birdie. The signature holes are the 17th and 18th.

Seventeen is a par 4 on the ocean, and it tees off going down the right along the Atlantic to a tucked-in green. It's 405 yards from the back tees. The 18th is a dogleg right and a beautiful driving hole, finishing with a well-bunkered and undulating green. Although a shot that is way left will be out on the beach, don't be afraid for your tee shot to be left; that's the perfect place.

A driving range and practice green are available here. Also, it has a pro shop, locker room, club rental, full restaurant and bar.

Fees range from $55 to $110, including cart. Summer afternoons are the cheapest times to play. Walking is allowed.

Around Charleston . . .

Fun Things To Do

It's important to stop at the **Charleston Visitor Reception & Transportation Center** at 375 Meeting Street when you first arrive in the area. You can park there and tour downtown without the headache of searching for elusive parking spaces. Also, you'll enjoy the video display and the quantity of free maps and brochures describing the spots you'll want to tour. Guided walking tours for the hearty, bus tours for the less adventurous, water tours by reservation or the famous carriage tours are our preference when we want someone to explain what it is we're seeing. The architecture and the culture of the past two centuries are preserved and displayed in a magnitude in Charleston that is found in few other areas. Among the churches, house museums and formal gardens are stories of earthquakes, fires, hurricanes and wars. The center is open daily from 8:30 AM to 5:30 PM.

Charles Towne Landing, on S.C. 171 between I-26 and U.S. 17, is an unusual state park. It's an interpretation of the first English settlement in South Carolina, which occurred on the plantation site in 1670. It was first established as a site for celebration of the state's tricentennial then later converted to a state park. The exhibits and the animals in natural habitat will interest the whole family. The park is open year round. Watch for more activity here in the future; excavations are expected to lead to additional exhibits and possible additions to the animal forest. For more information, you may call 556-4450.

FYI

Unless otherwise noted, the area code for all phone numbers in this chapter is 803.

The **Charleston Museum** at 360 Meeting Street is the oldest museum in America. It showcases the memorabilia of early Charlestonians and defines the social and natural history of the coastal region. A special Discover Me room will occupy your children for hours, as they can touch things as well as learn about toys and clothes from past children's lives. Call for information about hours and prices, 722-2996.

The Battery is a seaside park where you can walk or drive among the cannon, statues and monuments telling of people and events of the American Revolution and the Civil War. Once a significant defense site for the city, it now plays host to laughing children, biking athletes, strolling retirees and blushing brides.

Other activities in the Charleston area that are worth including in planning a golf trip are the numerous festivals. Whether you love seafood, music, crafts or any combination, you will find a festival that shows it all. We recently enjoyed B. B. King and a number of lesser-known groups during the popular annual jazz festival, where young and old spend the day in the park sunning and schmoozing and soaking up the brass vibrations.

One of the great parts of the Charleston experience still remains the beach activity on the neighboring islands, such as Isle of Palms, Sullivan's Island and Johns Island. Think about biking, walking, fishing, swimming or just relaxing with a book while watching the kids shovel sand over your feet.

If you really like nature, take a ferry to Bull Island and explore the **Cape Romain National Wildlife Refuge**. It's 20 miles north of Charleston and is a pristine wilderness of 64,000 acres home to dolphins, egrets, pelicans and herons including 250 species of birds. Call 881-4582 for information on Coastal Expeditions including a 38-passenger pontoon charter.

Where to Eat

We've found an abundance of great restaurants throughout the Charleston and Mt. Pleasant areas, on both sides of Shem Creek, the port for the area's fishing fleet. Our picks

Photo: The Charleston Area Convention & Visitors Bureau

Exploring Charleston's many beautifully restored homes is a
pleasant pastime when you're not golfing.

are often in downtown Charleston because it's such a neat town we want to make sure you enjoy it.

We offer our recommendations based on the quality of food, of course, as well as on the service and all-around dining experience, but also for the downtown atmosphere itself. It's only a few miles from wherever you will golf or stay. You can put your vehicle into a parking garage since street parking spaces are hard to find. Then walk around and get a feel for the place — the cobblestone streets, the beautifully restored buildings, the market in the town's center.

Late-night dinners are fashionable, and jazzy dessert cafes or watering holes are open into the wee hours for the crowd that mingles college students with fun-loving golfers and Charleston professionals, not to mention an occasional film star who happens to be on location.

Unless otherwise noted, restaurants are in Charleston proper. Refer to our Preface for an explanation of the pricing code.

82 Queen
$$-$$$ • 82 Queen St. • 723-7591

Fine wines accompany elegant dinners of Lowcountry foods served in a historic building created from two townhouses wrapped around a garden courtyard. It's one of the locals' favorite spots for lunch, after work socializing or dinner.

BJ's Broadstreet Cafe
$ • 17 Broad St. • 722-0559

Home of the BJ burger, this cafe is inside the Music Farm across from the Visitor's Center downtown. For a quick lunch on weekdays or a late night pizza treat, check the burgers or sandwiches from the barn or from the coup, or try chicken wings prepared with a special recipe and a choice of dips. Beers and juices are varied.

Bocci's Italian Restaurant
$-$$ • 158 Church St. • 720-2121

Some of the best crusty bread you will ever sample is made at Bocci's. Try to save room for the pasta with special sauces then for pastries galore. You could be in Northern Italy if you didn't step out into the bustling historic downtown of Charleston after a lusty lunch or dinner experience here.

California Dreaming Restaurant and Bar
$-$$$ • 1 Ashley Pointe Dr. • 766-1644

The view, the decor and the croissants drizzled with honey are enough to bring you back to this fine restaurant regularly. You might also choose a huge salad of many varieties, fried or blackened fish dinners or steaks cooked to perfection. We know someone who will drive an hour to Charleston just to have lunch here. When you see the lines waiting for dinner, you'll also have another clue that it's the place to see and be seen. Try to book in advance for dinner, and bring a big appetite and people who like to have fun.

Chef & Clef Restaurant
$-$$$ • 102 N. Market • 722-0732

This is a great place for a late Sunday morning champagne brunch while you listen to fine jazz. Dinner is good also, or stop by for dessert after a dinner elsewhere and a downtown walk. The different floors for different music styles are interesting and always popular with every age group.

East Bay Trading Company
$$-$$$ • 161 E. Bay St. • 722-0722

The atmosphere is casual and friendly set in a huge old warehouse where you can see several floors from your table or from the glass elevator. Food is very good here, and golfers will feel at home for happy hour and dinner. Choose a fish special of the day or any variety of seafood, steak or chicken. You can hang around the huge bar area and find a lot of people having fun.

L'Attitude South
$$-$$$ • 130 Mill St., Mt. Pleasant • 884-5005

A maverick waterfront kitchen, they call it, this almost-hidden restaurant overlooking Shem Creek offers happy hour and dinner daily and Sunday brunch. Sunset and creek views are spectacular, and the food preparation and service match just fine. A starter to try is the inside out yellow tomato sandwich with ciabatta bread and basil oil. You've never

Photo: Hilton Head Island Resort

The 18th hole on Pete Dye's course at Hilton Head Island
is one of the most famous in the Carolinas.

had *this* tomato sandwich at home. A typical Southern entree here is shrimp and andouille sausage over creamy grits with veal stock gravy. Or try the five-spiced duck breast with whipped sweet potatoes accompanied by chow-chow with tiny green bean and red onion salad. Cappuccino, espresso or cordials go great with Key lime pie to finish. We always look forward to a meal here.

Louis's Charleston Grill
$$$-$$$$ • 224 King St. • 577-4522

Nationally recognized as one of the country's best restaurants, Louis's provides a culinary experience beyond that of any ordinary dining room. You should choose this for one of your most special meals. Louis Osteen uses regional foods splashed with ingenious touches of Lowcountry tradition and prepared with his traditional French training. Take some extra time, and maybe a few extra bucks, and you'll savor the evening you spend with Louis.

One-Eyed Parrot
$-$$ • 1130 Ocean Blvd., Isle of Palms • 886-4360

Reservations and stress are unacceptable here. Go for the Caribbean style seafood, tender steaks, island-style rum punch or pina coladas. Stay for the fun. Lunch starts at the beach level at The Banana Cabana where you can go barefoot and sit in the sun on a beautiful beach. You may enjoy the cheeseburger of paradise or the seafood burrito. For dinner upstairs, begin with tapas (Spanish for "appetizer") such as fried artichoke hearts or conch fritters. Then try the parrot paella (medley of shrimp, chicken, sausage with yellow rice, peas, pimentos and tomato rouille). So much food and fun is ready for you here after golf on the two beautiful neighboring Wild Dunes courses. You'll understand why it's called paradise.

Saffron
$ • 333 E. Bay St. • 722-5588

We highly recommend the fresh homemade bread, such as Charleston sourdough, and some healthy and tasty dishes for breakfast or lunch. A great salad is the East-West kiwi salad that includes slivered chicken with hearts of palm, kiwi, mandarin orange and fresh pineapple on greens. Mediterranean specialties of roasted lamb or saffron chicken also are good and spicy. European pastries, croissants, danishes, muffins and other daily delights must go home with you on any trip here. For wholesale or retail goodies, check out the Saffron Bread Factory at 1001 Harborview Road on James Island, 762-7636.

Shem Creek Bar & Grill
$$ • 508 Mill St., Mt. Pleasant • 884-8102

Dine indoors or outside in the gazebo overlooking the tidal waterway, or just order from Sloppy John's, Shem Creek's oyster bar, for fresh shucked oysters and clams on the half shell. For lunch, dinner or weekend brunch, the daily specialties are fresh seasonal offerings such as she crab soup, seafood gumbo or cioppino (shrimp, oysters, scallops, fish, clams and mussels stewed with tomatoes, onions, bell peppers, garlic and wine over fettuccine). Shem grilled seafood is a specialty with Charleston red rice and fresh vegetables. If you've had your fill of seafood, try the grill thrill of filet mignon, ribeye steak or teriyaki chicken. The food and fun are great, and the view matches.

Squeaky's Tavern & Grill
$ • 5 Cumberland St. • 722-1541

Squeaky the turtle invites you for a "shelluva good time," and you might begin at turtle hours at 4 PM for special drink prices and to slow down, unwind, relax and come out of your shell. A light seafood or vegetable omelet is a nice dinner, or try fresh and delicious chicken livers with or without onions. Southern originals are dirty shrimp grits and their famous fried chicken. Top it all with a giant hot brownie sundae. Tuesday night jazz and blues jam sessions add to the reasons to enjoy this visit. If you ask locals about the Top 10 reasons to eat here, they'll probably give you 11 of them.

Sticky Fingers
$-$$ • 235 Meeting St. • 853-7427
U. S. 17 N, Mt. Pleasant • 856-9840
1200 N. Main St., Summerville • 875-7969

For ribs and barbecue ordered to go, catered or delivered overnight from a mail order catalog, Sticky Fingers can do it all. Included

Holes 16 and 17 on Tom Fazio's Harbor Course at Wild Dunes.

on the extensive menu are lunch salads and sandwiches or burgers with low calorie or no fat choices. We recommend a dinner special of barbecue pork or half a rotisserie chicken. Side dishes of dirty rice or cinnamon apples round out any meal nicely. The kids menu is sure to please. Be sure to take home a catalog and think about the luxury of receiving these sticky delicacies via FedEx in any city.

The Trawler
$$ • Shem Creek, Mt. Pleasant • 884-2560

Open daily for lunch, dinner or raw bar, this famous restaurant with a view of the creek specializes in the steam pot including every imaginable seafood or the famous fish stew and crab dip. A shellfish mixed grill or broiled sea scallops are among our favorites too, or choose delicious beef or chicken anytime in the middle of the huge seafood menu.

Vickery's
$-$$$ • 15 Beaufain St. • 577-5300

Many of the appetizers are large enough for an average eater's entree. Try something made with black beans and dirty rice, and go ahead and pour pepper gravy over your fries so you'll know you've been to the South for a meal. Lots of cayenne and Cuban flavored dishes are tempting. Save room for chocolate diplomattico or bourbon pecan pie for dessert. Micro, domestic, import and draft beers are more than you can name. Also, the wine list is varied, and the award winning double martinis are famous. The original Vickery's (plus two others) is in Atlanta, so if it's good enough for both of these Southern cities, it's worth a try for lunch, dinner or Sunday brunch of good things like Cuban Benedict or a big ugly biscuit and sausage gravy. You'll see a college crowd mixed with professionals and golfers of all ages.

Village Cafe
$$ • 415 Mill St., Mt. Pleasant • 884-8095

Light entrees are superb for lunch or dinner. Try the eggplant roasted pepper, mushroom and two-cheese lasagna with tomato basil pasta and smoked tomato sauce served with garlic olive oil. Or how about a salad of dungeness crab and grilled portabello mushroom over exotic greens with an herbed dijon vinaigrette. A larger entree is a pecan crust lamb topped with a maple vinaigrette served with a sweet onion tart and mashed new potatoes. Desserts are fabulous items like white chocolate hazelnut creme brulee. Low fat, cholesterol and sodium features are also offered (but, for heaven's sake, just skip a meal or two so you can have what you want here!).

Where to Stay

Your best trip to Charleston will include someone special and a stay in one of the historic bed and breakfast homes downtown. Man or woman cannot live on golf alone, and a little history tinged with romance adds to any experience. When it's too dark to golf any longer, it's time to enjoy a winter fireplace in your bedroom or a summer sunset from the veranda (you know we spell and pronounce it verandah in the Lowcountry) while you turn the clock back several hundred years. We also recommend a few nice hotels and some basic places for a quick golf trip with no frills.

Please call for information or to book reservations before arriving. You will find many venues filled during the height of summer tourist season and during some festival or convention weekends. Unless otherwise noted, accommodations are in Charleston proper. Refer to our Preface for an explanation of the pricing code.

The Ashley Inn Bed & Breakfast
$$$ • 201 Ashley Ave. • 723-1848

This historic inn, c. 1832, is close to the Charleston Visitor Center from where you can easily bike, walk or take a horse-drawn carriage to tour the downtown or drive quickly to any number of golf courses or beaches. The lovely pink house is an architectural treasure. Sausage soufflé, creamy Southern grits casserole with zucchini and cheddar biscuits, hazelnut peach syrup over crunchy (different!)

French toast are breakfasts here you will long remember. Also, the piazza setting overlooking the Charleston garden will be a treat during breakfast, afternoon tea or evening sherry. The six guest rooms and suites are furnished with antique four poster, pencil post or canopied rice beds. All have private bath, air conditioning and cable television.

Charleston Place
$$$$$ • 130 Market St. • 722-4900

In the heart of the historic district, this hotel stands out for its elegance and newness in a city filled with otherwise restored antiquity. Splurge on the club floors where you receive personalized service fit for royalty. Louis's Charleston Grill, one of the most noted restaurants in America, is in this hotel, along with a complete health club, indoor-outdoor pool and world-class boutiques including Polo, Gucci and many names you will recognize. The location is easily accessible from any golf course, and you will find the downtown attractions a nice diversion.

Hampton Inn-Riverview Hotel
$$-$$$ • 11 Ashley Pointe Dr. • 556-5200, (800) HAMPTON

This is a modern high-rise atypical of Charleston architecture but providing the standard quality and continental breakfast of a Hampton Inn, which we choose in many cities, along with a view of the Ashley River. Also, it's convenient to the popular California Dreaming Restaurant and not far from downtown for browsing or touring. It's near the main routes to all of the golf courses to boot.

Historic Charleston Bed and Breakfast
$$-$$$$ • 60 Broad St. • 722-6606

This organization represents more than 60 properties, all of which are private homes with owners who share their area's stories along with extraordinary beds and homemade Southern breakfasts. They include spacious and elegant suites in historic homes aged at least a century or two. The bed and breakfast inns are furnished with antiques and often have piazzas overlooking their own private garden or courtyard or maybe a lake, the Ashley River or the Charleston Harbor. Ask for the size, location and price that suits you.

Holiday Inn
$$-$$$ • U.S. Hwy. 17, Mt. Pleasant • 884-6000

Going above and beyond the clean and comfortable atmosphere at most Holiday Inns, this is an elegant property overlooking the harbor, just minutes away from Charleston or the golf courses in Mt. Pleasant. A pool, fitness center and sauna are available, and you will appreciate the concierge level service if you want to be treated accordingly.

Laurel Hill Plantation
$$-$$$ • 8913 U.S. Hwy. 17N., McClellanville • 887-3708

This country bed and breakfast inn is halfway between Charleston and Myrtle Beach, and the location is ideal for reaching golf courses a few miles in either direction. Overlooking the marsh, islands, waterways and the Atlantic Ocean, the plantation house is a restored version of the 1850 historic home that was destroyed in the 1989 hurricane. Four charming guest rooms with private baths are lovingly furnished with simple traditional antiques. The hearty country breakfast will be a great start to a day of golf, and the serene fishing pond will be a place to return for recuperation from any stress your day may have inflicted upon you. You could also hide away here for a long vacation and never think of busy city life.

Seabrook Island Resort
$$$$-$$$$$ • 1002 Landfall Way, Seabrook • 768-1000, (800) 845-2475

Ultimate golf, tennis, equestrian and senior citizen packages, along with villa rates, are among the choices you will have here. If you're looking for a full family vacation with a multitude of activities along a sun-drenched Southern island, choose this resort, and you'll never want to leave.

Twenty-Seven State Street Bed & Breakfast
$$-$$$$ • 27 State St. • 722-4243

This private residence was built in the early 1800s in the French quarter of the original walled city. The carriage house suites are furnished with antiques and reproductions and include kitchenette and private bath along with a spacious combination bedroom and living room. A veranda brings sea breezes from the harbor two blocks away. Fresh fruit and flowers, a large country breakfast in your suite, newspaper, cable television, phone and bicycles are included amenities. Paul and Joye Craven welcome you to their charming modern accommodation with old world flavor.

Wild Dunes Resort
$$$$ • Isle of Palms • 886-2279, (800) 845-8880

Boating, tennis, swimming, biking, dining and entertainment add to the golf amenities of this resort. The island is near Charleston but totally removed from the traffic or history. If you really want to play golf, and someone else in your party really doesn't, this resort is a perfect compromise with vacation villa rentals near all the choices for a leisurely stay.

Golf Equipment

Discount shopping for your golf equipment and accessories is popular in Charleston. Good choices that also have unusually wide selections for women are **Charleston Golf Center**, 1663 Savannah Highway, Charleston, 763-0800; **Pro Golf Discount**, 966 Houston Northcut, Mt. Pleasant, 881-2255; and **Edwin Watts**, 2037 Sam R. Henberg Boulevard, Charleston, 763-1995.

Golf Instruction

The best golf instruction will be found among the professionals at the top resorts. Call in advance to ask for an appointment. Other instruction is limited to **L.B.'s**, 6656 Dorchester Road, Charleston, 552-1717; and **The Practice Tee**, 3251 U.S. Highway 17 N., Mt. Pleasant, 884-1144.

Gullah Spoken Here

Gullah is the language still spoken by many natives of the Sea Islands of Beaufort. The roots of the Gullah speaking people have been traced to the west coast of Africa, from where some 10,000 slaves were believed to have originated, and much of the African rice coast culture survives in the language, the foods and the crafts of sweetgrass baskets.

Our friend, Kitty Green, owner and president of Gullah-N-Geechie Mahn Tours, will say, "De Gullah-N-Geechie Mahn Tours wish fa vite ya to de Sea Islandts ob Bufat, Sous Carolina," when she means that her company invites you to visit the Sea Islands of Beaufort, South Carolina. When you leave she will say, "We tanks ya!" None of this pronunciation is for lack of education on Kitty's part, or that of her guides or family. Place her in any big city and you will know she is well-traveled, educated and speaks as properly as anyone you will ever meet. The Gullah is a studied dialect, which she and her family have perfected for its historical value. The dialect is indigenous to the Sea Island, four miles from Beaufort and 30 miles from Hilton Head, where the African-American culture is carefully preserved as a celebration of its rich heritage. The dialect reflects the linguistic heritage

Beaufort Courses

Country Club of Beaufort at Pleasant Point
8 Barnwell Dr., Beaufort • 522-1605, (800) 869-1617
Championship Yardage: 6506
Slope: 118   Par: 72
Men's Yardage: 6112
Slope: 115   Par: 72
Ladies' Yardage: 4880
Slope: 120   Par: 72

Russell Breeden designed this 18-hole course in 1970. The private sea island community is set among lakes, saltwater marshes and a deepwater river just a few miles from the historic city of Beaufort. Fairways and greens are bermudagrass. Nature is on display here with occasional young marsh deer bounding along and almost 100 acres of lakes and wide salt marsh adding to the beauty and difficulty of play. Five- to 15-foot elevations sometimes bring a big surprise between tee and green.

The signature hole is the 18th — a slight dogleg left with a lagoon on the right and oaks on the left — a beautiful and difficult par 3 that returns to the clubhouse. The 7th hole requires a carry over water on the right and

offers a special challenge to a golfer who needs the roll. Some of the long par 4s are favorites for the long hitters, such as 10 where the drive should go straight and narrow followed by a creative approach shot that must avoid the sand traps and oak trees.

A driving range and a putting, chipping and sand practice area are available. You'll also find club rentals, a pro shop, bar and snack bar.

Walking is allowed. You can generally book about a week in advance, but if you have a big group, they'll be happy to work with you to book an earlier reservation. Rates begin at $24 for summer afternoon play, including cart.

The Golf Professionals Club
93 Francis Marion Cir., Beaufort • 524-3635
Champions Course
Championship Yardage: 6811
Slope: 124   Par: 72
Men's Yardage: 6430
Slope: 119   Par: 72
Ladies Yardage: 5241
Slope: 121   Par: 72

The Champions Course has the reputation of being demanding for its difficult doglegs of a people who were once so much removed from the mainland that their own culture was all that prevailed.

While you are visiting St. Helene you must see the Hallelujah Singers, nationally renowned for their performance in the movie *Forrest Gump*, who sing and narrate the Gullah culture. The group's originator and artistic director is Kitty's sister, Marlena Smalls, who is now called the Sea Island Lady of Forrest Gump. You can't leave this performance without goose bumps from its powerful emotional appeal. You'll also enjoy the nature tour, storytelling, plantation melodies, blues and jazz and demonstrations such as sweetgrass basket weaving, crabbing, shrimping and net making.

Visit the Penn Center, a national historic site that houses a museum. It's believed to be the oldest educational institution for black children in South Carolina and possibly in the country.

The Gullah House Restaurant is another important stop. Also owned by Kitty Green's family, the food includes "sandwishes," "plattas," "frittas," "grits-n-tings" and of course vegetables and corn bread the way it should be cooked. On weekend evenings, a healthy helping of blues or jazz goes with the food. Call 838-7516, 838-7560 or (800) 647-5573 for information on planning a complete group tour including accommodations and meals. Or visit during the annual Gullah Festival in May or the Heritage Days on St. Helena Island the second weekend in November. Call the Beaufort Chamber of Commerce, 524-3163, or the Hilton Head Chamber of Commerce, 785-3683, for schedules of festivals, dinner theater or other information.

and for requiring a number of placement shots. Fairways are somewhat narrow. The starting hole is the signature, a 90-degree dogleg left, 225 yards from the tee, then 200 yards to the green after a good tee shot.

Players Course

Championship Yardage: 5929
Slope: 104   Par: 72
Men's Yardage: 5659
Slope: 101   Par: 72
Ladies' Yardage: 5192
Slope: 107   Par: 72

The Players Course is a good recreational golf course for people of all abilities. The average golfer can make pars and an occasional birdie on this fun course. No. 18 is a great finishing hole with a well-bunkered elevated green.

Designed by Southern Turf Nurseries, the two 18-hole courses were built in 1969. Fairways are bermudagrass. Practice greens, driving range, pro shop, club rental, locker room and bar are available. New guest houses are at The Golf Professionals Club, and packages are offered.

Walking is allowed. One of the true bargain courses, greens fees include a cart and are $22 during afternoons and $25 during mornings year round. Tee times can be booked a couple of weeks in advance.

Ocean Creek Golf Course

90 B Ocean Creek Blvd., Fripp Island
• 838-1576
Championship Yardage: 6510
Slope: 131   Par: 71
Men's Yardage: 6094
Slope: 125   Par: 71
Ladies' Yardage: 4884
Slope: 119   Par: 71
Other Yardage: 5649
Slope: 121   Par: 71

This fabulous new 18-hole course, which opened in October 1995, was the first signature course design of Davis Love III. The rolling dunes and marshlands are on the southern tip of Fripp Island, just past the Ocean Point course. Encompassed within the course are the sites where scenes of the movies *Forrest Gump* and *Jungle Book* both were filmed. You won't recognize either, especially the 5th where *Forrest Gump's* Vietnam scenes were shot. The movies preceded the golf course.

Greens are tifdwarf and fairways are bermudagrass. Wooden bridges and walkways connect the fairways, and five holes are along the marsh. No. 1 is a par 5, a dogleg left with 495 yards where you play up to a small hill. From that point, you are about 175 yards to the pin on an undulating green, guarded on the front by a large trap. No. 3 is a 159-yard par 3 where you must shoot over a small creek, and its greens are undulating and guarded by the obligatory traps on the left and right. The water will only come into play if you have a short slice. It's a beautiful hole with palm trees in the back, and all the fairways are bordered by a mixture of palms, pines and old oaks; bunkers are clean white sand. No. 4 is the favorite hole of an assistant professional Todd Fields. He calls it a "do or die" situation. You can make eagle or birdie if you are confident, he says. It's 260 yards, and a crosswind can be expected. No. 6 is considered the signature hole, a par 3 surrounded by natural vegetation and salt marsh.

The clubhouse is done in tropical colors of melon and green like a splash of summer sherbet flavored in the Caribbean and flung across the South Carolina landscape. Palm trees and hibiscus wrapped around the course lend the vacation air to it.

Fripp Island is private, but tee times are available to resort guests far in advance. Don't be intimidated by the guard because you can visit the welcome center for a daily pass to the golf course.

A driving range, putting green and beverage cart are available. Walking is allowed.

Greens fees with cart range from $39 to $49, such a deal for a premier course. Play it now before it becomes so popular you can't get on it.

Ocean Point Golf Links

250 Ocean Point Dr., Fripp Island
• 838-1521
Championship Yardage: 6590
Slope: 129   **Par: 72**
Men's Yardage: 6060
Slope: 124   **Par: 72**
Ladies' Yardage: 4950
Slope: 113   **Par: 72**

The 18-hole George Cobb course was built in 1964. It was closed during the winter of 1996 for rebuilding and brought in the late 1996 and 1997 season in great shape. Mounding was added along with an emphasis on the views of the dunes along the Atlantic ocean. It's a private course open to resort guests, and attractive golf packages are available for every season. Greens and fairways are bermudagrass.

The 18th, a 486-yard par 5, is the signature hole. It's right on the ocean, bordered by the Fripp Inlet. Typical of an oceanside hole, it's usually windy here. Another classic hole is the 9th, a 365-yard par 4 that also borders the beach; you can expect the ocean breeze to affect the flight of your golf ball. Tight fairways are sandwiched by generous water and woods. Many of the holes have ocean views so beautiful they are a potential distraction to the golfing, but your best judgment is required to succeed on this course.

A practice green, driving range, rental clubs, pro shop, bar, restaurant and beverage cart are available. Private and group lessons are offered by the director of golf, the head professional and first assistant or by the second assistant, at varying price ranges per lesson or for a package of six lessons. Video and playing lessons also are available. Call for information about custom fitting also.

Walking is allowed here. Greens fees, including cart, range from $39 to $54. Ask about a summer afternoon delight. You can book well in advance of your requested tee time, usually at least 60 days.

On Fripp Island, tennis, boating, beach activities and fine dining are all within easy access, so you won't need to venture off the island unless you are easily bored by one of the world's most gorgeous exclusive golf resort experiences. You'll drive through Beaufort on the way here, and you will notice additional dining and touring available for any time before or after your island adventure.

FYI

Unless otherwise noted, the area code for all phone numbers in this chapter is 803.

INSIDERS' TIP

Plan your shot and select your club while approaching your ball. Ready golf is the only good etiquette.

Around Beaufort . . .

Fun Things to Do

Beaufort is such a small place that you can really walk around and find almost anything you need and any choice of food, especially in the historic area, which is the entire downtown. It's just minutes from Interstate 95 and a short distance from Hilton Head Island, although you won't know what a pretty and peaceful place this is unless you make a special trip here and spend a few days and nights. It's on the way to Fripp Island, but you'll surely miss the most charming part of the town and its views if you only pass through.

The city is centuries from any big city noise or clutter. We recommend visiting here on a sunny spring day when you have finished golfing nearby and have nothing else to do except relax on a veranda with a water view. House museums of the **Historic Beaufort Foundation** include the Verdier house, c. 1790, at 801 Bay Street, and the George Parsons Elliott home of 1844 located at 1004 Bay Street. Call 524-6334 for information about tours on varying days of the week. The Christmas season is an especially inviting time to enjoy candlelight or holiday events in the homes and area plantations. We also like it here in late September for **Bubba's Beaufort Shrimp Festival**, which includes marine exhibits, shrimp boats, music, family fun and unique cuisine.

Call the **Beaufort Chamber of Commerce** at 524-3163 or visit it at 1006 Bay Street for other information and to book a guided walking tour or join a horse and carriage ride, which will afford an excellent view of the historic district. You may also call **Carolina Buggy Tours** at 525-1300 for reservations or group tours in carriages drawn by the beautiful Belgian and Percheron draft horses. The architecture and the history in this lovely town are unmatched. Don't limit your visit to the historic area, as much other fine dining and accommodation options are available too.

The **Beaufort Museum** at 713 Craven Street, 525-7077, provides a series of permanent and changing exhibits on the history and culture of the area. It's in the Arsenal, the oldest civic building in the Lowcountry, built

in 1795 for the local militia. The **Parris Island Museum** is in the War Memorial Building on Parris Island just south of Beaufort. The displays here tell the story of Parris Island beginning with the French Huguenots in 1562, progressing to the Spanish and English colonists, then to the era when the Federal Navy built a yard and ending with the Marine Corps' establishment of a recruit depot. It's free and open daily. Call 525-2951 for information.

Hunting Island State Park is a large secluded barrier island near historic Beaufort. The historic 19th-century lighthouse offers a stunning view of the coastline and the semitropical flora and fauna. Call 838-2011 for information about park and interpretive center hours, nature programs and camping where 200 sites and 15 cabins are provided for the nature lover.

Where to Eat

Refer to our Preface for an explanation of the pricing code.

The Bank Waterfront Grill & Bar
$$ • 926 Bay St. • 522-8831

For fun, food and spirits, visit this historic waterfront landmark, which serves more than 70 menu items including fresh local seafood, steaks, burgers, pasta and huge specialty salads. The appetizer menu or "beginning balance" presents an extensive list ranging from jalapeno peppers to oysters on the half shell to mozzarella cheese sticks. An unusual sandwich is the salmon BLT. "Junior investors" are welcome too for their own size menu items. Chef specialties include Beaufort crabcakes, lobster pasta and frogmore stew. Try the "luscious liquid assets" whether you eat or not. They are items like kahlua, bananas and cream, any exotic flavor of colada or daiquiri or lenders lemonade (vodka, lemonade and Sprite). It's open every day for lunch and dinner, and the waterfront deck or upstairs bar are friendly spots for evening crowds to gather.

Blackstone's Groceries, Deli, Sundries
$ • 915 Bay St. • 524-4330

Breakfast or lunch is good at this deli in the middle of a sort of grocery store in down-

Make Your Headquarters Here

Imagine being a military helicopter pilot and living in Los Angeles. Imagine retiring from that and being a litigation attorney living outside Washington, D.C. Imagine that your spouse is a professional whose career also demands long hours and you barely see each other. Meet Gary and Sharon Groves who have been there and done that until they tired of the big city pressures and demanding careers. They imagined dropping all of that and sitting in a porch rocking chair overlooking the sailboats on the Beaufort waterfront. There you will find them daily where they are pouring an afternoon glass of wine to welcome incoming guests or chatting over Sunday morning coffee before the guests depart for the golf course.

Proprietors of the Cuthbert House Inn have many tales to tell of their busy city lives, but their eyes light up with the tales they savor telling of the past year's refurbishing of their historic bed and breakfast inn.

Antiques and reproductions now flavor the c. 1790 home, which John A. Cuthbert built for his bride four blocks away from its present location. The Cuthbert family suffered illnesses and deaths of children and had the house sawed in half to move it to the present location on a bluff overlooking the river. When it was put back together, the chimneys were built in the middle.

As the Civil War began and the town was occupied, homes in the area were made into barracks and hospitals. The Cuthbert House was headquarters for General Rufus Saxton who then purchased the house for $1,000 after the government confiscated the area property from the Southerners for nonpayment of taxes. The widowed Mrs. Saxon sold it to Colonel Wilson who added Victorian porticos and a back wing in the 1880s. The elderly Mrs. Cuthbert died a refugee.

Open a wide oversized door, built to accommodate the hoop skirts of the period, and tread across the beautifully preserved wide-board floors and reproduction Oriental carpets into one of the parlors that features a marble mantelpiece with carved names and initials left by Civil War Union soldiers. The marble matches that of a mantelpiece in the neighboring Secession House. General William Sherman stayed here during his march from Georgia to Columbia, South Carolina, as General Saxon's guest.

Most Beaufort houses of the period were T-shaped, so built to allow the daily winds to blow through the whole house. The patched-together pieces of the house, plus Gary's newly crafted additions of plumbing where needed, combine to produce an authentic antebellum experience suitable for today's needs. All of the refinishing is done by Sharon and Gary, including many long hours to strip years of paint layers from the gracefully curving banister.

The 10,500-square-foot house is listed on the National Register of Historic Places. Parlor suites with adjoining bedrooms feature lovely antiques and reproductions and enough space to spread out and stay for a long vacation. Also, two ground level apartment suites include two bedrooms, with a king or queen bed and two twin beds, casual furnishings, full kitchens and private entrances. Additional suites and a pub in the common area adjoining a parlor and conservatory will soon be ready. All six suites have private baths and outstanding views of the waterfront.

The front porch is a good place to read a book for a long leisurely rest. You'll appreciate the hospitality and enjoy meeting other visitors over Gary's special home-made Southern breakfast, which varies daily from pancakes to eggs, probably some stone ground grits brought in from Charleston, always with fresh fruit, coffee or tea and juice. Gary grew up learning to cook from his mother and grandmother and enjoys doing it so he gets it just the way he likes it.

It's a short walk to the downtown historic district where you can join a narrated carriage or walking tour or browse through shops and restaurants for an easy relaxing day. We highly recommend the Cuthbert House at 1203 Bay Street for a golf, corporate, romantic or combination getaway trip. For reservations and an unforgettable experience call 521-1315 or (800) 327-9275; fax 521-1314; better yet e-mail Sharon and Gary at cuthbert@hargray.com. All modern conveniences such as telephone, fax, television and e-mail are available during your stay here. Rates range from $125 to $185 depending on your choice of suite and number in your party. Children older than 12 are welcome. No pets and no smoking indoors, please.

town Beaufort. Try the smoked salmon plate with goat cheese, capers, onion, lemons and French bread. Deli sandwiches of any meat and cheese are good on crunchy oat bread or croissant. Beer and wine are available. You'll have fun eating here for a quick meal.

Boundary Street Club House
$-$$ • 2317 Boundary St. • 522-2115

The mission of the Clubhouse is for you to "escape the distractions of everyday life and relax, unwind and enjoy the company." For lunch start with a macho nacho or the ball game, which is a combination of many appetizers such as potato skins, buffalo wings and barbecue ribs with a variety of sauces. If you can continue, the house specialty prime rib is slow roasted and may be chosen chargrilled with garlic in sizes up to a sportsman cut of a pound. Fajitas, seafood or smothered chicken also are good main courses. Sporting combinations are available for a taste of it all. Extra innings are great desserts, and sharing is common. Lunch and dinner are served daily.

Dockside Restaurant
$ • 11th St. W., Port Royal • 524-7433

On Battery Creek, the views and atmosphere are great with the fresh local seafood and Lowcountry favorites. While waiting for your meal, overlooking the shrimp boat docks, you might want to try the jalapeno stuffed shrimp or sunset shrimp, which are sauteed in garlic butter with green peppers, onion, black olives, artichokes and tomatoes and served over linguine. A steamed seafood pot includes crab legs, shrimp, oysters and a half lobster at an incredible price. A non-seafood lover can appreciate the southwest chicken or a charcoal grilled New York strip sirloin a pound in size.

Dukes Bar-B-Q
$ • 3166 Boundary St. • 524-1128

The buffet at Dukes includes 30 items with country style vegetables, various salads, barbecue pork and fried or barbecue chicken. It's open Thursday, Friday and Saturday for lunch or dinner. This is a place for family dining and for filling big eaters economically with good down-home style cooking.

Firehouse Books & Espresso Bar
$ • 706 Craven St. • 422-2665

All day every day, this is a neat spot to enjoy a bookstore while sampling espresso, cappuccino, latte, juices or tea with sandwiches, baguettes, bagels or cheesecake. For a morning visit, light lunch, afternoon tea or just an anytime visit with a good golf book to read, it's a pleasant stop in the historic district.

The Gullah House Restaurant
$ • 859 Sea Island Pkwy., St. Helena Island • 838-2402

Near Beaufort and convenient to Hilton Head golf courses, the Gullah House will teach you a language of the old days on St. Helene Island as well as fill you with delicious homecooked meals and a serving of jazz and blues on Friday and Saturday nights. The West African people who originally lived on the island were isolated from the mainland to the point that they developed their own language, some of which is preserved today. For instance you might order "Smutta Steak" which is a country fried steak smothered with sliced potatoes, onions and gravy. (See our sidebar for more explanation of the language.) Go for the breakfast buffet on Saturday and Sunday or lunch and dinner Tuesday through Sunday. Enjoy the folklore while you're there. Kitty Green is the marketing mastermind here, and she will appreciate knowing where you read about the restaurant.

Ollie's Seafood Grille & Bar
$ • Lady's Island Marina • 525-6333

A new restaurant at the marina features local seafood with steamed shrimp and oysters as well as fresh-cut steaks. You can also enjoy she crab soup or frogmore stew (a combination of shrimp, sausage, potatoes, corn on the cob, onions, celery and Ollie's own special seasoning), and we recommend the SunShine rice with any entree. It's open daily for lunch and dinner, and it's popular with the seafaring crowd that arrives by boat and with those who come for the view of the water.

Where to Stay

Refer to our Preface for an explanation of the pricing code.

Bay Street Inn
$$-$$$$$ • 601 Bay St. • 522-0050, 524-7720

You'll recognize the waterfront antebellum mansion from the movie *The Prince of Tides*. It's on the Intracoastal Waterway in the heart of Beaufort's historic district. Eight rooms with private baths (seven with fireplaces) are filled with antiques and face the water. The library, living room and porches are inviting, and innkeepers Jeffrey and Leslee Peth will make you welcome. Formal gourmet breakfast is served in the dining room; evening fruit, chocolates and sherry top off the day. Bicycles are at your disposal for your tour of the lovely little town.

The Beaufort Inn
$$$-$$$$$ • 809 Port Republic St. • 521-9000

Built in 1907 by a prominent attorney and converted to a modern inn in 1930, the home has kept the history of local plantations to match the names of its 13 guest rooms while Debbie and Russell Fielden have expanded and restored the entire mansion. It's a block from the Intracoastal Waterway park in the center of the historic district. You will find the inn suitable for a luxury golf or family vacation and for a conference or a group luncheon or dinner meeting. All rooms have private bath, television and telephone plus individual thermostat; some have a Jacuzzi or wet bar. Children older than 8 are welcome; pets are not. A full service bar and extensive wine list are available. The formal dining room is open to the public as well as to inn guests for dinner and breakfast. Complimentary afternoon tea is served by reservation, and full Southern gourmet breakfast is included with accommodations. Inquire about golf or other activity packages.

Fripp Island Resort
$$$-$$$$$ • One Tarpon Blvd., Fripp Island • 838-3535, (800) 845-4100

Stay in an intimate villa, an oceanfront condo or a rambling oceanfront home, and enjoy the exclusive resort that has everything for you and your family for a vacation or business trip. Housing options include 250 villa and house choices. Ask for whatever size and style you like. Camp Fripp provides recreation, activities and natural adventures for sandpipers ages 3 to 5, inquisitive alligators ages 6 to 9 and island explorers ages 10 to 14. You only need to take your children, sunscreen and insect repellent (well, okay, and maybe a few items thrown into a suitcase). You'll have such a good golf vacation that the children can be allowed to decide where to return every year.

Begin your stay with the two championship golf courses, enough to make your vacation perfect. Then add 10 tennis courts, a deepwater marina, five year-round restaurants and three during the warm summer, seaside pools, fitness center, jogging and biking paths, camp-style recreation for children, and you've got a full-scale resort. No traffic jams, no noise, no stress, no neon signs, no pollution . . . shall we say more! The author of *The Prince of Tides* and *Beach Music* lives and writes on this island. Hollywood filmmakers have found

Sleep Where the Stars Slept

Remember the movie *The Prince of Tides*? Then you know the wonderful old town of Beaufort and Barbara Streisand and Nick Nolte. They stayed at The Rhett House Inn during the filming. You'll also feel at home here and enjoy the relaxed but elegant atmosphere. It's at 1009 Craven Street, just a block from the Intracoastal Waterway and minutes from the historic downtown.

Close-up

Fresh flowers, luscious soft robes (you can buy one to take home) and English or American antiques add to the charm of 10 guest rooms individually decorated and including television, telephone and private bath. Three also feature fireplaces, and several open onto a veranda (where the only smoking is allowed) where you may while away an hour or two in the hammock. Afternoon tea includes linzer tortes or homemade cookies on the veranda. Great coffee, homemade muffins and healthy Southern breakfasts of fruit and pancakes await you in the dining room in the morning, or you may choose a continental breakfast served in your room. You also may request a tray of tea or coffee in the garden or on the piazza or a picnic lunch to take with you.

Thomas Rhett and his wife, Caroline Barnwell, lived here before the Civil War. Marianne and Steve Harrison now own the inn. As with many charming inn owners in the South, they have retreated from the big city life, which for them was in the New York garment district. Small receptions, weddings, meetings and retreats are appropriate here, as are golf outings. The inn is so popular and successful that it has been reviewed in such magazines as *Bride*, *Country*, *Leisure*, *Elle* and *Vogue*. We rate it one of the best.

As elegant and special as the inn is, possibly the best part is the restaurant, called Caroline's on Craven. The chef, Casey Taylor, is well-known from his success in a popular upscale Charleston restaurant, and he recently was featured on a Discovery Channel special of "Great Chefs of the South." One acquaintance said she would eat here every night if she lived in Beaufort. Begin dinner with the Lowcountry egg roll, which is stuffed with oysters, country ham and leeks with horseradish sauce and tomato coulis. A yellow corn chowder or a seasonal Wadmalaw Island baby greens salad could follow. A special entree is pan seared scallops over creamy grits with apple smoked bacon, sage and cheddar gravy. Or try the fabulous honey-roasted game hen with wild rice, sauteed leeks and a wild mushroom gravy. Possibly you can then enjoy the big ice cream sandwich made with a homemade brownie large enough for a meal itself. It's all à la carte and well worth any extra you may pay for a superb dining experience.

Before or after dinner relax with new friends in the parlor and choose a book, cards, backgammon or compact disk from the library to enjoy in your room.

You're welcome for dinner at Caroline's Tuesday through Sunday with reservations without staying at the inn; however, we highly recommend just pretending that you're Southern aristocracy and staying here for a few days while golfing and escaping from the real world. The price ranges from $125 to $195, and queen, king or double beds are available.

Children older than 5 are welcome but no pets. Golf, tennis, swimming and massages will be arranged at your request.

Call 524-9030 or fax 524-1310 for reservations.

perfect settings of several varieties, and so will you.

TwoSuns Inn Bed & Breakfast
$$-$$$ • 1705 Bay St. • 522-1122

The charming inn is in a restored 1917 Neo-classic Revival-style grand home in a nationally landmarked historic district. The gracious resident owners are Carrol and Ron Kay. Five bayview queen or king guest rooms are complete with modern private baths and a casually elegant ambiance. Handcrafted window and bed ensembles, which Carrol sells, are unique to each room. Amenities include room phones, a parlor cable TV and VCR with video library and a self-serve guest refrigerator with snacks and soft drinks. Croquet and horseshoes are available on the front lawn. Van, carriage, walking, bicycle or boat tours of the historic downtown are convenient from here.

A full breakfast and daily afternoon tea and toddy hour are included. Each breakfast menu offers special entrees, fruit selection, juice and "lovin' from the oven," plus coffee from silver service and a wide tea selection. The inn is suitable for small meetings and special events.

Hilton Head Courses

Callawassie Island Club
S.C. Hwy. 6, 176 Callawassie Rd., Callawassie Island • 521-1533
Dogwood/Palmetto Course
Championship Yardage: 6822

Slope: 130	Par: 72
Men's Yardage: 6426	
Slope: 125	Par: 72
Ladies Yardage: 5166	
Slope: 123	Par: 72
Other Yardage: 6053	
Slope: 123	Par: 72

Magnolia/Dogwood Course
Championship Yardage: 6956

Slope: 138	Par: 72
Men's Yardage: 6514	
Slope: 132	Par: 72
Ladies' Yardage: 5237	
Slope: 126	Par: 72
Other Yardage: 6124	
Slope: 129	Par: 72

Palmetto/Magnolia Course
Championship Yardage: 6956

Slope: 132	Par: 72
Men's Yardage: 6462	
Slope 129	Par: 72
Ladies' Yardage: 5201	
Slope: 120	Par: 72
Other Yardage: 6035	
Slope: 124	Par: 72

The three nine-hole courses at Callawassie Island Club — to be played in tandem pairs to create an 18-hole round — were designed by Tom Fazio and built in 1986. Fazio says it's one of his best; of course, he likes all of his designs, as well he should.

Callawassie Island is an 880-acre sea island that sits among the marshlands between the Colleton and Chechessee rivers. A short drive from Charleston or Hilton Head and just past Beaufort, this island showcases a delightful piece of nature where birds and wildlife disregard your golfing, and your round is relaxed and easygoing but not necessarily easy.

The order of difficulty is Magnolia, Dogwood then Palmetto. The Dogwood is the newest, and its four finishing holes along the river lend dramatics to your game. Greens are tifdwarf, and fairways are bermudagrass. The signature hole at Callawassie is the par 4 No. 9 on the Magnolia Course, where you must hit over a marsh onto an island green. The 4th hole on the Dogwood is tough — a 450-yard par 4 with a wetlands hazard on the right that narrows your driving area. On 15 of Callawassie's 27 holes, you will encounter marshland or ponds.

Practice greens, a driving range, pro shop, rental clubs, locker room, bar and restaurant are available.

Greens fees range from $52 to $73, including cart. Walking is allowed for members only. Advance bookings are accepted up to 40 days before play.

By the way, if you've never seen a black river, spend an extra few hours and paddle a kayak along some barely discovered water where you will find nature like nowhere else. It could be within sight of I-95, and you still can hear not a sound — save an occasional chirp or splash. If you should find Tulifinny Joe's Outpost in Ridgeland (we'll give you the number — 726-5334 — to help in the search), where the best kayaks and guides hang out, be sure

Photo: Hilton Head Island Chamber of Commerce

Who can concentrate on putting with such a dramatic background?

to ask Leon, Judy or Em to tell you all about this location where the Waterway was born.

Country Club of Hilton Head
70 Skull Creek Dr. • 681-4653
Championship Yardage: 6919
Slope: 132   Par: 72
Men's Yardage: 6543
Slope: 128   Par: 72
Other Yardage: 6162
Slope: 124   Par: 72
Ladies Yardage: 5373
Slope: 123   Par: 72

Part of Hilton Head Plantation's complex, the 18-hole course was designed by Rees Jones and built in 1985. It features bermudagrass greens and fairways.

The 12th green is on the Intracoastal Waterway, and others run near it as well as along freshwater ponds and marshlands. Several holes are long par 5s, two of them measuring more than 575 yards each. For instance, No. 18 is 579 yards uphill from the back tees. All in all, you will encounter 13 doglegs as well as water hazards on 14 holes. Elevation changes are constant, including some tees, landing areas and greens. And what about that punch-bowl-shaped green on the 6th?

A practice green, driving range, pro shop, beverage cart and club rental are available.

The greens fees, including cart, range from

$55 to $73. Walking is not allowed. They do their best to accommodate advance tee times of as much as 120 days.

Golden Bear Golf Course at Indigo Run
72 Colonial Dr. • 689-2200
Championship Yardage: 7014
Slope: 129   Par: 72
Men's Yardage: 6643
Slope: 125   Par: 72
Other Yardage: 6184
Slope: 119   Par: 72
Ladies' Yardage: 4974
Slope: 120   Par: 72

The chief architect for this Nicklaus design was Bruce Borland. Fairways and greens are bermudagrass. Lagoons and freshwater wetlands are sprinkled among oak, cypress and pine forests around the fairways and greens. Mounding and elevation are minimal.

One of the most challenging holes is 446-yard No. 11, a long dogleg left with water to the left of the green. The par 5 15th, a dogleg right of 512 yards, has a substantial landing area for your tee shot. As long as you pass the trees on the right side of the fairway, you should have a somewhat easy shot to the green.

Practice greens, a driving range, pro shop, rental clubs, a bar and grill and a beverage cart all add up to an enjoyable golf excursion.

Greens fees range from $55 to $73, including cart. Individuals can book tee times 30 days in advance; if you book through a golf package, that time increases to 120 days. Walking is not allowed.

Hilton Head National Golf Club
1100 U.S. Hwy. 278,
Hilton Head
• 842-5900, (888) 955-1234
Championship Yardage: 6779

Slope: 132	Par: 72
Men's Yardage: 6260	
Slope: 125	Par: 72
Other Yardage: 5589	
Slope: 116	Par: 72
Ladies' Yardage: 4649	
Slope: 109	Par: 72

Gary Player designed this 18-hole course in 1989. Fairways and greens are bermudagrass, and the course is always in superb condition.

There is no residential development here, just marshland. The 9th is a tough hole due to its length, and you're almost always driving into the wind to an elevated green. Marshland lines the entire right side. The No. 17 signature hole is a par 3 with a fountain guarding the front. Other than the 17th, the narrow fairways and lack of marsh resemble a Northern course more than a typical Carolina layout.

A driving range, practice greens, pro shop, bar, restaurant and rental clubs are available.

Walking is not allowed. Greens fees are $40 to $85, including cart. Tee times can be made up to one year in advance.

Island West Golf Club
U.S. Hwy. 278 • 757-6660
Championship Yardage: 6803

Slope: 129	Par: 72
Men's Yardage: 6208	
Slope: 124	Par: 72
Ladies' Yardage: 4938	
Slope: 116	Par: 72

Fuzzy Zoeller designed the 18-hole course in 1992, and the architect was Clyde Johnston. The 150-acre coastal forest includes live oaks and tall pines around lush wetlands and richly colored bermudagrass greens and fairways.

The course caters to the novice as well as the veteran and exudes Fuzzy's trademark sense of fun. The forward tees are well-placed for ladies or juniors; on 12 holes they are in front or to the side of carry — over water or wetlands. Shooting from the back tees . . . well, you'll have the carry on those 12 holes to have the opportunity to test your skills. Island West starts with a par 5 that is not overly difficult and ends with a unique large double green on No. 8 and a beautiful No. 9. The signature hole is the 17th, which plays to the double green.

Practice greens, a driving range and beverage cart are available. The Southern-style clubhouse houses a bar and grill and a pro shop.

Book your tee time up to one year in advance of your game. Greens fees and cart range from $39 to $65. Walking is not allowed.

The Links at Stono Ferry
5365 Forest Oaks Dr.,
Hollywood
• 763-1817
Championship Yardage: 6606

Slope: 115	Par: 72
Men's Yardage: 6085	
Slope: 112	Par: 72
Other Yardage: 5710	
Slope: 111	Par: 72
Ladies' Yardage: 4928	
Slope: 119	Par: 72

Ron Garl designed this beautiful resort in 1989 as a Southern experience that can include a polo game after your round of great golf. It lies along the Intracoastal Waterway toward the mainland and has bermudagrass greens and fairways.

The signature hole is the 14th, a par 3 measuring 157 yards. The tee box is built out into the Intracoastal Waterway, and the carry is about 120 yards to the green over marsh and wetlands. Water is prevalent on the back nine and comes into play on five holes.

Practice greens, a driving range, pro shop, rental clubs, a bar and restaurant and a beverage cart are available.

The cost of a round is $25 on weekdays and $32 on weekends, and you can book tee times one week in advance. The cart fee is $15. Walking is not allowed.

Old South Golf Links
50 Buckingham Plantation Dr., Bluffton
• 785-5353
Championship Yardage: 6772
Slope: 129   Par: 72
Men's Yardage: 6354
Slope: 125   Par: 72
Other Yardage: 5779
Slope: 119   Par: 72
Ladies' Yardage: 4776
Slope: 123   Par: 71

This Clyde Johnston course is 18 holes of bermudagrass greens and fairways, and it's open to the public year round. It's easy to find on the mainland just before reaching Hilton Head Island.

Johnston's Old South golf links is a tribute to a man working within nature's guidelines. You will experience natural amenities and fabulous views playing this course. Johnston said, "The variety of the setting from oak forest to open pasture to tidal marsh provides an opportunity to vary the design elements and strategy of play." This all adds up to marvelous diversity. It's a popular and beautiful course featuring seven marsh-front holes and three spectacular island greens among live oaks scattered on rolling terrain. The clubhouse verandas overlook the large putting green and the lagoon, a reminder that you're in the Lowcountry, not in Scotland as the links might persuade you to believe.

The par 4 16th is the signature hole, with two carries over marsh. Lateral water hazards are characteristic. The 7th also requires two shots over water.

The course offers rental clubs, practice greens, a driving range, pro shop, bar, restaurant and beverage cart. Also, the Ken Venturi Training Center provides three-day sessions by instructors personally trained by the legendary golfer and teacher. The package includes half-day or full-day sessions with video swing analysis and stroke saver clinics plus golf daily and unlimited practice range use. For training information call 837-2500.

Walking is allowed after 2 PM. Bookings can be up to 60 days in advance. Cost ranges from $48 to $75, including cart.

Oyster Reef Golf Course
155 High Bluff Rd. • 681-7717
Championship Yardage: 7027
Slope: 131   Par: 72
Men's Yardage: 6440
Slope: 123   Par: 72
Other Yardage: 6071
Slope: 118   Par: 72
Ladies' Yardage: 5288
Slope: 118   Par: 72

Bermudagrass greens and fairways characterize the 18-hole Rees Jones course built in 1982 — part of the Hilton Head Plantation complex.

Nine ponds and 66 bunkers contribute to the fairness of the nicely laid out course where every hole is challenging. Doglegs are surrounded by mounds and fairway bunkers. Exact approach shots are required to the large greens with well-defined tiers. The 6th is the signature hole. It overlooks Port Royal Sound, and beautiful oak trees surround the green. It's a par 3 of 192 yards from the tips.

A chipping green, practice green and driving range and club rentals are available. You can also enjoy a pro shop, bar, restaurant and beverage cart. The locker room is for members only. Rates range from $63 to $79, including cart and greens fee. Walking is not allowed. You may call up to 90 days in advance to book a tee time.

Palmetto Dunes Golf Course
Palmetto Dunes Resort, 1 Trent Jones Ln.
• 785-1138

The three 18-hole courses provide an outstanding golf experience on Hilton Head. The oldest of the trio, the Robert Trent Jones course, involves a winding lagoon on 11 holes, and stray shots can easily find their way into one of the many fairway bunkers or lagoons. The Arthur Hills layout, heavily wooded with trademark elevation changes and rolling fairways provided by sand dunes, was overhauled and reopened in the fall of 1995. All greens were rebuilt, some tee areas expanded and the irrigation system reworked.

Unrestricted walking is allowed on all courses any time and any day. According to management, an increasing number of good players are asking to walk, keeping with golf tradition and reaping the fitness benefits.

Greens fees, including cart, begin at $36.75 and go to $74.50. Specials are available when booking through the resort. Advance bookings are accepted up to 30 days.

Arthur Hills Course

Championship Yardage: 6651

Slope: 127	**Par: 72**
Men's Yardage: 6122	
Slope: 120	**Par: 72**
Ladies' Yardage: 4999	
Slope: 113	**Par: 72**

The par 4 12th hole has water running along an entire side from tee to green. The par 5 13th hole, 507 yards from the blue tees, is built for the long driver — your tee shot must carry over water. Your second shot entails a fairway wood, but you must be careful because both fairway and green are guarded by a lake bordering the right side.

George Fazio Course

Championship Yardage: 6534

Slope: 126	**Par: 70**
Men's Yardage: 6239	
Slope: 123	**Par: 70**
Ladies' Yardage: 5273	
Slope: 117	**Par: 70**

This is a straightforward course with water only coming into play on six holes, which makes it forgiving though not easy. Bunkering is dramatic, and fairways are rolling. The fairways are open on the front nine but are more severe on the back nine. The finishing hole has a large bunker right off the tee that must be carried with your tee shot, and your second shot must also carry a bunker to a short fairway leading up to the green. This course has only two par 5s and three par 3s. The series of long par 4s will test your ability.

Robert Trent Jones Course

Championship Yardage: 6710

Slope: 123	**Par: 72**
Men's Yardage: 6148	
Slope: 119	**Par: 72**
Ladies' Yardage: 5425	
Slope: 117	**Par: 72**

Fairways are extensively bunkered, landing areas are generous and the water hazards are abundant on the way to the large well-trapped greens. A winding lagoon system comes into play on 11 of 18 holes here. You go out from the clubhouse to the left of the water, make the turn and return on the right side. The fairways are open and the greens are large. The majority of the holes on the back nine involve water; exceptions are the 10th, 11th, 16th and 18th. The signature is the 10th, a par 5 that plays into an ocean breeze and a spectacular ocean view.

The course was named to *Golf for Women* magazine's first list of the top 100 most "women friendly" golf courses nationwide in 1995.

Palmetto Hall Plantation

108 Fort Howell Dr. • 689-4100

The Arthur Hills course opened in 1991, the Robert Cupp course in 1993. Unrestricted walking is allowed on the Cupp course, a recent change that management is finding pleases many good golfers who respect the game's tradition. A luxurious 14,000-square-foot Lowcountry-style clubhouse complements the rich sense of history here. The new clubhouse features trophy cases and historic artifacts. Antiques and paintings add an elegant touch. A pro shop, men's and women's locker rooms and lounges are on the main level. The grill room is a typical gentlemen's club with English golf paintings. Upstairs a ballroom is divided into smaller banquet rooms for weddings or corporate parties.

Greens fees, including cart, range from $35 to $74.50. Bookings are accepted 60 days in advance.

Arthur Hills Course

Championship Yardage: 6918

Slope: 132	**Par: 72**
Men's Yardage: 6582	
Slope: 123	**Par: 72**
Other Yardage: 6257	
Slope: 117	**Par: 72**
Ladies' Yardage: 4956	
Slope: 119	**Par: 72**

This first course of the community was spread across the former site of a Civil War garrison. Oaks, pines, willow and lakes wrap the rolling curves of this course. Some greens are edged with bunkers, and water is involved in 12 of the 18 holes, providing a formidable challenge. The par 5 490-yard 5th hole, for instance, has water up the entire right side of the fairway, so all shots must be placed to the left. Save some strength for the signature par 4 434-yard 18th hole, which has water running all the way up the left side of the fairway.

Robert Cupp Course

Championship Yardage: 7079
Slope: 141 | **Par: 72**
Men's Yardage: 6522
Slope: 126 | **Par: 72**
Other Yardage: 6042
Slope: 120 | **Par: 72**
Ladies' Yardage: 5220
Slope: 126 | **Par: 72**

As with many courses along the South Carolina coast, this scenic course has a lot of water and sawgrass marshland, although they may not always come into play. Dense forests of oak and pine also wrap around the course. It is somewhat original with straight lines and sharp angles evolving from Cupp's computerized design. The geometric shape includes square greens, angular bunkers and pyramid-shaped mounding. The 6th hole is a par 5, 542 yards from the back tees. It doglegs left. A good second shot will be played to the right because the green is bordered by a pond on the left and rear. The 12th hole is a beautiful 208-yard par 3 with sand guarding the left front and side of the green.

Port Royal Golf Club

10A Graslawn Ave. • 686-8801

The three 18-hole courses offer enough variety to keep you interested for three good rounds any time. All fairways and greens are bermudagrass.

A pro shop, locker rooms, bar and restaurant, rental clubs, practice greens and driving range round out the resort's golf amenities.

Walking is allowed occasionally on all of these courses during the winter, but you should ask before making plans to walk. Fees range from $32 to $76, including cart and greens fees. The staff at this course is very helpful and will work with you to book an advance tee time whenever you call.

Barony Course

Championship Yardage: 6530
Slope: 124 | **Par: 72**
Men's Yardage: 6038
Slope: 122 | **Par: 72**
Ladies' Yardage: 5253
Slope: 115 | **Par: 72**

The Barony Course was built in 1963 and designed by George Cobb. The 12th on the Barony is a good par 4 measuring 428 yards. Water flanks the right and left of the fairway. Most of the greens are small with numerous bunkers, some deep and wide surrounding the greens. This course brings shot-making ability to the forefront and downplays long drives and iron shots.

Planters Row Course

Championship Yardage: 6520
Slope: 128 | **Par: 72**
Men's Yardage: 6009
Slope: 126 | **Par: 72**
Ladies' Yardage: 5126
Slope: 116 | **Par: 72**

Planters Row was built in 1983 and designed by Willard Byrd. On Planters Row, the hole to fear is the 12th. It's narrow, measures 424 yards and requires a carry over water to the green. The course ends with a 480-yard par 5, with woods to the left and water to the right of the fairway. A good shot will set up your pitch to the elevated green.

Robbers Row Course

Championship Yardage: 6711
Slope: 134 | **Par: 72**
Men's Yardage: 6188
Slope: 129 | **Par: 72**
Ladies' Yardage: 5299
Slope: 114 | **Par: 72**

The Robbers Row Course was designed by George Cobb and Pete Dye and built in 1967. It was recently redesigned by Pete Dye who added several water hazards. On Robbers Row take note of the 10th — a long, slight dogleg right that plays par 4 at 454 yards. Most greens are guarded by bunkers, thus requiring precise shot placement.

Rose Hill Country Club

One Clubhouse Dr., Bluffton • 842-3740
South-East
Championship Yardage: 6464
Slope: 124 | **Par: 72**
Men's Yardage: 6030
Slope: 121 | **Par: 72**
Ladies' Yardage: 5046
Slope: 119 | **Par: 72**
Other Yardage: 5579
Slope: 118 | **Par: 72**

East-West

Championship Yardage: 6808
Slope: 126   Par: 72
Men's Yardage: 6276
Slope: 121   Par: 72
Ladies' Yardage: 5103
Slope: 119   Par: 72
Other Yardage: 5640
Slope: 115   Par: 72

West-South

Championship Yardage: 6822
Slope: 127   Par: 72
Men's Yardage: 6300
Slope: 124   Par: 72
Ladies' Yardage: 5081
Slope: 118   Par: 72
Other Yardage: 5681
Slope: 118   Par: 72

The 27 holes designed by Gene Hamm are set along rolling terrain bordered by tall pines, live oaks and magnolias. The course combinations offer many challenges for golfers of all levels. Although it doesn't come into play on every shot, all but five holes have water around them. The West is the most played course. No. 1 on the West is a dogleg over water and is sometimes considered the signature hole. One of the tough holes is No. 2 on the West Course. It's 101 yards with water all along the left side, then cutting into the middle of the fairway so you must clear the water on your second shot. It has bermudagrass fairways and greens. The East Course is more open than the West and South, and it is slightly shorter. The South Course fairways are treelined, and greens are well bunkered.

No walking is allowed. Club rental, driving range, putting area, beverage cart and restaurant are provided. Book a week or two in advance. Greens fees range from $48 to $59 including cart.

Sea Pines Resort

11 Lighthouse Ln. • 842-8484,
(800) 925-4653

These three 18-hole courses are among the most popular on Hilton Head Island and offer preferred tee times and reduced rates to resort guests. Afternoon summer specials may offer you two courses for $125. That's a bargain. Afternoon summer specials at Harbour Town are $105. A more typical price is $164 or more, including cart. Enjoy a half-day school plus 18 holes of golf and cart on the Sea Marsh Course for $165. Eight hours of beginner golf instruction are also available for $200.

Harbour Town Golf Links

Championship Yardage: 6919
Slope: 136   Par: 71
Men's Yardage: 6119
Slope: 126   Par: 71
Ladies' Yardage: 5019
Slope: 117   Par: 71

The MCI Heritage Classic is played each April on Harbour Town — designed by Pete Dye and Jack Nicklaus in 1969. It's always ranked among the world's top golf courses. The well-protected greens are some of the smallest of any tournament course. The architects created some of the best par 3s you'll ever see. The par 4 18th hole is well-known in golf circles for its wind hazard off the sound.

Ocean Course

Championship Yardage: 6614
Slope: 125   Par: 72
Men's Yardage: 6213
Slope: 119   Par: 72
Ladies' Yardage: 5284
Slope: 111   Par: 72

The Ocean Course — the island's first course, and now its newest — was designed by George Cobb in 1962 and remodeled by Mark McCumber in 1995. Multiple tees accommodate all skill levels, and the restructuring preserved traditional beauty while modernizing. Various hazard placements add to the excitement, and the fabulous ocean vistas on the dramatic beachfront 15th are tough to beat.

Sea Marsh Course

Championship Yardage: 6515
Slope: 120   Par: 72
Men's Yardage: 6129
Slope: 117   Par: 72
Ladies' Yardage: 5054
Slope: 123   Par: 72

The Sea Marsh Course was designed by George Cobb in 1964 and remodeled in 1990 by Clyde Johnston. The Sea Marsh's varied layout often crosses lagoons or marshes. Fairways are wide, and oaks, pines and palmettos surround them. Medium-size greens are bunkered and slope from back to front, requiring exact approach shots. Distance shots are sometimes required, although the course is not lengthy.

Shipyard Golf Club
45 Shipyard Dr. • 689-5600

Three nine-hole layouts include the Brigantine, Clipper and Galleon courses. Fairways and greens are bermudagrass. Oaks, pines, magnolias, lagoons and ponds populate these courses and demand driving accuracy and putting delicacy. Water comes into play on 25 of the 27 holes.

Amenities include a practice putting and chipping green and a driving range. A pro shop, locker room, bar and restaurant, beverage cart and club rental are all on-site. The course also offers memberships.

Summer rates begin at $38 for late afternoon specials and increase to $80 during the spring season, including greens fees and cart. Walking is allowed after 5 PM during the summer.

Galleon Course

Championship Yardage: 3364

Slope: No rating	Par: 36

Men's Yardage: 3035

Slope: No rating	Par: 36

Ladies' Yardage: 2658

Slope: No rating	Par: 36

The Galleon is a George Cobb design. A nice par 3 is No. 5 — 179 yards and fronted by two bunkers that may come into play if your shot is short.

Fairways are defined by trees; they are of medium width allowing space to work the ball. The Galleon's second hole is its signature, a dogleg left, par 5, with a bunker to the left that can be carried by a long hitter. Then you have a chance to go for the elevated green, which has water in front and bunkers to left, front, right and rear. The uphill shot cannot be short or it falls back into the water.

Clipper Course

Championship Yardage: 3466

Slope: No rating	Par: 36

Men's Yardage: 3132

Slope: No rating	Par: 36

Ladies' Yardage: 2733

Slope: No rating	Par: 36

The only hole on this George Cobb design that doesn't involve water is the par 4 427-yard 6th.

This was the original back nine for the Galleon when the course began as an 18-hole layout. One of the Clipper's spectacular holes is the 9th, which doglegs left, has bunkers to the right of the fairway and one on the left corner that is difficult to carry. From there in, the hole is well-bunkered. The green is somewhat elevated and has bunkers 100 yards out and to the green. Shots that miss the green will be in these bunkers.

Brigantine Course

Championship Yardage: 3352
Slope: No rating   Par: 36
Men's Yardage: 2959
Slope: No rating   Par: 36
Ladies' Yardage: 2457
Slope: No rating   Par: 36

Tree lines also define the fairways here. The 5th hole, a par 3, is 180 yards from the back tee. A bunker circles the left back portion and around two-thirds of the green. It's a slight downhill shot with water from the tee to the green. A good carry is required.

Watch out for the 6th hole on this Willard Byrd design — a long par 4 with bunkers by the landing area and water on the left. Likewise, beware No. 9 — a par 5, 523 yards, with water running down the complete side of the fairway.

Private homes and rental condominiums surround this course but blend with the pines and don't distract from the golfing experience.

Around Hilton Head . . .

Fun Things To Do

Golf is indisputably the most important of the things you can do on Hilton Head Island. Tennis is especially significant too. Fishing, parasailing, skiing, horseback riding, miniature golf and, of course, dolphin watching and beach walking are also worthy of some vacation time. Shopping includes some unique boutiques and some good outlet malls, enough nice choices for the discriminating. Don't expect the neon resort atmosphere of Myrtle Beach with a zillion things to do or a college town with prolific nightlife like Charleston or Wilmington, North Carolina. Go for the sunsets and the sophisticated lifestyle of a privileged few. Just expect a memorable experience, and you've got it.

The **Family Circle Magazine Cup** features top women tennis players annually during late March or early April. Call 785-9602 for information. The **MCI Heritage Classic** features top golfers during the third week of April annually. Check out the **Hilton Head Celebrity Golf Tournament** every Labor Day weekend. For information on both golf events call 671-2448.

Where To Eat

Shrimp, oysters, crab and fish top the menu of local specialties. They're fresh today, and you can count on the hushpuppies and red rice to accompany the meal in many seafood restaurants. Some 200 restaurants also provide enough variety of international cuisine or basics to please any appetite. Here's a good start for sampling imported recipes or Lowcountry cooking in the resort atmosphere. Refer to our Preface for an explanation of the pricing code.

Aunt Chiladas Easy Street Cafe
$-$$$ • 69 Pope Ave. • 785-7700

Choose Mexican, Italian, seafood, steaks or just about anything else you can think of, and it's probably here in quantities for the whole family for lunch or dinner. Don't go with us if you don't want to be embarrassed during the all-you-can-eat crab leg feast, which can be quite lengthy, but, oh, so delicious. The owner's Italian mother makes great Italian entrees, and steaks are outstanding, even though the restaurant claims a Mexican theme.

FYI
Unless otherwise noted, the area code for all phone numbers in this chapter is 803.

INSIDERS' TIP

Take your practice swing while others are hitting.

Café at Wexford

$$ • Village at Wexford, U.S. 278
• 686-5969

A great choice for French cuisine, this cafe offers hot appetizers of escargot, traditional French soup in a crock with croutons and Swiss cheese or a slice of boneless duck stuffed with spinach, veal and cheese with bing cherry sauce. Pate or smoked Maine salmon are delicious cold appetizers. Entrees include sweetbreads sauteed in cream sauce with mushrooms and julienne strips of ham or crepes stuffed with chicken and mushrooms in a cream sauce with cheese. Daily specials are offered, and dinners are served with bread, salad, potatoes and vegetables.

Crazy Crab

$-$$$ • U.S. Hwy. 278 • 681-5021
$-$$$ • Harbour Town • 363-2722

Two locations are well-known by islanders and golfers, and everyone will send you there for lunch or dinner. Steamed seafood pots are usually a favorite. They have almost everything in them and require serious appetites. Dress is casual, and fun is a definite.

Damon's

$-$$ • The Village at Wexford, U.S. 278
• 785-6677

Barbecued ribs and prime rib are specialties here. The famous loaf of onion rings is such a tasty huge appetizer that you will miss your dinner if you don't share it with several people. Open for lunch or dinner, Damon's serves one of our favorite barbecue sandwiches too. Homemade rye bread is good, and you will never leave here hungry.

The Gaslight

$$$-$$$$ • 303 The Market Place
• 784-5814

The food and the menu are French, but the translation is adequate and the hospitality is Carolinian. Begin at the wine bar with selections from France or Cali-

Enjoy a relaxing stay on Kiawah Island.

fornia. Then try an hors d'oeuvre such as country pate or snails in the shell with garlic and white wine. The fish menu includes braised grouper, Atlantic salmon, imported Dover sole and mousse of snapper. The lamb tenderloin on a bed of curried leeks is also a specialty. Steaks and chicken breast are available if you are not adventurous with a menu. À la carte salads and vegetables are varied.

Harbourmaster's Waterfront
$$$-$$$$ • Shelter Cove Harbour, U.S. 278 • 785-3030

Fine dining in a dressy and elegant restaurant is a treat here. Linen napkins and proper service are a treat for special occasions. The rack of lamb is tender and mouthwatering, and the beef and fish are also good. Call for reservations for dinner only.

Il Cappuccino
$$ • 8 New Orleans Rd. • 785-5008

Northern, Southern and contemporary Italian cuisine are offered on an extensive menu, and the chefs will also be happy to accommodate special requests. Begin this feast with spinach gnocchi or roasted peppers with fresh mozzarella. Think about a Tuscany salad of baby greens, duck confit, walnuts and gorgonzola with walnut vinaigrette. Pasta choices are varied or pasta du jour is included with all non-pasta entrees. Pan-seared scallops and crab cannelloni both caught our attention. Veal, chicken or pork also are nice choices.

The Kingfisher
$$ • Shelter Cove Harbour, U.S. 278 • 785-4442

At the water's edge, this is one of our favorite Hilton Head restaurants, and it offers a view in a bustling center of activity. Happy hour is fun here daily in the harbour lounge or waterside deck, and shrimp, oysters and crab legs are a great deal. For dinner any day seafood is fabulous, including daily selections that can be grilled, blackened, Greek (sauteed with onions, artichoke hearts, black olives, garlic, sherry, lemon and feta cheese) herb encrusted or crab

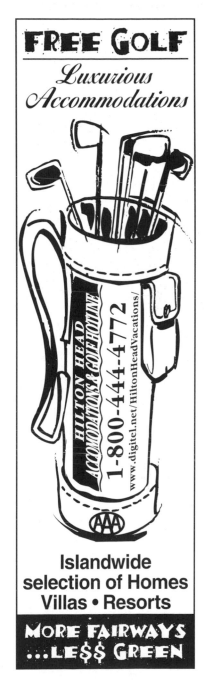

Dijon. Beef and poultry also are broiled or grilled to perfection.

La Pola's
$-$$ • Shelter Cove Harbour, U.S. 278 • 842-6400

Upstairs in a cozy indoor restaurant or on the porch, this choice Italian restaurant is the neighbor to The Kingfisher. Frozen drinks, beer and wine are varied. The view is spectacular and the food tantalizing. Artichoke fritters or fried calamari are great appetizers. Italian favorite entrees are good, and the specialties are culinary Olympic winners such as veal and artichoke hearts or chicken Chesapeake.

The Nantucket Seafood House
$$ • 26 New Orleans Rd. • 686-6339

Open for dinner daily, the menu and the dialect are exactly as you would expect in a Nantucket restaurant. Everything includes an "h" whether it's spelled that way or not. You might begin with an "appetizah" of stuffed quahogs which are "lahge clams baked with homemade stuffing." Then try the "grilled Edgahtown sahdfish" or the Ipswich fried clams flown directly in to this kitchen. If you want to stay land side, you will enjoy the 12-ounce aged "chahgrilled center cut N.Y. strip." Vegetable, potato, house salad and fresh bread accompanies any entree.

Old Oyster Factory
$$-$$$ • 101 Marshland Rd. • 681-6040

Seafood and steaks are served at the site of the island's original oyster cannery, a landmark experience and location. The atmosphere is casual overlooking the water. Happy hour and dinner are enjoyed here.

Tony Roma's
$-$$ • 840 William Hilton Pkwy. • 842- 4825

Famous in many states for the ribs and sauces, this place won't disappoint the pork or beef lover. Choose from Blue Ridge Smokies, Carolina honeys, bountiful beef or red hots. Soups, salads, appetizers, burgers, chicken or sandwiches also are good, but we go for the ribs or maybe a shrimp and rib combo. Side dishes include a good variety with especially tasty beans and slaw.

Where to Stay

Resorts are the best choices for Hilton Head visits, as you'll find the top golf courses are easily booked through the resort. Also you will enjoy the luxury and the amenities, not to mention superbly prepared food. The beaches in Hilton Head are usually private, unlike those in much of the Myrtle Beach area; therefore, the premium beach access, as well as the best golf course access, usually comes through the top-quality resorts. For Hilton Head Central Reservations call 785-9050 or (800) 845-7018. Refer to our Preface for an explanation of the pricing code.

Accommodations & Golf Hotline
$$-$$$ • 111A Marriott Center, Office Park Rd. • 686-6662, (800) 444-4772

This full-service rental company rents condos, homes and villas of one- to four-bedroom size throughout the island area and specializes in golf packages. Most of the packages include a round of free golf for four people once a day for seven days. Cart fee is additional. The condos hold the golf crown award given to the top five percent of the world's condos from Resort Condominium International, as well as AAA and three diamond approval. Call for a brochure with all the details.

Crown Plaza Resort
$$$-$$$$$ • 130 Shipyard Dr. • 842-2400, (800) 334-1881

At Shipyard Plantation Golf Course, this resort includes 340 rooms and suites, miles of beach, a complete fitness center, indoor and outdoor pools, the Van der Meer Racquet Club, two dining rooms, lounge and a camp for kids. You also have coffee and tea in-room and any luxury you could want.

Disney's Hilton Head Island Resort
$$-$$$$$ • Shelter Cove Harbour, U.S. 278 • 341-4100, (800) 859-8644

Nestled among live oaks on a 15-acre private island within Shelter Cover Harbour are 123 vacation villas where you may choose a studio or one-, two- or three-bedroom villa. Disney's Beach House is on the Atlantic Ocean with pool, snack bar, arcade,

living room and games. Also here is Ben & Stretch's workout room, the Big Strike arcade, the Broad Creek Mercantile and a community hall with games and video library. The resort includes two pools, fishing pier with gazebo, shopping and dining within walking distance. Golf and tennis are available in several nearby areas. Relax here and find your own magic.

Fairfield Inn
$$•SP9 Marina Side Dr. •842-4800, (800) TEE OFF4

Affordable lodging includes 14 two-room suites, and golf packages are available on any of 20 courses. Rates include cart. Complimentary continental breakfast is included for all guests. Amenities include an outdoor heated pool. Marriott hospitality meets affordable lodging here, and the convenience to golf course is superior.

Fiddler's Cove Beach & Racquet Club
$$-$$$ • 45 Folly Field Rd.
• 842-1611, (800) 321-1611

This affordable and convenient resort offers free tennis on 10 clay courts and free indoor racquetball. Some of the villas provide views of the lush fairways of the Port Royal Plantation golf course. Situated on the resort's 23 acres are comfortable two-bedroom villas, each with private balcony, a queen and two twin beds, two baths, living and dining rooms, fully equipped kitchen, color television, wet bar and washer/dryer. Also, you may enjoy two pools with heated spa and sundeck

INSIDERS' TIP

Always keep an extra ball, tees and ball marker in your pocket. You might need one when you'd least expect it.

plus a tot lot for the little ones. It's a short walk to a wide stretch of beach and a short drive to shops and restaurants.

Hampton Inn
$$$ • 1 Airport Rd. • 681-7900, (800) 426-7866

Hampton Inns the world over are dependable if you're looking for a comfortable place that is not an expensive luxury resort. Continental breakfast is quick to grab on the way to an early tee time. An outdoor pool and exercise room are offered. Refrigerators are in suites. Babysitting services may be booked.

Hilton Head Vacation Rentals
$$-$$$ • The Plaza at Shelter Cove • (800) 732-7671

More than 125 villas, condos and rental homes are managed by this company. As part of your rental package, the staff will arrange your tee time on any of the public or semiprivate courses.

Hyatt Regency Hilton Head
$$$$$ • 1 Hyatt Cir. • 785-1234, (800) 233-1234

The Hyatt has more than 500 rooms and provides a traditional quality accommodation. You can't go wrong here within the Palmetto Dunes complex. The hotel features a health club with massage, whirlpool and sauna, indoor and outdoor Olympic pools and a children's wading pool. Bikes and scooters are available; tennis and racquetball courts are here. Dining, dancing and live entertainment are part of the experience. Five golf courses will keep you swinging, and others on the island and mainland are minutes away.

Oceanfront Rentals
$$-$$$ • 11 New Orleans Rd. • 785-8161, (800) 845-6132

This company manages about 175 properties that include your choice of luxurious or budget-type vacation rentals in all areas of Hilton Head. Golf packages can be arranged when you rent a villa or home of any size — from one to eight bedrooms. Some properties are on the ocean; others

are on golf courses. Advance tee times are guaranteed on more than 30 area courses; free tennis, group rates and free accompanying non-golfer accommodations are offered.

Palmetto Dunes Resort
$$$$$ • 4 Queens Folly Rd. • 785-1161, (800) 845-6130

Access to five fabulous golf courses is the best reason for choosing to stay at Palmetto Dunes. Villas or vacation homes of one to six bedrooms are oceanside, on the harbor or on the fairway where you will enjoy the location, and your family will appreciate the boating, three miles of beachcombing, pools or tennis on 19 clay, four Supergrasse and two hard courts including eight lighted for night play. The 2,000 oceanfront acres of this sophisticated resort and residential community are adjacent to Shelter Cove Harbour, a Mediterranean-style village with retail stores and restaurants fronting a deepwater marina. Meeting and conference facilities also are superb.

Port Royal Village
$$$ • Port Royal Village • 681-9325, (800) 673-9385

Near the 54 holes of Port Royal Golf Club, this collection of vacation villas and townhouse rentals is near the beach as well; it also has a top-rated tennis complex. It has a pool and offers an hour a day at the racquet club. Tennis courts are of all three surfaces. The resort will package golf for you at several nearby courses in addition to the Port Royal Golf Club.

Vacations on Hilton Head
$$-$$$ • The Plaza at Shelter Cove • 686-3400, (800) BEACH ME

A central reservation service claiming to be the largest one on the island, this company will arrange accommodations including a golf package in any price range requested. Discount greens fees and guaranteed tee times can be arranged on any public or semiprivate course, and a variety of accommodations is available with or without other amenities.

Westin Resort & Villas
$$$$$ • Port Royal Plantation • 681-4000,
(800) 228-3000

More than 400 rooms in a luxurious facility stretching along the beach, spacious meeting rooms, cafe, restaurant and bar, tennis, pools and of course championship croquet and golf are all around you. This top-quality resort offers easy Southern charm and some of the best-prepared food you will ever find in a hotel setting.

Golf Equipment

Player's Golf is in the Shoppes on the Parkway and sells equipment, apparel and accessories; call 785-GOLF. **Nevada Bob's** is another large discount shop on the William Hilton Parkway, with better variety than the one in Myrtle Beach; call 686-GOLF. Also, **Las Vegas Discount Golf**, Buckingham Plantation Drive, 837-3399, is a new superstore that carries golf and tennis equipment.

Golf Instruction

One of the best places to study is where you can also play. The **Golf Academy of Hilton Head Island** helps you learn then helps you receive a discount on greens fees at Port Royal and Shipyard. A full-day program includes four hours of instruction with video analysis, then lunch and 18 holes of golf. The half-day includes a three-hour lesson with video analysis. Special programs are designed for women and juniors, and a mini program will analyze and correct flaws in your swing. Call 785-4540 or (800) 925-0467.

Private instruction is available at many of the other fine resorts, including a variety of quality programs at Sea Pines where you can also study during the morning and play on the Sea Marsh Course during the afternoon. Call 842-1454 for information on a full-day, half-day, beginner or short clinic.

South Carolina's Midlands

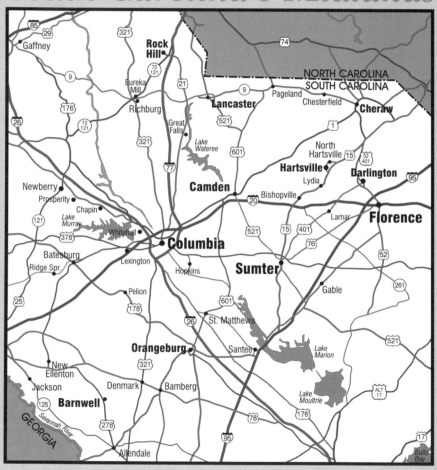

South Carolina's Midlands

South Carolina is consistently rated as one of the top (if not *the* top) golf destinations in the United States. Thus it should come as no great surprise that its capital city and environs boast a number of fine public courses as well as a few private ones that the public can play as part of an accommodations package.

In general, you'll find an interesting mix of traditional and modern layouts in the Midlands. Most of the facilities are first-class, and most courses are well-kept. Versions of bermudagrass predominate in the fairways, and common bermudagrass rules on the greens. Only a handful of courses maintain bentgrass greens.

Note that although we provide weekday and weekend greens fees (sometimes including cart) for each course, these costs are subject to change at any time. We suggest you ask about exact costs when you book a tee time.

Columbia is well-known for its volcanic summer heat. In fact, sometimes it's beyond volcanic. Greens tend to transition in June and October, so bear that in mind when planning a trip to the area. You should be able to play year round in Columbia, but spring and fall usually are the most comfortable seasons.

More than likely, many cities in America would gladly trade public courses with Columbia.

As in our North Carolina Mountains chapter, we have divided this chapter into regional sections to help you better negotiate the large area that makes up the Midlands.

Columbia Area Golf Courses

Charwood — The Country Club of Pineridge
4082 Bachman Rd., West Columbia
• 755-2000

Charwood — The Country Club of Pineridge offers three distinctly pleasing and pleasingly distinct nine-hole courses with plenty of variety and challenge. The rerouting and revision of some holes is now complete. Note the particularly interesting nuggets of sagacity and advice included on the score card for each hole.

Amenities include a practice green, practice range, pro shop, bar, snack bar and rental clubs.

You can walk these courses and book a round anytime. Approximate cost for 18 holes, including cart, is $22 weekdays, $26 weekends.

Charwood Course

Back Yardage: 2898	Par: 36
Middle Yardage: 2777	Par: 36
Ladies' Yardage: 2306	Par: 36

The Charwood Course, also known as the White Course, boasts tight fairways, so accu-

---

INSIDERS' TIP

Before you visit a course, always call to make sure it's open and is not hosting a big corporate outing or tournament.

GOLF COURSES IN SOUTH CAROLINA'S MIDLANDS

Name	Type	# Holes	Par	Slope	Yards	Walking	Booking	Cost w/ Cart
Beech Creek Golf Club	semiprivate	18	72	116	6397	restricted	anytime	$18-25
Bishopville Country Club	semiprivate	18	72	n/r	6448	anytime	anytime	$11.75-17
Bogeyville Golf Course	semiprivate	18	72	100	5514	anytime	anytime	$14-18
Calhoun Country Club	semiprivate	18	72	n/r	5954	restricted	anytime	$18-23
Cedar Creek Golf Club	semiprivate	18	72	119	6689	no	anytime	$25-35
Charwood								
Charwood Course	semiprivate	9	36	n/r	2898	anytime	anytime	$22-26
Ridgewood Course	semiprivate	9	36	n/r	3157	anytime	anytime	$22-26
Pinewood Course	semiprivate	9	36	n/r	3416	anytime	anytime	$22-26
Cheraw State Park	public	18	72	120	6129	anytime	anytime	$24-26
Chester Golf Club	public	18	72	n/r	6273	restricted	5 days	$24-31
Coldstream Golf Club	semiprivate	18	71	118	5733	restricted	10 days	$22-28
Cooper's Creek	semiprivate	18	72	115	6039	anytime	7 days	$22-28
Fox Creek	semiprivate	18	72	118	6493	restricted	anytime	25-30
Golden Hills Golf and Country Club	semiprivate	18	71	119	6011	anytime	2 days	$24-30
Green River Country Club	semiprivate	18	72	n/r	6257	restricted	anytime	$17-27
Houndslake Resort								
Azalea		9	36	n/a	3222	restricted	anytime	$30-35
Dogwood		9	36	n/a	3253	restricted	anytime	$30-35
Laurel		9	36	n/a	3350	restricted	anytime	$30-35
Highland Park Country Club	semiprivate	18	71	n/r	6100	anytime	anytime	$12

Name	Type	# Holes	Par	Slope	Yards	Walking	Booking	Cost w/ Cart
Hillcrest	public	18	72	114	6104	anytime	anytime	$20-22
Indian River	public	18	71	n/r	6052	restricted	anytime	$29-3
Lake Marion Golf Course	public/resort	18	72	113	6223	no	anytime	$25-37
Lakewood Links	semiprivate	18	72	116	6027	no	24 hours	$25-37
Lancaster Golf Club	public	18	72	n/r	6140	restricted	3 days	$29-32
LinRick	public	18	73	120	6293	anytime	2 days	$22-27
Mid-Carolina Club	semiprivate	18	72	116	6368	anytime	1 day	$25
Midland Valley Country Club	semiprivate	18	72	118	6182	anytime	anytime	$27-33
Northwoods	semiprivate	18	72	118	6485	restricted	7 days	$25-40
Oak Hills Golf and Country Club	public	18	72	117	6449	restricted	anytime	$32-37
Paw Paw Country Club	semiprivate	18	72	117	6649	anytime	anytime	$15-20
Persimmon Hill	public	18	72	117	6449	weekdays	anytime	$25
Pineview	semiprivate	18	72	116	6346	restricted	anytime	$16-27
Pocalla Springs	semiprivate	18	71	n/r	5882	anytime	anytime	$16
Sandy Pointe	public	18	72	116	6045	anytime	anytime	$18-25
Santee National	semiprivate	18	72	114	6125	restricted	anytime	$27-36
Sedgewood Country Club	public	18	72	n/r	6031	anytime	anytime	$15-20
Sweetwater Country Club	semiprivate	18	71	n/r	5830	anytime	7 days	$21-28
Timberlake Plantation	semiprivate	18	72	124	6226	anytime	7 days	$28-34
The Traces Golf Club	semiprivate	18	72	117	6449	restricted	anytime	$24-31
White Pines	public	18	72	111	5848	restricted	10 days	$24-31
White Plains Country Club	semiprivate	18	72	n/r	5874	restricted	3 days	$25-30

racy is key off the tee. This nine-hole track is relatively short and poses no major problems until you get to the greens, which are sloped and slick when firm.

Ridgewood Course

Championship Yardage: 3157	Par: 36
Men's Yardage: 2945	Par: 36
Ladies' Yardage: 2478	Par: 36

The Ridgewood Course, or Blue Course, is slightly more open than the Charwood Course. The fairways are flatter and wider. The ball must carry bunkers to reach the built-up greens, which are predominantly flat. If the rough has been allowed to grow up around the greens, then getting up and down will not be easy.

Pinewood Course

Back Yardage: 3416	Par: 36
Middle Yardage: 3074	Par: 36
Ladies' Yardage: 2580	Par: 37

The Pinewood Course (a.k.a. Rose Course) is the most interesting and modern of the trio at Charwood. Needless to say, because the course is a typical modern design, there are mounds. This nine offers the most variety and challenge, big elevation changes and some fun driving holes. The fairways are tight in places, and the holes are relatively longer than on the counterpart courses.

Coldstream Golf Club

Lake Murray Blvd., Irmo • 781-0114

Championship Yardage: 6155	
Slope: 122	Par: 71
Men's Yardage: 5733	
Slope: 118	Par: 71
Ladies' Yardage: 5047	
Slope: No rating	Par: 71

Coldstream, a Michael Mungo design, opened in 1975. Bermudagrass covers the fairways and greens. Some holes are flat, but most feature elevation changes. The course is part of a residential development near the shores of Lake Murray.

At Coldstream, we found narrow fairways, plenty of variety, a couple of spectacular holes and mostly small greens. Miss the green here and you may be in trouble: Your ball will roll into deep rough or bounce almost anywhere. Still, the relatively straightforward layout makes

for a fun round if you're playing at a relaxed pace. If your approach shots are accurate, you'll score well. You may enjoy the final hole on the front nine: a 196-yard par 3, which requires a downhill shot through a chute to a green backed by a series of hedges.

Amenities include a practice green, pro shop, bar, snack bar, occasional beverage cart and rental clubs.

Walking is allowed primarily on weekdays. You can book up to 10 days in advance. Approximate cost, including cart, is $23 weekdays, $28 weekends.

Cooper's Creek Golf Club

Country Rd., Pelion • 894-3666

Championship Yardage: 6582	
Slope: 120	Par: 72
Men's Yardage: 6039	
Slope: 115	Par: 72
Ladies' Yardage: 4565	
Slope: 99	Par: 73

Cooper's Creek opened in 1973. Red Chase designed the course. Bermudagrass covers the greens and fairways, and most of the track is set in wooded terrain with some significant elevation changes.

Cooper's Creek offers tremendous variety in a pleasant country atmosphere. Each hole has a character all its own. Some fairways are wide, others are narrow. Some holes are flat, others may remind you of a roller-coaster ride. The greens differ in size, shape and undulation. We found that the course is fair and not overly penal, although really awful shots will likely yield really awful results.

Make sure you bring your brain to this course: Cooper's Creek is a thinking player's track. Concentrate, take what the course gives you, and you'll have lots of fun. Seeing as the course is quite close to I-20 on the way to Augusta, Georgia, this would make a fun stop on the way to The Masters.

Amenities include a putting green, practice range, chipping green, locker room, snack bar and rental clubs.

If you're fit, the course is walkable, and you can walk anytime. You can book up to seven days in advance. Approximate cost, including cart, is $22 weekdays, $28 weekends.

FYI

Unless otherwise noted, the area code for all phone numbers in this chapter is 803.

Golden Hills Golf and Country Club

100 Scotland Dr., Lexington • 957-3355

Championship Yardage: 6461	
Slope: 126	**Par: 71**
Men's Yardage: 6011	
Slope: 119	**Par: 71**
Other Yardage: 5575	
Slope: 115	**Par: 71**
Ladies' Yardage: 4957	
Slope: 113	**Par: 71**

Golden Hills, a Ron Garl design, opened in 1987. Bermudagrass covers the fairways and greens, and most of the holes are set in woodland bordered by a residential development. The course combines undulating and flat terrain, and water hazards come into play on several holes.

Golden Hills used to be a pure links course, with tall, ball-eating rough bordering many of the fairways. The members apparently changed all that: What used to be rough is now fairway or light rough. But you'll still find plenty of tight holes, particularly on the back nine. Resist the temptation to swing the driver too much: In many instances, Golden Hills forces you to play target golf — the big stick may simply get you into big trouble.

As you drive up to the clubhouse, you come face to face with the terrifying 10th hole — a 361-yard par 4, requiring a 200- to 215-yard tee shot to a narrow downhill landing area fronted by a large pond. Once you've lobbed an accurate long iron down the fairway, you have to smack the ball about 140 yards over water to a thin green. You should feel very pleased to score par here.

The course boasts interesting variety; no two holes are the same. If you're up for a challenge that will test your brain as much as your swing, play Golden Hills. And as one member told us, "The course will give you all you want from the tips." (Note: "The tips" are the back tees, for those of you who might be unfamiliar with the jargon.)

Amenities include a practice green, pro shop, locker room, restaurant, pro shop, bar and rental clubs. The practice range is open to members only.

You can walk anytime, but it's a tough round on foot. Nonmembers can book two days in advance. Approximate cost, including cart, is $24 weekdays, $30 weekends.

Indian River

200 Congaree Hunt Dr., West Columbia • 955-0080

Championship Yardage: 6507	
Slope: No rating	**Par: 71**
Men's Yardage: 6052	
Slope: No rating	**Par: 71**
Other Yardage: 5586	
Slope: No rating	**Par: 71**
Ladies' Yardage: 4643	
Slope: No rating	**Par: 71**

Indian River, a Lyndell Young-designed course, opened in 1992. Bermudagrass covers the well-maintained greens and fairways. The course is undulating on the front nine and somewhat flatter on the back. The holes are bordered by pine forest, wetlands or both, and water comes into play on several holes.

Indian River boasts a Scottish links-style design in a serene and peaceful wooded environment. The mix works well: Indian River is one of the more popular public tracks in the Columbia area. A modern course, you'll find mounds off the tee, wide and rolling fairways, decent variety and some fine views. And for a modern course (typically replete with tricks and trappings), Indian River is fair. We found little trouble off the tee but plenty of challenge around the sizable greens — some of the most undulating in the entire Midlands area. Pat yourself on the back for reaching the green in regulation but realize that getting down in two will likely produce massive beads of perspiration on your sun-drenched forehead. It's important to look at pin placement and play your ball as close to the stick as possible if you plan to two-putt these greens.

Indian River is a worthwhile course to visit if you're in the area, particularly if you enjoy putting challenges.

INSIDERS' TIP

When you're on a green, fix your ball mark and one other. Pat down spike marks. Move around the edges, not the middle.

Amenities include a practice green, practice range, pro shop and snack bar.

You can walk the course anytime on the weekdays and after 2 PM on weekends, although it's not a particularly easy trek. You can book anytime. Approximate cost, including cart, is $28 weekdays, $35 weekends.

Indian Trail Golf Club
1304 Willis St., Batesburg • 532-9010

Championship Yardage: 3027	
Slope: No rating	Par: 36
Men's Yardage: 2867	
Slope: No rating	Par: 36
Ladies' Yardage: 2182	
Slope: No rating	Par: 36

Indian Trail opened in 1993. Tifton bermudagrass covers the fairways and greens, and the course winds through some wonderful wooded terrain in a peaceful country setting.

Indian Trail is the creation of Rudy Raborn, a Certified Public Accountant by day who has been moonlighting as a golf course owner and architect. Perhaps it's time for Mr. Raborn to leave his day job in the world of number-crunching and take up golf course layout full time.

To Raborn's credit, this pleasant and rolling nine-hole course boasts a truly competent design. The course will definitely make you think about your game and may even make you think of Robert Trent Jones: sensible use of water, bunkers and those "landing strip" tee boxes. The greens are primarily sloped but fair, as are the fairways, and the overall design is solid. To assure that you don't go home without a serious challenge, two of the greens slope away from the fairway.

The back nine is on the drawing board and should be ready sometime in 1997. If you're in the area, drop by this course for a pleasantly challenging surprise. And if you have a bad round, who knows . . . perhaps Mr. Raborn will help you take it out on the IRS (there must be some allowance for a tax deduction based on pain and suffering incurred on the golf course!).

Amenities include a practice range, putting green, tax form preparation, snack bar and rental clubs.

Walking is allowed anytime, and you can book anytime as well. Approximate cost, including cart, is $16 weekdays, $18 weekends.

LinRick Golf Course
356 Campground Rd., Columbia
• 754-6331

Championship Yardage: 6959	
Slope: 125	Par: 73
Men's Yardage: 6293	
Slope: 120	Par: 73
Other Yardage: 5255	
Slope: No rating	Par: 73
Ladies' Yardage: 5086	
Slope: No rating	Par: 73

LinRick Golf Course opened in 1971. This Russell Breeden design is operated by the Richland County Recreation Commission. Thus you might think of LinRick as Columbia's municipal course. Bermudagrass covers the greens and fairways. Eight lakes bring water into play on several holes.

You might be asking, "Why a funny name like LinRick?" Well, the course is named after Thomas S. Lynton and J. W. Derrick, two gentlemen who played significant roles with the recreation commission. Instead of calling the course the Lynton-Derrick Columbia and Richland County Municipal Golf Course Open to All, they slimmed it down to LinRick. Wise decision.

Nomenclature aside, LinRick is an outstanding public course. The Russell Breeden design features lots of water, wooded terrain, doglegs, plenty of challenge, picturesque holes and midsize greens. We have a sneaking suspicion that Russell Breeden must be fairly happy with this layout, particularly the final five holes — among the most challenging and picturesque in the Columbia area. We found wide fairways on the front nine and more narrow fairways on the back. The residents of Columbia should be proud; LinRick represents their city well.

Amenities include a practice range, putting green, pro shop, snack bar and rental clubs.

You can walk the course anytime. Book after 9 AM on Thursdays for the weekend and after 9 AM on Monday for a weekday. Approximate cost, including cart, is $17 weekdays, $27 weekends.

Fox Creek near Lydia is a varied course and a great example of what makes golf in South Carolina's Midlands so popular.

Mid-Carolina Club
3593 Kibler Bridge Rd., Columbia
• 364-3193
Championship Yardage: 6595
Slope: 122   **Par: 72**
Men's Yardage: 6368
Slope: 116   **Par: 72**
Other Yardage: 5791
Slope: 111   **Par: 72**
Ladies' Yardage: 5351
Slope: 123   **Par: 73**

Mid-Carolina is open to the public on weekdays only; on weekends, you must play with a member. Or better still, be a member. Greens and fairways are bermudagrass. The course is development-free and set in wooded terrain.

Mid-Carolina is a good example of a mature, well-maintained Russell Breeden design. Four sets of tees provide challenge for golfers of all levels. Some of the bunkers are larger than those on other Breeden-designed courses. Water comes into play on nearly half the holes, and it's most noticeable on three of the par 3s.

The course offers some dramatic elevation changes on the back nine. We overheard one regular player telling an assembled group that he had gone without his driver for the past 13 years in favor of a fourth wedge. His point is that you won't need to smack the ball a long way to score successfully at Mid-Carolina. The course plays less than 6600 yards from the tips. The premium here is on accuracy off the tee, not distance. This is particularly true on some of the dogleg holes and some of the tighter holes on the back nine.

Amenities include a practice range, putting green, chipping green, pro shop, snack bar and rental clubs.

You can walk the course anytime. The public can book up to a day in advance. Approximate cost, including cart, is $25.

Northwoods Golf Club

201 Powell Rd., Columbia • 786-9242

Championship Yardage: 6800

Slope: 122   Par: 72

Men's Yardage: 6485

Slope: 118   Par: 71

Other Yardage: 5936

Slope: 113   Par: 72

Ladies' Yardage: 4954

Slope: 116   Par: 72

Northwoods opened in 1990. Bermudagrass covers the fairways and greens. Some holes are set in wooded terrain, others are wide open. The course is hillier on the front nine than on the back — where there is more water.

Northwoods is a modern course designed by P. B. Dye, son of Pete Dye, one of the most famous and highly paid ex-insurance salesmen turned golf course architects in the world. If you've never played a Dye course and you're within striking distance of Columbia, then you must play here. Standing on some tees can be a mind-bending experience. Standing in the middle of the fairway can be a mind-bending experience. Standing in the middle of a bunker where the lip is above your head can be a mind-bending experience. You get the picture. There are some massive greens with equally massive undulations, uneven stances in the fairway and some incredible blind shots. Hit a perfect drive down the middle of the fairway on the 14th, and you're faced with a wedge into the green. The only problem is that you can't see the green, such is the size of the mound in between you, your ball and the green.

Did we mention the bunkers? At Northwoods they come in every shape and size, including a couple that could only have been created through the detonation of a large incendiary device. Have fun at Northwoods, but don't be surprised if the course beats you up — physically and mentally. We warned you!

The course is walkable for the very fit, and pedestrian play is allowed on weekdays and weekends after 1 PM. You can book up to seven days in advance. Approximate cost, including cart, is $25 weekdays, $40 weekends.

Oak Hills Golf and Country Club

7629 Fairfield Rd., Columbia • 735-9830, (800) 263-5218

Championship Yardage: 6894

Slope: 122   Par: 72

Men's Yardage: 6449

Slope: 117   Par: 72

Other Yardage: 5666

Slope: 111   Par: 72

Ladies' Yardage: 4829

Slope: 110   Par: 72

Oak Hills Golf and Country Club opened in 1991. Steve Melnick, who plays on the PGA Tour, and D. J. DeVictor teamed up to design this exciting modern track. The course is laid out on terrain that provides a good mix of open and wooded holes. Water frequently comes into play. In the last couple of years, the course added 1,452 tons of bunker sand, 648 tons of top soil and more than 140,700 square feet of sod. Bermudagrass covers the fairways and greens.

We found plenty of entertainment and variety at Oak Hills. Greens, fairways, bunkers and water hazards vary in dimension. However, the course provides excellent sight lines, so blind shots are few. Keep the ball in play off the tee and prepare to play an approach shot possibly from an uphill or downhill stance. Get the ball to the green, and the slope will challenge your abilities with the blade.

Many of the holes are majestically framed by trees. With four sets of tees, challenges abound for golfers of all abilities. Overall, the course is friendly, playable, pretty and popular. How can you go wrong?

INSIDERS' TIP

To speed up play, particularly when the course is busy, be generous with your "gimmee" putts. Players behind you will be irritated if you take two minutes lining up a three-footer.

Amenities include a practice green, practice range, pro shop, locker room, bar, restaurant, beverage cart and rental clubs. The yardage book inside the golf cart is an interesting touch.

Walking is restricted, but you may book anytime. Approximate cost, including cart, is $25 weekdays, $30 weekends.

Persimmon Hill Golf Club

4322 W. Southborough Rd., Saluda
• **275-2561**
Championship Yardage: 7063
Slope: 123   Par: 72
Men's Yardage: 6449
Slope: 117   Par: 72
Other Yardage: 5666
Slope: 112   Par: 72
Ladies' Yardage: 4829
Slope: 100   Par: 72

Persimmon Hill opened in 1962. The temperature on opening day — Labor Day — was 102. Russell Breeden designed this popular course. Bermudagrass covers the fairways and greens, and the design wanders through some wonderful and scenic pine forests.

The brochure for Persimmon Hill (an excellent name for a golf course, don't you think?) calls it "The Thrill on the Hill." The course boasts an excellent layout. Russell Breeden might even tell you that it's one of his better tracks. The land provides great variety, and the layout makes commendable use of the natural features. You won't find tremendous trouble off the tee, but you will need to think when playing around the spring-fed water hazards. The greens are large and rolling, and the bunkers are larger than we've seen on other Russell Breeden courses. Perhaps the course favors the long hitter. That's certainly the case on the monster 18th — a 630-yard par 5 (the longest hole in South Carolina). Once you've played Persimmon Hill, you'll understand why it's one of the most understated yet popular courses in the area.

Amenities include a practice range, putting green, pro shop, snack bar and rental clubs.

Walking is allowed primarily on weekdays. You can book anytime. Approximate cost, including cart, is $25.

Sedgewood Country Club

9560 Garner's Ferry Rd., Hopkins
• **776-2177**
Championship Yardage: 6810
Slope: No rating   Par: 72
Men's Yardage: 6031
Slope: No rating   Par: 72
Ladies' Yardage: 4841
Slope: No rating   Par: 72

Russell Breeden designed Sedgewood, which opened around 1965. Bermudagrass and native grasses cover the fairways and greens. The course is primarily flat on the front nine and somewhat more hilly on the back.

If you're a relaxed golfer who likes to play without a shirt on summer days and not pay a fortune — but who enjoys a challenge on a well-designed course — then Sedgewood is for you. Then there's the world's longest tee on the 18th hole: The tee box must stretch for more than 100 yards. If it's a hot day and you're on the putting surface, the sprinkler system — with sprinkler heads positioned squarely in the middle of the green — unexpectedly may cool you down. You'll find some fun holes on this course, but it could benefit from a revamp.

Amenities include a practice green, practice range, pro shop, snack bar and locker room, although the latter amenity doubles as an auxiliary maintenance storage facility.

The course is walkable anytime. You can play without a shirt anytime. You can drink beer anytime (if you're of legal age). You can book anytime too. Greens fees, including open-air cart, are $15 weekdays, $20 weekends.

Timberlake Golf Club

1700-A Amicks Ferry Rd., Chapin
• **345-9909**
Championship Yardage: 6703
Slope: 132   Par: 72
Men's Yardage: 6226
Slope: 124   Par: 72
Other Yardage: 5701
Slope: 117   Par: 72
Ladies' Yardage: 4829
Slope: 121   Par: 72

Timberlake Plantation, a Willard Byrd design, opened in 1987. Bermudagrass covers the fairways and greens. This well-maintained course winds around the wooded shoreline of

Lake Murray, and water hazards come into play on several holes.

Timberlake Plantation is a magnificent modern course without too many of the huge mounds, bunkers and other absurdities often found on contemporary layouts. Byrd created an awesome and varied track that is fairly tight off the tee box yet lots of fun around the sloped greens. If the rough is grown up any, you'll need to be particularly careful off the tee. Many of the holes are straightforward, but the last four seem more difficult and breathtaking. The crème de la crème is the 18th hole; Lake Murray guards the right side of the large green. Make par or birdie here and you'll have plenty to be happy about as you down a cold one at the 19th.

Timberlake provides an excellent example of how a modern course can be fun, challenging and visually appealing without being tricked-up. This course is a must-play if you're in the Columbia area.

There's a small marina adjacent to the new clubhouse, so you may be able to cruise up to the course in your power boat! Call Timberlake to inquire about specific details.

Amenities include a practice green, practice range, pro shop, locker room, snack bar, beverage cart and rental clubs. An inn and restaurant are slated for completion in 1997.

Walking is allowed anytime and is manageable if you're fit. You can book up to seven days in advance. Approximate cost, including cart, is $28 weekdays, $34 weekends.

Timberlake Plantation is a little tricky to find. Take I-26 toward Spartanburg. Take Exit 91 to Chapin and take a left into town. About a mile outside Chapin, the road forks; veer right, and proceed for about 6 miles. The course is on the right.

Courses Available Through Packages

The Columbia Metropolitan Convention and Visitors Bureau offers a number of package deals that feature some of the better public courses in Columbia as well as some out-standing private courses. Those in the Columbia Golf Promotion include Crickentree, Cooper's Creek, Fort Jackson (on the U.S. Army base), Northwoods, Oak Hills, Timberlake Plantation, Windemere and The Woodlands. Call (800) 264-4884 or 254-0479 for more information.

Aiken Area Golf Courses

In Aiken, you're so close to the home of The Masters that you can almost smell the azaleas at Amen Corner. Sadly, your percentage of chance to play at Augusta National is optimistically described as zero or less. Thankfully, golfing options abound in the Aiken area, which is home to some formidable new courses.

Aiken is in the heart of "Thoroughbred Country." This means that when golfers aren't playing golf, they're breeding and riding horses. Aiken's old and pretty downtown area boasts some fine restaurants. The area has always been a highly rated retirement center, so if the average age of the foursome in front of you is 92 and they're all taking the slow boat to the 19th hole, don't be surprised. Decent people all, they'll probably let you play through. You'll find a variety of courses around here, including young and fantastic Cedar Creek, venerable Midland Valley Country Club and wonderful Houndslake.

The soil is sandy, and pine forests dot the prevailing country scenery. You'll find bermudagrass on the greens and fairways.

FYI
Unless otherwise noted, the area code for all phone numbers in this chapter is 803.

Allendale County Golf Course
Rte. 1, Barton Rd., Allendale • 584-7117
Men's Yardage: 3789
Slope: No rating   **Par: 36**
Ladies' Yardage: 2736
Slope: No rating   **Par: 36**

Allendale County Golf Course, formerly Allendale County Country Club (a real hit with alliteration fans . . .), opened in 1952. The course was designed by Walker Smith, a millionaire with a glass eye who made his fortune in the hat business. Smith, a left-hander with a chronic and incurable slice, designed the course to suit the needs of a left-hander with a chronic and incurable slice. That is to say, a lot of holes play left. So if you're a left-hander and your stock shot is a big, booming out-of-control fade, you'll love Allendale County Golf Course.

The course was purchased in 1993 by Joe and Audrey Vuknic who spent many years running a course in the Hilton Head area. Allendale is being renovated. Set in rolling, fairly open terrain bordered by farmland and pine forests, the wide fairways provide a comfortable landing area off the tee. The small to midsize sloping greens, however, will test your ability to read putts. Some greens are protected by bunkers.

The Vuknics operate a small pro shop, bar and snack bar. There's also a practice putting green. Gone are the days when, according to local lore, Mr. Smith would instruct the greenskeeper to pull the flags out of the holes when a group he disliked was on the course. The atmosphere these days is friendly and relaxed. The calendar features five tournaments a year and a weekly captain's choice scramble where, as we discovered, the aristocracy of Allendale County is more than happy to lighten your wallet.

Walking is allowed anytime, and you won't need a tee time. Approximate cost for 18 holes, including cart, is $15. Rental clubs are available.

Bogeyville Golf Course
500 Bogeyville Rd., Bogeyville • 649-3366
Men's Yardage: 5514
Slope: 100   **Par: 72**
Ladies' Yardage: 4622
Slope: No rating   **Par: 72**

Bogeyville Golf Course opened at least 30 years ago. The H. D. Wyman-designed course features bermudagrass on both the fairways and greens. Some holes are set in wooded terrain; others are wide open. Water hazards come into play on some holes. The course offers challenging golf in a peaceful country setting. Terrain is undulating, particularly on the back nine.

We found Bogeyville (what a name for a golf course!) somewhat remote, though the many and varied golfers who were playing in the middle of the week in the heat of the day

apparently found it extremely accessible. You'll certainly find plenty of variety on this course, including some remarkable holes, such as a par 5 on the front nine that literally makes a U-turn. The front nine opens with a drivable par 4. Water and bunkers come into play on this mature course bordered by pine trees, water and thicket, although there's decidedly more water and thicket on the back nine. The greens are predominantly flat; make sure, however, that you keep them in front of you — disaster lurks behind some of the greens.

Walking is allowed anytime, and you may book anytime as well. Approximate cost, including cart, is $14 weekdays, $18 weekends.

Bogeyville is definitely off the beaten path. The following directions should help: From Aiken, take U.S. Highway 1 N. past I-20 and look for a signpost for the course on your left. Take an unimproved road for about 3 (bumpy) miles, and the course will appear on your right.

Cedar Creek Golf Club
2475 Club Dr., Aiken• 648-4206
Championship Yardage: 7206
Slope: 119   **Par: 72**
Men's Yardage: 6689
Slope: 119   **Par: 72**
Other Yardage: 6277
Slope: 115   **Par: 72**
Ladies' Yardage: 5231
Slope: 115   **Par: 72**

Cedar Creek, an Arthur Hills design, opened in 1992 and is part of a new upscale residential development. The fairways and greens are bermudagrass. Most holes are bordered by trees, and water, wasteland and creeks frequently come into play.

With Cedar Creek, Arthur Hills has given the golfing world a fine modern course. Challenges come from significant elevation changes, large hilly greens with surrounding bunkers, the occasional mound and some holes where you must hit the fairway or green. You may find yourself flirting with out-of-bounds on a few holes if you're wayward off the tee. For a modern course, the design is not overly tricked-up or difficult. If your last name is Daly and your first name is John, you'll want to play from the tips — a

Walking vs. Riding

If you join the United States Golf Association (and you should), you may receive the pamphlet *A Call to Feet*, urging more golfers to walk. In the pithily written document, the powers-that-be even refer to golf in a cart as "cart-ball". Pretty stern stuff from the men and women in Far Hills, New Jersey — home of the USGA — for whom golf "is a walking game."

An unscientific survey shows that most public courses in the Carolinas prefer that you use a cart when you play. The courses where walking is restricted far outnumber those where walking is unrestricted. Even on courses where walking is allowed, riders almost always outnumber the pedestrians. Many designers and architects, particularly in the last 10 years, have built courses where the only realistic option is to ride — especially true on courses built around a housing or condo development. Most modern courses feature significant distances between green and tee, making walking tedious if not impossible. The modern course that's walkable is a vanishing species. It's all quite sad.

Courses built earlier in the century are walkable and were built to be so. With the arrival of the cart, many of these courses laid ugly ribbons of asphalt or concrete to accommodate the buggy. Many of these same courses started telling customers when they could and could not walk. In addition to the unsightly cart path, the cart's boxy shape invades the beauty of the course. And if the cart is gas-powered, it's also smelly and noisy.

Photo: Lake Norman Magazine

Go ahead and walk — it's great exercise.

From our observations and experience, there are numerous myths and problems that surround the cart issue. Many will tell you that cart fees generate income, but that's rarely true when you consider the costs of buying or leasing the cart, insurance, electricity or gas, upkeep, storage and cleaning. Seeing as more people like to ride in carts than walk, the cart generates greens fee income, primarily due to laziness. It's an unfortunate fact that some people simply wouldn't play the game if they couldn't ride. Thus a portion of the greens fee covers part of the cost of keeping carts ready and available; even if you walk, you're probably still paying for a cart.

Many amateurs (and course rangers) will tell you that play is faster in a cart. That may be so when the course is deserted; but that's not always the case when the course is busy. During or after rain, most courses make you keep the cart on the path. Thus a twosome will be forced to drive to a point parallel with the ball, walk to where the ball lies, hit the shot, walk back and begin the process again. Under these circumstances, on a walkable course, two golfers walking will play faster than two golfers riding in a cart. Even a foursome of decent golfers will rarely delay a foursome that's riding.

And then there's the issue of aesthetics. The great golf course designers build courses so that the course is best viewed from the fairway, not the cart path. From the cart path, you're going to see woods, scrub and the backside of mounds. Walkers see the green complex and the fairway. Walkers see the golf course, not the cart path.

When you play golf, we think you should walk. In Scotland, where the game began, everyone walks. Courses are walkable, and the Scots know how to play in well under four hours. Most people we know play golf because it's a release from their indoor workplace. The game provides a well-deserved break from the office or factory, from traffic and from the concrete jungles where we work and shop. So why the great need and desire to ride in a cart on a cart path?

The Scots realized, and still realize, the tremendous health benefits of playing golf. Many a recovering heart-disease victim is told to take lessons from a golf pro and take to the links for four hours of gentle walking. If someone with a heart problem can walk a golf course, any physically healthy person can. On walkable courses, we've run into people who think that their poor knees mean that they have to ride in a cart. Garbage. The gentle yet beneficial exercise provided by walking the course can only help build up the leg and back muscles — which can only help ailing joints.

In the Carolinas, one of the only public-access golf courses with an established and well-run caddie program is Pinehurst Country Club. If you play there (you should at some stage in your life), take a caddie, for a caddie will make the course even more walkable, advise you where to aim and tell you which way a putt will break. A caddie will rake the bunker after you've made a mess, suggest what club might work and tell you exactly how far you are from the pin. This is pure golf, and caddies are part of what make Pinehurst so special. Wouldn't it be great if more public courses could follow Pinehurst's example?

Perhaps one day a course will sell its carts, blow up its cart paths, provide you with a walking bag or pull cart for free and restore a piece of tradition so sadly lacking in today's game. In this book, we've included information about walking so those of you who are dedicated to the traditional game can indulge in the benefits — spiritual and physical — provided by walking your round of golf.

---

whopping 7206 yards. Thankfully, Arthur Hills also remembered the short hitters in the world: There's a 1000-yard difference between the championship and men's tees. Comparatively speaking, you'll have more fun from the men's tees if you're a mid- to high handicapper.

If you're in the Aiken area, make sure you play this course. You may like it enough to plop down some cash for a house on the 18th! The course hosted the 1995 NCAA Division II National Championship and is a regular stop on the Powerbilt Tour.

Amenities at this top-notch facility include a practice green, practice range, pro shop, locker room, bar, beverage cart and rental clubs.

We do not recommend walking this course. You can book anytime, and the approximate cost, including cart, is $25 weekdays, $35 weekends.

Highland Park Country Club

Highland Park Ave., Aiken • 649-6029
Men's Yardage: 6100
Slope: No rating   **Par: 71**
Ladies' Yardage: 4911
Slope: No rating   **Par: 71**

Highland Park opened its golf course in 1903. Bermudagrass covers the fairways and greens. The layout winds through some pretty pine forest and is mostly flat.

Venerable Highland Park is just a three-putt from booming downtown Aiken. While wandering around this ancient course, we almost felt the presence of the ghosts of great golfers striding up the fairways, a fleet of doting caddies in their wakes.

Sadly, this excellent layout could use some sprucing up. If someone with a love for old traditional courses would revamp it, perhaps Highland Park could become one of the better tracks around. Still, if you're in the area and want to see a wonderful traditional layout and have some fun, take the time to play Highland Park.

Amenities include a practice green, pro shop, locker room and rental clubs.

You can walk anytime, and you won't need a tee time. Approximate cost, including cart, is $12.

Houndslake Country Club

1900 Houndslake Dr., Aiken • 648-3333

Houndslake Country Club is primarily a private club that offers playing privileges if you stay at the Guest House adjacent to the course. The Guest House itself is more than a hotel, offering more of a resort or corporate getaway-type ambiance. Otherwise, this course is for the members.

Joe Lee designed all three nine-hole courses at Houndslake. The first two opened in 1974; the third nine, in 1979. The courses are set in rolling terrain bordered by homes and pine trees. Lee is well-known in Florida, especially for his courses surrounding Disneyland near Orlando. You won't find Mickey or Daffy at Houndslake, but you will find three fine, mature courses that rival any in the Midlands for character and quality of design.

You can't go wrong with any of these courses. Adding to the challenge at Houndslake is a mysterious wind that bounces off the tall pine trees and creates a swirling tempest at times.

Amenities include a practice green, practice range, pro shop, bar, snack bar and rental clubs.

You can walk these courses and book a round with your reservation at the Guest House. Approximate cost for 18 holes, including cart, is $30 weekdays, $35 weekends.

Azalea Course

Championship Yardage: 3222	**Par: 36**
Slope: 118	
Men's Yardage: 3009	**Par: 36**
Slope: 114	
Ladies' Yardage: 2653	**Par: 36**
Slope: 121	

The Azalea Course is an interesting beginning to the trifecta, offering mostly straightforward holes with wide fairways and large greens. Fairways and greens are guarded by some large bunkers. This nine rewards solid driving and accurate iron play.

Dogwood Course

Championship Yardage: 3253	**Par: 36**
Slope: 120	
Men's Yardage: 2994	**Par: 36**
Slope: 116	
Ladies' Yardage: 2582	**Par: 36**
Slope: 120	

This second nine at Houndslake offers a little more challenge and elevation change. It features one of the most wonderful and picturesque par 5s in the Midlands — the 509-yard 7th. Smack it downhill off the tee toward a small lake, then decide whether you want to go for it or lay up off a downhill lie. Once you're on the large green, two-putting is a serious challenge. Play the course for this hole alone and you'll be quite happy. In places, this nine is a little narrower off the tee, with more out-of-bounds.

Laurel Course

Championship Yardage: 3350	**Par: 36**
Slope: 122	
Men's Yardage: 3047	**Par: 36**
Slope: 117	
Ladies' Yardage: 2642	**Par: 36**
Slope: 123	

The Laurel Course is the newest of the three courses, the most challenging and the least developed. If you liked the first two nines, you'll enjoy this course even more. Each hole is unique and fun, offering a variety of shot-making opportunities. The par 5 No. 7, just 435 yards from the white tees, is very reachable for the mid-handicapper.

Midland Valley Country Club

U.S. Hwy. 1, Aiken • 663-7332

Championship Yardage: 6870	
Slope: 126	**Par: 72**
Men's Yardage: 6182	
Slope: 118	**Par: 72**
Other Yardage: 5748	
Slope: 111	**Par: 72**
Ladies' Yardage: 5545	
Slope: 123	**Par: 74**

Midland Valley Country Club opened in 1965. The course was designed by Ellis Maples. Jim Ferree, who plays on the PGA SENIOR TOUR, is the director of golf. Greens and fairways are bermudagrass.

Midland Valley is one of the better courses in the Aiken area. We found an excellent traditional design and a well-maintained, mature track. If you haven't played an Ellis Maples course, definitely try this one. Attention is paid to details here: The course is meticulous, and yardage markers indicate the distance to the back, middle and front of the green. Towering pine trees and shrubs add to the ambiance, and water comes into play on a few holes.

Maples made excellent use of the sandy undulating terrain to produce a course with great variety and challenge. Maples courses are often defined by midsize sloped greens protected by a bunker or two. One of the bunkers will front roughly half of the green. Thus, pin placement can play a significant role in what type of approach shot you'll play. If the pin is behind the bunker, risk it and go for it, or play it safe and aim for the unprotected part of the green. You'll also find some fun and exciting driving holes where placement is often more important than pure brute strength. Fans of mature, traditional courses will love Midland Valley.

Amenities include a practice green, practice range, pro shop, locker room, bar, snack bar and rental clubs.

Walking is allowed anytime, although the elevation changes will test your stamina. You can book anytime as well. Approximate cost, including cart, is $27 weekdays, $33 weekends.

Paw Paw Country Club

600 George St., Bamberg • 245-4171
Championship Yardage: 7063
Slope: 123   Par: 72
Men's Yardage: 6449
Slope: 117   Par: 72
Other Yardage: 5666
Slope: 112   Par: 72
Ladies' Yardage: 4829
Slope: No rating   Par: 72

Paw Paw, a quality Russell Breeden layout, sits peacefully in the heart of Bamberg County. Bermudagrass covers the fairways

and greens. We found a predominantly flat track, with shallow greens and fairway bunkers providing most of the difficulties. The fairways are lined with old Midland pines. You'll see the occasional mound here, but the challenge off the tee is keeping the ball straight down some relatively narrow fairways. You'll also need to be accurate on your approach shot; if you miss the green here at Paw Paw, only a good chipping game will keep your score from ballooning. There's more water on the back nine than on the front.

Enjoy the difficult finishing hole — a 446-yard par 4 with just enough water to make you nervous. When you're looking for a straightforward yet challenging course, stop by Paw Paw.

Amenities include a practice range, putting green, pro shop and snack bar.

You can walk this course anytime if you wish, but it's truly a hike. You can book up to seven days in advance. Approximate cost, including cart, is $15 weekdays, $20 weekends.

Sweetwater Country Club

U.S. Hwy. 64, Barnwell • 259-5004
Championship Yardage: 6248
Slope: No rating   Par: 71
Men's Yardage: 5830
Slope: No rating   Par: 71
Ladies' Yardage: 4680
Slope: No rating   Par: 71

Sweetwater, a Russell Breeden design, opened in 1981. The course sits amid rolling terrain, although many of the fairways are flat. Bermudagrass covers the fairways and greens. Water comes into play on a few holes.

Sweetwater boasts a fine design that's undergoing some improvements. The course is fair and not tricked-up. We found decent variety in a relaxed and pretty setting. The fairways vary in width, and the greens vary in size and shape. A couple of greens are noticeably shallow; others are protected by large bunkers. Chipping areas are mown around the greens. Overall, Sweetwater is a thoroughly playable course.

INSIDERS' TIP

Park your cart or place you bag on the far side of the green so you can move along quickly when finished.

Amenities include a practice green, practice range, pro shop, handicap computer and snack bar.

Walking is allowed anytime. You can book seven days in advance. Approximate cost, including cart, is $21 weekdays, $28 weekends.

Santee-Cooper Area Golf Courses

The Santee-Cooper area (including Orangeburg, Santee, Sumter, Manning and Moncks Corner) is defined by two large bodies of water: Lake Marion and Lake Moultrie. The area is home to some fine golf courses. This zone's recreational atmosphere extends to golf. A number of individuals from northern climes come here from February through May as an alternative to Myrtle Beach and Florida. This may explain why Santee-Cooper is surprisingly rich in quality golf courses — and why you'll find plenty of golf package experts offering excellent winter and spring deals. We didn't see a bad course around here. The immediate area around Sumter is particularly strong. Why? Perhaps it's the presence of Shawn Weatherly, the 1980 Miss Universe. Perhaps it's the presence of Shaw Air Force Base. Or perhaps it's the water. Who knows.

Overall, you'll find courses from the modern to the traditional and back again. Spend a long weekend in the area playing golf; you won't be disappointed.

Packages are available through the Santee-Cooper Counties Promotion Commission, P.O. Drawer 40, Santee, South Carolina 29142, 854-2131.

Beech Creek Golf Club
1800 Sam Gillespie Blvd., Sumter
• 499-4653
Championship Yardage: 6805
Slope: 120   Par: 72
Men's Yardage: 6397
Slope: 116   Par: 72
Other Yardage: 5956
Slope: 111   Par: 72
Ladies' Yardage: 5247
Slope: 115   Par: 72

Beech Creek opened in 1990. James Goodson designed the course, which today is part of a residential development. The course is well-maintained and somewhat flat. Bermudagrass 419 covers the fairways, and putting surfaces are tiftdwarf.

You'll find plenty of variety on this well-designed modern course. Fairways vary from tight to expansive, and greens vary in size and shape. You'll also find mounds, out-of-bounds, water, pot bunkers and other trappings of the contemporary layout.

Beech Creek is popular with members of the United States Armed Forces stationed at Shaw Air Force Base. The track is one of a host of fine courses in the surprisingly golf-rich Sumter area. For $30 or less per round, including cart, the course is also a fine value.

Amenities at Beech Creek include a practice green, practice range, pro shop, snack bar, yardage book and rental clubs.

Walking is restricted on weekends. You can book anytime. Approximate cost, including cart, is $18 weekdays, $25 weekends.

Calhoun Country Club
U.S. Hwy. 176, St. Matthews • 823-2465
Championship Yardage: 6339
Slope: No rating   Par: 72
Men's Yardage: 5954
Slope: No rating   Par: 72
Ladies' Yardage: 4812
Slope: No rating   Par: 72

The front nine at Calhoun Country Club opened in 1959, and the back nine opened a year later. Ashby Gressette designed the course. Bermudagrass covers the fairways and greens. The layout winds through some fine woodlands, providing a peaceful country setting. The front nine is open and includes some wide fairways. The back nine is more narrow.

At Calhoun Country Club we found a fun and relatively straightforward course with plenty of elevation changes. The greens are mostly flat and slightly sloped; some are elevated and bunkered. Water comes into play on some holes, but overall, the course is not overly penal. Play Calhoun from the tips for the best challenge. On some of the tee shots, you'll be guiding the ball through a chute. The atmosphere at Calhoun is friendly and relaxed. However, if you're looking for an intense round,

Calhoun's design is strong and varied enough to provide a test.

Amenities at Calhoun include a practice green, practice range, pro shop, men's locker room and snack bar.

The course is walkable anytime except weekends when some restrictions apply. You can book anytime. Approximate cost, including cart, is $18 on weekdays and $23 on weekdays — an excellent value.

Crystal Lakes Golf Course
Dillon Park, Sumter • 775-1902
Men's Yardage: 5870
Slope: 110   Par: 72
Ladies' Yardage: 5560
Slope: No rating   Par: 72

Crystal Lakes is Sumter's muni. The Eddie Riccoboni-designed track opened in 1990. Bermudagrass covers the fairways and greens.

Just a smooth 3-iron from Shaw Air Force Base, you'll find Crystal Lakes, a small, well-designed nine-hole course that is popular with local golfers. (Yes, we know the true nine-hole course is an anomaly in this book, but this one is a great golfing deal for 18 holes, especially for beginning players.) If your backswing is interrupted by the sonic boom of an F-15 practicing low-altitude bombing runs, it's okay to take a mulligan.

Aeronautics aside, you'll find an aquatic environment on the first four holes. The 1st hole is a par 3 over water "infested" by one alligator. Otherwise, Crystal Lakes is a fun, low-pressure, flat, walkable, user-friendly golf course that is challenging enough to entertain the mid- to low handicapper.

After your round, if you're not too frazzled by the reptile, bunkers and low-flying, first-strike aircraft, you can relax with a jovial round of darts in the game room adjacent to the pro shop.

Amenities include a practice range, putting green, pro shop, snack bar and rental clubs.

You can and should walk this course anytime. You won't need a tee time. Approximate cost for 18 holes, including cart, is $14. You can walk 18 holes for $6 on weekdays.

FYI

Unless otherwise noted, the area code for all phone numbers in this chapter is 803.

Hillcrest Golf and Tennis Club
Old St. Matthew Rd., Orangeburg
• 533-6030
Championship Yardage: 6722
Slope: 119   Par: 72
Men's Yardage: 6104
Slope: 114   Par: 72
Ladies' Yardage: 5208
Slope: 107   Par: 72

The golf course at Hillcrest Golf and Tennis Club opened in 1972. Russell Breeden designed the primarily flat track. Trees define the fairways, and water comes into play on a few holes but rarely poses a serious threat.

Hillcrest is owned by the City of Orangeburg. Wouldn't it be nice if every town in North and South Carolina could boast a solid, well-designed muni like Hillcrest? We found a well-kept, well-marked, relatively straightforward course with plenty of variety and fun. Off the tee, the course is basically wide-open, with the occasional raised bunker lurking in the fairway. As you might expect with a Russell Breeden design, the greens are predominantly midsize, with a couple of bunkers protecting the putting surface. The greens are undulating but fair. The key to scoring well here is solidly hit, accurate approach shots.

Amenities include a practice green, practice range, pro shop, locker room, snack bar and rental clubs.

The course is walkable anytime. You can book anytime too. Approximate cost, including cart, is $20 weekdays, $22 weekends.

Lake Marion Golf Course
S.C. Hwy. 6, Santee • 854-2554,
(800) 344-6534
Championship Yardage: 6615
Slope: 117   Par: 72
Men's Yardage: 6223
Slope: 113   Par: 72
Ladies' Yardage: 5254
Slope: 112   Par: 72

Lake Marion Golf Course opened in 1979 and is part of the Santee-Cooper Resort. Eddie Riccoboni designed the course. Bermudagrass covers the greens and fairways. Pine trees border most holes, and water comes into play quite a bit.

At Lake Marion, we found a wonderful and friendly golf course with an understated charm usually found only at country club and private courses. This definitely is one of the must-play courses in this area and will be well worth the trip (the yardage book gives the distance from Chicago: 919 miles). Majestic pine trees frame equally majestic golf holes that offer both challenge and visual appeal. Design-wise, the brilliance of this traditional layout lies in the strategic placement of bunkers. Just one or two bunkers per hole are enough to guard the midsize to large greens. You'll have to think here and play sound, smart golf. You'll also have a lot of fun driving the ball from some of Lake Marion's elevated tees. Play your cards right on the greens and you'll make some birdies. This is the type of golf course that's fun to play more than once. Be sure to purchase the witty, entertaining and thoroughly useful yardage book.

Amenities at Lake Marion include a practice green, practice range, extensive pro shop, locker room, snack bar, occasional beverage cart and rental clubs.

You need to use a cart to play. You can book anytime. Approximate cost, including cart, is $35 weekdays and weekends.

Lakewood Links Golf Club
3600 Green View Pkwy., Sumter
• 481-5700
Championship Yardage: 6857
Slope: 123   Par: 72
Men's Yardage: 6027
Slope: 116   Par: 72
Ladies' Yardage: 5072
Slope: 116   Par: 72

Lakewood Links opened in 1989 and is part of a residential development. Common bermudagrass covers the fairways, and 328 bermudagrass is used on the greens. Porter Gibson designed the course. Houses and pine trees border the holes, and water comes into play on 11 of them.

Lakewood Links, as its name implies, is a links-style course with all the trappings of a modern layout built in tandem with a residential development. We found mounds; large, multilevel undulating greens; bunkers around the greens and in the fairways; out-of-bounds terrifyingly near the middle of the fairway; more mounds; and significant distances from tees to greens. The course is especially narrow on the back nine, so if you choose to break out your 300cc titanium-headed driver, make sure you bang it down the middle, otherwise you might be in for a long day. The par 4 10th hole is 461 yards from the back tees and 420 from the men's, yet the fairway at the 175-yard marker is just 25 yards wide. Therein lies the challenge of this course. You'll be entertained by the par 3s here. The course also features a significant number of doglegs.

Visually, the course is quite appealing. There are numerous ponds so packed with lilies, Monet would have felt like he was at home in Giverny.

Amenities at Lakewood include a practice green, practice range, extensive pro shop, locker room, snack bar, occasional beverage cart and rental clubs.

Use a cart to play here. You can book 24 hours in advance. Approximate cost, including cart, is $18 weekdays, $22 weekends.

Pineview
7305 Myrtle Beach Hwy., Gable • 495-3550
Championship Yardage: 7084
Slope: 122   Par: 72
Men's Yardage: 6346
Slope: 116   Par: 72
Other Yardage: 5951
Slope: 112   Par: 72
Ladies' Yardage: 5307
Slope: 119   Par: 72

Pineview, formerly known as Pineland Plantation, opened in 1968. Bermudagrass covers the greens and fairways. The Russell Breeden-designed layout is primarily flat and set in a pine forest.

Renovations have taken place at Pineview, and many improvements have been made, including a new clubhouse. The course includes all the classic Breeden touches: runway tee boxes, the occasional mound, slightly raised greens, one or two bunkers per green and putting surfaces that are more sloped than undulating. You won't encounter a lot of trouble off the tee, so if you're playing from the tips, go ahead and take out the big stick. Just make sure you put yourself in a good spot for your second shot. Water comes into play on a few holes at this relaxed and straightforward course that should continue to improve over the next few years.

Russell Breeden: Golf Course Architect

In South Carolina's Midlands, one architect's name pops up over and over again: Russell Breeden. We spoke with the enthusiastic and active designer who will turn 80 years old in 1997. He lives near Greenville, in Mauldin.

Off the tee, a Breeden course is fair. You'll find the occasional bunker, but you'll be able to hit the driver most of the time. Greens are sometimes sloped, sometimes undulating, but almost always protected by a bunker to the front left or front right and another off to one side. Greens are usually raised, and water often comes into play.

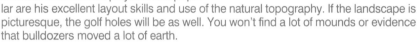

Close-up

Perhaps what makes many of Breeden's courses so playable and popu-lar are his excellent layout skills and use of the natural topography. If the landscape is picturesque, the golf holes will be as well. You won't find a lot of mounds or evidence that bulldozers moved a lot of earth.

Ironically, an architect that Breeden admires is Jack Nicklaus, one of the leading

---

Amenities at Pineview include a practice green, practice range, pro shop, snack bar and bar.

You can walk anytime on weekdays and on weekends after 2 PM. You can book any-time. Approximate cost, including cart, is $24 weekdays, $30 weekends.

Pocalla Springs Country Club
1700 U.S. Hwy. 15 S., Sumter • 481-8322

Championship Yardage: 6327	
Slope: No rating	**Par: 71**
Men's Yardage: 5582	
Slope: No rating	**Par: 71**
Ladies' Yardage: 4682	
Slope: No rating	**Par: 71**

The course at Pocalla Springs Country Club, an Eddie Riccoboni design, opened in 1955. Bermudagrass covers the fairways and greens. This layout winds along on primarily flat ground dotted with live oaks.

Pocalla Springs is a mature course that's popular with local golfers. You might take a look at the yardage from the back tees, giggle and think this is a silly track designed for "Oh honey, I'm hot today!" old-timers. Think again. According to the locals, Pocalla Springs' tight fairways, large greenside bun-kers and hard, smallish greens will flat out "eat your lunch."

You'll find five par 3s (in fact, you'll come face to face with one of them as you drive up to the clubhouse): The 14th is just 127 yards from the back tees, and the bunkers that sur-round and front the green each seem larger than the green itself — which is not much larger than a hot tub. Get the ball safely on the green and your birdie putt from the edge might be one of the shortest of your golfing life. Miss the green and you'd better know how to chip or use your sand wedge. You might want to pack away your driver in favor of a fourth wedge!

Amenities include a practice green, prac-tice range, pro shop, bar, restaurant, bever-age cart and rental clubs.

You can walk and book a round anytime. Approximate cost, including cart, is $16.

Santee National Golf Club
S.C. Hwy. 6, Santee • 854-3531

Championship Yardage: 6858	
Slope: 120	**Par: 72**
Men's Yardage: 6125	
Slope: 114	**Par: 72**
Other Yardage: 5415	
Slope: 116	**Par: 72**
Ladies' Yardage: 4748	
Slope: 116	**Par: 72**

Santee National opened in 1989 and is

proponents of modern design. Go figure. He also admires one of the hottest architects around: Tom Fazio, who lives in North Carolina.

Breeden began his golfing career as a golf course superintendent in Virginia. He "studied" golf under the Scotsman Fred Findlay — who also tutored notable architect George Cobb (see the related sidebar in our Upstate South Carolina chapter).

Breeden estimates that 75 of his designs grace courses spread across North and South Carolina, Virginia and Kentucky. Among his favorites are Persimmon Hill in the Columbia area, Possum Trot in Myrtle Beach, Lanier Country Club in Spartanburg and Sleepy Hole in Portsmouth, Virginia — a course that hosted an LPGA event for five years.

Using his experience as a former superintendent, Breeden takes pride in overseeing a course's development from initial design and layout through its opening. He's currently working on one of Charlotte's new public courses, Charlotte National, and says he's too busy to play these days.

If you've played a lot of golf in North and South Carolina, chances are you've played a Russell Breeden course. It's also a good bet that you enjoyed the course for its playability, fairness and quality of layout.

part of an upscale residential development called Chapel Creek Plantation. Porter Gibson designed the course. Bermudagrass covers the fairways, and bentgrass blankets the greens. Most holes are bordered by trees. Water, wasteland and creeks frequently come into play.

At Santee National, we found a modern yet fair course with outstanding variety. The front nine is relatively open; the back nine is more wooded and undulating than the front, which is fairly flat. The variety at Santee National makes it difficult to characterize the fairways and greens as large, medium or small. You'll see it all here! Big hitters off the tee will enjoy Santee National due to the lack of serious trouble spots adjacent to the fairways. The key to scoring well here is keeping your ball in play off the tee and hitting accurate approach shots as well as having a good day with the short game. Good chippers will have fun here. And, of course, because Santee National is modern, you'll find lots of mounds!

Amenities at Santee National include a practice green, practice range, pro shop, bar, restaurant, beverage cart and rental clubs.

Only members can walk. You can book anytime. Approximate cost, including cart, is $35 weekdays and weekends.

Pee Dee Country Golf Courses

Pee Dee Country (including Darlington, Florence, Dillon and Marion) boasts some fine golf courses in pleasant environments. You'll find a variety of layouts throughout the area and a cluster of particularly good courses around Florence and Darlington.

Golf packages are available through Pee Dee Golf, 332-2611, or Swamp Fox Golf, (800) 845-3538. These firms may be able to get you on some of the private courses in the area, including Ellis Maples' Country Club of South Carolina.

Bishopville Country Club
S.C. Hwy. 3, Bishopville • 428-3675
Championship Yardage: 6877
Slope: No rating	**Par: 72**
Men's Yardage: 6448	
Slope: No rating	**Par: 72**
Other Yardage: 5675	
Slope: No rating	**Par: 72**
Ladies' Yardage: 5620	
Slope: No rating	**Par: 73**

Bishopville Country Club opened in 1959. Bermudagrass covers the fairways and greens. Some holes are set in wooded terrain; others are wide open. The course is primarily flat. Water hazards come into play on a few holes. Improvements and renovations were completed in the fall of 1995. The course offers decent variety, sound design and the potential for a fun round.

Fairways at Bishopville are primarily wide and lack serious trouble spots, so feel free to take a big rip with the driver. Be careful, however, on the home-lined holes where the fairways narrow and the greens decrease in size. The 16th hole features what must surely be one of the smallest greens in the Carolinas.

Streams, overgrown trenches and water hazards come into play on a few holes but only pose a threat to the really wayward shot. The sloping greens are raised and flanked and protected by a variety of bunkers. A couple of the greens are domed. Large tufts of pampas grass are placed at potentially awkward positions around a few of the greens and provide a unique and potentially irritating hazard. Another interesting feature is a double green on the front nine.

Amenities at Bishopville include a practice range, putting green, chipping green, pro shop, snack bar and rental clubs.

Walking is allowed anytime. You can book anytime. Approximate cost, including cart, is $11.75 weekdays, $17 weekends.

Fox Creek Golf Club
S.C. Hwy. 151, Lydia • 332-0613
Championship Yardage: 6903
Slope: 123	**Par: 72**
Men's Yardage: 6493	
Slope: 118	**Par: 72**
Other Yardage: 5915	
Slope: 112	**Par: 72**
Ladies' Yardage: 5271	
Slope: 106	**Par: 72**

Fox Creek opened in 1987. According to the owners, a committee of architects designed the course. Bermuda 419 covers the fairways, and tifdwarf covers the greens. Most holes are set in rolling, wooded terrain, and water hazards frequently come into play.

Fox Creek has amazing variety. Perhaps the design committee was comprised of 18 individuals, each responsible for laying out a hole. The result is a track featuring just about

every design element in the book; believe us, you won't be bored at Fox Creek. In fact, you'll be challenged by the greens here. Tifdwarf is grainy, so make sure you take a look at the direction the grass is growing: It will affect your putt.

The course is completely house-free. You'll find yourself playing all sorts of shots as you navigate this wonderful track. Resist the temptation to hit the driver too much; keeping the ball in the right place at the right time is more important than pure distance.

You won't forget the 18th hole, a magnificent par 5 that doglegs left over water to a large two-tiered green. Overall, it's a playable and fun course, with distinct differences from hole to hole. We think you'll find it's well worth the trip.

Amenities include a practice range, putting and chipping greens, a pro shop, snack bar, rental clubs and the occasional beverage cart.

If you're fit, the course is walkable. However, walking is restricted to weekdays. You can book anytime. Approximate cost, including cart, is $20 weekdays, $25 weekends.

Governor's Run
665 Club Dr., Lamar • 326-5513
Championship Yardage: 6900
Slope: 130	**Par: 72**
Men's Yardage: 6211	
Slope: 121	**Par: 72**
Ladies' Yardage: 4900	
Slope: 110	**Par: 72**

Governor's Run originally opened as Lamar Country Club. A new back nine opened in January 1996. Eddie Riccoboni designed the front nine, which is relatively flat with some mild elevation changes. The back nine features more undulation, contour and water. Common bermudagrass covers the fairways, and bermudagrass 328 covers the greens. The course is set in a peaceful country environment.

The front nine is relatively wide open and features a sensible design with a lack of serious trouble. The greens are predominantly medium-size and sloped. Chipping areas surround many of the greens. Bunkers come into play on several holes. Overall, the course is relaxed, fun, straightforward and fair. You'll

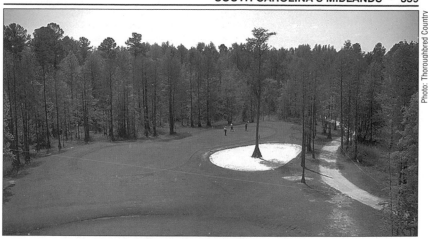

One of the challenges at Paw Paw Country Club's course is to keep the ball straight down some relatively narrow fairways.

enjoy driving the ball in this primarily wide-open design.

Amenities include a practice range, putting green, pro shop and snack bar. A new clubhouse features a bar and grill.

You can walk this course and book a round anytime. Approximate cost, including cart, is $14 weekdays, $18 weekends.

Sandy Point Golf Club

S.C. Hwy. 4, Hartsville • 335-8950
Championship Yardage: 6840
Slope: 122   **Par: 72**
Men's Yardage: 6045
Slope: 116   **Par: 72**
Ladies' Yardage: 5203
Slope: No rating   **Par: 73**

Sandy Point opened its J. B. Ammons design in 1982. Bermudagrass covers the fairways, and bentgrass covers the greens. The course is set in wooded terrain. The back nine features more of a links design than the front — a parkland design.

At Sandy Point, you'll find excellent variety, elevation changes and six holes where water comes into play. Most of the fairways are tight, so you'll need to be straight off the tee. If you play from the tips, you'll also need to be long with the big stick. Bunkers make you think about your approach shot. Once you reach the green, your short game

will be challenged by small, undulating greens. Sandy Point is popular with local golfers.

Amenities include a practice green, pro shop, locker room and snack bar.

You can walk anytime. You can book anytime too. Approximate cost, including cart, is $20 weekdays, $25 weekends.

The Traces Golf Club

4322 W. Southborough Rd., Florence • 662-7775
Championship Yardage: 7063
Slope: 123   **Par: 72**
Men's Yardage: 6449
Slope: 117   **Par: 72**
Other Yardage: 5666
Slope: 112   **Par: 72**
Ladies' Yardage: 4829
Slope: No rating   **Par: 72**

James Goodson designed The Traces Golf Club, which opened in 1991. Bermudagrass covers the fairways and greens. Some holes are set in wooded terrain; others are wide open. The course is primarily flat. Water hazards come into play on several holes. The Traces has hosted Nike Tour qualifying play as well as the Powerbilt Tour.

This course provides an excellent example of what a modern, popular golf course should be. Four sets of tees challenge all levels of golfer. The greens are massive and relatively easy to hit. There's potential trouble off the tee on some holes, but you'll be rewarded on most if you keep your ball in play. Mounds are present but don't get in the way. The scenery is pretty, especially on the back nine.

The key to scoring well here is a solid short game, particularly with your putter. You may hit a green and still have a 75-foot downhill slider. We watched one foursome on a par 3 hit decent but not perfect shots, all of which landed on the green. Getting the ball down in two was not as easy. The 12th and 13th holes are unforgettable. On No. 12, if you're playing from the back, you'll need all you have off the tee: The hole measures 471 yards. But the fairway is wide enough to be fair and allow you to hit the driver.

The facility is well-run. If you're in the area, make sure you play this course; it's worth the drive from Columbia.

Amenities include a practice range, practice green, chipping green, pro shop, snack bar, beverage cart and rental clubs.

The course is walkable, although the back nine is a trek; walking is restricted on the weekends. You can book anytime. Approximate cost, including cart, is $24 weekdays, $31 weekends.

Olde English District Golf Courses

Olde English District (including Cheraw, Camden, Chester and Lancaster) is so named because the area was a significant base for the British Army in the Revolutionary War. It's dotted with a number of fine golf courses. Cheraw State Park's modern course is probably the one you'll want to play the most. Two of the three Springs Industries-owned courses, in Lancaster and Chester, are fine traditional courses worth a visit.

Note: Courses in the Fort Mill area and to the north are reviewed in N.C.'s Charlotte Region chapter of this book.

Cheraw State Park
S.C. Hwy. 52, Cheraw • 537-0160, (800) 868-9630
Championship Yardage: 6928
Slope: 130   **Par: 72**
Men's Yardage: 6129
Slope: 120   **Par: 72**
Ladies' Yardage: 5408
Slope: No rating   **Par: 72**

Cheraw State Park boasts a modern course designed by Tom Jackson. And since it's part of the park, you can camp nearby should you be a golfer who prefers a night spent in a tent versus a dry, comfortable and air-conditioned motel room with a big TV and large selection of stations. Fairways are bermudagrass, and the greens are bentgrass, although they may be changed to bermudagrass in the near future. Laid out in a magnificent pine forest (with no houses in sight), the course is set on undulating terrain and poses several water hazards, including a significant lake.

FYI
Unless otherwise noted, the area code for all phone numbers in this chapter is 803.

In this age of wholesale government downsizing, Cheraw State Park is a rare example of successful government intervention. Based on this effort, we can only hope that the State of South Carolina's budget includes significant earmarks for additional golf courses!

We believe you'd be hard-pressed to find a better course in this area. Its modern design includes the obligatory mounds, big bunkers and water plus large, undulating greens that will test your sanity and patience. The course features a number of doglegs. Its variety is evident around the greens; you'll find different contours and extensive bunkering.

The backbreaker hole is the 13th, a 492-yard par 4 (that's not a misprint). The hole doglegs left down a hill. Assuming you hit your drive 325 yards, you'll be faced with a long and significantly downhill approach shot to a shallow green fronted by water and backed by a cavernous bunker. Hit it hot and you're flying over the green. Hit it fat and you're in the drink. Good luck!

Make a daytrip from Charlotte, Columbia or wherever; it will be worth it. It might be of interest to some golfers that Cheraw is the home of jazz great Dizzy Gillespie.

Amenities include a practice green, chipping green, pro shop, snack bar, practice range, locker room and rental clubs. The clubhouse is particularly impressive.

The course is a hike, but you can walk anytime. You can book up to a year in advance. Approximate cost, including cart, is $24 weekdays, $26 weekends.

Chester Golf Club

S.C. Hwy. 9, Chester • 581-5733
Championship: 6811
Slope: No rating	**Par: 72**
Men's Yardage: 6273	
Slope: No rating	**Par: 72**
Other Yardage: 5816	
Slope: 112	**Par: 72**
Ladies' Yardage: 5347	
Slope: No rating	**Par: 72**

Chester Golf Club, designed by Russell Breeden, opened in the early 1970s. The fairways are bermudagrass, and the greens are bentgrass. Holes are mixed between wooded terrain and flat, open stretches. Water hazards come into play on eight holes. The greens are slightly raised, sloped and undulating. As you might expect with a Breeden course, each green is strategically protected by a couple of bunkers.

Chester Golf Club is part of the Springs Industries triumvirate of golf courses. We think the track is one of Breeden's better designs in that it makes tremendous use of the land. Hole after hole is magnificently framed by a backdrop of mature pines and hardwoods.

Dare we recommend that you make the trip from Charlotte or Columbia? Yes, of course we do! We ran into a number of regulars in the pro shop who were justifiably enthusiastic about their course. There's plenty of variety here, without modern trickery. And there are no houses to avoid.

The course closes with a bang, as you must smack the ball a long way over water with your second shot, even with a good drive. The fairways vary in width, but the course allows and almost encourages you to bring out your big weapon on a few excellent driving holes. Chester is a thoroughly sensible and completely fair course in a wonderful setting.

Walking is allowed (and you should walk) on weekdays and after 1 PM on weekends.

You can book on Monday for the weekend. Approximate cost, including cart, is $24 weekdays, $31 weekends.

Green River Country Club

Country Club Rd., Chesterfield • 623-2233
Championship Yardage: 6706
Slope: No rating	**Par: 72**
Men's Yardage: 6257	
Slope: No rating	**Par: 72**
Ladies' Yardage: 5328	
Slope: No rating	**Par: 73**

The full 18-hole layout opened at Green River Country Club in 1982. The members designed the back nine; R. C. Goodson designed the front, which opened in roughly 1965. The course is set on rolling wooded terrain. Bermudagrass covers the fairways and greens.

The front nine at Green River is spectacularly understated and straightforward — you'll look at the course and think, "I'll devour this track." The fairways are wide open. A couple of holes bring water into play. Hit the driver on most holes but be accurate — your second shot will have to avoid bunkers and reach the right part of the green for a birdie attempt. You'll use almost every club in the bag, yet the course comes without all the trappings of the modern layout. Chipping areas flank the greens — a nice touch.

With your score card reading two under and a hot dog firmly planted in your stomach, it's time to tackle the back nine — somewhat different from the front, though still fair. For starters, there are many more doglegs. The fairways are more rolling though still fairly wide. The greens vary in shape and size. The most difficult hole on the course is a terrifying par 5 that features a pond at the bottom of a large downslope. (If possible, enlist the guidance of a member who knows how to score par.) Overall, the back nine is more challenging, primarily due to the elevation changes and all the water. Still, the course is a lot of fun; try to visit if you're in the area.

Amenities include a practice green, practice range, pro shop and snack bar.

Walking is allowed mostly on weekdays. You can book anytime. Approximate cost, including cart, is $17 weekdays, $27 weekends.

South Carolina's temperate climate makes for enjoyable golfing throughout the year.

Lancaster Golf Club

Airport Rd., Lancaster • 285-5239
Championship Yardage: 6553

Slope: No rating	**Par: 72**
Men's Yardage: 6140	
Slope: No rating	**Par: 72**
Ladies' Yardage: 5017	
Slope: No rating	**Par: 73**

The front nine at Lancaster Golf Club opened in the 1930s. The course added a back nine more recently. The course is one of three Springs Industries courses. Bermudagrass covers the fairways, and bentgrass covers the greens. *Architects of Golf* lists Donald Ross as the initial designer; Russell Breeden redesigned the track.

The course is well-kept and boasts a solid design that wanders through some beautiful woodlands. It's mainly flat, save a few minor elevation changes. The fairways are predominantly wide, and water only comes into play on three holes, including the 7th — an island green. Bunkers abound around the greens, so it's important to consider them if you play aggressively. Lancaster also boasts a golf ball-stealing fox.

Lancaster offers an on-site meeting and banquet facility. Other amenities include a practice range, practice green and snack bar.

Walking is restricted on the weekends. You can book up to three days in advance. Ap-proximate cost, including cart, is $29 week-days, $32 weekends.

White Pines

614 Mary Ln., Camden • 432-7442
Championship Yardage: 6373

Slope: 115	**Par: 72**
Men's Yardage: 5848	
Slope: 111	**Par: 72**
Ladies' Yardage: 4806	
Slope: 102	**Par: 72**

White Pines opened in 1969. We could not determine the designer, so drop us a line us if you know. Bermudagrass covers the greens and fairways. The layout is mostly open and hilly.

To score well at White Pines, you must keep your ball in play. To do so, avoid the numerous ditches and water hazards; they have a yen for dimpled eggs. The greens vary in size, and most are undulating. Some are raised, and all are protected in some fashion by bunkers. It helps to be accurate from tee to green. Overall, we found a relaxed setting for a fun round of golf.

Amenities include a practice range, putting green, pro shop, snack bar, locker room and rental clubs.

Walking is allowed primarily on weekdays. You can book up to 10 days in advance. Ap-proximate cost, including cart, is $24 week-days, $31 weekends.

White Plains Country Club
White Plains Church Rd., Pageland
• 672-7200

Championship Yardage: 6353

Slope: 117	Par: 72
Men's Yardage: 5874	
Slope: No rating	Par: 72
Ladies' Yardage: 4602	
Slope: No rating	Par: 72

White Plains, an Eddie Riccoboni design, opened in 1968. Bermudagrass covers the fairways, and bentgrass is used on the greens. The layout is open and undulating, with trees bordering the course and defining the fairways.

At this friendly course, we found a playable and mostly straightforward track. In the heat of summer, White Plains, due to its openness, becomes white hot. The layout is sensible yet challenging, short yet demanding. The fairways are generally wide enough to let you pull out the driver. Greens are fairly large and primarily flat yet gently sloped. You'll end up using most of the clubs in your bag. If you get in trouble, you can only blame yourself (or your clubs, your job or whatever political party you don't like). Overall, this is a fun course that can be as easygoing or as intense as you want it to be.

Amenities include a practice range, putting green, chipping green, pro shop, snack bar and rental clubs.

Walking is allowed primarily on weekdays. You can book up to three days in advance. Approximate cost, including cart, is $25 weekdays, $30 weekends.

Around the Midlands . . .

Fun Things To Do

There's plenty to see and do in the Midlands if you've left your clubs or desire to play golf behind. Don't believe it? Read on.

In Columbia, the **Greater Columbia Convention and Visitors Bureau** at 301 Gervais Street should be your first stop. There's plenty of information and advice as well as historical and audiovisual exhibits. This is also the site of the **South Carolina State Museum**. By appointment only, you can tour the **Governor's Mansion** (800 Richland Street)

on Tuesdays, Wednesdays and Thursdays. Call 737-3000.

On weekdays, you can tour the **State House** (734-2323), where the legislature of South Carolina convenes. The **Columbia Museum of Art**, 799-2810, is at the junction of Senate and Bull streets. There's also the **Movietonews Film Library**, 777-7000, in the McKissick Museum at The University of South Carolina .

The **Fort Jackson Museum**, 782-7668, in Fort Jackson is open from Tuesday through Sunday. And if you've got the kids with you, don't miss one of the finest zoos in the country: **Columbia Riverbanks Zoo**, 779-8730, is about a mile west of Columbia off I-126/U.S. Highway 76 (take the Greystone Riverbanks Exit). No one is admitted after 4 PM.

Two **steeplechase races** take place in Camden each year — one in the fall and one in the spring. **Camden** is a beautiful small town, with quaint shops and restaurants.

Cheraw is another picturesque town, with a number of historical buildings. Old **St. David's Episcopal Church** on Market Street, 537-3832, for example, dates back to 1770. **Cheraw State Park** on U.S. 1 offers camping, fishing, picnicking, lake swimming, rental boats, a bridle trail (that's horses, not newlyweds) and rental cottages. Call 537-3033 for more information.

If you're in **Aiken**, and you like horses, visit the **Thoroughbred Hall of Fame**, 649-7770, in Hopeland Gardens (the city park) at the junction of Whiskey Road and Dupree Place. You might also enjoy the **Aiken County Museum**, 642-2015.

For more information about the Aiken area, contact Thoroughbred Country, P.O. Box 850, Aiken, South Carolina, 29802, 649-2248.

If you're in the **Pee Dee** area on Labor Day, spend a day at the **Southern 500** NASCAR Race that's held at Darlington Raceway on Hartsville Highway, 393-5442 — the track they call "The Lady in Black." You might want to visit the **NMPA Stock Car Hall of Fame/Joe Weatherly Museum**, 393-2103, in Darlington on S.C. Highway 34 next to the raceway.

In **Florence**, there's the **Florence Air and Missile Museum** on U.S. Highway 301 N., 665-5118, the **Florence Museum** at Spruce

Street, 662-3351, and the **Francis Marion College Planetarium** on U.S. 301 N., 661-1362.

For more information about the Pee Dee area, contact the **Pee Dee Tourism Commission** at 669-0950.

In the **Santee-Cooper** area, **Lake Marion** and **Lake Moultrie** offer some of the best fishing and watersports opportunities in South Carolina. (There are fish camps dotted throughout the region for great dining).

In **Orangeburg**, visit the **Orangeburg Arts Center**, 536-4074, on Riverside Drive and the **Orangeburg National Fish Hatchery**, 534-4828, on U.S. Highway 21 bypass south of Orangeburg.

Sumter offers car racing at the **Sumter Speedway** on Wedgefield Road, 481-3499, the **Sumter County Museum** on North Washington Street, 775-0908, and the **Sumter Gallery of Art** on North Main Street, 775-0543.

For further information about the Santee-Cooper area, contact the **Santee-Cooper Counties Promotion Commission** at 854-2131. Call toll-free from outside South Carolina, (800) 227-8510.

Where to Eat

We're going to direct you to some restaurants that provide a welcome flair and diversion from the chain-run culinary scenery that tends to dominate this area. Refer to our Preface for an explanation of the pricing code.

Columbia Area

Blue Marlin
$$$ • 1200 Lincoln St., Columbia • 799-3838

Bill Duke's latest effort is this retro-ambiance restaurant with dark wood paneling and some of the best Lowcountry cooking you'll find outside the Lowcountry. You'll also find steaks and pasta on the menu. How about shrimp and grits for your out-of-town guests? Or you might try the deviled crab or the plump oysters. Finish the meal with a homemade cobbler. You won't need a reservation — and you should dress down, not up. Relax.

The Capitol Cafe
$ • 1210 Main St., Columbia • 765-0176

Just a smooth wedge from the shadow of the State Capitol building sits the Capitol Cafe where you'll feel like you've stepped back in time a few years. You get the sense that the comfortable booths have hosted many a heated political conversation or that quite a few "I'll scratch your back if you scratch mine . . . and pass the mustard" deals have been made here. The menu offers home favorites, ranging from toast to K.C. Sirloin steak (how's that for spanning the gastronomic gamut?). Conversation here centers of the fortunes of the University of South Carolina football team, debauchery, politics and the latest news from The Citadel.

Hennessy's Restaurant and Lounge
$$$ • Main and Blanding Sts., Columbia • 799-8280

At Hennessy's, you'll be instantly impressed with the fine ambiance created by white tablecloths and linens. This is a downtown restaurant where you can have a good old-fashioned culinary blowout. And you won't be disappointed. Begin with Oysters Rockefeller or Maryland crab cake. Move on to she-crab soup, then to Steak au Poivre or Shrimp Hennessy. Follow it all with something from the dessert tray. You won't be disappointed. There's also a variety of beer, wine and liquor. Go for it. But before you do, make a reservation.

Longhorn Steaks, Restaurant and Saloon
$$ • 902-A Gervais St., Columbia • 254-5100

This Texas-style eatery is perfect for a casual evening in a fun and laughter-filled environment. Devour a steak or try some uniquely prepared salmon — Longhorn style.

The Sherlock Holmes
$ • 1440 Main St., Columbia • 779-3659

Head down a short flight of stairs and you might think you're walking onto the set of "Cheers" — only this place is slightly smaller and without the highly paid actors. Relax with a cold beer or engage in somewhat raucous conversation. Or hunker down and munch a tasty lunch from the pub-fare menu. Sherlock's specialty is a juicy pot roast, thinly sliced, served on a French roll with melted Swiss cheese and accompanied by dipping sauce. Or you might try the veggie lasagna. Wash it down with a couple of Killian's Red ales. Good food, I presume, Watson?

Aiken Area

No. 10 Downing Street
$$$ • 241 Laurens St. S.W., Aiken • 642-9062

This is not an English restaurant, despite the fact that the previous owners named this place after the official residence of the Prime Minister of the United Kingdom due to their fondness for Sir Winston Churchill (a fellow alum of one of us). The ambiance of No. 10 is defined by the four cozy dining rooms with fireplaces. The culinary excellence is defined by a menu that changes monthly. No. 10 Downing Street is famous for lunchtime soups and desserts, rack of lamb and shrimp and scallop feta served over linguine. You'll also find an excellent range of fresh fish entrees. The restaurant offers a full wine list and liquor drinks too.

Olive Oils Restaurant
$$ • 233 Chesterfield St., Aiken • 649-3726

Italian fare dominates the menu at Olive Oils. You'll find staple basics such as lasagna, spaghetti, fettuccine and the like. But if you're feeling more adventuresome, try something like the Trout Italiano (baked trout served with anchovies, onions, carrots and a special selection of secret seasonings). Or have a go at the stuffed veal chops or the filet mignon. The menu also includes a full range of fresh seafood. Olive oils is open for dinner only.

Santee-Cooper Area

The Chestnut Grill
$$ • 1455 Chestnut St. N.E., Orangeburg • 531-1747

The Chestnut Grill used to be called Mr. Steak and, as that name implied, red meat is one of the more popular menu options. You'll find USDA choice steaks and prime rib plus tasty seafood and a remarkably extensive wine

list, a full range of beer and spirits. There's a children's menu as well.

Cole's Family Restaurant and Cafeteria
$$ • 1000 Broad St., Sumter • 773-5664

Cole's is somewhat something of a Sumter institution. It's one of those wonderful (and inexpensive) restaurants where you'll find large helpings of home cooked meals plus a number of super-friendly waitresses who probably served the parents of the current generation of Cole's attendees. Sit down and enjoy a hearty breakfast of bacon and pancakes, or settle in for a feast consisting of prime rib, steaks, seafood, chicken, Italian dishes and many a tasty pork chop. There's a banquet room and a full selection of basic beer and wine offerings. Breakfast is full service from 6 am to 10 am. The cafeteria option is open for lunch and dinner Monday to Saturday and for brunch on Sunday.

Georgio's Pizza
$$ • 344 Pinewood Rd., Sumter • 775-7325

Located in the spacious Savannah Plaza, Georgio's has been a local pizza and pasta hangout since 1978. Plenty of those locals have taken out one of the wonderful and extensive 5 ft. party subs that can be the centerpiece of any party. Or better still, you should sit down to a wonderful pizza with a thin crust and just about any type of topping imaginable. The menu says that the dough here is made from an "old recipe." That's what makes it so tasty.

There's a variety of subs and gyros in addition to a number of delicious pasta dishes ranging including lasagna and spaghetti. Try the souvlaki if you're not completely satiated with a large pizza. Or try some a salad or one of the other Greek or Italian items on the menu. Georgio's also offers a full beer and wine selection.

House of Pizza
$$ • 910 Calhoun Rd., Orangeburg • 531-4000

Greek-owned and operated, the "Kali Orexi" is a great place for pizza as well as subs, sandwiches, salads, gyros, souvlaki, shish kabob and baklava. Round out your meal with a draft beer or a glass of Italian wine. You'll find another House of Pizza at 1338 Grove Park Road.

Pee Dee Area

Corona
$$ • 2029 W. Evans St., Florence
• 665-6508

Mexican food in Florence? You better believe it! After your round of golf, what better way to spend your winnings on a large margarita followed by a really massive bowl of chips and salsa followed by a creme burrito. Your winnings don't have to be too great here for you to enjoy yourself to the max at what we believe might be the only Mexican restaurant in the Florence area. Corona also offers a full range of vegetarian dishes. It's open for lunch Monday and Friday and dinner every night of the week.

The Country Barn Restaurant
$ • S.C. Hwy. 151, Darlington • 395-2257

The Country Barn restaurant presents an array of country cooking in its Country Cooking BUFFET (their caps). It's open Thursday to Saturday evenings from 11 AM to 9 PM and from 11 AM to 3 PM on Sundays. Also sample the salad bar and dessert bar. Things get really exciting on Friday for the sumptuous seafood buffet. The Country Barn also claims to be a "BBQ Specialist." Bring all the appetite you can muster.

Town House Restaurant
$$-$$$ • 317 S. Irby, Florence • 669-5083

Open for lunch and dinner from Monday to Saturday and located next to the public library, the Town House Restaurant is a fine place for a full variety of standard favorites. There're grilled chicken, fried chicken, flounder, shrimp, juicy hamburgers, barbecue, steaks, sandwiches and tremendously greasy onion rings. We can't guarantee that you'll lose weight here, but you'll certainly leave full.

Olde English District

Lui's Inn Chinese Restaurant
$ • 807 Market St., Cheraw • 537-4889

You might not think of Cheraw as a place to find an outstanding, albeit small, Chinese

restaurant; but Lui's Inn fits the bill. Just a few minutes from the challenging golf course at Cheraw State Park, you'll find all your favorite Chinese dishes, such as hot and sour soup and General Chicken (he must have been the one who ran away). We suggest you try the surprisingly good shrimp curry. For those of you who love cheap (and tasty) Chinese cuisine, you'll be right at home.

The Paddock Restaurant and Pub
$$ • 514 Rutledge St., Camden • 432-3222

Camden is well known for its steeplechase, so it makes perfect sense that one of its better restaurants is called The Paddock. In addition to a range of drinking options, The Paddock offers a diverse menu that includes soups, salads, pizza, steaks, seafood (try the linguine in clam sauce) and chicken dishes — even lamb chops. If you can't find anything on the menu that excites you, you'd better check your pulse.

Where to Stay

There is no shortage of places to stay in the Midlands. Every motel chain you've ever heard of has a large presence, and you'll find some independent players as well. Refer to our Preface for an explanation of the pricing code.

Columbia Area

Adam's Mark Hotel
$$$$ • 1200 Hampton St., Columbia
• 771-7000

This large, full-service hotel is right in the heart of downtown Columbia. You'll find a spacious room complete with one king-size or two double beds, color cable TV and a concierge lounge where continental breakfast is served daily. You'll also find a pool and a Jacuzzi. On-site meeting facilities, a gift shop, secretarial services and a health club round out the amenities. Inquire about golf packages.

Claussen's Inn
$$$$ • 2003 Green St., Columbia
• 765-0440

Claussen's is a Columbia landmark. This bed and breakfast inn is in the heart of Five Points near the USC campus and the State

Capitol. Rates include continental breakfast and turndown service, with chocolates and complimentary wine, sherry and brandy in the lobby.

Courtyard by Marriott
$$ • 347 Zimalcrest Dr., Columbia
• 731-2300

This no-frills, down-to-earth lodging is convenient to Columbia's main thoroughfares. Amenities include a whirlpool, an outdoor pool, in-room coffee makers and ironing boards, cable TVs with pay-per-view movies plus a restaurant that's open for lunch and dinner. If you want to do some laundry, your detergent is free.

Embassy Suites
$$$$ • I-126 at Greystone Blvd., Columbia
• 252-8700

The seven-story atrium makes this one of the most visually arresting hotels in the Columbia area. There's a complimentary cocktail reception in the evening, and breakfast is included in your room rate. In the room, you'll find a coffee maker and color cable TV. The hotel offers golf packages.

Super 8 Motel
$ • 2516 Augusta Rd., West Columbia
• 796-4833

Clean, sensibly priced and convenient to Downtown Columbia and the University of South Carolina, West Columbia's Super 8 Motel boasts 88 rooms, which must make it popular among numerologists and bingo players everywhere. You'll find a choice of rooms, some with double beds, others with king-size beds. The room rate includes cable TV with free Showtime and ESPN, plus access to the swimming pool. Group rates and Senior Citizen discounts are available as well.

Super 8 Motel
$ • 5719 Fairfield Rd., Columbia
• 735-0008

Four miles from Downtown Columbia and 4 miles from Fort Jackson is Columbia's newest Super 8 Motel, built in mid-1996. Most importantly, it's less than 2 miles from one of Columbia's better public golf courses: Oak Hill.

Golf packages are available. The motel offers 43 rooms, including a Jacuzzi suite, whirlpool suite and several king suites. Non-smoking rooms are available. The price of admission here (which is reasonable) includes continental breakfast plus cable TV (with HBO and ESPN).

Aiken Area

Best Western Aiken
$$ • 3560 Richland Ave., Aiken • 649-3968

Within easy striking distance of beautiful downtown Aiken, this Best Western offers microwaves, TVs, refrigerators and coffee makers as well as VCRs and movie rentals. Some rooms even have Jacuzzis. Amenities include a lounge, continental breakfast and meeting facilities. Note that the price increases somewhat the week The Masters is played.

FYI

Unless otherwise noted, the area code for all phone numbers in this chapter is 803.

Comfort Suites Aiken
$$ • 3608 Richland Ave. W., Aiken • 641-1100

Tired after a long day in business meetings? Have a bad day on the course? Consider the small extra investment that will get you a Jacuzzi suite here. You'll also have a TV with cable in the room, and the price of admission includes access to the swimming pool and the weight room. The hotel offers full corporate meeting facilities.

Holley Inn
$$ • 235 Richland Ave., Aiken • 648-4265

When in Aiken, check out the charming Holley Inn — a place so old that the elevator is hand-operated, and the floorboards in the hallways are uneven. Relax in the courtyard or sip a drink in the bar. The service in the Holley Inn Restaurant will remind you of a bygone era — when hotel guests were treated like royalty.

Santee-Cooper Area

Best Western Orangeburg
$$ • 475 John C. Calhoun Dr., Orangeburg
• 534-7630

The Best Western Orangeburg is a modern and convenient motel. The moderate room rate includes continental breakfast, cable TV

Photo: Josh Gibson

Santee National's course offers outstanding variety.

with Showtime and access to the swimming pool. A conference room is also available should you want to organize a meeting.

Pee Dee Area

The Inn Downtown
$$ • 121 W. Palmetto St., Florence • 662-6341

The Inn Downtown is yet another of Florence's many hotels and motels offering good value. This 110-unit property offers spa-

cious rooms and suites, fax service, a restaurant that's open for lunch, a bar, transportation to the airport, banquet rooms and cable TV (with HBO and ESPN). As the name implies, the Inn Downtown is extremely close to downtown Florence.

Swamp Fox Inn
$ • I-95 and U.S. Hwy. 76, Florence • 665-0803

The Swamp Fox Inn is a self-confessed "mom and pop" hotel where you'll find a clean comfortable room at an extraordinary price. Along with your approximately $25, you'll be situated in one of the 60 rooms. You'll also get free cable TV (with HBO and ESPN) and access to the restaurant, which serves meals from six in the morning until nine at night. There's a pool, and the hotel can help with you golf packages to many of the fine collection of local courses.

Olde English District

Days Inn Cheraw
$ • 820 Market St., Cheraw • 537-5554

The Days Inn Cheraw offers a comfortable place to stay in the town that's best known in the jazz world as the birthplace of Dizzy Gillespie. You won't find much about Dizzy here at the Days Inn, but you will be provided with a clean room and all the cable TV (with HBO) you care to watch. Other amenities include an outdoor pool and a daily continental breakfast.

Holiday Inn of Camden
$$ • U.S. Hwys. 1 and 601, Lugoff
• 438-9441

The Holiday Inn Camden is actually just down the road in Lugoff, but it's near enough to Camden to warrant its name. The price of your room includes cable TV, access to an exercise room and a full breakfast buffet. If you're hungry, thirsty and in the mood for a dance, head for Plum's Restaurant and Lounge.

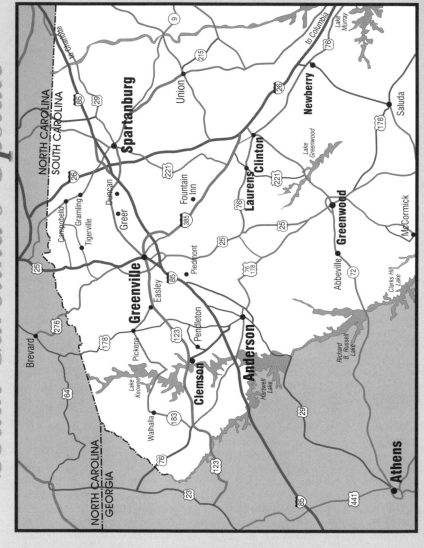

South Carolina's Upstate

South Carolina's Upstate

As you might expect in a state that's renowned for its high-quality golf courses, Upstate South Carolina is endowed with a fine portfolio of public-access tracks. First, for the sake of clarity, let's define the Upstate: We've included the Greenville-Spartanburg area all the way down to the Greenwood-Abbeville area that borders Georgia.

The Upstate possesses some fine scenery. The southern reaches of the Appalachian Mountains dip into this area, giving some of the courses a distinctly mountainous feel. The area around Greenville is lush and rolling, providing an excellent landscape for the golf course architect.

The Upstate is well-known for economic development and success. BMW recently built a massive factory in Greer. You can see it as you drive down I-85 from Spartanburg to Greenville. It's quite a sight. A number of enterprises have moved to the area or have sprung up as a direct result of the new facility. Aside from the manufacture of the chariot James Bond drove in the most recent 007 flick (a BMW Z3), the Upstate maintains a strong and diverse industrial base. Everywhere you go, it seems there's a factory or a distribution facility just around the corner. And more are coming. Fuji, for instance, just opened a plant outside Greenwood. Clearly, Upstaters are hard-working and prosperous.

They also like to play golf — on good courses. We played a number of fine tracks designed by notable architects Tom Jackson, Russell Breeden, Gary Player, P.B. Dye,

George Cobb and Willie B. Lewis. In fact, Breeden, Jackson and Lewis make their homes in the area, and George Cobb lived here.

The area course that's on everyone's must-play list is The Cliffs at Glassy, a Tom Jackson design north of Greenville. The Cliffs is private, but it's worth your while to try to make friends with a member. If you can't get on The Cliffs, don't worry — you'll find plenty of other high-quality courses in the area.

A note about greens fees: As with all courses in the Carolinas, where golf is a year-round activity, expect seasonal variations and occasional discounts.

FYI

Unless otherwise noted, the area code for all phone numbers in this chapter is 864.

Bonnie Brae Golf Course

1316 Fork Shoals Rd., Greenville
• 277-9838

Championship Yardage: 6579	
Slope: 115	**Par: 72**
Men's Yardage: 6255	
Slope: 113	**Par: 72**
Ladies' Yardage: 5468	
Slope: 116	**Par: 74**

Bonnie Brae Golf Course opened in 1961. According to staff, Charles Willimon designed the course, which is set on wooded and mostly undulating terrain. You'll find bermudagrass in the fairways and on the greens.

Charles Willimon may not be the best-known architect in the great golfing state of South Carolina. That doesn't matter. Bonnie Brae's course proves it doesn't require a big-name architect to create a fun, sensible and varied track: large, small and midsize greens in unique and interesting shapes; no two bun-

GOLF COURSES IN SOUTH CAROLINA'S UPSTATE REGION

Name	Type	# Holes	Par	Slope	Yards	Walking	Booking	Cost w/ Cart
Bonnie Brae Golf Course	semiprivate	18	72	113	6255	anytime	7 days	$24-27
Boscobel Golf Club	semiprivate	18	72	n/r	6184	anytime	2 days	$22-26
Carolina Springs Golf and CC								
Pines/Cedars Course	semiprivate	18	72	122	6248	anytime	5 days	$25-30
Pines/Willows Course	semiprivate	18	72	120	6416	anytime	5 days	$25-30
Cedars/Willows Course	semiprivate	18	72	117	6204	anytime	5 days	$25-30
Clemson University	public	18	72	n/a	6911	anytime	anytime	$32-44
Cobb's Glen Country Club	semiprivate	18	72	120	6470	restricted	2 days	$30-35
Cotton Creek Golf Club	semiprivate	18	72	113	6170	anytime	anytime	$20-25
Falcon's Lair	semiprivate	18	72	119	6444	anytime	7 days	$22-25
The Gauntlet Golf Club	semiprivate	18	72	130	6233	anytime	5 days	$25-30
Greer Golf and Country Club	public	18	72	116	5730	anytime	anytime	$25-28
Hickory Knob	public	18	72	n/r	5951	anytime	anytime	$22-26
Hunter's Creek								
Maple/Willow Course	semiprivate	18	72	n/r	6407	restricted	7 days	$26-35
Willow/Oak Course	semiprivate	18	72	n/r	6301	restricted	7 days	$26-35
Oak/Maple Course	semiprivate	18	72	n/r	6376	restricted	3 days	$26-35
Lakeview Golf Club	Semiprivate	18	72	110	6016	anytime	3 days	$20-23
Links O'Tryon	semiprivate	18	72	122	6230	restricted	2 days	$35-45
Oak Ridge Country Club	semiprivate	18	72	111	5487	anytime	2 days	$20-25
Parkland Golf Club	semiprivate	18	72	120	6140	anytime	anytime	$13-22
Peach Valley Golf Club	public	18	70	92	5925	anytime	anytime	$17-21
Pickens Country Club	semiprivate	18	72	117	5966	anytime	2 days	$25-30
River Chase	semiprivate	18	71	114	6086	anytime	anytime	$39-49
River Falls Plantation	semiprivate	18	72	121	6238	no	anytime	$32-41
Rolling Green Golf Club (27 holes)								
First & Second Nines	semiprivate	18	71	118	5635	anytime	7 days	$21-23
Southern Oaks Golf Club	semiprivate	18	72	115	6449	anytime	2-7 days	$27-32
Stoney Pointe	semiprivate	18	72	117	6129	anytime	7 days	$25-30
Summersett	semiprivate	18	72	108	5420	restricted	anytime	$21-26
Table Rock	resort/semiprivate	18	72	114	6038	anytime	anytime	$19-23
Village Green Country Club	public	18	72	117	5873	anytime	2 days	$20-25
Verdae Greens Golf Club	semiprivate/resort	18	72	118	6249	restricted	7 days	$35-45
Willow Creek Golf Course	public	18	72	n/r	6222	restricted	5 days	$29-34

kers look the same; fairways are wide in some places, narrow in others. It's difficult to characterize this course, which is why it's popular with local golfers.

Willimon's design starts off with a bang: a 457-yard par 4. Bunkers are strategically placed on quite a few holes and influence approach shots to the sloped greens. On some holes, the superintendent left chipping areas. Water comes into play on a few holes but won't ruin your day unless you're hitting the ball just terribly. There's nothing earth-shattering or jaw-dropping about this course, but it's certainly worth a look if you're in the mood for a relaxed round on a well-designed, mature track.

Amenities include a practice green, range, snack bar, rental clubs, an occasional beverage cart and a pro shop.

The course is walkable anytime. You can book a tee time seven days in advance. Approximate cost, including cart, is $24 weekdays and $27 on weekends.

Boscobel Golf Club
U.S. Hwy. 76, Pendleton • 646-3991
Championship Yardage: 6449
Slope: No rating   **Par: 72**
Men's Yardage: 6184
Slope: No rating   **Par: 72**
Other Yardage: 5776
Slope: No rating   **Par: 72**
Ladies' Yardage: 5023
Slope: No rating   **Par: 72**

Boscobel opened in the 1930s. *Architects of Golf* lists Fred Bolton as the original designer, although Russell Breeden worked on the course as well. You'll find bermudagrass fairways and bentgrass greens set on rolling terrain.

Boscobel is a mature course, with plenty of established trees. According to the locals, the course is "sneaky long" and plays every bit of its 6500 yards from the tips. You'll have to use all your clubs and marshal your short-game skills, considering the greens are predominantly small to midsize. You'll have plenty of tricky and downright difficult putts on these greens. The fairways vary in width. The front nine is hilly; the back is slightly flatter. And water is a factor on three holes. The course provides good value and is convenient to the Clemson area.

Amenities include a practice green, locker room, bar, snack bar and pro shop.

Walk anytime you wish. You won't need a tee time during the week, and you can book for the weekend on Thursday. Approximate cost, including cart, is $22 weekdays and $26 on weekends.

Carolina Springs Golf and Country Club
1680 Scuffletown Rd., Fountain Inn
• 862-3551

Pines/Cedars Course
Championship Yardage: 6676
Slope: 125   **Par: 72**
Men's Yardage: 6248
Slope: 122   **Par: 72**
Other Yardage: 5833
Slope: 116   **Par: 72**
Ladies' Yardage: 5084
Slope: 116   **Par: 72**

Pines/Willows Course
Championship Yardage: 6815
Slope: 123   **Par: 72**
Men's Yardage: 6416
Slope: 120   **Par: 72**
Other Yardage: 5988
Slope: 113   **Par: 72**
Ladies' Yardage: 5084
Slope: 119   **Par: 72**

Cedars/Willows Course
Championship Yardage: 6643
Slope: 121   **Par: 72**
Men's Yardage: 6204
Slope: 117   **Par: 72**
Other Yardage: 5773
Slope: 113   **Par: 72**
Ladies' Yardage: 4996
Slope: 113   **Par: 72**

Carolina Springs opened in 1968. Russell Breeden designed this course, with bermudagrass fairways and bentgrass greens set on hilly terrain. Most of the holes are wooded, while others are open. Improvements are currently under way.

This course is somewhat typical of a Russell Breeden track: It presents plenty of difficulties while appearing straightforward. Trouble off the tee comes in the form of the occasional raised bunker. But the fun really begins with approach shots. Most of the green complexes include one, two or three bunkers;

the midsize to large greens slope to reward the bold, and you can run the ball up to the pin on quite a few holes. Each hole presents its own decision-making challenges. Water comes into play on a few holes but should only affect the truly awful shot. Play the course from the tips and you'll have your hands full.

On first inspection, there isn't a massive difference between the three courses; play them in any combination for a wonderful round.

Amenities include a practice green, range, snack bar, rental clubs, a beverage cart and pro shop.

The course is walkable anytime. You can book a tee time five days in advance. Approximate cost, including cart, is $25 weekdays and $30 on weekends.

Cobb's Glen Country Club

2201 Cobbs Way, Anderson • 226-7688
Championship Yardage: 7002
Slope: 129   **Par: 72**
Men's Yardage: 6470
Slope: 120   **Par: 72**
Other Yardage: 5952
Slope: 115   **Par: 72**
Ladies' Yardage: 5312
Slope: 121   **Par: 72**

Cobb's Glen opened in 1975. As you might expect, George Cobb designed the course, with help from John LaFoy, on rolling terrain. Houses and woods border many holes. In the fairways, you'll find bermudagrass; on the greens, bentgrass.

We found Cobb's Glen a fun, well-designed and challenging course that's well worth a visit if you're in the Clemson/Anderson area. It's a hefty course from the back tees (more than 7000 yards), so you might want to play it from the middle or front if your last name isn't Daly and your first name isn't John. If the bermudagrass rough is at all long, the fairways are narrower than they look. Adding to the trouble off the tee are numerous fairway bunkers that are ready and willing to catch your ball. The greens are mostly large and undulating. These, too, are

heavily bunkered. Water comes into play on a few holes, but the woods that border most of the holes pose more of a hazard. Cobb's Glen is mature and has a traditional feel.

Amenities include a practice green, range, locker room, bar, snack bar, restaurant, rental clubs, an occasional beverage cart and a pro shop.

The course is walkable for the physically fit, and you can walk late in the day. You can book a tee time 48 hours in advance. Approximate cost, including cart, is $35 weekdays and $40 on weekends.

Cotton Creek Golf Club

640 Keltner Blvd., Spartanburg • 583-7084
Championship Yardage: 6653
Slope: 116   **Par: 72**
Men's Yardage: 6170
Slope: 113   **Par: 72**
Ladies' Yardage: 5070
Slope: 118   **Par: 72**

Cotton Creek Golf Club opened in 1968. Russell Breeden designed this course on slightly rolling terrain, with bermudagrass fairways and greens.

Cotton Creek is a somewhat typical Breeden design. The routing and overall layout are sound. You'll find the occasional raised bunker in the fairway. The green complexes feature two or three bunkers, a pampas grass bush here and there, slightly undulating putting surfaces and some small mounds. One interesting touch is the addition of grass bunkers — a rarity on a Breeden course. Overall, this track is open, straightforward and fun, providing a venue for an enjoyable round of golf in a country setting. Keep the ball in play, smack it to the middle of the medium-size greens, two-putt, and you'll leave with a smile on your face. The back nine is a little tighter and a bit more wooded.

Amenities include a practice green, range, chipping green, locker room, bar, snack bar, restaurant, rental clubs, a beverage cart and a pro shop.

The course is walkable anytime, and you

INSIDERS' TIP

Early in the morning or late in the evening can be the best times to see the subtleties in a golf course, as shadows highlight the contour of greens and fairways.

can book a tee time whenever you choose. Approximate cost, including cart, is $20 weekdays and $25 on weekends.

Falcon's Lair

1308 Falcon's Dr., Walhalla • 638-0000
Championship Yardage: 6955
Slope: 124	**Par: 72**
Men's Yardage: 6444	
Slope: 119	**Par: 72**
Other Yardage: 5913	
Slope: 113	**Par: 72**
Ladies' Yardage: 5238	
Slope: 123	**Par: 74**

Falcon's Lair, a Harry Bowers design, opened in 1991 and features bermudagrass fairways and bentgrass greens set on undulating terrain.

After graduating from Michigan State with degrees in park planning and turf grass science, Bowers joined Robert Trent Jones as an associate designer. He supervised several new designs and remodeled others. In 1991, Bowers and Curtis Strange built Odyssey Golf Course in Illinois.

Falcon's Lair demands accuracy off the tee. Several greens are tricky, and trouble spots exist on almost every hole. There are some extremely pretty holes on this course as well.

Amenities include a practice green, range, chipping green, locker room, snack bar and rental clubs.

You can walk anytime; book a tee time up to seven days in advance. Approximate cost, including cart, is $22 weekdays and $25 on weekends.

The Gauntlet Golf Club

253 Chinquapin Rd., Tigerville • 895-6758
Championship Yardage: 6713
Slope: 135	**Par: 72**
Men's Yardage: 6233	
Slope: 130	**Par: 72**
Other Yardage: 5543	
Slope: 124	**Par: 72**
Ladies' Yardage: 4545	
Slope: 119	**Par: 72**

The Gauntlet Golf Club, a P.B. Dye design, opened in 1992. Most holes are bordered by woods, and the course is very hilly. Fairways are bermudagrass; greens are bentgrass.

The Gauntlet is one-third of a triumvirate of perilous Carolinas golf courses including The Gauntlet at St. James Plantation in Southport, North Carolina, and Myrtle West Golf Club outside North Myrtle Beach.

Just a theory, but here goes: "P.B." in P.B. Dye stands for Pin Ball, which is what your ball will behave like if you miss the green just slightly or, on occasion, if you actually hit a green.

The Greenville version of The Gauntlet is set in the foothills of the Smoky Mountains and provides one of the greatest challenges in the Upstate — a challenge that borders on the absurd in places. Earth was moved. Sands were shifted. The sky was shaken. The golfing world has never been the same. No two holes are the same either, but they're all extensively difficult. Score par on most holes and you should be extremely pleased with yourself. Each hole has a name with an Arthur and The Knights of the Round Table motif. If the course beats you up in a particularly nasty fashion, our advice is to restore your sense of humor by renting *Monty Python and the Holy Grail*.

As you might expect with a modern course, there's plenty of mounds, bunkers, steep drop-offs, water, blind shots and uneven stances. Some holes defy description. The par 5 No. 16, a 521-yard monster, looks innocent enough off the tee, but that's because the shot is uphill to a flat landing area. From there, you can lay up to a series of terraced landing areas or go for it and fire away at a massive green divided by an elephant buried in the shallowest of graves. We tried to putt from one end to the other while keeping the ball on the green — and failed miserably. You've been warned.

The Greenville-Spartanburg area is full of fine courses, but we suggest you visit here for the experience of playing a Dye course. Whether or not you'll return depends on your ability to suck up mental anguish. It's hard to imagine semi-hallucinogenic thought processes that apparently went into designing the aptly named Gauntlet.

Amenities include a practice green, range, chipping green, snack bar, rental clubs, an occasional beverage cart and a pro shop.

You'll only add injury to insult if you try to walk this course, but you can if you want to. . . . You can book a tee time five days in advance. Approximate cost, including cart, is $25 weekdays and $30 on weekends.

Courses in Upstate South Carolina provide magnificent scenery and interesting elevation changes.

Greer Golf & Country Club

2990 Gap Creek Rd., Greer • 877-9279
Championship Yardage: 6321
Slope: 121   **Par: 72**
Men's Yardage: 5730
Slope: 116   **Par: 72**
Ladies' Yardage: 5083
Slope: 110   **Par: 72**

Greer Golf & Country Club opened nine holes in 1954. The club added nine more in 1965. There's no record of any one designer. Bermudagrass covers the fairways; bentgrass, the greens.

As mentioned in this chapter's introduction, Greer is known around the world as the site of a massive BMW automotive factory. However, this friendly town is also home to a decent golf course. The track is popular with locals, many of whom find time in their schedules to work out their beer drinking muscles in the clubhouse, which is well-equipped with a few card tables and a state-of-the-art (in 1954) television.

The course is relatively straightforward until you reach the undulating greens. The fairways are tree-lined. The course has a pleasant country ambiance, well-removed from the hustle and bustle of life in the rapidly expanding and booming Greenville-Spartanburg metropolis. Have fun.

Amenities include a practice green, range, locker room, bar, snack bar, restaurant, rental clubs, a beverage cart, small-screen TV and pro shop.

The course is walkable for the physically fit, and you can walk anytime. You'll need a tee time on the weekend. Approximate cost, including cart, is $25 weekdays and $28 on weekends.

Hickory Knob State Resort Park Golf Course

Rt. 1, Box 199-B, McCormick • 391-2450
Championship Yardage: 6560
Slope: No rating   **Par: 72**
Men's Yardage: 5951
Slope: No rating   **Par: 72**
Other Yardage: 4905
Slope: No rating   **Par: 72**
Ladies' Yardage: 4905
Slope: No rating   **Par: 72**

Hickory Knob State Resort Park Golf Course opened in 1982. Tom Jackson designed the course amid rolling wooded terrain. Fairways and greens are bermudagrass.

Hickory Knob is part of McCormick State Park. We found it to be an excellent course with plenty of challenges. Here's a good example of sound government! You won't find the abundance of mounds that typically defines a Tom Jackson course; the greatness lies in the variety. You'll find greens of all sizes and shapes. Some are sloped; others pitch and roll. Bunkering is extensive, and there's plenty of water, some of which comes from the picturesque lake bordering the course.

You won't have to bang the ball a mile here to score well, but you will need to keep it in play and take what the course gives you. You'll also have to carry the ball over water on a few occasions. Just the setting alone is worth the modest price of admission. The course is a touch remote, but you'll be rewarded with a fun round on an excellent course at a great price.

Amenities include a practice green, range, chipping green, locker room, bar, snack bar and pro shop.

You can walk and book a tee time at Hickory Knob whenever you choose. Approximate cost, including cart, is $22 weekdays and $26 on weekends.

Hunter's Creek
702 Hunter's Creek Blvd., Greenwood
• 223-9286

Maple/Willow Course
Championship Yardage: 7089
Slope: No rating	Par: 72
Men's Yardage: 6407	
Slope: No rating	Par: 72
Other Yardage: 5723	
Slope: No rating	Par: 72
Ladies' Yardage: 4977	
Slope: No rating	Par: 72

Willow/Oak Course
Championship Yardage: 6927
Slope: No rating	Par: 72
Men's Yardage: 6301	
Slope: No rating	Par: 72
Other Yardage: 5704	
Slope: No rating	Par: 72
Ladies' Yardage: 4931	
Slope: No rating	Par: 72

Oak/Maple Course
Championship Yardage: 6920
Slope: No rating	Par: 72
Men's Yardage: 6376	
Slope: No rating	Par: 72
Other Yardage: 5765	
Slope: No rating	Par: 72
Ladies' Yardage: 5000	
Slope: No rating	Par: 72

The Oak nine at Hunter's Creek Plantation opened in 1995. Tom Jackson designed the course. Many of the holes are open, others are bordered by woods. You'll find bermudagrass on the greens and fairways.

All three nines are now open at Hunter's Creek. All of the courses are a modern treat complete with mounds, tough greens, big tee shots and a variety of nasty bunkers. All three nines are extremely challenging from the back tees. If you're a fan of modern and difficult courses, take the challenge at Hunter's Creek.

Amenities include a practice green, range, chipping green, bar, snack bar, restaurant, rental clubs, a beverage cart and a pro shop.

The Oak nine is walkable. You can book a tee time seven days in advance. Approximate cost, including cart, is $26 weekdays and $35 on weekends.

Lakeview Golf Club
315 Piedmont Golf Course Rd., Piedmont
• 277-2680
Championship Yardage: 6455	
Slope: 116	Par: 72
Men's Yardage: 6016	
Slope: 110	Par: 72
Ladies' Yardage: 5036	
Slope: No rating	Par: 73

Lakeview Golf Course opened in 1954. In the fairways, you'll find 419 bermudagrass; the greens are 328 bermudagrass. Although we searched high and low, we could not determine who designed this course.

Lakeview offers a fun and relaxing round in a pleasant country setting. Like its neighbor, Bonnie Brae, the course is set on gently rolling terrain. Some of the holes are wide open, while others are set in woodland. One of the first things you'll notice, depending on the time of year, is that the first fairway is cross-cut — a landscaping touch evident from the elevated tee. The greens are small to medium-size and not overly undulating. The layout is predominantly straightforward: What you see is what you get. There's a distinct lack of water and heavy bunkering. Perhaps the back nine is a little tighter than the front. The course offers enough challenge and variety to keep the novice as well as the low-handicapper happy, which may explain its popularity.

Amenities include a practice green, range, chipping green, snack bar, rental clubs and a pro shop.

You can walk the course anytime. You won't need a tee time during the week, but you will need to call on Wednesday to book for the weekend. Approximate cost, including cart, is $20 weekdays and $23 on weekends.

Links O'Tryon

11250 New Cut Rd., Campobello
• 468-4995
Championship Yardage: 6728

Slope: 130	**Par: 72**
Men's Yardage: 6230	
Slope: 122	**Par: 72**
Other Yardage: 5539	
Slope: 113	**Par: 72**
Ladies' Yardage: 5051	
Slope: 114	**Par: 72**

Links O'Tryon, a Tom Jackson design, opened in 1987. The course is set on gently rolling terrain bordered by woods and houses. You'll find bermudagrass fairways and bentgrass greens.

Links O'Tryon is well-known in the Upstate as one of the area's finest courses. For three years running, the course was voted No. 1 in Upstate South Carolina by *GolfWeek* magazine.

The course offers many Tom Jackson links-type touches. It's somewhat forgiving, even rewarding. Many of the holes are quite memorable, including the 562-yard uphill par 5 No. 8, which requires considerable heft off the tee. The hole features a small and undulating green fronted by a large, deep bunker. No. 6, a 377-yard par 4 requires an excellent tee shot to avoid the trees on the left of the fairway.

FYI

Unless otherwise noted, the area code for all phone numbers in this chapter is 864.

Perhaps this course is less penal than other Jackson designs. The open aspect that defines most of this course as well as its proximity to the foothills of the Smoky Mountains mean that wind may be a factor, accentuating the "n'ae wind, n'ae golf" links effect.

But variety is key here. You'll have to place all of your shots to score well here, and no two holes are the same — a great example of why Tom Jackson is such a well-respected architect. Bunkers come in all shapes and sizes; some are plain massive. Jackson took a page out of Robert Trent Jones' book with a couple of cloverleaf bunkers that are fun to look at but no fun to be in. Water comes into

play on a few holes, but it shouldn't pose too much of a problem unless you're very wayward.

Amenities include a practice green, range, chipping green, locker room, bar, snack bar, restaurant, rental clubs, a beverage cart and a pro shop.

The front nine is more walkable, and you can walk after 2 PM. Book a tee time whenever you choose during the week, but you'll need to call after 1 PM on Thursday to schedule for the weekend. Approximate cost, including cart, is $35 weekdays and $45 on weekends.

Oak Ridge Country Club

5451 S. Pine St., Spartanburg • 582-7579
Championship Yardage: 6156

Slope: 121	**Par: 72**
Men's Yardage: 5487	
Slope: 111	**Par: 72**
Ladies' Yardage: 4491	
Slope: 112	**Par: 72**

Oak Ridge Country Club opened in 1980. George Cobb designed the course on picturesque rolling terrain. Fairways are 419 bermudagrass, and greens are bentgrass.

The course was remodeled in 1992. Much of the difficulty on this well-designed course comes from its hilly nature. At times, you might feel like you're on a mountain track. The greens vary in shape but are primarily midsize and sloped, with some subtle undulations. The combination scorecard/yardage book is a useful aid. You'll find bunkering in the fairways and around most of the greens. Keeping the ball in play on this somewhat short course is crucial, so you might want to leave your big stick in the trunk. The course narrows a touch on the back nine, and water comes into play on a few holes. You can't go wrong with a George Cobb design, so visit this course if you can. It's also an excellent value.

Amenities include a practice green, range, chipping green, snack bar, rental clubs, a beverage cart and pro shop.

The course is walkable for the physically fit, and you can walk anytime. You can book a tee time two days in advance. Approximate cost, including cart, is $20 weekdays and $25 on weekends.

Parkland Golf Club
295 E. Deadfall Rd., Greenwood
• 229-5086
Championship Yardage: 6520
Slope: 124   Par: 72
Men's Yardage: 6140
Slope: 120   Par: 72
Other Yardage: 5710
Slope: 114   Par: 72
Ladies' Yardage: 5130
Slope: 115   Par: 72

Parkland Golf Club opened in 1986. John Park designed the course on rolling wooded terrain, with bermudagrass greens and fairways.

Parkland is a fine country course — another example that proves you don't need a big name architect to create a formidable track. Overall, the layout is relatively flat and features a number of tricky holes surrounded by towering pine trees. Some of the holes are tight off the tee. Streams and ponds come into play, particularly on the back nine. You'll find a great deal of bunkering around the greens and an occasional bunker in the fairway. The greens undulate and vary in size. There's nothing tricked-up about this course; it exudes an old-style country club feel. Definitely play here if you can.

Amenities include a chipping green, snack bar and pro shop.

The course is walkable for the fit, and you can walk anytime. You won't need a tee time. Approximate cost, including cart, is $13 weekdays and $22 on weekends.

Peach Valley Golf Club
2363 Chesnee Hwy., Spartanburg
• 583-2244
Championship Yardage: 6225
Slope: 109   Par: 70
Men's Yardage: 5925
Slope: 92   Par: 70
Ladies' Yardage: No rating
Slope: 97   Par: 76

Peach Valley opened in 1960. The course is set on open and primarily flat terrain. In the fairways, you'll find bermudagrass; on the greens, bentgrass and bermudagrass. Who

designed this course? We don't know, and neither did anyone or any text source we consulted.

Peach Valley offers low-cost, worry-free, relaxed golf in a pleasant setting. Greens are raised and small to medium-size, with subtle slopes. The fairways are wide and open, so feel free to take out the boron-shaft, titanium-head big daddy you just purchased from the club maker in the pro shop and let it rip.

Amenities include a practice green, range, chipping green, snack bar, restaurant, rental clubs and a pro shop.

The course is walkable, you should walk here and can do so anytime (three cheers!). You also can book a tee time whenever you choose. Approximate cost, including cart, is $17 weekdays and $21 on weekends.

Pickens Country Club
1018 Country Club Rd., Pickens
• 878-6083
Championship Yardage: 6250
Slope: 120   Par: 72
Men's Yardage: 5966
Slope: 117   Par: 72
Ladies' Yardage: 4912
Slope: 115   Par: 72

Pickens Country Club opened in 1954 with nine holes; the club added a back nine in 1958. Willie B. Lewis designed the course. Woods border some of the holes, and most of the fairways are defined and delineated with evergreens and hardwoods. The course is set in rolling terrain; water only comes into play on a couple of holes. You'll find bermudagrass in the fairways and bentgrass on the greens.

At Pickens Country Club, we found a fine, mature, traditional layout. You won't find anything tricked-up or gimmicky here; it's fairly straightforward, the trees are mature and magnificent, there's barely a house in sight anywhere, and many of the holes sweep majestically right and left, giving you the feeling that you're on a country club track. You might ask yourself why today's modern courses aren't like this one.

Like a lot of older traditional designs, you'll find that the degree of trouble off the tee depends on the length of the rough: If it's long and shaggy, you'll need to keep your ball in the short grass. The greens are small, undulating and, according the staff, fast outside

Designer Profile: George Cobb

George Cobb (1914-1986) lived in Greenville, South Carolina, most of his life. He graduated with a degree in landscape architecture from the University of Georgia in 1937, then worked for the National Park Service until he entered the Marine Corps as an engineering officer in 1941.

A scratch golfer, Cobb was asked to build a course at Camp LeJeune. Cobb was so unsure of his abilities as an architect, he hired Fred Findlay to design the course; Cobb supervised the construction. After World War II, he entered private practice as a golf course architect and land planner. In the 1950s and '60s, he was a design consultant at Augusta National where he designed and built the par 3 course. Cobb was a close friend of Bobby Jones, and you'll find examples of his drawing skills in Jones' autobiography.

Photo: The Architects of Golf

Many Cobb-designed courses are private, and you'll find most of his public-access courses in resort areas. He tended to build long, difficult courses for private clubs but included more playability in his resort tracks. During the last 15 years of his career, he was assisted by John LaFoy. Many of Cobb's courses have hosted professional and amateur tournaments.

You'll find Cobb's work in Alabama, Florida, Georgia, Maryland, Minnesota, North and South Carolina, Tennessee, Virginia, West Virginia and the Bahamas.

George Cobb
—

In total, George Cobb worked on nearly 100 golf courses.

---

the summer months. They're probably harder than they look. You won't find an overabundance of bunkers, although some strategically placed sand and grass bunkers will make you think about your approach shot.

The course offers a yardage book that includes swing thoughts and golf tips on each page, including one tip that encourages you not to over-think . . . a classic example of yardage-book irony.

Amenities include a practice green, range, chipping green, locker room, bar, snack bar and pro shop.

You can walk anytime. Nonmembers can book a tee time two days in advance. Approximate cost, including cart, is $25 weekdays and $30 on weekends.

River Chase

459 Fairwood Blvd., Union • 427-3055
Championship Yardage: 6607
Slope: 121   **Par: 71**
Men's Yardage: 6086
Slope: 114   **Par: 71**
Ladies' Yardage: 5138
Slope: 103   **Par: 71**

River Chase, a fine Russell Breeden design that opened in 1976, is set in rolling wooded terrain, with bermudagrass greens and fairways.

You'll find there isn't much room off the tee, which makes the course play longer — as if it weren't long enough already (6607 yards from the tips). The green complexes are challenging and feature numerous bunkers and extreme undulations. It's a pretty course, relatively free of houses and other obstructions. Just keep the ball down the middle of the fairways and you'll be in great shape.

In 1995 the owners renovated the course and improved it tremendously, thus making it one of the better courses in the Union area of the Upstate.

Amenities include a practice green, range, locker room, snack bar and pro shop.

River Chase is walkable for the fit, and you can walk anytime. You can book a tee time whenever you choose. Approximate cost, including cart, is $39 weekdays and $49 on weekends.

River Falls Plantation
100 Player Blvd., Duncan • 433-9192

Championship Yardage: 6697	
Slope: 127	**Par: 72**
Men's Yardage: 6238	
Slope: 121	**Par: 72**
Other Yardage: 5702	
Slope: 116	**Par: 72**
Ladies' Yardage: 4928	
Slope: 125	**Par: 72**

Gary Player designed the golf course at River Falls Plantation, which opened in 1990. Most holes are bordered by woods, and some holes have a mountain feel. In the fairways, you'll find bermudagrass; on the greens, bentgrass.

Player routed the course exceedingly well, and the result is a track with a number of memorable holes. We found outstanding variety: It's the sort of course where, as the old saying goes, you'll have to use every club in your bag. You may be forced to plan a strategy on just about every hole. Some holes offer great elevation changes. Fairway widths vary a great deal, and on certain holes you'll want to throttle back with a long iron off the tee. On other holes, take out the big stick and fire away. Water frequently comes into play. The green complexes vary in size, shape and protection to the point where it's impossible to generalize. On certain holes, you might think of this course as a sort of kinder, gentler Pete Dye-type design. Definitely play this course if you're in the Upstate.

Amenities include a range, chipping green, locker room, snack bar, restaurant, rental clubs, a beverage cart and pro shop.

Walking is not allowed, but you can book a tee time whenever you choose. Approximate cost, including cart, is $32 weekdays and $41 on weekends.

Rolling Green Golf Club
386 Hester Shore Rd., Easley • 859-7716
First and Second Nines

Championship Yardage: 6116	
Slope: 118	**Par: 71**
Men's Yardage: 5635	
Slope: 118	**Par: 71**
Ladies' Yardage: 4546	
Slope: 115	**Par: 71**
### Second and Third Nines	
Championship Yardage: 6159	
Slope: No rating	**Par: 72**
Men's Yardage: 5705	
Slope: No rating	**Par: 72**
Ladies' Yardage: 4679	
Slope: No rating	**Par: 72**
### Third and First Nines	
Championship Yardage: 6083	
Slope: No rating	**Par: 71** .
Men's Yardage: 5610	
Slope: No rating	**Par: 71**
Ladies' Yardage: 4625	
Slope: No rating	**Par: 71**

Rolling Green offers 27 holes. The first nine at Rolling Green opened in 1968, the second nine opened two years later and the third opened in 1991. Willie B. Lewis designed the first nine holes; the owners, the Dacus family, designed the second and third nines. The course is set in rolling terrain and is bordered by woods. Water comes into play on a number of holes. You'll find bermudagrass in the fairways and bentgrass on the greens.

As you might expect from a course built in three stages, each section has its own character and feel. The front nine is relatively narrow and pretty yet straightforward. You won't find any significant water on the front nine. The greens are medium-size, sloped and protected by bunkers. Keep the ball in play and you'll have some fun. On the second nine, the bunkers seem a little deeper and a bit more menacing; the greens are a little larger. The layout retains the traditional feel of the first nine. Water also comes into play. The third nine offers a bit more variety; the fairways are defined and delineated by evergreen trees.

There are some significant elevation changes on the final nine plus a bit more water. Considering that the final nine is just a few years old, it feels remarkably mature. Overall, Rolling Green offers three fun, varied and interesting nine-hole layouts.

Amenities include a practice green, range, chipping green, locker room, bar, snack bar and pro shop.

You can walk anytime. Nonmembers can book a tee time seven days in advance. Approximate cost, including cart, is $21 weekdays and $23 on weekends.

Southern Oaks Golf Club
105 Southern Oaks Dr., Easley • 859-6698
Championship Yardage: 6701

Slope: 119	**Par: 72**
Men's Yardage: 6449	
Slope: 115	**Par: 72**
Other Yardage: 6044	
Slope: No rating	**Par: 72**
Ladies' Yardage: 5000	
Slope: 110	**Par: 72**

Willie B. Lewis designed Southern Oaks Golf Club, which opened in 1989. The course is set on gently rolling terrain and is predominantly open. Fairways are bermudagrass; greens, bentgrass.

An important fact about Southern Oaks: Head PGA professional Wayne Myers scored here what might be the world-record for 18 holes: 57. Obviously, Myers had numerous eagles and birdies during this impressive round, but don't think Southern Oaks is a pushover. This is one of the finest courses in the Greenville-Spartanburg metroplex, and it surely rates as one of Willie B. Lewis' best efforts.

The course is modern inasmuch as it was built fewer than 10 years ago, but the design borrows more from the traditional than from today's trickery and treachery. In many ways Southern Oaks reminded us of Tanglewood in Clemmons, North Carolina, without all the bunkers. Most of the holes are open, but each hole has a distinct character. There's usually plenty of room off the tee. The greens are midsize to large, with plenty of slope and/or undulation. Bunkers come into play on quite a few holes, and water poses a hazard on several holes as well. We think you'll enjoy the tee shot on the par 4 No. 3: You must clear nearly 200 yards of water to reach a peninsula landing area; the hole plays 465 yards from the back tees. There's also a 625-yard par 5 on the front nine. So make sure you bring your big stick and be ready to smack it a few holes, although some holes favor placement over distance off the tee. Overall, this is a must-play course if you're a fan of traditional yet challenging golf courses. Southern Oaks is an excellent value, especially if you walk.

Amenities include a practice green, range, chipping green, locker room, snack bar/grill, rental clubs and a pro shop.

A group of landscape architects owns the course, thus there's an understated emphasis on the landscaping, with plenty of young trees planted amid the shrubberies. Also, as you might expect, there's a strong emphasis on course maintenance.

The course is walkable, you should walk and you can walk anytime. You can book a tee time for the weekend on the preceding Thursday, seven days in advance for the weekdays. Approximate cost, including cart, is $27 weekdays and $32 on weekends.

FYI

Unless otherwise noted, the area code for all phone numbers in this guide is 864.

Stoney Pointe
709 Swing About Rd., Greenwood
• 942-0900
Championship Yardage: 6681

Slope: 125	**Par: 72**
Men's Yardage: 6129	
Slope: 117	**Par: 72**
Other Yardage: 5449	
Slope: 111	**Par: 72**
Ladies' Yardage: 4962	
Slope: 120	**Par: 72**

Stoney Pointe opened in 1991. Tom Jackson designed the course. It's open in some places and bordered by woods and houses in others. In the fairways, you'll find 419 bermudagrass; on the greens, you'll find bentgrass.

Stoney Pointe is a wonderful design and, for our money, it's one of Tom Jackson's best efforts. In places, the course has a links feel, with mounds bordering the fairways and un-

South Carolina boasts two excellent state park courses in Cheraw
and Hickory Knob. Tom Jackson designed both tracks.

dulations within them. Many are tight, with out-of-bounds and water lurking off the tee. The greens vary in size, and many are sloped and rolling. If the rough is tall, you must avoid it to score well. The yardage book/score card is a useful aid. As with many Jackson courses, bunkers come in all shapes, sizes and depths. If the rough is grown up around the greens, it will hamper your finesse pitches and chips. You'll also find some grass bunkers, just to make the course all the more difficult. Stoney Pointe is a fun and challenging course that we suggest you play more than once. It's also a good value.

Amenities include a practice green, range, chipping green, locker room, bar, snack bar, rental clubs and a pro shop.

You can walk anytime and book a tee time seven days in advance. Approximate cost, including cart, is $25 weekdays and $30 on weekends.

Summersett
111 Pilot Rd., Greenville • 834-4781
Championship Yardage: 6025

Slope: 114	**Par: 72**
Men's Yardage: 5420	
Slope: 108	**Par: 72**
Ladies' Yardage: 4910	
Slope: 119	**Par: 74**

Summersett opened in the late 1930s. *Architects of Golf* lists Tom Jackson as the individual who revamped the track in 1979. The course is set on undulating terrain, and you'll find bermudagrass fairways and bentgrass greens.

Summersett is short from the back tees (6025 yards), but it's also tight off the tee. Tom Jackson resisted the temptation to lengthen the course to absurd proportions. Instead, it appears the renovation made good use of the original routing, and the course was made more difficult by adding variable pitch and roll to the greens. There's plenty of variety here, and you'll discover it's most sensible to keep the driver in the bag, especially on the back nine.

With the foothills of the Smoky Mountains

bearing down from above, the course has a mountainous feel; the rolling terrain makes for some interesting tee shots. It's definitely worth a visit if you're looking for a good game on a short but sensible course.

Amenities include a practice green, chipping green, snack bar, rental clubs, a beverage cart and a pro shop.

You may walk the course anytime except weekends before 2 PM. You can book a tee time whenever you choose. Approximate cost, including cart, is $21 weekdays and $26 on weekends.

Table Rock Resort
171 Sliding Rock Rd., Pickens • 878-2030
Championship Yardage: 6514

Slope: 118	**Par: 72**
Men's Yardage: 6038	
Slope: 114	**Par: 72**
Ladies' Yardage: 5085	
Slope: 112	**Par: 72**

The golf course at Table Rock Resort was designed by Willie B. Lewis and opened in 1983. Table Rock is a mountain course; most of the holes are bordered by woods, while others are wide open, with a couple of shared fairways. You'll find common bermudagrass in the fairways and 328 bermudagrass on the greens. Water comes into play on a number of holes.

The owners and management at Table Rock have completed a number of improvements. The basic layout and design is sound, with some fine holes beautifully framed by trees. The atmosphere is fun and relaxing.

Many of the fairways are narrow, particularly on the back nine where the course is less open and more wooded. There are a couple of fun driving holes where you need to bang it through a chute. Locals advise keeping the driver in the bag unless you can keep it straight. The greens are primarily small, flat and interestingly shaped; the change-over to bentgrass may alter that. Most of the holes are flat, although a few include significant elevation changes. Water comes into play mainly in the form of pretty mountain streams that need be avoided: Take a picture, but don't let your ball anywhere near them. A couple of bunkers lurk here and there. But overall, Table Rock boasts a course with a lot of potential.

If you're fed up with golf, the resort offers horseback riding, walks, tennis or fishing in a stocked lake. Table Rock State Park is just a few minutes away.

Amenities include a practice green, range, chipping green, locker room, bar, snack bar, restaurant, rental clubs and an occasional beverage cart.

You can walk anytime, and the course is walkable for the fit. You can also book anytime. Approximate cost, including cart, is $19 weekdays and $23 on weekends.

Verdae Greens Golf Club

650 Verdae Blvd., Greenville • 676-1500
Championship Yardage: 6773
Slope: 126	**Par: 72**
Men's Yardage: 6249	
Slope: 118	**Par: 72**
Other Yardage: 5470	
Slope: No rating	**Par: 72**
Ladies' Yardage: 5012	
Slope: 116	**Par: 72**

Verdae Greens opened in 1990. Willard Byrd designed this track amid rolling terrain. Many holes are bordered by woods. In the fairways, you'll find bermudagrass; on the greens, you'll find Pencross bentgrass, one of the best and most durable putting surfaces grown.

Verdae Greens (an interesting name) is owned by Embassy Suites Hotels (note the large multistory Embassy Suites adjacent to the course. Call 676-9090 for reservations). Thus the course is a magnet for golfers on corporate outings, retreats and getaways.

Verdae Greens is home to one of the finest and prettiest golf courses in the Greenville-Spartanburg area: an excellent example of Willard Byrd's magic. The course hosts a Nike Tour event once won by Scott Gump. We found excellent variety and some serious challenges. Water comes into play often. The course is not overly long, but it's narrow and exacting in places. You'll need to play some target golf to score well. It's important to be in the right place at the right time. Bunkers lurk off the tee and around the greens, which

are relatively large but mercilessly undulating at times.

If you're a mid-handicapper, play from the "other" tees and you'll have a good time. If you're a corporate golfer, hit from the back tees, expense each sleeve of balls to the company account and be sure to write it off. This is a must-play course in the Greenville-Spartanburg area. A useful purchase is the witty yardage book: Heed its advice.

Amenities include a practice green, range, chipping green, bar, snack bar, restaurant, rental clubs, a beverage cart and pro shop.

The course is walkable for the fit and dedicated, and you can walk anytime on weekdays. You can book a tee time seven days in advance. Approximate cost, including cart, is $35 weekdays and $45 on weekends.

Village Green Country Club

S.C. Hwy. 176, Gramling • 472-2411
Championship Yardage: 6372
Slope: 122	**Par: 72**
Men's Yardage: 5873	
Slope: 117	**Par: 72**
Ladies' Yardage: 5280	
Slope: 123	**Par: 74**

Village Green Golf Course opened in approximately 1965. *Architects of Golf* lists Russell Breeden as the course designer; give an assist to Dan Breeden. In the fairways, you'll find bermudagrass; on the greens, bentgrass.

Village Green is a fine course — a playable and attractive track that provides good value for your hard-earned golfing dollar. The course features all the typical Breeden elements and includes a number of truly fine golf holes. There's a definite lack of hardship off the tee, and you'll have to plan your approach shot to avoid the bunkers and leave yourself a viable birdie putt. The back nine is slightly hillier. As the shadows lengthen at the end of the day, the subtle undulations in the green will become more evident. To score well, keep the ball in the fairway and avoid the deep rough around the greens. True to Breeden form, the course becomes a little tougher as you come home. Village Green is worth a visit.

Oh, and call ahead on the 9th and 18th tees for your Kenburger and adult beverage from Ken's Grill.

Amenities include a practice green, range,

chipping green, bar, snack bar/grill (Ken's), rental clubs, a beverage cart and pro shop.

You can walk anytime (yeah!). No advance tee times are necessary during the week, but book on Thursday for the weekend. Approximate cost, including cart, is $20 weekdays and $25 on weekends.

The Walker Course at Clemson University

110 Madren Center Dr., Clemson
• 656-0236
Championship Yardage: 6911

Slope: 137	**Par: 72**
Men's Yardage: 6560	
Slope: 129	**Par: 72**
Other Yardage: 5934	
Slope: 121	**Par: 72**
Ladies' Yardage: 4667	
Slope: 103	**Par: 72**

The Walker Course at Clemson University is the official course of Clemson. D.J. DeVictor designed the course. In the fairways, you'll find bermudagrass; on the greens, you'll find bentgrass. The course is set in primarily open and rolling terrain.

Clemson welcomes you not to Death Valley but to the Walker Course, an amenity made possible primarily through the donations of several wealthy orange-clad alumni. DeVictor designed an impressive and challenging course with plenty of trouble for the wayward. From many of the holes, the university is clearly visible.

The most difficult hole is the 9th, a par 4 that plays 460 yards from the "Tiger" tees. A creek cuts across the middle of the fairway, meaning the longer hitter might have to lay up. You're then faced with 200 yards over water to an undulating green set in a bowl. You should be proud with a par here. If you're a die-hard "my blood runneth orange" Clemson fan, then you'll love the 17th hole, a moderately difficult par 3 that's shaped like a tiger paw. Only at Clemson.

Overall, the course offers tremendous variety. DeVictor made good use of the land to create a number of truly challenging holes. Most of the greens are undulating. There isn't

a great deal of trouble off the tee unless you're quite wayward. The greens are predominantly large and undulating. Bunkers and other hazards are placed to make you think quite hard — play the percentage shot and you'll be in great shape. Unless you're a superstar all-American, play the course from the white tees for the most fun.

The Walker Course at Clemson is the newest course in the Upstate, it's one of the prettiest, and it's a course you should play — even if you graduated from the universities of Georgia or South Carolina.

You'll enjoy the local color on the right flank of the 7th hole where the odor of fresh ordure from the university's Department of Agriculture facility creates a uniquely pungent olfactory hazard.

Ironically, the Walker Course is barely walkable even if you are fit. But you are allowed to walk at anytime. Approximate cost, including cart, is $32 weekdays and $42 on weekends.

FYI
Unless otherwise noted, the area code for all phone numbers in this guide is 864.

Willow Creek Golf Course

205 Sandy Run, Greer
• 476-6492
Championship Yardage: 6698

Slope: No rating	**Par: 72**
Men's Yardage: 6222	
Slope: No rating	**Par: 72**
Other Yardage: 5640	
Slope: No rating	**Par: 72**
Ladies' Yardage: 4846	
Slope: No rating	**Par: 72**

Willow Creek Golf Course, a Tom Jackson design, opened in summer 1995. The course combines open holes and some bordered by woods. Water frequently comes into play. You'll find bermudagrass in the fairways and Crenshaw bentgrass on the greens.

Danner-Eller enterprises owns Willow Creek. (This combination also owns the Hermitage Golf Course in Old Hickory outside of Nashville, Tennessee — host to the Sara Lee Classic on the LPGA Tour). Needless to say, it doesn't hurt to have the area's hottest architect, Tom Jackson, as the big-name designer.

Willow Creek demonstrates that Jackson is not a cookie-cutter designer. The course is

Designer Profile: Tom Jackson

Born in Pennsylvania in 1941, Tom Jackson is one of the busiest architects in the Carolinas, and with good reason: He has built some of the finest new public courses in our area.

Close-up

Jackson graduated with a degree in ornamental horticulture from the State University of New York at Farmingdale. He also earned a degree in landscape architecture from the University of Georgia.

In 1965, Robert Trent Jones hired Jackson to build several courses in the Southeast. Three years later, he joined George Cobb and eventually started his own firm in 1971. From his base in Greenville, Jackson has designed or remodeled more than 50 courses, and more are on the way. His best-known effort is a private course north of Greenville called The Cliffs at Glassy. This has been rated as the fourth most beautiful course in America by *Golf Digest*. You'll find Jackson's work in Alabama, Florida, Georgia and South Carolina.

Jackson aims to build roughly six or seven courses a year. And when he's not supervising course construction, he's playing golf to a six-handicap. Jackson has two sons who are now active in the business as associates.

Photo: The Architects of Golf

Tom Jackson
—

Jackson builds courses to meet his clients' needs and desires, but his designs emphasize playability, particularly on public courses. Play a Jackson course from the tips and you'll likely find it difficult; play it from forward tees and the course will be manageable. Jackson employs some of the characteristics of a modern course, including big mounds, undulating greens and large bunkers, but you won't find tricked up or completely impossible designs. You will find that his courses are among the more aesthetically pleasing — particularly those without houses.

If you believe that the greatest indication of an architect's prowess is the popularity of his or her courses with the people who plop down hard-earned cash to play them, you'll find Jackson's quite remarkable. We think you'll always enjoy a round on a Tom Jackson course, regardless of your score, and you'll be tempted to play it over and over again.

flatter and apparently less penal than some of Jackson's other tracks: The mounds bordering the fairways aren't quite as large. Still, the course has a links feel, and if the wind is blowing, you're in for a challenge. The tee boxes are massive and, clearly, built to withstand the expected heavy play. The greens are also large, and the influence of the bunkering and slope of the green will vary depending on pin placement.

Based on the looks of the clubhouse and the track record of the ownership, there's an initial commitment to make this course one of the better facilities in the area; this should be achieved once the course has had some time to grow and mature.

Amenities include a practice green, range, chipping green, locker room, snack bar, restaurant, rental clubs and a pro shop. There's no beverage cart, because your cart is the beverage cart: The course supplies you with your own personal cooler.

The course is not especially walkable, but you're allowed to walk on weekdays. You can book a tee time five days in advance. Approximate cost, including cart, is $29 weekdays and $34 on weekends.

Around Upstate South Carolina ...

Fun Things To Do

While you're driving through the Greenville-Spartanburg area in the reckless pursuit of golfing nirvana, you might begin to feel somewhat awed by the sheer volume of industry. On I-85, construction crews busily prepare new interchanges and add lanes in an effort to support all the traffic produced by the area's pulsing industrial base. People work hard here. And when their work is done, they like to play. And many of them play golf on the fine selection of aforementioned courses.

A visitor to this area might wonder what there is to do besides view factories from arterial roads or play golf. Well, you'd be surprised. Downtown **Greenville** has undergone a fine renovation, and you'll find all sorts of eclectic opportunities for dining and drinking. The **NFL's Carolina Panthers** spend summer camp at **Wofford College** in Spartanburg. There's dirt track stock-car racing at the speedway in Gaffney. But most importantly, minor league glove-dropping ice hockey is coming to the Greenville-Spartanburg area for the 1997-98 season.

Here are just a few activities you might find interesting.

For starters, **Tours Around Greenville South** (TAGS), 123 W. Broad Street, Greenville, 467-8088, is a volunteer organization that assists visitors in seeing Greenville's special attractions. Give 'em a call; they'll point you in the right direction.

The **Greenville Braves**, AA affiliate of Major League Baseball's Atlanta Braves franchise, play at Greenville Municipal Stadium on Mauldin Road, Greenville, 299-3456. Take Exit 46 from I-85.

If you strike out at the ball park, a real hit, especially with the kids, is the **Greenville Zoo**, 150 Cleveland Park Drive, Greenville, 467-4310. You'll find 14 acres of exotic animal kingdom, featuring lions and other big cats, miniature deer, kangaroos, tortoises and myriad wild beasts roaming about in a natural setting. Go ahead and make your day (and your kids' day too) with a visit to Dirty Harry, the resident boa constrictor.

Another educational attraction is **Roper Mountain Science Center**, 504 Roper Mountain Road, Greenville, 281-1188. All types of fun and scientifically oriented activities await the entire family. There are observatory/planetarium shows, hands-on exhibits and nature trails. Go to the intersection of I-385 and Roper Mountain Road.

For more information about activities and events in the Greenville area, contact or stop by **The Greater Greenville Convention & Visitors Center**, 206 N. Main Street, Greenville, 233-0461. Or you may also call or write **Discover Upcountry Carolina Association**, P.O. Box 3116, Greenville 29602, (800) 849-4766.

In **Spartanburg**, there's plenty to do when you're not playing golf. Anyone interested in historic homes should see the **Thomas Price House**, Road 200, Woodruff. It was built in 1795 and was the centerpiece of the Thomas Price Plantation; the house is brick with a steep gambrel roof and inside end chimneys. Call 476-2483 for more information.

Cowpens National Battlefield, 4001 Chesnee Highway near Gaffney, 461-2828, was the site of one of the more important battles in American history. On a grim January day in 1781, Gen. Daniel Morgan and his militia beat up a group of British soldiers in less than an hour. Part of the National Park System operates a visitors center, auto trail, walking trail and picnic area. If you're a member of a YMCA, you can get more fit than you already are at the **Spartanburg YMCA**, 226 S. Pine Street, 85-0306. This branch is the largest single-unit YMCA in the Southeast and features two indoor pools, basketball and handball courts, Nautilus equipment and a cardiac-rehab center.

For more information about Spartanburg, call the **Spartanburg Convention and Visitors Bureau**, 594-5050.

Where to Eat

There's no shortage of places to eat in the Greenville-Spartanburg area. We've mentioned that Upstaters are a hard-working lot; we've noted that they like to play golf. Well, they also like to eat, as evidenced by the plentiful locally owned proprietorships where local folk have been feasting for years. You'll find all your favorite chain restaurants plus an excellent variety of ethnic- and regional-fare establishments, including Chinese, Italian and down-home country-style favorites, to name a few.

Annie's Natural Cafe
$$ • 121 S. Main St., Greenville • 271-4872

Annie's has a sort of European flair and atmosphere. Coupled with the great selection of foods health-conscious folks and vegetarians will savor, such as veggie lasagna and herbal tea, this place is a wonderfully unique addition to the downtown Greenville eating scene.

The Blue Ridge Brewing Company
$$ • 217 N. Main St., Greenville • 232-4677

Walk in the door, head straight for the bar and ask yon fair bartender for a pint of Colonel Paris Pale Ale, an outstanding hand-crafted beer. Then look around to discover this relatively new establishment has an Old World feel and a trendy, well-to-do younger clientele — although beer lovers of all sizes, shapes and ages seem to enjoy themselves here.

Sample other fine pints, including Dove Field Wheat, Strumhouse Scottish Red Ale and the Rainbow Trout Amber Ale. There's an abundance of food as well — basic appetizers, soups, salads and sandwiches plus some interesting pub-type entrees, including pan-seared trout and a half-rack of brewhouse ribs. There's smoked-salmon pizza too. For brewpub lovers, this is heaven.

Country Earl's Chompin' & Stompin'
$$ • I-385 at Exit 31, Simpsonville • 967-8569

You'll get good, hearty country cookin' here at Country Earl's, in addition to a full evening of country entertainment. Indulge in fried chicken, beef tips, chicken and gravy and all your favorite fixins. And enjoy various bands, clogging exhibitions and all types of dancing to work off your meal. Tour-bus groups are welcome to come chomp and stomp.

Le Baron Restaurant
$$ • 2600 E. Main St., Spartanburg • 579-3111

Le Baron's tag line invites you to, "Discover the difference between eating out and real dining pleasure." This enormous restaurant with banquet facilities for up to 500 hungry souls offers a full menu featuring fresh seafood, charcoal broiled steaks, succulent prime rib and a host of veal dishes. There's live entertainment on Saturday evenings as well. And if you need catering services, call Le Baron's in-house service: Sophie's Choice. Who chose that name?

Little Pigs Barbeque
$ • 414 Montague Ave., Greenwood • 229-1314

Owner Barbara Sprouse and her staff want you to enjoy what she refers to as the best barbeque in town. This popular establishment serves plates and sandwiches in the traditional way, replete with fries, slaw and hushpuppies — all the essentials of the barbeque experience. But there's also fare here for the non-pork eaters. There's homemade chicken salad, hamburgers, hot dogs, chef salads, barbequed chicken, roast beef, club sandwiches and fish plates.

INSIDERS' TIP

Unless otherwise instructed, play "real" golf — play the ball where it lies.

Papa Sam's Breakfast Nook
$ • 191 E. St. John St., Spartanburg
• 582-6655

Twenty-four hours a day, seven days a week, you can get breakfast at Papa Sam's. On the menu you'll find the standard fare with pancakes, waffles, eggs cooked to order and even some sandwiches, biscuits, toast, orange juice, grapefruit juice and other sundry items. But the item you must order is the famous (on East St. John Street anyway) Trashcan Omelette. This work of art is stuffed full of ham, American and Swiss cheeses, mushrooms, onions, peppers and probably anything else you might want. Adjacent to the breakfast section of the restaurant is a bigger restaurant featuring a full menu of prime rib, steaks, seafood and other standards. It's also home to the famous (again, on East St. John Street) Monster Burger, which is enormous.

Peter David's Fine Dining
$$ • 921 Grove Rd.,
Greenville • 242-0404

Peter David's offers an elegant atmosphere and affordable prices. Menu items include fresh seafood, beef, veal and a value-priced wine selection. The establishment is a member of the Blue Plate Society.

Longhorn Steaks
$$ • 1793 E. Main St., Spartanburg
• 585-9400

On U.S. 29, also called E. Main Street near Hillcrest Mall, this version of the popular chain offers all that folks have come to expect from a Longhorn. Begin your meal with a beer and some sizzling appetizers, then delve into a thick and juicy steak cooked to your specifications. If steak is not your cup of tea, devour a chicken dish or try Longhorn's famous salmon. Round out the meal with another brew or a Texas-size bowl of ice cream.

Stefano's Authentic Italian Cuisine
$$ • 1560 Union St., Spartanburg
• 591-1941

Stefano's proclaims that it's Spartanburg's premier Italian restaurant. It's certainly worth a visit if you're a lover of Northern Italian cuisine. This large restaurant specializes in banquets and catering. You'll find your favorite pasta dishes as well as some unique recipes featuring chicken, veal and fresh fish. Wash down your Veal Valdostana with a bottle of Valpolicella and top it off with tiramisu.

Yoder's Dutch Kitchen
$$ • S.C. Hwy. 72 E., Abbeville • 459-5556

It may come as some surprise to you that one of the top 10 Pennsylvania Dutch restaurants in the country is right here in the thriving submetropolis known as Abbeville. Yoder's declares itself a "nice place to bring your family or friends" — except on Sunday, Monday and Tuesday when the restaurant is closed. There's a smorgasbord-style buffet, so if you're particularly hungry, you can indulge all you want here. Also try the lunch buffet Wednesday through Saturday. In addition to the tasty Pennsylvania Dutch treats, you can purchase whole pies, apple butter and cinnamon-nut rolls.

FYI
Unless otherwise noted, the area code for all phone numbers in this guide is 864.

Where to Stay

With all the business activity in the Greenville-Spartanburg area, it's very important to book a room before you arrive, particularly for the weekday. Try to call up to two weeks in advance of your arrival if you can.

Best Western Spartan Inn & Conference Center
$$ • I-85 Bus. and S.C. Hwy. 9,
Spartanburg • 578-5400

This comfortable and accessible (right off I-85) Best Western underwent a complete

---

INSIDERS' TIP

If you're a mid- to high-handicapper and you're more than 200 yards from the green, try an approach shot and leave yourself a pitching wedge to the green. This will often lead to lower scores.

Photo: S.C. Parks, Recreation & Tourism

The Hickory Knob course at McCormick State Park is fun and challenging.

renovation just four years ago and is popular among the business traveler set. This hotel offers 122 rooms with free cable TV. There's a business center, banquet and meeting rooms, a tennis court and an outdoor pool. Corporate rates are available. After a busy day of golf and/or business, retire to Bigoli's Restaurant and Lounge.

Courtyard by Marriott
$$ • 110 Mobile Dr., Spartanburg
• 585-2400

Designed by business travelers for business travelers, Spartanburg's version of the well-known and popular Courtyard concept is perfect for the person coming to the Upstate to close a deal. But it's also an excellent place for the golfer. The restaurant offers a great breakfast buffet and serves a solid sandwich and dinner menu. Choose a guest room or indulge in a suite. You'll find that the prices are a good value.

Holiday Inn Express
$$ • At McAlister Square Mall, 27 S. Pleasantburg Dr., Greenville • 232-3339

This Holiday Inn Express is off I-385 and U.S. 291, two blocks from the Palmetto International Exposition Center and close to McAlister Square Mall. Breakfast is included in your room rate. Amenities include fax and other business services and cable TV.

Holiday Inn Greenwood
$$ • 1014 Montague Ave., Greenwood
• 223-4231

The Holiday Inn Greenwood offers 100 remodeled rooms as well as a courtyard with a pool and decks. It's a good value, particularly if you make use of the corporate, group and special weekend rates; kids and teens stay free. A free full breakfast and local calls are included in your room rate, and fax and copy services are available. After a round of Greenwood-area golf, relax in Simon's Bar and Grill. Or take in the bountiful Sunday brunch before

you venture forth onto the links for your Sunday afternoon round.

Holiday Inn North
$$$ • I-85 and S.C. Hwy. 9, Spartanburg
• 578-5400

The Holiday Inn in Spartanburg is well-known as a good place to stay and eat. There are 122 recently renovated rooms and suites; you'll get free cable with HBO, ESPN and CNN. There's a business center for the business traveler as well as meeting rooms. The hotel offers corporate rates. If you're there for golf or for business, unwind on the tennis court, by the pool or in Bleachers! Sports Bar and Grill.

Hyatt Regency Greenville
$$$$ • 220 N. Main St., Greenville
• 235-1234

Enter the spacious atrium lobby and you'll immediately be at ease in this outstanding hotel right downtown. There are 327 guest rooms, with amenities that include cable TV with ESPN and coffee makers. Many of the rooms have fine views. There's also a pool, health club and a full-service business center.

Pettigru Place
$$$ • 302 Pettigru St., Greenville
• 242-4529

In the heart of downtown, Pettigru Place offers five individually decorated guest rooms, each with private bath. Gourmet breakfast is included in the tab.

The Phoenix
$$ • 246 N. Pleasantburg Dr., Greenville
• 233-4651

The Phoenix is a full-service inn, with outdoor dining in the Courtyard Grille plus romantic dining in the Palms Restaurant. There's dancing and entertainment in The Bar. The Phoenix exudes a much more intimate setting than the typical motel. In-room amenities include cable TV with ESPN and a full bathroom in each suite.

INSIDERS' TIP

Take a putting lesson from your PGA pro, buy a putter that fits your build and watch a lot of strokes drop off your score.

Residence Inn by Marriott

$$$ • 9011 Fairforest Rd., Spartanburg

• 576-3333

The Residence Inn chain tends to cater to the person who is staying in an area for an extended period; weekly and monthly rates are available. Residence Inn Spartanburg offers one- and two-bedroom suites, a fully equipped kitchen, a living room with a fireplace, cable TV with free HBO, complimentary breakfast and a swimming pool.

Advertisers Index

Index